Lecture Notes in Computer Science 1158

Edited by G. Goos, J. Hartmanis and J. van Leeuwen

Springer
Berlin
Heidelberg
New York
Barcelona
Budapest
Hong Kong
London
Milan
Paris
Santa Clara
Singapore
Tokyo

Stefano Berardi Mario Coppo (Eds.)

Types for Proofs and Programs

International Workshop, TYPES '95
Torino, Italy, June 5-8, 1995
Selected Papers

Springer

Series Editors

Gerhard Goos, Karlsruhe University, Germany

Juris Hartmanis, Cornell University, NY, USA

Jan van Leeuwen, Utrecht University, The Netherlands

Volume Editors

Stefano Berardi
Mario Coppo
Università degli Studi di Torino, Dipartimento di Informatica
Corso Svizzera 185, I-10149 Torino, Italy
E-mail: {berardi/coppo}@di.unito.it

Cataloging-in-Publication data applied for

Die Deutsche Bibliothek - CIP-Einheitsaufnahme

Types for proofs and programs : selected papers / International Workshop TYPES '95, Torino, Italy, June 5 - 8, 1995. Stefano Berardi ... (ed.). - Berlin ; Heidelberg ; New York ; Barcelona ; Budapest ; Hong Kong ; London ; Milan ; Paris ; Santa Clara ; Singapore ; Tokyo : Springer, 1996
(Lecture notes in computer science ; Vol. 1158)
ISBN 3-540-61780-9
NE: Berardi, Stefano [Hrsg.]; International Workshop TYPES <3, 1995, Torino>; GT

CR Subject Classification (1991): F.4.1, F.3.1, D.3.3, I.2.3

ISSN 0302-9743
ISBN 3-540-61780-9 Springer-Verlag Berlin Heidelberg New York

Typesetting: Camera-ready by author
SPIN 10549802 06/3142 - 5 4 3 2 1 0 Printed on acid-free paper

Preface

This book is a selection of papers presented at the third annual workshop held under the auspices of the ESPRIT Basic Research Action 6453 *Types for Proofs and Programs.* It took place in Torino, Italy, from the 5th to the 8th of June 1995. Eighty people attended the workshop.

We thank the European Community for the funding which made the workshop possible. We thank Franco Barbanera, Luca Boerio, and Ferruccio Damiani, who took care of the local arrangements. Finally, we thank the following researchers who acted as referees: P. Audebaud, T. Altenkirch, F. Barbanera, G. Barthe, U. Berger, I. Beylin, T. Coquand, C. Cornes, P. Curmin, M. Dezani, P. Dybjer, H. Geuvers, E. Giménez, U. Herbelin, M. Hofmann, F. Honsell, Z. Luo, L. Magnusson, V. Padovani, H. Persson, C. Paulin-Mohring, I. Polack, A. Ranta, M. Ruys, A. Saibi, T. Schreiber, H. Schwichtenberg, K. Slind, J. Smith, M. Stefanova, Y. Takayama, T. Tammet, D. Terrasse, J. von Plato.

This volume is a follow-up to *Types for Proofs and Programs '93*, LNCS 806, edited by H.Barendregt and T.Nipkow and *Types for Proofs and Programs '94*, LNCS 996, edited by P. Dybjer, B. Nordstrom, and J. Smith. *Types for Proofs and Programs* is a continuation of ESPRIT Basic Research Action 3245 *Logical Frameworks: Design, Implementation and Experiments.* Papers from the annual workshops of these projects are collected in the books *Logical Frameworks* and *Logical Environments.* Both volumes were edited by G. Huet and G. Plotkin and published by Cambridge University Press.

Torino July 1996

Stefano Berardi and Mario Coppo

Contents

Introduction

The papers in these proceedings focus on various aspects of the development of computer-aided systems for formal reasoning using logical frameworks based on type theory. The most important applications we are interested in are the mechanization of mathematics and the realization of powerful tools for real software development. A logical framework provides a formalism in which a large class of theories can be represented. This is important since experience has shown that different aspects of mathematics and computer science are better represented using different theories. Moreover an implementation of the framework provides a proof system for each of the theories represented in it.

Type theory is a formalism in which theorems and proofs, specifications and programs can be represented in a uniform way. In particular, a type can be understood both as a proposition and as a specification, and a term having that type can be seen both as a proof of that proposition and as a program meeting that specification. A characteristic feature of type theory is that it supports constructive reasoning, a kind of reasoning frequently used in computer science, but very little developed so far inside computer-aided systems. The logical frameworks based on type theory which have been designed and tested during the TYPES project are Alf, Coq, and LEGO. They follow the same leading ideas but differ in the type theory on which they are based and in some choices regarding implementation. A related logical framework is Isabelle, which is based on higher order logic.

We expect these tools will soon help researchers in mathematics and computer science in developing software and checking its correctness, as systems like Mathematica or Maple already do in the more restricted field of symbolic computing. As compared to these latter, computer-aided systems for formal reasoning are less advanced at present, but are intended to be of broader use since they will help in any situation where logical or mathematical reasoning is required.

The papers in these proceedings deal with the three main aspects of the project: foundations of type theory and logical frameworks, implementation, and applications.

In the group of foundational papers, Barthe and Ruys and Barendregt develop an equational description of a proof checking algorithm, which is a basic tool in a logical framework. Barthe studies the possibility of including the notions of inheritance and overloading in type theory. Berger and Schwichtenberg give an example of extraction of a program from a classical proof. Cederquist and Negri describe the formalization in type theory of a central result of mathematical analysis. Coquand and Smith explain how to derive a typical logical result inside a constructive formalism. Curmin introduces an algorithm for the extraction of a program from a constructive proof. Stefanova and Geuvers introduce a new class of models for the calculus of construction, the formalism upon which the

Coq system is based. Hofmann and Padovani solve two interesting open problems in type theory. Von Plato, finally, presents a methodological reflexion on the translation of mathematical concepts and results in our constructive setting.

Another group of papers deals more closely with implementation aspects. Cornes and Terrasse describe a possible implementation of inductive reasoning in Coq. Magnusson describes an implementation of a proof-checking algorithm in Alf. Smith and Tammet investigate the theoretical background of a complex proof search algorithm. Ranta's paper is a (mostly theoretical) study of an algorithm for translating a symbolic proof in English.

The remaining papers are on the side of the applications. Under this heading we classify both large-scale testing, like examples of development of theoretical computer science within our systems, and industrial applications. Beylin and Dybjer develop in Alf a basic result in category theory. Dybjer also formalizes in Alf a part of the type theory on which Alf itself is based. Giménez reports on an industrial application: a formal correctness proof for the alternating bit protocol developed in Coq. Honsell and Miculan encode dynamic logic in Coq. Finally, Paulin-Mohring develops a correctness proof for a multiplier circuit in Coq using streams.

Implicit Coercions in Type Systems

Gilles Barthe

CWI, PO Box 94079, 1090 GB Amsterdam, The Netherlands.
Email:gilles@cwi.nl

Abstract. *We propose a notion of pure type system with implicit coercions. In our framework, judgements are extended with a context of coercions Δ and the application rule is modified so as to allow coercions to be left implicit. The setting supports multiple inheritance and can be applied to all type theories with Π-types. One originality of our work is to propose a computational interpretation for implicit coercions. In this paper, we demonstrate how this interpretation allows a strict control on the logical properties of pure type systems with implicit coecions.*

1 Introduction

The increasing importance of mathematical software has been accompanied by a drift of mainstream mathematics towards mathematical logic and the foundations of mathematics. Before mathematical software, formal systems were generally seen both by logicians and mathematicians as safe heavens into which mathematics could theoretically be embedded. With powerful mathematical software, there is now a genuine interest in developing mathematics within a formal system (see e.g. [7, 13]). This radical change in the relationship between mathematics and mathematical logic calls for a new strategy in the design of formal systems. New criteria such as comfort, efficiency and suitability to implementation, have to be taken into account when assessing the value of formal systems. The new challenge is to provide formal systems for *feasible formal mathematics*. Despite an early proposal by N.G. de Bruijn ([8]), much remains to be done in this direction. There are still notable differences between formal and informal mathematics:

- *at the level of reasoning:* the level of detail required in formal proofs is much greater than the level of detail in informal proofs; reasoning in a formal system requires every single step to be decomposed in terms of primitive rules.
- *at the level of language:* formal mathematics requires extreme rigour in the formulation of statements. Commonly used mathematical expressions, such as $x \in G$, where G is a group, are not always well-formed in a formal language because it is often required that the expression on the right hand side of $\in$ should be a set. Hereafter we shall refer to this problem as implicit syntax.

While the first problem has been partially solved by a variety of tools (tactics, inductionless induction, partial reflection and decision procedures), the problem of implicit syntax has received little attention in the context of proof-checking[1].

The goal of this paper is to contribute to the study of implicit syntax in proof-checking. In this paper, we focus on one specific aspect of implicit syntax, namely *implicit coercions*; by implicit coercions, we refer to a grammatical convention which allows to apply a map $f : A \rightarrow B$ to an element a of A' whenever there is a coercion from A' to A. We propose a notion of pure type system with implicit coercions (PTSC for short) whose judgements are of the form $\Delta|\Gamma \vdash M : A$ where Δ is a set of legal terms. Elements of Δ, which are called *coercions*, specify which are the arguments that can be omitted in an expression. A typical derivation is

$$\frac{i : \mathbb{N} \rightarrow \mathbb{Z}| \vdash 3 : \mathbb{N} \quad i : \mathbb{N} \rightarrow \mathbb{Z}| \vdash \mathsf{minus} : \mathbb{Z} \rightarrow \mathbb{Z}}{i : \mathbb{N} \rightarrow \mathbb{Z}| \vdash \mathsf{minus}\ 3 : \mathbb{Z}}$$

The derivation is valid because $i : \mathbb{N} \rightarrow \mathbb{Z}$ is assumed as an implicit coercion (of course, there are suitable rules to introduce coercions in a context). One of the novelties of our approach is to give a computational interpretation of implicit coercions. We define a (conditional) reduction relation $\rightarrow_\epsilon$ which makes coercions explicit. There are several advantages in having such a relation:

1. the equational theory of the type system is rich enough to identify terms which should be identified (such as minus 3 and minus $(i\ 3)$);
2. expliciting a term is viewed as a computational process interacting with β-reduction;
3. by identifying suitable terms, $\rightarrow_\epsilon$ forces pure type systems with implicit coercions to be conservative extensions of pure type systems.

We shall show that under certain conditions $\rightarrow_\epsilon$ is normalising (i.e. the use of implicit coercions can be removed from any derivation) and confluent (i.e. there is essentially an unique way of making a term explicit). The relevance of these properties will be discussed in Section 3.2.

Related work The use of implicit coercions or subtyping in proof-checking has been considered by several authors (see [1, 3, 4] for the former and [2, 5, 14, 15] for the latter). In [4], the author reports on a medium-scale example of formalisation of mathematics using implicit coercions. See also [10, 16] for work on overloading and implicit syntax respectively.

Contents of the paper The paper is organised as follows: in the next section, we give an informal motivation of the syntax of pure type systems with implicit coercions by giving an abstract definition of implicit syntax. In section 3, we present the syntax for pure type systems with implicit coercions. In order to look at interesting examples, we consider pure type systems with Σ-types. In section 4, we exemplify the use of our syntax in the formalisation of algebra. In section 5, we study the basic meta-theory of implicit coercions and show that

[1] Some of the concepts involved in implicit syntax such as overloading and argument synthesis have been thoroughly investigated in the context of programming languages ([9, 18, 19]).

pure type systems with implicit coercions provide an implicit syntax for pure type systems. Possible extensions to our work are discussed in section 6. Section 7 contains some final remarks.

Acknowledgements I would especially like to thank P. Aczel for many discussions on classes and on the formalisation of mathematics. The paper has also benefited from comments from A. Bailey, A. Saibi and the anonymous referees. This work was partially carried out at the Universities of Manchester and Nijmegen with the financial support of the Esprit project 'Types: Types for programs and proofs'.

2 What is implicit syntax?

In this section, we give an abstract definition of the concept of implicit syntax. There are two fundamental assumptions about implicit syntax:

1. it is meant to improve (not to increase) the expressivity of a formal system;
2. it should not affect the theory of the formal system.

To fix ideas, we shall make the ideas precise in the abstract setting of formal systems.

Definition 1 *A formal system as a triple* $(A, =_A, \mathsf{Thm})$ *where* A *is a set of expressions,* $=_A$ *is an equality relation on* A *and* Thm *is a binary relation on* A.

For example, every pseudo-context Γ of a pure type system λS determines a formal system $\mathsf{F}_{\lambda S}(\Gamma)$ by taking A to be the set of Γ-terms, $=_A$ to be β-equality and Thm_A to be the typing relation :.

Definition 2 *An implicit syntax for a formal system* $\mathbb{A} = (A, =_A, \mathsf{Thm}_A)$ *consists of a formal system* $\mathbb{B} = (B, =_B, \mathsf{Thm}_B)$ *and a map* $e : B \to A$ *such that:*

1. $A \subseteq B$;
2. *for every* $b \in B$, $b =_B e(b)$;
3. *for every* $a_1, a_2 \in A$, $a_1 =_A a_2 \quad \Leftrightarrow \quad a_1 =_B a_2$;
4. *for every* $a_1, a_2 \in A$, $(a_1, a_2) \in \mathsf{Thm}_A \quad \Leftrightarrow \quad (a_1, a_2) \in \mathsf{Thm}_B$;
5. *for every* $b_1, b_2 \in B$, $(b_1, b_2) \in \mathsf{Thm}_B \quad \Leftrightarrow \quad (e(b_1), e(b_2)) \in \mathsf{Thm}_A$.

The definition is meant to capture idea is that B should contain more terms than A (requirement 1) and that every term in B could be translated into a term in A with the same meaning (requirement 2). Moreover, $=_B$ (resp. Thm_B) should coincide with $=_A$ (resp. Thm_A) on A (requirements 3 and 4) and e should preserve the logical structure of the formal system (requirement 5).

The emphasis of this paper will be on showing that PTSCs are an implicit syntax for PTSs (this will be stated precisely in Section 9). We believe this perspective to be fundamental for proof-checking as it provides a means to ensure that PTSCs have a suitable logical interpretation.

3 Pure type systems with implicit coercions

In this section, we define a deductive system for pure type systems with implicit coercions. In order to treat interesting examples, we consider an extension of pure type systems with Σ-types. However, our approach is independent from type constructors (we only need a function space former) and does not require the presence of Σ-types.

3.1 Syntax

Definition 3 *1. A pure type system is specified by a quadruple*

$$\lambda S = (\mathsf{Sort}, \mathsf{Axiom}, \mathsf{Rule}_\Pi, \mathsf{Rule}_\Sigma)$$

where Sort *is a set,* Axiom $\subseteq$ Sort $\times$ Sort *and* $\mathsf{Rule}_\Pi, \mathsf{Rule}_\Sigma \subseteq$ Sort $\times$ Sort $\times$ Sort.

2. The set of pseudo-terms *of a pure type system* $\lambda S = (\mathsf{Sort}, \mathsf{Axiom}, \mathsf{Rule}_\Pi, \mathsf{Rule}_\Sigma)$ *is given by the following abstract syntax:*

$$T = V|\mathsf{Sort}|\Pi V : T.T|\lambda V : T.T|TT|\Sigma V : T.T|\mathsf{pair}(T,T)|\mathsf{fst}\ T|\mathsf{snd}\ T$$

where V is a fixed set of variables.

3. A pseudo-coercion *is a pair of the form $(\lambda y : B.t, B \to C)$ where $\lambda y : B.t$ and $B \to C$ are pseudo-terms. Sets of pseudo-coercions are usually denoted by Δ.*

4. The closure *Δ^+ of a set Δ of pseudo-coercions: it is the least set such that*

$$\lambda x : A_1.c_n(c_{n-1}(\ldots(c_1 x)\ldots)) : A_1 \to B_n \quad \in \Delta^+$$

whenever $(c_i : A_i \to B_i) \in \Delta$ for $i = 1, \ldots, n$ and $A_{i+1} =_\beta B_i$ for $i = 1, \ldots, n-1$.

5. Let Δ be a set of pseudo-coercions. The relation $\to_{\epsilon(\Delta)}$ is defined on pseudo-terms as the compatible closure of $t\ u \to_{\epsilon(\Delta)} t\ (i\ u)$, where it is assumed that $i \in \Delta^+$. $\twoheadrightarrow_{\epsilon(\Delta)}$ (resp. $=_{\epsilon(\Delta)}$) is defined as the reflexive, transitive (resp. reflexive, symmetric and transitive) closure of $\to_{\epsilon(\Delta)}$.

6. A pseudo-context *is a sequence of the form*

$$\lambda y : B_1.t_1 : B_1 \to C_1, \ldots, \lambda y : B_m.t_m : B_m \to C_m | x_1 : A_1, \ldots, x_n : A_n$$

where the $\lambda y : B_i.t_i : B_i \to C_i$'s are pseudo-coercions, the x_i's are variables and the A_i's are pseudo-terms. Pseudo-contexts are usually written as $\Delta|\Gamma$.

7. A judgement *is a triple of the form $(\Delta|\Gamma, M, A)$ where $\Delta|\Gamma$ is a pseudo-context and M, A are pseudo-terms.*

8. The derivability relation $\vdash$ is defined by the rules of Table 1.

Few explanations seem in order to justify our syntax: all the rules except (Entry), (Method) and the conversion rules are straightforward adaptations of the rules for pure type systems. The (Method) rule introduces implicit syntax in the system by allowing to apply $f : \Pi x : A.B$ to elements of several types (in

(Axiom)	$\mid \vdash c : s$	if $(c, s) \in$ Axiom
(Start)	$\dfrac{\Delta \mid \Gamma \vdash A : s}{\Delta \mid \Gamma, x : A \vdash x : A}$	if $x \notin \Gamma$
(Weakening)	$\dfrac{\Delta \mid \Gamma \vdash t : A \quad \Delta \mid \Gamma \vdash B : s}{\Delta \mid \Gamma, x : B \vdash t : A}$	if $x \notin \Gamma$
(Product)	$\dfrac{\Delta \mid \Gamma \vdash A : s_1 \quad \Delta \mid \Gamma, x : A \vdash B : s_2}{\Delta \mid \Gamma \vdash \Pi x : A.B : s_3}$	if $(s_1, s_2, s_3) \in \mathsf{Rule}_\Pi$
(Application)	$\dfrac{\Delta \mid \Gamma \vdash t : \Pi x : A.B \quad \Delta \mid \Gamma \vdash u : A}{\Delta \mid \Gamma \vdash tu : B[u/x]}$	
(Abstraction)	$\dfrac{\Delta \mid \Gamma, x : A \vdash t : B \quad \Delta \mid \Gamma \vdash \Pi x : A.B : s}{\Delta \mid \Gamma \vdash \lambda x : A.t : \Pi x : A.B}$	
(Sum)	$\dfrac{\Delta \mid \Gamma \vdash A : s_1 \quad \Delta \mid \Gamma, x : A \vdash B : s_2}{\Delta \mid \Gamma \vdash \Sigma x : A.B : s_3}$	if $(s_1, s_2, s_3) \in \mathsf{Rule}_\Sigma$
(Pairing)	$\dfrac{\begin{array}{c}\Delta \mid \Gamma \vdash t_1 : A \quad \Delta \mid \Gamma \vdash t_2 : B[t_1/x] \\ \Delta \mid \Gamma \vdash \Sigma x : A.B : s\end{array}}{\Delta \mid \Gamma \vdash \mathsf{pair}(t_1, t_2) : \Sigma x : A.B}$	
(First Projection)	$\dfrac{\Delta \mid \Gamma \vdash t : \Sigma x : A.B}{\Delta \mid \Gamma \vdash \mathsf{fst}\ t : A}$	
(Second Projection)	$\dfrac{\Delta \mid \Gamma \vdash t : \Sigma x : A.B}{\Delta \mid \Gamma \vdash \mathsf{snd}\ t : B[\mathsf{fst}\ t/x]}$	
(Entry)	$\dfrac{\Delta \mid \Gamma \vdash c : C \quad \Delta' \mid \Gamma' \vdash t : A \to B}{\Delta, t : A \to B \mid \Gamma \vdash c : C}$	PROVISO
(Method)	$\dfrac{\Delta \mid \Gamma \vdash t : \Pi x : A.B \quad \Delta \mid \Gamma \vdash u : A'}{\Delta \mid \Gamma \vdash tu : B[i\ u/x]}$	if $(i, A'' \to A_0) \in \Delta^+$ with $A =_\beta A''$
(β-conversion)	$\dfrac{\Delta \mid \Gamma \vdash c : C \quad \mid \Gamma' \vdash C : s \quad \mid \Gamma' \vdash C' : s}{\Delta \mid \Gamma \vdash c : C'}$	if $C =_\beta C'$ and $\Gamma \to_{\epsilon(\Delta)} \Gamma'$
(ϵ-conversion)	$\dfrac{\Delta \mid \Gamma \vdash c : C \quad \Delta \mid \Gamma \vdash C' : s}{\Delta \mid \Gamma \vdash c : C'}$	if $C \downarrow_{\epsilon(\Delta)} C'$

Table 1. RULES FOR DERIVATIONS IN PURE TYPE SYSTEMS WITH IMPLICIT COERCIONS

fact to all the types which are linked to A by a pseudo-coercion). Note that the predicate of the conclusion is $B[i\ u/x]$ rather than $B[u/x]$ because we do not know if the latter is legal. The (Entry) rule enables new coercions to be introduced provided a certain PROVISO is satisfied. The role of the PROVISO is discussed in Subsection 3.2. As for the conversion rules, there are two rules: one for β-conversion and one for ϵ-conversion. The choice for these rules is given in Subsection 3.3.

3.2 The coherence and conservativity properties

In Section 2, we made two fundamental assumptions for implicit syntax and formalised these assumptions in Definition 2. Here we see how to instantiate the definition to the framework of pure type systems with implicit coercions.

In our context, the translation map from implicit to explicit syntax has an obvious candidate namely ϵ-reduction. We would like that for every legal contexts

$\Delta|\Gamma$ and $|\Gamma'$ such that $\Gamma \twoheadrightarrow_{\epsilon(\Delta)} \Gamma'$, the set of legal $\Delta|\Gamma$-terms (with $\beta\epsilon(\Delta)$-equality) is an implicit syntax for the set of legal Γ'-terms (with β-equality). This is a consequence of the following two properties:

1. for every derivation $\Delta|\Gamma \vdash M : A$, there exists a derivation $|\Gamma' \vdash M' : A'$ with $\Gamma \twoheadrightarrow_{\epsilon(\Delta)} \Gamma'$, $M \twoheadrightarrow_{\epsilon(\Delta)} M'$ and $A \twoheadrightarrow_{\epsilon(\Delta)} A'$;
2. for every derivations $\Delta|\Gamma \vdash M : A$, $|\Gamma' \vdash M' : A'$ and $|\Gamma'' \vdash M'' : A''$ such that $\Gamma \twoheadrightarrow_{\epsilon(\Delta)} \Gamma', \Gamma''$, $M \twoheadrightarrow_{\epsilon(\Delta)} M', M''$ and $A \twoheadrightarrow_{\epsilon(\Delta)} A', A''$ one has $\Gamma' =_\beta \Gamma''$, $M' =_\beta M''$ and $A' =_\beta A''$.

We respectively call them the *conservativity* property and the *coherence* property. The role of the proviso is to ensure that both properties hold. In order to simplify the problem, we require coercions to be closed.

Definition 4 - *A pseudo-coercion* $\lambda x : A.t : A \to B$ *is* simple *if* $\lambda x : A.t$ *and* $A \to B$ *are closed.*
- *A set* Δ *of pseudo-coercions is* coherent *if all coercions are simple and*
  1. $\forall(\lambda x : A.i, A \to B), (\lambda x' : A'.i', A' \to B') \in \Delta^+.$
  $$A =_\beta A' \quad \wedge \quad B =_\beta B' \quad \Rightarrow i\,[x'/x] =_\beta j$$
  2. $\forall(\lambda x : A.i, A \to B) \in \Delta^+. \quad A =_\beta B \quad \Rightarrow \quad i =_\beta x$

The entry rule is now formulated as

$$\frac{\Delta|\Gamma \vdash c : C \qquad |\vdash t : A \to B}{\Delta, t : A \to B|\Gamma \vdash c : C} \text{ if } \Delta \cup \{t, A \to B\} \text{ is coherent.}$$

Note that for the sake of simplicity we require coercions to be fully explicit, i.e. to be derivable in the empty context.

3.3 The conversion rule

The conversion rule is split in two (see Table 1). There is a β-conversion rule which allows to convert fully explicit types (i.e. types which are derivable in a context with no pseudo-coercions) and an ϵ-conversion rule which allows to convert types which are related by ϵ-reduction. There are two reasons for such a choice:

- it seems natural to postpone computations until the term is fully explicit. With this view, reduction is a succession of two processes, *explicitation* (i.e. ϵ-reduction) and *computation* (i.e. β-reduction).
- it is unclear what may be the effects of a very general conversion rule, such as

$$\frac{\Delta|\Gamma \vdash c : C \;\; \Delta|\Gamma \vdash C' : s}{\Delta|\Gamma \vdash c : C'} \text{ if } C =_{\beta\epsilon(\Delta)} C'$$

4 Implicit coercions at work

In this section, we exemplify the use of implicit coercions in the formalisation of mathematics.

4.1 Formalising algebra with implicit coercions

The Calculus of Constructions with strong sums $CC\Sigma$ has two sorts, $*$ and $\Box$, related by the axiom $* : \Box$. The rules for products are $(*,*)$, $(\Box,*)$, $(*,\Box)$, $(\Box,\Box)$. The rules for sums are $(*,*,*)$ and $(\Box,*,\Box)$. The system is Church-Rosser, strongly normalising, consistent and has decidable type-checking. In $CC\Sigma$, it is possible to define several basic algebraic types, such as sets, groupoids, monoids... We give some of these definitions here. For the sake of simplicity, we take $Set = *$.

$$
\begin{aligned}
Gpd &= \Sigma T : Set.\Sigma o : T \to T \to T.\mathsf{AxGpd}\ o \\
AbGpd &= \Sigma T : Set.\Sigma o : T \to T \to T.(\mathsf{AxGpd}\ o) \wedge (\mathsf{Comm}\ o) \\
Mon &= \Sigma T : Set.\Sigma o : T \to T \to T.\Sigma e : T.\mathsf{AxMon}\ o\ e \\
AbMon &= \Sigma T : Set.\Sigma o : T \to T \to T.\Sigma e : T.(\mathsf{AxMon}\ o\ e) \wedge (\mathsf{Comm}\ o) \\
Grp &= \Sigma T : Set.\Sigma o : T \to T \to T.\Sigma e : T.\Sigma i : T \to T.\mathsf{AxGrp}\ o\ e\ i \\
AbGrp &= \Sigma T : Set.\Sigma o : T \to T \to T.\Sigma e : T.\Sigma i : T \to T.(\mathsf{AxGrp}\ o\ e\ i) \wedge (\mathsf{Comm}\ o)
\end{aligned}
$$

where Comm o is the proposition stating that o is commutative and AxGpd, AxMon and AxGrp respectively state the axioms of groupoids, monoids and groups. The canonical maps between these types, as shown in figure 1, yield a coherent set Δ of coercions. The context of coercions Δ can be used to formalise algebra.

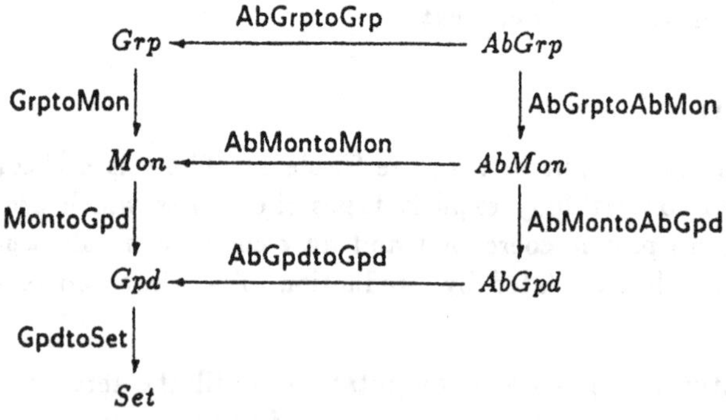

Fig. 1. Basic coercions for algebra

For example, we can apply comp $\equiv \lambda G : Gpd.\mathsf{fst}\ (\mathsf{snd}\ G)$ to monoids, groups... If moreover we define Op2 as $\lambda T : Set.T \to T \to T$ then comp G is of type Op2 G whenever $G : Monoid$, $G : Group$...

4.2 Typical features of implicit coercions

They include:

- *uniformity:* we do not have any restriction on the domain and codomain of a coercion. This enables us to treat in an identical manner canonical coercions of a different nature, such as the one from naturals to integers or the one from groups to sets;
- *multiple inheritance:* there can be several coercions maps with the same domain and there might be more than one path between two types. For example, one can have four coercion maps $f : A \rightarrow B$, $g : B \rightarrow C$, $h : A \rightarrow B'$ and $i : B' \rightarrow C$ provided $g \circ f$ and $i \circ h$ are extensionally equal.
- *top-down introduction of coercions:* it is possible to introduce a coercion $f : A \rightarrow B$ and then a coercion $g : B \rightarrow C$. In fact, coercions can be introduced in any order. This solves the problem of "super-type" which occurs when coercions are required to be built up in a tree-like manner. In our syntax, there is no problem in defining the natural, then the integers and declaring a coercion from natural to integers, then build the rationals and declare a coercion from integers to rationals...
- *splitting a coercion:* it is possible to "split" a coercion $f : A \rightarrow B$ into two coercions $g : A \rightarrow C$ and $h : C \rightarrow B$ provided f and $h \circ g$ are extensionally equal. This allows to postpone the introduction of new notions until they are needed. For example, one does not need to introduce the notion of monoid before the notion of group in order to split the coercion from groups to groupoids into a coercion from groups to monoids and from monoids to groupoids;
- *back and forth coercions:* it is possible to have two coercions $f : A \rightarrow B$ and $g : B \rightarrow A$ provided the maps are mutually inverse. Back and forth coercions allow for equivalent representations of a same mathematical object to be used without any major bureaucratic difficulty. This is very convenient for re-usability as experience shows that different users chose different but equivalent representations of a same mathematical object. However, the absence of η-conversion limits significantly the usefulness of back and forth coercions, as seen in the next subsection.

4.3 Limitations of implicit coercions

Our syntax for implicit coercions suffers from some limitations and should be considered as a preliminary step towards a theory of implicit syntax. We try to discuss some of these limitations briefly.

Re-usability The definition of the closure of a set of coercions does not allow for an immediate re-use of methods as can be seen in the following example. Assume we have a two types ColourPoint and Point with an implicit coercion i : ColourPoint $\rightarrow$ Point. If we have a map move : Nat $\times$ Point $\rightarrow$ Point and c : ColourPoint, then we will not have movepair(n, c) : Point for every natural number n. This choice has been made deliberately for the simplicity of the syntax. Besides, we can always define another implicit coercion from Nat $\times$ ColourPoint to Nat $\times$ Point.

Efficient proof-checking The conversion rules are rather inefficient for proof-checking because they require computations to be postponed until terms are fully explicit. We conjecture it can be solved by considering a more general form of conversion. In fact, the essential property to prove the coherence and conservativity properties is that for every application of conversion

$$\frac{\Delta|\Gamma \vdash c : C \quad \Delta|\Gamma \vdash C' : s}{\Delta|\Gamma \vdash c : C'}$$

and derivations $|\Gamma_1 \vdash C_1 : s_1$ and $|\Gamma_1' \vdash C_1' : s_1'$ with $\Gamma \twoheadrightarrow_{\epsilon(\Delta)} \Gamma_1, \Gamma_1'$ and $C \twoheadrightarrow_{\epsilon(\Delta)} C_1, C_1'$, one has $C_1 =_\beta C_1'$.

The coherence requirement The definition of coherent set of pseudo-coercions requires equality up to β-conversion. In practice, natural sets of pseudo-coercions do not respect equality up to β-conversion. For example, the swapping maps $\mathsf{swap}_1 : (A \times B) \rightarrow (B \times A)$ and $\mathsf{swap}_2 : (B \times A) \rightarrow (A \times B)$ where A and B are closed types do not form a coherent set of coercions. However, this fact is closely related to the choice of β-equality as the primitive notion of equality for pure type systems. In our view, it is a problem of pure type systems not of implicit coercions.

Polymorphic and general coercions The restriction to simple coercions is a serious one. In practice, one might want to consider polymorphic coercions (of closed type $\Pi \mathbf{x} : \mathbf{A}.B \rightarrow C$) or even general coercions (of possibly open type $\Pi \mathbf{x} : \mathbf{A}.B$. For example, one might want to define the coercion collapse : $\Pi T : \mathsf{Type}.List\ T \rightarrow Multiset\ T$ which transforms a list of elements of an arbitrary set into a multi-set by forgetting the ordering.

Unfortunately, the formulation of the proviso for polymorphic coercions becomes quite intrinsic and is left as a subject for future work.

5 The coherence and conservativity properties

In this section, we prove that implicit coercions have the coherence and conservativity properties. Before we establish some preliminary results.

5.1 The rule $(Entry - A)$

The set of derivable judgements remains unchanged if one considers the restricted entry rule $(Entry - A)$

$$\frac{\Delta| \vdash c : s \mid \vdash t : A \rightarrow B}{\Delta, t : A \rightarrow B| \vdash c : s} \quad \text{if } (c, s) \in \mathsf{Axiom} \text{ and } \Delta \cup \{t, A \rightarrow B\} \text{ is coherent}$$

The set of derivable judgements remains unchanged if we replace $(Entry)$ by $(Entry - A)$. The proof proceeds by induction on the derivations and uses induction loading: we prove that if $\Delta|\Gamma \vdash M : A$ is derivable and $\Delta' \supseteq \Delta$ is coherent, then $\Delta'|\Gamma \vdash M : A$ in the system with $(Entry - A)$.

5.2 Normal forms

We introduce the notion of $\epsilon(\Delta)$-normal form. Because of possible loops in the graph of coercions, we are forced to consider a slightly weaker notion than usual. We start with some preliminary results.

Definition 5 *$M \twoheadrightarrow_{\epsilon(\Delta|\Gamma)} N$ if there exists A such that $\Delta|\Gamma \vdash M, N : A$ and $M \twoheadrightarrow_{\epsilon(\Delta)} N$.*

The following fact is easy to establish but nevertheless important.

Lemma 6 *If $\Delta|\Gamma \vdash M : A$ and $\Delta|\Gamma \vdash N : B$ with $M \twoheadrightarrow_{\epsilon(\Delta)} N$, then $\Delta|\Gamma \vdash N : A$.*

The above lemma gives an alternative definition of $\twoheadrightarrow_{\epsilon(\Delta|\Gamma)}$.

Definition 7 *A term M is in $\epsilon(\Delta|\Gamma)$-normal form if*

- *there exists A such that $\Delta|\Gamma \vdash M : A$;*
- *if $M \twoheadrightarrow_{\epsilon(\Delta|\Gamma)} P$, then there exists N such that $P \twoheadrightarrow_{\epsilon(\Delta|\Gamma)} N$ and $N \twoheadrightarrow_{\beta} M$.*

We will show that a term is in $\epsilon(\Delta|\Gamma)$-normal form if it is typable in a context without coercions. As usual, we say M has $\epsilon(\Delta|\Gamma)$-normal form N if N is in $\epsilon(\Delta|\Gamma)$-normal form, $\Delta|\Gamma \vdash M : A$ and $M \twoheadrightarrow_{\epsilon(\Delta|\Gamma)} N$. The notion of normal form and reduction on contexts is defined recursively. We write, somewhat loosely, $\Gamma, x : A \twoheadrightarrow_{\epsilon(\Delta)} \Gamma', x : A'$ if $\Gamma \twoheadrightarrow_{\epsilon(\Delta)} \Gamma'$ and $A \twoheadrightarrow_{\epsilon(\Delta|\Gamma)} A'$.

5.3 Coherence

We show that that the coherence property holds.

Proposition 8 (Coherence) *Let $\Delta|\Gamma \vdash M : A$ be a derivable judgement. Let M_1, M_2 be $\epsilon(\Delta|\Gamma)$-normal forms for M. Then $M_1 =_\beta M_2$.*

Proof: the proposition is proved by induction on the structure of the terms. The only interesting case is when $M = M_1 M_2$. By induction hypothesis, M_1 and M_2 have at most one $\epsilon(\Delta|\Gamma)$-normal form up to convertibility. Assume M has two $\epsilon(\Delta|\Gamma)$-normal forms N and P. We show they are β-convertible. First, note that there exist coercions $i_1, \ldots, i_n, j_1, \ldots, j_m$ such that $N = N_1\ (i_1\ (\ldots\ (i_n\ N_2)\ldots))$ and $P = P_1\ (j_1\ (\ldots\ (j_p\ P_2)\ldots))$, where N_k and P_k are $\epsilon(\Delta|\Gamma)$-normal forms of M_k $(k = 1, 2)$. By generation lemma, $\Delta|\Gamma \vdash N_1', P_1' : \Pi x : A.B$ and $\Delta|\Gamma \vdash N_2', P_2' : A'$ with A' linked to A. Again by generation, $\Delta|x : A' \vdash i_1\ (\ldots\ (i_n\ x)\ldots) : A' \to A$ and $\Delta|x : A' \vdash j_1\ (\ldots\ (j_p\ x)\ldots) : A' \to A$. Both terms have a $\epsilon(\Delta, x : A')$-normal form, say I and J respectively, with $\Delta|x : A' \vdash I, J : A' \to A$. By coherence, we know $I =_\beta J$. Hence $I[N_2'/x] =_\beta J[P_2'/x]$ and $N_1'\ (I[N_2'/x]) =_\beta P_1'\ (J[P_2'/x])$.

5.4 Conservativity

To prove conservativity, we use induction loading.

Proposition 9 (Conservativity) *Assume $\Delta|\Gamma \vdash M : A$ is a derivable judgement. Then*

- *Γ, M and A have an $\epsilon(\Delta|\Gamma)$-normal form;*
- *for every $\epsilon(\Delta|\Gamma)$-normal forms Γ', M' and A' of Γ, M and A, the judgement $|\Gamma' \vdash M' : A'$ is derivable.*

The result is proved by induction on the derivations.

5.5 Decidability of type-checking

Definition 10 - *Let Δ be a set of pseudo-coercions. A pure type system has* decidable type-checking *for Δ if for every context $\Delta|\Gamma$ and pair of pseudo-terms (M, A), it is decidable if $\Delta|\Gamma \vdash M : A$ is derivable.*
- *A pure type system has decidable type-checking if it has decidable type-checking for all sets of pseudo-coercions.*
- *A pure type system has decidable type-checking for the standard syntax (STC) if it has decidable type-checking for the empty set of pseudo-coercions.*

The latter property is named so because derivation in the context without coercions correspond exactly to derivations in the standard syntax.

Lemma 11 *Assume $\Delta|\Gamma \vdash M : A$, $\Gamma' \twoheadrightarrow_{\epsilon(\Delta)} \Gamma$, $M' \twoheadrightarrow_{\epsilon(\Delta)} M$ and $A' \twoheadrightarrow_{\epsilon(\Delta)} A$. Then $\Delta|\Gamma' \vdash N' : A'$.*

We can advocate Proposition 9 and Lemma 11 to prove decidability of type-checking.

Proposition 12 *$\Delta|\Gamma \vdash M : A$ is derivable iff Δ is a coherent set of coercions and there exist Γ', M' and A' such that $|\Gamma' \vdash M' : A'$ is derivable, $\Gamma \twoheadrightarrow_{\epsilon(\Delta)} \Gamma'$, $M \twoheadrightarrow_{\epsilon(\Delta)} M'$ and $A \twoheadrightarrow_{\epsilon(\Delta)} A'$.*

One strategy to check whether $\Delta|\Gamma \vdash M : A$ is derivable is therefore to compute all possible legal $\epsilon(\Delta)$ reductions of Γ, M and A. This is achieved by defining for every term M its set $\mathsf{Exp}_{\Delta}(M)$ of possible explicitations of M relative to a set of pseudo-coercions Δ. In the sequel, we let $\Delta^{\bullet}$ be the smallest subset of Δ^{+} containing:

- all the pseudo-coercions $c : A \rightarrow B$ of Δ such that $A \neq_{\beta} B$;
- all the pseudo-coercions $\lambda x : A_1.c_n(c_{n-1}(\ldots(c_1 x)\ldots)) : A_1 \rightarrow B_n$ where for $i = 1, \ldots, n$, $c_i : A_i \rightarrow B_i$ are pseudo-coercions in Δ and
  - $A_{i+1} =_{\beta} B_i$ for $i = 1, \ldots, n-1$,
  - $A_i \neq_{\beta} B_j$ for $i \leq j$.

In other words, $\Delta^\bullet$ is the set of pseudo-coercions which do not contain any loop. $\mathsf{Exp}_\Delta(M)$ is defined inductively on the structure of the terms:

$$\begin{aligned}
\mathsf{Exp}_\Delta(x) &= \{x\} \\
\mathsf{Exp}_\Delta(s) &= \{s\} \\
\mathsf{Exp}_\Delta(\Pi x : A.B) &= \{\Pi x : A'.B' \mid A' \in \mathsf{Exp}(A) \ \wedge \ B' \in \mathsf{Exp}_\Delta(B)\} \\
\mathsf{Exp}_\Delta(\Sigma x : A.B) &= \{\Sigma x : A'.B' \mid A' \in \mathsf{Exp}(A) \ \wedge \ B' \in \mathsf{Exp}_\Delta(B)\} \\
\mathsf{Exp}_\Delta(\lambda x : A.b) &= \{\lambda x : A'.b' \mid A' \in \mathsf{Exp}(A) \ \wedge \ b' \in \mathsf{Exp}_\Delta(b)\} \\
\mathsf{Exp}_\Delta(M\ N) &= \{M'(i\ N') \mid M' \in \mathsf{Exp}_\Delta(M),\ N' \in \mathsf{Exp}_\Delta(N) \text{ and } (i, A \to B) \in \Delta^\bullet\} \\
\mathsf{Exp}_\Delta(\langle a, b\rangle) &= \{\langle a', b'\rangle \mid a' \in \mathsf{Exp}(a) \ \wedge \ b' \in \mathsf{Exp}_\Delta(b)\} \\
\mathsf{Exp}_\Delta(\mathsf{fst}\ M) &= \{\mathsf{fst}\ M' \mid M' \in \mathsf{Exp}_\Delta(M)\} \\
\mathsf{Exp}_\Delta(\mathsf{snd}\ M) &= \{\mathsf{snd}\ M' \mid M' \in \mathsf{Exp}_\Delta(M)\}
\end{aligned}$$

where it is assumed that x is a variable and s is a sort. Note that $\mathsf{Exp}_\Delta(M)$ is finite and contains all the possible legal reducts of M.

Lemma 13 *$\Delta|\Gamma \vdash M : A$ is derivable iff Δ is a coherent set of coercions and $|\Gamma' \vdash M' : A'$ is derivable for some $\Gamma' \in \mathsf{Exp}_\Delta(\Gamma)$, $M' \in \mathsf{Exp}(M)$ and $A' \in \mathsf{Exp}_\Delta(A)$.*

We have a procedure to check whether a judgement with implicit coercions is derivable in provided that:

- STC holds;
- it is decidable whether a set Δ of coercions is coherent;
- the closure $\Delta^\bullet$ of a coherent set of coercions Δ can be computed effectively.

Note that the last two requirements are automatically fulfilled when the domains and codomains of the coercions are normalising.

Definition 14 *A pure type system with implicit coercions is standard strongly normalising (SSN) if for every derivable judgement $|\Gamma \vdash M : A$, the term M is strongly normalising w.r.t. $\to_\beta$.*

We have:

Theorem 15 *A pure type system with implicit coercions has decidable type-checking (and type-synthesis) if it has STC and SSN.*

In [17], L.S. van Benthem Jutting has proved that type-checking and type-synthesis are decidable for a normalising pure type system with finitely many sorts. It follows:

Corollary 16 *The systems of the λ-cube with implicit coercions have decidable type-checking and type-synthesis.*

6 Possible extensions and related work

In this section, we put our work into a more general perspective by looking at some related work. We also discuss the possibility of using implicit coercions to define subtyping.

6.1 Implicit coercions with principal typing

P. Aczel and A. Bailey have recently suggested an alternative approach to implicit coercions. Their approach is based on type systems with type-casting and principal types such as the type system of Lego. Principal types are crucially used in the method rule: if $i : A' \rightarrow A$ is a coercion, $f : A \rightarrow B$ and $a :: A'$ (where :: denotes principal typing), then $f\ a : B$. If $a : A$ but not $a :: A'$, then $f\ a$ will not be legal. However, one will be able to type-cast a and apply it to f. In other words, $f\ (a : A) : B$. In our view, their approach is extremely syntactic and does not fully reflect the mathematical intuition behind the use of implicit coercions. However their approach has the considerable advantage to yield a simple and efficient type-checking algorithm.

6.2 Records

G. Betarte and A. Tasistro have recently provided an alternative solution to the problem of implicit syntax based on dependent records ([5, 6]). Roughly speaking, record types correspond to Σ-types and coercions correspond to projections. The specific structure of the coercions has the pleasant effect to simplify the coherence problem and to allow for coercions between records with free variables. Moreover, the problem of conversion seems to disappear. Because of the obvious advantages of their approach, it would be interesting whether their results can be carried over to the framework of pure type systems.

6.3 Classes

The original motivation for our work was to enhance proof-checkers with a notion similar to that of type class as it is used in Gofer ([11, 12]) or Haskell ([10]). Although our work shares many motivations with type classes as developed in these languages, the actual formalisms of type classes and implicit coercions are quite distinct. It makes it difficult to compare formalisms.

6.4 Subtyping

The type system for implicit coercions remains strongly typed in the sense that every term has at most one type (provided the pure type system is functional). One might consider replacing the Method rule with a subsumption rule

$$\frac{\Delta|\Gamma \vdash M : A}{\Delta|\Gamma \vdash M : A'} \text{ if } (t : A \rightarrow A') \in \Delta$$

and redefine $\epsilon(\Delta)$-reduction as the compatible closure of $t \rightarrow_{\epsilon(\Delta)} it$ if $i \in \Delta^+$. In this way, one would obtain type systems with subtyping. It would be interesting to see whether the coherence and conservativity conditions hold for this new syntax.

6.5 Implementation

This work originates from previous work with Peter Aczel on formalising Galois theory in Lego. In absence of a mechanism to handle multiple inheritance, we realised that the syntax was becoming too heavy and the number of identifiers was becoming disproportionate very rapidly. This led us to consider the possibility of implementing implicit coercions in Lego; this was done by September 1993. However, this implementation only supports single inheritance. It would be nice to have an implementation of the syntax proposed in this paper.

7 Conclusion

In this paper, we have presented a modified syntax for pure type systems which allows for a uniform treatment of implicit coercions. The syntax enjoys some important properties and has proved useful in the formalisation of mathematics in Lego ([4]). However, the syntax also suffers from some severe limitations. Future research should concentrate on the possility of overcoming some of these limitations, especially the one to simple coercions.

In the longer term, it seems important to understand the interaction between inheritance, subtyping and argument synthesis in order to be able to bring the flexibility of expression in formal systems close to the one of informal mathematics. Such a program, if completed, would constitute a definite step towards feasible formal mathematics.

References

1. P. Aczel. A notion of class for type theory. Note, 1995.
2. D. Aspinall and A. Compagnoni. Subtyping dependent types. In *Proceedings of LICS'96*. IEEE Computer Society Press, 1996. To appear.
3. A. Bailey. Lego with classes. Note, 1995.
4. G. Barthe. Formalising algebra in type theory: fundamentals and applications to group theory. Manuscript. An earlier version appeared as technical report CSI-R9508, University of Nijmegen, under the title 'Formalising mathematics in type theory: fundamentals and case studies', 1995.
5. G. Betarte and A. Tasistro. Extension of Martin-Löf's theory of types with record types and subtyping: motivation, rules and type checking. Manuscript, 1995.
6. G. Betarte and A. Tasistro. Formalisation of systems of algebras using dependent record types and subtyping: an example. Manuscript, 1995.
7. R.L. Constable, S.F. Allen, H.M. Bromley, W.R. Cleaveland, J.F. Cremer, R.W. Harper, D.J. Howe, T.B. Knoblock, N.P. Mendler, P. Panangaden, J.T. Sasaki, and S.F. Smith. *Implementing Mathematics with the NuPrl Development System*. Prentice-Hall, inc., Englewood Cliffs, New Jersey, first edition, 1986.

8. N.G. de Bruijn. The mathematical vernacular, a language for mathematics with typed sets. In R. Nederpelt, H. Geuvers, and R. de Vrijer, editors, *Selected papers on Automath*, volume 133 of *Studies in Logic and the Foundations of Mathematics*, pages 865–935. North-Holland, Amsterdam, 1994.
9. C.A. Gunter and J.C. Mitchell. *Theoretical Aspects of Object-Oriented Programming: Types, Semantics and Language Design*. The MIT Press, 1994.
10. P. Hudak, S.L. Peyton Jones, P.L. Wadler, Arvind, B. Boutel, J. Fairbairn, J. Fasel, K. Guzman, K. Hammond, J. Hughes, T. Johnsson, R. Kieburtz, R.S. Nikhil, W. Partain, and J. Peterson. Report on the functional programming language Haskell, version 1.2. *Special Issue of SIGPLAN Notices*, 27, 1992.
11. M. Jones. Introduction to Gofer. Included as part of the Gofer distribution. Available by anonymous `ftp` from `nebula.cs.yale.edu` in the directory `pub/haskell/gofer`, 1991.
12. M. Jones. A system of constructor classes: overloading and implicit higher-order polymorphism. *Journal of Functional Programming*, pages 1–25, January 1995.
13. Z. Luo. *Computation and Reasoning: A Type Theory for Computer Science*. Number 11 in International Series of Monographs on Computer Science. Oxford University Press, 1994.
14. Z. Luo. Coercive subtyping. Draft, 1995.
15. F. Pfenning. Refinement types for logical frameworks. In H. Geuvers, editor, *Informal Proceedings of TYPES'93*, pages 285–299, 1993. Available from http://www.dcs.ed.ac.uk/lfcsinfo/research/types-bra/proc/index.html.
16. R. Pollack. Implicit syntax. In G. Huet and G. Plotkin, editors, *Informal Proceedings of First Workshop on Logical Frameworks, Antibes*, May 1990.
17. L. S. van Benthem Jutting. Typing in pure type systems. *Information and Computation*, 105(1):30–41, July 1993.
18. P. Wadler and S. Blott. How to make ad hoc polymorphism less ad hoc. In *Proceedings of POPL'89*, pages 60–76. ACM Press, 1989.
19. A. Wikström. *Functional Progrmmaming using Standard ML*. Interntional Series in Computer Science. Prenctice Hall, 1987.

A Two-Level Approach Towards Lean Proof-Checking

Gilles Barthe*, Mark Ruys and Henk Barendregt

Faculty of Mathematics and Informatics
University of Nijmegen, The Netherlands
email: gilles@cwi.nl,{markr,henk}@cs.kun.nl

Abstract. *We present a simple and effective methodology for equational reasoning in proof checkers. The method is based on a two-level approach distinguishing between syntax and semantics of mathematical theories. The method is very general and can be carried out in any type system with inductive and oracle types. The potential of our two-level approach is illustrated by some examples developed in Lego.*

1 Introduction

The main actions in writing mathematics consist of defining, reasoning and computing (symbolically; this is also called 'equational reasoning'). Whereas defining and reasoning are reasonably well captured by an interactive proof-developer, the formalization of computations has caused problems. This paper studies the possibilities of a partial automation of equational reasoning, which is from the authors' experience, one of the most recurrent source of problems in formalizing mathematics using a proof-developer [5, 25]. We describe several methods using elementary techniques from universal algebra which provides an efficient tool to solve problems of an equational nature in any type theory with inductive types and term-rewriting (inductive types are required for a formalization of universal algebra, in particular for the formalization of the type of terms of a signature).

Our main goal is to solve equational problems of the form $a =_{\mathcal{A}} b$, where $\mathcal{A}$ is a model of a given equational theory $\mathcal{S} = (\Sigma, E)$, a and b are (expressions for) elements of $\mathcal{A}$, and $=_{\mathcal{A}}$ is the equality relation of the carrier of $\mathcal{A}$. To do so, we use two naming principles:

for satisfiability: we recast the problem $a =_{\mathcal{A}} b$ in a syntactic form $[\![\ulcorner a \urcorner]\!]^{\mathcal{A}}_{\alpha} =_{\mathcal{A}} [\![\ulcorner b \urcorner]\!]^{\mathcal{A}}_{\alpha}$ where α is an assignment and $\ulcorner a \urcorner$ and $\ulcorner b \urcorner$ are two Σ-terms such that

$$[\![\ulcorner a \urcorner]\!]^{\mathcal{A}}_{\alpha} = a \quad \text{and} \quad [\![\ulcorner b \urcorner]\!]^{\mathcal{A}}_{\alpha} = b$$

where $[\![\_]\!]^{\mathcal{A}}_{\alpha}$ denotes the α-interpretation of Σ-terms into the model $\mathcal{A}$. (Note that such terms always exist and one can even find optimal terms). By the

* Current address: Department of Software Technology, CWI, Amsterdam, The Netherlands.

soundness theorem, the latter problem follows from $\mathcal{S} \vdash \ulcorner a \urcorner = \ulcorner b \urcorner$ (we use this informal notation to state that $(\ulcorner a \urcorner, \ulcorner b \urcorner)$ is a theorem of $\mathcal{S}$). If $\mathcal{S}$ is equivalent to a canonical term-rewriting system $\mathcal{R}$, then the last problem can be solved automatically by taking the $\mathcal{R}$-normal forms of $\ulcorner a \urcorner$ and $\ulcorner b \urcorner$ and check whether they are equal. We internalize the whole informal process using *oracle types* [7]; the rewrite system is grafted to the type theory in such a way that the conversion rule itself is changed and checking whether $[\ulcorner a \urcorner] = [\ulcorner b \urcorner]$ (the equality here is Leibniz equality) boils down to a reflexivity test, which can be done by the proof checker.

for extensionality: often we need a proof object for statements of the form

$$s =_{\mathcal{A}} t \quad \Rightarrow \quad \phi(s) =_{\mathcal{A}} \phi(t) \tag{1}$$

where s, t and $\phi(x)$ be (expressions for) elements of $\mathcal{A}$. If this is done in the way taught in books on logic (applying several times the axioms of equational logic) a proof object for this fact becomes rather large: quadratic in the size of the expression 'ϕ'. However, using the naming principle one can solve (1) by proving the meta-result

$$s =_{\mathcal{A}} t \quad \Rightarrow \quad [\![\ulcorner \phi \urcorner]\!]^{\mathcal{A}}_{\alpha\,(x:=s)} =_{\mathcal{A}} [\![\ulcorner \phi \urcorner]\!]^{\mathcal{A}}_{\alpha\,(x:=t)}$$

for all $\ulcorner \phi \urcorner$. This result has a proof of fixed size.

In this paper, we shall give a detailed presentation of these methods (and some minor variants) and demonstrate with non-trivial examples that they provide a suitable tool for a partial automation of equational reasoning in proof-checking. The distinctive features of our approach are:

- it applies to type systems where equality is treated axiomatically (intensional frameworks) and with proof-objects; the only requirement is the presence of (first-order) inductive types and so-called oracle types;
- the size of the implementation of the proof-checker is kept fairly small; the whole process can be carried out within the proof-checker;
- the proof-checker is built upon formal systems whose meta-theory is easy to understand.

The paper is organized as follows: in section 2, we introduce the relevant mathematical background for the subsequent parts of the paper. In section 3, we specify the nature of equational reasoning and delimit the range of equational problems whose resolution can be automated. In section 4, we discuss the possible approaches to the automation of equational reasoning and present our own solution in terms of oracle types. In section 5, we present a preliminary implementation of the two-level approach in Lego. Large parts of the paper are of expository nature; they have been included because (i) the material we present has never been presented elsewhere with a view to use it for our specific purpose (ii) the main contribution of this paper is to specify the problem and device a methodology to solve it (but the methodology does not use any new technique).

The two-level approach was grew out from earlier work by P. Aczel and the first author on the formalization of (universal) algebra in type theory. The applications of universal algebra for equational reasoning were realized later by the first author and presented at the HISC meeting in Amsterdam in March 1994 (see [5, 4]). After the completion of this work, H. Elbers and the first author have developed further the two-level approach and provided an automatic procedure to solve equational problems in Lego [6]. The work presented in this paper bears some similarities with the work of the NuPrl team on reflection [11, 16], although the specific use of naming principles to automate equational reasoning seems to be new.

Acknowledgments Thanks to P. Aczel, H. Elbers and H. Geuvers for useful discussions on the two-level approach. Thanks to J. Harrison for his comments on an earlier version of the draft. This work was partially supported by the ESPRIT project 'TYPES: Types for Programs and Proofs'.

2 Mathematical Background

In this section, we review some standard material on equational logic and term-rewriting. During the last few years, there has been an explosion in the number of variants of equational logic: many-sorted, order-sorted, conditional... We shall only be concerned with the simplest formalism, unsorted equational logic. For convenience, we separate the presentation in two parts; the first part is concerned with syntax, equational deduction and term-rewriting. The second part is devoted to semantics. See [10, 18] for a longer introduction to the notions involved.

2.1 Equational Logic and Term-Rewriting

The basic notions of universal algebra are those of signature and equational theory. As the notions are standard, we give them without any further comment.

Definition 1 - *A* signature *is a pair* $\Sigma = (F_\Sigma, \mathsf{Ar})$ *where* F_Σ *is a set of function symbols and* $\mathsf{Ar} : F_\Sigma \to \mathbb{N}$ *is the arity map.*

- *Let* Σ *be a signature. Let* V *be a fixed, countably infinite set of variables. The set* T_Σ *of* Σ-terms *is defined as follows:*
  - *if* $x \in V$, *then* $x \in T_\Sigma$,
  - *if* $f \in F_\Sigma$ *and* $t_1, \ldots, t_{\mathsf{Ar} f} \in T_\Sigma$, *then* $f(t_1, \ldots, t_{\mathsf{Ar} f}) \in T_\Sigma$.
- *A map* $\theta : T_\Sigma \to T_\Sigma$ *is a* Σ-substitution *if for every* $f \in F_\Sigma$ *and* Σ*-terms* $t_1, \ldots, t_{\mathsf{Ar} f}$ *we have* $\theta(f(t_1, \ldots, t_{\mathsf{Ar} f})) = f(\theta t_1, \ldots, \theta t_{\mathsf{Ar} f})$.
- *The relation* $\leq$ *is defined by* $t, t' \in T_\Sigma$, $t \leq t'$ *if there exists* θ *such that* $\theta t = t'$. *The pre-order induced by* $\leq$ *is denoted by* $T_\Sigma^{\leq}$.
- *The set* $\mathsf{var}(s)$ *of variables of a term* s *is defined inductively as follows:*
  - *if* $x \in V$, *then* $\mathsf{var}(x) = \{x\}$,
  - $\mathsf{var}(f(t_1, \ldots, t_{\mathsf{Ar} f})) = \bigcup_{1 \leq i \leq n} \mathsf{var}(t_i)$.

– *if s and t are Σ-terms and u is an occurrence of s, $s[u \leftarrow t]$ is the term obtained by replacing the subterm of s at u by t.*

Note that every (partial) map $\theta : V \to T_\Sigma$ yields a *Σ-substitution* in an obvious way. We shall sometimes refer to such maps as partial substitutions. The standard terminology can be carried over to partial substitutions, so we will also talk about partial renamings.

Equational Logic. A *Σ-equation* is a pair of Σ-terms (s,t), usually written as $s \doteq t$.

Definition 2 *An* equational theory *is a pair $\mathcal{S} = (\Sigma, E)$ where Σ is a signature and E is a set of Σ-equations.*

The rules for equational deduction are given in the following table:

Rules for equational deduction	
$\dfrac{}{s \doteq s}$	Reflexivity
$\dfrac{s \doteq t}{t \doteq s}$	Symmetry
$\dfrac{s \doteq t \quad t \doteq u}{s \doteq u}$	Transitivity
$\dfrac{s_1 \doteq t_1 \ldots s_n \doteq t_n}{f(s_1,\ldots,s_n) \doteq f(t_1,\ldots t_n)}$	Compatibility
$\dfrac{s \doteq t}{\theta s \doteq \theta t}$	Instantiation

where θ is a substitution.

Definition 3 *Let $\mathcal{S} = (\Sigma, E)$ be an equational theory. A Σ-equation $s \doteq t$ is a* theorem *of $\mathcal{S}$ (written $\mathcal{S} \vdash s \doteq t$) if it is deducible from E using the rules for equational deduction.*

Term-Rewriting. Let Σ be a signature.

Definition 4 *A Σ-*rewrite rule *is a pair of Σ-terms (s,t), usually written $s \to t$, such that s is a non-variable term and* $\mathsf{var}(t) \subseteq \mathsf{var}(s)$. *A Σ-*rewrite system *is a set of rewrite rules.*

As usual, we talk about rewrite rules and rewrite systems when there is no risk of confusion. Note that every Σ-rewrite system $\mathcal{R}$ induces an equational theory $(\Sigma, \mathcal{R})$, simply by seeing rewrite rules as equations. By *abus de notation*, we shall denote this equational theory by $\mathcal{R}$.

Let $\mathcal{R}$ be a rewrite system and s and t be two Σ-terms. We say that s *one step $\mathcal{R}$-rewrites* to t (notation $s \to_{\mathcal{R}} t$) if there exist an occurrence u of s, a rewrite rule (l,r) in $\mathcal{R}$ and a Σ-substitution θ satisfying $s/u = \theta l$ and $t = s[u \leftarrow \theta r]$.

We let $\twoheadrightarrow_{\mathcal{R}}$ and $\leftrightarrow_{\mathcal{R}}$ be respectively the reflexive transitive and the reflexive, symmetric and transitive closure of $\to_{\mathcal{R}}$. Finally, $s \downarrow_{\mathcal{R}} t$ if there exists u such that $s \twoheadrightarrow_{\mathcal{R}} u$ and $t \twoheadrightarrow_{\mathcal{R}} u$. Note that $\downarrow_{\mathcal{R}} \subseteq \leftrightarrow_{\mathcal{R}}$.

Definition 5 *A rewrite system $\mathcal{R}$ is* confluent *if* $\downarrow_{\mathcal{R}} = \leftrightarrow_{\mathcal{R}}$ *and* terminating *if there is no infinite reduction sequence* $t \rightarrow_{\mathcal{R}} t_1 \rightarrow_{\mathcal{R}} t_2 \rightarrow_{\mathcal{R}} \cdots$. *A rewrite system is* canonical *if it is both confluent and terminating.*

Proposition 6 *Let $\mathcal{R}$ be a confluent rewrite system.*

$$(s \downarrow_{\mathcal{R}} t) \quad \Leftrightarrow \quad (s \leftrightarrow_{\mathcal{R}} t) \quad \Leftrightarrow \quad \mathcal{R} \vdash s \doteq t \ .$$

Remark. Algebraic structures are usually described equationally rather than as term-rewriting systems. However, some of them can be turned into term-rewriting systems using the Knuth-Bendix completion procedures [18].

2.2 The Semantics of Equational Logic and the Completeness Theorem

Equational theories are syntactical descriptions of mathematical objects. The objects satisfying these descriptions are the mathematical structures themselves. In this section, we define a semantics for equational theories. As we are interested in using universal algebra to solve the problem of equational reasoning in type theory, our semantics is ultra-loose, i.e. the equality relation between terms is interpreted as an arbitrary equivalence relation rather than as the underlying equality of the model.

Definition 7 *An Σ-*algebra *$\mathcal{A}$ for a signature Σ consists of a set A, an equivalence relation $=_{\mathcal{A}}$ on A and for each function symbol f of arity n, a function $f^{\mathcal{A}} : A^n \to A$ such that for every $(a_1, \ldots, a_n), (a'_1, \ldots, a'_n) \in A^n$,*

$$a_1 =_{\mathcal{A}} a'_1, \ldots, a_n =_{\mathcal{A}} a'_n \quad \Rightarrow \quad f^{\mathcal{A}}(a_1, \ldots, a_n) =_{\mathcal{A}} f^{\mathcal{A}}(a'_1, \ldots, a'_n) \ .$$

For implementation purposes, we us a slightly modified definition of assignment and satisfiability. Of course, the resulting semantics is equivalent to the standard one.

Definition 8 *An $\mathcal{A}$-*assignment *is a partial map $\alpha : V \rightharpoonup A$ with a non-empty, finite domain.*

Any $\mathcal{A}$-assignment can be extended inductively to a partial function $[\![\_]\!]^{\mathcal{A}}_{\alpha}$ on the set of Σ-terms:

$$\begin{aligned} [\![x]\!]^{\mathcal{A}}_{\alpha} &\simeq \alpha x && \text{if } x \in \mathsf{dom}\ \alpha \\ [\![f(t_1, \ldots, t_n)]\!]^{\mathcal{A}}_{\alpha} &\simeq f^{\mathcal{A}}([\![t_1]\!]^{\mathcal{A}}_{\alpha}, \ldots, [\![t_n]\!]^{\mathcal{A}}_{\alpha}) \ . \end{aligned}$$

Definition 9 *Let $\mathcal{A}$ be a Σ-algebra. Two $\mathcal{A}$-assignments α and β are* compatible *if* $\mathsf{dom}\ \alpha = \mathsf{dom}\ \beta$ *and* $\alpha x =_{\mathcal{A}} \beta x$ *for all* $x \in \mathsf{dom}\ \alpha$.

The following lemma shows that compatible assignments satisfy the same equations.

Lemma 10 (Compatibility lemma) *Let $\mathcal{A}$ be a Σ-algebra. Let α and β be two compatible $\mathcal{A}$-assignments. Let t be a Σ-term such that* $\mathsf{var}(t) \subseteq \mathsf{dom}\ \alpha$. *Then* $[\![t]\!]_\alpha^\mathcal{A} =_\mathcal{A} [\![t]\!]_\beta^\mathcal{A}$.

We write $\mathcal{A} \models s \doteq t$ if for all $\mathcal{A}$-assignments α such that $\mathsf{var}(s) \cup \mathsf{var}(t) \subseteq \mathsf{dom}\ \alpha$,

$$[\![s]\!]_\alpha^\mathcal{A} =_\mathcal{A} [\![t]\!]_\alpha^\mathcal{A} \ .$$

Definition 11 *Let $\mathcal{S} = (\Sigma, E)$ be an equational theory. A Σ-algebra $\mathcal{A}$ is a $\mathcal{S}$-model if $\mathcal{A} \models s \doteq t$ for all the equations $s \doteq t$ in E.*

We say that $\mathcal{S} = (\Sigma, E)$ *semantically entails* a Σ-equation $s \doteq t$ (notation $\mathcal{S} \models s \doteq t$) if $\mathcal{A} \models s \doteq t$ for every $\mathcal{S}$-model $\mathcal{A}$. The fundamental theorem of equational logic establishes the compatibility between syntax and semantics.

Theorem 12 (Soundness/Completeness) *For every Σ-equation $s \doteq t$,*

$$\mathcal{S} \vdash s \doteq t \quad \Leftrightarrow \quad \mathcal{S} \models s \doteq t \ .$$

The completeness result is proved by constructing the term-model $T_\mathcal{S}$ as the quotient of T_Σ by the provability relation $\sim_\mathcal{S}$. The crucial fact that we shall exploit later is that for every term s and t,

$$\mathcal{S} \vdash s \doteq t \quad \Leftrightarrow \quad [s] = [t]$$

where $[\_] : T_\Sigma \to T_\mathcal{S}$ is the canonical map assigning to every term its equivalence class under the provability relation.

3 The Naming Principles

In this section, we define a methodology to solve equational problems in type theory. Our methodology is very flexible and can be carried out in any type system with inductive types. In particular, it can be carried out in the underlying type systems of Lego [20], Coq [13], Alf [21] and NuPrl [12].

3.1 Specifying the Problem to be Solved

Our first task is to fix the boundaries of the problem to be solved. In its most general form, equational reasoning is concerned with determining whether two elements s and t of a set V of values are related by an equality relation R. Naturally, the problem is far too general to have an automated solution. Yet there is a well-understood branch of mathematical logic, namely equational logic, which is concerned with equational theories, i.e. first-order languages with a single (binary) predicate symbol $=$. Equational logic provides the *right level of generality* to tackle the problem of equational reasoning for several reasons:

1. the problem is general enough: a wide collection of mathematical theories can be presented equationally, for example the theories of monoids, groups and rings;

2. one might expect an useful and automated solution to the problem: in some cases, it is possible to provide an algorithm to test whether an equation of a given theory $\mathcal{S}$ is a theorem of this theory;
3. this work can provide a theoretical foundation to integrate computer algebra systems and proof checkers: computer algebra systems, with their impressive power, are mostly concerned with equational theories.

This justifies the following choice for the form of an equational problem.

The problem. *Let $\mathcal{S}$ be an equational theory. Let $\mathcal{A}$ be a model of $\mathcal{S}$. Let a and b be expressions for elements of $\mathcal{A}$. Does $a =_{\mathcal{A}} b$?*

Note that the problem makes sense within a type system with inductive types as one can formalize all basic notions of universal algebra in such a system. Here are a few examples of equational problems.

Example 13 – *Let $\mathbb{Z}_n$ be the ring of integers modulo n, where $n \geq 3$. Does $2(n-1) = 0$?*
- *Let $\boldsymbol{D}_8$ be the dihedral group with eight elements. Let $\sigma, \tau \in \boldsymbol{D}_8$. Does $\tau\sigma = \sigma^3\tau$? Here the problem is quantified over all elements of $\boldsymbol{D}_8$.*
- *Let $(M, =_M, \circ_M, e_M)$ be a monoid. Let $x, y \in M$. Does $(x \circ_M e) \circ_M y =_M x \circ_M y$? Here the problem is quantified over all $x, y \in M$ and monoids M.*

To solve the problem, we will first relate it to equational logic and then use equational logic to solve the problem automatically.

For the remaining of this section, we work with the formalization of universal algebra in the type system. In particular, an equational theory is an inhabitant of the type of equational theories, and a model of a theory is an inhabitant of the type of models of this theory. To alleviate the presentation, we will still use the ordinary language of universal algebra.

In the sequel, we let $\mathcal{S} = (\Sigma, E)$ be a fixed equational theory and $\mathcal{A}$ be a model of $\mathcal{S}$.

3.2 Equational Logic, Local Equational Logic and Equational Reasoning

Equational logic is *global* in the sense that it is used to determine whether a $\mathcal{S}$-equation $s \doteq t$ is true in all models of $\mathcal{S}$, i.e. whether $\mathcal{S} \models s \doteq t$. In contrast, equational reasoning is *local*, in the sense that one is also interested whether a given equality holds in a specific model, i.e. $a =_{\mathcal{A}} b$ for some specific a and b in a specific model $\mathcal{A}$ of $\mathcal{S}$. An intermediate formal system is *local equational logic*, a variant of equational logic whose deductive system allows to infer whether $\mathcal{A} \models s \doteq t$ for a specific model $\mathcal{A}$ of $\mathcal{S}$. One could even go one step further and develop a formal system to infer whether $[\![s]\!]_\alpha^{\mathcal{A}} =_{\mathcal{A}} [\![t]\!]_\alpha^{\mathcal{A}}$ in a specific model $\mathcal{A}$ and for a specific assignment α. This last problem, which we call the *local satisfiability problem* is in fact a special instance of equational reasoning. If we analyse the logical formulations of local satisfiability and semantical entailment, we see that the latter represents an uniform notion of the former[2]. One concludes that *the goal of equational logic is to know whether an uniform collection of equational problems is satisfied.*

Local satisfiability is a very common form of equational problem. However, not all equational problems arising in the formalization of mathematics are concerned with local satisfiability. An equally important instance of equational problem is the *extensionality problem:* given a $\mathcal{S}$-term t, a model $\mathcal{A}$ of $\mathcal{S}$ and two interpretations α, β in $\mathcal{A}$, does $[\![t]\!]_{\alpha}^{\mathcal{A}} =_{\mathcal{A}} [\![t]\!]_{\beta}^{\mathcal{A}}$? In fact, those two problems (local satisfiability and extensionality) form the core of equational reasoning.

3.3 The Naming Principles

As outlined in the previous subsection, there is a divergence between equational logic as a formal system and equational reasoning as it occurs in mathematics. We have

a goal: an equational problem, i.e. an equality $a =_{\mathcal{A}} b$;
some tools: equational logic, which can be used to solve a local satisfiability problem, and the compatibility lemma, which can be used to solve an extensionality problem.

The difficulty in applying the tools to solve the goal is that equational problems are essentially of a semantical nature while equational logic is designed to solve syntactical problems. In order to apply equational logic to equational reasoning, one must perform a preliminary manipulation on equational problems, so that they present themselves in a form which is amenable to be solved by equational logic. What is needed here is a *naming principle* which transforms a semantical equational problem into a local satisfiability problem or an extensionality problem. For the clarity of the discussion, we will therefore distinguish between the *naming principle for satisfiability* (for short NPS) and the *naming principle for extensionality* (for short NPE). One fundamental feature of these naming principles is that they do not require any extension of the type system; indeed, the naming principles are a special instance of conversion rules. We introduce these principles below.

The Naming Principle for Satisfiability. The aim of the naming principle for satisfiability is to recast a local equation $a =_{\mathcal{A}} b$ into an equation of the form $[\![s]\!]_{\alpha}^{\mathcal{A}} =_{\mathcal{A}} [\![t]\!]_{\alpha}^{\mathcal{A}}$, where

- s and t are terms of the theory T,
- $[\![s]\!]_{\alpha}^{\mathcal{A}} \twoheadrightarrow a$,
- $[\![t]\!]_{\alpha}^{\mathcal{A}} \twoheadrightarrow b$.

[2] By the soundness/completeness theorem, $\mathcal{S} \models s \doteq t$ is equivalent to the collection of local satisfiability problems $([\![s]\!]_{\alpha}^{\mathcal{A}} =_{\mathcal{A}} [\![t]\!]_{\alpha}^{\mathcal{A}})_{(\mathcal{A} \in \mathcal{M}, \alpha \in \mathcal{V}(\mathcal{A})}$ where $\mathcal{M}$ is the collection of $\mathcal{S}$-models and for $\mathcal{A} \in \mathcal{M}$, $\mathcal{V}(\mathcal{A})$ is the set of $\mathcal{A}$-assignments.

Of course, the equation to be solved has not changed; what has changed is the way to look at it. The equation in its second form makes it clear that the problem to be solved is an instance of an uniform collection of equational problems, as defined in the previous section. The advantage of this switch of perspective is that the equation in its second form is more amenable to be solved by standard syntactic tools. Indeed, $[\![s]\!]^{\mathcal{A}}_{\alpha} =_{\mathcal{A}} [\![t]\!]^{\mathcal{A}}_{\alpha}$ is an immediate consequence of $\mathcal{S} \vdash s \doteq t$. This yields a semi-complete[3] method to prove $a =_{\mathcal{A}} b$:

1. apply the NPS; this reduces the equational problem to one of the form $[\![s]\!]^{\mathcal{A}}_{\alpha} =_{\mathcal{A}} [\![t]\!]^{\mathcal{A}}_{\alpha}$;
2. apply any method available to prove $\mathcal{S} \vdash s \doteq t$.

Of course, the efficiency of the method depends on the choice of s and t[4]. Fortunately, there is always an optimal application of the NPS.

Definition 14 *Let $\mathcal{A}$ be a model of $\mathcal{S}$. Let a be an element of $\mathcal{A}$. The* pre-order of codes *of a is the sub-pre-order of $T^{\leq}_{\Sigma}$ whose elements are the terms t for which there exists an assignment α such that $[\![t]\!]^{\mathcal{A}}_{\alpha} \twoheadrightarrow a$.*

For every element a of $\mathcal{A}$, the pre-order of codes of a has a top element (unique up to renaming), called the *optimal code* of a. We write $\ulcorner a \urcorner$ for the optimal code of a.

Similarly, we can define a *code for an equational problem* $a =_{\mathcal{A}} b$ to be an equation $s \doteq t$ such that for some assignment α, $[\![s]\!]^{\mathcal{A}}_{\alpha} \twoheadrightarrow a$ and $[\![t]\!]^{\mathcal{A}}_{\beta} \twoheadrightarrow b$. Every equational problem $a =_{\mathcal{A}} b$ has an *optimal code* $\ulcorner a \urcorner \doteq \ulcorner b \urcorner$ (one can verify that $\ulcorner a \urcorner$ and $\ulcorner b \urcorner$ are optimal codes for a and b respectively) with the two properties:

- $\ulcorner a \urcorner \doteq \ulcorner b \urcorner$ is a code for $a =_{\mathcal{A}} b$;
- $\mathcal{S} \vdash \ulcorner a \urcorner \doteq \ulcorner b \urcorner$ if and only if $\mathcal{S} \vdash s \doteq t$ for some code $s \doteq t$ of $a =_{\mathcal{A}} b$.

The conclusion is that one can define an algorithm which performs the optimal choice for the NPS. In the sequel, it is understood that the NPS is always applied for such an optimal choice.

The Naming Principle for Extensionality. The aim of the naming principle for extensionality is to recast a local equation $a =_{\mathcal{A}} b$ into an equation $[\![t]\!]^{\mathcal{A}}_{\alpha} =_{\mathcal{A}} [\![t]\!]^{\mathcal{A}}_{\beta}$, where

- t is a term of the theory T,
- $[\![t]\!]^{\mathcal{A}}_{\alpha} \twoheadrightarrow a$,
- $[\![t]\!]^{\mathcal{A}}_{\beta} \twoheadrightarrow b$.

[3] The method can fail even if the equational problem is true.

[4] Indeed, some uses of the NPS can be less than judicious. Every equational problem $a =_{\mathcal{A}} b$ can be reduced by the NPS to $[\![s]\!]^{\mathcal{A}}_{\alpha} =_{\mathcal{A}} [\![t]\!]^{\mathcal{A}}_{\alpha}$ where s and t are distinct variables and α is any assignment satisfying $\alpha s = a$ and $\alpha t = b$. In order to solve the problem according to the proposed method, we must now solve $\mathcal{S} \vdash s \doteq t$. This only holds if the theory is inconsistent!

In the second form, the equation can be immediately deduced from $\alpha x =_{\mathcal{A}} \beta x$ for all $x \in \mathsf{var}(t)$. As for the NPS, the method is only semi-complete. Yet it is a very important tool for formal proof development. Indeed, the standard representation of sets in most type systems uses the so-called setoids; consequently all the reasoning takes place with book equalities and extensionality matters do come up very often. As for the NPS, the NPE can be applied optimally. Indeed, one can find for every equational problem $a =_{\mathcal{A}} b$ a term t (the *optimal code* for NPE) such that

- there exist two assignments α and β such that $[\![t]\!]_{\alpha}^{\mathcal{A}} \twoheadrightarrow a$ and $[\![t]\!]_{\beta}^{\mathcal{A}} \twoheadrightarrow b$;
- for every term t' and assignments δ and γ such that $[\![t']\!]_{\delta}^{\mathcal{A}} \twoheadrightarrow a$ and $[\![t']\!]_{\gamma}^{\mathcal{A}} \twoheadrightarrow b$, there exists a substitution θ such that $\theta t' \twoheadrightarrow t$.

Note that it is possible to extend the naming principle for extensionality to formulae. Details will appear in [25].

Combining Both Principles. In the previous subsections, we have considered two different naming principles which can be used to solve equational problems. However, the method that we have described disregards the possibility of using assumptions present in the context. In fact, the NPS is too weak to be useful in this more general case. For example, if one has to prove in a monoid M that

$$(a \circ b) \circ c =_{\mathcal{A}} a' \circ (b \circ c) \tag{2}$$

for some elements a, a', b and c of M such that $a =_{\mathcal{A}} a'$, the NPS reduces the problem to

$$[\![(x \cdot y) \cdot z]\!]_{\gamma}^{\mathcal{A}} =_{\mathcal{A}} [\![x' \cdot (y \cdot z)]\!]_{\gamma}^{\mathcal{A}} \tag{3}$$

for a suitable assignment γ. Moreover, one cannot invoke the NPE principle to reduce equation (3) further. However, one can combine the NPS and the NPE to obtain a powerful naming principle (NPSE) which can be used to solve equational problems in a context. This new principle takes as input an equational problem $a =_{\mathcal{A}} b$ and returns as output an equation $[\![s]\!]_{\alpha}^{\mathcal{A}} = [\![t]\!]_{\beta}^{\mathcal{A}}$ where s and t are two terms s and t and α and β are two assignments such that

- $[\![s]\!]_{\alpha}^{\mathcal{A}} \twoheadrightarrow a$,
- $[\![t]\!]_{\beta}^{\mathcal{A}} \twoheadrightarrow b$,
- $\mathsf{dom}\ \alpha = \mathsf{dom}\ \beta$ and $\alpha x = \beta x$ for every $x \in \mathsf{dom}\ \alpha$.

As for the NPS, the equation follows from $\mathcal{S} \vdash s \doteq t$. With this new principle, equation (2) can be reduced to $[\![(x \cdot y) \cdot z]\!]_{\alpha}^{\mathcal{A}} =_{\mathcal{A}} [\![x \cdot (y \cdot z)]\!]_{\beta}^{\mathcal{A}}$ and $\alpha x = \beta x$ for suitable α and β. This shows that the NPSE is stronger than the combination of the NPS and the NPE. However, it is difficult to find an optimal use of the NPSE for obvious reasons. Fortunately, one can recover the power of the NPSE from the NPS by grafting a simple procedure on top of the NPE. The procedure, called *collapsing procedure* (or CP for short),

- takes as input a problem of the form $[\![s]\!]^{\mathcal{A}}_{\alpha} = [\![t]\!]^{\mathcal{A}}_{\alpha}$ and two variables x and y in the domain of α,
- returns as output the problems $[\![s[y/x]]\!]^{\mathcal{A}}_{\alpha} = [\![t[y/x]]\!]^{\mathcal{A}}_{\alpha}$ and $\alpha x = \alpha y$.

The benefits of the CP are similar to those of the NPSE. For example, the CP can be called to reduce equation (3) into the two problems

$$[\![(x \cdot y) \cdot z]\!]^{\mathcal{A}}_{\gamma} =_{\mathcal{A}} [\![x \cdot (y \cdot z)]\!]^{\mathcal{A}}_{\gamma}$$
$$\gamma x =_{\mathcal{A}} \gamma x' \ .$$

The CP provides an easy means to make use of the optimal naming of an equational problem via the NPS. Unfortunately, there does not seem to be any obvious counterpart for making use of the optimal naming of an equational problem via the NPE[5].

4 Oracle Types

4.1 How to Automate Equational Reasoning?

As mentioned earlier, the naming principles do not solve equational problems. A naming principle is a special kind of conversion rule which recasts an equational problem into a specific form. Here these specific forms are local satisfiability and extensionality problems. The point is the naming principles make apparent terms of an equational theory. In the special case where we look at a local satisfiability problem, the equational problem will become of the form $[\![s]\!]^{\mathcal{A}}_{\alpha} =_{\mathcal{A}} [\![t]\!]^{\mathcal{A}}_{\alpha}$. By the soundness/completeness theorem, the equality is a consequence of $\mathcal{S} \vdash s \doteq t$. Reducing an equational problem to a problem of the form $\mathcal{S} \vdash s \doteq t$ is useful because we dispose of techniques to determine whether an equation is in the deductive closure of an equational theory:

using computer algebra systems. Current computer algebra systems are excellent at equational reasoning. They have various clever algorithms to compute all kinds of equations at a symbolic (syntactical) level. We could use such a system to compute $s \doteq t$ and, if this succeeds, we let our proof checker assume the statement as an axiom. This is what we call the *external believing* way.

using term-rewriting. Another technique to check $\mathcal{S} \vdash s \doteq t$ is of course term-rewriting: if $\mathcal{S}$ can be completed into a confluent and terminating term-rewriting system $\mathcal{R}$, we can look at the normal form of s and t with respect to the completion of $\mathcal{S}$. For such theories, equational reasoning can be partially

[5] Consider a monoid H and three elements a, b, c of H such that $a \circ b =_H a' \circ b'$. The optimal use of the NPE on

$$(a \circ b) \circ c =_H (a' \circ b') \circ c$$

will yield the two subproblems $a =_H a'$ and $b =_H b'$. Indeed, the NPE will be applied with $(x \circ y) \circ z$ as code whereas it would have been better to take $x \circ y$ as code.

automated by using the naming principle and importing in some way term-rewriting into the type theory as done for example in [9]. We call this method the *internal believing* way, because the problem is solved without any outside help. This is the method proposed in this paper.

the autarkic way. We might want to define a map nf which assigns to every term its normal form in $\mathcal{R}$ and to show that for every term t and assignment α, we have $[\![t]\!]_\alpha^{\mathcal{A}} =_{\beta\iota} [\![\mathsf{nf}\ t]\!]_\alpha^{\mathcal{A}}$. In order to check $s \doteq t$, we just have to verify $(\mathbf{nf}\ s) = (\mathbf{nf}\ t)$, where $=$ denotes Leibniz equality. This comes down to a reflexivity test. This method is called the *autarkic* way because it does not involve any change to the type theory or the proof-checker. It must be said that this method seems currently too inefficient to be used in practice.

Most proposals in the literature opt for the external believing approach [2, 15, 17]. Indeed, the external believing way has an obvious advantage: hybrid systems offer a shortcut to integrate term-rewriting in proof checking. However, the approach has two disadvantages:

- proof checkers are based on well-understood languages whose logical and computational status are well understood. It is not always the case for computer algebra systems.
- proof checkers generate from scripts proof-objects; if the computer algebra system is used as an oracle, then all calculations performed by the computer algebra system have to be taken as axioms by the proof checker. Such a process threatens the reliability of the hybrid system[6].

One can remedy to these two problems by using the computer algebra system not as an oracle but as a guide, as done in [15]. In this case, the answer of the computer algebra system is used to solve an equation. We call this method the *skeptic* way because the proof-checker does not trust the computer algebra system. This technique is superior over the external believing one in that it eliminates the holes in the proof-terms. Moreover, the problem of the reliability of the computer algebra system is circumvented. However the skeptic way seems unfeasable in a proof-checker such as Lego because of the absence of tactics.

4.2 The Internal Believing Approach via Oracle Types

In this section, we introduce oracle types. The formalism, which is based on algebraic, inductive and quotient types, is well-suited for the introduction of canonical term-rewriting systems. We refer the reader to [7] for a general scheme for oracle types and focus on a specific example of oracle type used to solve equational problems for groups. It consists of two types:

- an inductive type $\underline{G}$ corresponding to the set of terms of the signature of groups,

[6] Sometimes the user has to make sure that the necessary side conditions are satisfied. For example, several computer algebra systems will state that $(\sqrt{x})^2$ equals x, without bothering about the condition that $x \geq 0$.

- the quotient G of $\underline{G}$ by the deductive closure of the theory of groups; G is defined as an algebraic type, i.e. equality between inhabitants of G is forced by the rewrite rules.

Both types are related by a map $[\_] : \underline{G} \to G$ which assigns to every term its equivalence class under the provability relation. There is an axiom to reflect the universal property of quotients as it is used in the completeness theorem: an equation $s \doteq t$ holds in every group if $[s] = [t]$. If we work in ECC [19], the rules are:

$$\frac{}{\vdash \underline{G} : \Box_0} \qquad \frac{}{\vdash \underline{e} : \underline{G}} \qquad \frac{}{\vdash \underline{i} : \underline{G} \to \underline{G}} \qquad \frac{}{\vdash \underline{o} : \underline{G} \to \underline{G} \to \underline{G}}$$

$$\frac{}{\vdash G : \Box_0} \qquad \frac{}{\vdash e : G} \qquad \frac{}{\vdash i : G \to G} \qquad \frac{}{\vdash o : G \to G \to G}$$

$$\frac{}{\vdash \underline{a} : \mathbb{N} \to \underline{G}} \qquad \frac{}{\vdash a : \mathbb{N} \to G} \qquad \frac{\Gamma \vdash b : \underline{G}}{\Gamma \vdash [b] : G} \qquad \frac{\Gamma \vdash p : [a] = [b]}{\Gamma \vdash \mathbf{noconf}\ p : a =_{\underline{G}} b}$$

$$\frac{\Gamma \vdash C : \Box_0 \quad \begin{array}{c}\Gamma \vdash f_e : C \\ \Gamma \vdash f_a : \mathbb{N} \to C\end{array} \quad \begin{array}{c}\Gamma \vdash f_i : \underline{G} \to C \to C \\ \Gamma \vdash f_o : \underline{G} \to \underline{G} \to C \to C \to C\end{array}}{\epsilon^C\ [f_a, f_e, f_i, f_o] : \underline{G} \to C}$$

$$\frac{\Gamma \vdash a : A \quad \Gamma \vdash B : s}{\Gamma \vdash a : B} \qquad \text{if } A \to_{\beta\chi\iota\rho} B \text{ or } B \to_{\beta\chi\iota\rho} A$$

where $=_{\underline{G}}$ is the (impredicatively defined) deductive closure of the theory of groups, $[\_]$ is a new constructor and $\mathbb{N}$ are the inductively defined natural numbers. The computational content of the system is given by β-reduction and the following reduction relations:

- ι-reduction; let $\mathbf{f} = (f_a, f_e, f_i, f_o)$. The rules are

$$\begin{aligned}
\epsilon^C\ [\mathbf{f}]\ (a\ i) &\to_\iota f_a\ i \\
\epsilon^C\ [\mathbf{f}]\ e &\to_\iota f_e \\
\epsilon^C\ [\mathbf{f}]\ (i\ x) &\to_\iota f_i\ x\ (\epsilon^C\ [\mathbf{f}]\ x) \\
\epsilon^C\ [\mathbf{f}]\ (o\ x\ y) &\to_\iota f_o\ x\ y\ (\epsilon^C\ [\mathbf{f}]\ x)\ (\epsilon^C\ [\mathbf{f}]\ y)
\end{aligned}$$

- ρ-reduction; the rules correspond to the Knuth-Bendix completion of the axioms of groups:

$$\begin{aligned}
o\ e\ x &\to_\rho x & i\ e &\to_\rho e \\
o\ x\ e &\to_\rho x & o\ (o\ x\ (i\ y))\ y &\to_\rho x \\
o\ x\ (o\ y\ z) &\to_\rho o\ (o\ x\ y)\ z & o\ (o\ x\ y)\ (i\ y) &\to_\rho x \\
o\ (i\ x)\ x &\to_\rho e & i\ (i\ x) &\to_\rho x \\
o\ x\ (i\ x) &\to_\rho e & i\ (o\ x\ y) &\to_\rho o\ (i\ y)\ (i\ x)
\end{aligned}$$

- χ-reduction; for every $x, y : \underline{G}$,

$$[\underline{o}\; x\; y] \rightarrow_{\chi} o\, [x]\, [y]$$
$$[\underline{i}\; x] \rightarrow_{\chi} i\, [x]$$
$$[\underline{e}] \rightarrow_{\chi} e$$

Note that the rules we present here are in fact a subset of the usual rules for *congruence* types.

5 Formalization in Lego

Type theory based proof checkers such as Alf, Coq and Lego are expressive enough for the two-level approach described above to be developed within the system itself. We present an implementation of the two-level approach in Lego. The reason to choose Lego is that it allows for the user to input its own rewrite rules, thus offering the possibility to implement oracle types.

5.1 Formalization of Equational Logic

Formalizing equational logic in Lego is relatively easy. There are no major difficulties in developing the whole theory along the lines of section 2. We can define a type of signatures as

```
Signature == <T:Type> T -> nat
```

where `nat` is the inductively defined type of natural numbers. The set of (n-tuples of) terms over a set of variables is defined as an inductive type. Equations are defined as pairs of terms and equational theories as signatures together with a predicate over the type of equations. One can even formalize the deductive closure of a set of equations by formalizing first the notion of simultaneous substitution. It is equally easy to define the semantics of equational logic. The definitions of algebra, assignment, satisfaction and model are immediate adaptations of the definitions introduced in section 3. See [25] for a more detailed presentation of our implementation of universal algebra in Lego.

5.2 Formalization of the Naming Principles

Lego does not offer support for the naming and extensionality principles[7]. Yet they are special instances of conversion rules, so they can be performed manually using the `Equiv` command. We present three examples, one using the NPE, a second using the CP and the third one using the NPS. These examples are meant to give an idea of the method used. To understand them fully, the reader should read first Appendix B. In each case, the proofs turn out to be remarkably short.

[7] An extension of the Lego system is proposed in [6] to solve this problem.

Note that in our implementation we did not use (nor need) specifications of equational theories.

First, we give an example where the NPE is used to solve an equational problem. Here `G` is an algebra for the signature of groups, `obj G` is an element of its carrier, `times` is the multiplication on `G` and `inv` is the inverse on `G`. `TIMES` and `INV` are function symbols of the signature of groups. `int` is the interpretation function which, given an assignment `rho`, assigns a symbol of the signature to an element of `G` whose set of variables is contained in the domain of `rho`. Note that `[x:A]b` stands for $\lambda x{:}A.b$, `{x:A}B` for $\Pi x{:}A.B$, `<x:A>B` for $\Sigma x{:}A.B$, `Set` stands for the type of setoids, `Eq` for the equality of a `Set`, `el` for the elements of a `Set`, `obj` for the elements of a model and `Q` is Leibniz equality.

```
Lego> Goal {x,y,z:obj G} (Eq x y) ->
                          (Eq (times (inv x) z) (times (inv y) z));
Goal
  ?0 : {x,y,z:obj G}(Eq x y)->Eq (times (inv x) z) (times (inv y) z)
Lego> intros;
intros (4)
  x : obj G
  y : obj G
  z : obj G
  H : Eq x y
  ?1 : Eq (times (inv x) z) (times (inv y) z)
Lego> rho == necons x (necons y (base z));
defn  rho = necons x (necons y (base z))
      rho : nelist (obj G)
Lego> t   == TIMES (INV (VAR ZeroN)) (VAR TwoN);
defn  t = TIMES (INV (VAR ZeroN)) (VAR TwoN)
      t : termGr
Lego> u   == TIMES (INV (VAR  OneN)) (VAR TwoN);
defn  u = TIMES (INV (VAR OneN)) (VAR TwoN)
      u : termGr
Lego> Equiv Eq (int G rho t) (int G rho u);
Equiv
  ?2 : Eq (int G rho t) (int G rho u)
Lego> Refine SubstitutionLemma G ZeroN;
Refine by  SubstitutionLemma G ZeroN
  ?9 : Eq (int G rho (TFV sig ZeroN)) (int G rho (VAR OneN))
Lego> Refine H;
Refine by  H
Discharge..  rho H z y x
*** QED ***
```

Note that the NPE yields the goal ?2. The `SubstitutionLemma` is used to obtain ?9 is a specific instance of the compatibility lemma. The next example uses the CP procedure. Here we are working in a context in which `times_assoc` states that `times` is associative. The CP procedure is called by the term `CP`.

```
Lego> Goal {a,b,b',c:obj G} (Eq b b') ->
            Eq (times a (times b c)) (times (times a b') c);
Goal
  ?0 : {a,b,b',c:obj G} (Eq b b') ->
                         (Eq (times a (times b c)) (times (times a b') c)
Lego> intros;
intros (5)
  a : obj G
  b : obj G
  b' : obj G
  c : obj G
  H : Eq b b'
  ?1 :Eq (times a (times b c)) (times (times a b') c)
Lego> rho == necons a (necons b (necons b' (base c)));
defn  rho = necons a (necons b (necons b' (base c)))
      rho : nelist (obj G)
Lego> t   == TIMES (VAR ZeroN) (TIMES (VAR OneN) (VAR ThreeN));
defn  t = TIMES (VAR ZeroN) (TIMES (VAR OneN) (VAR ThreeN))
      t : termGr
Lego> u   == TIMES (TIMES (VAR ZeroN) (VAR TwoN)) (VAR ThreeN);
defn  u = TIMES (TIMES (VAR ZeroN) (VAR TwoN)) (VAR ThreeN)
      u : termGr
Lego> Equiv Eq (int G rho t) (int G rho u);
Equiv
  ?1 : Eq (int G rho u) (int G rho u)
Lego> Refine CP G OneN (VAR TwoN);
Refine by  CP G OneN (VAR TwoN)
  ?9 : Eq (int G rho (TFV sig OneN)) (int G rho (VAR TwoN))
  ?10 : Eq (int G rho (Subst t OneN (VAR TwoN)))
          (int G rho (Subst u OneN (VAR TwoN)))
Lego> Refine H;
Refine by  H
?10 : ...
Lego> Refine times_assoc;
Refine by  times_assoc
Discharge..  rho H c b' b a
*** QED ***
```

The final example uses the NPS. Oracle types are used to give a short proof of an equality on groups. In the sequel, `Q_refl` is a proof of the reflexivity of Leibniz equality, `comm` and `conj` respectively denote the commutator and the conjugate of two elements. For comparison, we have included a traditional proof of this fact in appendix B.

```
Goal {x,y,z:obj G} Eq (conj (comm x y) z) (comm (conj x z) (conj y z));
  intros;
  rho == necons x (necons y (base z));
  t   == CONJ (COMM (VAR ZeroN) (VAR OneN)) (VAR TwoN);
  u   == COMM (CONJ (VAR ZeroN) (VAR TwoN)) (CONJ (VAR OneN) (VAR TwoN));
  Equiv Eq (int G rho t) (int G rho u);
  Refine Soundness;
```

```
Refine Q_refl;
Save comm_conj;
```

6 Conclusions

We have developed a simple, flexible and rather efficient method to solve equational problems in type theory. The main ingredients of our method are a two-level formalization of universal algebra based on oracle types. The approach chosen in this paper is also intimately related to the design of hybrid systems and can be seen as an attempt to lay the foundations for a theoretical understanding of the interaction between proof checkers and computer algebra systems. In the future, it seems worthwhile to try to extend the framework to equational theories which do not yield a confluent terminating term-rewriting system. A longer term goal related to this research is the understanding of computer algebra algorithms. A full understanding of their nature as term-rewriting systems is necessary to see whether a type system with (a reasonable variant of) oracle types can provide a theoretical framework in which the integration of proof checkers and computer algebra systems can be justified.

References

1. A. Bailey. *Representing algebra in Lego*, M.Sc. thesis, University of Edinburgh, October 1993.
2. C. Ballarins, K. Homann and J. Calmet. *Theorems and algorithms: an interface between Maple and Isabelle*, in the proceedings of ISSAC'95.
3. H.P. Barendregt. *Typed λ-calculi*, Handbook of logic in computer science, Abramsky and *al* eds, OUP 1992.
4. G. Barthe. *Towards a mathematical vernacular*, manuscript, presented at the HISC workshop, Amsterdam, March 1994.
5. G. Barthe. *Formalising mathematics in type theory: fundamentals and case studies*, manuscript, June 1994, submitted for publication.
6. G. Barthe and H. Elbers. *Towards lean proof checking*, to appear in the proceedings of DISCO'96, Lecture Notes in Computer Science, Springer-Verlag, 1996. An extended version will appear as a CWI technical report.
7. G. Barthe and H. Geuvers. *Congruence types*, to appear in the proceedings of CSL'95, 1995.
8. G. Barthe, M. Ruys and H. Barendregt. *A two-level approach towards lean proof-checking*, to appear as a CWI technical report, 1996.
9. V. Breazu-Tannen. *Combining algebra and higher-order types*, in the proceedings of LICS'88, pp 82-90, IEEE, 1988.
10. P. Cohn. *Universal algebra*, Mathematics and its Applications, Vol. 6, D. Reidel, 1981.
11. R. Constable. *Metalevel Programming in Constructive Type Theory*, Logic and Algebra of Specification, F. Bauer and *al* eds, NATO Asi Series, 1994.
12. R. Constable and *al*. *Implementing mathematics with the NuPrl proof development system*, Prentice Hall, 1986.

13. G. Dowek and *al.* *The Coq proof assistant user's guide* Technical Report, INRIA, November 1993.
14. H. Elbers. *A machine-assisted construction of the real numbers*, M.Sc. thesis, University of Nijmegen, September 1993.
15. J. Harrison and L. Théry. *Extending the HOL theorem prover with a computer algebra system to reason about the reals*, in proceedings of HOL'93, LNCS, 1993.
16. D. Howe. *Automating reasoning in an implementation of constructive type theory*, Ph.D. thesis, Cornell University, 1988.
17. P. Jackson. *Exploring abstract algebra in constructive type theory*, in the proceedings of CADE-12, LNAI 814, June 1994.
18. J.W. Klop. *Term-rewriting systems*, in Handbook of logic in computer science (volume 2), Abramsky and *al* eds, OUP 1992.
19. Z. Luo. *Computation and reasoning: a type theory for computer science*, OUP, 1994.
20. Z. Luo and R. Pollack. *LEGO proof development system: user's manual*, Technical Report, University of Edinburgh, May 1992.
21. L. Magnusson and B. Nordström. *The Alf proof editor and its proof engine*, in the proceedings of Types for Proofs and Programs, LNCS 806, May 1993.
22. P. Martin-Löf. *An intuitionistic theory of types*, Bibliopolis, 1984.
23. R. Nederpelt and *al.* *Selected papers on AUTOMATH*, North-Holland, 1994.
24. B. Nordström, K. Petersson and J. Smith. *Programming in Martin-Löf's type theory*, OUP, 1990.
25. M.P.J. Ruys. Ph.D. thesis, University of Nijmegen, forthcoming (1996).

A Formalization of Universal Algebra

The reader is referred to [8] for the formalization in Lego. It can be obtained via WWW at `http://www.cs.kun.nl/fnds/papers/two-level.shtml`[8], together with the complete set of Lego files to reproduce the examples. For an elaboration on formalizing mathematics (and universal algebras) in type theory, see [25].

B Examples

This appendix contains examples of equational problems solved using our approach. To keep the presentation simple, we introduce the group axioms without using an equational theory. Note that because of the two-level approach, the number of Lego commands of the proof `comm_conj` is very small (in essence only four). This in contrast to the traditional proof `comm_conj_hand`. Because of a lot of applications of the transitivity of equality and the group axioms, the proof explodes up to a few pages of Lego commands. The former proof can be found at same location mentioned in the previous appendix.

[8] The same files are also available by anonymous FTP from `ftp.cs.kun.nl`. Look at the directory `/pub/CSI/CompMath.Found` and its descenders.

```
(* Define the signature and the terms of a Group. *)

[sigGr  : Signature                     = ...]
[termGr : SET                           = term sigGr]
[VAR    : nat -> termGr                 = TFV sigGr]
[ONE    : termGr                        = ...]
[INV    : termGr -> termGr              = ...]
[TIMES  : termGr-> termGr -> termGr = ...]
[DIV    : termGr-> termGr -> termGr = ...];

(* Let G be a group, satisfying the group axioms. *)

[G            : Algebra sigGr                     ];
[one          : obj G                             = ...]
[inv          : (obj G) -> (obj G)                = ...]
[times        : (obj G) -> (obj G) -> (obj G) = ...];
[one_ident    : identity times one                ]
[inv_invers   : inverse times one inv             ]
[times_assoc  : associative times                 ];

(* Show y = z  ->  z ((x/y) y) = z ((x/z) z) *)

Goal {x,y,z:obj G} (Eq y z) -> Eq (times (times y (times x (inv y))) z)
                                  (times (times z (times x (inv z))) z);
  intros;
  rho == necons x (necons y (base z));
  t  == TIMES (TIMES (VAR OneN) (DIV (VAR ZeroN) (VAR OneN))) (VAR TwoN);
  u  == TIMES (TIMES (VAR TwoN) (DIV (VAR ZeroN) (VAR TwoN))) (VAR TwoN);
  Equiv Eq (int G rho t) (int G rho u);
  Refine SubstitutionLemma G OneN;
  Refine H;
Save Example_1;

(* Show b = b'  ->  a (b c) = (a b') c *)

Goal {a,b,c,d:obj G} (Eq b d) -> Eq (times a (times b c))
                                    (times (times a d) c);
  intros;
  rho == necons a (necons b (necons c (base d)));
  t   == TIMES (VAR ZeroN) (TIMES (VAR OneN) (VAR TwoN));
  u   == TIMES (TIMES (VAR ZeroN) (VAR ThreeN)) (VAR TwoN);
  Equiv Eq (int G rho t) (int G rho u);
  Refine CP G OneN (VAR TwoN);
  Refine H;
  Refine Times_assoc;
Save Example_2;

(* ==================================================================
   Use Oracle Types to implement term rewriting.                    *)
```

```
[FreeGroup : SET];

[varFg   : nat -> FreeGroup];
[oneFg   : FreeGroup];
[invFg   : FreeGroup -> FreeGroup];
[timesFg : FreeGroup -> FreeGroup -> FreeGroup];

(* Define the Knuth-Bendix completion of the group equations. *)

[ [x,y,z : FreeGroup]

   timesFg oneFg x                 ==> x
|| timesFg x oneFg                 ==> x
|| timesFg (invFg x) x             ==> oneFg
|| timesFg x (invFg x)             ==> oneFg
|| invFg oneFg                     ==> oneFg
|| timesFg (timesFg x (invFg z)) z ==> x
|| timesFg (timesFg x y) (invFg y) ==> x
|| timesFg x (timesFg y z)         ==> timesFg (timesFg x y) z
|| invFg (invFg z)                 ==> z
|| invFg (timesFg z y)             ==> timesFg (invFg y) (invFg z)
];

[class : termGr -> FreeGroup = ...];

[Soundness : {s,t:termGr} {rho:el (Assignment G)}
             (Q (class s) (class t)) -> Eq (int G rho s) (int G rho t)];

(* ---------------------------------------------------------------------
   The conjugate of a commutator equals the commutator of the conjugates.

   Define the commutator [x,y] == (x y)/(y x)
   and the conjugate       x*y  == y (x/y)                              *)

[comm [x,y : obj G]  : obj G  = times (times x y) (inv (times y x))]
[COMM [x,y : termGr] : termGr = TIMES (TIMES x y) (INV (TIMES y x))]
[conj [x,y : obj G]  : obj G  = times y (times x (inv y))]
[CONJ [x,y : termGr] : termGr = TIMES y (TIMES x (INV y))];

(* Show [x,y]*z = [x*z,y*z] using the two-level approach. *)

Goal {x,y,z:obj G} Eq (conj (comm x y) z) (comm (conj x z) (conj y z));
  intros;
  rho == necons x (necons y (base z));
  t   == CONJ (COMM (VAR OneN) (VAR OneN)) (VAR TwoN);
  u   == COMM (CONJ (VAR OneN) (VAR TwoN)) (CONJ (VAR OneN) (VAR TwoN));
  Equiv Eq (int G rho t) (int G rho u);
  Refine Soundness;
  Refine Q_refl;
Save comm_conj;
```

The Greatest Common Divisor: A Case Study for Program Extraction from Classical Proofs

U. Berger H. Schwichtenberg

Yiannis Moschovakis suggested the following example of a classical existence proof with a quantifier–free kernel which does not obviously contain an algorithm: the gcd of two natural numbers a_1 and a_2 is a linear combination of the two. Here we treat that example as a case study for program extraction from classical proofs. We apply H. Friedman's A–translation [3] followed by a modified realizability interpretation to extract a program from this proof. However, to obtain a reasonable program it is essential to use a refinement of the A–translation introduced in Berger/Schwichtenberg [1, 2]. This refinement makes it possible that not all atoms in the proof are A–translated, but only those with a "critical" relation symbol. In our example only the divisibility relation $\cdot|\cdot$ will be critical.

Let $a, b, c, i, j, k, \ell, m, n, q, r$ denote natural numbers. Our language is determined by the constants $0, 1, +, *$, function symbols for the quotient and the remainder denoted by $q(a, c)$ and $r(a, c)$, a 4–ary function denoted by $\text{abs}(k_1 a_1 - k_2 a_2)$ whose intended meaning is clear from the notation and an auxiliary 5–ary function f which will be defined later. We will express the intended meaning of these function symbols by stating some properties (lemmata) $v_1, \dots, v_6$ of them; these will be formulated as we need them.

Theorem.

$$\forall a_1, a_2 (0 < a_2 \to$$

$$\exists k_1, k_2 (\text{abs}(k_1 a_1 - k_2 a_2) | a_1 \wedge \text{abs}(k_1 a_1 - k_2 a_2) | a_2 \wedge 0 < \text{abs}(k_1 a_1 - k_2 a_2))).$$

Proof. Let a_1, a_2 be given and assume $0 < a_2$. The ideal (a_1, a_2) generated from a_1, a_2 has a least positive element c, since $0 < a_2$. This element has a representation $c = \text{abs}(k_1 a_1 - k_2 a_2)$ with $k_1, k_2 \in \mathbf{N}$. It is a common divisor of a_1 and a_2 since otherwise the remainder $r(a_i, c)$ would be a smaller positive element of the ideal.

The number $c \in (a_1, a_2)$ dividing a_1 and a_2 is the greatest common divisor since any common divisor of a_1 and a_2 must also be a divisor of c.

The least element principle and <-induction.

In order to formally write out the proof above we need to make explicit the instance of the induction scheme used implicitly in the least element principle.

The least element principle w.r.t. a measure μ says

$$\exists\vec{k}\, M(\vec{k}) \to \exists\vec{k}\, (M(\vec{k}) \wedge \forall\vec{\ell}[\mu(\vec{\ell}) < \mu(\vec{k}) \to M(\vec{\ell}) \to \bot])$$

(in our example $M(k_1, k_2) \equiv 0 < \mathrm{abs}(k_1 a_1 - k_2 a_2)$ and $\mu(k_1, k_2) \equiv \mathrm{abs}(k_1 a_1 - k_2 a_2)$). In order to reduce this to the induction scheme we use the fact that the formula above is classically equivalent to

$$\forall\vec{k}\, (M(\vec{k}) \to \forall\vec{\ell}[\mu(\vec{\ell}) < \mu(\vec{k}) \to M(\vec{\ell}) \to \bot] \to \bot) \to \forall\vec{k}(M(\vec{k}) \to \bot)$$

i.e. the principle of $<$*-induction* for the complement of M, $N(\vec{k}) := M(\vec{k}) \to \bot$. We can write this as

$$\mathrm{Prog}(N) \to \forall\vec{k}\, N(\vec{k}),$$

where

$$\mathrm{Prog}(N) := \forall\vec{k}(\forall\vec{\ell}[\mu(\vec{\ell}) < \mu(\vec{k}) \to N(\vec{\ell})] \to N(\vec{k})).$$

In the formal treatment of our example it will be more convenient to use the least element principle in the form of $<$–induction.

To prove $<$–induction we assume that N is progressive,

$$w_1 \colon \mathrm{Prog}(N),$$

and prove $\forall\vec{k}\, N(\vec{k})$. This is achieved by proving $\forall n B(n)$, where

$$B(n) := \forall\vec{k}(\mu(\vec{k}) < n \to N(\vec{k})),$$

and using $B(n)$ with $n := \mu(\vec{k}) + 1$. We prove $\forall n B(n)$ by (zero–successor) induction.

Base. $B(0)$ follows easily from the lemma

$$v_1 \colon \forall m(m < 0 \to \bot)$$

and Efq: $\bot \to N(\vec{k})$. Efq is not needed if (as in our example) N is a negation.

Step. Let n be given and assume w_2: $B(n)$. To show $B(n+1)$ let $\vec{k}$ be given and assume w_3: $\mu(\vec{k}) < n + 1$. We will derive $N(\vec{k})$ by using the progressiveness of N, w_1, at $\vec{k}$. Hence we have to prove

$$\forall\vec{\ell}(\mu(\vec{\ell}) < \mu(\vec{k}) \to N(\vec{\ell})).$$

So, let $\vec{\ell}$ be given and assume further w_4: $\mu(\vec{\ell}) < \mu(\vec{k})$. From w_4 and w_3: $\mu(\vec{k}) < n + 1$ we infer $\mu(\vec{\ell}) < n$ (using an arithmetical lemma). Hence, by induction hypothesis w_2: $B(n)$ at $\vec{\ell}$ we get $N(\vec{\ell})$.

Detailed proof of the theorem.

Now we repeat the proof of the theorem in some more detail using $<$-induction. As always in classical logic, we may view the proof as an indirect one, deriving a contradiction from the assumption that the claim is false. So let a_1, a_2 be given and assume $v_0\colon 0 < a_2$ and

$$u\colon \forall k_1,k_2(\text{abs}(k_1a_1 - k_2a_2)|a_1 \to \text{abs}(k_1a_1 - k_2a_2)|a_2 \to 0 < \text{abs}(k_1a_1 - k_2a_2) \to \bot).$$

We have to prove $\bot$ which will be achieved by proving $\forall k_1, k_2(0 < \text{abs}(k_1a_1 - k_2a_2) \to \bot)$ by $<$-induction and then specializing this formula to $k_1, k_2 = 0, 1$ and using the assumption $v_0\colon 0 < a_2(= \text{abs}(0a_1 - 1a_2))$.

The principle of $<$-induction is used with

$$N(k_1, k_2) := 0 < \text{abs}(k_1a_1 - k_2a_2) \to \bot \quad \text{and} \quad \mu(k_1, k_2) := \text{abs}(k_1a_1 - k_2a_2).$$

We have to show that N is progressive. To this end let k_1, k_2 be given and assume

$$u_1\colon \forall \ell_1, \ell_2(\mu(\ell_1, \ell_2) < \mu(k_1, k_2) \to N(\ell_1, \ell_2)).$$

We have to prove $N(k_1, k_2)$. So, assume $u_2\colon 0 < \mu(k_1, k_2)$. We have to show $\bot$. This will be achieved by using the (false) assumption u at k_1, k_2. We have to prove $\mu(k_1, k_2)|a_1$ and $\mu(k_1, k_2)|a_2$. Informally, one would argue "if, say, $\mu(k_1, k_2)\not| a_1$ then the remainder $r_1 := r(a_1, \mu(k_1, k_2))$ is positive and less than $\mu(k_1, k_2)$. Furthermore we can find ℓ_1, ℓ_2 such that $r_1 = \mu(\ell_1, \ell_2)$. Altogether this contradicts the assumption u_1". More formally, to prove $\mu(k_1, k_2)|a_1$ we use the lemma

$$v_2\colon \forall a, q, c, r(a = qc + r \to (0 < r \to \bot) \to c|a)$$

at a_1, $q_1 := q(a_1, \mu(k_1, k_2))$ (the quotient), $\mu(k_1, k_2)$ and r_1. We have to prove the premises

$$a_1 = q_1\mu(k_1, k_2) + r_1 \quad \text{and} \quad 0 < r_1 \to \bot$$

of the instantiated lemma v_2. Here we need the lemmata

$$v_3\colon \forall a, c(0 < c \to a = q(a, c)c + r(a, c)),$$
$$v_4\colon \forall a, c(0 < c \to r(a, c) < c)$$

specifying the functions quotient and remainder. Now the first premise follows immediately from lemma v_3 and $u_2\colon 0 < \mu(k_1, k_2)$. To prove the second premise, $0 < r_1 \to \bot$, we assume $u_3\colon 0 < r_1$ and show $\bot$. First we compute ℓ_1, ℓ_2 such that $r_1 = \mu(\ell_1, \ell_2)$. This is done by some auxiliary function f, defined by

$$f(a_1, a_2, k_1, k_2, q) := \begin{cases} qk_1 - 1, & \text{if } k_2a_2 < k_1a_1 \text{ and } 0 < q; \\ qk_1 + 1, & \text{otherwise.} \end{cases}$$

f satisfies the lemma

$$v_5\colon \forall a_1, a_2, k_1, k_2, q, r(a_1 = q \cdot \mu(k_1, k_2) + r \to r = \mu(f(a_1, a_2, k_1, k_2, q), qk_2)).$$

Hence we let $\ell_1 := f(a_1, a_2, k_1, k_2, q_1)$ and $\ell_2 := q_1k_2$. Now we have $\mu(\ell_1, \ell_2) = r_1 < \mu(k_1, k_2)$ by v_5, u_2 and v_4, as well as $0 < r_1 = \mu(\ell_1, \ell_2)$ by u_3 and v_5. Therefore, we get $\bot$ by u_1 at ℓ_1, ℓ_2 (using some equality lemmata). This completes the proof of $\mu(k_1, k_2)|a_1$. $\mu(k_1, k_2)|a_2$ is proved similarly using the lemma

$$v_6\colon \forall a_1, a_2, k_1, k_2, q, r(a_2 = q \cdot \mu(k_1, k_2) + r \to r = \mu(qk_1, f(a_2, a_1, k_2, k_1, q))).$$

The refined A–translation.

The proof of the principle of <–induction and the proof of the theorem were given in such a detail that it is now easy to formalize them completely. Only some arguments concerning $<$ and $=$ were left implicit. We will now briefly recall the term extraction process described in [1, 2] in general, and will see that we don't need to worry about these omissions.

Let $\forall\vec{x}_1 C_1, \ldots, \forall\vec{x}_\ell C_\ell$ be Π–formulas (i.e. C_i quantifier free) and $A_1, \ldots, A_m$ quantifier free formulas (in our example $C_1 \equiv 0 < a_2$ ($\vec{x}_1$ is empty), $A_1 \equiv \text{abs}(a_1k_1 - a_2k_2)|a_1$, $A_2 \equiv \text{abs}(a_1k_1 - a_2k_2)|a_2$, $A_3 \equiv 0 < \text{abs}(a_1k_1 - a_2k_2)$). Assume we have a classical proof of

$$\forall\vec{a}(\forall\vec{x}_1 C_1 \to \ldots \to \forall\vec{x}_\ell C_\ell \to \exists\vec{k}(A_1\wedge, \ldots, \wedge A_m)),$$

i.e., a deduction

$$d[u\colon \forall\vec{k}(A_1 \to \ldots \to A_m \to \bot), v_1\colon \forall\vec{x}_1 C_1, \ldots, v_\ell\colon \forall\vec{x}_\ell C_\ell,]\colon \bot.$$

To keep the derivation short we allow auxiliary lemmata

$$v_{\ell+1}\colon \forall\vec{x}_{\ell+1} C_{\ell+1}, \ldots, v_n\colon \forall\vec{x}_n C_n$$

asserting true Π–formulas. So, in fact, we have

$$d[u, v_1, \ldots, v_n]\colon \bot.$$

We sketch the main steps leading from this derivation to an intuitionistic proof of

$$A := \exists^*\vec{k}(A_1 \wedge \ldots \wedge A_m)$$

($\exists^*$ is the constructive existential quantifier) and hence to terms computing a witness $\vec{k}$.

1. Let $L := \{A_1 \to \ldots \to A_m \to \bot, C_1, \ldots, C_n\}$. Determine inductively the L*–critical* relation symbols as follows: If $(\vec{D}_1 \to P_1) \to \ldots \to (\vec{D}_m \to P_m) \to R(\vec{t})$ is a positive subformula of a formula in L, and for some i, $P_i \equiv \bot$ or $P_i \equiv Q(\vec{s})$ where Q is L–critical, then R is L–critical too.

2. For each formula F let its A*–translation* F^A be the formula obtained from F by replacing $\bot$ by A and each subformula $R(\vec{s})$, where R is L–critical, by $(R(\vec{s}) \to A) \to A$. Find derivations

$$d_u\colon \forall\vec{k}(A_1 \to \ldots \to A_m \to \bot)^A, \quad \text{and} \quad d_{v_i}[v_i\colon \forall\vec{x}_i C_i]\colon \forall\vec{x}_i C_i^A$$

following the recipe given in [2].

3. Replace in $d[u, v_1, \ldots, v_n]\colon \bot$ each formula by its A–translation. We obtain a derivation

$$d_A[u_A, v_{1A}, \ldots, v_{nA}]\colon A,$$

where $u_A: \forall \vec{k}(A_1^A \to \ldots \to A_m^A \to A)$ and $v_{iA}: \forall \vec{x}_i C_i^A$ (induction axioms are replaced by new induction axioms for the A–translated formulas). Furthermore replace in the derivation above the free assumptions by the derivations constructed in step 2. We get the translated derivation

$$d^{\mathrm{tr}}[v_1, \ldots, v_n] := d_A[d_u, d_{v_1}, \ldots, d_{v_n}]: A.$$

4. Apply Kreisel's modified realizability interpretation [4] to extract a finite list of terms
$$\vec{r} := (d^{\mathrm{tr}})^{\mathrm{ets}}$$
such that $A_1[\vec{r}/\vec{k}] \wedge \ldots \wedge A_m[\vec{r}/\vec{k}]$ is provable from $v_1, \ldots, v_6$.

Comments.

- Term extraction commutes with the logical rules, e.g. $(d_1 d_2)^{\mathrm{ets}} = d_1^{\mathrm{ets}} d_2^{\mathrm{ets}}$, and substitution, i.e.
$$(d^{\mathrm{tr}})^{\mathrm{ets}} \equiv (d_A[d_u, d_{v_1}, \ldots, d_{v_n}])^{\mathrm{ets}} \equiv d_A^{\mathrm{ets}}[d_u^{\mathrm{ets}}, d_{v_1}^{\mathrm{ets}}, \ldots, d_{v_n}^{\mathrm{ets}}].$$
By the latter we may first extract terms from the derivations $d_A, d_{v_1}, \ldots, d_{v_n}$ and also from the proof of $<$–induction separately, and then substitute these terms into the terms extracted from $d_A[u_A, v_{1A}, \ldots, v_{nA}]: A$.
- Assume that we have fixed some system of lemmata $\forall \vec{x}_1 C_1, \ldots, \forall \vec{x}_n C_n$ and computed the L-critical relation symbols according to step 1. Then it's clear that we may use any other true $\to \forall$–formula D as a further lemma, provided D does neither contain $\bot$ nor any L–critical relation symbol. The simple reason is, that in this case $D^A \equiv D$. In the sequel we will call such formulas D *harmless*.

Computing the L–critical relation symbols.

Now we come back to our example. Let us repeat the main lemmata used in the proofs of the principle of $<$–induction and the theorem.

$$\begin{aligned}
&v_0: 0 < a_2,\\
&v_1: \forall m(m < 0 \to \bot),\\
&v_2: \forall a, q, c, r(a = qc + r \to (0 < r \to \bot) \to c|a),\\
&v_3: \forall a, c(0 < c \to a = q(a,c)c + r(a,c)),\\
&v_4: \forall a, c(0 < c \to r(a,c) < c),\\
&v_5: \forall a_1, a_2, k_1, k_2, q, r(a_1 = q \cdot \mu(k_1, k_2) + r \to r = \mu(f(a_1, a_2, k_1, k_2, q), qk_2)),\\
&v_6: \forall a_1, a_2, k_1, k_2, q, r(a_2 = q \cdot \mu(k_1, k_2) + r \to r = \mu(qk_1, f(a_2, a_1, k_2, k_1, q))).
\end{aligned}$$

The only critical relation symbol w.r.t. $v_0, \ldots, v_6$ is $\cdot|\cdot$. Since the parts of our proofs which were left implicit concerned neither $\cdot|\cdot$ nor $\bot$, they may be viewed as applications of harmless lemmata (in the sense of the second comment) and hence won't cause problems.

Formal derivations.

We now spell out the derivation term $d[u, v_0, v_1, \dots, v_6]\colon \bot$ formalizing the proof of the theorem. We use the following abbreviations.

$$\begin{aligned}
\mu(\vec{k}) &:= \mathrm{abs}(k_1 a_1 - k_2 a_2), \\
q_i(\vec{k}) &:= q(a_i, \mu(\vec{k})), \\
r_i(\vec{k}) &:= r(a_i, \mu(\vec{k})), \\
\vec{\ell}_1(\vec{k}) &:= f(a_1, a_2, k_1, k_2, q_1(\vec{k})), q_1(\vec{k})k_2, \\
\vec{\ell}_2(\vec{k}) &:= q_2(\vec{k})k_1, f(a_2, a_1, k_2, k_1, q_2(\vec{k})), \\
N(\vec{k}) &:= 0 < \mu(\vec{k}) \to \bot, \\
\mathrm{Prog} &:= \forall \vec{k}(\forall \vec{\ell}[\mu(\vec{\ell}) < \mu(\vec{k}) \to N(\vec{\ell})] \to N(\vec{k})), \\
B(n) &:= \forall \vec{k}(\mu(\vec{k}) < n \to N(\vec{k})).
\end{aligned}$$

Recall that, using the abbreviations above, u denotes the assumption

$$u\colon \forall \vec{k}(\mu(\vec{k})|a_1 \to \mu(\vec{k})|a_2 \to N(\vec{k})).$$

The derivations below are given in a natural deduction calculus and are written as typed λ–terms according to the well–known Curry–Howard correspondence. By e we will denote (different) subderivations of d which derive a harmless formula from harmless assumptions. There is no need to make them explicit since they will disappear in the term extraction process. The derivation of the theorem is given by

$$d \equiv d_{<-\mathrm{ind}}^{\mathrm{Prog} \to \forall \vec{k}\, N(\vec{k})} d_{\mathrm{prog}}^{\mathrm{Prog}} 0 1 (e^{0<\mu(0,1)}[v_0]),$$

where

$$\begin{aligned}
d_{<-\mathrm{ind}} &\equiv \lambda w_1^{\mathrm{Prog}} \lambda \vec{k}.\mathrm{Ind}_{n,B(n)} d_{\mathrm{base}} d_{\mathrm{step}} (\mu(\vec{k}) + 1)\vec{k} e^{\mu(\vec{k})<\mu(\vec{k})+1}, \\
d_{\mathrm{base}} &\equiv \lambda \vec{k}, w_0^{\mu(\vec{k})<0}, \tilde{w}_0{}^{0<\mu(\vec{k})}.v_1 \mu(\vec{k}) w_0, \\
d_{\mathrm{step}} &\equiv \lambda n, w_2^{B(n)}, \vec{k}, w_3^{\mu(\vec{k})<n+1}.w_1 \vec{k}(\lambda \vec{\ell}, w_4^{\mu(\vec{\ell})<\mu(\vec{k})}.w_2 \vec{\ell}(e^{\mu(\vec{\ell})<n}[w_4, w_3])),
\end{aligned}$$

$$\begin{aligned}
d_{\mathrm{prog}} &\equiv \lambda \vec{k}, u_1^{\forall \vec{\ell}(\mu(\vec{\ell})<\mu(\vec{k}) \to N(\vec{\ell}))}, u_2^{0<\mu(\vec{k})}.u\vec{k} d_{\mathrm{div}_1}^{\mu(\vec{k})|a_1} d_{\mathrm{div}_2}^{\mu(\vec{k})|a_2} u_2, \\
d_{\mathrm{div}_i} &\equiv v_2 a_i q_i(\vec{k}) \mu(\vec{k}) r_i(\vec{k}) (e^{a_i = q_i(\vec{k})\mu(\vec{k}) + r_i(\vec{k})}[v_3, u_2]) d_{\not<_i}^{0<r_i(\vec{k}) \to \bot}, \\
d_{\not<_i} &\equiv \lambda u_{3,i}^{0<r_i(\vec{k})}.u_1 \vec{\ell}_i(\vec{k}) (e^{\mu(\vec{\ell}_i(\vec{k}))<\mu(\vec{k})}[v_5, u_2, v_4]) (e^{0<\mu(\vec{\ell}_i(\vec{k}))}[u_{3,i}, v_5]).
\end{aligned}$$

A–translation and term extraction.

Preparation. We let

$$A := \exists^* \vec{k}(\mu(\vec{k})|a_1 \wedge \mu(\vec{k})|a_2 \wedge 0 < \mu(\vec{k})),$$

where $\vec{k} \equiv k_1, k_2$. In the modified realizability interpretation every formula F is mapped to a finite list $\tau(F)$ of finite types over nat, such that if d derives F then d^{ets} has type $\tau(F)$. For instance $\tau(A) = \vec{\text{nat}} := (\text{nat}, \text{nat})$. Using some obvious abbreviations to denote finite sequences of types — for instance $\text{nat} \to \vec{\text{nat}} \to \vec{\text{nat}}$ abbreviates (ρ, ρ), where $\rho \equiv \text{nat} \to \text{nat} \to \text{nat} \to \text{nat}$ — we compute the types of some further formulas.

$$\begin{aligned}
\tau(N(\vec{k})^A) = \tau(\bot^A) = \tau(A) = \vec{\text{nat}}, \\
\tau(\text{Prog}^A) = \vec{\text{nat}} \to (\vec{\text{nat}} \to \vec{\text{nat}}) \to \vec{\text{nat}}, \\
\tau(B(n)^A) = \tau(a|c^A) = \vec{\text{nat}} \to \vec{\text{nat}}.
\end{aligned}$$

If F neither contains $\bot$ nor $\cdot|\cdot$ then $\tau(F^A) = \tau(F) = ()$ and hence the sequence of extracted terms of a derivation of F is empty too. Furthermore note that $(\text{Ind}_{n,B(n)^A})^{\text{ets}} \equiv \vec{R}$ where $\vec{R} \equiv (R_1, R_2)$ are simultaneous primitive recursion operators of type

$$\vec{R}\colon (\vec{\text{nat}} \to \vec{\text{nat}}) \to (\text{nat} \to (\vec{\text{nat}} \to \vec{\text{nat}}) \to (\vec{\text{nat}} \to \vec{\text{nat}})) \to \text{nat} \to (\vec{\text{nat}} \to \vec{\text{nat}})$$

with

$$\begin{aligned}
R_i\vec{y}\vec{f}0 = y_i, \\
R_i\vec{y}\vec{f}(z+1) = f_i z(R_1\vec{y}\vec{f}z)(R_2\vec{y}\vec{f}z).
\end{aligned}$$

Now we are prepared to compute the extracted terms. To make the relation between the derivations and their extracted terms as clear as possible we denote the finite list of object- (or function-) variables corresponding to the assumption w_i by $\vec{w}_i$ etc. According to step 3 and step 4 and the comment the extracted terms are given by

$$(d^{\text{tr}})^{\text{ets}} \equiv (d^{\text{tr}}_{<\text{-ind}})^{\text{ets}}(d^{\text{tr}}_{\text{prog}})^{\text{ets}}01$$

where

$$\begin{aligned}
(d^{\text{tr}}_{<\text{-ind}})^{\text{ets}} &\equiv \lambda\vec{w}_1^{\vec{\text{nat}}\to(\vec{\text{nat}}\to\vec{\text{nat}})\to\vec{\text{nat}}}\lambda\vec{k}.\vec{R}(d^{\text{tr}}_{\text{base}})^{\text{ets}}(d^{\text{tr}}_{\text{step}})^{\text{ets}}(\mu(\vec{k})+1)\vec{k}, \\
(d^{\text{tr}}_{\text{base}})^{\text{ets}} &\equiv \lambda\vec{k}.d^{\text{ets}}_{v_1}\mu(\vec{k}), \\
(d^{\text{tr}}_{\text{step}})^{\text{ets}} &\equiv \lambda n, \vec{w}_2^{\vec{\text{nat}}\to\vec{\text{nat}}}, \vec{k}.\vec{w}_1\vec{k}(\lambda\vec{\ell}.\vec{w}_2\vec{\ell}),
\end{aligned}$$

$$\begin{aligned}
(d^{\text{tr}}_{\text{prog}})^{\text{ets}} &\equiv \lambda\vec{k}, \vec{u}_1^{\vec{\text{nat}}\to\vec{\text{nat}}}.d^{\text{ets}}_u\vec{k}(d^{\text{tr}}_{\text{div}_1})^{\text{ets}}(d^{\text{tr}}_{\text{div}_2})^{\text{ets}}, \\
(d^{\text{tr}}_{\text{div}_i})^{\text{ets}} &\equiv d^{\text{ets}}_{v_2}a_iq_i(\vec{k})\mu(\vec{k})r_i(\vec{k})(\vec{u}_1\vec{\ell}_i(\vec{k})).
\end{aligned}$$

It remains to compute d^{ets}_u, $d^{\text{ets}}_{v_1}$ and $d^{\text{ets}}_{v_2}$.

$$d_u\colon \forall\vec{k}(((\mu(\vec{k})|a_1 \to A) \to A) \to ((\mu(\vec{k})|a_2 \to A) \to A) \to 0 < \mu(\vec{k}) \to A),$$

$$d_u \equiv \lambda\vec{k}, u_4^{(\mu(\vec{k})|a_1\to A)\to A}, u_5^{(\mu(\vec{k})|a_2\to A)\to A}, u_6^{0<\mu(\vec{k})}.$$

$$u_5(\lambda u_8^{\mu(\vec{k})|a_2}.u_4(\lambda u_7^{\mu(\vec{k})|a_1}.\exists^{*+}_A\vec{k}u_7u_8u_6)).$$

Here we used the $\exists^*$-introduction axiom

$$\exists_A^{*+}: \forall \vec{k}(\mu(\vec{k})|a_1 \to \mu(\vec{k})|a_2 \to 0 < \mu(\vec{k}) \to A)$$

with $(\exists_A^{*+})^{\mathrm{ets}} \equiv \lambda \vec{k}.\vec{k}$. We obtain

$$d_u^{\mathrm{ets}} \equiv \lambda \vec{k}, \vec{u}_4^{\,\mathrm{n\vec{a}t}\to\mathrm{n\vec{a}t}}, \vec{u}_5^{\,\mathrm{n\vec{a}t}\to\mathrm{n\vec{a}t}}.\vec{u}_5(\vec{u}_4\vec{k}).$$

The computation of $d_{v_1}^{\mathrm{ets}}$ is easy:

$$\begin{aligned} &d_{v_1}: \forall m(m < 0 \to A), \\ &d_{v_1} \equiv \lambda m, u_9^{m<0}.\mathrm{Efq}_A(v_1 m u_9), \\ &d_{v_1}^{\mathrm{ets}} \equiv \lambda m \vec{0} \end{aligned}$$

(instead of $\vec{0}$ any terms of type $\mathrm{n\vec{a}t}$ would do). The control structure of the extracted program is introduced by $d_{v_2}^{\mathrm{ets}}$:

$$\begin{aligned} &d_{v_2}: \forall a, q, c, r(a = qc + r \to (0 < r \to A) \to (c|a \to A) \to A), \\ &d_{v_2} \equiv \lambda a, q, c, r, u_{10}^{a=qc+r}, u_{11}^{0<r\to A}, u_{12}^{c|a\to A}. \\ &\qquad g_{0<r} u_{11}(\lambda u_{13}^{0<r\to\bot}.u_{12}(v_2 aqcru_{10}u_{13})), \end{aligned}$$

where

$$g_{0<r}: (0 < r \to A) \to ((0 < r \to \bot) \to A) \to A$$

is a derivation with extracted terms

$$g_{0<r}^{\mathrm{ets}} \equiv \lambda \vec{x}, \vec{y}.\mathbf{if}\ \ 0 < r\ \ \mathbf{then}\ \ \vec{x}^{\mathrm{n\vec{a}t}}\ \ \mathbf{else}\ \ \vec{y}^{\mathrm{n\vec{a}t}}\ \ \mathbf{fi}.$$

Hence

$$d_{v_2}^{\mathrm{ets}} \equiv \lambda a, q, c, r, \vec{u}_{11}^{\,\mathrm{n\vec{a}t}}, \vec{u}_{12}^{\,\mathrm{n\vec{a}t}}.\mathbf{if}\ \ 0 < r\ \ \mathbf{then}\ \ \vec{u}_{11}\ \ \mathbf{else}\ \ \vec{u}_{12}\ \ \mathbf{fi}.$$

The final program.

If we plug d_u^{ets}, $d_{v_1}^{\mathrm{ets}}$ and $d_{v_2}^{\mathrm{ets}}$ into the program pieces we obtain

$$(d^{\mathrm{tr}})^{\mathrm{ets}} \equiv (d^{\mathrm{tr}}_{<-\mathrm{ind}})^{\mathrm{ets}}(d^{\mathrm{tr}}_{\mathrm{prog}})^{\mathrm{ets}} 01$$

where, letting $\vec{w}_1 \equiv \vec{w}_1^{\,\mathrm{n\vec{a}t}\to(\mathrm{n\vec{a}t}\to\mathrm{n\vec{a}t})\to\mathrm{n\vec{a}t}}$ and $\vec{w}_2 \equiv \vec{w}_2^{\,\mathrm{n\vec{a}t}\to\mathrm{n\vec{a}t}}$,

$$\begin{aligned} (d^{\mathrm{tr}}_{<-\mathrm{ind}})^{\mathrm{ets}} &=_{\alpha\beta\eta} \lambda \vec{w}_1 \lambda \vec{k}'.\vec{R}(\lambda \vec{k}.\vec{0})(\lambda n, \vec{w}_2, \vec{k}.\vec{w}_1\vec{k}\vec{w}_2)(\mu(\vec{k}') + 1)\vec{k}', \\ (d^{\mathrm{tr}}_{\mathrm{prog}})^{\mathrm{ets}} &=_{\beta} \lambda \vec{k}, \vec{u}_1^{\,\mathrm{n\vec{a}t}\to\mathrm{n\vec{a}t}}.(d^{\mathrm{tr}}_{\mathrm{div}_2})^{\mathrm{ets}}((d^{\mathrm{tr}}_{\mathrm{div}_1})^{\mathrm{ets}}\vec{k}), \\ (d^{\mathrm{tr}}_{\mathrm{div}_i})^{\mathrm{ets}} &=_{\beta} \lambda \vec{u}_{12}^{\,\mathrm{n\vec{a}t}}.\mathbf{if}\ \ 0 < \vec{r}_i(\vec{k})\ \ \mathbf{then}\ \ \vec{u}_1\vec{\ell}_i(\vec{k})\ \ \mathbf{else}\ \ \vec{u}_{12}\ \ \mathbf{fi} \end{aligned}$$

and hence

$$\begin{aligned} (d^{\mathrm{tr}}_{\mathrm{prog}})^{\mathrm{ets}} =_{\beta} \lambda \vec{k}, \vec{u}_1^{\,\mathrm{n\vec{a}t}\to\mathrm{n\vec{a}t}}.\ &\mathbf{if}\ \ 0 < r_2(\vec{k})\ \ \mathbf{then}\ \ \vec{u}_1\vec{\ell}_2(\vec{k})\ \ \mathbf{else} \\ &\mathbf{if}\ \ 0 < r_1(\vec{k})\ \ \mathbf{then}\ \ \vec{u}_1\vec{\ell}_1(\vec{k})\ \ \mathbf{else} \\ &\vec{k}\ \ \mathbf{fifi}. \end{aligned}$$

Therefore we get, using the fact that $\mu(0,1) = a_2$,

$$(d^{\mathrm{tr}})^{\mathrm{ets}} =_\beta \quad \vec{R}(\lambda\vec{k}.\vec{0}) \\ (\lambda n, \vec{w}_2^{\,\mathrm{n\bar{a}t}\to\mathrm{n\bar{a}t}}, \vec{k}.\ \ \mathbf{if}\ \ 0 < r_2(\vec{k})\ \ \mathbf{then}\ \ \vec{w}_2\vec{\ell}_2(\vec{k})\ \ \mathbf{else} \\ \mathbf{if}\ \ 0 < r_1(\vec{k})\ \ \mathbf{then}\ \ \vec{w}_2\vec{\ell}_1(\vec{k})\ \ \mathbf{else} \\ \vec{k}\ \ \mathbf{fifi}) \\ (a_2+1)01$$

To make this algorithm more readable we may write it in the form $(d^{\mathrm{tr}})^{\mathrm{ets}} = \vec{h}(a_2+1,0,1)$, where

$$\vec{h}(0,\vec{k}) := \vec{0}, \\ \vec{h}(n+1,\vec{k}) := \ \ \mathbf{if}\ \ 0 < r_2(\vec{k})\ \ \mathbf{then}\ \ \vec{h}(n,\vec{\ell}_2(\vec{k}))\ \ \mathbf{else} \\ \mathbf{if}\ \ 0 < r_1(\vec{k})\ \ \mathbf{then}\ \ \vec{h}(n,\vec{\ell}_1(\vec{k}))\ \ \mathbf{else} \\ \vec{k}\ \ \mathbf{fifi}.$$

As an example let us try out the extracted algorithm to compute coefficients k_1, k_2 such that $\gcd(66,27) = |k_1 \cdot 66 - k_2 \cdot 27|$.

$\vec{h}(28,0,1)$ $\quad \mu(0,1) = 27$

$0 < r_1 = 12 \quad q_1 = 2$

$\underbrace{q_1k_1}_{0} \pm 1, \quad \underbrace{q_1k_2}_{2} \quad -1$, if $k_2a_2 < \underbrace{k_1a_1}_{0}$ No

$1, \quad 2$

$\vec{h}(27,1,2)$ $\quad \mu(1,2) = 12$

$0 < r_1 = 6 \quad q_1 = 5$

$\underbrace{q_1k_1}_{5\cdot 1} \pm 1, \quad \underbrace{q_1k_2}_{5\cdot 2} \quad -1$, if $\underbrace{k_2a_2}_{2\cdot 27} < \underbrace{k_1a_1}_{1\cdot 66}$ Yes

$4, \quad 10$

$\vec{h}(26,4,10)$ $\quad \mu(4,10) = |4\cdot 66 - 10\cdot 27| = |264 - 270| = 6$

$6|66$

$0 < r_2 = 3 \quad q_2 = 4$

$\underbrace{q_2k_1}_{4\cdot 4}, \quad \underbrace{q_2k_2}_{4\cdot 10} \pm 1 \quad -1$, if $\underbrace{k_1a_1}_{4\cdot 66=264} < \underbrace{k_2a_2}_{10\cdot 27=270}$ Yes

$16, \quad 39$

$\vec{h}(25,16,39)$ $\quad \mu(16,39) = |16\cdot 66 - 39\cdot 27| = |1056 - 1053| = 3$

$3|66$

$3|27$

Result: $16, 39$

Note that, although $3 = |16\cdot 66 - 39\cdot 27|$ is the least positive element of the ideal $(66,27)$, the coefficients 16, 39 are not minimal. The minimal coefficients are 2, 5.

Remarks.

- As one sees from this example the recursion parameter n is not really used in the computation but just serves as a counter or more precisely as an upper bound for the number of steps until both remainders are zero. This will always happen if the induction principle is used only in the form of the least element principle (or, equivalently, $<$-induction) and the relation symbol $<$ is not critical. Because then in the extracted terms of $<$-induction, the step $(d^{\mathrm{tr}}_{\mathrm{step}})^{\mathrm{ets}} \equiv \lambda n, \vec{w}_2^{\,\vec{\mathrm{nat}}\to\vec{\mathrm{nat}}}, \vec{k}.\vec{w}_1\vec{k}(\lambda\vec{\ell}.\vec{w}_2\vec{\ell})$ has in its kernel no free occurrence of n.

- If one removes n according to the previous remark it becomes clear that our gcd algorithm is similar to Euklid's. The only difference lies in the fact that we have kept a_1, a_2 fixed in our proof whereas Euklid changes a_1 to a_2 and a_2 to $r(a_1, a_2)$ provided $r(a_1, a_2) > 0$ (using the fact that this doesn't change the ideal).

- There is an interesting phenomenon which may occur if we extract a program from a classical proof which uses the least element principle. Consider as a simple example the wellfoundedness of $<$,

$$\forall g^{\mathrm{nat}\to\mathrm{nat}} \tilde{\exists} k(g(k+1) < g(k) \to \bot).$$

  If one formalizes the classical proof "choose k such that $g(k)$ is minimal" and extracts a program one might expect that it computes a k such that $g(k)$ is minimal. But this is impossible! In fact the program computes the least k such that $g(k+1) < g(k) \to \bot$ instead. This discrepancy between the classical proof and the extracted program didn't show up in our gcd example since there was only one $c = \mu(k) > 0$ such that c divides a_1 and a_2, whereas in the example above there may be different $c = g(k)$ such that $g(k+1) < g(k) \to \bot$.

Implementation.

The gcd example has been implemented in the interactive proof system MINLOG. We show the term which was extracted automatically from a derivation of the theorem.

```
(lambda (a1)
 (lambda (a2)
  ((((((nat-rec-at '(arrow nat (arrow nat (star nat nat))))
       (lambda (k1) (lambda (k2) (cons n000 n000))))
     (lambda (n)
      (lambda (w)
       (lambda (k1)
        (lambda (k2)
         ((((if-at '(star nat nat))
            ((<-strict-nat 0) r2))
```

```
            ((w l21) l22))
            ((((if-at '(star nat nat))
              ((<-strict-nat 0) r1))
              ((w l11) l12))
             (cons k1 k2))))))))
  ((plus-nat a2) 1))
 0)
1)))
```

Here we have manually introduced **r1, r2, l11, l12, l21, l22** for somewhat lengthy terms corresponding to our abbreviations r_i, $\vec{\ell}_i$. The unbound variable n000 appearing in the base case is a dummy variable used by the system when it is asked to produce a realizing term for the instance $\bot \to \exists k A(k)$ of ex–falso–quodlibet. In our case, when the existential quantifier is of type nat one might as well pick the constant 0 (as we did in the text).

Acknowledgements. We would like to thank Monika Seisenberger and Felix Joachimski for implementing the refined A–translation and doing the gcd example in the MINLOG system.

References

[1] Ulrich Berger and Helmut Schwichtenberg. Program development by proof transformation. In H. Schwichtenberg, editor, *Proof and Computation*, volume 139 of *Series F: Computer and Systems Sciences*, pages 1–45. NATO Advanced Study Institute, International Summer School held in Marktoberdorf, Germany, July 20 – August 1, 1993, Springer Verlag, Berlin, Heidelberg, New York, 1995.

[2] Ulrich Berger and Helmut Schwichtenberg. Program extraction from classical proofs. In D. Leivant, editor, *Logic and Computational Complexity, International Workshop LCC '94, Indianapolis, IN, USA, October 1994*, volume 960 of *Lecture Notes in Computer Science*, pages 77–97. Springer Verlag, Berlin, Heidelberg, New York, 1995.

[3] Harvey Friedman. Classically and intuitionistically provably recursive functions. In D.S. Scott and G.H. Müller, editors, *Higher Set Theory*, volume 669 of *Lecture Notes in Mathematics*, pages 21–28. Springer Verlag, Berlin, Heidelberg, New York, 1978.

[4] Georg Kreisel. Interpretation of analysis by means of constructive functionals of finite types. In A. Heyting, editor, *Constructivity in Mathematics*, pages 101–128. North–Holland, Amsterdam, 1959.

Extracting a Proof of Coherence for Monoidal Categories from a Proof of Normalization for Monoids

Ilya Beylin and Peter Dybjer

Department of Computing Science
Chalmers University of Technology
Göteborg, Sweden

Abstract. This paper studies the problem of coherence in category theory from a type-theoretic viewpoint. We first show how a Curry-Howard interpretation of a formal proof of normalization for monoids almost directly yields a coherence proof for monoidal categories. Then we formalize this coherence proof in intensional intuitionistic type theory and show how it relies on explicit reasoning about proof objects for intensional equality. This formalization has been checked in the proof assistant ALF.

1 Introduction

Mac Lane [18, pp.161–165] proved a coherence theorem for monoidal categories. A basic ingredient in his proof is the normalization of object expressions. But it is only one ingredient and several others are needed too.

Here we show that almost a whole proof of this coherence theorem is hidden in a Curry-Howard interpretation of a proof of normalization for monoids.

The second point of the paper is to contribute to the development of constructive category theory in the sense of Huet and Saibi [16], who implemented part of elementary category theory in the proof assistant Coq. Here we extend the scope of constructive category theory to the area of coherence theorems (cf. also [9]). We have formalized our proof in Martin-Löf type theory and implemented it in the proof assistant ALF. An interesting aspect of this formalization is that the problem of reasoning about explicit proofs of equality in the object language (arrows in a free monoidal category) reduces to reasoning about explicit proofs of equality in the metalanguage (proof objects for intensional equality I).

The paper is organized in the following way. In Section 2 we prove a normalization theorem for monoids. In Section 3 we introduce the notion of a monoidal category and prove coherence for it. In Section 4 we show how the proof can be formalized in intuitionistic type theory. Section 5 contains a few remarks about the implementation in ALF. Section 6 is about related work.

The ALF-implementation can be found on the web [11]. More discussion and a comparison with an implementation of the same proof in HOL can be found in Agerholm, Beylin, and Dybjer [2].

2 Normalization for Monoids

Let M be the set of binary words with variables in the set X, that is, the least set such that

$$\begin{aligned} e &\in M \\ x &\in M \quad \text{for any } x \in X \\ a \otimes b &\in M \quad \text{for any } a, b \in M \end{aligned}$$

Write $a \sim b$ if a and b are congruent with respect to associativity ($a \otimes (b \otimes c) \sim (a \otimes b) \otimes c$) and unit laws ($e \otimes a \sim a$ and $a \otimes e \sim a$). Hence $M/\sim$ is a free monoid generated by X.

Moreover, the subset N of normal binary words is the least set such that $e \in N$ and if $n \in N$ and $x \in X$ then $n \otimes x \in N$.

We shall analyze the proof of the following "obvious" normalization theorem (see Hedberg [13]):

Theorem 1. *There is a function (algorithm)* $Nf : M \to N$*, such that* $a \sim b$ *iff* $Nf(a) = Nf(b)$.

A simple way to construct such a function is by using that N^N together with function composition and the identity function forms a monoid. So let $Nf(a) = [\![a]\!](e)$, where $[\![\,]\!] : M \to N^N$ is defined by

$$\begin{aligned} [\![e]\!](n) &= n \\ [\![x]\!](n) &= n \otimes x \\ [\![a \otimes b]\!](n) &= [\![b]\!]([\![a]\!](n)) \end{aligned}$$

The theorem now follows from the following two lemmas:

Lemma 2. *If* $a \sim b$ *then* $[\![a]\!] = [\![b]\!]$ *and* $Nf(a) = Nf(b)$.

Proof. By induction on the proof of $a \sim b$.

Lemma 3. $a \sim Nf(a)$.

Proof. $a \sim e \otimes a \sim [\![a]\!](e) = Nf(a)$ using the following auxiliary lemma:

Lemma 4. $n \otimes a \sim [\![a]\!](n)$.

Proof. By induction on a.

In the next section we shall see how a kind of Curry-Howard interpretation of this proof yields a proof of coherence for monoidal categories.

3 Coherence for Monoidal Categories

3.1 Monoidal Categories

Definition 5. A *monoidal category* consists of a category $\mathcal{C}$; a bifunctor $\otimes : \mathcal{C} \times \mathcal{C} \to \mathcal{C}$; an object e; and three natural isomorphisms

$$\begin{aligned} \alpha_{a,b,c} &: a\otimes(b\otimes c) \longrightarrow (a\otimes b)\otimes c \\ \lambda_a &: e\otimes a \longrightarrow a \\ \rho_a &: a\otimes e \longrightarrow a \end{aligned}$$

such that the following diagrams (called the coherence conditions) commute:

$$\begin{array}{ccccc} a\otimes(b\otimes(c\otimes d)) & \xrightarrow{\alpha} & (a\otimes b)\otimes(c\otimes d) & \xrightarrow{\alpha} & ((a\otimes b)\otimes c)\otimes d \\ \downarrow{\scriptstyle id\otimes\alpha} & & & & \uparrow{\scriptstyle \alpha\otimes id} \\ a\otimes((b\otimes c)\otimes d) & & \xrightarrow[\alpha]{\qquad\qquad} & & (a\otimes(b\otimes c))\otimes d \end{array}$$

$$\begin{array}{ccc} a\otimes(e\otimes b) & \xrightarrow{\alpha} & (a\otimes e)\otimes b \\ & {\scriptstyle id\otimes\lambda}\searrow \quad \swarrow{\scriptstyle \rho\otimes id} & \\ & a\otimes b & \end{array}$$

Mac Lane's [18, pp 158-159] definition contained a third coherence condition $\lambda_e = \rho_e$ which was later proved to be redundant by Kelly. Our proof of coherence does not use this condition.

Definition 6. The category $\mathcal{M}$ has elements (binary words) of M as objects. Its Hom-sets are equivalence classes of arrow expressions. The arrow expressions are inductively generated as follows:

$$\begin{array}{rll} g \circ f : a \longrightarrow c & \text{if } g : b \longrightarrow c \text{ and } f : a \longrightarrow b \\ id : a \longrightarrow a & \text{if } a \text{ is an object} \\ f\otimes g : a\otimes b \longrightarrow a'\otimes b' & \text{if } f : a \longrightarrow a' \text{ and } g : b \longrightarrow b' \\ \alpha : a\otimes(b\otimes c) \longrightarrow (a\otimes b)\otimes c & \text{if } a, b, c \text{ are objects} \\ \alpha^{-1} : (a\otimes b)\otimes c \longrightarrow a\otimes(b\otimes c) & \text{if } a, b, c \text{ are objects} \\ \lambda : e\otimes a \longrightarrow a & \text{if } a \text{ is an object} \\ \lambda^{-1} : a \longrightarrow e\otimes a & \text{if } a \text{ is an object} \\ \rho : a\otimes e \longrightarrow a & \text{if } a \text{ is an object} \\ \rho^{-1} : a \longrightarrow a\otimes e & \text{if } a \text{ is an object} \end{array}$$

Equivalence of arrow expression is the congruence relation inductively generated by associativity and identity laws (making $\mathcal{M}$ a category with composition $\circ$ and identity id); the interchange laws (making $\otimes$ a bifunctor); laws making α, λ and ρ natural isomorphisms with inverses α^{-1}, λ^{-1}, and ρ^{-1} respectively; and finally the two coherence conditions. (See also the ALF implementation of $\mathcal{M}$ in section 4.)

We will use arrow expressions to denote arrows in $\mathcal{M}$.

Proposition 7. *(i) $\mathcal{M}$ is a free monoidal category generated by X. (ii) $\mathcal{M}$ is a groupoid, that is, all its arrows are isomorphisms. (iii) There is an arrow $f : a \longrightarrow b$ in $\mathcal{M}$ iff $a \sim b$ in M.*

Proof. (i) $\mathcal{M}$ is a free monoidal category by construction.

(ii) follows directly by induction on arrows of $\mathcal{M}$.

(iii) By induction on f and, in the other direction, on the proof that $a \sim b$.

3.2 The Coherence Theorem

Theorem 8. *If $f, f' : a \longrightarrow b$ are arrows in $\mathcal{M}$ then $f = f'$.*

Before we prove the theorem we note that it implies the coherence theorem as formulated by Mac Lane. He defines a category $\mathcal{W}$ which has the same objects as $\mathcal{M}$ (when $X = \{\square\}$). Moreover, there is a unique arrow between two binary words in $\mathcal{W}$ iff the two words have the same length. So $\mathcal{W}$ is a preorder with every arrow invertible. Mac Lane's coherence theorem ([18, p 162, theorem 1]) states that $\mathcal{W}$ is a free monoidal category. But our theorem entails that $\mathcal{M}$ is isomorphic to $\mathcal{W}$ so Mac Lane's theorem is a corollary.

Proof of Theorem 8. Let $\mathcal{N}$ be the set N considered as a discrete category. The coherence theorem follows immediately from the categorical counterparts of Lemmas 2 and 3: that Nf can be extended to a functor $Nf : \mathcal{M} \to \mathcal{N}$ (Lemma 9) and that there is a natural isomorphism $\nu_a : a \cong Nf(a)$ (Lemma 10). Indeed, if $f, f' : a \longrightarrow b$, then $f = \nu_b^{-1} \circ id \circ \nu_a = f'$ because of naturality of ν:

$$\begin{array}{ccc} a & \overset{f}{\underset{f'}{\rightrightarrows}} & b \\ {\scriptstyle \nu_a}\downarrow & \text{(nat)} & \downarrow{\scriptstyle \nu_b} \\ Nf(a) & \underset{id}{\longrightarrow} & Nf(b) \end{array}$$

Lemma 9. *The functions $Nf : M \to N$ and $[\![\,]\!] : M \to N^N$ can be extended to functors $Nf : \mathcal{M} \to \mathcal{N}$ and $[\![\,]\!] : \mathcal{M} \to \mathcal{N}^{\mathcal{N}}$.*

Proof. Follows immediately from Lemma 2.

Lemma 10. *There is a natural isomorphism $\nu_a : a \cong Nf(a)$.*

Proof. Let

$$\nu_a : a \xrightarrow{\lambda^{-1}} e \otimes a \xrightarrow{\xi_a^e} [\![a]\!]e$$

where ξ is an auxiliary natural isomorphism constructed in Lemma 11.(For typographical reasons we write its components as ξ_a^n rather than $\xi_{n,a}$.) Then naturality of ν follows from the naturality of ξ:

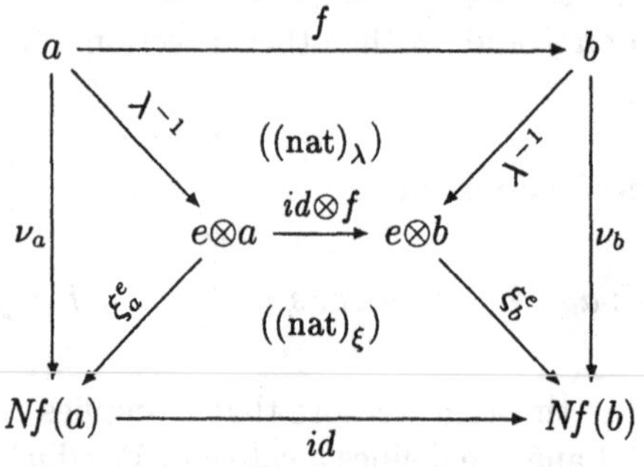

Lemma 11. *There is a natural isomorphism* $\xi^n_a : n{\otimes}a \cong [\![a]\!](n)$.

Proof. ξ^n_a is defined by recursion on a:

$$\begin{aligned}
\xi^n_{a\otimes b} &: n{\otimes}(a{\otimes}b) \xrightarrow{\alpha} (n{\otimes}a){\otimes}b \xrightarrow{\xi^n_a \otimes id} [\![a]\!](n){\otimes}b \xrightarrow{\xi^{[\![a]\!]n}_b} [\![b]\!]([\![a]\!](n)) = [\![a{\otimes}b]\!]n \\
\xi^n_e &: n{\otimes}e \xrightarrow{\rho} e \\
\xi^n_x &: n{\otimes}x \xrightarrow{id} n{\otimes}x
\end{aligned}$$

There is a dual definition of $(\xi^n_a)^{-1}$.

We prove that ξ^n_a is natural in a by induction on arrow expressions in $\mathcal{M}$. (Naturality in n is trivial, since $\mathcal{N}$ is a discrete category.) We justify each case of the induction by a commuting diagram. In these we indicate explicitly when we have used an induction hypothesis (ind), a coherence equation (coh), functoriality (fun) of ⊗, or naturality (nat). When there is no explicit indication we have simply unfolded the definition of ξ or used a basic category law.

Case $g \circ f$.

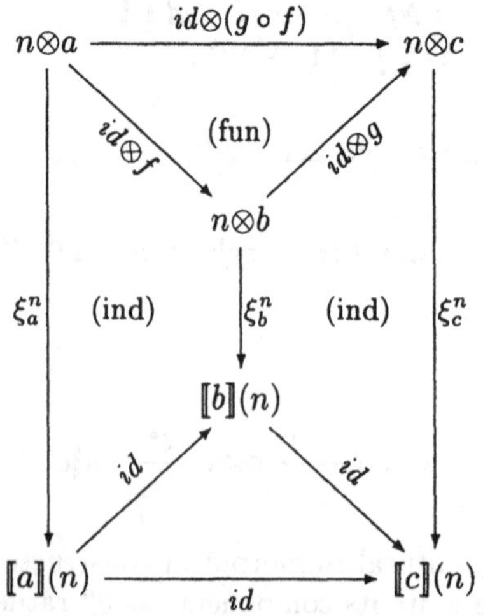

Case id .

$$n\otimes a \xrightarrow{id\otimes id} n\otimes a$$

$$\xi_a^n \Big\downarrow \quad (fun) \quad \Big\downarrow \xi_a^n$$

$$[\![a]\!](n) \xrightarrow{id} [\![a]\!](n)$$

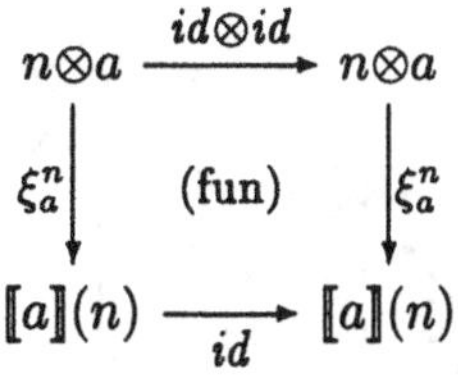

Case f⊗g .

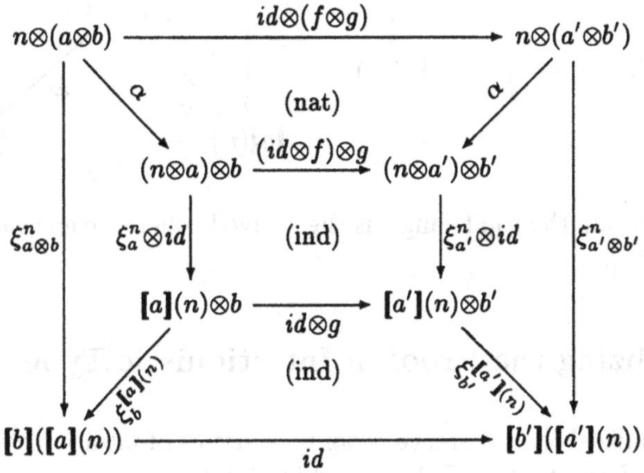

Case α .

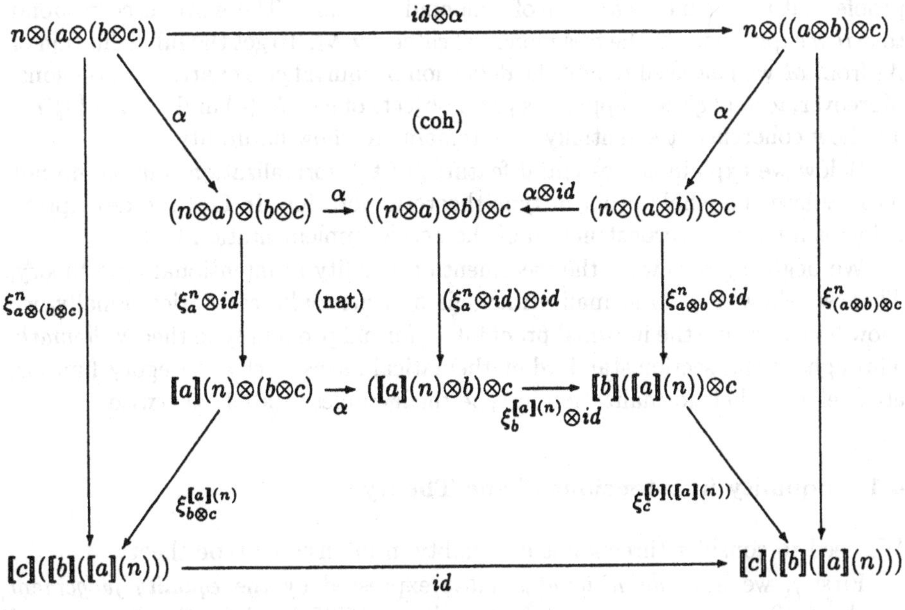

Cases λ *and* ρ .

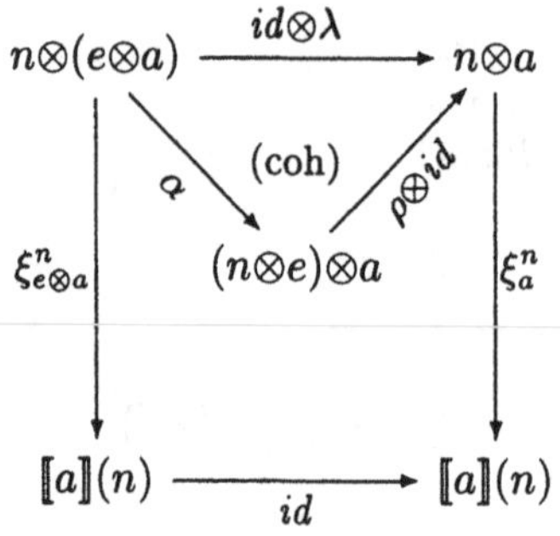

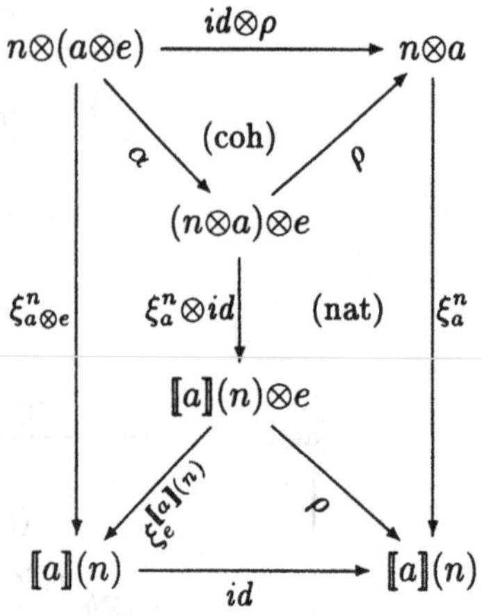

In the last diagram the top triangle is the derived coherence equation (9) in Mac Lane [18, p 159].

4 Formalizing the Proof in Intuitionistic Type Theory

We have formalized the coherence proof in Martin-Löf intuitionistic type theory using the proof assistant ALF developed in Göteborg by Coquand, Magnusson, Nordlander, and Nordström [3].

When we formalize the free monoid in type theory we introduce explicit proofs that two elements a and b of a monoid are equal. These proofs correspond to arrow expressions in the free monoidal category $\mathcal{M}$. To get the full definition of $\mathcal{M}$ from M we just need to add the definition of equivalence of arrow expressions. Moreover, ν_a and ξ_a^n will appear as proof objects of $a \sim Nf(a)$ and $n \otimes a \sim [\![a]\!](n)$. To show coherence it essentially only remains to show naturality.

Below we explain the essential features of the formalization, but we do not recapitulate the whole proof in type-theoretic notation. In fact the description below is a rational reconstruction of the actual implementation [11].

We begin by reviewing the treatment of equality in intensional type theory. Then we show how to formalize monoids and monoidal categories. Finally, we show how to refine the informal proof into a formal proof in type theory. *Remark.* Throughout this section standard mathematical terms, such as category, functor, etc., refer to their formalization in type theory unless stated otherwise.

4.1 Equality in Intensional Type Theory

We need to consider three kinds of equality in intensional type theory.

Firstly, we have *definitional equality* expressed by the *equality judgement* $a = b : A$. Two expressions are definitionally equal iff they have the same normal form. Definitionally equal objects can be substituted for each other everywhere:

$$\frac{a = b : A \qquad \mathcal{J}[a]}{\mathcal{J}[b]},$$

where $\mathcal{J}[x]$ is an arbitrary judgement depending on x.

Secondly, we have basic *intensional equality* expressed by the *equality proposition* $I(A, a, b)$. This relation is inductively generated by the reflexivity axiom:

$$\frac{a : A}{r : I(A, a, a)}$$

(We often simplify notation by omitting some arguments. For example, the proper form of r is $r(A, a)$.) We have the following rule of substitutivity of intensional equality:

$$\frac{c : I(A, a, b) \qquad d : P(a)}{\textit{I-elim}(c, d) : P(b)}$$

Note that the conclusion depends on the *proof* c of equality. There is a definitional equation for *I-elim:*

$$\textit{I-elim}(r, d) = d$$

I is an *intensional* equality, since we cannot prove

$$(\forall x : A)\ I(B, f(x), g(x)) \rightarrow I(A \rightarrow B, f, g).$$

It is often necessary to introduce a special equivalence relation which will play the role of equality on a certain set (a *book equality* in AUTOMATH terminology). Extensional equality of functions in a set $A \rightarrow B$ is one example. We shall follow Hofmann [14] and call such pairs of sets and equivalence relations *setoids.* It is necessary to work with setoids, since one cannot form a new set by taking the quotient of a set with respect to the equivalence relation. In intuitionistic type theory the term *set* is reserved for something which is inductively generated by "constructors" in much the same way as a "datatype" in a functional programming language.

Furthermore, given two setoids $\langle A, \sim_A \rangle$ and $\langle B, \sim_B \rangle$, we will be interested in pairs of functions from A to B and proofs that the function preserves equivalence. We call such pairs *setoid-maps* (or just *maps*).

4.2 Monoids

A *monoid* in type theory can now be defined as a setoid $\langle M, \sim_M \rangle$ with an element e and a binary map $\circ$, such that the laws expressing that e is a unit and $\circ$ is associative are satisfied up to $\sim_M$.

We call a monoid *strict* if $\sim_M$ is intensional equality I. The terminology is intended to suggest that the distinction between strict and non-strict monoids in type theory is reminiscent of the distinction between strict and non-strict categorical notions, such as strict and relaxed monoidal categories in category theory, where a strict monoidal category is one where the monoidal laws hold up to equality and not only up to isomorphism [18].

4.3 The Normalization Proof for Monoids

There is no difficulty in principle in formalizing the normalization proof for monoids. See also Hedberg [13]. A minor point is that we define N as the set of lists with elements in X and introduce an explicit injection $J : N \to M$. (There are no "true" subsets in type theory.) Hence the normalization function is defined as follows:

$$Nf(a) = J([\![a]\!](e)).$$

4.4 Monoidal Categories

We follow Aczel [1], Huet and Saibi [16], and Dybjer and Gaspes [10] and formalize a notion of category in intuitionistic type which does not have equality of objects as part of the structure. A *category* thus consists of a *set* of objects, but *setoids* of arrows indexed by pairs of objects. There is a family of identity arrows indexed by objects (that is, a *function* that to each object assigns a arrow), and a family of composition maps indexed by three objects.

Hence the object part of a *functor* is a *function* between object sets, whereas the arrow part is a *map* between Hom-setoids in the appropriate way.

A *natural transformation* is defined as a family of arrows together with a proof of commutativity of the naturality diagram. Two natural transformations are *equal* iff their arrow components are extensionally equal. We can prove that functors and natural transformations under this equality form a category.

We have thus gone through all notions that the definition of a *monoidal category* refers to. Hence it is also clear how to define this notion inside type theory. In Figure 1 we show the implementation of $\mathcal{M}$ and of the coherence proposition in ALF.

One can show that our formalization of monoidal categories is adequate with respect to the standard set-theoretic definition in the following sense. The essential idea is to use the naive interpretation in classical set theory of Martin-Löf type theory [8]. But we need to interpret the Hom-setoids as Hom-sets of equivalence classes rather than as set-theoretic setoids, and similarly for the interpretation of maps.

4.5 The Coherence Proof

Since there are no subsets in type theory, there are no subcategories either. So analogously to the monoid case we have to construct $\mathcal{M}$ and $\mathcal{N}$ independently and then define an injection functor $J : \mathcal{N} \to \mathcal{M}$. The objects of $\mathcal{N}$ are elements of N and the arrows are proofs of intensional equality:

$$\mathcal{N}(m,n) = I(N,m,n) \qquad [m,n : N]$$

We define J on arrows by equality elimination:

$$J(h) = \textit{I-elim}(h, id_{Jm}) : \mathcal{M}(Jm, Jn) \qquad [m,n : N;\ h : \mathcal{N}(m,n)],$$

Definition of $\mathcal{M}$

the object part

$\mathrm{Obj} \in \mathbf{Set}$
$\quad \mathrm{Var} \in (x \in \mathrm{X})\ \mathrm{Obj}$
$\quad \otimes \in (A, B \in \mathrm{Obj})\ \mathrm{Obj}$
$\quad \mathrm{e} \in \mathrm{Obj}$

the arrow part

$\mathrm{Hom} \in (A, B \in \mathrm{Obj})\ \mathbf{Set}$
$\quad \iota \in (A \in \mathrm{Obj})\ \mathrm{Hom}(A, A)$
$\quad \mathrm{o} \in (g \in \mathrm{Hom}(B, C); f \in \mathrm{Hom}(A, B))\ \mathrm{Hom}(A, C)$
$\quad \otimes \in (f \in \mathrm{Hom}(A, A'); g \in \mathrm{Hom}(B, B'))\ \mathrm{Hom}(\otimes(A, B), \otimes(A', B'))$
$\quad \lambda \in (A \in \mathrm{Obj})\ \mathrm{Hom}(\otimes(\mathrm{e}, A), A)$
$\quad \rho \in (A \in \mathrm{Obj})\ \mathrm{Hom}(\otimes(A, \mathrm{e}), A)$
$\quad \alpha \in (A, B, C \in \mathrm{Obj})\ \mathrm{Hom}(\otimes(A, \otimes(B, C)), \otimes(\otimes(A, B), C))$
$\quad \lambda' \in (A \in \mathrm{Obj})\ \mathrm{Hom}(A, \otimes(\mathrm{e}, A))$
$\quad \rho' \in (A \in \mathrm{Obj})\ \mathrm{Hom}(A, \otimes(A, \mathrm{e}))$
$\quad \alpha' \in (A, B, C \in \mathrm{Obj})\ \mathrm{Hom}(\otimes(\otimes(A, B), C), \otimes(A, \otimes(B, C)))$

equivalence relation on the arrows

$== \in (f, g \in \mathrm{Hom}(A, B))\ \mathbf{Set}$
$\quad \mathrm{refE} \in ==(f, f)$
$\quad \mathrm{symE} \in (==(f, f'))\ ==(f', f)$
$\quad \mathrm{transE} \in (==(f, f'); ==(f', f''))\ ==(f, f'')$

o-laws

$\quad \alpha\mathrm{o} \in ==(\mathrm{o}(\mathrm{o}(h, g), f), \mathrm{o}(h, \mathrm{o}(g, f)))$
$\quad \lambda\mathrm{o} \in ==(\mathrm{o}(\iota(B), f), f)$
$\quad \rho\mathrm{o} \in ==(\mathrm{o}(f, \iota(A)), f)$
$\quad \mathrm{oE} \in (==(g, g'); ==(f, f'))\ ==(\mathrm{o}(g, f), \mathrm{o}(g', f'))$

⊗-laws

$\quad \otimes\mathrm{E} \in (==(f, f'); ==(g, g'))\ ==(\otimes(f, g), \otimes(f', g'))$
$\quad \otimes\iota \in ==(\otimes(\iota(A), \iota(B)), \iota(\otimes(A, B)))$
$\quad \otimes\mathrm{o} \in ==(\otimes(\mathrm{o}(g, f), \mathrm{o}(g', f')), \mathrm{o}(\otimes(g, g'), \otimes(f, f')))$

naturality conditions

$\quad \mathrm{nat}\alpha \in ==(\mathrm{o}(\otimes(\otimes(f, g), h), \alpha(A, B, C)), \mathrm{o}(\alpha(A', B', C'), \otimes(f, \otimes(g, h))))$
$\quad \mathrm{nat}\lambda \in ==(\mathrm{o}(f, \lambda(A)), \mathrm{o}(\lambda(A'), \otimes(\iota(\mathrm{e}), f)))$
$\quad \mathrm{nat}\rho \in ==(\mathrm{o}(f, \rho(A)), \mathrm{o}(\rho(A'), \otimes(f, \iota(\mathrm{e}))))$

isomorphism

$\quad \mathrm{iso}\alpha' \in ==(\mathrm{o}(\alpha(A, B, C), \alpha'(A, B, C)), \iota(\otimes(\otimes(A, B), C)))$
$\quad \mathrm{iso}\alpha \in ==(\mathrm{o}(\alpha'(A, B, C), \alpha(A, B, C)), \iota(\otimes(A, \otimes(B, C))))$
$\quad \mathrm{iso}\lambda' \in ==(\mathrm{o}(\lambda(A), \lambda'(A)), \iota(A))$
$\quad \mathrm{iso}\lambda \in ==(\mathrm{o}(\lambda'(A), \lambda(A)), \iota(\otimes(\mathrm{e}, A)))$
$\quad \mathrm{iso}\rho' \in ==(\mathrm{o}(\rho(A), \rho'(A)), \iota(A))$
$\quad \mathrm{iso}\rho \in ==(\mathrm{o}(\rho'(A), \rho(A)), \iota(\otimes(A, \mathrm{e})))$

coherence conditions

$\quad \mathrm{coh}_{\mathrm{penta}} \in (A, B, C, D \in \mathrm{Obj}$
$\qquad)==(\mathrm{o}(\otimes(\alpha(A, B, C), \iota(D)),$
$\qquad\qquad \mathrm{o}(\alpha(A, \otimes(B, C), D), \otimes(\iota(A), \alpha(B, C, D)))),$
$\qquad\quad \mathrm{o}(\alpha(\otimes(A, B), C, D), \alpha(A, B, \otimes(C, D))))$
$\quad \mathrm{coh}_{\mathrm{tri}} \in (A, C \in \mathrm{Obj}$
$\qquad)==(\mathrm{o}(\otimes(\rho(A), \iota(C)), \alpha(A, \mathrm{e}, C)), \otimes(\iota(A), \lambda(C)))$

Statement of Coherence theorem

$\mathrm{Coherence} \in (A, B \in \mathrm{Obj}; f, g \in \mathrm{Hom}(A, B))\ ==(f, g)$

Fig. 1. Excerpts of the ALF code

which implies that $J(h)$ must be an identity arrow. However, the equality $J(h) = id_{Jn}$ is ill-typed unless h has already type $\mathcal{N}(n,n)$.

Moreover, when we define the arrow part of the functor $[\![\ ]\!] : \mathcal{M} \to \mathcal{N}^{\mathcal{N}}$, we cannot simply put

$$[\![f]\!]_n = id_{[\![a]\!](n)} = id_{[\![b]\!](n)} \qquad [a, b : M;\ f : \mathcal{M}(a,b)]$$

as in the informal account, since we do not have the *definitional* equality $[\![a]\!](n) = [\![b]\!](n)$. The point is that even though $[\![f]\!]_n = id$ for any fixed f and n, we cannot write the general statement.

Instead we use proof objects which witness the ***propositional equality*** in N:

$$[\![f]\!]_n : \mathcal{N}([\![a]\!](n), [\![b]\!](n)) \qquad [a, b : M;\ n : N;\ f : \mathcal{M}(a,b)]$$

We also have to verify that this family of arrows is natural in n.

This phenomenon forces a slight modification in the formalization of the proof of naturality of ξ. All base cases go through exactly as in the informal account, but the induction steps need to be modified.

Consider first the left diagram for the case of composition in the informal proof above:

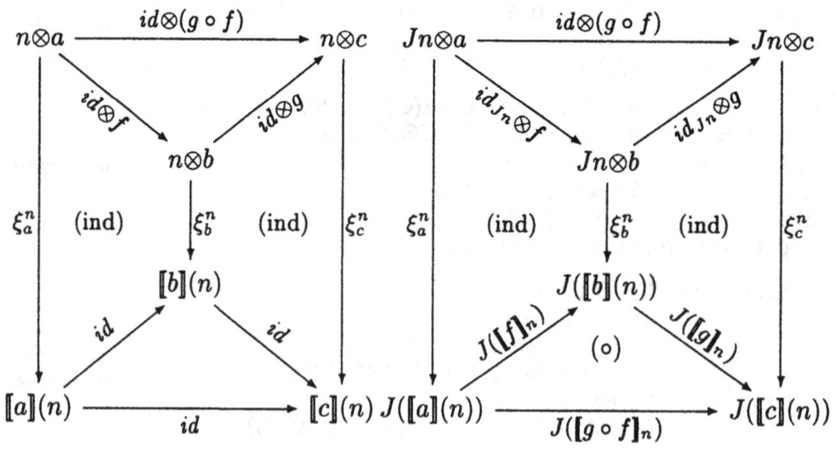

informal version   type-theoretic version

Note the difference between the two lower triangles. Previously commutativity followed directly from the identity law. But in the type-theoretic formalization we have to appeal to the functoriality of J and $[\![\ ]\!]$.

We next consider the case for multiplication:

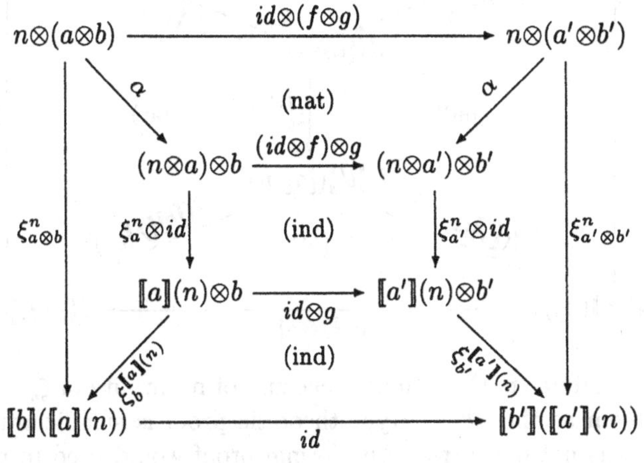

informal version

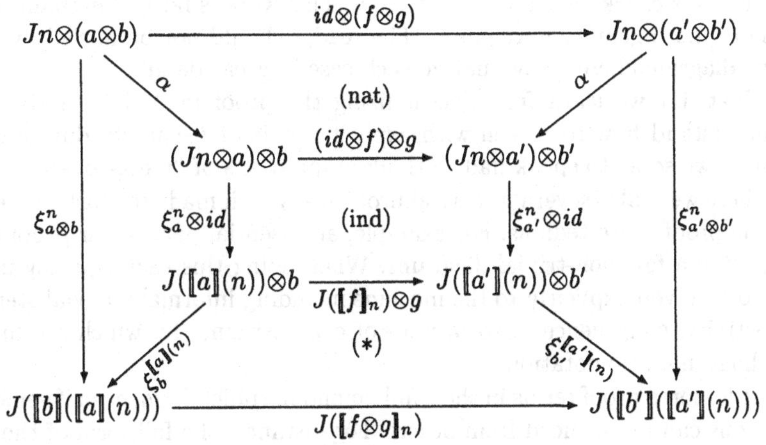

type-theoretic version

The difference is in the lower trapezium (*). To prove that it commutes we

analyze the type-theoretic version into

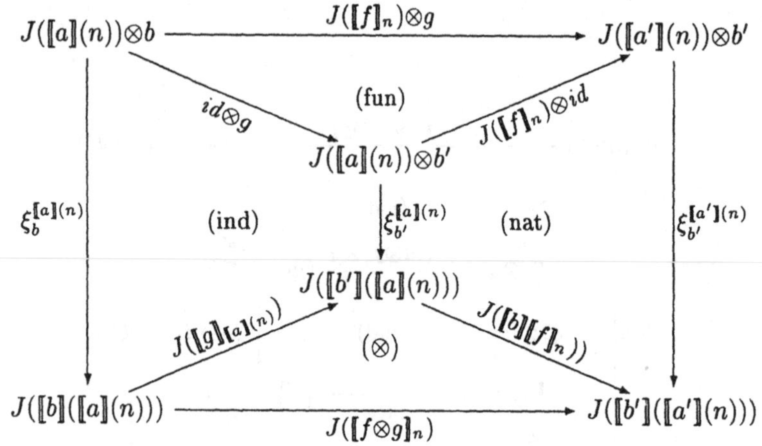

The right trapezium (nat) commutes because of naturality of ξ_b^n in n.

It may seem as though the type-theoretic proof is significantly more complex, but this is not quite true. Any formal proof would need to perform some reasoning about substitutivity of equality, which is not explicitly represented in the diagram from the informal proof.

5 Experience of the ALF-Implementation

The basic message of this paper is that a proof of coherence for monoidal categories is implicit in a proof of normalization for monoids. The additional work just involves checking the naturality of ν. This work is fairly "mechanical" for a human – no ingenuity is required. The reader should not be misled by the size of the diagrams here, they analyze each case in great detail.

What did we learn from mechanizing the proof in ALF? Firstly, we had to understand how to reason with explicit proofs of I-equality during diagram chasing, we so as to speak had to think of questions of "meta-coherence".

There were also several practical problems, which made the task of mechanizing the proof quite tedious. For example, an essential part of our proof consists in chasing a few non-trivial diagrams. When doing this each equality inference had to be given explicitly to the machine including informally trivial steps using transitivity, congruence, associativity of composition, etc. which are hidden in the diagrammatic notation.

ALF stores proof terms in their full "monomorphic" form, even if some subexpressions can be deduced from others. For instance, the full form of the oE-rule (congruence of == with respect to composition) is

$$\frac{A,B,C\ :Obj \qquad g,g'\ :Hom(B,C) \qquad f,f'\ :Hom(A,B) \qquad p\ :\ ==(B,C,g,g') \qquad q\ :\ ==(A,B,f,f')}{==(A,C,o(A,B,C,g,f),o(A,B,C,g',f'))}$$

Only the last two parameters (p and q) matter here, the others are not controlled by the user and usually hidden (cf. the compact definition on Figure 1). In our application the superfluous parts of terms tended to dominate (the internal representation of a term was sometimes 20 times bigger than the "polymorphic" term displayed on the screen).

6 Related Work

Discussions with Martin Hyland and John Power revealed that the extracted proof is essentially a logical version of the proof of coherence for bicategories (in the special case of monoidal categories) given in the recent paper by Gordon, Power, and Street [12]. Their proof relies on Street's bicategorical Yoneda lemma. In our case a proof with similar structure was instead discovered by using the Curry-Howard interpretation which makes explicit the connection between the *formal proof* of normalization and the proof of coherence.

The present work can be seen as an application of a certain approach to normalization in logical calculi: so-called "reduction-free" normalization [5, 7, 6, 4]. The idea is to construct an appropriate model of the calculus and a function which inverts the interpretation function. Here the appropriate model is the category $\mathcal{N}^{\mathcal{N}}$ and inversion is application to unit. Another proof of coherence in this style is Lafont's for *cccs* [17].

We would also like to mention the proof of coherence for monoidal categories by Huet [15]. In contrast to ours his approach is reduction-based and uses the method of Knuth-Bendix completion from rewriting theory.

Acknowledgement. The first author was supported by a grant from the Swedish Institute. The second author was supported in part by the ESPRIT projects TYPES and CLICS-II, by TFR (the Swedish Technical Research Council), and by the Isaac Newton Institute for Mathematical Sciences.

References

1. P. Aczel. Galois: a theory development project. A report on work in progress for the Turin meeting on the Representation of Logical Frameworks, 1993.
2. S. Agerholm, I. Beylin, and P. Dybjer. A comparison of HOL and ALF formalizations of a categorical coherence theorema. In *Theorem Proving in Higher Order Logic (HOL'96).* Springer LNCS, 1996. To appear.
Available on `http://www.cs.chalmers.se/~ilya/FMC/hol_alf.ps.gz`.
3. T. Altenkirch, V. Gaspes, B. Nordström, and B. von Sydow. A user's guide to ALF. Draft, January 1994.
4. T. Altenkirch, M. Hofmann, and T. Streicher. Categorical reconstruction of a reduction free normalization proof. In D. Pitt, D. E. Rydeheard, and P. Johnstone, editors, *Springer LNCS 953, Category Theory and Computer Science, 6th International Conference, CTCS '95, Cambridge, UK,* August 1995.

5. U. Berger and H. Schwichtenberg. An inverse to the evaluation functional for typed λ-calculus. In *Proceedings of the 6th Annual IEEE Symposium on Logic in Computer Science, Amsterdam*, pages 203–211, July 1991.
6. C. Coquand. From semantics to rules: a machine assisted analysis. In E. Börger, Y. Gurevich, and K. Meinke, editors, *Proceedings of CSL '93, LNCS 832*, 1993.
7. T. Coquand and P. Dybjer. Intuitionistic model constructions and normalization proofs. Preliminary Proceedings of the 1993 TYPES Workshop, Nijmegen, 1993.
8. P. Dybjer. Inductive sets and families in Martin-Löf's type theory and their set-theoretic semantics. In *Logical Frameworks*, pages 280–306. Cambridge University Press, 1991.
9. P. Dybjer. Internal type theory. In *TYPES '95, Types for Proofs and Programs*, Lecture Notes in Computer Science. Springer, 1996.
10. P. Dybjer and V. Gaspes. Implementing a category of sets in ALF. Manuscript, 1993.
11. Formal proof of coherence theorem. Home page. `http://www.cs.chalmers.se/~ilya/FMC/`.
12. R. Gordon, A. J. Power, and R. Street. Coherence for tricategories. In *Memoirs of the American Mathematical Society*. To appear.
13. M. Hedberg. Normalizing the associative law: an experiment with Martin-Löf's type theory. *Formal Aspects of Computing*, pages 218–252, 1991.
14. M. Hofmann. Elimination of extensionality and quotient types in Martin-Löf's type theory. In *Types for Proofs and Programs, International Workshop TYPES'93, LNCS 806*, 1994.
15. G. Huet. Initiation à la Théorie des Catégories. Notes de cours du DEA Fonctionnalité, Structures de Calcul et Programmation donné à l'Université Paris VII en 1983-84 et 1984-85, 1987.
16. G. Huet and A. Saibi. Constructive category theory. In *Proceedings of the Joint CLICS-TYPES Workshop on Categories and Type Theory, Göteborg*, January 1995.
17. Y. Lafont. *Logique, Categories & Machines. Implantation de Langages de Programmation guidée par la Logique Catégorique.* PhD thesis, l'Universite Paris VII, January 1988.
18. S. Mac Lane. *Categories for the Working Mathematician.* Springer-Verlag, 1971.

A Constructive Proof of the Heine-Borel Covering Theorem for Formal Reals

Jan Cederquist[1] and Sara Negri[2]

[1] Department of Computing Science
University of Göteborg
S-412 96 Göteborg, Sweden
e-mail ceder@cs.chalmers.se

[2] Dipartimento di Matematica Pura ed Applicata
Via Belzoni 7 - 35131 Padova, Italy
Department of Computing, Imperial College
180 Queen's Gate, SW7 2BZ London, U.K.
e-mail negri@pdmat1.math.unipd.it

Abstract. The continuum is here presented as a formal space by means of a finitary inductive definition. In this setting a constructive proof of the Heine-Borel covering theorem is given.

1 Introduction

It is well known that the usual classical proofs of the Heine-Borel covering theorem are not acceptable from a constructive point of view (cf. [vS, F]). An intuitionistic alternative proof that relies on the fan theorem was given by Brouwer (cf. [B, H]). In view of the relevance of constructive mathematics for computer science, relying on the connection between constructive proofs and computations, it is natural to look for a completely constructive proof of the theorem in its most general form, namely for intervals with real-valued endpoints.

By using formal topology the continuum, as well as the closed intervals of the real line, can be defined by means of finitary inductive definitions. This approach allows a proof of the Heine-Borel theorem that, besides being constructive, can also be completely formalized and implemented on a computer. Formal topology can be expressed in terms of Martin-Löf's type theory; a complete formalization of formal topology in the ALF proof editor has been given in [JC]. A development of mathematical results in formal topology will then be a preliminary work for a complete formalization of these results. On the basis of the present work, the first author has implemented the proof of the Heine-Borel theorem for rational intervals.

Moreover, here as elsewhere (see for instance [C, C2, N, NV]), the use of a pointfree approach allows to replace non-constructive reasoning by constructive proofs.

We point out that a proof similar in spirit to our work was given by Martin-Löf in [ML].

The paper is organized as follows: in Section 2 we provide all the preliminary definitions on formal topology to make the exposition self-contained; in Section 3 the continuum is defined as a formal space by means of an inductive definition, equivalent to the one given in [NS] but more suitable for our purpose. As an aside, the definition provides an explicit description of its Stone compactification (cf. [N]). Formal reals are also proved to be equivalent to real numbers à la Bishop. In the following section, the formal space of a closed interval with rational endpoints is defined. Formal intervals are then proved to coincide, when considered in the extensional way as sets of points, with the usual intervals of the real line. Finally, the Heine-Borel covering theorem is proved and the same is done, without any substantial difference, for intervals with real-valued endpoints.

2 Preliminaries

We recall here the basic theoretical background concerning formal topology. Further general information can be found in [S, SVV], whereas in [N, NV] the constructive character of this approach to topology is testified by applications to constructive pointfree proofs. In [NS], the theory of real numbers in the framework of formal topology is developed, but we also provide here all the definitions needed.

Formal topologies were introduced by Per Martin-Löf and Giovanni Sambin ([S, S1]) as a constructive approach to (pointfree) topology, in the tradition of Johnstone's version of the *Grothendieck topologies* [J] and Fourman and Grayson's *Formal Spaces* [FG], but using simpler technical devices and a constructive set theory based on Martin Löf's constructive type theory.

The definition of a formal topology is obtained by abstracting from the definition of a topological space $\langle X, \Omega(X)\rangle$, without mentioning the points. Since a point-set topology can always be presented using one of its bases, the abstract structure that we will consider is a commutative monoid $\langle S, \cdot_S, 1_S\rangle$ where the set S corresponds to the base of the point-set topology $\Omega(X)$, $\cdot_S$ corresponds to the operation of intersection between basic subsets, and 1_S corresponds to the whole collection X.

In a point-set topology any open set is obtained as a union of elements of the base, but union does not make sense if we refuse reference to points; hence we are naturally led to think that an open set may directly correspond to a subset of the set S. Let c^* denote the element of the base which corresponds to the formal basic open c. Since there may be many different subsets of basic elements whose union is the same open set, we need an equivalence relation $\cong_S$ between two subsets U and V of S such that $U \cong_S V$ holds if and only if the opens $U^* \equiv \bigcup_{a\in U} a^*$ and $V^* \equiv \bigcup_{b\in V} b^*$ are equal. For this purpose we introduce an infinitary relation $\lhd_S$, called *cover*, between a basic element a of S and a subset U of S whose intended meaning is that $a \lhd_S U$ when $a^* \subseteq U^*$. The conditions we require of this relation are a straightforward rephrasing of the analogous set-theoretic situation.

Besides the notion of cover, we introduce a predicate $Pos_S(a)$ $[a \in S]$ to express positively (that is without using negation) the fact that a basic open is not empty.

Definition 1 Formal topology. A *formal topology* over a set S is a structure

$$\mathcal{S} \equiv \langle S, \cdot_S, 1_S, \lhd_S, Pos_S \rangle$$

where $\langle S, \cdot_S, 1_S \rangle$ is a commutative monoid with unit, $\lhd_S$ is a relation, called *cover*, between elements and subsets of S such that, for any $a, b \in S$ and $U, V \subseteq S$, the following conditions hold:

$$\text{(reflexivity)} \qquad \frac{a \in U}{a \lhd_S U}$$

$$\text{(transitivity)} \ \frac{a \lhd_S U \qquad U \lhd_S V}{a \lhd_S V} \qquad \text{where} \quad U \lhd_S V \equiv (\forall u \in U)\ u \lhd_S V$$

$$(\cdot\ \text{- left}) \qquad \frac{a \lhd_S U}{a \cdot_S b \lhd_S U}$$

$$(\cdot\ \text{- right}) \qquad \frac{a \lhd_S U \qquad a \lhd_S V}{a \lhd_S U \cdot_S V} \qquad \text{where} \quad U \cdot_S V \equiv \{u \cdot_S v \mid u \in U, v \in V\}$$

and Pos_S is a predicate on S, called *positivity predicate*, satisfying:

$$\text{(monotonicity)} \ \frac{Pos_S(a) \qquad a \lhd_S U}{(\exists b \in U)\ Pos_S(b)}$$

$$\text{(positivity)} \qquad a \lhd_S \{a\}^+ \qquad \text{where} \quad U^+ \equiv \{b \in U \mid Pos_S(b)\}\ .$$

All the conditions, except positivity, are a straightforward rephrasing of the preceding intuitive considerations. One reason to introduce positivity is that any non-positive basic open is covered by everything. Indeed, when Pos_S is a decidable predicate, positivity is equivalent to

$$\frac{\neg Pos_S(a)}{a \lhd_S \emptyset}$$

and this will be the case both for the topology of formal reals and for the topology of intervals with rational endpoint. Technically, positivity also allows proof by cases on $Pos_S(a)$ for deductions involving covers (for a detailed discussion cf. [SVV]).

We point out that we can dispense with the unit in the definition of formal topology without any substantial difference in the development of the theory. This choice will be pursued in the sequel.

In order to connect our pointfree approach to classical point-set topology, the notion of point has to be recovered. Since we reverse the usual conceptual order between points and opens, and take the opens as primitive, points will be defined as particular, well behaved, collections of opens. We recall here the definition of a (formal) point of a formal topology:

Definition 2. Let $\mathcal{A} \equiv \langle S, \cdot, 1, \lhd, Pos \rangle$ be a formal topology. A subset α of S is said to be a *formal point* if for all $a, b \in S$, $U \subseteq S$ the following conditions hold:

1. $1 \in \alpha$;
2. $\dfrac{a \in \alpha \quad b \in \alpha}{a \cdot b \in \alpha}$;
3. $\dfrac{a \in \alpha \quad a \lhd U}{(\exists b \in U)(b \in \alpha)}$;
4. $\dfrac{a \in \alpha}{Pos(a)}$.

In order to maintain the usual intuition on points, in the sequel we will write $\alpha \Vdash a$ (α forces a, or α is a point in a) in place of $a \in \alpha$. Moreover, when a singleton set occurs we will sometimes omit curly brackets, and write $a \lhd b$ for $a \lhd \{b\}$, and $U \cdot b$ for $U \cdot \{b\}$.

3 The Continuum as a Formal Space

Formal real numbers can be obtained as formal points of a suitable formal topology based on the rationals (cf. [NS]). We are adopting here a somewhat different approach to formal reals in comparison with the one given in [NS]. We have the same monoid operation and positivity predicate, and the covering relations are equivalent, but we dispense with the unit. By this approach we avoid adding top and bottom to the rational numbers. The following definition was proposed by Thierry Coquand in order to make inductive arguments easier. Technically, it is a *finitary inductive definition*, since each rule involved has only finitely many premises (cf. [A]). In fact, we do not need to close under the cover rules. Moreover, as we will see, the definition provides a simple presentation of the Stone compactification for the cover (cf. [N]).

Definition 3. The *formal topology of formal reals* is the structure

$$\mathcal{R} \equiv \langle Q \times Q, \cdot, \lhd, Pos \rangle ,$$

where Q is the set of rational numbers, $S \equiv Q \times Q$ is the Cartesian product. The monoid operation is defined by $(p, q) \cdot (r, s) \equiv (max(p, r), min(q, s))$; the cover $\lhd$ is defined by

$$(p, q) \lhd U \equiv (\forall p', q')(p < p' < q' < q \rightarrow (p', q') \lhd_f U) ,$$

where the relation $\lhd_f$ is inductively defined by

1. $\dfrac{q \leq p}{(p, q) \lhd_f U}$;
2. $\dfrac{(p, q) \in U}{(p, q) \lhd_f U}$;

3. $$\frac{(p,s) \lhd_f U \quad (r,q) \lhd_f U \quad p \le r < s \le q}{(p,q) \lhd_f U};$$

4. $$\frac{(p',q') \lhd_f U \quad p' \le p < q \le q'}{(p,q) \lhd_f U}.$$

The positivity predicate is defined by

$$Pos(p,q) \equiv p < q\ .$$

According to the intuitive set-theoretic reading of the definition of formal topology, the above definition amounts to the following: A basic open (p,q) is covered by a family U of basic opens if and only if all (p',q') strictly included in (p,q) are included in the union of a finite subfamily of U. The rest of this section will be devoted to proving that the above definition really defines a formal topology whose formal points correspond to constructive real numbers.

The usual definition of formal point of a formal topology, given in Section 2, specializes to the following one when considering the formal topology of formal reals $\mathcal{R}$.

Definition 4. A subset α of S is a *formal point of* $\mathcal{R}$ if it satisfies

1. $(\exists p,q)(\alpha \Vdash (p,q))$;
2. $$\frac{\alpha \Vdash (p,q) \quad \alpha \Vdash (p',q')}{\alpha \Vdash (p,q)\cdot(p',q')};$$
3. $$\frac{\alpha \Vdash (p,q) \quad (p,q) \lhd U}{(\exists (p',q') \in U)(\alpha \Vdash (p',q'))};$$
4. $$\frac{\alpha \Vdash (p,q)}{Pos(p,q)}.$$

We observe here that, since $Pos(p,q)$ is decidable, the fourth rule is provable from the third. Let $Pt(\mathcal{R})$ denote the formal points of $\mathcal{R}$, called *formal reals*.

We will now prove that both $\lhd$ and $\lhd_f$ are covers, the latter being the Stone compactification of the former.

Proposition 5. *The relation $\lhd_f$ is a cover.*

Proof. Before proving the cover rules for $\lhd_f$, we observe that the rule of $\cdot$ - right follows from the rule of *localization* $\frac{a \lhd U}{a \cdot b \lhd U \cdot b}$ since the base is a semilattice.

Reflexivity: By definition.

Transitivity: Suppose $(p,q) \lhd_f U$ and $U \lhd_f V$. Then it is straightforward by induction on the derivation of $(p,q) \lhd_f U$ that $(p,q) \lhd_f V$.

$\cdot$ - Left: By the fourth axiom since $p \le max(p,r)$ and $min(q,s) \le q$.

Localization: Suppose $(p,q) \lhd_f U$. Then we prove, by induction on the derivation of $(p,q) \lhd_f U$, that $(p,q)\cdot(r,s) \lhd_f U\cdot(r,s)$. We first observe that we can assume $r < s$, because if $s \le r$ the claim follows trivially by the first rule. If $(p,q) \lhd_f U$ is derived by the first or the second axiom the claim is trivial.

Suppose it is derived by the third axiom with the assumptions $p \leq t < v \leq q$, $(p,v) \lhd_f U$ and $(t,q) \lhd_f U$. If $s \leq t$ then $min(v,s) = min(q,s)$ and therefore $(p,v)\cdot(r,s) = (p,q)\cdot(r,s)$. From $(p,v) \lhd_f U$, by induction hypothesis, we have $(p,v)\cdot(r,s) \lhd_f U\cdot(r,s)$ thus $(p,q)\cdot(r,s) \lhd_f U\cdot(r,s)$. If $v \leq r$ then $max(t,r) = max(p,s)$ and the conclusion follows as above by applying inductive hypothesis to the premiss $(t,q) \lhd_f U$. Otherwise $max(t,r) < min(v,s)$ and we have, by induction hypothesis and the same rule, $(p,q)\cdot(r,s) \lhd_f U\cdot(r,s)$. If it comes from $(p',q') \lhd_f U$, with $p' \leq p < q \leq q'$, then by induction hypothesis we get $(p',q')\cdot(r,s) \lhd_f U\cdot(r,s)$ and since $max(p',r) \leq max(p,r)$ and $min(q,s) \leq min(q',s)$ we obtain by the same rule $(p,q)\cdot(r,s) \lhd_f U\cdot(r,s)$. □

Moreover we have the following essential result:

Proposition 6. *The relation $\lhd_f$ is a Stone cover, i.e., a cover with the property that, for arbitrary $(p,q) \in S$ and $U \subseteq S$, $(p,q) \lhd_f U$ implies the existence of a finite subset U_0 of U such that $(p,q) \lhd_f U_0$.*

Proof. Suppose $(p,q) \lhd_f U$. Then we can find a finite subset U_0 of U such that $(p,q) \lhd_f U_0$ by induction on the derivation of $(p,q) \lhd_f U$. □

The following lemma is used to prove that $\lhd$ is a cover.

Lemma 7. *Suppose $(p,q) \lhd_f U$, $U \lhd V$ and let $p < p' < q' < q$. Then $(p',q') \lhd_f V$.*

Proof. By induction on the derivation of $(p,q) \lhd_f U$. If $p \geq q$ and $p < p' < q' < q$ we have $(p',q') \lhd_f U$ by axioms 1 and 4. If $(p,q) \in U$ then by the assumption $U \lhd V$ we have $(p,q) \lhd V$ and therefore if $p < p' < q' < q$, $(p',q') \lhd_f V$. If $p \leq r < s \leq q$, $(p,s) \lhd_f U$ and $(r,q) \lhd_f U$ we distinguish two cases according to the position of r,s with respect to p',q'. In the first case $r < p'$ or $q' < s$, in the second $p' \leq r < s \leq q'$. Suppose $r < p'$, then $r < p' < q' < q$ so from the assumptions $(r,q) \lhd_f U$ and $U \lhd V$ we get, by induction hypothesis, $(p',q') \lhd_f V$. If $q' < s$ we conclude symmetrically. If $p' \leq r < s \leq q'$ we can find r', s' such that $r < r' < s' < s$. Therefore we have $p < p' < s' < s$ and $r < r' < q' < q$. By induction hypothesis the former, together with $(p,s) \lhd_f U$ and $U \lhd V$ gives $(p',s') \lhd_f V$ and the latter together with $(r,q) \lhd_f U$ and $U \lhd V$ gives $(r',q') \lhd_f V$. Since $p' \leq r' < s \leq q'$ we get the conclusion $(p',q') \lhd_f V$. If $(p,q) \lhd_f U$ is derived by the fourth rule we just apply induction hypothesis to the premiss and the fourth rule again. □

Proposition 8. *The relation $\lhd$ is a cover.*

Proof. Reflexivity: Let $(p,q) \in U$, then $(p,q) \lhd_f U$ and so if $p < p' < q' < q$ we have $(p',q') \lhd_f U$. Therefore $(p,q) \lhd U$.

Transitivity: Let $p < p' < q' < q$. Then there exist p'' and q'' such that $p < p'' < p' < q' < q'' < q$ and $(p'',q'') \lhd_f U$. By the lemma above we have $(p',q') \lhd_f V$ and therefore $(p,q) \lhd V$.

$\cdot$ - Left: Suppose $(p,q) \lhd U$, then $(p,q)\cdot(r,s) \lhd U$ follows directly from the definitions since $max(p,r) < p' < q' < min(q,s)$ implies $p < p' < q' < q$.

$\cdot$ - Right: Straightforward from the validity of $\cdot$ - right for $\lhd_f$. □

Finally, it is straightforward to prove monotonicity and positivity for Pos, thus completing the proof that $\mathcal{R}$ is a formal topology.

We will now prove that the cover $\lhd_f$ is the Stone compactification of the cover $\lhd$. We point out that this result is not needed in the proof of the Heine-Borel theorem.

Proposition 9. *If $(p,q) \lhd U$ and U is finite, then $(p,q) \lhd_f U$.*

Before proving Proposition 9, observe we can assume that, for all $(r,s) \in U$, $Pos((p,q)\cdot(r,s))$ holds. In fact, if this is not the case, from $(p,q) \lhd U$ we have $(p,q) \lhd ((p,q)\cdot U)^+$, and from $(p,q) \lhd_f ((p,q)\cdot U)^+$, by $\cdot$ - left and transitivity, $(p,q) \lhd_f U$. The following lemmas will allow a proof of Proposition 9 by induction on the number of elements of U.

Lemma 10. *For positive (p,q), $(p,q) \lhd_f (r,s)$ implies $r \le p < q \le s$.*

Proof. By induction on the derivation of $(p,q) \lhd_f (r,s)$. If $(p,q) \lhd_f (r,s)$ is derived by the first or the second axiom, the claim holds trivially. If it is derived by the third axiom from $p \le u < v \le q$, $(p,v) \lhd_f (r,s)$, $(u,q) \lhd_f (r,s)$, then by induction hypothesis we have $r \le p < v \le s$, $r \le u < q \le s$ and therefore $r \le p < q \le s$. If it follows from $p' \le p < q \le q'$ and $(p',q') \lhd_f (r,s)$ by the fourth axiom, then by induction hypothesis $r \le p' < q' \le s$ and therefore $r \le p < q \le s$. □

Corollary 11. $(p,q) \lhd (r,s)$ *implies* $(p,q) \lhd_f (r,s)$.

Proof. Let $(p,q) \lhd (r,s)$. Then, for all p',q' such that $p < p' < q' < q$, we have $r \le p' < q' \le s$, and therefore $r \le p < q \le s$, hence $(p,q) \lhd_f (r,s)$. □

Lemma 12. *Suppose that $p < q$ and $(p,q) \lhd U$, where U is finite and for all $(r,s) \in U$, $Pos((p,q),(r,s))$ holds. Then there exists $(p_1,q_1) \in U$ such that $p_1 \le p < q_1$.*

Proof. Let (p_1,q_1) be an element of U such that p_1 is the smallest (with respect to the usual order of the rational numbers) of all the first projections of elements of U. Then $p_1 \le p$. In fact, for all $(p',q') \in U$, $p_1 \le max(p',p) < min(q',q) \le q$, that implies $U \cdot (p,q) \lhd_f (p_1,q)$. Since $(p,q) \lhd U\cdot(p,q)$, we have by transitivity $(p,q) \lhd (p_1,q)$, and therefore, by Corollary 11 and Lemma 10, we get $p_1 \le p < q$. Then, by the assumption that for, all $(r,s) \in U$, $Pos((p,q)\cdot(r,s))$ holds, we have $p_1 \le p < q_1$. □

Lemma 13. *Suppose that $(p,q) \lhd_f U$, and let $p < u < q$. Then there exists $(r,s) \in U$ such that $r < u < s$.*

Proof. Straightforward by induction on the derivation of $(p,q) \lhd_f U$. □

Corollary 14. *Suppose that $(p,q) \lhd U$, and let $p < u < q$. Then there exists $(r,s) \in U$ such that $r < u < s$.*

Proof. If $p < u < q$, there exist p', q' such that $p < p' < u < q' < q$ and therefore $(p', q') \lhd_f U$. Then the conclusion follows by Lemma 13. □

Lemma 15. *Suppose that* $(p,q) \lhd U$, *and let* $(r,s) \in U$ *with* $\neg Pos((p,q)\cdot(r,s))$. *Then* $(p,q) \lhd U \setminus \{(r,s)\}$.

Proof. From $(p,q) \lhd U$ we have, by positivity and $\cdot$ - right, $(p,q) \lhd (U\cdot(p,q))^+$. Since $\neg Pos((p,q)\cdot(r,s))$ holds, we have $(U\cdot(p,q))^+ \subseteq (U \setminus \{(r,s)\})\cdot(p,q)$ and therefore $(p,q) \lhd (U \setminus \{(r,s)\})\cdot(p,q)$, thus a fortiori $(p,q) \lhd U \setminus \{(r,s)\}$. □

Proof of Proposition 9. The proof is by induction on the number of elements of U. If $U = \{(r,s)\}$ the claim follows by Corollary 11. Suppose the result holds for $|U| = n$ and suppose that $(p,q) \lhd U_{n+1}$, where $|U_{n+1}| = n+1$. By Lemma 12 there exists $(p_1,q_1) \in U_{n+1}$ such that $p_1 \le p < q_1$. If $q \le q_1$ then $p_1 \le p < q \le q_1$ and therefore $(p,q) \lhd_f (p_1,q_1)$, so by reflexivity and transitivity $(p,q) \lhd_f U_{n+1}$. Otherwise $q_1 < q$, hence by Corollary 14 there exists $(p_2,q_2) \in U_{n+1}$ such that $p_2 < q_1 < q_2$. So we can find r, s such that $q_1 < r < s < q_2$. Since $p \le r$ and $(p,q) \lhd U_{n+1}$, $(r,q) \lhd U_{n+1}$. From $q_1 < r$, we have $\neg Pos((r,q)\cdot(p_1,q_1))$ and therefore, by Lemma 15, we have $(r,q) \lhd U_{n+1} \setminus \{(p_1,q_1)\}$, so that by induction hypothesis $(r,q) \lhd_f U_{n+1} \setminus \{(p_1,q_1)\}$. Then a fortiori $(r,q) \lhd_f U_{n+1}$. Since $(p,s) \lhd_f \{(p_1,q_1),(p_2,q_2)\}$, we also have $(p,s) \lhd_f U_{n+1}$ and therefore $(p,q) \lhd_f U_{n+1}$. □

We conclude this section with observing that formal reals offer an alternative approach to constructive analysis; they have been used in the treatment of the Hahn-Banach theorem (cf. [CCN]) and of the Cantor and Baire theorems (cf. [N1], [NS]). Moreover, we can show that they are equivalent to real numbers à la Bishop. First we recall the following (cf. [Bi]):

Definition 16. A *real number* is a sequence of rational numbers $(x_n)_n$ such that

$$|x_m - x_n| \le m^{-1} + n^{-1} \quad (m, n \in \mathbb{N}^+) .$$

Two real numbers, $(x_n)_n$ and $(y_n)_n$, are equal if

$$|x_n - y_n| \le 2n^{-1} \quad (n \in \mathbb{N}^+) .$$

We have:

Proposition 17. *There exists a bijective correspondence between formal reals and real numbers à la Bishop.*

Proof. Let α be a formal real. By the rules in Definition 4, α contains arbitrarily small intervals, in particular (p,q) with $q - p \le 2/3$. Since $\frac{2x+y}{3} < \frac{x+2y}{3}$ again by the rules in Definition 4, $\alpha \Vdash (x,y)$ implies $\alpha \Vdash (x, \frac{x+2x}{3}) \lor \alpha \Vdash (\frac{2x+y}{3}, y)$. Now we can recursively generate a sequence of intervals $((x_n, y_n))_n$, by case-analysis:

$$(x_1, y_1) \equiv (p,q)$$

$$(x_{i+1}, y_{i+1}) \equiv \begin{cases} (x_i, \frac{x_i+2y_i}{3}) \text{ if } \alpha \Vdash (x_i, \frac{x_i+2y_i}{3}) \\ (\frac{2x_i+y_i}{3}, y_i) \text{ if } \alpha \Vdash (\frac{2x_i+y_i}{3}, y_i) . \end{cases}$$

It can be verified that the sequences $(x_n)_n$ and $(y_n)_n$ are real numbers according to Definition 16.

Conversely, if $(x_n)_n$ is a real number à la Bishop, then the set defined by

$$\alpha \equiv \bigcup_{n \in \mathbb{N}^+} \{(p,q) : p < x_n - 2/n < x_n + 2/n < q\}$$

is a formal real.

Moreover the correspondence thus established is bijective. □

4 The Formal Space $[a,b]$

Given two rational numbers a, b such that $a < b$, we will define a formal space whose formal points are the formal points of $\mathcal{R}$ between a and b. We will follow the standard way to build, from an open U of a space X, a space classically corresponding to the closed subspace $X \backslash U$. Indeed, we will define a cover relation $\lhd_{[a,b]}$ and the intended meaning of $(p,q) \lhd_{[a,b]} U$ is that the part of (p,q) inside the closed interval $[a,b]$ is covered by U. By classical set-theoretic reasoning we have that $(p,q) \cap [a,b] \subseteq \cup U$ is the same as

$$(p,q) \subseteq (\cup U) \cup \{(r,a) \mid r < a\} \cup \{(b,s) \mid b < s\} .$$

An interval (p,q) is then positive in the space $[a,b]$ iff the part of (p,q) inside $[a,b]$ is positive. This justifies the following:

Definition 18. Let $\mathcal{R} \equiv \langle Q \times Q, \cdot, \lhd, Pos \rangle$ be the formal topology of formal reals and let $[a,b]$ be defined by

$$[a,b] \equiv \langle Q \times Q, \cdot, \lhd_{[a,b]}, Pos_{[a,b]} \rangle$$

where the relation $\lhd_{[a,b]}$ is defined by

$$(p,q) \lhd_{[a,b]} U \equiv (p,q) \lhd U \cup \{(r,a) \mid r < a\} \cup \{(b,s) \mid b < s\} ,$$

and the predicate $Pos_{[a,b]}$ is defined by

$$Pos_{[a,b]}(p,q) \equiv Pos((p,q) \cdot (a,b)) .$$

In the sequel we will use the notation $\mathcal{C}[a,b]$ for $\{(r,a) \mid r < a\} \cup \{(b,s) \mid b < s\}$ and we will understand $\mathcal{C}[a,b]$ as the complement of $[a,b]$.

By the following proposition and by the immediate verification that $Pos_{[a,b]}$ is a positivity predicate, the above does indeed define a formal topology.

Proposition 19. *The relation $\lhd_{[a,b]}$ is a cover.*

The proposition follows from the following lemma:

Lemma 20. *Let $\lhd$ be a cover on the base S and let $V \subseteq S$. Then the relation $\lhd_V$ defined by*

$$a \lhd_V U \equiv a \lhd U \cup V$$

is a cover.

Proof. Reflexivity, transitivity, $\cdot$ - left are straightforward, and $\cdot$ - right follows from the fact that in general $(U \cup V) \cdot (W \cup V) \lhd (U \cdot W) \cup V$. □

As in Section 3, the general definition of formal point of a formal topology can be specialized to $[a, b]$:

Definition 21. A subset α of S is a *formal point of* $[a, b]$ if it satisfies

1. $(\exists p, q)(\alpha \Vdash (p, q))$;
2. $\dfrac{\alpha \Vdash (p, q) \quad \alpha \Vdash (p', q')}{\alpha \Vdash (p, q) \cdot (p', q')}$;
3. $\dfrac{\alpha \Vdash (p, q) \quad (p, q) \lhd_{[a,b]} U}{(\exists (p', q') \in U)(\alpha \Vdash (p', q'))}$;
4. $\dfrac{\alpha \Vdash (p, q)}{Pos_{[a,b]}(p, q)}$.

As was the case in Definition 4 the fourth rule is provable from the third, since $Pos_{[a,b]}(p, q)$ is decidable. We will denote with $Pt([a, b])$ the collection of formal points of $[a, b]$, called *formal reals of the interval* $[a, b]$.

We recall here the definition of order for $Pt(\mathcal{R})$ (cf. [NS]):

$$\alpha < \beta \equiv (\exists (p, q), (r, s) \in S)(\alpha \Vdash (p, q) \ \&\ \beta \Vdash (r, s) \ \&\ q < r) ;$$

$$\alpha \leq \beta \equiv \neg(\beta < \alpha) .$$

Let $\bar{a}$ denote the formal point $\{(p, q) \,|\, p < a < q\}$, corresponding to the rational a. Then we have $\alpha < \bar{a} \Leftrightarrow (\exists (p, q) \in S)(\alpha \Vdash (p, q) \ \&\ q < a)$.

The following proposition says that the formal space $[a, b]$ really corresponds to the closed interval $[a, b]$, i.e., the definition of the formal space $[a, b]$ is correct:

Proposition 22. $\alpha \in Pt([a, b]) \Leftrightarrow \alpha \in Pt(R) \ \&\ \bar{a} \leq \alpha \leq \bar{b}$.

Proof. $\Rightarrow$: Let $\alpha \in Pt([a, b])$. It is immediate that $\alpha \in Pt(R)$ since $(p, q) \lhd U$ implies $(p, q) \lhd_{[a,b]} U$. To show that $\bar{a} \leq \alpha$, suppose $\alpha < \bar{a}$. Then by definition $(\exists (p, q) \in S)(\alpha \Vdash (p, q) \ \&\ q < a)$ and therefore $\neg Pos_{[a,b]}(p, q)$, against the assumption. Hence $\bar{a} \leq \alpha$. The inequality $\alpha \leq \bar{b}$ is proved symmetrically.

$\Leftarrow$: Let $\alpha \in Pt(R) \ \&\ \bar{a} \leq \alpha \leq \bar{b}$. Clauses 1 and 2 are obvious.

3. Let $\alpha \Vdash (p, q)$ and $(p, q) \lhd_{[a,b]} U$. Then there exists $(r, s) \in U \cup \mathcal{C}[a, b]$ such that $\alpha \Vdash (r, s)$. Since $Pos_{[a,b]}(r, s)$ holds, it cannot be $(r, s) = (r, a)$ or $(r, s) = (b, s)$ and therefore $(r, s) \in U$. □

5 The Heine-Borel Covering Theorem for $[a, b]$

Here we will prove the Heine-Borel covering theorem asserting that any open cover of a closed and bounded interval has a finite sub-cover. We will use the notation $[a, b] \lhd_{[a,b]} U$ for $(\forall p, q)((p, q) \lhd_{[a,b]} U)$, meaning that U covers the whole space $[a, b]$.

Theorem 23. *The formal space* $[a,b]$ *is compact, i.e.*

$$[a,b] \lhd_{[a,b]} U \Rightarrow (\exists U_0 \subseteq_\omega U)([a,b] \lhd_{[a,b]} U_0) .$$

The proof uses the following lemma:

Lemma 24. $[a,b] \lhd_{[a,b]} U \Leftrightarrow (\exists r,s)(r < a < b < s \;\&\; (r,s) \lhd_f U \cup C[a,b])$.

Proof. $\Rightarrow$: By the hypothesis $[a,b] \lhd_{[a,b]} U$, in particular there exist p, q such that $p < a < b < q$ and $(p,q) \lhd_{[a,b]} U$. Then by definition

$$(\forall p', q')(p < p' < q' < q \rightarrow (p',q') \lhd_f U \cup C[a,b]) .$$

By choosing r and s such that $p < r < a < b < s < q$, we can thus conclude $(\exists r,s)(r < a < b < s \;\&\; (r,s) \lhd_f U \cup C[a,b])$.

$\Leftarrow$: Observe that $(r,s) \lhd_f U \cup C[a,b]$ implies $(r,s) \lhd U \cup C[a,b]$, that is $(r,s) \lhd_{[a,b]} U$. If $r < a < b < s$, for all (p,q), $(p,q) \lhd \{(p,a),(r,s),(b,q)\}$ holds, and therefore $(p,q) \lhd_{[a,b]} \{(r,s)\}$. The claim follows by transitivity of $\lhd_{[a,b]}$. □

Proof of Theorem 23. Suppose $[a,b] \lhd_{[a,b]} U$. Then by Lemma 24 there exists r and s such that $r < a < b < s \;\&\; (r,s) \lhd_f U \cup C[a,b]$ and by Proposition 6 there exists a finite subset W_0 of $U \cup C[a,b]$ such that $(r,s) \lhd_f W_0$. Now, since W_0 is a finite subset of $U \cup C[a,b]$, we can find a finite subset U_0 of U such that $W_0 \subseteq_\omega U_0 \cup C[a,b]$. We get $(r,s) \lhd_f U_0 \cup C[a,b]$. So, by Lemma 24 again, $[a,b] \lhd_{[a,b]} U_0$. □

6 The Formal Space $[\alpha,\beta]$

Generalizing the formal space $[a,b]$ that corresponds to an interval with rational endpoints, we will define the formal space $[\alpha,\beta]$, with α and β formal reals with $\alpha < \beta$, that corresponds to an interval with real endpoints. The cover for the formal space $[\alpha,\beta]$ is defined starting from $\lhd$, similarly to the cover for $[a,b]$:

Definition 25. Let $\lhd_{[\alpha,\beta]}$ be the relation defined by

$$(p,q) \lhd_{[\alpha,\beta]} U \;\equiv (p,q) \lhd U \cup C[\alpha,\beta] ,$$

where $C[\alpha,\beta] \equiv \{(r,a) \mid r < a < \alpha\} \cup \{(b,s) \mid \beta < b < s\}$.

Proposition 26. *The relation* $\lhd_{[\alpha,\beta]}$ *is a cover.*

The proof is immediate by Lemma 20.

Definition 27. A subset γ of S is a *formal point of* $[\alpha,\beta]$ if it satisfies

1. $(\exists p,q)(\gamma \Vdash (p,q))$;
2. $\dfrac{\gamma \Vdash (p,q) \quad \gamma \Vdash (p',q')}{\gamma \Vdash (p,q)\cdot(p',q')}$;

3. $$\frac{\gamma \Vdash (p,q) \quad (p,q) \lhd_{[\alpha,\beta]} U}{(\exists (p',q') \in U)(\gamma \Vdash (p',q'))} \; ;$$

4. $$\frac{\gamma \Vdash (p,q)}{p < q \;\&\; \alpha < \bar{q} \;\&\; \bar{p} < \beta} \; .$$

We remark that the property $p < q \;\&\; \alpha < \bar{q} \;\&\; \bar{p} < \beta$ of the basic neighbourhood (p,q) expresses the fact that (p,q) has positive intersection with the interval $[\alpha,\beta]$. Nevertheless, we do not call it a positivity predicate, since the property of positivity does not seem to be constructively valid for this predicate.

The collection of formal points of $[\alpha,\beta]$ will be denoted $Pt([\alpha,\beta])$. As in the case of the formal space $[a,b]$ we have:

Proposition 28. $\gamma \in Pt([\alpha,\beta]) \;\Leftrightarrow\; \gamma \in Pt(R) \;\&\; \alpha \le \gamma \le \beta$.

Proof. $\Rightarrow$: If $\gamma \in Pt([\alpha,\beta])$ it is immediate to show $\gamma \in Pt(R)$ since $(p,q) \lhd U$ implies $(p,q) \lhd_{[\alpha,\beta]} U$. Now suppose $\gamma < \alpha$. Then by definition

$$(\exists (p_\gamma,q_\gamma),(p_\alpha,q_\alpha) \in S)(\gamma \Vdash (p_\gamma,q_\gamma) \;\&\; \alpha \Vdash (p_\alpha,q_\alpha) \;\&\; q_\gamma < p_\alpha) \; .$$

From $\gamma \Vdash (p_\gamma,q_\gamma)$, by the fourth rule, we obtain that $\alpha < \bar{q}_\gamma$ which contradicts $\bar{q}_\gamma < \bar{p}_\alpha < \alpha$. Hence $\alpha \le \gamma$. We obtain $\gamma \le \beta$ symmetrically.

$\Leftarrow$: 1 and 2 are direct.

3. Let $\gamma \Vdash (p,q)$ and $(p,q) \lhd_{[\alpha,\beta]} U$. By definition we have $(p,q) \lhd U \cup \mathcal{C}[\alpha,\beta]$ and by the third rule for $Pt(\mathcal{R})$ we get $(\exists (p',q') \in U \cup \mathcal{C}[\alpha,\beta])(\gamma \Vdash (p',q'))$. If $\gamma \Vdash (p',q')$, by the fourth rule for $Pt([\alpha,\beta])$ (which is proved below), $\alpha < \bar{q}'$ and $\bar{p}' < \beta$ and therefore $(p',q') \in U$. Hence $(\exists (p',q') \in U)(\gamma \Vdash (p',q'))$.

4. Let $\gamma \Vdash (p,q)$. Then by the fourth rule for $Pt(\mathcal{R})$ we have $p < q$. If $\gamma \Vdash (p,q)$ we also have $\gamma < \bar{q}$ and since $\alpha < \gamma$ we get $\alpha < \bar{q}$. The inequality $\bar{p} < \beta$ is proved symmetrically. □

7 The Heine-Borel Covering Theorem for $[\alpha,\beta]$

Here we will prove the Heine-Borel covering theorem for closed intervals with real-valued endpoints. We introduce the notation:

$$[\alpha,\beta] \lhd_{[\alpha,\beta]} U \equiv (\forall p,q)((p,q) \lhd_{[\alpha,\beta]} U) \; .$$

Theorem 29. *The formal space* $[\alpha,\beta]$ *is compact, i.e.*

$$[\alpha,\beta] \lhd_{[\alpha,\beta]} U \Rightarrow (\exists U_0 \subseteq_\omega U)([a,b] \lhd_{[\alpha,\beta]} U_0) \; .$$

The proof uses the following lemma:

Lemma 30. $[\alpha,\beta] \lhd_{[\alpha,\beta]} U \Leftrightarrow (\exists r,s)(\bar{r} < \alpha < \beta < \bar{s} \;\&\; (r,s) \lhd_f U \cup \mathcal{C}[\alpha,\beta])$.

Proof. $\Rightarrow$: Given $[\alpha,\beta] \lhd_{[\alpha,\beta]} U$, there exist p, q such that $\bar{p} < \alpha < \beta < \bar{q}$ and $(p,q) \lhd_{[\alpha,\beta]} U$. By definition

$$(\forall p', q')(p < p' < q' < q \rightarrow (p', q') \lhd_f U \cup \mathcal{C}[\alpha,\beta]) .$$

Now we can choose r, s such that $\bar{p} < \bar{r} < \alpha < \beta < \bar{s} < \bar{q}$. Hence we obtain $(\exists r, s)(\bar{r} < \alpha < \beta < \bar{s}\ \&\ (r,s) \lhd_f U \cup \mathcal{C}[\alpha,\beta])$.

$\Leftarrow$: Choose (r,s) such that $\bar{r} < \alpha < \beta < \bar{s}$ and $(r,s) \lhd_f U \cup \mathcal{C}[\alpha,\beta]$. For any a, b with $\bar{r} < \bar{a} < \alpha < \beta < \bar{b} < \bar{s}$ we get, for all (p,q), $(p,q) \lhd_f \{(p,a),(r,s),(b,q)\}$. We have $(p,a) \lhd_f U \cup \mathcal{C}[\alpha,\beta]$ because if $p < a$ then $(p,a) \in U \cup \mathcal{C}[\alpha,\beta]$ otherwise $(p,a) \lhd_f U \cup \mathcal{C}[\alpha,\beta]$ by axiom. By symmetry we have $(b,q) \lhd_f U \cup \mathcal{C}[\alpha,\beta]$, and therefore, by transitivity, $(p,q) \lhd_f U \cup \mathcal{C}[\alpha,\beta]$. This also means that $(p,q) \lhd_{[\alpha,\beta]} U$ and, since (p,q) is arbitrary, $[\alpha,\beta] \lhd_{[\alpha,\beta]} U$. □

Proof of Theorem 29. Suppose $[\alpha,\beta] \lhd_{[\alpha,\beta]} U$. Then, by Lemma 30, there exist r and s such that $\bar{r} < \alpha < \beta < \bar{s}\ \&\ (r,s) \lhd_f U \cup \mathcal{C}[\alpha,\beta]$ and by Proposition 5 there exists a finite subset W_0 of $U \cup \mathcal{C}[a,b]$ such that $(r,s) \lhd_f W_0$. Then we can find a finite subset U_0 of U such that $W_0 \subseteq_\omega U_0 \cup \mathcal{C}[\alpha,\beta]$ and we get $(r,s) \lhd_f U_0 \cup \mathcal{C}[\alpha,\beta]$. Using Lemma 30 again, $[\alpha,\beta] \lhd_{[\alpha,\beta]} U_0$. □

8 Acknowledgements

We wish to thank Thierry Coquand and Jan Smith for helpful suggestions and remarks.

References

[A] P. Aczel. *An Introduction to Inductive Definitions*, in *Handbook of Mathematical Logic*, J. Barwise ed., North-Holland (1977) 739–782.

[B] L. E. J. Brouwer. *Die intuitionistische Form des Heine-Borelschen Theorems*, in *L. E. J. Brouwer Collected Works*, A. Heyting ed., North-Holland, Amsterdam (1975) vol. 1, 350–351, 1926C.

[Bi] E. Bishop. "Foundations of Constructive Analysis", Mc Graw Hill, 1967.

[JC] J. Cederquist. *A machine assisted formalization of pointfree topology in type theory*, Chalmers University of Technology and University of Göteborg, Sweden, Licentiate Thesis (1994).

[CCN] J. Cederquist, T. Coquand, S. Negri *Helly-Hahn-Banach in formal topology*, forthcoming.

[C] T. Coquand. *An intuitionistic proof of Tychonoff's theorem*, The Journal of Symbolic Logic vol. 57, no. 1 (1992) 28–32.

[C2] T. Coquand. *Constructive Topology and Combinatorics*, proceeding of the conference Constructivity in Computer Science, San Antonio, LNCS 613 (1992) 159–164.

[FG] M. P. Fourman, R.J. Grayson. *Formal Spaces*, in "The L. E. J. Brouwer Centenary Symposium", A. S. Troelstra and D. van Dalen (eds), North-Holland, Amsterdam (1982) 107–122.

[F] M. Franchella. "L. E. J. Brouwer pensatore eterodosso. L'intuizionismo tra matematica e filosofia", Guerini Studio (1994).

[H] A. Heyting. "Intuitionism, an introduction", North-Holland (1971).

[J] P. T. Johnstone. "Stone Spaces", Cambridge University Press (1982).

[M] L. Magnusson, "The Implementation of ALF - a Proof Editor based on Martin-Löf's Monomorphic Type Theory with Explicit Substitution", Chalmers University of Technology and University of Göteborg, PhD thesis (1995).

[ML] P. Martin-Löf. "Notes on Constructive Mathematics", Almqvist & Wiksell, Stockholm (1970).

[ML1] P. Martin-Löf. "Intuitionistic type theory", notes by Giovanni Sambin of a series of lectures given in Padua, June 1980, Bibliopolis, Napoli (1984).

[N] S. Negri. *Stone bases, alias the constructive content of Stone representation*, "Logic and Algebra", A. Ursini and P. Aglianò eds., Dekker, New York (1996) 617–636.

[N1] S. Negri. "Dalla topologia formale all'analisi", Ph.D. thesis, University of Padua (1996).

[NS] S. Negri, D. Soravia. *The continuum as a formal space*, Rapporto Interno n.4, 17-7-95, Dipartimento di Matematica Pura e Applicata, Università di Padova.

[NV] S. Negri, S. Valentini. *Tychonoff's theorem in the framework of formal topologies*, The Journal of Symbolic Logic (in press).

[NPS] B. Nordström, K. Peterson, J. Smith, "Programming in Martin-Löf's Type Theory", Oxford University Press (1990).

[S] G. Sambin. *Intuitionistic formal spaces – a first communication*, in Mathematical logic and its applications, D. Skordev ed., Plenum (1987) 187–204.

[S1] G. Sambin. *Intuitionistic formal spaces and their neighbourhoods*, in "Logic Colloquium 88", R. Ferro et al. eds., North-Holland, Amsterdam (1989) 261–285.

[SVV] G. Sambin, S. Valentini, P. Virgili. *Constructive Domain Theory as a branch of Intuitionistic Pointfree Topology*, Theoretical Computer Science (in press).

[vS] W. P. van Stigt. "Brouwer's Intuitionism", Studies in the History and Philosophy of Mathematics, vol. 2, North-Holland (1990).

An Application of Constructive Completeness

Thierry Coquand and Jan M. Smith

Department of Computing Science,
Chalmers University of Technology and Univ. of Göteborg,
S-41296 Göteborg, Sweden.
e-mail: {coquand, smith}@cs.chalmers.se

Introduction

The completeness theorem for first-order logic is one of the basic result of classical model theory. It states that a first-order sentence is provable if and only if it holds in all models, or, in a relativised form, that a first-order sentence is derivable in a theory if and only if it holds in any model of the theory. This expresses a strong relation between syntax and semantics and can be used to give elegant semantical proofs of purely syntactical properties. One typical use is for proving conservativity results: to prove that a first-order theory T_2 is a conservative extension of a theory T_1, it is enough to show that any model of T_1 can be extended to a model of T_2. It follows then directly that a formula derivable in T_2 holds in any model of T_1, and hence, by the completeness theorem, is also derivable in T_1.

The usual proofs of the completeness theorem, by Gödel and Henkin, are not constructive. In this paper, we explore one possible effective version of this theorem for first-order intuitionistic logic, that uses topological models in a point-free setting, following Sambin [10]. The truth-values, instead of being simply booleans, can be arbitrary open sets of a given topological space. There are two advantages with considering this more abstract notion of model. The first is that, by using formal topology, we get a remarkably simple completeness proof; it seems indeed simpler than the usual classical completeness proof. The second is that this completeness proof is now constructive and elementary. In particular, it does not use any impredicativity and can be formalized in intuitionistic type theory; this is of importance for us, since we want to develop model theory in a computer system for type theory. Formal topology has been developed in the type theory implementation ALF [1] by Cederquist [2] and the completeness proof we use has been checked in ALF by Persson [9].

In view of the extreme simplicity of this proof, it might be feared that it has no interesting applications. We show that this is not the case by analysing a conservativity theorem due to Dragalin [4] concerning a non-standard extension of Heyting arithmetic. We can transpose directly the usual model theoretic conservativity argument, that we sketched above, in this framework. It seems likely that a direct syntactical proof of this result would have to be more involved.

The first part of this paper presents a definition of topological models, Sambin's completeness proof, and an alternative completeness proof; we also discuss how Beth models relate to our approach. The second part shows how to use this in order to give a proof of Dragalin's conservativity result; our proof is different from his and, we believe, simpler.

In [8] a stronger conservativity result is proved, using more sophisticated methods based on sheaf semantics.

1 Intuitionistic Model Theory

A *formal topology* $T = \langle S, \cdot, 1, \lhd \rangle$ is a commutative idempotent monoid $\langle S, \cdot, 1 \rangle$ with a covering relation $\lhd$, that is, a relation which satisfies the following rules.

Reflexivity

$$\frac{a \in U}{a \lhd U}$$

Transitivity

$$\frac{a \lhd U \quad U \lhd V}{a \lhd V}$$

$\cdot$ -left

$$\frac{a \lhd U}{a \cdot b \lhd U}$$

Stability

$$\frac{a \lhd U \quad b \lhd V}{a \cdot b \lhd U \cdot V}$$

where $U \lhd V$ means that every element of U is covered by V. Intuitively, the elements of S are the basic open sets and the multiplication $\cdot$ corresponds to intersection. An open set is represented by a set of basic open sets; in traditional topology with points, this corresponds to that an open set can be represented as the union of a set of basic open sets. For the details of formal topology in a type theoretic setting, we refer to Sambin [11].

1.1 Topological interpretations

A *formal topological interpretation* of a first order language consists of the following.

- A topology $T = \langle S, \cdot, 1, \lhd \rangle$.
- A set D, the domain of the interpretation.
- To each individual constant a an element $[\![a]\!]$ in D and to each function constant f^n of arity n a function $[\![f^n]\!]$ in $D^n \to D$.
- To each relation R^n of arity n a function $[\![R^n]\!]$ that gives an open set to each element in D^n.

Given an assignment ρ of an element in D to each variable, we associate an element $[\![t]\!]_\rho$ in D to each term t by

$$[\![x]\!]_\rho = \rho(x)$$
$$[\![a]\!]_\rho = [\![a]\!]$$
$$[\![f^n(t_1,\ldots,t_n)]\!]_\rho = [\![f^n]\!]([\![t_1]\!]_\rho,\ldots,[\![t_n]\!]_\rho)$$

We can now associate an open set $[\![A]\!]_\rho$ to each formula A by induction as follows.

1. $[\![R(t_1,\ldots,t_n)]\!]_\rho = [\![R^n]\!]([\![t_1]\!]_\rho,\ldots,[\![t_n]\!]_\rho)$
2. $[\![\top]\!]_\rho = \{1\}$
3. $[\![\bot]\!]_\rho = \emptyset$
4. $[\![A\&B]\!]_\rho = [\![A]\!]_\rho \cdot [\![B]\!]_\rho$
5. $[\![A \vee B]\!]_\rho = [\![A]\!]_\rho \cup [\![B]\!]_\rho$
6. $[\![A \supset B]\!]_\rho = \{s \in S : \{s\} \cdot [\![A]\!]_\rho \lhd [\![B]\!]_\rho\}$
7. $[\![\exists x B(x)]\!]_\rho = \bigcup_{d\in D}[\![B(d)]\!]_\rho$
8. $[\![\forall x B(x)]\!]_\rho = \{s \in S : (\forall d \in D)(s \lhd [\![B(d)]\!]_\rho)\}$

In this definition, $[\![B(d)]\!]_\rho$ is an abbreviation of $[\![B(x)]\!]_{\rho[x:=d]}$, where the assignment $\rho[x := d]$ is obtained from ρ by giving the variable x the value d.

We say that a formula A is *valid* in an interpretation if $1 \lhd [\![A]\!]_\rho$ holds for every assignment ρ. A *model* of a set Γ of formulas is an interpretation in which all formulas of Γ are valid.

A topological interpretation can be seen as a generalization of the ordinary classical notion of interpretation in the sense that the two truth values *true* and *false* are replaced by the much richer structure of an arbitrary topological space. Topological interpretations of intuitionistic propositional logic were considered already in the thirties by Tarski [12].

Gödel and Kreisel [6] have showed that a constructive completeness proof for predicate logic is impossible with the usual intuitive definition of validity in all structures, which, in fact, turns out to be the same as validity in all Beth models; see Troelstra [13]. But by weakening the interpretation of absurdity by allowing it to possibly hold in some nodes of a Beth model, it is possible to prove completeness [15, 3]. Beth models where $k \Vdash \bot$ is not ruled out are called *exploding*; and the reason why Gödel and Kreisel's argument is not applicable on exploding models is the fact that $k \Vdash \bot$ is in general not decidable.

The formal formulation of topological models automatically includes the exploding ones: there might be basic open sets which are covered by the empty set, that is, the interpretation of absurdity; and in general it is not decidable whether $a \lhd \emptyset$ holds. We will describe in more detail below how an exploding Beth model can easily be formulated in a point-free setting. This is in contrast to the traditional approach to topological models where it seems difficult to directly introduce exploding models: in order to represent the forcing relation, a covering relation must be introduced [14].

We can now prove the following soundness theorem, where $A_1,\ldots,A_n \vdash A$ means that A is derivable from $A_1,\ldots,A_n$ in intuitionistic predicate logic, formulated in natural deduction.

Theorem 1. *If* $A_1, \ldots, A_n \vdash A$, *then* $[\![A_1]\!]_\rho \cdot \ldots \cdot [\![A_n]\!]_\rho \lhd [\![A]\!]_\rho$ *holds for every topological interpretation and for every assignment* ρ.

Proof. Straightforward by induction on the length of the derivation; for details, see Sambin [10]. □

When $n = 0$, $[\![A_1]\!]_\rho \cdot \ldots \cdot [\![A_n]\!]_\rho$ should be understood as the full space S; hence we get as a corollary that if A is a logical truth, then $[\![A]\!]_\rho$ covers the whole space, or equivalently, $1 \lhd [\![A]\!]_\rho$.

1.2 The completeness proof

We let $\vdash_T$ denote the derivability relation of some arbitrary first-order theory T. The next theorem expresses completeness.

Theorem 2. *If* $[\![A_1]\!]_\rho \cdot \ldots \cdot [\![A_n]\!]_\rho \lhd [\![A]\!]_\rho$ *holds for every topological interpretation of the theory* T *and every assignment* ρ, *then* $A_1, \ldots, A_n \vdash_T A$.

The proof of the completeness is by constructing a topology that is universal in the sense that $[\![A_1]\!]_\rho \cdot \ldots \cdot [\![A_n]\!]_\rho \lhd [\![A]\!]_\rho$ holds for the topology and every assignment ρ if and only if $A_1, \ldots, A_n \vdash_T A$.

The universal model is a term model, that is, the domain is the set of terms of the language and a term is interpreted as itself. The topology of the interpretation is obtained from the monoid $\langle L, \cdot, 1\rangle$ of formulas with provable equivalence as equality

$$A = B \text{ if and only if } \vdash_T A \leftrightarrow B,$$

and the operation $\cdot$ defined by

$$A \cdot B \;=\; A \& B.$$

The unit of the monoid is defined by $1 = \top$. Clearly, the operation $\cdot$ is well defined, that is, if $A = A'$ and $B = B'$ then $A \cdot B = A' \cdot B'$.

A is covered by a set U if and only if every proposition C that can be proved from each of the formulas in U can also be proved from A:

$$A \lhd U \;=\; (\forall C)((\forall D \in U)(D \vdash_T C) \Rightarrow A \vdash_T C).$$

This definition is the standard *Dedekind-MacNeille completion* [7] by which an arbitrary partial ordering can be extended to a complete ordering.

The open set associated with an atomic proposition is defined to be the set of formulas which proves it:

$$[\![R^n]\!](t_1, \ldots, t_n) \;=\; \{A : A \vdash_T R^n(t_1, \ldots, t_n)\}.$$

We call the topology $\mathcal{L} = \langle L, \cdot, 1, \lhd\rangle$, the *Tarski-Lindenbaum topology.* We write $[\![A]\!]$ for $[\![A]\!]_\rho$ when ρ is the identity assignment.

From the definition of covering and that $[\![\bot]\!] = \emptyset$ we get that $A \lhd \emptyset$ if and only if $A \vdash_T \bot$; hence, $A \lhd \emptyset$ is in general not decidable.

The open set $[\![A]\!]$ associated to a formula A is the set of all formulas which prove it:

Lemma 3. *For the Tarski-Lindenbaum topology,*
$B \lhd [\![A]\!]$ *if and only if* $B \vdash_T A$.

Proof: By a straightforward induction on the length of the formula A; for details, see Sambin [10]. □

Now completeness follows: if for every topology $[\![A_1]\!]_\rho \cdot \ldots \cdot [\![A_n]\!]_\rho \lhd [\![A]\!]_\rho$ holds for all assignments ρ, then, in particular, it holds for the Tarski-Lindenbaum topology and the identity assignment; hence, by the lemma, $A_1, \ldots, A_n \vdash_T A$. This remarkably simple proof should be compared with Henkin's proof for first order classical logic; but, of course, the notion of model used here is weaker than the usual one. The usual completeness proof for ordinary topological interpretations of intuitionistic logic is based on similar ideas as Henkin's proof.

1.3 Henkin Topology

We now define another covering relation on the monoid $\langle L, \cdot, 1\rangle$ of formulas with provable equivalence modulo a first-order theory T as equality. This covering is defined by an infinitary inductive definition:

$$\frac{A \in U}{A \lhd U}$$

$$\frac{A \vdash_T \bot}{A \lhd U}$$

$$\frac{A \vdash_T A' \qquad A' \lhd U}{A \lhd U}$$

$$\frac{A \vdash A_1 \vee A_2 \qquad A_1 \lhd U \qquad A_2 \lhd U}{A \lhd U}$$

$$\frac{A \vdash \exists x\, B \qquad B(t) \lhd U \text{ for all terms } t}{A \lhd U}$$

It is straightforwardly proved by induction that this defines a formal topology. We call this topology the *Henkin* topology associated to the first-order theory T. For a classical first-order theory, the points of this formal topology are exactly the Henkin sets, that is, maximal consistent extensions of the theory T. It is easy to prove

Lemma 4. *For the Henkin topology,* $A \lhd B$ *if and only* $A \vdash_T B$.

As for the Tarski-Lindenbaum topology, we have

Theorem 5. *For the Henkin topology,*
$B \lhd [\![A]\!]$ *if and only if* $B \vdash A$.

Hence, we get another completeness proof.

By induction, if $A \lhd U$ in the Henkin topology, then $A \lhd U$ in the Tarski-Lindenbaum topology. In fact, the converse implication does not hold.

1.4 Connection with Beth models

There are two versions of exploding models, one for Kripke models [15] and one for Beth models [3]. We shall explain how exploding Beth models can be seen as particular cases of topological models.

First we reformulate the notion of *spread* in the context of formal topology. We use variables $u, v, \ldots$ for finite sequences of integers. We write concatenation by juxtaposition, and $v \leq u$ means that v is of the form $un_1 \ldots n_p$, where possibly p may be 0 (in which case $u = v$.) We say that u and v are incompatible if and only if neither $u \leq v$ nor $v \leq u$ holds. A spread S is then a decidable inhabited set of sequences of integers such that

1. if $v \leq u$ and $v \in S$, then $u \in S$,
2. if $u \in S$, then there exists n such that $un \in S$.

To each spread S we associate a formal space $X(S)$ defined as follows. As a semi-lattice, $X(S)$ is formed by the disjoint union of S and an extra element Δ. The product operation is defined by

- $u \cdot v = v$ if $v \leq u$,
- $u \cdot v = \Delta$ if u and v are incompatible,
- $x \cdot y = \Delta$ if x or y is Δ.

The covering relation $u \lhd U$ is inductively defined by the clauses

- $\Delta \lhd U$,
- η-inference: $u \lhd U$ if $u \in U$,
- ζ-inference: $un \lhd U$ if $u \lhd U$,
- $\mathcal{F}$-inference: $u \lhd U$ if $un \lhd U$ for all n.

The three last rules were used by Brouwer in connection with his analysis of the bar theorem [5].

Notice that all elements of S are *positive* for this notion of covering: if $u \lhd U$ and $u \in S$, then U is inhabited. This follows from the second clause of the definition of a spread.

A non-exploding Beth model over the spread S corresponds exactly to a topological model over the space $X(S)$ and we have $u \lhd [\![A]\!]$ if and only if $u \Vdash A$. An exploding Beth model is a model where we allow $u \Vdash \bot$ for some $u \in S$. The corresponding notion of space is obtained as follows. Given a subset $E \subseteq S$, we define a new space $Y(S)$ by adding to the inductive definition of $u \lhd U$ the clause that $u \lhd U$ if $u \in E$; in particular we have $u \lhd \emptyset$ if $u \in E$. The semilattice structure of $Y(S)$ is the same as the one of $X(S)$. We can then verify that the equivalence $u \in [\![A]\!]$ if and only if $u \Vdash A$ still holds. The result of Gödel and Kreisel on the impossibility of getting a completeness theorem with non-exploding Beth models can be formulated as the fact that in order to get a completeness theorem, it is essential to consider *non*-decidable subsets E. The universal model used in the completeness proof above is not a Beth model, but we have a similar situation since $\{u \ : \ u \lhd \emptyset\}$ is not decidable.

2 Application to a Conservativity Result

The conservativity result we present is due to Dragalin [4].

2.1 Non-standard arithmetic

We first extend the language of first-order intuitionistic arithmetic, HA, with a new constant ∞ and for each numeral $\overline{n}$ add the axiom

1. $\overline{n} < \infty$

Clearly, this extension is conservative over HA: only a finite number of the new axioms can appear in a derivation; so if we just replace ∞ with a sufficiently big numeral in the derivation, we obtain a derivation in HA. We denote this extension by HA^∞.

We next extend HA^∞ with a new predicate $\mathsf{F}(x)$, expressing that x is a standard, or feasible, number. For the new predicate we add the axiom

2. $\mathsf{F}(0)$
3. $\neg\mathsf{F}(\infty)$
4. $x = y \wedge \mathsf{F}(x) \supset \mathsf{F}(y)$
5. $y < x \wedge \mathsf{F}(x) \supset \mathsf{F}(y)$
6. Let f be an arbitrary function constant of HA. Then

$$\mathsf{F}(x_1) \wedge \cdots \wedge \mathsf{F}(x_n) \supset \mathsf{F}(f(x_1, \ldots, x_n))$$

7. Induction scheme for standard numbers:

$$A(0) \wedge \forall x(\mathsf{F}(x) \wedge A(x) \supset A(s(x))) \supset \forall x(\mathsf{F}(x) \supset A(x))$$

where $A(x)$ is an arbitrary formula of the extended language.

From now on we let $\lhd$ denote the covering relation of an arbitrary model for HA^∞. We define an interpretation of F by

$$[\![\mathsf{F}(t)]\!]_\rho = \bigcup_{n \in N} [\![t = \overline{n}]\!]_\rho$$

In this interpretation the above axioms are all validated:

Lemma 6. *Let P be any of the above axioms about* F. *Then* $1 \lhd [\![P]\!]$ *in any model of* HA^∞.

Proof. The proof is straightforward and almost the same as the corresponding part of the proof by Dragalin [4]. □

We let $\mathsf{HA}^\infty\mathsf{F}$ denote HA extended with these axioms. Our main result is the following.

Theorem 7. $\mathsf{HA}^\infty\mathsf{F}$ *is conservative over* HA.

Proof. It is enough to prove that $\mathsf{HA}^\infty\mathsf{F}$ is conservative over HA^∞. So let A be a formula of HA which is derivable in $\mathsf{HA}^\infty\mathsf{F}$, that is, there is a finite conjunction Γ of axioms about F such that $\mathsf{HA}^\infty + \Gamma \vdash A$. By theorem 1 we have that $\Gamma \lhd [\![A]\!]$ holds in every model of HA^∞. By lemma 6 we then obtain $1 \lhd [\![A]\!]$ in every model of HA^∞; hence, by theorem 2, $\mathsf{HA}^\infty \vdash A$. □

Let $\mathsf{PA}^\infty\mathsf{F}$ denote first-order classical arithmetic, PA, extended by the above axioms. We then have

Corollary 1 $\mathsf{PA}^\infty\mathsf{F}$ *is conservative over* PA.

The proof of the corollary is by Gödel's double negation interpretation. Let A^* denote the double negation interpretation of the formula A and Ax the set of axioms above about ∞ and F. Let A be a formula in the language of PA such that $PA + Ax \vdash A$. Since $\Gamma \vdash B$ implies $\Gamma^* \vdash B^*$ for any set Γ of formulas and any formula B, we get $\mathsf{HA} + Ax^* \vdash A^*$. Hence, by the lemma below, $\mathsf{HA}^\infty\mathsf{F} \vdash A^*$. By theorem 7, we then get $\mathsf{HA} \vdash A^*$. Since $\mathsf{PA} \vdash A^* \supset A$ we obtain $\mathsf{PA} \vdash A$. □

Lemma 8. *Let P be any of the axioms in* $\mathsf{PA}^\infty\mathsf{F}$. *Then* $\mathsf{HA}^\infty\mathsf{F} \vdash P^*$.

The only non-trivial case is when P is an instance of the induction scheme in $\mathsf{HA}^\infty\mathsf{F}$. So P^* is

$$A^*(0) \wedge \forall x(\neg\neg\mathsf{F}(x) \wedge A^*(x) \supset A^*(s(x))) \supset \forall x(\neg\neg\mathsf{F}(x) \supset A^*(x))$$

for some formula $A(x)$. Since all double negated interpreted formulas are stable, we have $\vdash \neg\neg A^*(x) \supset A^*(x)$ which implies $\vdash (\mathsf{F}(x) \supset A^*(x)) \supset (\neg\neg\mathsf{F}(x) \supset A^*(x))$. Hence, P^* follows from P. □

Since the arguments of the paper are effective, the proof of this corollary can be seen directly as an algorithm that, given a proof of a sentence in $\mathsf{PA}^\infty\mathsf{F}$, transforms this into a proof of the same sentence in PA. A formalization of the proof in the type theory system ALF [1] would then directly give a computer implementation of the transformation algorithm.

References

1. Thorsten Altenkirch, Veronica Gaspes, Bengt Nordström, and Björn von Sydow. *A User's Guide to ALF*. Chalmers University of Technology, Sweden, May 1994.
2. Jan Cederquist. A machine assisted formalization of pointfree topology in type theory. Licentiate thesis, Chalmers University of Technology and University of Göteborg, Sweden, 1994.
3. H.C.M. de Swart. An intuitionistically plausible interpretation of intuitionistic logic. *Journal of Symbolic Logic*, 42:564–578, 1977.
4. Albert G. Dragalin. An explicit boolean-valued model for non-standard arithmetic. *Publ. Math. Drebecen*, 42:369–389, 1993.
5. M. Dummett. *Elements of intuitionism*. Clarendon Press, Oxford, 1977.
6. G. Kreisel. On weak completeness of intutionistic predicate logic. *Journal of Symbolic logic.*, 27:139–158, 1962.

7. H. M. MacNeille. Partially ordered sets. *Transactions of AMS*, 42, 1937.
8. Ieke Moerdijk and Erik Palmgren. Minimal models of heyting arithmetik. Technical Report Report U.U.D.M 1995:25, Dept. of Mathematics, Uppsala University, Sweden, June 1995.
9. Henrik Persson. A formalization of a constructive completeness proof for intuitionistic predicate logic. Draft, Chalmers University of Technology, Göteborg, September 1995.
10. G. Sambin. Pretopologies and completeness proofs. *Journal of Symbolic Logic*, 60:861–878, 1995.
11. Giovanni Sambin. Intuitionistic Formal Spaces - A First Communication. In *The Proceedings of Conference on Logic and its Applications, Bulgaria*. Plenum Press, 1986.
12. A. Tarski. Der Aussagenkalkül und die Topologie. *Fundamenta Mathematicae*, 31:103–134, 1938.
13. A. S. Troelstra. *Choice Sequences, a Chapter of Intuitionistic Mathematics*. Clarendon Press, 1977.
14. A. S. Troelstra and D. van Dalen. *Constructivism in Mathematics. An Introduction*, volume II. North-Holland, 1988.
15. Wim Veldman. An intuitionistic completeness theorem for intuitionistic predicate logic. *Journal of Symbolic Logic*, 41:159–166, 1976.

Automating Inversion of Inductive Predicates in Coq

Cristina Cornes[1] and Delphine Terrasse[2]

[1] INRIA Rocquencourt, B.P. 105, 78153 Le Chesnay, Cedex France
Email: Cristina.Cornes@inria.fr
[2] INRIA Sophia-Antipolis, 2004 route des Lucioles, BP 93 Sophia Antipolis Cedex France Email:Delphine.Terrasse@inria.fr

Abstract. An inductive definition of a set is often informally presented by giving some rules that explain how to build the elements of the set. The closure property states that any object is in the set *if and only if* it has been generated according to the formation rules. This is enough to justify case analysis reasoning: we can read the formation rules backwards to derive the necessary conditions for a given instance to hold. The problem of inversion consists in finding out these conditions.
In this paper we address the problem of deriving inversion lemmas in logical frameworks based on Type Theory that have been extended with inductive definitions at the primitive level. These frameworks associate to each inductive definition a case analysis principle corresponding to the closure property. In this formal context, inversion lemmas can be seen as derived case analysis principles. Though they are intuitively simple they are curiously hard to formalize.
We relate first inversion to completion in logic programming. Then we discuss two general algorithms to generate inversion lemmas. They are presented in the proof assistant system Coq [8] but they can be adapted to any other proof assistant having a similar notion of inductive definition.

1 Introduction

An inductive definition of a set is often informally presented by giving some rules (so-called "constructors") that explain how to build the elements of the set. An object belongs to the set *if and only if* it has been generated according to the rules. A basic example is the set of natural numbers, with two formation rules '$0 \in nat$' and '*if* $n \in nat$ *then* $(S\ n) \in nat$'. We can also define relations inductively. A simple example is the relation *less or equal*, noted $\leq$, over natural numbers with two constructors $\leq_0$ and $\leq_S$:

$$\frac{}{0 \leq n}\leq_0 \qquad\qquad \frac{n \leq m}{(S\ n) \leq (S\ m)}\leq_S$$

An inductively defined relation is usually identified with the smallest set closed under a set of rules, or equivalently the set of formulas obtained by finite applications of the rules and axioms. Formally, an inductively defined relation is the least fixedpoint of a monotone operator over a complete lattice. It can be more constructively characterised in terms of ordinal powers of this monotone operator (Tarski's theorems)[1]. An element of such a relation *must* have been built from one of the introduction rules (constructors) of the relation. This last statement is sufficient to justify case analysis reasoning. We can deduce for example: $if\ \ (S\ n) \leq (S\ m)\ \ then\ necessarily\ \ n \leq m$ because the only possible final rule is $\leq_S$.

This kind of reasoning occurs frequently. Assume, for example, that $\mathcal{P}$ is a property about natural numbers and that we want to prove the proposition: $\forall n, m \in nat,\ \ if\ (S\ n) \leq m\ \ then\ (\mathcal{P}\ n\ m)$. Then we may need to use the facts that $m = (S\ m_0)$ and $n \leq m_0$ for some $m_0 \in nat$. This is necessarily true because the only constructor whose conclusion matches $(S\ n) \leq m$ is $\leq_S$. We are implicitly doing *inversion* on the instance $(S\ n) \leq m$ when deducing these facts.

To develop this proof in a formal system one step of the formal proof will require the following obvious *inversion* principle: $if\ \ (S\ n) \leq m\ \ then\ \ \exists m_0 \in nat.\ m = (S\ m_0) \wedge n \leq m_0$. Another example of such principle is '$(S\ n) \leq 0\ is\ false$' stating that a proof *can not* be built by any application of the rules. Hence, given an instance of an inductively defined relation, the problem of inversion is to find out the assumptions and structural conditions under which this instance can be derived.

There exist various formal systems (first, second or higher order logics, type systems, etc) in which natural reasoning can be formalized. They differ in their expressiveness and in the choice of the underlying logic. The theorem provers and proof assistants that implement some of these formal systems allow to check mechanically the correctness of proofs and may even help to develop proofs interactively.

The status of inversion principles varies from one system to the other. They might be coded within the formal system as inference rules or have to be proved in the system. Consider for example the fragment of predicate calculus corresponding to Horn clauses. The associated theorem prover implements the resolution procedure and can be augmented with the "negation as failure" inference rule, whereby $\sim P$ can be inferred when every proof search for P fails. In this case the constructors of the relation $\leq$ are Horn clauses. The negation as failure meta rule allows to deduce that $(S\ n) \leq 0$ *is false* as a consequence of (first-order) unification failure. The validity of this rule is given in the meta theory using Clark's completion lemma (see section 2). In this simple framework, inversion is coded *in* the proof engine and justified at the meta level.

In higher order logical frameworks the notion of inductive definition can be formalized naturally through higher order quantification. In these frameworks, propositions and proofs can be uniformly represented by simply typed λ terms. One possibility to deal with inductive definitions in type systems is to use polymophism to describe recursive types like in the systems F, F_ω and the Calculus of Constructions (CoC in short) [6]. This latter system allows all dependencies between terms and types. Hence, the structural induction principles associated with recursive types can also be represented using both "polymophism" and "dependent types" dimensions. Nevertheless, these induction principles cannot be derived from axioms of the theory. Another solution is to extend the type system with a *primitive* notion of inductive types. The Calculus of Inductive Constructions [17, 15, 8] (*CIC* in short) and the Extended Calculus of Constructions [12] are extensions of the CoC with inductive types. Another example is Martin-Löf's Intuitionistic Type Theory [14]. In these systems, to invert a given instance (e.g. $(S\ n) \leq (S\ m)$) a specific inversion principle can be *formalized and proved* (e.g. $if\ (S\ n) \leq (S\ m)\ then\ n \leq m$). This task may become hard and tedious when dealing with complex predicates and has to be automated.

Th. Coquand proposed in [4] another approach to deal with inductive definitions in type theory. He has introduced a pattern matching mechanism at the primitive level that can be combined with recursion to provide an alternative to the notion of induction principle. In this context, inversion is automatically performed by the (higher order) unification procedure. Inversion principles lie at the meta level justifying some aspects of the proof engine (as in logic programming). However the higher order unification used in the type checking algorithm is not decidable and the meta theory is not yet well established.

In this paper, we address the problem of deriving automatically inversion principles in the *CIC*. We hope that the analysis and methods discussed will provide a good support to solve the treatment of inversion in other systems having a similar notion of inductive types.

The plan of the paper is as follows. Section 2 describes the problem of inversion in logic programming. Section 3 presents the basic concepts of the *CIC* as implemented in the proof assistant Coq. Readers familiar with the *CIC* are suggested to read only the paragraph about notations. Section 4 is the heart of the paper. First, it addresses the problem of proving discrimination and injectivity properties of constructors of inductive types. Then, it describes two methods to deal with inversion in the *CIC* and discusses how they could be extended. We explain how to generate automatically the statement of inversion lemmas together with their proofs. Finally in section 5 we draw conclusions.

2 Related Work

In logic programming a relation is defined by a set of Horn clauses, belonging to a *logic program*. The proof search procedure is resolution. In order to derive negative information on a relation R, this procedure can be augmented with the *negation as failure* inference rule. This rule is justified using the notion of *completed program* (called *completed data base* in [3]). The proof that a given instance of a relation is inconsistent is not obtained from the initial logic program, but from the completed one in a particular equality theory.

Suppose that $(R\ \bar{t}) \leftarrow L_1 \wedge \ldots \wedge L_m$ is a program clause where $\bar{t}$ is a sequence of terms and $L_1 \ldots L_m$ are literals. Let '=' denote the equality relation we shall describe later on, and $\bar{x}$ be new variables not appearing in the clause. Then, the previous clause is equivalent to: $(R\ \bar{x}) \leftarrow \bar{x} = \bar{t} \wedge L_1 \wedge \ldots \wedge L_m$.

If $\bar{y}$ denotes the variables of the original clause, this is also equivalent to the following *general form of the clause*: $(R\ \bar{x}) \leftarrow (\exists \bar{y})(\bar{x} = \bar{t} \wedge L_1 \wedge \ldots \wedge L_m)$ $(*)$.

Now, suppose R is defined with $k \geq 1$ clauses of the form: $(R\ \bar{x}) \leftarrow E_i$ where $1 \leq i \leq k$. The E_i are existentially quantified conjunctions of literals such as $(*)$. The *completed definition of* R is then:

$$(\forall \bar{x})(R\ \bar{x}) \leftrightarrow (E_1 \vee E_2 \vee \ldots \vee E_k).$$

The only-if part of this definition is just the k general form of the clauses grouped as a single implication. The if-half part is the completion law for R. The following axiom schemas about the equality relation are needed to ensure that constants and functors have free interpretations:

1. $f(\bar{x}) \neq g(\bar{y})$ for f, g any pair of distinct functors;
2. $f(\bar{x}) = f(\bar{y}) \rightarrow \bar{x} = \bar{y}$ for f any functor;
3. $\tau(x) \neq x$ where $\tau(x)$ is any term structure in which x occurs free.

Schema 1 requires that different functors are different data constructors, and schema 2 that constructed objects are equal only if they are constructed from equal components (functors are injections). Schema 3 is a finiteness condition that ensures that objects are obtained by finite application of the functors. Adding reflexivity, symmetry and transitivity of the equality to these axiom schemas, and the substitution schema: $x = y \rightarrow (W(x) \leftrightarrow W(y))$ (W any well formed formula) yields the definition of the *equality theory*.

The *completion* of a logic program is the collection of completed definitions of the relations concerned, together with the equality theory.

3 Inductive Definitions in Coq

The Coq system [8] is an implementation of the *CIC* (a complete description of *CIC* can be found in [15, 17]). For sake of clarity we work with Coq axiomatisation language called "vernacular" instead of the concrete syntax of *CIC* terms. The sorts are *Prop* (the sort of propositions), *Set* (the sort of sets), *Typeset* (*Set* : *Typeset*) and *Type* (*Prop* : *Type*). The terms are variables, applications $(M\ N)$, λ-abstractions $[x : T]M$, product types and universal formulas $(x : T)P$, functional types and logical implication $T \rightarrow P$ (which is an abbreviation for $(x : T)P$ when x has no free occurrence in P) and three other constructs to deal with inductive definitions: terms for inductive types, for constructors and for elimination operators.

• **Inductive** *id* : A := c_1 : T_1 |... | c_k : T_k. denotes the *smallest set* of type A closed under the constructors
$c_1 : T_1 \ldots c_k : T_k$.

• < T > **Match** e **of** $e_1 \ldots e_n$ **end** denotes a recursion operator w.r.t. e returning a value of type T.

• < T > **Case** e **of** $e_1 \ldots e_n$ **end** denotes a pattern matching operator w.r.t. e returning a value of type T.

Data types are specified in Coq like in programming languages by a set of constructors with their respective types. For instance we can define the natural numbers by:

```
Inductive nat : Set := O: nat | S: nat->nat.
```

This `Inductive` command defines `nat` to be the smallest set closed under the constructors `O` and `S`. A condition of positivity is required on the type of constructors to ensure the existence of such a set (see [15] for more details). Thus this command declares the objects `nat:Set`, the constructors `O:nat` and `S:nat->nat` and some elimination operators. These operators may be either recursion or case analysis operators. The former ones allow to define recursive functions or to prove properties by induction:

```
nat_ind : (P:nat->Prop)  (P O) -> ((m:nat)(P m)->(P (S m))) -> (n:nat)(P n)
nat_rec : (P:nat->Set)   (P O) -> ((m:nat)(P m)->(P (S m))) -> (n:nat)(P n)
nat_rect: (P:nat ->Type) (P O) -> ((m:nat)(P m)->(P (S m))) -> (n:nat)(P n)
```

They are dependent and curried versions of the recursion operator of Gödel's system T. The difference between them lies in the sort of P. Thus `nat_ind` allows to prove properties by induction on natural numbers, `nat_rec` is used to define functions by recursion on natural numbers and `nat_rect` allows to define propositions or sets by recursion on natural numbers. The concrete syntax `Match` denotes the use of any of these recursion principles. As expected the case analysis operators, which focus only on the closure property, are less expressive than recursion principles:

```
nat_case : (P:nat->Set) (P O) -> ((m:nat) (P (S m))) -> (n:nat)(P n)
```

Note that there is no inductive hypothesis. Case analysis over `Prop` or `Type` are also available. The concrete syntax `Case` denotes the use of case analysis operators. Elimination principles are not only logical operators but have a computational behaviour given by the ι-reduction:

<T>Case O of f_o f_s end $\rhd_\iota$ f_o	<T>Match O of f_o f_s end $\rhd_\iota$ f_o
<T>Case (S n) of f_o f_s end $\rhd_\iota$ (f_s n)	<T>Match (S n) of f_o f_s end $\rhd_\iota$ (f_s n <T>Match n of f_o f_s end)

These reduction rules are part of Coq definitional equality in addition to β-reduction and δ-expansion (constant unfolding). This reduction is known to enjoy the properties of confluence and termination [17]. Type checking operates modulo this definitional equality.

Case analysis principles express the closure property with respect to the constructors, whereas recursion principles express the minimality property, ensuring the finiteness of inductive objects and the termination of recursively defined functions. Now let us see an example of non-recursive function:

```
Definition is_zero : nat->Prop := [n:Prop]
  <Prop>Case n of
        (* O *)   True
        (* S n *) [_:nat]False end.
```

This command defines a propositional function by case analysis on natural numbers. The `Case` operator has two branches, one for each constructor of `nat`, and `<Prop>` indicates the type of the result. The function `is_zero` returns the proposition `True` when applied to `0` and `False` when applied to an argument of the form `(S n)`. This possibility of defining a proposition or a set by pattern matching over an inductive set I is called *strong elimination* and is possible only if I is a *small inductive type*[3] (see [15] for a precise description).

In Coq we can also define inductive families or predicates. The relation $\leq$ of our example can be defined as a binary predicate between natural numbers:

```
Inductive Le : nat->nat->Prop :=
   Le_0 : (n:nat)(Le 0 n)
|  Le_S : (n,m:nat) (Le n m)->(Le (S n) (S m)).
```

This definition states that there are two constructors namely `Le_0` and `Le_S` corresponding to the rules $\leq_0$ and $\leq_S$ of the example. The type of each constructor can be read as an inference rule. As the types of the constructors satisfy the positivity condition, the defined relation is the smallest one closed under the constructors. As for inductive sets, the system derives elimination principles that allow to prove properties by induction or case analysis on proofs of the relation. For example, the case analysis operator of `Le` is:

```
Le_case : (P:nat->nat->Prop)
            ((n:nat)(P 0 n)) ->
             ((n,m:nat)(Le n m)->(P (S n) (S m)))
              -> (n,n0:nat)(Le n n0)->(P n n0)
```

This principle is suitable to prove a property `(P n m)` by case analysis on a proof of `(Le n m)` but not by case analysis on a proof of `(Le (S n) m)`. Here we need the following more specific case analysis principle:

```
Le_inv : (P:nat->nat->Prop) (n,m:nat)
           ((m0:nat)(Le n m0)->(P n (S m0)))
            ->(Le (S n) m)->(P n m)
```

We will see that this is the *inversion principle* of `(Le (S n) m)` and that inversion lemmas can be seen as derived case analysis principles.

Inductive predicates (or families) may have *parameters* and *indexes*. Parameters are global arguments inside the definition. For example, consider the type of arrays (lists of a certain length):

```
Inductive array [A:Set] : nat->Set :=
   nil: (array A 0)
|  cons: (n:nat) A -> (array A n) -> (array A (S n)).
```

The argument between brackets is a parameter and is global to the definition. For each set A we have defined the family $array_A : nat \to Set$ of arrays of

[3] An inductive type is small if all its constructors are small. $(I\ t_1 \ldots t_s)$ is a *small type of constructor* and $(x : T)C$ is a small type of constructor if T has type *Prop* or *Set* and C is also a small type of constructor. Unrestricted strong elimination leads to paradoxes [17].

elements of A. The family $array_A$ depends (is indexed) on naturals. Thus, `array` has two arguments: the first is a parameter while the second is an *index*. We say that a type is *dependent* if it has an index.

In Coq we can also define mutually inductive types but for sake of simplicity we are going to consider only non-mutual inductive definitions.

This concludes our brief survey on inductive definitions in Coq. The following paragraph defines the notations we shall use in the rest of the paper.

Notations: The empty sequence of terms is ϵ. Let $\bar{a} = a_1 \dots a_n$ and $\bar{b} = b_1 \dots b_n$ be two non empty sequences of terms with the same length. We define the term $\bar{a} = \bar{b} \equiv a_1 = b_1 \wedge \dots \wedge a_n = b_n$ where $=$ denotes the equality predicate `eq` (see section 4.1), $|\bar{a}| \equiv n$, $\bar{a}^i \equiv a_1 \dots a_i$, $(\bar{a})_i \equiv a_i$.

Let $\bar{x} \equiv x_1 \dots x_n$ be a sequence of variables, $\bar{A} \equiv A_1 \dots A_n$ be a sequence of terms, and let M be a term. We define the following abbreviations:

$$
\begin{aligned}
(\bar{x} : \bar{A})M &\equiv (x_1 : A_1) \dots (x_n : A_n)M \\
[\bar{x} : \bar{A}]M &\equiv [x_1 : A_1] \dots [x_n : A_n]M \\
(M\ \bar{A}) &\equiv (\dots((M\ A_1)\ A_2)\dots)\ A_n) \\
(\exists \bar{x} : \bar{A})M &\equiv (Ex\ [x_1 : A_1]\ (Ex\ [x_2 : A_2]\ (\dots (Ex\ [x_n : A_n]\ M)\dots).
\end{aligned}
$$

We denote by $(\bar{x} : \bar{T})$ or $(x_1 : T_1)..(x_n : T_n)$ or Γ and Δ contexts of variable declarations and by [] the empty context. The forward extension of Γ with the declaration $x{:}T$ is written $(x{:}T){::}\Gamma$. The abbreviation $\exists\Gamma$ stands for the existential formula $(\exists \bar{x}^{n-1} : \bar{T}^{n-1})T_n$ whenever Γ is the non-empty context $(\bar{x}^n : \bar{T}^n)$. The abbreviation $(\exists\Gamma, M)$ is defined by cases on the structure of Γ: $(\exists[\,], M) \equiv M$ and $(\exists(\bar{x}^n : \bar{T}^n), M) \equiv \exists(\bar{x}^n : \bar{T}^n)$.

`Typewriter` style is used in the paper for the vernacular syntax of Coq and small style for technical remarks. Programs are presented in an ML-sytle programming language and **bold face** style in programs is used for keywords.

4 Dealing with Inversion in Coq

In Horn clauses provers the completion lemma lies at the metalevel justifying some aspects of the proof engine. Inversion principles in Coq can be seen as completion lemmas but they must be proved at the object level. The following remarks sketch the main aspects involved in proving inversion lemmas in Coq. We stress the differences with the logic programming context:

1. **The status of equality.** In logic programming equality lies at the metalevel and is used by the unification procedure. In Coq it is defined at "object level" as the smallest reflexive relation:
   `Inductive eq [A:Set; x:A] : A->Prop := refl_equal : (eq A x x).`
   This means that for each set A and each element a in A, the predicate $=_{A,a}$ corresponds to the set of objects equal to a. We write the application $(eq\ T\ t_1\ t_2)$ in concrete implicit syntax: $t_1 = t_2$. Thus we can write `O=(S O)` in Coq (though there is no proof). This relation satisfies symmetry, transitivity and substitutivity properties. Note that `eq` relates terms of the *same* type only. Thus `nil=(cons O (S O) nil)` is wrongly typed because `nil` is of type `(array O)` and `(cons O (S O) nil)` is of type `(array (S O))`.

2. **The status of axiom schemas for equality.** In Coq the axiom schemas of section 2 are not true in general. But when they concern constructors of inductive types they express well known freeness properties: axiom 1 is the *non-confusion* or *discriminating property* ($\sim 0 = (S\ n)$), axiom 2 is the *injection property* ($(S\ n) = (S\ m) \rightarrow n = m$). Axiom 3 is finiteness condition that ensures together with axiom 1 that constructors always generate new objects ($\sim n = (S\ n)$). In logic programming these properties lie at the metalevel while in Coq they may be *proved* in the system.
3. **The status of completion lemmas.** In the *CIC* some elimination principles are associated to inductive definitions, making explicit the closure and minimality properties. Instead of adding the axiom $(\forall \bar{x})(R\ \bar{x}) \rightarrow (E_1 \vee E_2 \vee \ldots \vee E_k)$ we are interested in *deriving* it from these primitive elimination principles. Consider for example the completion lemma for `Le`:
$$(n, m : nat)\ (Le\ n\ m) \leftrightarrow$$
$$n = O \quad \vee \quad (\exists\, n_1, m_1 : nat)\ (Le\ n_1\ m_1) \wedge n = (S\ n_1)\ \wedge m = (S\ m_1)$$
This lemma involves the closure property of `Le` but not the minimality property. Imagine that we had defined `Le` to be the set obtained by possibly infinite applications of the constructors rules: `Le` would still satisfy the completion lemma. Given a proof of a certain instance of `Le` we can use the if-part to destruct the instance performing some inversion. The if-part can be seen as another formulation of the "case" schema for `Le`. This can be generalized to any relation R and conveys the intuition that the proof of inversion lemmas does not need any inductive hypothesis and can be done just by using the case analysis operator. This is important because inversion methods apply both to inductive and coinductive types. The only-if part of the completion lemma follows from the constructors and does not concern inversion.
4. **Dependent completion lemmas.** In logic programming there are no terms to denote proofs. In Coq proofs and propositions can be uniformly represented. This leads to a *dependent* version of Clark's completion lemma containing conditions on the proofs H and H_1 :
$$(n, m : nat)\ (H : (Le\ n\ m))\ \ n = O \wedge H = (Le\_0\ m)$$
$$\vee\ (\exists\, n_1, m_1 : nat)(\exists H_1 : (Le\ n_1\ m_1))$$
$$n = (S\ n_1) \wedge m = (S\ m_1) \wedge H = (Le\_S\ n_1\ m_1\ H_1) \quad (**).$$
It states that any term H of type $(Le\ n\ m)$ is built either from the constructor *Le_0* or from*Le_S*.

In conclusion, a set of tools for automating inversion in Coq requires a certain notion of equality, some tactics for proving automatically discrimination and injectivity properties, and tools to state and prove inversion lemmas. As we shall see there are several ways to state inversion lemmas. The main difficulty to find the correct statement is that a *global* analysis of the predicate is necessary because a given instance may be proved with several constructors.

This section is organized as follows. In 4.1 we briefly present how to prove discrimination and injection lemmas to simplify equalities between objects of non-dependent types. In section 4.2 we discuss two possible definitions of an equality for family types. We discuss the discrimination and injection lemmas in this case. The rest of section 4 presents and discusses two different approaches to state and prove inversion lemmas in Coq.

4.1 Equality for Inductive Sets

The substitutivity property of the equality `eq` defined above is coded in Coq by the induction principle `eq_ind` derived by the system, `eq_ind : (A:Set)(x:A) (P:A->Prop)(P x)->(y:A)x=y->(P y)`. We recognize here Leibniz's equality: if two elements are equal no predicate can discriminate them.

Discrimination and injection properties (e.g. `~O=(S O)` and `(S n)=(S m)->n=m`) can be seen as particular cases of equality inversion lemmas.

To prove `~O=(S O)` we apply the elimination principle of the equality using the predicate `is_zero` defined in section 3 as discriminator.

To prove `(S n)=(S m)-> n=m`, consider *pred* to be the predecessor function (called *injector*) and *f_equal* to be the congruence lemma for equality: f_equal : $(A, B : Set)(f : A \to B)(x, y : A)x = y \to (f\ x) = (f\ y)$. Then, if $(S\ n) = (S\ m)$ by *f_equal* we have $(pred\ (S\ n)) = (pred\ (S\ m))$, and thus $n = m$ by conversion.

The idea of these proofs can be generalised to any inductive type T defined by: *Inductive* T : *Set* := $c_1 : (\bar{w}_1 : \bar{W}_1)T \mid \ldots \mid c_k : (\bar{w}_k : \bar{W}_k)T$ and can be implemented into a tactic that automatically proves this kind of goals. Nevertheless the automatic generation of the injector term presents some difficulties when dealing with dependent types. Consider the example of arrays defined in section 3. Suppose we want to prove the following injectivity property: $(m, n : nat)(a, b : (array\ n))(cons\ n\ m\ a) = (cons\ n\ m\ b) \to a = b$. The injector *tail* expects an argument in $(array\ n)$ to yield the result in $(array\ (pred\ n))$. Hence, to build *tail* automatically we need also to generate mechanically the function *pred*. If we had an equality $\mathcal{E}q$ that might compare any pair of elements of the same family then we could use the idea of the proof above to generate the injection lemma: $(m, n : nat)(a, b : (array\ n))(cons\ n\ m\ a) = (cons\ n\ m\ b) \to (\mathcal{E}q\ a\ b)$. We discuss two possible definitions of such an equality $\mathcal{E}q$ in section 4.2.

Injection and discriminaton lemmas may be combined into simplification procedures for equalities between arbitrary structured terms of an inductive type. A detailed discussion on automatic tactics to prove this kind of lemmas can be found in [9].

4.2 Equality for Inductive Families

Let I be a family of types with some elements $a : (I\ \bar{t})$ and $b : (I\ \bar{t}')$. In this section we are going to state a new equality $\mathcal{E}q$ to compare a and b even if t and t' are not the same. One motivation for such an equality is to extend the injection tactics to dependent types, another one would be to state ***dependent inversion lemmas***. Careful readers should have noticed that the constraints $H = (Le\_0\ m)$ and $H = (Le\_S\ n_1\ m_1\ H_1)$ in lemma (**) in page 6 are not well typed if $=$ denotes the predicate `eq`. Such constraints should be expressed in terms of an equality for family types. For sake of clarity we are going to discuss the case of families of arity one. The ideas and comments can be easily generalized to indexed families of arity n.

Dependent equalities. This approach consists in generalizing the identity predicate to indexed families of sets. The equality for families of arity one is:

```
Inductive EqDep1 [U:Set; P:U->Set; p:U; x:(P p)] : (q:U)(P q)->Prop
        := refl_EqDep1 : (EqDep1 U P p x p x).
```

For example, if a : $(array\ n)$ and b : $(array\ m)$ then to to compare a and b we write: $(EqDep1\ nat\ array\ n\ a\ m\ b)$. As `eq`, `EqDep1` is reflexive, transitive and symmetric. The substitutivity schema is coded by the elimination principle `EqDep1_ind` that is derived by the system. Thus this equality can also be used as a rewrite rule. Note that an equality $(EqDep1\ nat\ array\ n\ a\ m\ b)$ may be inconsistent for two reasons: either n and m are different (then so are a and b), or n and m are equal but a and b are not. To extend the discrimination tactic to deal with dependent equalities we need to prove the inversion lemmas of `EqDep1`:

```
Lemma EqDep1_p1: (U:Set) (P:U->Set) (u,w:U) (u1:(P u)) (w1:(P w))
                 (EqDep1 U P u u1 w w1) -> u=w.

Lemma EqDep1_p2: (U:Set) (P:U->Set) (u:U) (u1, w1:(P u))
                 (EqDep1 U P u u1 u w1) -> u1=w1.
```

The lemma `EqDep1_p1` can be proved using `EqDep1_ind` while `EqDep1_p2` is equivalent to the elimination principle `EqDep1_K2`:

```
Definition EqDep1_K2 := (U:Set) (P:U->Set) (u:U) (u1:(P u))
     (Q:(P u)->Prop) (Q u1) -> (w1:(P u)) (EqDep1 U P u u1 u w1) -> (Q w1).
```

which is not provable in the *CIC* (Streicher [16]). This situation generalizes to any arity: given a dependent equality $EqDep_n$ there are $n+1$ inversion lemmas and only one $(EqDep_n\_p_1)$ is provable in the system. The main drawback of this approach is that an equality predicate is needed for *each* arity n.

Iterated pairs. This approach (due to C.Murthy) consists in using Σ-types and the predicate `eq` to compare objects of dependent types. In Coq the Σ-type is defined as:

```
Inductive sigS [U:Set; P:U->Set] : Set := existS : (x:U)(P x) -> (sigS U P).
```

`projS1` and `projS2` are respectively the first and the second projection. For example if $a : (array\ n)$ and $b : (array\ m)$ then we can write $(existS\ nat\ array\ n\ a) = (existS\ nat\ array\ m\ b)$ to mean that a and b are equal (recall that $=$ denotes `eq`). For binary families we apply the constructor `existS` twice. The Σ-types provide a uniform way to compare elements of dependent types avoiding extra predicate definitions.

Suppose we have $(existS\ nat\ array\ n\ a) = (existS\ nat\ array\ m\ b) \vdash (Q\ n\ a)$. We cannot use elimination of the equality to substitute a for b in Q because none of the pairs occur in the goal. Nevertheless we can sometimes use projections to transform the goal and make appear a pair so that elimination on `eq` performs the expected rewriting. For example we can transform the goal into: $pr = (existS\ nat\ array\ m\ b) \vdash (Q\ (projS1\ pr)\ (projS2\ pr))$, where pr denotes $(existS\ nat\ array\ n\ a)$. Now the elimination of the equality rewrites a into b. This technique can be automated and solves many usual cases but it does not solve the problem in the general case. In particular, it does not work when several arguments depend on the same index[4].

A more general approach consists in using the injectivity property of the constructor **existS** w.r.t. both arguments to derive the equalities about indexes and use them. Once again, the injectivity property w.r.t. the first argument can be derived in the theory, while the other:

```
Lemma inj_pair2 : (U:Set) (P:U->Set) (p:U) (x,y:(P p))
                  (existS U P p x)=(existS U P p y) -> x=y.
```

is independent because it is equivalent to Streicher's axiom `EqDep1_K2`. Adding it as an axiom yields a consistent theory [16] in which injection lemmas for iterated pairs can be proved.

The discrimination (injection) tactic can be reduced to discriminating (injecting) the indexes.

Remarks: From the logical point of view using iterated pairs or dependent equalities are equivalent notions (i.e. `(existS U P p x)=(existS U P p y)<->(EqDep1 U P p x q y)`). Thus, we can deduce that `inj_pair2` and `EqDep1_p2` are also equivalent therefore adding one or the other as axiom yields the same theory.

Equality over iterated pairs seems the correct approach to extend injection and discrimination tactics because no extra predicates are necessary and it captures the notion of equality we expect.

4.3 Inversion Lemmas as Completion Lemmas

Let I be an inductive predicate. This method generates and proves an *inversion lemma* of the form:
$I_{inv} : (\bar{x} : \bar{T})(I\ \bar{x}) \rightarrow (I\_inv\_fun\ \bar{x})$ where I_inv_fun is a predicate that expresses the constraints that $\bar{x}$ must satisfy for the instance $(I\ \bar{x})$ to hold. This approach is an adaptation of Clark's completion method for logic programming (section 2). In logic programming the inversion predicate I_inv_fun is always stated as a disjunction of existential formulas. In Coq we can use computational power

[4] Example: suppose our goal is $(Q\ n\ a\ a)$ and we want to rewrite only the first occurrence of a into b. Then we can transform the goal into $(Q\ (projS1\ (n,a))\ (projS2\ (n,a))\ a)$ but we cannot eliminate the equality because the abstraction $[pr : (sigS\ nat\ array)]\ (Q\ (projS1\ pr)\ (projS2\ pr)\ a)$ is wrongly typed.

of the theory to define the inversion predicate by appropriate case analysis on arguments. For example [5]:

```
Definition Le_inv_fun : nat->nat ->Prop :=
 [n,m:nat] <Prop>Case n of
   (* O *)     True
   (* S n1 *) [n1:nat](Ex [m1:nat]  m=(S m1) /\ (Le n1 m1)) end.
```

Other formulations of inversion predicates can make deeper nested case analysis or match the arguments in a different order. They are all equivalent from the semantical point of view: they all state the necessary conditions on two natural numbers n and m such that $(Le\ n\ m)$ holds. From the computational point of view they are very different and this is reflected in the size of the proof of the inversion lemma. In any case inversion predicates only use case analysis and not recursion.

To illustrate how inversion works in Coq suppose we have already proved the following inversion lemma:

```
Lemma Le_inv : (n,m:nat)(Le n m) -> (Le_inv_fun n m).
```

We are going to formalize the proposition $\forall n, m \in nat,\ \ if\ (S\ n) \leq m\ \ then\ (\mathcal{P}\ n\ m)$ and try to invert the instance $(S\ n) \leq m$. The development of the proof is done by means of tactics. For the sake of conciseness we omit the context of hypothesis from one step to the other unless it is modified. We define $\mathcal{P}$ as a variable and we state the goal in Coq:

```
Coq < Variable P: nat->nat->Prop.
Coq < Theorem ex: (n,m:nat)(Le (S n) m) -> (P n m).
```

We apply the tactic `Intros` to introduce the hypotheses in the context and obtain the following goal:

```
  n : nat
  m : nat
  H : (Le (S n) m)
  ============================
   (P n m)
```

Now we would like to reason by case analysis on `H` to deduce that `m` should be equal to `(S x)` for a certain `x:nat`. For that we use the inversion lemma. We apply the tactic `Generalize (Le_inv (S n) m H)` to enforce the goal with the necessary conditions:

```
     :
  ============================
   (Le_inv_fun (S n) m)->(P n m)
```

Now `Simpl` reduces `(Le_inv_fun (S n) m)` to the expected premisses:

[5] Recall that $(Ex\ [x : T]\ P)$ denotes in Coq the existential formula $(\exists x : T)P$.

```
  :
==============================
  (Ex [m1:nat]m=(S m1)/\(Le n m1))->(P n m)
```

After having eliminated the existential quantifier and broken the conjunction we get the following goal:

```
  :
==============================
  m=(S x)->(Le n x)->(P n m)
```

The hypothesis `m=(S x)` and `(Le n x)` are the expected result of inverting `H:(Le (S n) m)` and can be used to continue the proof.

We would like to have an automatic tool that generates the statement of the inversion predicate and proves the inversion lemma, particularly for large predicate definitions. The following two sections are devoted to the generation of inversion predicates and proofs of inversion lemmas.

The Generation of the Inversion Predicate. Given an inductive predicate a wide range of inversion predicates can be obtained just by varying the order in which case analysis is done. The suitability of an inversion predicate is relative to the instance to be inverted. For example, to invert `(Le (S n) m)` we need an inversion predicate that matches the first argument yielding the constraints corresponding to `m` whereas to invert `(Le n O)` we need to match the second argument. When all the arguments of the instance are instantiated, as in `(Le (S n) O)`, the order of matchings is not important.

The algorithm we present to generate inversion predicates considers both the predicate definition and the instance to invert for deciding which arguments to match. It works in a similar fashion to Augustsson's algorithm for compiling pattern matching [2]. It is an adaptation of the algorithm presented in [13] for ProPre to a simpler context (inversion predicates are not recursive and so there is no termination condition to check). Let I be the following inductive predicate:

$$\mathit{Inductive}\ I\ :(\bar{x}:\bar{A})\mathit{Set}\ :=\ c_1:(\bar{w_1}:\bar{W_1})(I\ \bar{a_1})|\ \ldots\ |\ c_k:(\bar{w_k}:\bar{W_k})(I\ \bar{a_k}).$$

Then the inversion predicate for an instance $(I\ \bar{t})$ is the term:

$$[\bar{x}:\bar{A}\,]\ \mathit{build\_tree}\ \ (\bar{x}:\bar{A})\ \ \{<\bar{a_1},\ (\bar{x_1}:\bar{W_1})>;\ldots;<\bar{a_k},\ (\bar{x_k}:\bar{W_k})>;\ <\bar{t},\ []>\}_{true}$$

where the function *build_tree* builds a term (Clark's disjunction or a nested case analysis expression) which expresses the constraints that $\bar{x}$ should satisfy for the instance $(I\ \bar{x})$ to hold. For example, let $\Gamma_0 = [n:\mathit{nat}]$ and $\Gamma_S = [n, m : \mathit{nat},\ H : (Le\ n\ m)]$, then the inversion predicate for `(Le (S n) m)` is built as:

`[x1,x2:nat]`

$$\mathit{build\_tree}\ \ (x1, x2:\mathit{nat})\ \ \{<0\ n, \Gamma_0>;\ \ <(Sn)\ (Sm), \Gamma_S>;\ \ <(Sn)\ m,\ \ []>\}_{true}$$

The first argument of *build_tree* is the context of variables to match. The second is a sequence of pairs of the form $<\bar{patt_i}, \Gamma_i>$. The intuition is that Γ_i contains the constraints concerning the variables occurring in the sequence of terms $\bar{patt_i}$ (that we call *patterns*). The algorithm starts with a sequence containing information about the instance to invert in the **last** pair and about the constructors in the others. The booolean mark *true* explicits that the last pair of the sequence is dummy (i.e. it comes from the instance to invert) and must be used for information purposes only. A sequence marked *false* has no dummy pair.

Figure 1 presents an outline of a naive algorithm (see [9] for a complete presentation and discussion). The algorithm is defined recursively on the context and the sequence. It inspects in parallel from left to right the patterns in the pairs to decide when to match. When the context of variables to match is empty the algorithm translates the pairs of the sequence into constraints in Coq and terminates.

Some general comments about the algorithm. In the following we say that a term t is *in constructor form* if it is an application $(c\ \bar{t})$ where c is a constructor of an inductive type. A sequence is *complete* if the first pattern of all pairs is in constructor form. We call *guide* the first pattern of the last pair of a sequence marked *true* (a sequence marked $false$ has no guide).

• The constraints are generated in step 1. They can be either **False** (step 1a) or a disjunction where each term is either **True** or an existential formula (step 1b).

• Case expressions are generated only when the sequence is complete (step 2(a)i). The problem splits then in k subproblems, one for each branch of the case (i.e. one for each constructor), and *build_tree* is called recursively on a subsequence. Subsequences are computed by a function *Sieve* that given a sequence of pairs and a constructor c filters those pairs of the form $<(c\ \bar{t})\bar{p},\ \Gamma>$ and transforms them into $<\bar{t}\bar{p},\ \Gamma>$ discarding c. It sets the mark to $false$ whenever the last row of a marked sequence is not filtered.

• If the guide pattern is in constructor form but there is a pair with a variable as first pattern then the algorithm calls itself recursively with a "completed" sequence (step 2(a)ii). The function *Complete* replaces each pair of sequence $<x\bar{p},\ \Gamma>$ where x is a variable symbol of type T for set of pairs corresponding to a covering set for x[6].

• When no matching is possible then the contexts in the pairs are extended with a new constraint and *build_tree* applies recursively with the rest of the patterns (step 2b). The function *Extend* generates constraints due to non-linearity of variables.

• Finally if the sequence is non-empty and marked $false$ the case corresponds to some constructors of I that do not lead to a proof of the instance we wanted to invert. The algorithm can choose to translate the sequence into a constraint and stop or continue as in step 3 forgetting the conditions about the guide.

Proving the Inversion Lemma. The algorithm of the previous section builds an inversion predicate *I_inv_fun* suitable to invert an instance $(I\ \bar{t})$. To prove the inversion lemma: $(\bar{x} : \bar{A})(I\ \bar{x}) \rightarrow (I\_inv\_fun\ \bar{x})$ we reason by cases on the proof of $(I\ \bar{x})$. The proof of the branches strongly depends on the structure of the inversion predicate. The inversion predicate may be Clark's disjunction when no constructors appear in $\bar{t}$ or a (possibly nested) case analysis expression. We do

[6] To compute the covering set it looks up all the constructors of T of type $(\bar{x}_i : \bar{T}_i)T'$ such that T and T' are convertible without doing any unification. The function fails to find a covering set whenever applied to a non closed instance of a dependent type. This is an important difference with respect to Coquand's algorithm of pattern matching [4] that performs unification.

1. (a) $build\_tree\ []\ \{\}_{mark} = \mathbf{False}$

   (b) $build\_tree\ []\ \{<\epsilon, \Gamma_1>; \ldots <\epsilon, \Gamma_q>\}_{mark} =$
   if $mark$ **then** $\bigvee_{j=1}^{j=q-1}(\exists\Gamma_j, \mathbf{True})$ **else** $\bigvee_{j=1}^{j=q}(\exists\Gamma_j, \mathbf{True})$

2. $build\_tree\ (v:T)::\Delta\ \{<t_1\ \bar{p_1},\ \Gamma_1>; \ldots; <t_q\ \bar{p_q},\ \Gamma_q>; <t\ \bar{p}, \Gamma>\}_{true} =$
   (a) **if** $constructor\_form(t)$ **and**
   (for $1 \le i \le q$. $constructor\_form(t_i)$ **or** $variable(t_i)$) **then**
   i. **if** for $1 \le i \le q$. $constructor\_form(t_i)$ **then**

   let $[c_1 : (\bar{x_1} : \bar{W_1})(T\ \bar{a_1}); \ldots; c_k : (\bar{x_k} : \bar{W_k})(T\ \bar{a_k})] = constructors\_of\, T$ **and**
   $part_{c_j} = Sieve(c_j\ \ \{<t_1\ \bar{p_1},\ \Gamma_1>; \ldots; <t_q\ \bar{p_q},\ \Gamma_q>; <t\ \bar{p}, \Gamma>\}_{true})_{1\le j\le k}$
   in **<Prop>Case** v **of**
   $[\bar{x_1} : \bar{W_1}]\ build\_tree\ \ (\bar{x_1} : \bar{W_1})::\Delta\ \ part_{c_1}$
   ⋮
   $[\bar{x_k} : \bar{W_k}]\ build\_tree\ \ (\bar{x_k} : \bar{W_k})::\Delta\ \ part_{c_k}$
   end

   ii. **else** $build\_tree\ (v:T)::\Delta$
   $(Complete\ T\ \ \{<t_1\ \bar{p_1},\ \Gamma_1>; \ldots; <t_q\ \bar{p_q},\ \Gamma_q>;\ <(c\ \bar{u})\ \bar{p}, \Gamma>\}_{true})$
   (b) **else** $build\_tree\ \Delta\ \{<\bar{p_1},\ (Extend\ <t_1\bar{p_1}, \Gamma_1>\ v)>; \ldots;$
   $<\bar{p_q},\ (Extend\ <t_q\bar{p_q}, \Gamma_q>\ \ v)>;\ <\bar{p}, \Gamma>\}_{true}$

3. $build\_tree(v:T)::\Delta\ \ \{<\bar{p_1},\ \Gamma_1>; \ldots; <\bar{p_q},\ \Gamma_q>\}_{false} =$
   may generate constraint or keep on matching

Fig. 1. Algorithm for generating an inversion predicate w.r.t. an instance.

not give the proofs here (see [9]). Yet note that the deeper the case analysis tree is the shorter and simpler the proof of the lemma becomes, because the application of $\vee_{intro}$ is replaced by reduction and the number of $\exists_{intro}$ and $\wedge_{intro}$ decreases.

The size of the proof with Clark's disjunction is determined by the number of constructors of I. If I has $n+1$ constructors, then we will have at least $\frac{n(n+1)}{2}$ applications of the $\vee\_intro$. We need the same number of applications of $\vee_{elim}$ when using the lemma.

4.4 Inversion Lemmas as Case Lemmas

This approach (due to C.Murthy) consists in deriving an appropriate case schema for the instance to invert, in which equalities are made explicit. The previous approach requires a static analysis of the predicate definition whereas the method we briefly present here has a 'call by need' point of view. The statement and the proof of the inversion lemmas are generated together during the proof development process.

We are going to illustrate this method by proving the example goal already stated in 4.3, writing the script in a naive way. We do not redisplay subgoals which do not change after the current command execution.

```
  n : nat
  m : nat
  H : (Le (S n) m)
  ============================
   (P n m)
```

To simulate pattern matching we are going to use equalities between new variables and arguments of the relation `Le`. We first introduce reflexivity axioms on those arguments. Reflexivity axioms appear then in the second branch of the cut and are trivially solved. The `Idtac` tactic leaves the first branch unchanged.

```
ex < Cut (S n)=(S n)/\m=m ; [Idtac | Split;Trivial].
1 subgoal
    :
  ============================
   (S n)=(S n)/\m=m->(P n m)
```

We build now the predicate on which we want to eliminate the proof of `(Le (S n) m)`. The application of this predicate to the arguments `(S n)` and `m` has to be convertible with the goal.

```
ex < Change (([u,v:nat](u=(S n)/\v=m)->(P n m)) (S n) m).
1 subgoal
    :
  ============================
   ([u,v:nat]u=(S n)/\v=m->(P n m) (S n) m)
```

Now we eliminate the hypothesis `H:(Le (S n) m)` thereby generating 2 subgoals, one for each introduction rule of the `Le` relation. The equality constraints model unification during the elimination process. As we do not need induction hypotheses we use only the case analysis principle. The tactic `Case` applies this principle. Then we introduce the hypothesis. The result of `Case H; Intros` is the following:

```
2 subgoals
    :
  n0 : nat
  H0 : O=(S n)/\n0=m
  ============================
   (P n m)
subgoal 2 is:
 (P n m)
```

The first goal corresponds to the rule `Le_O` which does not match `H`, so the equality constraints are inconsistent. It can be trivially solved with discrimination after having broken the conjunctions by elimination of the '∧' connective.

```
ex < Elim H0; Intros.
2 subgoals
    :
  H1 : O=(S n)
  H2 : n0=m
  ============================
   (P n m)
subgoal 2 is:
 (P n m)
ex < Discriminate H1.
1 subgoal
    :
  H0 : (Le n0 m0)
  H1 : (S n0)=(S n)/\(S m0)=m
  ============================
   (P n m)
```

The rule `Le_S` matches `H`, so the constraints are consistent. Here again we destruct `H1` to have two separate equality constraints and we add them to the context. The result of `Elim H1;Intros` is:

```
    :
  H2 : (S n0)=(S n)
  H3 : (S m0)=m
  ============================
   (P n m)
```

The last step consists in generating by injection some equalities on variables in order to rewrite. Here only one equality can be deduced. We apply `Injection H2; Intros` and we obtain:

```
    :
  H0 : (Le n0 m0)
    :
  H3 : (S m0)=m
  H4 : n0=n
  ============================
   (P n m)
```

Now we are left with the necessary conditions (`H0, H3, H4`) for the instance `(Le (S n) m)` (`H`) to hold. More precisely we have performed inversion.

We can see easily that this method can be automated and integrated in a single tactic that builds the proof of the inversion lemma. This tactic has been implemented in Coq V5.10 and is called `Derive Inversion_clear`. It generates and stocks the inversion lemma associated to a given hypothesis H. It also uses discriminations to erase inconsistent branches, injections to simplify equalities, and rewriting to propagate them when they hold on variables (e.g. the lemma `Le_inv` in page 6 has been generated with this tactic). The resulting lemma can then be applied in any context to any hypothesis specializing H, thanks to the tactic `Use Inversion`.

4.5 Comparing the two methods

The two methods described above allow to invert the same set of instances but they build completely different proof terms.

The first approach uses strong elimination to define the inversion predicate by pattern matching on the arguments. The proof of the inversion lemma is shorter as applications of the rules $\vee_{intro}$ and $\vee_{elim}$ are replaced by reductions. The worst case (in terms of the size of the proof) is when the inversion predicate is Clark's disjunction. This method is useful when arguments of the predicates are elements of a small inductive type to take advantage of the pattern matching mechanism. It generates the inversion predicate suitable for an instance $(I\ \bar{t})$ by inspecting both the constructors of I and $\bar{t}$. The predicate obtained can be reused to invert any instance $(I\ \bar{t'})$ provided $\bar{t'}$ has instantiated arguments at least in the same positions as $\bar{t}$ has.

The second approach does not need strong elimination. It treats all the cases in a uniform manner using only injection and discrimination lemmas instead of the pattern matching mechanism. The size of the pattern tree in the first approach corresponds to the number of injections and discriminations used to simplify the equations. In order to reduce the size of the inversion proof it is important to implement injection and discrimination tactics taking advantage of reduction. The second approach does not make any global analysis of the predicate definition. Thus it is simpler to implement than the first one but reusability is much less frequent because the inversion lemma is specialized to a given instance.

4.6 Extending the methods

We give here some ideas about possible extensions.

1. We have described how to invert predicates of arity $A_1 \rightarrow \ldots \rightarrow A_n \rightarrow Prop$ where $A_i : Set \quad i : 1..n$.
   Predicates of type $(x_1 : A_1)(x_2 : A_1(x_1))..(x_n : A_n(x_1..x_{n-1}))Prop$ having some arguments of dependent type may be inverted as well. It suffices to determine before generating an equality constraint, whether the objects to compare have a non-dependent or a dependent type. In the first case the algorithm generates the constraint using `eq`. In the second one, it computes the dependencies and uses either a dependent equality or an equality between iterated pairs (as in section 4.2) to express the constraint.
2. The methods allow to derive *non-dependent* inversion principles. Imagine we have a goal `(P m H)` under the hypothesis `H:(Le O m)`. Then the inversion of `H` derives the constraints concerning `m` but not `H`. Yet the constraint about `H` might be interesting to rewrite the goal into `(P m (Le_O m))`. The second method could easily generate a *naive* dependent inversion lemma if it proves the lemma using the dependent version of the case analysis principle of `Le` (instead of the non-dependent one). A more useful dependent inversion lemma would explicitly state the constraint $(0, m, H) = (0, m, (Le\_\ 0\ m))$ among the constraints.

3. Inversion, injection and discrimination lemmas assume only the closure property of the type w.r.t. the constructor rules and their proof does not need any inductive hypotheses. E. Giménez proposed in [10] an extension to the *CIC* with coinductive types. A coinductive definition characterizes the maximal set closed under some introduction rules. Thus all the methods we have described extend in a straightforward way to coinductive types.
4. The methods use the equality **eq** to state the constraints. In fact they could use any substitutive relation. For example to take advantage of proof reduction they could use a *concrete equality* (i.e. a *boolean* function that reduces to **true** whenever it is applied to syntactically equal terms and to **false** otherwise). Thus injections and discriminations could be replaced by reduction. To use concrete equalities as rewrite rules a principle of substitutivity should be derived for each concrete equality.

5 Conclusion and Future Work

We have related the problem of inversion to that of completion in programming logic. We have presented two general algorithms to generate inversion lemmas in logical frameworks based on Type Theory extended with inductive definitions at the primitive level. The ideas have been presented for the Coq system but can be adapted to any other proof assistant having a similar notion of inductive definition.

The algorithms have pointed out that inversion principles are derived case analysis principles. Their proofs use only the closure property of the inductive predicate (under the constructor rules) and not the minimality property. Thus they extend directly to coinductive types. We have also discussed some problems that arise to state and prove discrimination and injection lemmas for constructors of dependent families.

The first algorithm has been implemented in an experimental version of Coq. It generates quite general inversion lemmas and short proofs, but it makes a global analysis of the predicate definition. The second (elaborated and implemented by C. Murthy) is part of the current version of Coq. It has been used in significant proof developments concerning both inductive and coinductive types and revealed to be helpful [11]. It produces an inversion lemma suitable for a given instance without any global analysis. This makes it easy to implement and comfortable to the user but the lemmas are hard to reuse with different instances. We think that the first algorithm is worth to be implemented only for optimization reasons to reduce the size of the proofs. It would be interesting to study whether inversion proofs generated by the second method remain of a reasonable size and how often a shorter proof may be obtained with the first one.

We have presented naive hints to generate dependent inversion lemmas. We have used them to provide Coq with a tactic that performs dependent inversion in a primitive manner. Further work remains to be done in this direction. We have not addressed the problem of automating finiteness lemmas of the form

$x \neq \tau(x)$ for objects of inductive types. Nevertheless this kind of automatic tool would be useful sometimes to generate more accurate inversion lemmas.

Acknowledgements

We are grateful to E. Giménez and Ch. Paulin for many helpful suggestions. We also thank Joëlle Despeyroux, G. Dowek, H. Goguen, G. Huet, C. Muñoz, and C. Murthy for their careful reading and comments on previous drafts.

References

1. P. Aczel: An Introduction to Inductive Definitions. The Handbook of Mathematical Logic, J. Barwise ed., North-Holland, (1992) 739-782
2. L. Augustsson: Compiling Pattern Matching. In J.P. Jouannaud, ed., Conference on Functional Programming Languages and Computer Architecture (LNCS 201), pages, 368-381, Nancy, France, 1985.
3. K. Clark: Negation as Failure. Logic and Databases, Ed.H. Gallaire, J.Minker. Plenum Press New York, pp.293-322, 1978.
4. T. Coquand : Pattern Matching with Dependent Types. Informal Proceedings Types for Proofs and Programs, June 1992.
5. T. Coquand, J.M.Smith: What is the status of pattern matching in type theory. El Wintermöte, pp.112-114, June 1993.
6. T. Coquand , G. Huet: The Calculus of Constructions. Information and Computation. Vol. 76, Nos. 2/3, February/March 1988.
7. C. Cornes: Inversion des Prédicats Inductifs. Université Paris VII, Rapport de stage de DEA Informatique Fondamentale. 1993.
8. C. Cornes et al: The Coq Proof Assistant Reference Manual, Version 5.10. Projet Coq, Inria-Rocquencourt and CNRS-ENS Lyon, France.
9. C. Cornes, D. Terrasse: Inverting Inductive Predicates in Coq. Rapport de Recherche I.N.R.I.A. to appear.
10. E. Giménez: Codifying guarded definitions with recursive schemes. In BRA Workshop on Types for Proofs and Programs, June 1994. LNCS 996 (1994) 39-59.
11. E. Giménez: The implementation of coinductive types in Coq: an experiment with the Alternating Bit Protocol. In BRA Workshop Types for Proofs and Programs, Turin, June 1995. To appear in the LNCS series.
12. Z. Luo : Computation and Reasoning: A Type Theory for Computer Science. 1994. Oxford University Press.
13. P. Manoury, M. Simonot: Automatizing Termination Proofs of Recursively Defined Functions. Theoretical Computer Science. Vol. 135, pp.319-343, 1994.
14. P. Martin-Löf : Intuitionistic Type Theory. Bibliopolis, Napoli, 1984.
15. Ch. Paulin-Mohring: Inductive Definitions in the System Coq: Rules and Properties. Proceedings of the International Conference on Typed Lambda Calculi and Applications (TLCA), Springer-Verlag LNCS 664 (1992) 328–345.
16. T. Streicher: Semantical Investigations into Intensional Type Theory. LMU München. Habilitationsschrift. 1993
17. B. Werner: Une Théorie des Constructions Inductives. Thèse Université Paris VII, May 1994.

First Order Marked Types

Philippe Curmin

Laboratoire de Logique Mathématique
Paris VII University
curmin@logique.jussieu.fr

Abstract. We present a simple notion of marking of first order formulas, which enables to optimize program extraction from intuitionistic Natural Deduction proofs. It gives a way to mark some parts of a proof depending on the marking of its conclusion. Thus it allows to remove useless code from the extracted λ-terms. We define a notion of realizability by which we prove the correctness of programs extracted from marked proofs. We also detail a proof-marking algorithm.

1 Introduction

One of the main drawbacks of the *proofs as programs* paradigm is the unefficiency of programs extracted from proofs. Indeed some proofs express algorithms, but not all algorithms (and in some cases not the "good" ones) can be extracted from proofs in a given syntax. And anyway proofs contain parts which correspond to useless code in programs. The following question arose with the development of *proofs as programs* interactive systems : how to optimize those programs which can be written from proofs ? This question is linked to the more general one : how to define a notion of "algorithmic irrelevance" or "algorithmic uselessness" in a given logic ?

A first solution is to encode this notion in the logic itself : by adding a kind of modality to formulas without (useful) algorithmic meaning, as the $\diamond$ symbol in the PX system [5] or the sort *Prop* for non-informative propositions in the Calculus of Constructions [8]. This approach could be called "static" because the status useful/useless for the computation has to be chosen a priori for each formula and can not be changed. For example in the Calculus of Constructions, the status of an hypothesis may not be switched from *Prop* to *Spec* or other way round, in different subproofs. Moreover, the logic is changed and one has to cope with these modalities when writting a proof, though they have no proper logical meaning.

A second solution is to define some kind of "decoration" of the proofs : for example, the *projection method* of Y. Takayama [9],[6] gives a means to choose (*a marking*) between the existential quantifiers in strictly positive position in a specification. The marked existential quantifiers correspond to the only witnesses which should be computed by the program.

In the *pruning method* of S. Berardi [1] a dummy constant (with a dummy type) replaces useless subterms of a typed λ-term. In both cases the approach is "dynamic" because the algorithmic status of a formula is not part of it, and because they give algorithms to compute the "decoration" of a proof (a typed λ-term in [1]).

We may also make a distinction between the "semantics" of the last two methods. In [9] *q-realizability* is used and a successful marking corresponds to a projection in the realizer of the specification. Hence only *redundancies* in the conclusion of a proof can be eliminated and for example optimizations can not be made on the right handside of a modus-ponens. In [1] *observational equivalence* is proved between any typed λ-term and any of its *prunings* of the same type as the term. So *prunings* with an altered type are not given any interpretation.

We present here a *dynamic* optimization procedure for programs (λ-terms) extracted from first order intuitionistic Natural deduction proofs. We do not use *modified realizability* as in [9] and so we are enabled to mark any subformula (not only strictly positive ones as in [9]) in a formula as computationally useless and to seek optimizations in any part of a proof. An hypothesis may be marked as informative in some subproof and as non-informative in another subproof. Any extraction rule has its optimized versions : for example we obtain all possible simplifications of recursion on integers and in particular its optimization to iteration. We can also "forget" all subterms corresponding to proofs of absurdity, and all subterms corresponding to proofs of equalities. We do not replace useless parts in terms by dummy constants as in [1], but we directly erase them. Yet we can describe the behaviour of the optimized extracted terms, using a notion of *realizability* which enables us to interpret any marked formula. We detail a *marking algorithm* of proofs which not only yields simplifications in the result computed by the extracted program (elimination of *redundancies* as in [9]), but also optimizes the intermediate computations : in particular it is able to put marks in a proof even if its conclusion is not marked. Moreover, our algorithm can deal with undetermined marks : when we do not know in advance whether an hypothesis in a proof corresponds to a useful argument in the extracted program or is only a *side condition*, the algorithm will answer to the question.

2 First order natural deduction

We now introduce a *first order natural deduction system* with only $\rightarrow, \wedge$ as connectors, quantifiers $\forall, \exists$ and equality. We use $\perp$ to denote absurdity and the negation of a formula A is represented by $(A \rightarrow \perp)$. We abbreviate $A \rightarrow (B \rightarrow C)$ by $A,\ B \rightarrow C$.

We also give introduction and elimination rules for two specific unary predicate symbols *Bool* and *Nat*, which respectively represent the data types of booleans and integers. We use constants symbols $\underline{T}$,$\underline{F}$ for boolean values, the constant symbol $\underline{0}$ for zero and the function symbol $\underline{s}$ for the successor function.

New function symbols should be added to that language to represent functions over the data types (like <u>not</u>, <u>+</u>, <u>×</u>, <u>mod</u>...).

A context Γ is a set of indexed formulas F^x s.t. distinct formulas have distinct indexes. Indexes are used to distinguish several occurrences of the same formula. We write the abbreviation Γ, A^x for $\Gamma \cup \{A^x\}$ with the implicit hypothesis that $A^x \notin \Gamma$.

The inference rules are the following :

<u>Rules for connectors and quantifiers</u> :

$\Gamma, A^x \vdash A$ axiom

$$\frac{\Gamma, A^x \vdash B}{\Gamma \vdash A \rightarrow B} \rightarrow \mathrm{I} \qquad \frac{\Gamma \vdash A \rightarrow B \quad \Gamma \vdash A}{\Gamma \vdash B} \rightarrow \mathrm{E}$$

$$\frac{\Gamma \vdash A \quad \Gamma \vdash B}{\Gamma \vdash A \wedge B} \wedge \mathrm{I} \qquad \frac{\Gamma \vdash A \wedge B}{\Gamma \vdash A} \wedge \mathrm{E}_l \qquad \frac{\Gamma \vdash A \wedge B}{\Gamma \vdash B} \wedge \mathrm{E}_r$$

$$\frac{\Gamma \vdash A}{\Gamma \vdash \forall \mathrm{x}\, A} \forall \mathrm{I}\ (*) \qquad \frac{\Gamma \vdash \forall \mathrm{x}\, A}{\Gamma \vdash A[\tau/\mathrm{x}]} \forall \mathrm{E}$$

$$\frac{\Gamma \vdash A[\tau/\mathrm{x}]}{\Gamma \vdash \exists \mathrm{x}\, A} \exists \mathrm{I} \qquad \frac{\Gamma \vdash \exists \mathrm{x}\, A \quad \Gamma \vdash \forall \mathrm{x}\, (A \rightarrow C)}{\Gamma \vdash C} \exists \mathrm{E}\ (*)$$

(*) if x is not free in the conclusion sequent.

<u>Absurdity rule</u> :

$$\frac{\Gamma \vdash \bot}{\Gamma \vdash A} \quad \text{for any formula } A$$

<u>Equational reasoning</u> :

$$\Gamma \vdash \tau = \tau \ \mathit{Refl} \qquad \frac{\Gamma \vdash \tau = \theta}{\Gamma \vdash \theta = \tau} \mathit{Sym} \qquad \frac{\Gamma \vdash \tau = \xi \quad \Gamma \vdash \xi = \theta}{\Gamma \vdash \tau = \theta} \mathit{Trans}$$

$$\frac{\Gamma \vdash \tau_1 = \theta_n \quad \dots \quad \Gamma \vdash \tau_n = \theta_n}{\Gamma \vdash \xi[\tau_1/\mathrm{x}_1, \dots, \tau_n/\mathrm{x}_n] = \xi[\theta_1/\mathrm{x}_1, \dots, \theta_n/\mathrm{x}_n]} \mathit{Comp}$$

$$\frac{\Gamma \vdash A[\tau/\mathrm{x}] \quad \Gamma \vdash \tau = \theta}{\Gamma \vdash A[\theta/\mathrm{x}]} \mathrm{Eq}$$

(Where $\tau, \tau_i, \theta, \theta_i, \xi, \xi_i$ are any first order terms and x, x_i any first order variables, with $1 \leq i \leq n$ and n any integer.)

Rules for *Bool* and *Nat* :

$$\Gamma \vdash Bool(\underline{T}) \;\; Bool\,\mathrm{I}_T \qquad \Gamma \vdash Bool(\underline{F}) \;\; Bool\,\mathrm{I}_F$$

$$\frac{\Gamma \vdash Bool(\tau) \quad \Gamma \vdash A[\underline{T}/\mathrm{x}] \quad \Gamma \vdash A[\underline{F}/\mathrm{x}]}{\Gamma \vdash A[\tau/\mathrm{x}]} \; Bool\,\mathrm{E}$$

$$\Gamma \vdash Nat(\underline{0}) \;\; Nat\,\mathrm{I}_0 \qquad \frac{\Gamma \vdash Nat(\tau)}{\Gamma \vdash Nat(\underline{s}\tau)} \; Nat\,\mathrm{I}_s$$

$$\frac{\Gamma \vdash Nat(\tau) \quad \Gamma \vdash A[\underline{0}/\mathrm{x}] \quad \Gamma \vdash \forall \mathrm{z}\,(Nat(\mathrm{z}),\, A[\mathrm{z}/\mathrm{x}] \rightarrow A[\underline{s}\mathrm{z}/\mathrm{x}])}{\Gamma \vdash A[\tau/\mathrm{x}]} \; Nat\,\mathrm{E}$$

In what follows, when we say that a sequent $\Gamma \vdash A$ is *provable* we mean that it is provable in the system detailed above.

3 First order marked types

We now introduce *marks* which specify the algorithmic interpretation of a formula : when we want to erase the algorithmic content of a subformula, we mark it with $\{0\}$. Thus for example from the implication $A \rightarrow B$ we get a "degenerated" implication $A\{0\} \rightarrow B$ which is the type of a "function" whose first argument is erased, and from the conjunction $A \wedge B$ we get "degenerated" conjunctions $A\{0\} \wedge B$ and $A \wedge B\{0\}$ which are respectively types of a "pair" without left or right component.

Formally, *marked formulas* are inductively defined as follows :

- $A\{0\}$ is a marked formula, for any formula A
  0 is called the *trivial* mark
- $A\{1\}$ is a marked formula if A is atomic
- if $A\{\mu\}$ and $B\{\nu\}$ are marked formulas then
  - ◇ if $\nu \neq 0$ then $(A \rightarrow B)\{\mu \rightarrow \nu\}$ is a marked formula
  - ◇ if μ, ν are not both 0 then $(A \wedge B)\{\mu \wedge \nu\}$ is a marked formula
  - ◇ if $\mu \neq 0$ then $(\forall \mathrm{x}\, A)\{\mu\}$ is a marked formula
  - ◇ $(\exists \mathrm{x}\, A)\{\exists \mu\}$ is a marked formula.

We note 1_A the unique mark for A without occurrences of 0.

This syntax is rather loose : we may put marks inside formulas instead of outside, i.e. attached to subformulas and even only to atomic subformulas. We may also write explicitely only trivial marks. By convention, the scope of a mark inside a formula is the smallest possible.

For example, a marked formula like $(\forall x\,(Nat(x) \rightarrow \exists y\,(Nat(y) \wedge P(x,y))))$ $\{1 \rightarrow \exists(1 \wedge 0)\}$ can be written $\forall x\,(Nat(x)\{1\} \rightarrow \exists y\,(Nat(y)\{1\} \wedge P(x,y)\{0\}))$ or $\forall x\,(Nat(x) \rightarrow \exists y\,(Nat(y) \wedge P(x,y)\{0\}))$.

Marked derivations are built with the following marked typing rules, where the usual correspondance between proofs and λ-terms is modified according to marks. The language we use to extract programs from marked proofs is an extension of pure λ-calculus.

A marked context $\Gamma\{\delta\}$ is a context Γ together with a partial function δ which associates a mark $\delta(x)$ to every indexed formula F^x in Γ such that $F\{\delta(x)\}$ is a marked formula. By $\Gamma\{0\}$ we mean that the formulas of Γ are all marked with 0. We do not write contexts explicitely when they are the same on all premisses of a rule and left unchanged by it.

Let μ, ν be any *non trivial marks* and ρ, ρ_1, ρ_2 be any marks.

Erasing rule :

$\Gamma\{0\} \vdash A\{0\}$ if $\Gamma \vdash A$ is provable

Marked rules for connectors and quantifiers :

$\Gamma\{\delta\}, A^x\{\mu\} \vdash x : A\{\mu\}$ axiom

$$\frac{\Gamma\{\delta\}, A^x\{\mu\} \vdash t : B\{\nu\}}{\Gamma\{\delta\} \vdash \lambda x\, t : A\{\mu\} \rightarrow B\{\nu\}} \rightarrow\text{I (1)} \qquad \frac{\Gamma\{\delta\}, A^x\{0\} \vdash t : B\{\nu\}}{\Gamma\{\delta\} \vdash t : A\{0\} \rightarrow B\{\nu\}} \rightarrow\text{I (2)}$$

$$\frac{\Gamma\{\delta\} \vdash t : A\{\mu\} \rightarrow B\{\nu\} \quad \Gamma\{\delta\} \vdash u : A\{\mu\}}{\Gamma\{\delta\} \vdash (t\ u) : B\{\nu\}} \rightarrow\text{E (1)}$$

$$\frac{\Gamma\{\delta\} \vdash t : A\{0\} \rightarrow B\{\nu\} \quad \Gamma\{0\} \vdash A\{0\}}{\Gamma\{\delta\} \vdash t : B\{\nu\}} \rightarrow\text{E (2)}$$

$$\frac{\vdash t : A\{\mu\} \quad \vdash u : B\{\nu\}}{\vdash \langle t, u \rangle : A\{\mu\} \wedge B\{\nu\}} \wedge\text{I (1)} \qquad \frac{\Gamma\{0\} \vdash A\{0\} \quad \Gamma\{\delta\} \vdash u : B\{\nu\}}{\Gamma\{\delta\} \vdash u : A\{0\} \wedge B\{\nu\}} \wedge\text{I (2)}$$

$$\frac{\Gamma\{\delta\} \vdash t : A\{\mu\} \quad \Gamma\{0\} \vdash B\{0\}}{\Gamma\{\delta\} \vdash t : A\{\mu\} \wedge B\{0\}} \wedge\text{I (3)}$$

$$\frac{\vdash t : A\{\mu\} \wedge B\{\nu\}}{\vdash \pi_l(t) : A\{\mu\}} \wedge\text{E}_l\text{ (1)} \qquad \frac{\vdash t : A\{\mu\} \wedge B\{0\}}{\vdash t : A\{\mu\}} \wedge\text{E}_l\text{ (2)}$$

$$\frac{\vdash t : A\{\mu\} \wedge B\{\nu\}}{\vdash \pi_r(t) : B\{\nu\}} \wedge\text{E}_r\ (1) \qquad \frac{\vdash t : A\{0\} \wedge B\{\nu\}}{\vdash t : B\{\nu\}} \wedge\text{E}_r\ (2)$$

$$\frac{\vdash t : A\{\mu\}}{\vdash t : (\forall \mathrm{x}\, A)\{\mu\}} \forall\text{I}\ (*) \qquad \frac{\vdash t : (\forall \mathrm{x}\, A)\{\mu\}}{\vdash t : A[\tau/\mathrm{x}]\{\mu\}} \forall\text{E}$$

$$\frac{\vdash t : A[\tau/\mathrm{x}]\{\mu\}}{\vdash EI(t) : (\exists \mathrm{x}\, A)\{\exists\mu\}} \exists\text{I}\ (1) \qquad \frac{\Gamma\{0\} \vdash A[\tau/\mathrm{x}]\{0\}}{\Gamma\{\delta\} \vdash ei : (\exists \mathrm{x}\, A)\{\exists 0\}} \exists\text{I}\ (2)$$

$$\frac{\vdash t : (\exists \mathrm{x}\, A)\{\exists\mu\} \qquad \vdash u : \forall \mathrm{x}\,(A\{\mu\} \rightarrow C\{\nu\})}{\vdash EE(t,u) : C\{\nu\}} \exists\text{E}\ (*)$$

(*) if x is not free in the conclusion sequent.

A second marked rule for ∃E is obtained by taking $\mu = 0$.

Marked absurdity rule :

$$\frac{\Gamma\{0\} \vdash \bot\{0\}}{\Gamma\{\delta\} \vdash @ : A\{\mu\}} \text{Abort}$$

for any marked formula $A\{\mu\}$ with $\mu \neq 0$ (@ is a new λ-constant).

Marked rules for equational reasoning :

$$\frac{\Gamma\{\delta\} \vdash A[\tau/\mathrm{x}]\{\mu\} \qquad \Gamma\{0\} \vdash \tau = \theta\{0\}}{\Gamma\{\delta\} \vdash A[\theta/\mathrm{x}]\{\mu\}} \text{Eq} \qquad \Gamma\{\delta\} \vdash id : \tau = \tau\{1\}$$

(*id* is a constant in our λ-calculus)

Marked rules for *Bool* and Nat :

$$\Gamma\{\delta\} \vdash T : Bool(\underline{T})\{1\} \quad Bool\,\text{I}_T \qquad \Gamma\{\delta\} \vdash F : Bool(\underline{F})\{1\} \quad Bool\,\text{I}_F$$

$$\frac{\vdash t : Bool(\tau)\{1\} \qquad \vdash u : A[\underline{T}/\mathrm{x}]\{\mu\} \qquad \vdash v : A[\underline{F}/\mathrm{x}]\{\mu\}}{\vdash if\,(t,u,v) : A[\tau/\mathrm{x}]\{\mu\}} Bool\,\text{E}$$

$$\Gamma\{\delta\} \vdash 0 : Nat(\underline{0})\{1\} \quad Nat\,\text{I}_0 \qquad \frac{\vdash t : Nat(\tau)\{1\}}{\vdash s(t) : Nat(\underline{s}\tau)\{1\}} Nat\,\text{I}_s$$

$$\frac{\vdash t : Nat(\tau)\{1\} \ \vdash u : A[\underline{0}]\{\mu\} \ \ \vdash v : \forall \mathrm{z}\,(Nat(\mathrm{z})\{\rho_1\},\, A[\mathrm{z}]\{\rho_2\} \rightarrow A[\underline{s}\mathrm{z}]\{\mu\})}{\vdash Nop\,(t,u,v) : A[\tau]\{\mu\}} Nat\,\text{E}$$

(Where for any term σ $A[\sigma]$ abbreviates $A[\sigma/\mathrm{x}]$.)

$$\text{with} \begin{cases} Nop = Nrec \text{ if } \rho_1 = 1 \text{ and } \rho_2 = \mu \\ Nop = Nit \text{ if } \rho_1 = 0 \text{ and } \rho_2 = \mu \\ Nop = Ncase_1 \text{ if } \rho_1 = 1 \text{ and } \rho_2 = 0 \\ Nop = Ncase_2 \text{ if } \rho_1 = \rho_2 = 0. \end{cases}$$

The operators *Nop* correspond to the possible simplifications of recursion over integers: recursion may be simplified either to iteration (*Nit*) or to case analysis on integers ($Ncase_1$ and $Ncase_2$).

The reduction of λ-terms $\triangleright$ is the transitive closure of the one step reduction $\triangleright_1$ defined itself as the contextual closure of the following rules :

$$\begin{array}{ll} (\lambda x\, t \;\; u) \triangleright_1 t[u/x] & \\ \pi_l(<t,u>) \triangleright_1 t & \pi_r(<t,u>) \triangleright_1 u \\ EE(EI(t),u) \triangleright_1 (u\; t) & EE(ei,\, u) \triangleright_1 u \\ if\,(T,u,v) \triangleright_1 u & if\,(F,u,v) \triangleright_1 v \\ Nop\,(0,u,v) \triangleright_1 u & Nrec\,(s(t),u,v) \triangleright_1 (v\; t\; Nrec\,(t,u,v)) \\ & Nit\,(s(t),u,v) \triangleright_1 (v\; Nit\,(t,u,v)) \\ & Ncase_1\,(s(t),u,v) \triangleright_1 (v\; t) \\ & Ncase_2\,(s(t),u,v) \triangleright_1 v \end{array}$$

Our typing system with marks enjoys *subject reduction* and *strong normalization*, but we will not prove these properties here.

Any marked derivation whose conclusion formula is not marked with 0 can be reduced to a derivation in *Curry style first order typed λ-calculus* : one just erases all subformulas marked with 0 and all subproofs of formulas marked with 0 (and all rules which use them, like $\rightarrow$ E (2)). This simple transformation provides an embedding from the marked system to *First Order Typed Λ-calculus* : if t is typable of type $A\{\mu\}$ ($\mu \neq 0$) then t is also typable (without marks) of type A' where A' is obtained from $A\{\mu\}$ by removing all subformulas marked with 0. Hence strong normalization for our system is straightforwardly deduced from strong normalization for some version of First Order Typed Λ-calculus.

The interest of this system lies in the possibility of marking parts of a specification and thus erasing parts of the related program. As a basic example, we take a specification F of a program for the predecessor function: $\forall x \in Nat\, \exists y \in Nat\, \exists b \in Bool\,((b = \underline{T} \rightarrow (x = \underline{0} \wedge y = \underline{0})) \wedge (b = \underline{F} \rightarrow \underline{s}y = x))$. Were $\forall x \in D\; C$ and $\exists x \in D\; C$ respectively abbreviate $\forall x\,(D(x) \rightarrow C)$ and $\exists x\,(D(x) \wedge C)$, for any data type D and any formula C. Let $P(x,y)$ be the subformula $\exists b \in Bool\,((b = \underline{T} \rightarrow (x = \underline{0} \wedge y = \underline{0})) \wedge (b = \underline{F} \rightarrow \underline{s}y = x))$ of F.

Let $t_0 = \lambda n\, Nrec\,(n,\, EI\,(<0,u>), \lambda m\, \lambda h\, EI\,(<m,v>))$ with $u = EI(<T, <\lambda d <id, id>, @>>)$ and $v = EI(<F, <@, \lambda d\, id>>)$: t_0 is typable of type $F\{1_F\}$ in our system, in the marked context $\Gamma = \{(\neg \underline{T} = \underline{F})\{0\}\}$. This term is not the expected program, because for any integer n it computes both an integer m and a witness for $P(n,m)$, but as it is extracted from a proof of F we already know that m is the predecessor of n. So the subterms u and v are *redun-*

dant and a better program would be $t_1 = \lambda n\, Nrec(n, EI(\underline{0}), \lambda m \lambda h\, EI(m))$. However, as the recursive argument h is not used in t_1, we can further optimize our program and get the term $t_2 = \lambda n\, Ncase_1(n, EI(\underline{0}), \lambda m\, EI(m))$. This optimization can be done in one go and directly at the proof level : we just mark the specification F to precise that the subformula $P(\mathrm{x}, \mathrm{y})$ has no algorithmic content. Indeed t_2 is of type $\forall \mathrm{x} \in Nat\, \exists \mathrm{y} \in Nat\, P(\mathrm{x}, \mathrm{y})\{0\}$ in the context Γ.

4 Realizability

For any λ-term t and any formula A we define a relation $t \Vdash^{\sigma}_{\Gamma} A$ for "t realizes A", depending both on a context Γ and on an application σ from all first order variables to closed terms, which will be called a *closure*. Any closure σ is trivially generalized to an application from first order terms to closed terms, from formulas to closed formulas and from contexts to closed contexts (in the last two cases σ is of course only applied to *free variables*). We denote by $\sigma[\mathrm{x} \leftarrow \tau]$ the closure which is like σ on all variables but x and applies x to the closed term τ.

The relation $t \Vdash^{\sigma}_{\Gamma} A\{\mu\}$ is defined for any λ-term t, any context Γ and any marked formula $A\{\mu\}$ (with $\mu \neq 0$) :

If $\sigma\Gamma \vdash \bot$ is provable then $t \Vdash^{\sigma}_{\Gamma} A\{\mu\}$ for any t, A, μ.

Otherwise, we proceed by induction on the length of A :

- $t \Vdash^{\sigma}_{\Gamma} Nat(\tau)\{1\} \Leftrightarrow$ $t \simeq_\beta s^n(0)$ and $\sigma\Gamma \vdash \sigma\tau = \underline{s}^n\underline{0}$ is provable for some integer n

  (where $s^n(0)$ abbreviates $\underbrace{s(\dots s}_{n\ times}(0)\dots)$ and $\underline{s}^n\underline{0}$ abbreviates $\underbrace{\underline{s}\dots\underline{s}}_{n\ times}\ \underline{0})$
- $t \Vdash^{\sigma}_{\Gamma} Bool(\tau)\{1\} \Leftrightarrow \begin{cases} t \simeq_\beta T \text{ and } \sigma\Gamma \vdash \sigma\tau = \underline{T} \text{ is provable} \\ \text{or} \\ t \simeq_\beta F \text{ and } \sigma\Gamma \vdash \sigma\tau = \underline{F} \text{ is provable} \end{cases}$
- $t \Vdash^{\sigma}_{\Gamma} (\tau = \tau)\{1\} \Leftrightarrow t \simeq_\beta id$
- $t \Vdash^{\sigma}_{\Gamma} A\{\mu\} \rightarrow B\{\nu\} \Leftrightarrow$ if $\sigma\Gamma \vdash \sigma A$ *is provable* then $(t\ u) \Vdash^{\sigma}_{\Gamma} B\{\nu\}$ for any u s.t. $u \Vdash^{\sigma}_{\Gamma} A\{\mu\}$
- $t \Vdash^{\sigma}_{\Gamma} A\{0\} \rightarrow B\{\nu\} \Leftrightarrow$ if $\sigma\Gamma \vdash \sigma A$ *is provable* then $t \Vdash^{\sigma}_{\Gamma} B\{\nu\}$
- $t \Vdash^{\sigma}_{\Gamma} A\{\mu\} \wedge B\{\nu\} \Leftrightarrow \pi_l(t) \Vdash^{\sigma}_{\Gamma} A\{\mu\}$ and $\pi_r(t) \Vdash^{\sigma}_{\Gamma} B\{\nu\}$
- $t \Vdash^{\sigma}_{\Gamma} A\{0\} \wedge B\{\nu\} \Leftrightarrow \sigma\Gamma \vdash \sigma A$ *is provable* and $t \Vdash^{\sigma}_{\Gamma} B\{\nu\}$
- $t \Vdash^{\sigma}_{\Gamma} A\{\mu\} \wedge B\{0\} \Leftrightarrow t \Vdash^{\sigma}_{\Gamma} A\{\mu\}$ and $\sigma\Gamma \vdash \sigma B$ *is provable*
- $t \Vdash^{\sigma}_{\Gamma} \forall \mathrm{x}\, A\{\mu\} \Leftrightarrow t \Vdash^{\sigma[\mathrm{x}\leftarrow\tau]}_{\Gamma} A\{\mu\}$ for any closed term τ

- $t \Vdash^{\sigma}_{\Gamma} \exists x A\{\exists\mu\} \Leftrightarrow$ $t \simeq_\beta EI(u)$ and $u \Vdash^{\sigma[x\leftarrow\tau]}_{\Gamma} A\{\mu\}$ and $\sigma\Gamma \vdash \sigma(A[\tau/x])$ is provable for some λ-term u and some closed term τ
- $t \Vdash^{\sigma}_{\Gamma} (\exists x A)\{\exists 0\} \Leftrightarrow$ $t \simeq_\beta ei$ and $\sigma\Gamma \vdash \sigma(A[\tau/x])$ *is provable* for some closed term τ

From this definition we infer the following properties, for any λ-terms t, t', any first order terms τ, θ and any marked formula $A\{\mu\}$ $(\mu \neq 0)$:

1. if $t \Vdash^{\sigma}_{\Gamma} A\{\mu\}$ and $t \simeq_\beta t'$ then $t' \Vdash^{\sigma}_{\Gamma} A\{\mu\}$
2. if $\sigma\Gamma \vdash \sigma B$ is provable then $t \Vdash^{\sigma}_{(\Gamma\cup\{B\})} A\{\mu\}$ iff $t \Vdash^{\sigma}_{\Gamma} A\{\mu\}$

The following lemma states the *adequation* of the realizability relation $\Vdash$ to the typability relation:

Lemma 4.1 *Let $\Gamma\{\delta\} \vdash t : A\{\mu\}$ be a sequent derivable in the marked typing system. Let $\Gamma = \{A_1^{x_1};\ldots;A_n^{x_n}\} \cup \Gamma'$ for some integer n ($n = 0$ is possible) where $\delta(x_i) \neq 0$ for $1 \leq i \leq n$ and $\delta(x) = 0$ for all indexed formulas $F^x \in \Gamma'$. Let σ be any closure.*

For any $w_1, \ldots, w_n$ s.t. $w_i \Vdash^{\sigma}_{\Gamma} A_i\{\delta(x_i)\}$ for every $1 \leq i \leq n$
we have $t[w_1/x_1, \ldots, w_n/x_n] \Vdash^{\sigma}_{\Gamma} A\{\mu\}$.

This lemma is proved by induction on the height of a derivation d of $\Gamma\{\delta\} \vdash t : A\{\mu\}$ (we detail only a few cases of the induction) :

We suppose that $\sigma\Gamma \vdash \bot$ is not provable, because otherwise the result is trivial, hence we suppose that d does not end with the absurdity rule.

If d is an axiom then $t = x_i$, $A = A_i$, $\delta(x_i) = \mu$ and the result is given by hypothesis on w_i.

Otherwise, the last rule in d has premisses and we can apply the induction hypothesis on the derivations of these premisses (we shorten $t[w_1/x_1, \ldots, w_n/x_n]$ to $t[\overline{w}/\overline{x}]$) :

- If d has the form
$$\frac{\begin{matrix}\vdots\\ \Gamma\{\delta\}, A^y\{\mu\} \vdash t : B\{\nu\}\end{matrix}}{\Gamma\{\delta\} \vdash \lambda y\, t : A\{\mu\} \to B\{\nu\}} \to_{\mathrm{I}}(1)$$
by induction hypothesis, for any u s.t. $u \Vdash^{\sigma}_{\Delta} A\{\mu\}$: $t[\overline{w}/\overline{x}, u/y] \Vdash^{\sigma}_{\Delta} B\{\nu\}$ with $\Delta = \Gamma \cup \{A^y\}$
hence $((\lambda y\, t)[\overline{w}/\overline{x}]\ u) \Vdash^{\sigma}_{\Delta} B\{\nu\}$ by property (**1**) above
hence by property (**2**) above :
if $\sigma\Gamma \vdash \sigma A$ is provable then $((\lambda y\, t)[\overline{w}/\overline{x}]\ u) \Vdash^{\sigma}_{\Gamma} B\{\nu\}$ for any u s.t. $u \Vdash^{\sigma}_{\Gamma} A\{\mu\}$

and $(\lambda y\, t)[\overline{w}/\overline{x}] \Vdash^{\sigma}_{\Gamma} A\{\mu\} \to B\{\nu\}$ by definition of the relation.

- If d has the form $$\dfrac{\Gamma\{\delta\}, A^{y}\{0\} \vdash t : B\{\nu\}}{\Gamma\{\delta\} \vdash t : A\{0\} \to B\{\nu\}} \to \text{I}\ (2)$$

  by induction hypothesis, $t[\overline{w}/\overline{x}] \Vdash^{\sigma}_{\Delta} B\{\nu\}$
  hence by property **(2)** above :
  $t[\overline{w}/\overline{x}] \Vdash^{\sigma}_{\Gamma} B\{\nu\}$ if $\sigma\Gamma \vdash \sigma A$ is provable
  hence $t[\overline{w}/\overline{x}] \Vdash^{\sigma}_{\Gamma} A\{0\} \to B\{\nu\}$ by definition.

- If d ends with $\to$ E (1) $$\dfrac{\overset{\vdots\, d_1}{\Gamma\{\delta\} \vdash t : A\{\mu\} \to B\{\nu\}} \qquad \overset{\vdots\, d_2}{\Gamma\{\delta\} \vdash u : A\{\mu\}}}{\Gamma\{\delta\} \vdash (t\ u) : B\{\nu\}}$$

  the sub-derivation d_1 gives us $t[\overline{w}/\overline{x}] \Vdash^{\sigma}_{\Gamma} A\{\mu\} \to B\{\nu\}$
  and from d_2 we get $u[\overline{w}/\overline{x}] \Vdash^{\sigma}_{\Gamma} A\{\mu\}$
  hence $(t\ \ u)[\overline{w}/\overline{x}] \Vdash^{\sigma}_{\Gamma} B\{\nu\}$ if $\sigma\Gamma \vdash \sigma A$ is provable
  but d_2 also yields a proof of $\Gamma \vdash A$ from which we get a proof of $\sigma\Gamma \vdash \sigma A$.
  In the case of $\to$ E (2) no term is extracted from the sub-derivation d_2, which is only needed to give a proof of $\sigma\Gamma \vdash \sigma A$ ...

- If d ends with $\exists$E $$\dfrac{\overset{\vdots\, d_1}{\vdash t : (\exists x\, A)\{\exists\mu\}} \qquad \overset{\vdots\, d_2}{\vdash u : \forall x\,(A\{\mu\} \to C\{\nu\})}}{\vdash EE\,(t, u) : C\{\nu\}} \exists\text{E}\ (*)$$

  If $\mu \neq 0$:
  By induction hypothesis on d_2 and condition $(*)$: $u[\overline{w}/\overline{x}] \Vdash^{\sigma}_{\Gamma} A[\tau/x]\{\mu\} \to C\{\nu\}$ for any closed term τ
  by induction hypothesis on d_1, there is some v and some closed term τ s.t. $t[\overline{w}/\overline{x}] \simeq_{\beta} EI\,(v)$ and $v \Vdash^{\sigma}_{\Gamma} A[\tau/x]$ and $\sigma\Gamma \vdash \sigma(A[\tau/x])$ is provable
  hence $(u[\overline{w}/\overline{x}]\ \ v) \Vdash^{\sigma}_{\Gamma} C\{\nu\}$
  hence $EE\,(t, u)\,[\overline{w}/\overline{x}] \Vdash^{\sigma}_{\Gamma} C\{\nu\}$ by property **(1)**.
  If $\mu = 0$:
  By induction hypothesis on d_2 and condition $(*)$: $u[\overline{w}/\overline{x}] \Vdash^{\sigma}_{\Gamma} C\{\nu\}$ if $\sigma\Gamma \vdash \sigma(A[\tau/x])$ is provable for some closed term τ
  by induction hypothesis on d_1, there is some closed term τ s.t. $t[\overline{w}/\overline{x}] \simeq_{\beta} ei$ and $\sigma\Gamma \vdash \sigma(A[\tau/x])$ is provable
  hence $EE\,(t, u)\,[\overline{w}/\overline{x}] \Vdash^{\sigma}_{\Gamma} C\{\nu\}$ by property **(1)**.

The correctness of programs extracted from marked proofs is an immediate corollary of the *adequation lemma* :

Here we have only *Nat* and *Bool* as data types but we may easily extend our system by adding rules for lists, trees... For any data type D we call *elements* of D the closed logical terms associated to it : the elements of *Bool* are $\underline{T}, \underline{F}$

and the elements of *Nat* are of the form $\underline{s}^n\underline{0}$ for some integer n. If $\underline{c}$ denotes an element of D then c denotes its canonical representation in λ-calculus i.e. the unique normal term s.t. $\vdash c : D(\underline{c})\{1\}$ is derivable.

Proposition 4.2 *Let* $A(\mathrm{x}_1,\ldots,\mathrm{x}_n,\mathrm{y})$ *be any formula having only* $\mathrm{x}_1,\ldots,\mathrm{x}_n,\mathrm{y}$ *as free variables. If* $\Gamma\{0\}\vdash t : \forall \mathrm{x}_1 \in D_1 \ldots \forall \mathrm{x}_n \in D_n\, \exists \mathrm{y} \in D\, A(\mathrm{x}_1,\ldots,\mathrm{x}_n,\mathrm{y})\{0\}$ *is derivable and* Γ *is a closed context s.t.* $\Gamma \vdash \bot$ *is not provable, then* t *is* correct *with respect to its marked specification i.e. for any closed terms* $\underline{c_1},\ldots,\underline{c_n}$ *s.t.* $\underline{c_i}$ *is an element of* D_i *for any* $1 \leq i \leq n$, *there is some element* $\underline{c}$ *of* D *s.t.*
$(t\ c_1 \ldots c_n) \simeq_\beta EI(c)$ *and* $\Gamma \vdash A[\underline{c_1}/\mathrm{x}_1,\ \ldots,\ \underline{c_n}/\mathrm{x}_n,\ \underline{c}/\mathrm{y}]$ *is provable.*

5 Proof marking

It is easy to show that from any proof π in the system of section **2** we can get a marked proof simply by putting the mark 0 on every Harrop subformula in π (here Harrop formulas are defined as usual but atomic formulas of the form $D(\tau)$ where D is a data type are not considered as Harrop). But we are looking for a stronger proof marking procedure.

Given a proof and a mark for its conclusion, we want to mark automatically the whole proof, and then extract an optimized program. Moreover, we may not precise entirely the mark of the conclusion and ask our marking algorithm to give us values for these undetermined marks.

For this purpose we extend our notion of mark by allowing variables to occur in marks. *Marking variables* will be written $m_1,\ldots,m_i,\ldots$ and we get the new definition of marked formulas from the previous one simply by replacing the condition "not 0" by the condition "neither 0 nor a variable".

A *marked version* of a proof π is a marked proof which gives π back when all marks are erased in it. Let π be a proof of a sequent $\Gamma \vdash A$ and δ,μ be respectively a distribution of marks for the context Γ and a mark for A : we call a *marking problem* and write (π,δ,μ) a proof identical to π but with conclusion decorated with δ,μ. A *solution* of (π,δ,μ) is a marked version of π whose conclusion is of the form $\Gamma\{\mathit{sub}\circ\delta\}\vdash A\{\mathit{sub}(\mu)\}$, where *sub* is a substitution which instanciates μ and the marks $\delta(x)$ to constant marks.

We define a marking procedure *MP* which takes a marking problem as input and either returns a solution of it or fails. *MP* uses an auxiliary procedure *Mark* which propagates marks bottom-up in a partially marked proof P. *Mark* is defined by induction on the height of P :

1. If the last rule of P is not marked and μ is neither 0 nor a variable (in all cases *Mark* goes on with the proofs of the premisses) :

- If π ends with the introduction of a connector, *Mark* just decomposes μ according to that connector.

- If π ends with an elimination rule except $\forall$E, *Mark* introduces *marking variables* for each formula in the premisses which is not in the conclusion. Every marking variable introduced has to be new i.e. not already occuring in the partially marked proof. As marks in contexts are simply copied by *Mark* from conclusion to premisses, we omit contexts in what follows...

For $\to$E :
$$\frac{\vdots \quad \vdots}{\frac{\vdash A \to B \qquad \vdash A}{\vdash B\{\mu\}}} \overset{Mark}{\Longrightarrow} \frac{\vdots \quad \vdots}{\frac{\vdash A\{m_i\} \to B\{\mu\} \qquad \vdash A\{m_i\}}{\vdash B\{\mu\}}}$$

For *Nat* E :
$$\frac{\vdash N(\tau) \qquad \vdash A[\underline{0}] \qquad \vdash \forall z\,(N(z), A[z] \to A[\underline{s}z])}{\vdash A[\tau]\{\mu\}} \overset{Mark}{\Longrightarrow}$$

$$\frac{\vdash N(\tau)\{1\} \qquad \vdash A[\underline{0}]\{\mu\} \qquad \vdash \forall z\,(N(z)\{m_i\}, A[z]\{m_{i+1}\} \to A[\underline{s}z]\{\mu\})}{\vdash A[\tau]\{\mu\}}$$

- If π ends with the absurdity rule, every formula in the premisse is marked with 0.
- With any other rule *Mark* just copies μ on the premisse.

- If P is an axiom then marks for A on both sides of the sequent have to be equal. So for each axiom reached with different marks for A on both sides, *Mark* produces a pair of marks to unify, which we call a *constraint.* The new constraint is added to those already produced by *Mark*.

$$(\Gamma, A^x)\{\delta\} \vdash A\{\mu\} \text{ with } \begin{cases} \mu \text{ not a variable} \\ \mu \neq 0 \\ \delta(x) \neq \mu \end{cases} \overset{Mark}{\Longrightarrow} \textit{constraint } (\delta(x), \mu)$$

2. If μ is either 0 or a variable, the proof is left unchanged by *Mark*...

3. If the last rule of P is already marked, *Mark* just goes on with the proofs of the premisses, unless it is a partially marked instance of *Nat* E of the form :

$$\frac{\ldots \quad \ldots \quad \forall z\,(N(z)\{\rho_1\}, A[z]\{\rho_2\} \to A[\underline{s}z]\{\mu\})}{\vdash A[\tau]\{\mu\}} \text{ with } \begin{cases} \rho_2 \text{ not a variable} \\ \rho_2 \neq 0 \\ \rho_2 \neq \mu \end{cases}$$

in that case *Mark* produces the constraint (ρ_2, μ) and goes on with the premisses.

Mark returns a partially marked proof P' (because some subproofs may have their conclusion marked with a variable) and a set of constraints $\mathcal{C}$. If all constraints in $\mathcal{C}$ have a solution i.e. if there is a unifier σ for $\mathcal{C}$, then σ instanciates some of the marking variables in P' and allows us to apply *Mark* on the corresponding subproofs. If not, the whole marking procedure fails.

Hence the following definition of *MP* (where *ident* is the identity substitution on marking variables and *triv* instanciates every marking variable to 0) :

```
MP( (π, δ, μ) ) = begin
                    P := (π, δ, μ) ;
                    sub := ident ;
                    repeat
                      Mark(P) ; (* returns C and P' *)
                      if C unifiable
                        then begin
                               σ := mgu of C ;
                               sub := σ o sub ;
                               P := σ(P')
                             end
                        else begin
                               return( Fail ) ;
                               exit ;
                             end
                    until C = ∅ ;
                    return( triv(P) ) ;
                    return( triv o sub )
                  end.
```

6 Properties of the marking algorithm

1. *MP* terminates :

If $\mathcal{C}$ is not empty then there is some axiom $(\Gamma, A^x)\{\delta\} \vdash A\{\rho\}$ in P with $\delta(x) \neq \rho$ or some marked instance of *Nat* E with $\rho_2 \neq \mu$ (see point **3** of the definition of *Mark*). Either the constraints in $\mathcal{C}$ do not unify, and *MP* terminates with *Fail*, or *Mark* is applied again on $\sigma(P)$. But then $\sigma(\delta(x)) = \sigma(\mu)$ (or $\sigma(\rho_2) = \sigma(\mu)$) and the axiom $(\Gamma, A^x)\{\sigma \circ \delta\} \vdash A\{\sigma(\rho)\}$ (or the marked instance of *Nat* E) in $\sigma(P)$ will not produce any constraint any more. Hence the number of repetitions of the loop repeat-until in *MP* is bounded by the number of axioms and instances of *Nat* E in π.

If we use *linear unification* for the unification step in *MP* then we can bound the computation time needed to solve each constraint by the length of the principal formula in the axiom or *Nat* E rule which produced it. We can bound the computation time for *Mark* by the number of nodes in the proof. Hence the marking algorithm is *quadratic* in the size of the proof (defined as the product of the number of nodes in the proof by the maximum length of a formula in the proof).

2. The solution computed by *MP* is the best one :

It is obvious that when MP succeeds, its output is a solution of the marking problem given as input. But we can also prove that the solution computed is in some sense the *minimum* one. For this purpose we define an ordering on marked proofs :

Constant marks can be ordered in the following way :

- $0 \leq_m \mu$ for any mark μ
- $1 \leq_m 1$
- for any connector c :
  $(\mu_1 \; c \; \nu_1) \leq_m (\mu_2 \; c \; \nu_2)$ iff $\mu_1 \leq_m \mu_2$ and $\nu_1 \leq_m \nu_2$

This ordering on marks induces an ordering on marked versions of the same proof :

$$\frac{\vdots \pi_1' \quad \cdots \quad \vdots \pi_k'}{\Gamma\{\delta\} \vdash A\{\mu\}} R \leq_p \frac{\vdots \pi_1'' \quad \cdots \quad \vdots \pi_k''}{\Gamma\{\delta'\} \vdash A\{\mu'\}} R \quad \text{iff } \mu = 0 \text{ or } \begin{cases} \mu \leq_m \mu' \\ \\ \delta(x) \leq_m \delta'(x) \\ \text{for any } F^x \in \Gamma \\ \\ \pi_i' \leq_p \pi_i'' \text{ for } 1 \leq i \leq k \end{cases}$$

When C is empty, the partially marked proof P produced by iteration of *Mark* is a kind of "skeleton" of a solution for the input. We mean that any solution is obtained from P by instanciation of all the marking variables occuring in P. Why ? Simply because *Mark* produces exactly the conditions (constraints) which any solution must satisfy. The algorithm returns $triv(P)$ which is obviously the smallest instanciation of P and hence the smallest solution for the ordering $\leq_p$.

3. The algorithm is *complete* i.e. it will terminate whenever the marking problem given in input has a solution.

4. The relation between the ordering $\leq_p$ on marked proofs and the reduction of extracted terms is stated by the following proposition :

Proposition 6.1 *Suppose d a derivation of $\Gamma\{\delta\} \vdash t : A\{\mu\}$ and f a derivation of $\Gamma\{\gamma\} \vdash u : A\{\nu\}$. Suppose $d \leq_p f$. If $u \rhd_1 u'$ and f' is a derivation of $\Gamma\{\gamma\} \vdash u' : A\{\nu\}$ then there is some term t' s.t. $t \rhd_1 t'$ or $t = t'$ and there is a derivation d' of $\Gamma\{\delta\} \vdash t' : A\{\mu\}$ s.t. $d' \leq_p f'$.*

This proposition is proved by a straightforward induction on the height of f. When $\mu = \nu$ and $\delta = \gamma$ we know by realizability that t and u have the same *input-output behaviour* but as an immediate corollary of the proposition we also know that any computation of u can be done by t with at most the same number of reduction steps. Hence in a broad sense t is an *optimization* of u. And our marking algorithm may be used to optimize the extraction of a program from a given proof : take a proof π of a specification F in a context Γ, choose marks for F and the formulas of Γ, apply MP and finally extract a program from the marked proof obtained. The extracted program is assured to be correct relatively to its specification and to be the best possible one relatively to our notion of proof marking.

7 Conclusion

The technique we detailed may very easily be suited to more powerful typing systems. For example we may add *course-of-value induction* for integers and use marking to forget in the extraction proofs of formulas (of the form $\tau < \sigma$) which just state that some argument in a recursive call is decreasing. Extension to *Second Order Typed Λ-calculus* (for example to the system *FA2* exposed in [7]) is also straightforward and enables to encode the many marked versions of first order deduction rules (in particular rules for the existential quantifier and rules for induction over integers, lists, trees...) using only the marked rules for implication and second order quantification. We implemented our proof-marking algorithm for *FA2* as part of a program extraction process added to an interactive proof editor designed by Ch. Raffalli. We are still working on a precise characterization of the optimizations produced by our algorithm.

References

1. S. Berardi, *Pruning Simply Typed λ-terms*, Technical Report, Turin University, 1993.
2. S. Berardi and L. Boerio, *Using Subtyping in Program Optimization*, Proceedings of TLCA '95, Edinburgh, April 1995, LNCS, Springer-Verlag.
3. L. Boerio, *Extending Pruning Techniques to Polymorphic Second Order λ-Calculus*, Proceedings of ESOP '94, Edinburgh, Avril 1994, LNCS 788, D. Sannella (ed.), Springer-Verlag, pp. 120-134.
4. C. Goad, *Computational Uses of the Manipulation of Formal Proofs*, Stanford Technical Report CS-80-819, 1980.
5. S. Hayashi and H. Nakano, PX : A Computational Logic, The MIT Press, 1988.
6. S. Hayashi and Y. Takayama "Lifschitz's Logic of Calculable Numbers and Optimizations in Program Extraction", 1994, LNCS 792, Springer Verlag.
7. J.L. Krivine and M. Parigot, Programming with proofs, *J. Inform. Process. Cybern. EIK* 26 (1990) 146-167.
8. Ch. Paulin-Mohring, *Extracting F_ω's Programs from Proofs in the Calculus of Constructions*, in: Association for Computing Machinery, editor, Sixteenth Annual ACM Symposium on Principles of Programming Languages, 1989.
9. Y. Takayama, *Extraction of Redundancy-free Programs from Constructive Natural Deduction Proofs*, Journal of Symbolic Computation, 1991, 12, 29-69.

Internal Type Theory

Peter Dybjer

Department of Computing Science
Chalmers University of Technology
Göteborg, Sweden

Abstract. We introduce *categories with families* as a new notion of model for a basic framework of dependent types. This notion is close to ordinary syntax and yet has a clean categorical description. We also present categories with families as a generalized algebraic theory. Then we define categories with families formally in Martin-Löf's intensional intuitionistic type theory. Finally, we discuss the *coherence problem* for these *internal categories with families.*

1 Introduction

In a previous paper [8] I introduced a general notion of *simultaneous inductive-recursive definition* in intuitionistic type theory. This notion subsumes various reflection principles and seems to pave the way for a natural development of what could be called "internal type theory", that is, the construction of models of (fragments of) type theory in type theory, and more generally, the formalization of the metatheory of type theory in type theory.

The present paper is a first investigation of such an internal type theory. We introduce *categories with families* to model a basic framework of dependent types and show how to formalize them in intensional intuitionistic type theory.

One goal is to represent Hofmann's setoid model of type theory [11, 13] in type theory. He also used a categorical notion of model of dependent types (Cartmell's categories with attributes) but worked in ordinary set-theoretic metalanguage. The setoid model of type theory can be viewed as a formalization of the standard "intuitive" model of type theory. It also justifies the rules of extensional type theory [16] and certain rules for quotient formation.

Our categorical approach to internal type theory can be contrasted to the syntactic approach by Pollack [19]. He formalized the syntax of dependent type theory in type theory and proved syntactic properties such as Church-Rosser.

The plan of the paper is as follows. In section 2 we introduce categores with families and their formalization as a generalized algebraic theory. In section 3 we show how to formalize some basic categorical notions in type theory, and then use these to define categories with families in type theory. We first give an abstract presentation and then show how to derive a system of inference rules. In section 4 we state a coherence problem for internal categories with families and propose how to solve it by constructing a model of normal forms.

2 Categories with Families

2.1 Basic Definitions

Categories with families (cwfs) are variants of Cartmell's *categories with attributes* [12, 18]. The point of the reformulation is to get a more direct link to the syntax of dependent types. In particular we avoid reference to pullbacks, which give rise to a conditional equation when formalized in a straightforward way. Cwfs can therefore directly be formalized as a generalized algebraic theory with clear similiarities to Martin-Löf's *substitution calculus* for type theory [17].

Let Fam be the category of families of sets. An *object* is a family of sets $(B(x))_{x \in A}$ and a *morphism* with source $(B(x))_{x \in A}$ and target $(B'(x'))_{x' \in A'}$ is a pair consisting of a function $f : A \to A'$ and a family of functions $g(x) : B(x) \to B'(f(x))$ indexed by $x \in A$.

The components of a cwf are named after the corresponding syntactic notions.

Definition 1. A *category with families* consists of the following four parts:

- A base *category* C. Its objects are called *contexts* and its morphisms are called *substitutions*.
- A *functor* $T : C^{op} \to Fam$. We write $T(\Gamma) = (\Gamma \vdash A)_{A \in Type(\Gamma)}$, where Γ is an object of C, and call it the family of *terms* indexed by *types* in context Γ. Moreover, if γ is a morphism of C then the two components of $T(\gamma)$ interpret substitution in types and terms respectively. We write $A[\gamma]$ for the application of the first component to a type A and $a[\gamma]$ for the application of the second component to a term a.
- A *terminal object* $[]$ of C called the *empty context*.
- A *context comprehension* operation which to an object Γ of C and a type $A \in Type(\Gamma)$ associates an object $\Gamma; A$ of C; a morphism $p : \Gamma; A \to \Gamma$ of C (the *first projection*); and a term $q \in \Gamma; A \vdash A[p]$ (the *second projection*). The following universal property holds: for each object Δ in C, morphism $\gamma : \Delta \to \Gamma$, and term $a \in \Delta \vdash A[\gamma]$, there is a unique morphism $\theta = \langle \gamma, a \rangle : \Delta \to \Gamma; A$, such that $p \circ \theta = \gamma$ and $q[\theta] = a$.

Throughout the paper we shall freely use "polymorphic" notation for improving readability. Without this convention we should for example have included indices for the projections and written $p_{\Gamma,A}$ and $q_{\Gamma,A}$ instead of just p and q.

A basic example of a cwf is obtained by letting C be the category of sets, $Type(\Gamma)$ be the set of Γ-indexed small sets, and

$$\Gamma \vdash A = \prod_{\gamma \in \Gamma} A(\gamma)$$

$$A[\delta](\gamma) = A(\delta(\gamma))$$

$$a[\delta](\gamma) = a(\delta(\gamma))$$

$$[] = 1$$

$$\Gamma; A = \sum_{\gamma \in \Gamma} A(\gamma)$$

Given a cwf we can recover the structure of a category with attributes. For example, the diagram

$$\begin{array}{ccc} \Delta; A[\gamma] & \xrightarrow{\langle \gamma \circ p, q \rangle} & \Gamma; A \\ {\scriptstyle p}\downarrow & & \downarrow{\scriptstyle p} \\ \Delta & \xrightarrow[\gamma]{} & \Gamma \end{array}$$

is a pullback, and terms $a \in \Gamma \vdash A$ are in one-to-one correspondence with sections $\langle id, a \rangle : \Gamma \to \Gamma; A$ of first projections $p : \Gamma; A \to \Gamma$.

Conversely, given a category with attributes we can recover the structure of a cwf. The terms can be recovered from sections of projections and substitution can be recovered from pullbacks.

Definition 2. Let (C, T) denote a cwf with base category C and functor T. A *morphism of cwfs* with source (C, T) and target (C', T') is a pair (F, σ), where $F : C \to C'$ is a functor and $\sigma : T \to T'F$ is a natural transformation, such that terminal object and context comprehension are preserved on the nose.

Definition 3. A pair of morphisms of cwfs

$$(C, T) \underset{(G, \tau)}{\overset{(F, \sigma)}{\rightleftarrows}} (C', T')$$

form an *equivalence of cwfs* iff

$$C \underset{G}{\overset{F}{\rightleftarrows}} C'$$

form an equivalence of categories with unit η and counit ϵ, such that

$$\begin{array}{ccc} T & \xrightarrow{\sigma} & T'F \\ {\scriptstyle T\eta}\downarrow & \swarrow{\scriptstyle \tau F} & \\ TGF & & \end{array} \qquad \begin{array}{ccc} TG & \xleftarrow{\tau} & T' \\ & {\scriptstyle \sigma G}\searrow & \downarrow{\scriptstyle T'\epsilon^{-1}} \\ & & T'FG \end{array}$$

commute.

Remark. There are alternative notions of cwf and morphism of cwfs which avoid reference to chosen structure and where preservation is up to isomorphism.

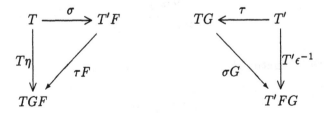

2.2 The Generalized Algebraic Theory of Categories with Families

The next step is to formalize cwfs as a *generalized algebraic theory* in the sense of Cartmell [5]. Generalized algebraic theories generalize many-sorted algebraic theories and are based on a framework of dependent types. They have four parts:

- A list of *sort symbols* with dependent typings.
- A list of *operator symbols* with dependent typings.
- A list of *equations* between well-formed *sort expressions* (not needed here).
- A list of *equations* between well-formed *terms*.

Cwfs make precise what it means to be a model of a generalized algebraic theory. Expressing the notion of a cwf as a generalized algebraic theory can hence be seen as a syntactic reflection process and a step towards internal type theory.

We present sort and operator symbols by their typing rules. As before, we use polymorphic notation and write $\delta \circ \gamma$ instead of the proper $\delta \circ_{\Theta,\Delta,\Gamma} \gamma$, etc.

Rules for the Category *C*

Sort symbols:

$$Context : Sort$$

$$\frac{\Delta, \Gamma : Context}{\Delta \to \Gamma : Sort}$$

Operator symbols:

$$\frac{\Theta, \Delta, \Gamma : Context \qquad \gamma : \Delta \to \Gamma \qquad \delta : \Theta \to \Delta}{\gamma \circ \delta : \Theta \to \Gamma}$$

$$\frac{\Gamma : Context}{id : \Gamma \to \Gamma}$$

Equations:

$$(\gamma \circ \delta) \circ \theta = \gamma \circ (\delta \circ \theta)$$
$$id \circ \gamma = \gamma$$
$$\gamma \circ id = \gamma$$

Rules for the Functor *T*

Sort symbols:

$$\frac{\Gamma : Context}{Type(\Gamma) : Sort}$$

$$\frac{\Gamma : Context \qquad A : Type(\Gamma)}{\Gamma \vdash A : Sort}$$

Operator symbols:

$$\frac{\Delta, \Gamma : Context \qquad A : Type(\Gamma) \qquad \gamma : \Delta \to \Gamma}{A[\gamma] : Type(\Delta)}$$

$$\frac{\Delta, \Gamma : Context \quad A : Type(\Gamma) \quad a : \Gamma \vdash A \quad \gamma : \Delta \to \Gamma}{a[\gamma] : \Delta \vdash A[\gamma]}$$

Equations:

$$A[\gamma \circ \delta] = A[\gamma][\delta]$$
$$A[id] = A$$
$$a[\gamma \circ \delta] = a[\gamma][\delta]$$
$$a[id] = a$$

Rules for the Terminal Object

Operator symbols:

$$[] : Context$$

$$\frac{\Gamma : Context}{<> : \Gamma \to []}$$

Equations

$$<> \circ \gamma = <>$$
$$id_{[]} = <>$$

Rules for Context Comprehension

Operator symbols:

$$\frac{\Gamma : Context \qquad A : Type(\Gamma)}{\Gamma; A : Context}$$

$$\frac{\Delta, \Gamma : Context \quad A : Type(\Gamma) \quad \gamma : \Delta \to \Gamma \quad a : \Delta \vdash A[\gamma]}{<\gamma, a> : \Delta \to \Gamma; A}$$

$$\frac{\Gamma : Context \qquad A : Type(\Gamma)}{p : \Gamma; A \to \Gamma}$$

$$\frac{\Gamma : Context \qquad A : Type(\Gamma)}{q : \Gamma; A \vdash A[p]}$$

Equations:

$$\begin{aligned} p \circ \langle\gamma, a\rangle &= \gamma \\ q[\langle\gamma, a\rangle] &= a \\ \langle\delta, a\rangle \circ \gamma &= \langle\delta \circ \gamma, a[\gamma]\rangle \\ id_{\Gamma;A} &= \langle p, q\rangle \end{aligned}$$

This completes the description of the generalized algebraic theory of cwfs. Note the correspondence between sort symbols and judgement forms and between operator symbols and inference rules of a substitution calculus for dependent types. But note also that there are no sort symbols which correspond to equality judgements and no operator symbols which correspond to general equality rules. Instead general equality reasoning is inherited from the metalanguage.

Reflecting the Rules for an Arbitrary Generalized Algebraic Theory

The generalized algebraic theory of cwfs is a categorical formulation of the basic framework of dependent types. It corresponds to those rules of a standard presentation which deal with formation of contexts, with substitution, and with assumption. These rules underly both generalized algebraic theories and intuitionistic type theory.

We can reflect the rules of an arbitrary generalized algebraic theory as an extension of the generalized algebraic theory of cwfs. For example, the rules of a generalized algebraic theory which introduces a sort of natural numbers and the sort of proofs of equality of natural numbers

$$N : sort$$

$$\frac{m, n : N}{I(m, n) : sort}$$

are reflected by the rules

$$\frac{\Gamma : Context}{N : Type(\Gamma)}$$

$$\frac{\Gamma : Context \qquad m, n : \Gamma \vdash N}{I(m, n) : Type(\Gamma)}$$

We could even reflect the generalized algebraic theory of cwfs itself, and add the following operator symbols:

$$\frac{\Gamma : Context}{\text{`}Context\text{'}(\Gamma) : Type(\Gamma)}$$

$$\frac{\Gamma : Context \qquad \text{`}\Delta\text{'}, \text{`}\Gamma\text{'} : \text{`}Context\text{'}(\Gamma)}{\text{`}\Delta\text{``} \rightarrow \text{'}_{\Gamma}\text{`}\Gamma\text{'} : Type(\Gamma)}$$

etc. Note the difference between the sort *Context* of contexts and the operator symbol '*Context*' of reflected contexts.

Such a game of reflection is quite pointless, since ultimately we have to understand what it means to be a model of a generalized algebraic theory in terms of, say, classical set theory anyway. The main point of the paper (see section 3) is to show an alternative explanation in terms of intuitionistic type theory.

Rules for the Cartesian Product of a Family of Types

We can also extend our generalized algebraic theory with various operator symbols and equations corresponding to the inference rules of intuitionistic type theory. As an example we give the rules for Π:

Operator symbols:

$$\frac{\Gamma : \mathit{Context} \qquad A : \mathit{Type}(\Gamma) \qquad B : \mathit{Type}(\Gamma; A)}{\Pi(A, B) : \mathit{Type}(\Gamma)}$$

$$\frac{\Gamma : \mathit{Context} \quad A : \mathit{Type}(\Gamma) \quad B : \mathit{Type}(\Gamma; A) \quad b : \Gamma; A \vdash B}{\lambda(b) : \Gamma \vdash \Pi(A, B)}$$

$$\frac{\Gamma : \mathit{Context} \quad A : \mathit{Type}(\Gamma) \quad B : \mathit{Type}(\Gamma; A) \quad c : \Gamma \vdash \Pi(A, B) \quad a : \Gamma \vdash A}{\mathit{app}(c, a) : \Gamma \vdash B[\langle id, a\rangle]}$$

Equations:

$$\begin{aligned}
\Pi(A, B)[\gamma] &= \Pi(A[\gamma], B[\langle \gamma \circ p, q\rangle]) \\
\lambda(b)[\gamma] &= \lambda(b[\langle \gamma \circ p, q\rangle]) \\
\mathit{app}(c, a)[\gamma] &= \mathit{app}(c[\gamma], a[\gamma]) \\
\mathit{app}(\lambda(b), a) &= b[\langle id, a\rangle] \\
\lambda(\mathit{app}(c[p], q)) &= c
\end{aligned}$$

The three first of the five equations represent the laws for substitution under Π, λ, and *app*. The fourth and fifth represent β and η-conversion respectively.

It is straightforward to formalize the other rules of type theory too.

3 Internal Categories with Families

3.1 Formalizing some Basic Categorical Notions in Type Theory

The definition of a cwf refers in particular to the notions of category, functor, and the category *Fam*. Therefore we shall first formalize these notions in intuitionistic type theory, and then use them to get a notion of cwf in intuitionistic type theory – an *internal cwf*.

But before doing this we shall briefly discuss the simpler problem of how to define ordinary algebraic notions, such as monoids, in type theory.

Remark. Throughout the rest of the paper we work in intuitionistic type theory and standard mathematical terms, such as category, functor, etc., will henceforth refer to a notion in type theory, unless stated otherwise.

Monoids in Type Theory. A monoid in the ordinary sense consists of a set M, a binary composition function $\circ$ on M and an element id, such that composition is associative and id is an identity with respect to composition. A naive way to interpret this in type theory would be to say that M is a set in the sense of type theory and $\circ$ is a function in the sense of type theory, that is, an algorithm. Furthermore, we could require that associativity and identity laws are valid as intensional identities (I-sets).

But this yields a too restrictive notion. For example, one way to define a free monoid is to quotient the set of binary trees (S-expressions). But since quotienting is not an operation on sets in type theory this construction would then not yield a monoid in type theory.

So instead we let the carrier of a monoid be a *setoid* $\mathcal{M}$, that is, a set M with an equivalence relation $\sim_M$, and $\circ$ be a *(setoid-)map*, that is, a function between the underlying sets which respects the equivalence relations. Furthermore associativity and identity laws have to be valid with respect to $\sim_M$.

Formally, a setoid is a quintuple $\mathcal{A} = \langle A, \sim_A, \mathit{ref}_A, \mathit{trans}_A, \mathit{sym}_A \rangle$. When we use a calligraphic letter to stand for a setoid, the corresponding italic letter will stand for its carrier, and *ref*, *trans*, *sym* (with an italic letter as a subscript) stand for the proofs of reflexivity, transitivity, and symmetry, respectively.

Categories and Functors in Type Theory. We follow Aczel [1] and Huet and Saibi [15] and define a *category* to have a *set* of objects, but hom-*setoids*. We shall not need to refer to equality of objects. The object part of a functor is a function between the object sets and the morphism part is a family of maps between the hom-setoids, such that the functor laws are satisfied with respect to the equivalence relation in the hom-setoid.

Setoids and maps under extensional equality $\sim_{ext}$ form a category in type theory which plays the role of the category of sets in ordinary category theory.

For the description of an implementation (in Coq) of category theory along these lines we refer to Huet and Saibi [15].

Setoid-Indexed Families of Setoids in Type Theory.

Definition 4. Let $\mathcal{A}$ be a setoid. An *$\mathcal{A}$-indexed family of setoids* consists of

- a family $\mathcal{B}$ of setoids indexed by the set A;
- a *reindexing* map $\iota(P) : \mathcal{B}(x') \to \mathcal{B}(x)$ whenever $P : x \sim_A x'$.

This family is *coherent* provided

- $\iota(\mathit{ref}_A) \sim_{ext} id$ (the identity map);
- $\iota(\mathit{trans}_A(P, P')) \sim_{ext} \iota(P) \circ \iota(P')$ (composition of maps);
- $\iota(P)$ is an isomorphism with inverse $\iota(\mathit{sym}_A(P))$ in the category of setoids.

Definition 5. Let $\mathcal{B}$ be an $\mathcal{A}$-indexed family of setoids and let $\mathcal{B}'$ be an $\mathcal{A}'$-indexed family with reindexings ι and ι', respectively. A *morphism* between these two families consists of

– a map $f : A \to A'$;
– an A-indexed family of maps $g(x) : B(x) \to B'(f(x))$ for $x : A$.

Such a morphism is *coherent* if the following diagram commutes in the category of setoids:

$$
\begin{array}{ccc}
B(x') & \xrightarrow{g(x')} & B'(f(x')) \\
\Big\downarrow \iota(P) & & \Big\downarrow \iota'(f(P)) \\
B(x) & \xrightarrow[g(x)]{} & B'(f(x))
\end{array}
$$

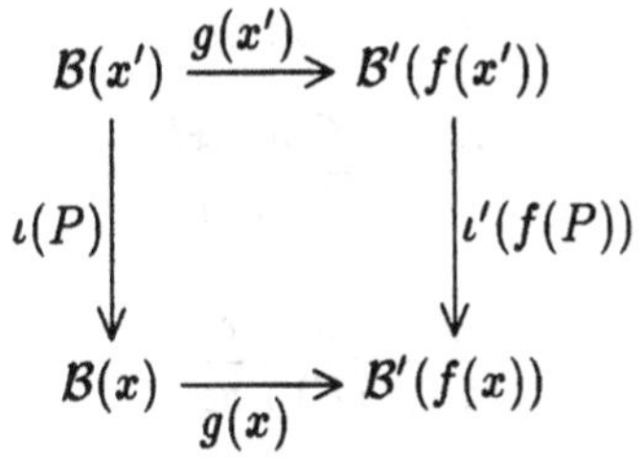

whenever $P : x \sim_A x'$.
    Two *morphisms* (f, g) and (f', g') are *equivalent* iff $P : f \sim_{ext} f'$ and

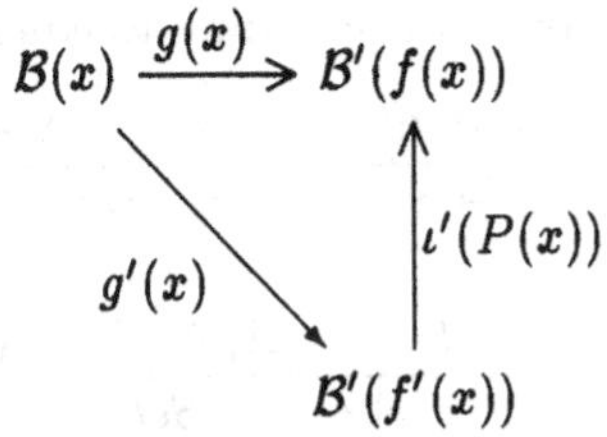

commutes in the category of setoids.

It is useful to note that the type-theoretic notion of a setoid is related to the category-theoretic notion of a *groupoid*. The underlying set of a setoid corresponds to the set of objects of the groupoid and the sets of equivalence proofs correspond to the homsets of a groupoid. The explicit proofs of reflexivity, transitivity, and symmetry in a setoid correspond to identity, composition, and inverse in a groupoid. Moreover, a setoid-indexed family of setoids is similar to a groupoid-indexed family of groupoids defined as a functor and the coherence conditions correspond to functoriality. Similarly, for morphisms, where the coherence condition corresponds to naturality.

Internal Cwfs. We are now ready to reinterpret Definition 1 (section 2.1) of cwfs using our type-theoretic definition of the categorical notions. For the purpose of defining internal cwfs we require that objects of *Fam* are coherent setoid-indexed families of setoids and that morphisms of *Fam* are coherent morphisms up to equivalence of morphisms as defined in the previous section.

3.2   Formal Rules for Internal Categories with Families

We present the formal rules for internal cwfs in a similar style as the generalized algebraic theory of cwfs in section 2.2. All formal rules are derived systematically from the abstract presentation of internal cwfs as outlined in the previous section.

The fundamental novelty is that among these rules there are general rules for equality reasoning, which have no counterpart among the sort and operator symbols of the generalized algebraic theory of cwfs.

So in addition to the four set constructors corresponding to the four sort symbols:

$$Context : Set$$

$$\frac{\Delta, \Gamma : Context}{\Delta \to \Gamma : Set}$$

$$\frac{\Gamma : Context}{Type(\Gamma) : Set}$$

$$\frac{\Gamma : Context \qquad A : Type(\Gamma)}{\Gamma \vdash A : Set}$$

there are three set constructors corresponding to equality judgements:

$$\frac{\Delta, \Gamma : Context \qquad \gamma, \gamma' : \Delta \to \Gamma}{\Delta \to \gamma \sim \gamma' \in \Gamma : Set}$$

$$\frac{\Gamma : Context \qquad A, A' : Type(\Gamma)}{\Gamma \vdash A \sim A' : Set}$$

$$\frac{\Gamma : Context \qquad A : Type(\Gamma) \qquad a, a' : \Gamma \vdash A}{\Gamma \vdash a \sim a' \in A : Set}$$

There is no set constructor for context equality, since our base category has a *set* and not a setoid of objects (contexts). We note the similarity to Martin-Löf's substitution calculus [17] which (unlike Ehrhard's [10], Curien's [7], and Ritter's [20]) lacks a judgement for context equality.

The element constructors in the definition can be divided into three kinds:

- Those which correspond to operator symbols of the generalized algebraic theory of cwfs, such as the rules for composition, identity, and substitution.
- General rules for equality reasoning.
- Those which correspond to the equations of the generalized algebraic theory of cwfs. These rules need to be modified to take into account explicit reasoning about equality.

We do not have space to display all these rules and shall therefore limit our discussion to the most interesting of the second and the third kind.

Among the general rules for equality there are the rules of reflexivity, transitivity, and symmetry for the three forms of equality judgement. There are also congruence rules for each operation. Of particular interest is the rule of type equality, which in the traditional formulation of type theory is written

$$\frac{\Gamma : Context \quad A, A' : Type(\Gamma) \quad \Gamma \vdash A = A' \quad \Gamma \vdash a : A'}{\Gamma \vdash a : A},$$

If we apply our definition of setoid-indexed family of setoids to the family of terms indexed by types, the reindexing function gives rise to the following rule:

$$\frac{\Gamma : Context \quad A, A' : Type(\Gamma) \quad P : \Gamma \vdash A \sim A' \quad a : \Gamma \vdash A'}{\iota(P, a) : \Gamma \vdash A}$$

Note the similarity with the typing rule in Curien's *explicit syntax* [7].

We also have equality rules for ι coming from the coherence conditions for objects of Fam:

$$\frac{\Gamma : Context \qquad A : Type(\Gamma) \qquad a : \Gamma \vdash A}{\iota ref : \Gamma \vdash \iota(ref, a) \sim a \in A}$$

$$\frac{\Gamma : Context \; A, A', A'' : Type(\Gamma) \; P : \Gamma \vdash A \sim A' \; P' : \Gamma \vdash A' \sim A'' \; a : \Gamma \vdash A''}{\iota trans : \Gamma \vdash \iota(trans(P, P'), a) \sim \iota(P, \iota(P', a)) \in A}$$

and also equalities expressing that $\iota(sym(P))$ is the inverse of $\iota(P)$.

Another rule comes from the coherence condition for morphisms of Fam and states that substitution in terms commutes with applications of type equality:

$$\frac{\Delta, \Gamma : Context \quad A, A' : Type(\Gamma) \quad P : \Gamma \vdash A \sim A' \quad a : \Gamma \vdash A' \quad \gamma : \Delta \rightarrow \Gamma}{\iota sub : \Delta \vdash \iota(P[\gamma], a[\gamma]) \sim \iota(P, a)[\gamma] \in A[\gamma]}$$

The third kinds of rules correspond to the equations of the generalized algebraic theory of cwfs. But to show the well-typedness of some of these rules we need to appeal to the type-equality law. For example, the two equations

$$A[id] = A$$
$$a[id] = a$$

are replaced by

$$\frac{\Gamma : Context \qquad A : Type(\Gamma)}{Subid : \Gamma \vdash A[id] \sim A}$$

$$\frac{\Gamma : Context \qquad A : Type(\Gamma) \qquad a : \Gamma \vdash A}{subid : \Gamma \vdash a[id] \sim \iota(Subid, a) \in A[id]}$$

Note the explicit dependence on the proof *Subid* in the second rule.

3.3 Examples of Internal Categories with Families

The Internal Cwf of Setoids. Hofmann [13] showed that the category of setoids has finite limits (and much more!). This result is unproblematic to represent in type theory. Therefore we can also construct an internal cwf of setoids as follows. Let C be an arbitrary category with finite limits. It gives rise to an internal cwf, where the category of contexts is C itself, where types in context Γ are objects of the slice category C/Γ, and where terms are sections. Substitution in types and terms is interpreted using the pullback functor. Moreover, proofs of type equality are interpreted as isomorphisms in the slice category. Reindexing is interpreted by composition with this isomorphism so that the coherence conditions follow from the laws of associativity and identity, etc.

The Internal Cwf $\mathcal{D}$ of Derivations. The simplest way to get a syntactic cwf is to turn the definition of an internal cwf in the previous section into a big mutual inductive definition of the seven families of sets corresponding to the seven forms of judgements in a substitution calculus. (To get a non-trivial cwf we should also include some basic type constructors.)

The elements of these sets are best thought of as *derivations* in a substitution calculus. Alternatively, they can be viewed as terms in explicit syntax [7].

Note also that the definition of a cwf in section 2.1 (or its presentation as a generalized algebraic theory in section 2.2) does not directly show how to generate free such categories. In contrast the definition of an internal cwf yields a straightforward construction of free internal cwfs.

An Internal Cwf from Ordinary Syntax of Dependent Types. One can also define a free cwf from a standard formulation of a substitution calculus based on *raw expressions*. Objects of the base category are pairs of raw contexts and derivations of "correct context" judgements, etc. The detailed proof that this indeed yields an internal cwf is non-trivial.

An Internal Cwf $\mathcal{N}$ of Normal Derivations. The basic idea is that a normal derivation of a term is one which is built up by the rules of thinning and of assumption. If we think of derivations as terms in an explicit syntax, then we note that such derivations correspond to de Bruijn numbers: zero comes from assuming the last variable and successor corresponds to the rule of thinning. Moreover, a normal substitution is a sequence of normal terms.

Explicitly, we have the following inductive clauses for generating normal derivations:

$$[\,] : Context$$

$$\frac{\Gamma : Context \qquad A : Type(\Gamma)}{\Gamma; A : Context}$$

$$\frac{\Gamma : Context}{\langle\rangle : \Gamma \to [\,]}$$

$$\frac{\Delta, \Gamma : Context \quad A : Type(\Gamma) \quad \gamma : \Delta \to \Gamma \quad a : \Delta \vdash A[\gamma]}{\langle\gamma, a\rangle : \Delta \to \Gamma; A}$$

$$\frac{\Gamma : Context \qquad A : Type(\Gamma)}{0 : \Gamma; A \vdash A[p]}$$

$$\frac{\Gamma : Context \qquad A, B : Type(\Gamma) \qquad a : \Gamma \vdash B}{s(a) : \Gamma; A \vdash B[p]}$$

(To get a non-trivial cwf we should again include some basic type constructors.)

Note that the operations $\_[\_]$ and p appear in the inductive clauses and hence we have a *simultaneous inductive-recursive definition* [8] of the sets of normal derivations and the cwf-operations on them.

We can prove that we get an internal cwf $\mathcal{N}$ by interpreting equality of types, terms, and substitutions as I-equality. This result has been implemented in ALF, a proof checker for intensional intuitionistic type theory [2].

4 The Coherence Problem for Internal Cwfs

Categorical interpretations of type theory can be divided into those which interpret type equality as isomorphism, such as Seely's lccc-interpretation [21], and those which interpret it as true equality, such as Cartmell's category with attributes interpretation. In either case a coherence problem arises. In order to interpret syntax in an lccc we have to make sure that two different derivations of the same judgement have the same interpretation. A proof of this was given by Curien [7]. On the other hand interpreting syntax in categories with attributes is relatively straightforward [13]. But here a coherence problem arises when one already has an lccc and wants to construct a category with attributes. For this purpose Hofmann [12] adapted a method due to Bénabou [3] for constructing a split fibration from an arbitrary fibration.

There is also a coherence problem for internal type theory. Proofs of type equality appear in terms and it is sometimes essential to know that the term does not depend on this particular proof. Formally:

Conjecture 1 *Coherence: if* $P, P' : \Gamma \vdash A' \sim A$ *and* $a : \Gamma \vdash A$ *then* $\Gamma \vdash \iota(P, a) \sim \iota(P', a) \in A'$ *in an internal cwf.*

(Note that we do not want to refer to equality between equality proofs in an internal cwf, so we cannot simply ask whether P and P' are "equal".)

This coherence proposition can be proved as a corollary to the following:

Conjecture 2 *Normalization: there is an equivalence of internal cwfs:*

$$\mathcal{D} \underset{(I,i)}{\overset{(N,\nu)}{\rightleftarrows}} \mathcal{N}$$

The upper arrow is a normalizing *cwf-morphism and the lower an* inclusion of normal forms.

The two crucial properties of normalization are (i) that two convertible terms have identical normal forms and (ii) that a term is convertible to its normal form [6]. In our case property (i) is a consequence of the fact that equality in $\mathcal{N}$ is the basic I-equality in type theory. Property (ii) is a consequence of the equivalence of $\mathcal{D}$ and $\mathcal{N}$ and can be expressed as follows. Let

$$\widehat{\Gamma} = (IN)(\Gamma)$$
$$\widehat{\gamma} = (IN)(\gamma)$$
$$\widehat{A} = (i \circ \nu)(A)$$
$$\widehat{a} = (i \circ \nu)(a)$$

be the normal forms of Γ, γ, A, a, respectively, in $\mathcal{D}$. Then there is an isomorphism

$$\eta_\Gamma : \Gamma \to \widehat{\Gamma}$$

which is natural

$$\Delta \to \gamma \sim \eta_\Gamma^{-1} \circ \widehat{\gamma} \circ \eta_\Delta \in \Gamma$$

and for each $A : Type(\Gamma)$, there is a proof

$$E_A : \Gamma \vdash A \sim \widehat{A}[\eta_\Gamma]$$

and for each $a : \Gamma \vdash A$,

$$\Gamma \vdash a \sim \iota(E_A, \widehat{a})[\eta_\Gamma] \in A$$

To prove that coherence follows from normalization we instantiate a to $\iota(P, a)$ and $\iota(P', a)$ respectively in the last equation. We get

$$\Gamma \vdash \iota(P, a) \sim \iota(E_A, \iota(\widehat{P, a}))[\eta_\Gamma] \in A'$$

$$\Gamma \vdash \iota(P', a) \sim \iota(E_A, \iota(\widehat{P', a}))[\eta_\Gamma] \in A'$$

Since $\iota(\widehat{P, a})$ and $\iota(\widehat{P', a})$ are I-equal the coherence proposition follows.

Unfortunately, we have only been able to give an informal sketch of the normalization proof. This is not satisfactory, since this is a proof in intuitionistic type theory which involves the manipulation of large terms in explicit syntax and it is difficult to carry out these manipulations safely by hand. As mentioned above we did manage to completely formalize the internal cwfs $\mathcal{D}$ and $\mathcal{N}$ in the proof assistant ALF, but we failed to prove their equivalence. In fact, the construction of $\mathcal{N}$ was a major undertaking which took the present version of ALF to the limits of its capability with very slow responses. We believe that the equivalence proof should be feasible with an improved proof assistant. Alternatively, a different construction of $\mathcal{N}$ might make the proof more manageable.

5 Related Work

The present paper is a revised version of a paper that appears in the proceedings of the *Joint CLICS-TYPES Workshop on Categories and Type Theory, Göteborg, January 1995* [9]. Much useful information on cwfs can also be found in the lecture notes on "Syntax and Semantics of Dependent Types" by Martin Hofmann [14]. He uses ordinary set-theoretic cwfs as the central semantic notion and gives several examples. He also discusses the relationship with other categorical notions of model for dependent types and gives a detailed proof of the equivalence of cwfs and categories with attributes.

Cwfs have also been used in recent unpublished work on "Tarski Semantics for Type Theory" by Per Martin-Löf (lecture at the meeting *Twenty-Five Years of Constructive Type Theory", Venice, October, 1995*).

The reader is also referred to the paper by Beylin and Dybjer [4] which shows how related phenomena appear in another proof of coherence in type theory.

Acknowledgements. The author is grateful for support from the ESPRIT BRA's TYPES and CLICS-II, from TFR (the Swedish Technical Research Council), and from The Isaac Newton Institute for Mathematical Sciences.

References

1. P. Aczel. Galois: a theory development project. A report on work in progress for the Turin meeting on the Representation of Logical Frameworks, 1993.
2. T. Altenkirch, V. Gaspes, B. Nordström, and B. von Sydow. A user's guide to ALF. Draft, January 1994.
3. J. Bénabou. Fibred categories and the foundation of naive category theory. *Journal of Symbolic Logic*, 50:10–37, 1985.
4. I. Beylin and P. Dybjer. Extracting a proof of coherence for monoidal categories from a proof of normalization for monoids. This volume.
5. J. Cartmell. Generalized algebraic theories and contextual categories. *Annals of Pure and Applied Logic*, 32:209–243, 1986.
6. T. Coquand and P. Dybjer. Intuitionistic model constructions and normalization proofs. *Mathematical Structures in Computer Science*, 1996. To appear.
7. P.-L. Curien. Substitution up to isomorphism. *Fundamenta Informaticae*, 19(1,2):51–86, 1993.
8. P. Dybjer. Universes and a general notion of simultaneous inductive-recursive definition in type theory. In *Proceedings of the 1992 Workshop on Types for Proofs and Programs*, 1992.
9. P. Dybjer and R. Pollack, editors. *Informal Proceedings of the CLICS-TYPES Workshop on Categories and Type Theory*, Programming Methodology Group, Göteborg University and Chalmers University of Technology, Report 85, 1995.
10. T. Ehrhard. *Une sémantique catégorique des types dépendents: Applications au Calcul des Constructions.* PhD thesis, Université Paris VII, 1988.
11. M. Hofmann. Elimination of extensionality and quotient types in Martin-Löf's type theory. In *Types for Proofs and Programs, International Workshop TYPES'93, LNCS 806*, 1994.
12. M. Hofmann. Interpretation of type theory in locally cartesian closed categories. In *Proceedings of CSL*. Springer LNCS, 1994.
13. M. Hofmann. *Extensional concepts in intensional type theory.* PhD thesis, University of Edinburgh, 1995.
14. M. Hofmann. Syntax and semantics of dependent types. In A. Pitts and P. Dybjer, editors, *Semantics and Logics of Computation.* Cambridge University Press, 1996. To appear.
15. G. Huet and A. Saibi. Constructive category theory. In *Proceedings of the Joint CLICS-TYPES Workshop on Categories and Type Theory, Göteborg*, January 1995.
16. P. Martin-Löf. Constructive mathematics and computer programming. In *Logic, Methodology and Philosophy of Science, VI, 1979*, pages 153–175. North-Holland, 1982.
17. P. Martin-Löf. Substitution calculus. Notes from a lecture given in Göteborg, November 1992.
18. A. M. Pitts. Categorical logic. In *Handbook of Logic in Computer Science.* Oxford University Press, 1997. Draft version of article to appear.
19. R. Pollack. *The Theory of Lego A Proof Checker for the Extended Calculus of Constructions.* PhD thesis, University of Edinburgh, 1994.
20. E. Ritter. *Categorical Abstract Machines for Higher-Order Typed Lambda Calculi.* PhD thesis, Trinity College, Cambridge, September 1992.
21. R. A. G. Seely. Locally cartesian closed categories and type theory. *Proceedings of the Cambridge Philosophical Society*, 95:33–48, 1984.

An Application of Co-Inductive Types in Coq: Verification of the Alternating Bit Protocol

Eduardo Giménez *

LIP URA CNRS 1398, ENS Lyon
46, Allée d'Italie 69364 Lyon Cedex 07, France
email : egimenez@ens-lyon.fr

Abstract. We describe an experience concerning the implementation and use of co-inductive types in the proof editor Coq. Co-inductive types are recursive types which, opposite to inductive ones, may be inhabited by infinite objects. In order to illustrate their use in Coq, we describe an axiomatisation of a calculus of broadcasting systems where non-ending processes are represented using infinite objects. This calculus is then used for developing a verification proof of the alternating bit protocol.

1 Introduction

Several previous attempts to set a mathematical framework for modeling have shown that the consideration of infinite mathematical objects could be useful (if not necessary) for modeling non-well-founded computations and other circular phenomena related with them [9, 18, 1]. This consideration was the starting point for us to explore possible extensions of type theory (in particular the Calculus of Constructions) for describing and reasoning about infinite objects, that could enable the application of interactive proof editors like the system Coq [4] to the verification of communicating systems. The purpose of this paper is to report an experiment of program verification carried out in a prototype extension of the system Coq that allows the introduction of infinite objects. The extension of the Calculus of Construction underlying it has been already described in [7]. Here we are concerned rather with the practical possibilities and limitations of the prototype.

The example chosen for the experiment is the verification of the alternating bit protocol, a simple communication system in which a process tries to send messages to another one through an unreliable medium. In order to describe the protocol we represented in Coq a variant of CBS [17], a CCS-like calculus for describing broadcasting systems developed by K. Prasad. The complete development is available within the contributions of the version V5.10 of Coq.

The plan of the paper is as follows. In the next section, we present a short tutorial about co-inductive types in Coq, illustrating how infinite objects can be introduced through some simple examples. In Section 3 we briefly introduce Prasad's Calculus of Broadcasting Systems, discussing some alternatives in the representation

* This research was partially supported by ESPRIT Basic Research Action "Types for Proofs and Programs" and by Programme de Recherches Coordonnées and CNRS Groupement de Recherche "Programmation".

of processes. In Section 4 we will present the description of the protocol and the main problems raised by its specification and verification. Finally, Section 5 draws the conclusions of the experiment and relate it to previous work.

2 Co-inductive types in Coq

We assume that the reader is rather familiar with inductive types. These types are characterised by their *constructors*, which can be regarded as the basic methods to build up the elements of the type. It is implicit in the definition of an inductive type that its elements are the result of a *well-founded* application of its constructors. Co-inductive types arise from relaxing this implicit condition and admitting an element of the type to be produced by a non-ending but effective process of construction, defined in terms of the basic methods characterising the type. So, we can consider the wider notion of types defined by constructors (let us call them *recursive types*) and classify them into inductive and co-inductive ones, depending on whether or not we consider non-ending methods as admissible for constructing elements of the type. Note that in both cases we obtain a "closed type", whose all elements are predetermined in advance (by the constructors). When we know that a is an element of a recursive type (no matter if it is inductive or co-inductive), what we know is that it is the result of applying one of the basic forms of construction allowed for the type. So the more primitive elimination rule for a recursive type is case analysis, i.e. considering which constructor could have been used to introduce an element of the type. In the case of inductive sets, the additional knowledge that they are well-founded provide us with a more powerful elimination rule, say, the principle of induction. This principle is obviously not valid for co-inductive types, since it is just the expression of the extra knowledge attached to inductive ones.

An example of an inductive type is the type of natural numbers, whose constructors are zero and the successor function. We can introduce this type in Coq by the following command:

```
Coq < Inductive Set nat := O: nat| S: nat ⇒ nat.
nat_ind is defined
nat_rec is defined
nat_rect is defined
nat is defined
```

The principles of induction on natural numbers *nat_ind*, *nat_rec* and *nat_rect* corresponding to the sorts *Prop*, *Set* and *Type* are automatically generated by the system. These principles are added to the (basic) form of elimination given by case analysis. We will not go further in what concerns inductive types, since we assume the reader to be rather familiar with these concepts. A description of the different principles of induction available in Coq can be found in [12, 4].

An example of a co-inductive type is the type of infinite sequences formed with elements of type A, also called streams. In Coq, it can be introduced through the following definition:

```
Coq < CoInductive Set Stream:= cons: A ⇒ (Stream A) ⇒ (Stream A).
Stream is defined
```

As was already mentioned, there are no principles of induction for co-inductive sets. The only elimination rule for streams is case analysis. This principle can be used, for example, to define the destructors $hd : (Stream\ A) \Rightarrow A$ and $tl : (Stream\ A) \Rightarrow (Stream\ A)$:

```
Coq < Definition hd := [x : (Stream A)]Case x of [a:A][s:(Stream A)]a end.
Coq < Definition tl  := [x : (Stream A)]Case x of [a:A][s:(Stream A)]s end.
```

The syntax for case expressions may be a little bit cumbersome for those not familiarised with Coq's notation. The expression **Case** x **of** G **end** defines an element of type Q by case analysis on an element x of a recursive type R. In the most general case Q may be a parametrised type depending on the elements of R, and then the object defined by the case expression has type $(Q\ x)$. The list of terms G corresponds to the cases of the analysis, and each one is a function whose arguments represent the components of an object built with the respective constructor. The reduction rule associated with this expression is the expected one:

$$\texttt{Case}\ (\texttt{cons}\ a\ s)\ \texttt{of}\ h\ \texttt{end} \Longrightarrow (h\ a\ s)$$

At this point the reader should have realised that we have left unexplained what is a "non-ending but effective process of construction" of a stream. In the widest sense, a method of construction is effective if we can eliminate any case analysis of it. In this sense, the following ways of introducing a stream are not acceptable.

$$zeros = (cons\ 0\ (tl\ zeros))$$
$$filter\ p\ (cons\ a\ s) = \text{if}\ \ (p\ a)\ \ \text{then}\ \ (cons\ a\ (filter\ p\ s))\ \ \text{else}\ \ (filter\ s)$$

The former it is not valid since the stream can not be eliminated to obtain its tail. In the latter, a stream is naively defined as the result of erasing from another (arbitrary) stream all the elements which does not verify a certain property P. This does not always makes sense, for example it does not when there is no element in the stream verifying P, in which case we can not eliminate it to obtain its head. On the contrary, the following definitions are acceptable methods for constructing a stream :

$$(from\ n) = (cons\ n\ (from\ (S\ n)))$$
$$alter = (cons\ true\ (cons\ false\ alter)).$$

The first one introduces a stream containing all the natural numbers greater than a given one, and the second the stream which infinitely alternates the booleans true and false.

In general, it is not evident to realise when a definition can be accepted or not. However, there is a class of definitions that can be easily recognised as being valid: those where all the recursive calls of the method are done after having explicitly mentioned which is (at least) the first constructor to start building the element, and where no other functions apart from constructors are applied to recursive calls. This class of definitions is called *guarded-by-constructors* definitions [3, 7]. The methods *from* and *alter* are examples of definitions which are guarded by constructors. The definition of the function *filter* is not, because there is no constructor to guard the recursive call in the *else* branch. Neither is the one of *zeros*, since there is a function applied to the recursive call which is not a constructor.

Guarded definitions are exactly the kind of non-ending process of construction which are allowed in Coq. The way of introducing a guarded definition in Coq is using the special command `CoFixpoint`. This command verifies that the definition introduces an element of a coinductive type, and checks if it is guarded by constructors. If we try to introduce the definitions above, *from* and *alter* will be accepted, while *zeros* and *filter* will be rejected giving some explanation about why.

`Coq < CoFixpoint` *from* : **nat** $\Rightarrow$ (*Stream nat*) := [n : **nat**](*cons* n (*from* (S n)))
from **is defined**

The elimination of a stream introduced by a `CoFixpoint` definition is done lazily, i.e. its definition can be expanded only when it occurs at the head of an application which is the argument of a case expression. Isolately, it is considered as a canonical expression which is completely evaluated.

What can be proven about a stream using only case analysis is just what can be proven unfolding its method of construction a finite number of times. But this is not always sufficient. Consider for example the following method for appending two streams:

`Coq < CoFixpoint` *conc* : (*Stream A*) $\Rightarrow$ (*Stream A*) $\Rightarrow$ (*Stream A*)
:= [s_1, s_2 : (*Stream A*)](*cons* (*hd* s_1) (*conc* (*tl* s_1) s_2)).

Informally speaking, we expect that for all pair of streams s_1 and s_2, (*conc* s_1 s_2) defines "the same" stream as s_1, in the sense that if their definitions would be unfolded up to the infinite, they would yield definitionally equal normal forms. However, no finite unfolding of the definitions gives definitionally equal terms. Their equality can not be proved just using case analysis. The weakness of the elimination principle proposed for infinite objects is in strong contrast with the strength of the inductive elimination principles, but this is not actually surprising. It just means that we can not expect to prove very interesting things about infinite objects doing finite proofs. To take advantage of infinite objects, we have to consider infinite proofs as well. For example, if we want to catch up the equality between (*conc* s_1 s_2) and s_1, then we have first to introduce the type of the *infinite* proofs of equality between streams. This is a co-inductive type, whose elements are build up from a unique constructor, requiring a proof of the equality of the heads of the streams, and an infinite proof of the equality of their tails.

`Coq< CoInductive` *Eq* : (*Stream A*) $\Rightarrow$ (*Stream A*) $\Rightarrow$ *Prop* :=
eqst : $\forall s_1, s_2$:(*Stream A*). (*hd* s_1) = (*hd* s_2) $\Rightarrow$ (*Eq* (*tl* s_1) (*tl* s_2)) $\Rightarrow$ (*Eq* s_1 s_2)

Now the equality of both streams can be proved introducing an infinite object of type (*Eq* s_1 (*conc* s_1 s_2)) by a `CoFixpoint` definition.

`Coq < CoFixpoint` *prf* : $\forall s_1, s_2$:(*Stream A*). (*Eq* s_1 (*conc* s_1 s_2))
:= [s_1, s_2 : (*Stream A*)] (*eqst* s_1 (*conc* s_1 s_2) (*refl_equal* (*hd* s_1)) (*prf* (*tl* s_1) s_2))

Instead of giving an explicit definition, we can use the proof editor of Coq to help us in the construction of the proof. A tactic `Cofix` allows to place a `CoFixpoint` definition inside a proof. This tactic introduces a variable in the context which has the same type as the current goal, and its application stands for a recursive call in the construction of the proof. Once the proof is finished, the proof term is checked to verify that all recursive calls are guarded by constructors.

3 The Calculus of Broadcasting Systems

After this brief introduction to co-inductive types, we turn to the representation of the calculus of processes that will be used to describe the protocol. This calculus is essentially Prasad's Calculus of Broadcasting Systems (CBS) as it is presented in [16], plus the possibility of having several transmission channels as well as failures in the communications.

3.1 Representation of Processes

CBS is a CCS-like calculus for describing communications among several processes running in parallel. The mode of communication is by broadcasting, i.e. when one process speaks on a certain channel, all other processes listening to the same channel can hear. This is a typical situation in communications by waves transmitted through the air, where processes may transmit on different wave frequencies. The communication is synchronic. At a meeting point, each process can choose either to speak or to hear on certain channel. If several processes speak at the same time, then the data is lost, and no process in the system hear what is said.

After a meeting, the processes evolve deterministically. The only non determinism lies in the choice of each process between hearing or speaking. We will denote $c\{a!p|x?q\}$ the process which may choose either to say a on channel c to become the process p, or to hear a value v on channel c to become $q[x/v]$. So x is considered to be bound in the subexpression $x?q$. We will also admit that a process may remain blocked waiting for hearing a value, such process is denoted $c\{x?q\}$. These are the basic process communicating agents that are considered in the calculus. Two processes p and q can be launched in parallel, and the result of this operation is also considered as being a process, denoted $(p \mid\mid q)$. From this informal explanation, it seems natural to represent the type of processes by the following co-inductive type:

Section ***Process*.**
Variable ***Channel***, A : ***Set*.**

CoInductive *Set Process* :=
  TALK   : *Channel* ⇒ *A* ⇒ *Process* ⇒ (*A* ⇒ *Process*) ⇒ *Process* |
  LISTEN : *Channel* ⇒ (*A* ⇒ *Process*) ⇒ *Process* |
  PAR   : *Process* ⇒ *Process* ⇒ *Process*.

In Coq, a **Variable** declaration correspond to the introduction of a general parameter relative to all the definitions after the declaration in the scope of the current **Section**, somewhat like the expression *let A be a set* ... frequently used in mathematical text books. After the section is closed, these parameters are abstracted away from the definitions. For the type of processes, the set of channels they transmit on and the the type A of the messages they sent are general parameters.

Remark that a (basic) process is like a tree representing all the possible situations it could run into. For this reason the type is co-inductive, since we do not want to exclude a priori the possibility for a process to evolve infinitely. If we want to describe processes that may have a finite life, we could add another constructor NIL : *Process* representing a dead process.

The processes originally considered in [16] did not have channels. Instead of this, an extra constructor of processes allows to enclose several ones speaking the same language A into a box. A box can be put in parallel with other boxes speaking a different language B, provided that two functions for translating from one language to the other are given. This choice in the representation can be reflected introducing the following set former :

CoInductive *Process*: *Set* $\Rightarrow$ *Set* :=
  TALK   : $\forall A : Set.\ A \Rightarrow (Process\ A) \Rightarrow (A \Rightarrow (Process\ A)) \Rightarrow Process$ |
  LISTEN : $\forall A : Set.\ (A \Rightarrow (Process\ A)) \Rightarrow (Process\ A)$ |
  PAR   : $\forall A : Set.\ (Process\ A) \Rightarrow (Process\ A) \Rightarrow (Process\ A)$ |
  TRANS : $\forall A, B : Set.\ (A \Rightarrow B) \Rightarrow (B \Rightarrow A) \Rightarrow (Process\ B) \Rightarrow (Process\ A)$.

Note that under this view, the general parameter A in the definition of the type of processes becomes an index, because *Process* occurs applied to a variable different from A in the type of TRANS. This impredicative definition is perfectly admissible in Coq but, as it will be shown in section 3.2, the choice of indexing the type by the channels would lead us to some annoying situations during the proof. We therefore prefer to keep the first representation proposed, using channels instead of the constructor TRANS.

3.2 Operational Semantics

The intuitive semantics suggested in the previous section can be formally described introducing for each channel a transition relation $P \xrightarrow{w}_c Q$ between processes labeled by an *action* w and a channel c. The possible actions are the *transmission* or the *reception* of certain message on the channel. We will write $!v$ the action of transmitting and $?v$ the action of receiving certain message $v : A$. Figure 1 lists the rules defining the transition relation on a reliable channel. The rules for the basic agents are straightforward, just note that processes do not care about reception actions on those channels different from the one they are listening to. To obtain a transmission from two processes in parallel it is necessary that one speaks and the other listens. Two processes in parallel hear a message if each one hear it. The communication is perfect: only one process speaks at a time, and its message reach the receivers.

$c\{x?Q\} \xrightarrow{?v}_c (Q\ v)$	$c'\{a!P \mid x?Q\} \xrightarrow{?v}_c c'\{a!P \mid x?Q\}, c \neq c'$	
$c\{a!P \mid x?Q\} \xrightarrow{!a}_c P$	$c\{a!P \mid x?Q\} \xrightarrow{?v}_c (Q\ v)$	$c'\{x?Q\} \xrightarrow{?v}_c c'\{x?Q\},\ c \neq c'$
$\dfrac{P \xrightarrow{!v}_c P' \quad Q \xrightarrow{?v}_c Q'}{(P \parallel Q) \xrightarrow{!v}_c (P' \parallel Q')}$	$\dfrac{P \xrightarrow{?v}_c P' \quad Q \xrightarrow{!v}_c Q'}{(P \parallel Q) \xrightarrow{!v}_c (P' \parallel Q')}$	$\dfrac{P \xrightarrow{?v}_c P' \quad Q \xrightarrow{?v}_c Q'}{(P \parallel Q) \xrightarrow{?v}_c (P' \parallel Q')}$

Figure 1: Communication on reliable channels

Let us consider now that the medium is such that a message sent through the channel may be lost without the sender realises about this fact. It is possible to model this situation by lifting the type of messages transmited with a special value τ representing "noise", a failure in the communication. A transmission action can now be either transmitting a message, as before, or transmitting noise. To give meaning to the action of transmitting noise, the rules in Figure 1 are extended with the rules in Figure 2. These rules specify that a talking process may fail its transmition without it realises about this fact, and that in order to obtain a loosy transmission from two processes in parallel, the message of at least one of them must be lost.

	$c\{a!P \mid x?Q\} \xrightarrow{!r}_c P$	
$\dfrac{P \xrightarrow{!r}_c P'}{(P \parallel Q) \xrightarrow{!r}_c (P' \parallel Q)}$	$\dfrac{Q \xrightarrow{!r}_c Q'}{(P \parallel Q) \xrightarrow{!r}_c (P \parallel Q')}$	$\dfrac{P \xrightarrow{!r}_c P' \quad Q \xrightarrow{!r}_c Q'}{(P \parallel Q) \xrightarrow{!r}_c (P' \parallel Q')}$

Figure 2: Communication on unreliable channels

These transition relations are described in Coq as inductive predicates. First, the type of actions has to be introduced.

Inductive *Set Signal* := *Noise* : *Signal* | *Clear* : $A \Rightarrow$ *Signal*.
Inductive *Set Action* := *Transmit* : *Signal* $\Rightarrow$ *Action* | *Receive* : $A \Rightarrow$ *Action*.

Then, the transition relations for reliable and unreliable channels are introduced as two different inductive predicates *SafeProcTrans* and *UnrelProcTrans*, each one parametrised by the channel c where the action is produced. Both relations are inductive, which means that a transmission is meaningful only for those systems in which there is a finite number of processes running in parallel. For the sake of space we do not present their whole definitions here, but just some of the introduction rules of *UnrelProcTrans*.

Inductive *UnrelProcTrans* [c : *Channel*] : *Process* $\Rightarrow$ *Action* $\Rightarrow$ *Process* $\Rightarrow$ *Set*
  := *uttalk*$_1$: $\forall f : A \Rightarrow$ *Process*. $\forall v : A$. $\forall p$:*Process*.
      (*UnrelProcTrans* c (TALK $c\ v\ p\ f$) $!v\ p$) |
  utpar$_1$: $\forall p_1, p_2, q_1, q_2$:*Process*. $\forall v : A$.
      (*UnrelProcTrans* $c\ p_1\ !v\ p_2$) $\Rightarrow$
      (*UnrelProcTrans* $c\ q_1\ ?v\ q_2$) $\Rightarrow$
      (*UnrelProcTrans* c (PAR $p_1\ q_1$) $!v$ (PAR $p_2\ q_2$)) |
...

Let us fix some useful terminology. A *trace* from p is a non-ending transition path of transmission actions

$$p \xrightarrow{!w_0, \nabla_0}_{c_0} p_0 \xrightarrow{!w_1, \nabla_1}_{c_1} p_1 \xrightarrow{!w_2, \nabla_2}_{c_2} \cdots$$

where the transitions are labeled not only by actions but also by proofs $\nabla_0, \nabla_1, \ldots$ of the transitions. So a trace represents a possible future for p, i.e,. a way in which things may happen. A *discourse* is a stream of signals $w_0, w_1, \ldots$ labeling the transmissions of a trace, and describes the conversation among the processes that an external observer would hear. The transition proofs labeling a trace can be used to describe properties about the communications. For example, consider a communicating system $(p \parallel q)$ in which two process are running in parallel. The property "p succeeds in sending its message to q" can be introduced as the following inductive predicate on transition proofs:

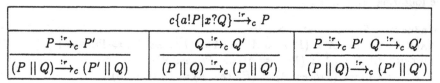

Inductive *LeftTalksSafely* $[c : Channel]$
$: (p : Process)(w : Action)(q : Process)(UnrelProcTrans\ c\ \ p\ w\ q) \Rightarrow Prop :=$
$lts : \forall p_1, p_2, q_1, q_2 : Process.\ \forall v : A.$
$\forall H_1 :(UnrelProcTrans\ c\ p_1\ !v\ p_2)).\ \forall H_2 :(UnrelProcTrans\ c\ q_1\ ?v\ q_2)).$
$(LeftTalksSafely\ \ c\ (\text{PAR}\ p_1\ q_1)\ \ !v\ \ (\text{PAR}\ p_2\ q_2)\ \ (utpar_1\ p_1\ p_2\ q_1\ q_2\ v\ H_1\ H_2))$

Another way of specifying this predicate is as a propositional function defined by case analysis on the transition proof, which associates the absurd proposition *False* to all the proofs except to those built with $utpar_1$.

3.3 Properties about Eventualities

Before turning our attention to the verification of the alternating bit protocol, we introduce some properties about communicating processes which will be used in the proof. Let us start assuming a function which associates to each channel c of the communicating system a certain labeled transition relation $p \xrightarrow{w}_c q$.

```
Section Eventuality_Properties.
Variable  ⟶ : Channel ⇒ Process ⇒ Action ⇒ Process ⇒ Set.
```

1. Certain Eventuality. When studying a communicating process, we are most of the time interested in studying its evolution if we constraint the future in certain way, i.e., we are interested not in all possible traces of the process but just in those where some property about the communications will eventually happen. Examples of this kind of "hypothesis about the future" that could be interesting are : *there will be a clear transmission*, or *someone will eventually talk on channel c*, or *we know that in the process* $(p \parallel q)$ *the sub-process p will not talk forever.* A wide class of these hypothesis can be thought as an instance of the following (second order) property: *P will eventually fail*, where P is a property about the transmissions of the system. In order to characterise this property in an abstract way, let us imagine a transition tree whose nodes are processes, and where the children of a given node q are all the processes q' such that $q \xrightarrow{w}_c q'$ for some action w. Thus, the branches of this tree are all the possible traces from the root. Assume a predicate P about transmitions. The property *P will eventually fail* can be thought of as a property about the future of a certain process p, this future being represented by the discourse s that will be heard from it. We may define this property saying that a proof of eventually $\neg P$ is a proof that the biggest transition tree that can be constructed starting from p and such that all its transitions verify P is well-founded. This is expressed through the following inductive definition:

Section **Certain_Eventuality.**
Variable $P : \forall c : \textbf{Channel}.\ \forall w : \textbf{Signal}.\ \forall p, q : \textbf{Process}.\ p \xrightarrow{w}_c q \Rightarrow \textbf{Prop}.$

Inductive *Evt*: $Process \Rightarrow (Stream\ Signal) \Rightarrow Prop :=$
$notyet : \forall p : Process.\ \forall s :(Stream\ Signal).$
$(\exists q_0 : Process.\ \exists c_0 : Channel.\ p \xrightarrow{!(hd\ s)}_{c_0} q_0)$
$\Rightarrow (\ \forall c : Channel.\ \forall q : Process.\ \forall t : p \xrightarrow{(!hd\ s)}_c q.$
$(P\ c\ (hd\ s)\ p\ q\ t) \Rightarrow (Evt\ q\ (tl\ s))\ ) \Rightarrow (Evt\ p\ s).$

End Certain_Eventuality.

Remark that this is an inductive type with only one (recursive) constructor. The only way to complete the construction of an element of it is that any path from the root reaches a process whose all sons are generated from communications not verifying P. When this situation is reached, the proof can be finished by absurdity, since any way of going deeper in the transition tree lead us into a contradiction with the hypothesis that P holds. The constructor also requires that there is at least one son q_0 of the process, so that if we are able of constructing an absurdity, this can be only with respect to the hypothesis that P holds.

2. Cyclic Eventuality. We could constraint the future even more, imposing not only that the property P will eventually fail, but also that this fact is cyclic, i.e. that it will always re-happen later on. To describe this property we have first to introduce the notion of a *witness* of the failure of P. A witness of $\neg P$ from p_0 is a process p_n accessible from p_0 at which the property P fails to happen for the first time. A proof that p_n is a witness consists in constructing a finite transition path

$$p_n \;{}_{c_n}\!\xleftarrow{!w_n,\nabla_n}\; p_{n-1} \cdots {}_{c_1}\!\xleftarrow{!w_1,\nabla_1}\; p_0 \;{}_{c_0}\!\xleftarrow{!w_0,\nabla_0}\; p$$

such that $(P\ c_i\ w_i\ p_{i-1}\ p_i\ \nabla_i)$ holds for all $i = 1, \ldots n-1$, and does not hold for $i = n$. The type of such transition paths can be defined inductively as follows:

Section Cyclic_Eventuality.
Variable P $:\forall c : \mathtt{Channel}.\ \forall w : \mathtt{Signal}.\ \forall p, q : \mathtt{Process}.\ p \xrightarrow{*}_c q \Rightarrow \mathtt{Prop}.$

Inductive *Witness* [*pn* : *Process*; *rs* : (*Stream Signal*)]
: *Process* $\Rightarrow$ (*Stream Signal*) $\Rightarrow$ *Prop* :=

start : $\forall p$:*Process*. $\forall cn$:*Channel*. $\forall wn$:*Signal*. $\forall t : p \xrightarrow{!wn}_{cn} pn.$
$(\neg(P\ cn\ wn\ p\ pn\ t)) \Rightarrow (Witness\ pn\ rs\ p\ (cons\ wn\ rs))$

| *goback* : $\forall p$:*Process*. $\forall s$:(*Stream Signal*).
$\forall c$:*Channel*. $\forall w$:*Signal*. $\forall q$:*Process*. $\forall t : p \xrightarrow{!w}_c q.$
$(P\ c\ w\ p\ q\ t) \Rightarrow (Witness\ pn\ rs\ q\ s)$
$\Rightarrow (Witness\ pn\ rs\ p\ (cons\ w\ s)).$

Remark that the chain of transitions is constructed backwards, starting from the witness p_n and climbing up in the transition tree until the root is reached. The general parameter rs corresponds to the discourse of p_n, what remains after erasing the initial segment $w_1, \ldots w_n$ from the discourse of p_0.

Once we have introduced this notion, we can say that $\neg P$ is a cyclicly eventuality from p if P will eventually fail from p, and it will eventually fail again from any witness q of its failure from p, and again from any witness of its failure from q, and so on forever. To put it in other words, the witnesses of the failure determine a frontier cutting the tree, such that any node at this frontier is the root of a tree which can be cut again, generating a second frontier, all whose nodes are roots of trees that can be cut once more, etc. This image gives rise to the following co-inductive definition:

CoInductive *CycEvt*: *Process* ⇒ (*Stream Signal*) ⇒ *Prop* :=

cycdet : ∀*p* :*Process*. ∀*s* :(*Stream Signal*). (*Evt P p s*) ⇒
(∀*q* :*Process*. ∀*rs* :(*Stream Signal*). (*Witness q rs p s*) ⇒ (*CycEvt q rs*))
⇒ (*CycEvt p s*).

End Cyclic_Eventuality.

It is important to require that P will eventually fail from p, otherwise we could prove that it will re-fail again from any witness just by absurdity from the hypothesis that there exists a witness of its failure.

Before defining the last eventuality property, let us introduce here a theorem about cyclic eventualities that will be necessary in the next section for the verification proof. The theorem states that if a property $\neg P$ is a cyclic eventuality from p, and we know a witness q of the failure of *another* property Q from p, then the property $\neg P$ is also a cyclic eventiality from q.

Variables P, Q :∀c :**Channel**. ∀w :**Signal**. ∀p, q :**Process**. $p \xrightarrow{!w}_c q \Rightarrow$ **Prop**.
Theorem *StillHappens* :
∀*p*, *q* :*Process*. ∀*ss*, ss_1 :(*Stream Signal*).
(*Witness Q q* ss_1 *p ss*) ⇒ (*CycEvt P p ss*) ⇒ (*CycEvt P q* ss_1).
Proof ...

The proof follows just by a straightforward induction on the proof that q is a witness, using the fact that if the property $\neg P$ is a cyclic eventuality from p, and $p \xrightarrow{w}_c q$, then $\neg P$ is a cyclic eventuality also from q. A constructive proof of this latter property requires the decidability of P.

3. Series of Eventualitues. A generalisation of the notion of cyclic eventuality consists in saying that is not always the same property P that comes to fail again somewhere in the future, but that there is in fact an infinity of properties $(P\ b_1)$, $(P\ b_2), \ldots$, depending on values $b_1, b_2, \ldots$ of certain type B that will fail one after the other. A slight modification of the previous definition allows us to introduce this new kind of eventualities. P is regarded as a function which associates to each b_i a certain property about the communications, and the stream $b_1, b_2, \ldots$ is introduced as an argument of the property.

Section Serial_Eventuality.
Variable B :**Set.**
Variable P :B ⇒∀c :**Channel**. ∀w :**Signal**. ∀p, q :**Process**. $p \xrightarrow{!w}_c q \Rightarrow$ **Prop**.

CoInductive *SerEvt* : (*Stream B*) ⇒ *Process* ⇒ (*Stream Signal*) ⇒ *Prop* :=

serdet : ∀*s* :(*Stream B*). ∀*p* :*Process*. ∀*ss* :(*Stream Signal*).
(*Evt* (*P* (*hd s*)) *p ss*) ⇒
(∀*q* :*Process*. ∀*rss* :(*Stream Signal*).
(*Witness* (*P* (*hd s*)) *q rss p ss*) ⇒ (*SerEvt* (*tl s*) *q rss*))
⇒ (*SerEvt s p ss*).

End Serial_Eventuality.
End Eventuality_Properties.

After this property we close the section concerning eventuality properties, abstracting away the transition relation $\longrightarrow$ from all the definitions above.

4 The alternating bit protocol

In this section we finally go into the verification of the protocol. Only the main ideas of the proof will be presented, the reader interested in the details may consult the whole proof at the *"contributions"* directory of the system Coq [4].

4.1 Description of the Protocol

The problem to be solved is the following one: a process has to communicate to another a stream of messages through an unreliable channel, so that all the messages of the stream are correctly received and in the same order they were sent. Once the receiver receives a message, it re-sends it on a reliable channel to whoever may need it. We also assume that, even though some of the messages may be lost in the unreliable channel, it is always possible to obtain a successful transmition after a finite number of attempts. The solution of this problem is well-known and consists in letting both the sender and the receiver to keep a bit which allows to re-synchronise the communication when a message is lost. The sender attaches its current bit to the messages it sends, so that the receiver can compare it with its own bit. Each time the receiver hears a message with the same bit it holds it is sure that it has got the next message to repeat, so it re-transmits this message on the safe channel. Then, it sends its current bit as acknowledgment to the sender, which is programmed to repeat the same message until the acknowledgment it receives corresponds to the bit it has.

In this example, the general parameters in the definition of the type of processes are instantiated with the following inductive types [2]:

`Inductive` *Set Channel* := $chnl_1$: *Channel* | $chnl_2$: *Channel*.
`Inductive` *Set Act* := *Send* : *bool* $\Rightarrow$ *A* $\Rightarrow$ *Act* | *Ack* : *bool* $\Rightarrow$ *Act* |
Relay : *A* $\Rightarrow$ *Act*.

The channel communicating the sender and the receiver is unreliable, but the one on which the receiver repeats the messages is not. This hypothesis is modeled defining the transition relation of the system by case analysis on the channel on which the action is performed, so that the relation *UnrelProcTrans* is associated to the former and the relation *SafeProcTrans* to the latter (cf. Section 3.2):

`Definition` *Trans* := [*c* : *Channel*]`Case` *c* `of` *UnrelProcTrans* *SafeProcTrans* `end`

The following descriptions of the sender and the receiver correspond to a (a slight modification of) the programs in lazy ML proposed for them in [16]. The sender is described using two mutually dependent guarded definitions, which differentiates the state of sending a message and the state of waiting for an acknowledgment:

[2] For the sake of readability, these general parameters will be systematically omitted in the rest of the section, writing *Process* instead of (*Process Channel Act*), TALK instead of (TALK *Channel Act*), etc.

```
CoFixpoint SEND : bool ⇒ (Stream A) ⇒ Process :=
[b :bool][s : (Stream A)](TALK chnl1 (Send b (hd s)) (SENDING b s) [v : Act](SEND b s))

with SENDING : bool ⇒ (Stream A) ⇒ Process :=
[b :bool][s : (Stream A)]
   (TALK chnl1 (Send b (hd s))  (SENDING b s)
         [v : Act]Case v of [b1 : bool][a : A](SENDING b s)
                            [b1 : bool]if (eqbool b1 b) then (SEND (not b) (tl s))
                                        else (SEND b s)
                            [a : A](SENDING b s) end ).
```

The receiver is also introduced through (three) mutually dependent guarded definitions. Each function of the block respectively corresponds to the state of waiting for the sender's next message, retransmitting this message on channel two, and sending an acknowledgment for it.

```
CoFixpoint ACKING : bool ⇒ Process :=
[b :bool](LISTEN chnl1 [v : Act]Case v of
                               [b1 : bool][a : A]if (eqbool b1 (not b))
                                                 then (OUT (not b) a) else (ACK b)
                               [b1 : bool](ACKING b)
                               [a : A](ACKING b end)

with OUT : bool ⇒ A ⇒ Process
     := [b1 : bool][a : A](TALK chnl2 (Relay a) (ACK b1) [v : Act](OUT b1 a)).

with ACK : bool ⇒ Process
        := [b : bool](TALK chnl1 (Ack b) (ACKING b) [v : Act](ACK b))
```

The description of the protocol just consists in putting the processes SENDING and ACK in parallel, both starting with the same bit. At the beginning there is a synchronisation phase in which the first message of the sender is not taken into consideration by the receiver[3], so the sender is programmed to send its first message twice.

```
Definition ABP : bool ⇒ (Stream A) ⇒ Process
     := [b : bool][s : (Stream A)](PAR (SENDING b) (cons (hd s) s)) (ACK b)).
```

4.2 A verified CBS simulator

In [16] an interpreter simulating CBS process in Lazy ML is proposed. The input of the interpreter is a stream of *oracle trees* determining which process talks at each meeting point, and its output is the resulting discourse of the process. It can be run interactively using a lazy functional language, so that each time the user enters an oracle tree, she learns which message is broadcasted. Before building the proof, we used this interpreter to gain a better understanding of the protocol. As a by-side

[3] This is not strictly necessary, but it simplifies the proof.

product of the expertiment, we also validated it in Coq using the `Program` family of tactics [11]. These tactics provide assistance to the user in the task of verifying already-written programs with respect to certain initial specification of them. The proof consisted in showing that the stream of messages yielded by the interpreter is actually a discourse, i.e., that it actually comes from a trace of the process. This proof is also available within the contributions of the version V5.10 of Coq.

4.3 The formal proof

The intuition about the correctness of the protocol arises from the transition diagram in Figure 3, which schematises the possible states in the communication process. This diagram shows that, starting from State 1, the processes always come back into this state, provided that two requirements are satisfied:

1. Channel one is fair, i.e. each of the process is capable of sending a value clearly after a finite number of attempts. This avoids the system to be blocked looping in states 2, 3, 4 and 5, or between states 4 and 5.
2. When the receiver wants to talk, it will eventually do it. In other words, both processes are scheduled equitably. This avoids infinite loops in states 3 and 4.

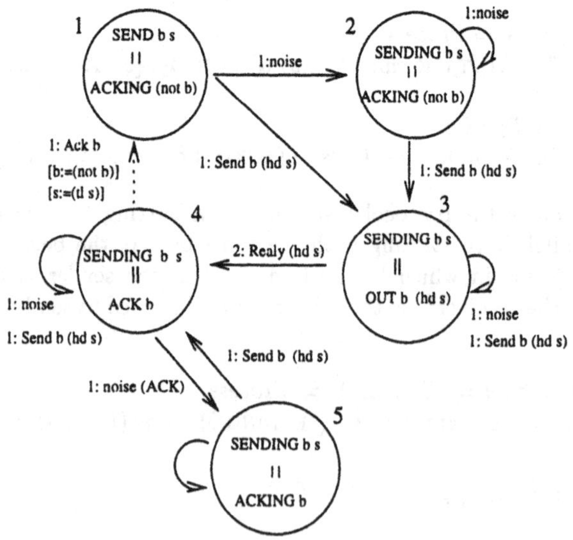

Figure 3 : The states of the protocol.

These constraints on the possible evolutions of the system can be expressed using the notion of cyclic eventuality described in the previous section, where the property that will eventually fail is that either the signal performed is τ or the property *LeftTalksSafely* defined in section 3.2 is satisfied. This amounts to say that we are excluding those traces containing infinite communications made of failed and/or sender's transmitions. The constraint are only for channel one, so if the action is on channel two we consider that the property has failed. Thus, we define the restriction on the traces as the following predicate *Restriction*:

Definition *TransConditions* :=
  [c :*Channel*][w : (*Signal Act*)][p, q : *Process*]
    Case c **of** [t : (*UnrelProcTrans* p !w q)]$w = \tau \vee$ (*LeftTalksSafely* $chnl_1$ p !w q t)
            [t : (*SafeProcTrans* p !s q)]*True* **end**

Definition *Restriction* := (*CycEvt Trans TransConditions*).

The property to be verified is that any discourse satisfying the restriction above contains (in order) the stream of messages (*Relay* s_0), (*Relay* s_1), ... on channel two, where $s_0, s_1, \ldots$ is the stream of input messages of the sender. This property can be expressed as an instance of the property *SerEvt* introduced in section 3.3, where the general parameter B corresponds to the type of messages A, and the i-th property to fail is the negation that the message (*Relay* s_i) has been heard on channel two.

Definition *MessageLost* :=
  [a : A][c :*Channel*][w : *Signal*][p, q : *Process*]
      [t : (*UnrelProcTrans* c p w q)]$\neg(c = chnl_2 \wedge w =$ (*Clear* (*Relay* b))).

Definition *InTrace* := (*SerEvt Trans A MessageLost*).

Theorem *ABP_Correctness* : $\forall b$:*bool*. $\forall s$:(*Stream A*). $\forall ss$:(*Stream Signal*).
          (*Restriction* (ABP b s) ss) $\Rightarrow$ (*InTrace* s (ABP b s) ss).

The verification theorem is a corollary of the following lemma, using the fact that ABP re-transmits the head of the stream twice:

Lemma *cycle* : $\forall b$:*bool*. $\forall s$:(*Stream A*). $\forall ss$:(*Stream Signal*).
      (*Restriction* (PAR (SENDING b s) (ACK b)) ss) $\Rightarrow$
          (*InTrace* (*tl* s) (PAR (SENDING b s) (ACK b)) ss).

The method used in the proof of *cycle* combines guarded definitions and a form of reasoning which is quite reminiscent of Brouwer's *principle of bar induction* [6]. Let us consider again that all the possible traces from (ABP b s) verifying the restriction are arranged in a tree. Such a tree can be associated to what Brouwer called a *spread*, and the property *Restriction* to the corresponding *spread-law*. The steps of our proof consists in showing the following facts:

1. Eventually the first message of the stream will be heared. In terms of the principle of bar induction, this corresponds to the requirement of showing that there is a property which *bars* the spread.
2. Any witness q of this fact is an instance (ABP (*not* b) (*tl* s)) of the process at the top of the tree[4]. This property is proved by induction on the proof that q is a

[4] Is in order to obtain this property that we have chosen to start the protocol at State 4. However, note that this choice obliges us to add a dummy message at the beginning of the stream, because at the first transmition the sender will be waiting for the acknowledgment of a "previous" (inexistent!) message to start repeating the next one (see Figure 3).

witness. This induction amounts to prove that it satisfies the other two premises required in the bar induction principle:
 - it follows from the one barring the spread (base case);
 - it is "hereditary upwards" through the branches of the tree (inductive case).

3. The restriction still holds for the stream of signals starting from the (unique) witness of the fact that the first message has been repeated on channel two. This fact enables us to grasp the (infinite!) proof of the lemma as a cyclic repetition of the approximation of it carried out upon here. The infinite repetition of barrings of the spread in which the proof consists corresponds to an infinite application of the only constructor of the property *SerEvt*, which is described through a guarded definition using the command `CoFixpoint`.

Step one: the tree is barred. Assume a boolean b, a stream of messages s, a process p and a stream of signals ss. The first step of the proof is expressed by the following theorem:

Theorem $Bar_{4,5}$:
$$(Restriction\ p\ ss)$$
$$\Rightarrow (p = (\text{PAR}\ (\text{SENDING}\ b\ s)\ (\text{ACK}\ b)) \vee p = (\text{PAR}\ (\text{SENDING}\ b\ s)\ (\text{ACKING}\ b)))$$
$$\Rightarrow (Evt\ \ Trans\ (MessageLost\ (hd\ (tl\ s)))\ p\ ss).$$

As was already said, the first message of the stream will not be taken into consideration by the receiver, but loosing the second message (the message at the head of the tail of messages) is a property determined to fail. The proof is by induction on the proof of the certain eventuality contained in the restriction, using three other similar lemmas for the previous sates. The lemma Bar_i corresponding to state $i = 1 \ldots 3$ is:

Lemma Bar_i : $(Evt\ Trans\ TransConditions\ p\ ss)$
$$\Rightarrow (p = \ldots \textit{the state } i \ldots) \Rightarrow (Evt\ \ Trans\ \ (MessageLost\ (hd\ s))\ p\ ss).$$

The proofs of all these lemmas are very similar. The general structure consists in analysing which are the possible states the process could run into, and using the local restriction to show that it will break through those situations that could block it. The statement of theorem $Bar_{4,5}$ is a bit different from those of its lemmas. States 4 and 5 have to be considered at once, and the proof needs the fact that the restriction is an eventuality not only *certain* but *cyclic*. The sureness of the restriction is used to prove that, after some looping between states 4 and 5, the receiver finally sends its acknowledgment clearly. However, it is necessary to show that the restriction still holds after this, so that the hypothesis necessary to apply the lemma for State 1 can be fullfiled. In other words, if the process is in the acknowledgment phase, the receiver has to speak clearly twice to send the message on channel two: one to break through this phase and then once more on channel two.

Studying the possible situations that a fixed process p could evolve into amounts to find the possible instances for c, w and q that could satisfy $p \xrightarrow{c}_w q$. Fortunately, this problem (which may be terribly tedious when doing manually) can be automatically solved in the V5.10 of Coq using the so-called *inversion tactics* [5]. The aid provided by these tactics is quite remarkable, and save us several hours of dealing with boring proofs. So the proofs of these lemmas are quite long (about 60 Coq tactics each one) but they present no difficulties.

The fact that most of these proofs consist in inverting the transition predicate explains why also the alternative of using boxes proposed in Section 3 for the representation of processes had to be discharged. If we would consider the language spoken as an index of the type of processes, so we should have done in the transition predicates, and in this case inversion tactics would not work. This is due to the fact that these tactics can not deal with the inversion of predicates where the type of some of its indexes depend on previous indexes of the predicate (cf. [5]).

Step two: there is a unique witness. Assumme a boolean b, a stream of messages s, two process p, q and two streams of signals ss, rss. The second requirement is expressed by this theorem:

Theorem $who\_is\_the\_witness_{4,5}$:
$(Witness\ Trans\ (MessageLost\ (hd\ (tl\ s)))\ q\ rss\ p\ ss)$
$\Rightarrow(\ p = (\text{PAR}\ (\text{SENDING}\ b\ s)\ (\text{ACK}\ b))\ \vee\ p = (\text{PAR}\ (\text{SENDING}\ b\ s)\ (\text{ACKING}\ b))\ )$
$\Rightarrow\ (q = (\text{PAR}\ (\text{SENDING}\ (not\ b)\ (tl\ s))\ (\text{ACK}\ (not\ b)))).$

stating which is the only possible witness of the fact that the message has been correctly received. The proof is by induction on the proof that q is a witness, analysing the possible forms this witness could take if we start from p. It also need similar lemmas for the previous states. The lemma corresponding to state $i = 1 \ldots 3$ is:

Lemma $who\_is\_the\_witness_i$:
$(Witness\ Trans\ (MessageLost\ (hd\ s))\ q\ rss\ p\ ss)$
$\Rightarrow(p = \ldots\ the\ state\ i \ldots) \Rightarrow(q = (\text{PAR}\ (\text{SENDING}\ b\ s)\ (\text{ACK}\ b))).$

Step three: and so on forever. In order to close the description of the infinite proof with a recursive call, it must be shown that the restriction still holds for the stream of signals remaining from the (unique) witness at which the first message is repeated on channel two. This property follows from the lemma *StillHappens* referred in section 3.3. This lemma requires *MessageLost* to be decidable, and this follows straightforwardly form the decidability of *LeftTalksSafely*.

5 Concluding Remarks and Related Works

We have illustrated the use of co-inductive types in a prototype version of Coq through a case of study. In our opinion, the best advantage of this prototype is to combine a simple and direct way of describing co-inductive types and infinite objects with a safe way of reasoning about them. Other proofs systems which allow to reason about infinite objects are Alf [10] and Isabelle [14]. The main differences with the former is that Alf does not prevent the user from the introduction of non-sense definitions, since the verification of the guarded condition is up to him. Another difference is that in Alf type conversion may diverge when working with infinite objects. This is because non-ending methods of construction are not considered as canonical expressions, so testing the equality of two infinite objects may lead to an infinite unfolding of their definitions. In Isabelle, co-inductive types can be encoded as greatest fixed points of monotone operators, and the way of introducing infinite objects is through co-recursive operators [13, 15]. This encoding gives exactly the same strength than using guarded definitions [7]. There exists packages for working with (co)inductive types, which automatise part of this encoding and derives a co-recursive operator associated with the type. However, infinite objects have to be encoded by hand in terms of this co-recursor, which, in our opinion, is a rather tedious task in practice, because it makes the codification of the type explicit again.

A verification proof of the alternating bit protocol in Coq has been previously developed by M. Bezem and J.F. Groote [2]. Their proof is based on a completely different formalism (the process algebra μCRL). We share with [2] the use of a (co)algebraic language for describing process, but the way of giving semantics to the language is different. In that work an axiomatic approach is followed, stating properties about the equality of the process algebra, while here we we have followed a style closer to natural semantics, where the meaning is given using a transition relation. It is remarkable that the the size of our proof is almost a third of the proof in [2]. In our opinion, one of the facts that could explain this difference of size is that in [2] the equality of the algebra is represented in Coq as Leibniz's propositional equality. This choice leads to a proof requiring a lot of rewriting, and unfortunately Coq still lacks of powerful rewriting tactics. On the contrary, the use of a transition relation specified as an recursive predicate allowed us to take advantage of Coq's specialised tactics for reasoning about recursive types, for example to deduce constraints about the subprocesses of a given one using inversion tactics (cf. 4.3). Other process models that have been experimented in Coq are based on I/O automata, see for example [8].

The complete development of the proof took us about a month of work and yields 70 Kb of source code. At least half of the time was invested in looking for good axiomatisations of CBS in Coq. This experiment gives us also the opportunity for testing some of the new features of the version V5.10 of Coq. We have already mentioned the important help provided by inversion tactics and proof reconstruction facilities. Among the main technical difficulties detected is the absence of simple mechanisms to handle the theories defined, for example simple ways of instantiating, hiding and inferring their general parameters. Also, some of the new features of Coq -like the possibility of extending the grammar and the pretty printer- still lacks of some form of assistance from the system to take full advantage of them.

References

1. P. Aczel. *Non-Well-Founded Sets*, volume 14 of *CLSI Lecture Notes*. Stanford University, 1988.
2. M. Bezem and J. Groote. A Formal verification of Alternating Protocol in the Calculus of Constructions. Technical Report 88, Departament of Philosophy, University of Utrecht, 1993.
3. T. Coquand. Infinite objects in Type Theory. In Henk Barendregt, Tobias Nipkow, editor, *Types for Proofs and Programs*, pages 62–78. LNCS 806, 1993.
4. C. Cornes et al. The Coq Proof assistant user's guide - Version V5.10. Technical Report 0177, INRIA, 1995.
5. C. Cornes and D. Terrasse. Automatizing Inversion Predicates in Coq. In *BRA Workshop on Types for Proofs on Programs*, 1995. In this book.

6. M. Dummett. *Elements of Intuitionism*. Oxford University Press, 1977.
7. E. Giménez. Codifying guarded definitions with recursive schemes. In *BRA Workshop on Types for Proofs and Programs (TYPES'94)*, LNCS 996, pages 39–59, 1994.
8. L. Helmink, M.P.A. Sellink, and F.W. Vaandrager. Proof-Checking a Data Link Protocol. In Henk Barendregt, Tobias Nipkow, editor, *Types for Proofs and Programs*, pages 127–165. LNCS 806, 1993.
9. G. Kahn and D. MacQueen. Coroutines and networks of parallel processes. *Information Processing 77*, pages 993–998, 1977.
10. L. Magnusson and B. Nordström. The ALF proof editor and its proof engine. In *Nijmegen Workshop on Types for Proofs and Programs*, 1993.
11. C. Parent. Synthesizing proofs from programs in the Calculus of Inductive Constructions. In *Mathematics for Programs Constructions'95*, LNCS 947, pages 351–379, 1995.
12. C. Paulin-Mohring. Inductive definitions in the system Coq : Rules and Properties. In M. Bezem, J.F. Groote, editor, *Proceedings of the TLCA*, 1993.
13. L. Paulson. Co-induction and Co-recursion in Higher-order Logic. Technical Report 304, Computer Laboratory, University of Cambridge, 1993.
14. L. Paulson. The Isabelle reference manual. Technical Report 283, Computer Laboratory, University of Cambridge, 1993.
15. L. Paulson. A fixed point approach to implementing (co)inductive definitions. Technical Report 304, Computer Laboratory, University of Cambridge, 1995.
16. K.V.S. Prasad. Programming with broadcasts. In E. Best, editor, *CONCUR'93*, pages 173–187. LNCS 715, 1993.
17. K.V.S. Prasad. A Calculus of Broadcasting Systems. To appear in *Science of Computer Programming*, 1995.
18. H.P. Sanders. *A Logic of Functional Programs with an Application to Concurrency*. PhD thesis, Chalmers University of Göteborg, 1992.

Conservativity of Equality Reflection over Intensional Type Theory

Martin Hofmann

Fachbereich Mathematik
TH Darmstadt
Schloßgartenstraße 7
D-64289 Darmstadt
Germany

Abstract. We investigate the relationship between intensional and extensional formulations of Martin-Löf type theory. We exhibit two principles which are not provable in the intensional formulation: uniqueness of identity and functional extensionality. We show that extensional type theory is conservative over the intensional one extended by these two principles, meaning that the same types are inhabited, whenever they make sense. The proof is non-constructive because it uses set-theoretic quotienting and choice of representatives.

1 Extensional and intensional type theory

A distinctive feature of Martin-Löf's type theories is the presence of two notions of equality: judgemental equality and propositional equality. Judgemental equality applies to both terms and types and is written as a judgement $\Gamma \vdash M = N : \sigma$ and $\Gamma \vdash \sigma = \tau$ *type*. The inference rules for these judgements include congruence rules for all the type and term formers and computational rules like the β and possibly the η-rule for function types. The present study applies to dependent type theories with at least Π-types, Σ-types, identity types, and natural numbers (to have a base type). For simplicity we assume an η-rule for the Π-types. In [6] we also deal with the absence of the η-rule.

Propositional equality only applies to terms and is itself a type (of equality proofs). That is, we have a type $Id_\sigma(M, N)$ in context Γ whenever $M, N : \sigma$.

$$\frac{\Gamma \vdash \sigma\ \mathit{type} \quad \Gamma \vdash M : \sigma \quad \Gamma \vdash N : \sigma}{\Gamma \vdash Id_\sigma(M, N)\ \mathit{type}} \ \textsc{Id-Form}$$

The formulation of equality as a type allows internal reasoning about equality, for example a propositional equality can be established by induction (**N**-elimination) so as to show $x{:}\mathbf{N} \vdash Id_{\mathbf{N}}(x, Suc^x(0))$ *true* where $Suc^x(0)$ means the x-fold application of the successor function to 0 defined by **N**-elimination. Here and in the sequel we write $\Gamma \vdash \sigma$ *true* to mean $\Gamma \vdash \sigma$ *type* and $\Gamma \vdash M : \sigma$ for some term M. Type annotations to Id and other type and term formers may be left out where appropriate.

Propositional equality is introduced via reflexivity, i.e. if $M : \sigma$ then we have a canonical element $\mathit{Refl}_\sigma(M) : \mathit{Id}_\sigma(M, M)$.

$$\frac{\Gamma \vdash M : \sigma}{\Gamma \vdash \mathit{Refl}_\sigma(M) : \mathit{Id}_\sigma(M, M)} \quad \text{ID-INTRO}$$

This, together with the congruence rules for judgemental equality gives that $M = N : \sigma$ always entails that $\mathit{Id}_\sigma(M, N)$ is inhabited (namely by $\mathit{Refl}_\sigma(M)$).

Now one would like to express that this is the only inhabitant of the identity type, i.e. one might wish the rule

$$\frac{\Gamma \vdash P : \mathit{Id}_\sigma(M, N)}{\Gamma \vdash P = \mathit{Refl}_\sigma(M) : \mathit{Id}_\sigma(M, N)} \quad \text{ID-UNI}$$

However, for this rule to "type-check" we need to identify propositional and judgemental equality. This is achieved by the equality reflection rule

$$\frac{\Gamma \vdash P : \mathit{Id}_\sigma(M, N)}{\Gamma \vdash M = N : \sigma} \quad \text{REFLECTION}$$

This axiomatisation of propositional equality is the one used in Martin-Löf's earlier works [8] and in many proof-theoretic studies on his type theories. The type theory based on this axiomatisation is called *extensional type theory*, TT_E for short, because by rule REFLECTION the judgemental equality becomes extensional. For instance, since as argued above $x{:}\mathbf{N} \vdash \mathit{Id}_{\mathbf{N}}(x, \mathit{Suc}^x(0))$ *true* we obtain by REFLECTION that $x{:}\mathbf{N} \vdash x = \mathit{Suc}^x(0) : \mathbf{N}$ which clearly is an extensional equality.

Equality reflection (REFLECTION) is intuitively appealing because it is valid in most models, in particular in the set-theoretic interpretation of type theory, and also because it leads to a single notion of equality in type theory. A serious disadvantage of extensional type theory is that judgemental equality and as a consequence type checking, i.e. the question whether a given judgement $\Gamma \vdash M = N : \sigma$ or $\Gamma \vdash M : \sigma$ holds, are undecidable. Intuitively, this is so, because a syntax-directed decision procedure for these judgements would have to "guess" the proof term P in the premise to rule REFLECTION. As any Π^0_1 statement in Heyting arithmetic can be encoded as a certain identity type, inhabitation of identity types is at least as complex as provability of such statements. A rigorous proof of undecidability using recursively inseparable sets is given in [6]. Therefore, extensional type theory is not really in line with the Curry-Howard isomorphism because terms do not correspond to proofs, only typing derivations do. Other shortcomings of extensional type theory are that in the presence of a universe U non-normalising terms become typeable in inconsistent contexts (for example the fixpoint combinator may be typed in $d{:}\,U, p{:}\,\mathit{Id}_U(d, d \to d)$) and—of a more aesthetic nature—that rule REFLECTION does not fit into the pattern of introduction and elimination rules. See, however, [10] for a formulation of REFLECTION as an η-like rule.

Probably for these reasons Martin-Löf has later on restricted judgemental equality to definitional expansion (definitional equality) and replaced rules ID-UNI and REFLECTION by his famous identity elimination rule which is motivated by the view of the identity type as an inductive family with sole constructor *Refl*.

The use of this elimination principle is described in detail in [9]. It is shown there, how it entails that propositional equality satisfies a Leibniz principle, that is if $x{:}\sigma \vdash \tau[x]$ *type* and $P : Id_\sigma(M_1, M_2)$ and $N : \tau[M_1]$ then one can construct a term $Subst_{\sigma,\tau}(M_1, M_2, P, N) : \tau[M_2]$. This Leibniz principle in turn allows one to show that propositional equality is an equivalence relation, i.e. if $P : Id(M_1, M_2)$ then we can construct $Sym(P) : Id(M_2, M_1)$ and for $Q : Id(M_2, M_3)$ we get $Trans(P, Q) : Id(M_1, M_3)$. Furthermore, it entails that *Id* is respected by all functions, i.e. if $U : \sigma \to \tau$ then we find $Resp(U, P) : Id(F\ M_1, F\ M_2)$.

Surprisingly, the intensional and extensional formulations of type theory have never been compared in the literature (to the best of our knowledge). This is the purpose of the present work. We first identify two principles which are provable in the extensional theory, but not in the intensional one and then embark on the proof that extensional type theory is conservative over the intensional one with these two principles added. We only sketch the formal argument here and refer the reader to [6] for a detailed proof.

We use a monomorphic presentation of type theory, i.e. terms with explicit type annotations, as in [9, Part III], however, without using a so-called Logical Framework, see also Sect. 3.

The material in this paper is mostly taken from the author's PhD dissertation [6]. However, some simplifications (in particular the assumption of η-conversion for Π-types) have been made, and the example in Section 2 is new.

1.1 Functional extensionality

Suppose that $\Gamma \vdash U, V : \Pi x{:}\sigma.\tau$ and $\Gamma, x{:}\sigma \vdash P : Id_\tau(U\ x\ , V\ x)$. In extensional type theory we can conclude $\Gamma \vdash Id_{\Pi x:\sigma.\tau}(U, V)$ *true* using REFLECTION, the congruence rule for λ, and η. In intensional type theory this is, however, in general not possible. A formal semantic argument for this may be found in [10]; intuitively one may argue that otherwise in the special case where Γ is empty we could deduce $Id_{\Pi x:\sigma.\tau}(U, V)$ *true* (from the existence of P above), but an identity type in the empty context can only be inhabited by a canonical element *Refl*(−), so U and V must be definitionally equal, which does not follow from the existence of the proof P which may have been obtained using induction. To achieve this principle called *functional extensionality* we add to intensional type theory a family of constants $Ext_{\sigma,\tau}(U, V, P)$ obeying the rule

$$\frac{\begin{array}{c}\Gamma \vdash U, V : \Pi x{:}\sigma.\tau \\ \Gamma, x{:}\sigma \vdash P : Id_\tau(U\ x, V\ x)\end{array}}{\Gamma \vdash Ext_{\sigma,\tau}(U, V, P) : Id_{\Pi x:\sigma.\tau}(U, V)} \quad \text{EXT-FORM}$$

1.2 Uniqueness of identity

Let $M, N : \sigma$ and $P, Q : Id_\sigma(M,N)$ be two proofs that M, N are propositionally equal. In extensional type theory it is an immediate consequence of ID-UNI that $Id_{Id_\sigma(M,N)}(P,Q)$ *true*. Streicher has conjectured in [10] that this is in general not the case in intensional type theory and in [7] this has actually been proved by a semantic argument. So again, we are led to extend our axiomatisation of propositional equality in an intensional setting. It turns out that it is enough to consider the case where Q is in canonical form so that we introduce a family of constants

$$\frac{\Gamma \vdash M : \sigma \qquad \Gamma \vdash P : Id_\sigma(M,M)}{\Gamma \vdash \mathit{IdUni}_\sigma(M,P) : Id_{Id_\sigma(M,M)}(P, \mathit{Refl}_\sigma(M))} \quad \text{ID-UNI-I}$$

to achieve *uniqueness of identity*. Axioms like EXT-FORM and ID-UNI-I introduce non-canonical elements of all types in the empty context (not only of identity types). The constant ID-UNI-I can be endowed with an obvious reduction rule which eliminates all of its instances in closed terms of basic type. Things are more serious with EXT-FORM since no reasonable reduction rule for these constants is known. However, in [5] we discuss a possibility for eliminating these non-canonical elements by translating the identity type into suitable equivalence relations. For the present work we shall simply regard *Ext* and *IdUni* as families of constants.

1.3 The intensional type theory $\mathbf{TT}_I$

It is also noticed in [10] that in the presence of uniqueness of identity the elimination operator for *Id* can be defined in terms of its particular instance *Subst* mentioned above. Therefore, we shall take *Subst* as a primitive and define *intensional type theory* (TT_I for short) as dependent type theory with rules ID-FORM, ID-INTRO, EXT-FORM, ID-UNI-I, and the following two rules for *Subst*.

$$\frac{\begin{array}{l}\Gamma \vdash P : Id_\sigma(M_1, M_2)\\ \Gamma, x{:}\sigma \vdash \tau[x]\ \mathit{type} \qquad \Gamma \vdash N : \tau[M_1]\end{array}}{\Gamma \vdash \mathit{Subst}_{\sigma,\tau}(M_1, M_2, P, N) : \tau[M_2]} \quad \text{LEIBNIZ}$$

$$\frac{\Gamma \vdash \mathit{Subst}_{\sigma,\tau}(M, M, \mathit{Refl}_\sigma(M), N) : \tau[M]}{\Gamma \vdash \mathit{Subst}_{\sigma,\tau}(M, M, \mathit{Refl}_\sigma(M), N) = N : \tau[M]} \quad \text{LEIBNIZ-COMP}$$

Recall that TT_E refers to extensional type theory defined by rules ID-UNI and REFLECTION above. Recall also that from *Subst* one may define operators *Sym*, *Trans*, and *Resp*, witnessing that *Id* is an equivalence relation compatible with function application.

In order to distinguish the intensional from the extensional type theory we write $\vdash_I$ and $\vdash_E$ for the two respective judgement relations.

The operators of TT_I are definable in TT_E, for example *Subst* is simply the identity in TT_E. More formally, we can define a "stripping map" $|-|$ by

$|Subst_{\sigma,\tau}(M_1, M_2, P, N)| := |N|$
$|IdUni_{\sigma}(M, P)| := Refl_{Id_{|\sigma|}(|M|,|M|)}(Refl_{|\sigma|}(|M|))$
$|Ext_{\sigma,\tau}(U, V, P)| := Refl_{\Pi x:|\sigma|.|\tau|}(|U|)$
homomorphically extended to all other terms, types, contexts, and judgements

Notice that $\Gamma = |\Gamma|$ if Γ does not contain *Subst* , *Ext*, or *IdUni* . This mapping enjoys the following trivial soundness property

Proposition 1 *If $\Gamma \vdash_I J$ then $|\Gamma| \vdash_E |J|$ for all contexts Γ and judgements J.*

2 Conservativity of TT_E over TT_I

We are now interested in a converse of the above proposition; more precisely, we shall establish the following conservativity property.

Theorem 2 *If $\Gamma \vdash_I \sigma$ type and $|\Gamma| \vdash_E M : |\sigma|$ for some M then there exists M' such that $\Gamma \vdash_I M' : \sigma$.*

Before sketching the proof of this theorem we shall illustrate its strength by an example suggested by Thomas Schreiber. The crux of this example is to show how the lack of equality reflection in TT_I can be inconvenient when one wants to actually program with dependent types rather than use type dependency merely to express constructive predicate logic.

We assume a type Bool with two canonical elements true : Bool and false : Bool. We use the following slightly unconventional elimination rule which is expressible in terms of the usual one, see [9, Ch. 21]

$$\frac{\begin{array}{l}\Gamma, b{:}\,\mathsf{Bool} \vdash \sigma\ type\\ \Gamma \vdash B : \mathsf{Bool}\\ \Gamma, p{:}\,Id_{\mathsf{Bool}}(B, \mathsf{true}) \vdash T : \sigma[\mathsf{true}/b]\\ \Gamma, p{:}\,Id_{\mathsf{Bool}}(B, \mathsf{false}) \vdash E : \sigma[\mathsf{false}/b]\end{array}}{\Gamma \vdash \mathsf{if}'_{[b:\mathsf{Bool}]\sigma}(B, [p{:}\,Id_{\mathsf{Bool}}(B, \mathsf{true})]T, [p{:}\,Id_{\mathsf{Bool}}(B, \mathsf{false})]E) : \sigma[B/b]}\ \textsc{Bool-E}$$

Notice that the free variables b in σ and p in T, E, respectively, become bound in the if′ expression. This elimination operator comes with the following two computation rules:

$$\frac{\Gamma \vdash \mathsf{if}'_{[b:\mathsf{Bool}]\sigma}(\mathsf{true}, [p{:}\,Id_{\mathsf{Bool}}(\mathsf{true}, \mathsf{true})]T, [p{:}\,Id_{\mathsf{Bool}}(\mathsf{true}, \mathsf{false})]E) : \sigma[\mathsf{true}/b]}{\begin{array}{l}\Gamma \vdash \mathsf{if}'_{[b:\mathsf{Bool}]\sigma}(\mathsf{true}, [p{:}\,Id_{\mathsf{Bool}}(\mathsf{true}, \mathsf{true})]T, [p{:}\,Id_{\mathsf{Bool}}(\mathsf{true}, \mathsf{false})]E) =\\ \quad T[Refl_{\mathsf{Bool}}(\mathsf{true})/p] : \sigma[\mathsf{true}/b]\end{array}}\ \textsc{Bool-C-T}$$

$$\frac{\Gamma \vdash \mathsf{if}'_{[b:\mathsf{Bool}]\sigma}(\mathsf{false}, [p{:}\,Id_{\mathsf{Bool}}(\mathsf{false}, \mathsf{true})]T, [p{:}\,Id_{\mathsf{Bool}}(\mathsf{false}, \mathsf{false})]E) : \sigma[\mathsf{false}/b]}{\begin{array}{l}\Gamma \vdash \mathsf{if}'_{[b:\mathsf{Bool}]\sigma}(\mathsf{false}, [p{:}\,Id_{\mathsf{Bool}}(\mathsf{false}, \mathsf{true})]T, [p{:}\,Id_{\mathsf{Bool}}(\mathsf{false}, \mathsf{false})]E) =\\ \quad E[Refl_{\mathsf{Bool}}(\mathsf{false})/p] : \sigma[\mathsf{false}/b]\end{array}}\ \textsc{Bool-C-F}$$

Suppose that we are given a type Loc of locations together with an equality function $\mathsf{eq} : \mathsf{Loc} \to \mathsf{Loc} \to \mathsf{Bool}$ and a proof term

$$\mathsf{eq\_correct} : \Pi l, l' : \mathsf{Loc}. Id_{\mathsf{Loc}}(l, l') \leftrightarrow Id_{\mathsf{Bool}}(\mathsf{eq}\ l\ l', \mathsf{true})$$

witnessing that eq is indeed an equality function on Loc. The terms eq and eq_correct may either be implemented or declared in some ambient context Γ. Furthermore, we assume a type Data depending on Loc, i.e. we have $\Gamma \vdash \mathsf{Data}(M)$ *type* whenever $\Gamma \vdash M : \mathsf{Loc}$. We make the definition

$$\mathsf{Store} = \Pi l : \mathsf{Loc}. \mathsf{Data}(l)$$

and our aim is to find a term

$$\mathsf{update} : \Pi l_0 : \mathsf{Loc}. \Pi d : \mathsf{Data}(l_0). \Pi s : \mathsf{Store}. \mathsf{Store}$$

which given l_0, d, s returns a store whose value at l_0 equals d and $(s\ l)$ at $l \neq l_0$. In TT_E we can easily construct such an update function by

$$\begin{array}{l} \mathsf{update} = \lambda l_0 : \mathsf{Loc}. \lambda d : \mathsf{Data}(l_0). \lambda s : \mathsf{Store}. \lambda l : \mathsf{Loc}. \\ \quad \mathsf{if'}_{[b:\mathsf{Bool}]\mathsf{Data}(l)}(\mathsf{eq}(l_0, l)\ , \\ \qquad [p : Id_{\mathsf{Bool}}(\mathsf{eq}(l_0, l), \mathsf{true})]d\ , \\ \qquad [p : Id_{\mathsf{Bool}}(\mathsf{eq}(l_0, l), \mathsf{false})](s\ l)) \end{array}$$

The important point here is that in TT_E we have $\mathsf{Data}(l_0) = \mathsf{Data}(l)$ in the presence of $p : Id(\mathsf{eq}(l_0, l), \mathsf{true})$ by virtue of eq_correct. Therefore, we have $d : \mathsf{Data}(l)$ and the first branch of the if′ expression type-checks.

Write

$$\mathsf{update\_type} = \Pi l_0 : \mathsf{Loc}. \Pi d : \mathsf{Data}(l_0). \Pi s : \mathsf{Store}. \mathsf{Store}$$

and for $f : \mathsf{update\_type}$

$$\begin{array}{l} \mathsf{update\_spec}(f) = \\ \quad (\Pi l_0 : \mathsf{Loc}. \Pi d : \mathsf{Data}(l_0). \Pi s : \mathsf{Store}. Id_{\mathsf{Data}(l_0)}(f\ l_0\ d\ s\ l_0\ , d)) \times \\ \quad (\Pi l_0 : \mathsf{Loc}. \Pi d : \mathsf{Data}(l_0). \Pi l : \mathsf{Loc}. (Id_{\mathsf{Loc}}(l, l_0) \to \bot) \to Id_{\mathsf{Data}(l)}(f\ l_0\ d\ s\ l\ , s\ l)) \end{array}$$

where $\bot$ is the empty type. We can readily establish

$$\Gamma \vdash_E \mathsf{update\_spec}(\mathsf{update})\ \mathit{true}$$

using if′ and equality reasoning.

Now assuming that Loc and Data already make sense in intensional type theory we can apply the conservativity theorem to the type

$$\sigma = \Sigma f : \mathsf{update\_type}. \mathsf{update\_spec}(f)$$

giving us an update function in TT_I which also satisfies update_spec. Coming up with such a function is not too difficult, indeed we may choose

$\mathsf{update'} = \lambda l_0{:}\,\mathsf{Loc}.\lambda d{:}\,\mathsf{Data}(l_0).\lambda s{:}\,\mathsf{Store}.\lambda l{:}\,\mathsf{Loc}.$
$\quad \mathsf{if'}_{[b:\mathsf{Bool}]\mathsf{Data}(l)}(\mathsf{eq}(l_0, l)\ ,$
$\qquad [p{:}\,Id_{\mathsf{Bool}}(\mathsf{eq}(l_0,l), \mathsf{true})]Subst_{\,\mathsf{Loc},\mathsf{Data}}(l_0, l\ ,\ ((\mathsf{eq\_correct}\ l_0\ l).2\ p)\ ,\ d)\ ,$
$\qquad [p{:}\,Id_{\mathsf{Bool}}(\mathsf{eq}(l_0,l), \mathsf{false})](s\ l))$

where the projection .2 yields the $\leftarrow$-part of **eq_correct**, hence the first argument to *Subst* is of type $Id_{\mathsf{Loc}}(l_0, l)$. The conservativity theorem does not necessarily give us this very update function, but we can also use it to obtain a proof of correctness of the latter. To that end we consider the type

$$\sigma = \mathsf{update\_spec}(\mathsf{update'})$$

We have $|\sigma| = \mathsf{update\_spec}(\mathsf{update})$ so $\Gamma \vdash_E |\sigma|\ true$ and hence $\Gamma \vdash_I \sigma\ true$ giving us the desired correctness proof for our particular function $\mathsf{update'}$. Constructing such proof directly requires quite some effort as the function in question contains an instance of *Subst*. In this case the author has been able to construct such a proof using the Lego system. This revealed that the use of *Ext* can be avoided here and that *IdUni* is only used for the particular type Loc. As observed by Michael Hedberg *IdUni* is definable from Martin-Löf's elimination rule for types with decidable equality (such as Loc) so that this example can be carried out in pure intensional Martin-Löf type theory without the additional constants *Ext* and *IdUni*.

It was pointed out by one of the referees that in the presence of pattern-matching like in ALF [1] the complicated equality reasoning in the example can be avoided if one replaces **eq** and **eq_correct** by a single constant

$$\mathsf{eq'} : \Pi l, l'{:}\,\mathsf{Loc}.Id_{\mathsf{Loc}}(l, l') + (Id_{\mathsf{Loc}}(l, l') \to \bot)$$

One may then define **update** by pattern matching over $\mathsf{eq'}(l, l_0)$ and in the positive case we may then assume that l and l_0 are *judgementally* equal. It is not clear, however, how this technique can be applied in general, in particular, the example in [6] and briefly mentioned in Section 3 does not seem to be amenable to a simple development using pattern-matching.

Proof of Thm. 2 (Sketch). The proof is based on two main ingredients. First, we observe that a consequence of this conservativity property is that types σ and σ' which are equal in TT_E must be isomorphic in TT_I. To see this consider the type

$$\begin{aligned}\rho := \Sigma f{:}\,\sigma \to \sigma'.\Sigma f^{-1}{:}\,\sigma' \to \sigma.&\\ Id(\lambda x{:}\,\sigma.f^{-1}(f\ x), \lambda x{:}\,\sigma.x) \times Id(\lambda x{:}\,\sigma'.f(f^{-1}\ x), \lambda x{:}\,\sigma'.x)&\end{aligned}$$

If $\vdash_E |\sigma| = |\sigma'|$ then $|\rho|$ is inhabited by two instances of the identity function together with two instances of reflexivity. So a proof of Theorem 2 must embody a construction of these isomorphisms. Now the only way to deduce judgemental type equalities in TT_E is by using congruence rules and REFLECTION in the case of type formers containing terms like the identity type. So we can compute these isomorphisms directly by induction on the structure of any two types σ and σ' without using conservativity in the first place.

The second ingredient is a general method for establishing conservativity between type theories. Generalising from Thm. 2 we call an extension $\mathbf{T}'$ of some type theory $\mathbf{T}$ *conservative* over $\mathbf{T}$ if whenever a type of $\mathbf{T}$ is inhabited in $\mathbf{T}'$ then it is already inhabited in $\mathbf{T}$.

Proposition 3 *Let* $\mathbf{T}$ *be a type theory and* $\mathbf{T}'$ *an extension of* $\mathbf{T}$. $\mathbf{T}'$ *is conservative over* $\mathbf{T}$ *if and only if there exists a model* $\mathbf{Q}$ *of* $\mathbf{T}'$, *hence of* $\mathbf{T}$, *such that the interpretation of* $\mathbf{T}$ *in this model is full (surjective).*

Proof. Suppose that σ is a type of $\mathbf{T}$ such that σ is inhabited in $\mathbf{T}'$ by some term M. The interpretation of M in $\mathbf{Q}$ yields a "semantic term" of the interpretation of σ in $\mathbf{Q}$ which by fullness gives a term of type σ in $\mathbf{T}$. For the converse we let $\mathbf{Q}$ be the term model of $\mathbf{T}'$

At this level of generality the argument is too informal so as to be of direct use. It only serves us as a guideline which the reader is invited to bear in mind. The theories $\mathbf{T}$ and $\mathbf{T}'$ are TT_I and TT_E, respectively, where a slight complication results from the fact that TT_E is not literally an extension of TT_I, but that we have an interpretation of one in the other, namely the stripping map. The role of "models" is played by *categories with families* in the sense of Dybjer [2, 4] or any other category-theoretic notion of model for type theory. For the purpose of this abstract it suffices to know that such a structure provides domains of interpretation for contexts, types, and terms[1], and comes with semantic type and term formers operating on these semantic objects. An interpretation function can then be defined which maps syntactic contexts, types, terms to their semantic companions and translates syntactic type and term formers into the corresponding semantic ones. Judgemental equality is then modelled by set-theoretic equality of semantic objects. Factoring the syntax by judgemental equality yields a particular model: the term model. The interpretation of the syntax in a some model induces a unique structure preserving map from the term model to this model. The model $\mathbf{Q}$ we use is a quotient of the term model of TT_I by propositional equality where in addition we identify types and contexts which are canonically isomorphic in the sense described above, i.e. which become equal in TT_E.

Let us now look at some of the details. In order to define the canonical isomorphisms between types one also needs to consider isomorphisms between contexts to get the inductive definition through. In order to specify those we extend propositional equality to contexts and context morphisms (substitutions) using Σ-types. It turns out that for this extension the same combinators as for ordinary propositional equality can be defined. Then by simultaneous induction on contexts and types we construct possibly undefined "isomorphism candidates" between any two contexts and types. That is, for contexts Γ, Δ we have a (possibly undefined) context morphism (a $|\Delta|$-tuple of terms) $co_{\Gamma,\Delta} : \Gamma \to \Delta$

[1] ... and substitutions, but we gloss over this point here.

which if defined possesses an inverse up to propositional equality. For types $\Gamma \vdash_I \sigma$ *type*, $\Delta \vdash_I \tau$ *type* we have a (possibly undefined) term

$$\Gamma, x{:}\sigma \vdash_I ty_{\Gamma,\Delta,\sigma,\tau}[x] : \tau[co_{\Gamma,\Delta}]$$

which—if defined—is an isomorphism w.r.t. propositional equality. We use square brackets to denote (generalised) substitution, i.e. if $f : \Gamma \to \Delta$ and $\Delta \vdash \sigma$ *type* then $\Gamma \vdash \sigma[f]$ *type* and similarly for other judgements. The isomorphism between contexts of different length is always undefined and between contexts of the same length it is obtained from the isomorphisms between types. An isomorphism between types can only be defined if they share the same outermost type former. In the case of Π and Σ-types the isomorphism is the obvious lifting of the isomorphism for the respective components. Functional extensionality is used to verify the isomorphism property in the case of Π-types. The interesting case is where σ and τ are identity types. For simplicity we assume that they are both in the same context and over the same type. I.e. let $\Gamma \vdash_I M_1, M_2, N_1, N_2 : \rho$ and put $\sigma = Id_\rho(M_1, M_2)$ and $\tau = Id_\rho(N_1, N_2)$. The isomorphism

$$\Gamma, p{:}\, Id_\rho(M_1, M_2) \vdash_I ty_{\Gamma,\Gamma,\sigma,\tau}[p] : Id_\rho(N_1, N_2)$$

is defined iff M_1, N_1 and M_2, N_2 are propositionally equal. In this case we pick $\Gamma \vdash_I P_1 : Id_\rho(M_1, N_1)$ and $\Gamma \vdash_I P_2 : Id_\rho(M_2, N_2)$ and set

$$ty_{\Gamma,\Gamma,\sigma,\tau}[p] := Trans\,(Trans\,(Sym\,(P_1), p), P_2)$$

Notice that in this case *ty* is defined w.r.t. some arbitrary choice of these proofs P_i. The isomorphism property is readily established using *IdUni*.

Having defined these isomorphisms we construct a model of TT_E in which

- contexts are equivalence classes of contexts, two contexts being identified if the isomorphism between them is defined,
- types in context $[\Delta]_\sim$ are equivalence classes of pairs (Γ, σ) where $\Gamma \in [\Delta]_\sim$, and $\Gamma \vdash_I \sigma$ *type*, and two such pairs are identified if the corresponding *ty*-isomorphism is defined,
- terms of type $[(\Delta, \tau)]_\sim$ are equivalence classes of triples (Γ, M, σ) where $(\Gamma, \sigma) \in [(\Delta, \tau)]_\sim$, and $\Gamma \vdash_I M : \sigma$, and two such triples (Γ, M, σ) and (Γ', N', σ') are identified if

  $$\Gamma \vdash Id_{\sigma'}(ty_{\Gamma,\Gamma',\sigma,\sigma'}[M]\,,\, M'[co_{\Gamma,\Gamma'}]) \text{ } true$$

  i.e., if M and M' with suitably adjusted source and target are propositionally equal in TT_I.

We have used here the notation $[-]_\sim$ for equivalence classes associated to a representative.

Now we prove that this structure, which we call **Q**, does indeed form a model of TT_E and that in particular the required semantic type and term formers are given by applying their syntactic companions (in TT_I) to equivalence classes. Here *Ext* and *IdUni* are used to show that various settings are independent of the choice of representatives and thus are well-defined on equivalence classes. For example, if $[(\Gamma, M, \sigma)]_\sim$ and $[(\Gamma', N', \sigma')]_\sim$ are two semantic terms of (semantic) type $[(\Delta, \sigma)]_\sim$ then we define the associated identity type as the equivalence class of the pair of Γ and

$$\Gamma \vdash Id_{\sigma'}(ty_{\Gamma,\Gamma',\sigma,\sigma'}[M]\ ,\ M'[co_{\Gamma,\Gamma'}])\ type$$

Since we have defined equality of terms in **Q** precisely as inhabitedness of this type the rule REFLECTION is valid in **Q**. Uniqueness of identity is required here to show that this setting is independent of the chosen representatives (Γ, M, σ) and (Γ', N', σ').

The above can be summarised by the following diagram of structure preserving maps between models.

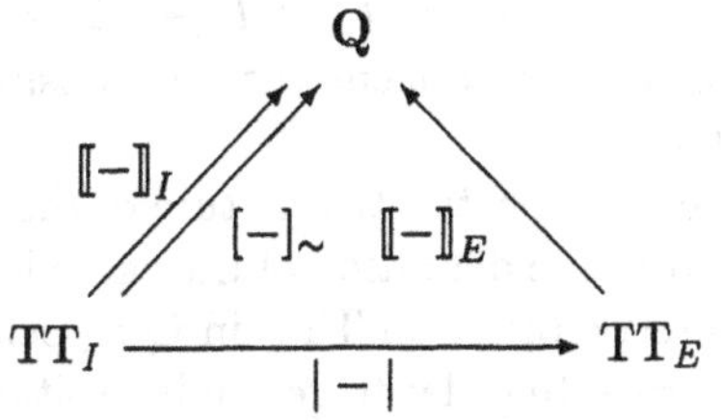

where TT_I and TT_E refer to the term models of the respective type theories. $[\![-]\!]_I$ and $[\![-]\!]_E$ denote the interpretations of TT_I and TT_E in **Q**, which being a model for TT_E also models TT_I. Finally, $[-]_\sim : \mathrm{TT}_I \to \mathbf{Q}$ is the projection map associating equivalence classes which is structure preserving by definition of **Q**.

By induction on derivations or—more elegantly—by an initiality argument we find that all three structure preserving maps from TT_I to **Q** are equal, more precisely, we have

$$[-]_\sim = [\![-]\!]_I = [\![-]\!]_E \circ |-| \tag{1}$$

Intuitively, we can now argue that the interpretation of TT_I in **Q** is surjective because we have characterised it as the projection associating equivalence classes and then apply Prop. 3. More formally, suppose that $\Gamma \vdash_I \sigma$ and $|\Gamma| \vdash_E M : |\sigma|$. Let $[\![M]\!]_E = [(\Gamma', M', \sigma')]_\sim$ be the interpretation of M in **Q**. By definition, we have $\Gamma' \vdash_I M' : \sigma'$. Moreover, by Eqn. 1 we find

$$[\Gamma]_\sim = [\![|\Gamma|]\!]_E = [\Gamma']_\sim$$

and

$$[(\Gamma, \sigma)]_\sim = [\![|(\Gamma, \sigma)|]\!]_E = [(\Gamma', \sigma')]_\sim$$

This in turn implies that $co_{\Gamma,\Gamma'}$ and $ty_{\Gamma,\Gamma',\sigma,\sigma'}$ are defined. Therefore, we have

$$\Gamma \vdash_I ty^{-1}{}_{\Gamma,\Gamma',\sigma,\sigma'}[M'[co_{\Gamma,\Gamma'}]] : \sigma$$

giving the desired inhabitant of σ in TT_I. □

We remark that we can even show that the stripping of the thus constructed inhabitant of σ is equal to M in TT_E by showing that the stripping map respects the equality in **Q** and thus lifts to a structure preserving map from **Q** to TT_E which again by initiality must be a left inverse to $[\![-]\!]_E$. We refer to [6] for details.

3 Discussion

Although relatively complex, the described method is fairly robust w.r.t. extensions of the type theory. For it to be extensible to a new type former it is enough that this type former admits an action on propositional isomorphisms. In [6] we demonstrate this by adding quotient types and a universe. We remark, however, that this condition is not met in the presentation of type theory using the Logical Framework in the sense of [9, Part III]. The reason is that there we can have variables of type $Set \to Set$ which act as completely unspecified type formers. Nevertheless, it is plausible that Thm. 2 continues to hold in this case. A possible proof could use a one-step definition of the isomorphism candidates by which for example the isomorphism $ty_{\Gamma,\Gamma,\sigma,\tau}$ would be defined iff there exists a context Δ, a type ρ, and context morphisms $f, g : \Gamma \to \Delta$ such that $\Gamma \vdash_I \sigma = \rho[f]$, $\Gamma \vdash_I \tau = \rho[g]$, and f, g are (component-wise) propositionally equal. We leave the details to a future paper.

We also point out the non-constructive nature of the proof. Not only has the axiom of choice been used in the definition of the canonical isomorphisms *co* and *ty*; more seriously the interpretation of TT_E in $\mathbf{Q}$ associates equivalence classes to contexts, types, and terms. In order to get an inhabitant of type σ in the proof above we must arbitrarily choose a representative of the corresponding class. We have done so implicitly by writing $[\![M]\!]_E = [(\Gamma', M', \sigma')]_\sim$. So the present proof does not directly give rise to an algorithm which effectively computes an inhabitant of σ from a derivation of $|\sigma|$ *true* in TT_E. Now such algorithm trivially exists by Markov's principle, that is we simply try out all possible terms and derivations and from the non-constructive proof of existence we know that this search always succeeds. But of course, one would like a more efficient algorithm which makes use of the given derivation in TT_E. It is, however, not clear whether the described argument gives rise to one such. An idea would be to carry out the construction of $\mathbf{Q}$ in some "setoid model" where quotients come with a canonical choice of representatives. This is, however, not possible using a semantics which interprets judgemental equality as set-theoretic extensional equality as we have done.

It appears that a constructivisation of the result could give rise to tactics facilitating theorem proving in TT_I, the idea being that parts of a proof or program development could be carried out in TT_E. The resulting derivation would then be automatically translated into TT_I. In [6] we give a proof in TT_E of a theorem of Mendler's stating that the dependent sum (Σ) preserves limits of ω-chains. Although the proof in TT_E is relatively straightforward it was despite considerable effort so far not possible to obtain a fully formal development in TT_I. The reason was that in this case one has to prove a property about a term which contains instances of *Subst* inside a primitive recursion over natural numbers rather than just booleans as in the case of the update function above. Given sufficient time and energy one could certainly push this proof through, but a systematic treatment based on the conservativity result would seem to save much work in such cases.

We remind the reader that the conservativity result applies to intensional type theory with functional extensionality and uniqueness of identity added. Another issue is the conservativity of the latter two over pure intensional type theory or rather the characterisation of those types and contexts for which they are conservative. This question remains unanswered and is left for future research. A brief discussion of the topic may be found in [6].

Judgemental equality has played a minor role in the present proof and it appears that the whole development would go through if TT_I was replaced by a type theory without judgemental equality at all and rules like β or LEIBNIZ-COMP replaced by corresponding constants of identity types in the style of IDUNI. The construction of the model **Q** would remain unchanged since propositionally equal objects are identified in **Q**, some care has to be taken, however, with the extension of propositional equality to contexts.

This generalisation would also answer affirmatively the question of conservativity of the original TT_I over this new type theory without judgemental equality.

Acknowledgement. I wish to thank Thomas Streicher and the anonymous referees for suggesting improvements of an earlier draft.

References

1. Thorsten Altenkirch, Veronica Gaspes, Bengt Nordström, and Björn von Sydow. *A User's Guide to ALF.* Chalmers University of Technology, Sweden, May 1994. Available on the WWW: file://ftp.cs.chalmers.se/pub/users/alti/alf.ps.Z.
2. Peter Dybjer. Internal type theory. In *Proc. BRA TYPES workshop, Torino, June 1995, Springer LNCS*, 1996. To appear.
3. Solomon Feferman. Theories of finite type. In Jon Barwise, editor, *Handbook of Mathematical Logic*, chapter D.4. North-Holland, 1977.
4. Martin Hofmann. Syntax and sematnics of dependent types. In P. Dybjer and A. M. Pitts, editors, *Semantics and Logics of Computation.* Cambridge University Press, 199?
5. Martin Hofmann. Elimination of extensionality for Martin-Löf type theory. In H. Barendregt and T. Nipkow, editors, *Types for Proofs and Programs.* Springer, 1994. LNCS 806.
6. Martin Hofmann. *Extensional Concepts in Intensional Type Theory.* PhD thesis, Univ. of Edinburgh, 1995.
7. Martin Hofmann and Thomas Streicher. A groupoid model refutes uniqueness of identity proofs. In *Proceedings of the 9th Symposium on Logic in Computer Science (LICS), Paris*, 1994.
8. Per Martin-Löf. *Intuitionistic Type Theory.* Bibliopolis·Napoli, 1984.
9. B. Nordström, K. Petersson, and J. M. Smith. *Programming in Martin-Löf's Type Theory, An Introduction.* Clarendon Press, Oxford, 1990.
10. Thomas Streicher. *Semantical Investigations into Intensional Type Theory.* Habilitationsschrift, LMU München, 1993.

A Natural Deduction Approach to Dynamic Logic*

Furio Honsell[1] and Marino Miculan[1,2]

[1] Dipartimento di Matematica e Informatica, Università di Udine
Via delle Scienze 206, I-33100 Udine, Italy. {honsell,miculan}@dimi.uniud.it
[2] Dipartimento di Informatica, Università di Pisa
Corso Italia 40, I-56100 Pisa, Italy. miculan@di.unipi.it

Abstract. Natural Deduction style presentations of program logics are useful in view of the implementation of such logics in interactive proof development environments, based on type theory, such as LEGO, Coq, etc. In fact, ND-style systems are the kind of systems which can take best advantage of the possibility of reasoning "under assumptions" offered by proof assistants generated by Logical Frameworks. In this paper we introduce and discuss sound and complete proof systems in Natural Deduction style for representing various "truth" consequence relations of Dynamic Logic. We discuss the design decisions which lead to adequate encodings of these logics in Coq. We derive in Dynamic Logic a set of rules representing a ND-style system for Hoare Logic.

Introduction

Computerized proof assistants are very useful, and probably necessary, in using logical systems for reasoning about programs. In fact, the amount of (often trivial and repetitive) routine details involved in using program logics renders error-prone the activity of a human prover.

Type Theories, such as the Edinburgh Logical Framework [9, 3] or the Calculus of Inductive Constructions [5, 27] were especially designed, or can be fruitfully used, as a general logic specification language, i.e. as a Logical Framework (LF). Thus they can streamline the process of generating interactive proof development environments tailored to the peculiarities of any given logics. In fact, any interactive proof development environment for these type theories (LEGO [16], Coq [14] and ELF [21]), can be readily turned into one for a specific logic, as soon as we fix a suitable environment corresponding to the encoding of the logic. Although these editors are not as efficient as some of those especially designed for a specific logic, nevertheless Logical Frameworks can be very useful for at least three reasons. First of all, they provide a common medium for integrating different systems. Hence LF-derived editors rival special purpose

* Work partially supported by the Esprit BRP no.6453, *Types for Proofs and Programs*, and italian MURST 40%-60% grants. Some of the results of this papers have been communicated by the second author at the TYPES Annual Meeting in Båstad, 1994.

editors when efficiency can be increased by integrating independent logical systems. Secondly, LF-generated editors are *natural.* A user of the original logic can transfer immediately to them his practical experience and "trade tricks,". They do not force upon the user the overhead of unfamiliar indirect codings, as would editors derived from FOL editors, via an encoding. On the contrary, it is a frequent experience that encodings in Logical Frameworks provide the "ultimate" or "normative" formalization of the logical system under consideration. The specification methodology of Logical Frameworks, in fact, forces the user to make precise all tacit conventions. Thirdly, Logical Frameworks are based on Type Theory presented in Natural Deduction style via the analogy "judgements as types". Therefore, they naturally allow the user of an LF-generated editor to reason "under assumptions" and go about in developing a proof the way mathematicians normally reason: using hypotheses, formulating conjectures, storing and retrieving lemmata, often in top-down, goal-directed fashion. This feature offered by Logical Frameworks urges the designer/implementor of an editor for a given object logic, to look for a presentation of the logic which can take best advantage of the possibility of manipulating assumptions.

The crucial concept involved in discussing the notion of assumption for a given logic is that of *consequence relation* (CR) [2]. CR's are abstract representations of logical dependencies between assumptions and conclusions. They play a crucial rôle in stating and proving adequacies of encodings in Logical Frameworks. Usually, a logic gives rise to more than one CR. For instance, in FOL we have the *validity* CR and the *truth* CR, according to how we understand free variables in assumptions. In *modal logics* further CR's arise, according to whether we focus on *frames* or *worlds.* Usually, CR's differ on the form of "deduction theorem" that they yield. Truth CR's are those which yield the simplest deduction theorems. Validity CR's are best suited for capturing the notion of *derivabilty* from sets of *axioms* and hence the notion of *theoremhood.* Many more different CR's can be defined for program logics if we take into account the possibility of restricting attention to interesting subclasses of models.

Before building an editor for a given logic, the designer/implementor has to clarify two equally important, apparently orthogonal, issues. Which CR is the one to focus on? Which style of presentation is best for actually "using" the logic, e.g. Hilbert, Natural Deduction (ND) or Gentzen (sequent) style? In the methodology of Logical Frameworks, answering the first question amounts to decide which *judgements* to encode. Experience shows that ND-style systems representing truth CR's, are best suited for exploiting the reasoning power of assumptions provided by Logical Frameworks.

In this paper we investigate logical systems for Dynamic Logic (DL) in view of their encoding in the interactive proof development environment Coq. Similarly to what happens for FOL, both validity and truth CR's arise for DL, and program logics in general. Sound and (relative) complete systems for representing the validity CR's restricted to *finite* sets of assumptions, can be readily derived from any Hilbert systems for DL [1, 8, 15]. But, surprisingly, little attention has been payed so far, in the literature, to "truth CR's" for program logics. Hence, in line with the remark above, in this paper we introduce and discuss Natural Deduction style systems for representing truth CR's.

In developing ND-style systems for DL, one of the most delicate and complicated issues one has to deal with, is that of free logical variables versus program identifiers. New difficulties arise when we consider derivations under assumptions, since assumptions on program variables enforce local constraints on the environments of subderivations. However, the type-theoretic metatheory provided by Logical Frameworks, which allows to express schematic (i.e. generalized) assumptions, provides interesting solutions to these difficulties. Another problematic issue arises in connection with "infinitary rules". Logical Frameworks, such as Coq, offer also in this case a remarkable metatheoretic solution. Since they embody the power of a higher order intuitionistic logic of inductive definitions, many recursive functions can be defined in them. Other difficulties arise in connection with "rules of proof" (i.e. rules which can be applied only to premises which depend on *no* assumptions), or with "proper sequent-style" rules, such as Scott's rule (i.e. rules which modify substantially the structure of *all* the assumptions). Some of these problematic side conditions in the rules can be internalized in the framework at the expense of a slight modification of the basic judgment, exploiting again the possibility of using schematic premises in rules.

In the encodings, we exploit thoroughly the higher-order features provided by Logical Frameworks.

In this paper, for the sake of simplicity we consider only the datatype of natural numbers.

The paper is organized as follows. In Section 1 we introduce sound and complete ND-style systems with respect to the truth CR for Dynamic Logic (DL) over the first order language of Peano Arithmetic. Encodings of these systems in type theory are given in Section 2. In Section 3 we describe the derivation of an impure ND-style system for the truth CR of Hoare Logic. In Section 4 we compare our work with the *KIV System* (which is a special purpose editor for DL [23]) and an implementation of Hoare Logic in the Cambridge HOL [6]. Final remarks appear in Section 5. In Appendix A we give the syntax and semantics of Peano Arithmetic (PA), Hoare Logic and DL. In Appendix B we give the notion of *Consequence Relation* and related basic logical notions. Throughout the paper we use standard proof theoretic notions and notations (see e.g. [22]). Terminology and notations concerning Logical Frameworks are as in [9].

The Coq code of these implementations and examples is available at the URL `http://www.dimi.uniud.it/~miculan/DL`. The authors are grateful to the referees for their useful remarks on an earlier version of the paper.

1 ND-style Proof Systems for Dynamic Logic

Dynamic Logic (see App.A for definitions) has been thoroughly investigated from the model theoretic point of view. Not as much attention, however, has been payed to its proof theory or to the possibility of representing consequence relations different from that of *validity*. The relevant concept being that of *theoremhood*, the proof systems considered have been mainly Hilbert-style systems [7, 8, 15, 26]. There is only one remarkable exception, albeit unpublished, of ND-style System for Deterministic DL due to C. Stirling [25] (see Sect.5).

Besides absolute validity and absolute truth, various CR's can be introduced according to the class of models that one focuses on. Since in this paper we focus on the language of Peano Arithmetic (PA), we consider two classes of models: the class of *all* first-order structures which are models of PA, and that consisting only of the standard model (denoted by N). Truth and validity CR's for DL are defined by suitably specializing the following general definition:

Definition 1 Truth and Validity on First-Order Structures. Let L be a first-order language, and let Γ range over sets of formulæ, p over formulæ of L.

1. Let $\mathcal{M}$ be a first-order model for L (see Appendix A);
   – the *truth CR* $\models^L_{\mathcal{M}}$ *wrt* $\mathcal{M}$ is the relation defined by
   $$\Gamma \models^L_{\mathcal{M}} p \iff [\![\Gamma]\!]_{\mathcal{M}} \subseteq [\![p]\!]_{\mathcal{M}};$$
   – the *validity CR* $\models\!\!\models^L_{\mathcal{M}}$ *wrt* $\mathcal{M}$ is the relation defined by
   $$\Gamma \models\!\!\models^L_{\mathcal{M}} p \iff ([\![\Gamma]\!]_{\mathcal{M}} = \mathbb{S}_{\mathcal{M}} \Rightarrow [\![p]\!]_{\mathcal{M}} = \mathbb{S}_{\mathcal{M}}).$$
2. The *(absolute) truth CR* is the relation $\models^L \stackrel{\text{def}}{=} \bigcap_{\mathcal{M}} \models^L_{\mathcal{M}}$; the *(absolute) validity CR* is the relation $\models\!\!\models^L \stackrel{\text{def}}{=} \bigcap_{\mathcal{M}} \models\!\!\models^L_{\mathcal{M}}$, where $\mathcal{M}$ ranges over all first-order models for L. □

We introduce a ND-style system for $\models$, $\mathcal{S}_{\text{ND}}(\text{DL})$, by adding to the usual ND-style system for Peano Arithmetic [22] the rules in Fig.1. By p^t_x we denote the formula obtained by replacing all occurrences of x, which are not bound by the $\forall$-quantifier, with t (possibly α-converting p in order to avoid capturing free variables in t). The set of variables in p whose occurrences are not all bound by $\forall$ is denoted by $\text{FV}(p)$. We write Natural Deduction rules and proofs in the *linearized* notation, hence "$\pi : \Gamma \vdash p$" denotes a proof tree π whose premises and conclusion are Γ and p respectively. The system is *infinitary* system, i.e. Γ is possibly an infinite set.

The system $\mathcal{S}_{\text{ND}}(\text{DL})$ is sound and complete with respect to the truth CR:

Theorem 2. $\forall \Gamma, p : \Gamma \vdash_{\mathcal{S}_{\text{ND}}(\text{DL})} p \iff \Gamma \models p.$

A proof can be obtained by modifying suitably the proof of Theorem 3.15 in [8]; see [20] for further details.

The system $\mathcal{S}_{\text{ND}}(\text{DL})$ is indeed a ND-style system, since there are introduction rules for each program constructor and the corresponding elimination rules are induced by the introduction rules. The rules for equality and the quantifier are more involved than the usual ones for FOL, due to the presence of commands. Reflexivity of equality can be encoded immediately, but the rules of congruence have to be rephrased with care: derivations like $[x := 0]\,(x = 0), x =$

$$:=\text{-I}\ \frac{\Gamma, y = t \vdash p^y_x}{\Gamma \vdash [x := t]p}\ y \notin \mathrm{FV}(\Gamma, p, t) \qquad :=\text{-E}\ \frac{\Gamma_1 \vdash [x := t]p \quad \Gamma_2, p^y_x, y = t \vdash q}{\Gamma_1, \Gamma_2 \vdash q}\ y \notin \mathrm{FV}(\Gamma_2, p, q, t)$$

$$;\text{-I}\ \frac{\Gamma \vdash [c_1][c_2]p}{\Gamma \vdash [c_1; c_2]p} \qquad ;\text{-E}\ \frac{\Gamma \vdash [c_1; c_2]p}{\Gamma \vdash [c_1][c_2]p}$$

$$^*\text{-I}\ \frac{\{\Gamma_n \vdash [c]^n p \mid n \in \mathbb{N}\}}{\bigcup_n \Gamma_n \vdash [c^*]p} \qquad ^*\text{-E}\ \frac{\Gamma \vdash [c^*]p}{\Gamma \vdash [c]^n p}\ n \in \mathbb{N} \qquad \text{where } [c]^0 p = p,\ [c]^{n+1} p = [c]\,[c]^n p$$

$$?\text{-I}\ \frac{\Gamma, b \vdash p}{\Gamma \vdash [b?]p} \qquad ?\text{-E}\ \frac{\Gamma_1 \vdash [b?]p \quad \Gamma_2 \vdash b}{\Gamma_1, \Gamma_2 \vdash p}$$

$$+\text{-I}\ \frac{\Gamma_1 \vdash [c_1]p \quad \Gamma_2 \vdash [c_2]p}{\Gamma_1, \Gamma_2 \vdash [c_1 + c_2]p} \qquad +\text{-E}\ \frac{\Gamma \vdash [c_1 + c_2]p}{\Gamma \vdash [c_i]p}$$

$$\forall\text{-I}\ \frac{\Gamma \vdash p}{\Gamma \vdash \forall x p}\ x \notin \mathrm{FV}(\Gamma) \qquad \forall\text{-E}\ \frac{\Gamma_1 \vdash \forall x p \quad \Gamma_2, p^y_x, y = t \vdash q}{\Gamma_1, \Gamma_2 \vdash q}\ y \notin \mathrm{FV}(\Gamma_2, \forall x p, t, q)$$

$$\textsc{CongrId}\ \frac{\Gamma_1 \vdash p \quad \Gamma_2 \vdash x = y}{\Gamma_1, \Gamma_2 \vdash p^y_x}\ y \notin \mathrm{FV}(p) \qquad \textsc{Congr}\ \frac{\Gamma_1 \vdash p^{t_1}_x \quad \Gamma_2 \vdash t_1 = t_2}{\Gamma_1, \Gamma_2 \vdash p^{t_2}_x}\ p \text{ is command-free}$$

Fig. 1. The system $\mathcal{S}_{\mathrm{ND}}(\mathrm{DL})$.

$1 \vdash [x := 0]\,(1 = 0)$ have to be prevented. To this end, we introduce two rules: CONGR and CONGRID. CONGR can be applied only to command-free formulæ, i.e. formulæ where no command appears (see App.A). CONGRID, can be applied to any formula, since it merely replaces all occurrences of an identifier with a new identifier.

The non traditional form of $\forall$-elimination is due to the fact that, in general, the quantified formula p may contain commands, and therefore not all occurrences of a bound variable can be replaced by a term. For instance, $\forall x. [x := 0]\,(x = 0)$ holds, but its naïve instantiation $[1 := 0]\,(1 = 0)$ is clearly meaningless. A correct formulation of instantiation of quantified variables is in fact one of the most difficult technical issues to deal with in encoding DL. In Hilbert systems this is usually achieved by replacing, whenever required, any program c with the equivalent "normal form" $z_1 := x_1; \ldots; z_n := x_n; c'; x_1 := z_1; \ldots; x_n := z_n$ where the x_i's are all the identifiers appearing in c, the z_i's are fresh and c' is obtained from c by replacing the x_i's with z_i's (see [8]). This solution is clearly cumbersome if we want to use practically the formal system. The problematic nature of instantiation of quantifiers lies, as in the case of the congruence rules, in the different nature of pure logical identifiers and program variables. In fact, the property "$s \in [\![p^t_x]\!] \iff s[x \mapsto [\![t]\!]s] \in [\![p]\!]$" does not hold for DL.

Our solution to the instantiation problem is to replace the bound variable x with a fresh variable y, and to assume $y = t$ in the minor premise. The usual $\forall$-elimination rule is derivable in the case of command-free predicates.

The infinitary nature of rule *-I is essential for achieving the completeness of $\vdash_{\mathcal{S}_{\mathrm{ND}}(\mathrm{DL})}$ with respect to the full $\models$ and not only to $\models \cap(\mathcal{P}_{<\omega}(\mathbb{P}) \times \mathbb{P})$. In fact, proofs in finitary systems can take into account only a *finite* number of assumptions, and since DL does not satisfy compactness (consider e.g. the set $\{[x := x-1]^n\, x \neq 0 \mid n \in \mathbb{N}\} \cup \{\neg\,[(x := x-1)^*]\, x \neq 0\}$), we can easily find a true consequence which is underivable in any finitary system (e.g. $\{[x := x-1]^n\, x \neq 0 \mid n \in \mathbb{N}\} \models [(x := x-1)^*]\, x \neq 0$).

The useful, albeit "impure", $[\cdot]$-intro rule $\frac{\emptyset \vdash p}{\emptyset \vdash [c]p}$ and Scott's rule Sc$\frac{\Gamma \vdash p}{[c]\Gamma \vdash [c]p}$ (where $[c]\,\Gamma \stackrel{\text{def}}{=} \{[c]\,p \mid p \in \Gamma\}$) are clearly admissible for $\mathcal{S}_{\text{ND}}(\text{DL})$.

Focusing on consequences true in all models of Peano Arithmetic, the system $\mathcal{S}_{\text{ND}}(\text{DL})$ rules out many interesting consequences which are true when reasoning about real programs which utilize as datatype the real integers. For instance, the formula $p \stackrel{\text{def}}{=} \langle (x := x - 1)^* \rangle\, (x = 0)$ is not valid: take any nonstandard model $\mathcal{N}^*$, and consider the state s such that $s(x) = \nu$, ν a nonstandard integer; then, $s \notin [\![p]\!]_{\mathcal{N}^*}$. The same happens with the **while**-termination formula $\langle \textbf{while}\ x > 0\ \textbf{do}\ x := x - 1 \rangle\, (x = 0)$. This is the reason for focusing on the sole standard model of arithmetic and the associated CR's $\models_{\mathbf{N}}$, $\vDash_{\mathbf{N}}$.

In order to represent $\models_{\mathbf{N}}$, we extend the standard ND-style system $\mathcal{S}_{\text{ND}}(\text{DL})$ to a hybrid Natural Deduction-Modal system, namely $\mathcal{S}^a_{\text{ND}}(\text{DL})$, by adding either the *convergence rule* or the equivalent dual *induction principle rule*:

$$\textsc{Conver}\ \frac{\emptyset \vdash p^{x+1}_x \supset \langle c \rangle\, p \quad \Gamma \vdash p^t_x}{\Gamma \vdash \langle c^* \rangle\, p^0_x}\ x \notin \text{FV}(c)$$

$$\textsc{Induc}\ \frac{\emptyset \vdash [c]\,p \supset p^{x+1}_x \quad \Gamma \vdash [c^*]\,p^0_x}{\Gamma \vdash p^t_x}\ x \notin \text{FV}(c)$$

Both rules are "impure" in the sense of Avron [2], and are proof-rules, since the first premise is a theorem. One can easily see that $\vdash_{\mathcal{S}^a_{\text{ND}}(\text{DL})} \langle (x := x - 1)^* \rangle\, (x = 0)$ and $\vdash_{\mathcal{S}^a_{\text{ND}}(\text{DL})} \langle \textbf{while}\ x > 0\ \textbf{do}\ x := x - 1 \rangle\, (x = 0)$. Indeed, $\mathcal{S}^a_{\text{ND}}(\text{DL})$ is sound and complete with respect to the standard model of integers.

Theorem 3. $\forall \Gamma, p : \Gamma \vdash_{\mathcal{S}^a_{\text{ND}}(\text{DL})} p \iff \Gamma \models_{\mathbf{N}} p$.

A proof can be readily derived from that of Th.2.

It is interesting to notice that the rule $*$-I is enough to recover the full power of the ω-rule of infinitary first order logic:

Theorem 4. *Let p be any command-free formula; then, the ω-rule* $\frac{\{\Gamma \vdash p^n_x \mid n \in \omega\}}{\forall x p}$ *is derivable in* $\mathcal{S}^a_{\text{ND}}(\text{DL})$.

Proof. (Sketch) The proof relies upon the fact that command iteration is nondeterministic, hence $\forall x p$ is equivalent to $y = 0 \supset [y := y + 1^*]\, p^y_x$ (y fresh). Each premise p^n_x in the ω-rule can be rendered by means of the formula $y = 0 \supset [y := y + 1]^n\, p^y_x$ (y fresh); applications of $*$-I and Induc yield the ω-rule. □

Instead of introducing proof rules, we could have used alternatively *non-interference* judgments *à la* Reynolds [24] as side conditions of the rules. These are judgments which generalize side-conditions such as $x \notin \text{FV}(A)$. See [20] for further details.

2 Encoding ND-style Systems for DL

In this section we apply and generalize the methodology developed in [9, 3] and define an encoding of $\mathcal{S}_{\text{ND}}(\text{DL})$ and of $\mathcal{S}^a_{\text{ND}}(\text{DL})$ within the Calculus of Inductive Constructions, as it is implemented by the Coq V5.10 proof assistant [14].

$\mathsf{X}, \mathsf{Te}, \mathsf{B}, \mathsf{C}, \mathsf{P}$	$: \mathsf{Set}$	isId	$: \mathsf{X} \to \mathsf{Te}$	$[\cdot]\cdot$	$: \mathsf{C} \to \mathsf{P} \to \mathsf{P}$
$\neg_b$	$: \mathsf{B} \to \mathsf{B}$	$0, 1$	$: \mathsf{Te}$	$*$	$: \mathsf{C} \to \mathsf{C}$
$\supset_b, \wedge_b$	$: \mathsf{B} \to \mathsf{B} \to \mathsf{B}$	$+, *$	$: \mathsf{Te} \to \mathsf{Te} \to \mathsf{Te}$	$?$	$: \mathsf{B} \to \mathsf{C}$
$\neg$	$: \mathsf{P} \to \mathsf{P}$	$=_b, <_b$	$: \mathsf{Te} \to \mathsf{Te} \to \mathsf{B}$	$;, +$	$: \mathsf{C} \to \mathsf{C} \to \mathsf{C}$
$\supset, \wedge$	$: \mathsf{P} \to \mathsf{P} \to \mathsf{P}$	$=, <$	$: \mathsf{Te} \to \mathsf{Te} \to \mathsf{P}$	$:=$	$: \mathsf{X} \to \mathsf{Te} \to \mathsf{C}$

Fig. 2. Representation of $\mathcal{L}(\mathrm{DL})$ in $\Sigma(\mathrm{DL})$ (some constructors).

An important difference with respect to the encoding of HOL in [9] is that we can no longer treat on a par object language identifiers and metalanguage schematic variables (see [3] for similar difficulties in handling Hoare Logic). In fact, the presence of identifiers in formulæ standing for left-hand values which cannot be substituted for, forces us to introduce a specific type for identifiers. Therefore, substitutions of terms for identifiers cannot be handled any mor "for free" by the metalanguage, using *higher order syntax*. Nevertheless, we can still handle at the metalevel substitution of identifiers for identifiers.

2.1 The Encoding of $\mathcal{S}_{\mathrm{ND}}(\mathrm{DL})$: the Signature $\Sigma(\mathrm{DL})$

Syntax. Each syntactic category is represented by an inductive set (denoted by the same name in this font), and each syntactic constructor is represented by a functional constant (Fig.2). There is also a function $\mathsf{b2p} : \mathsf{B} \to \mathsf{P}$, defined by induction on the syntax, which embeds propositional formulæ into formulæ. When clear form the context, it will be omitted for sake of readability. Applications of $\mathsf{b2p}$ are computable (Simplifable) in the Coq environment.

Let $\xi : \mathbb{B} \cup \mathbb{X} \cup \mathbb{T} \cup \mathbb{C} \cup \mathbb{P} \to \mathsf{B} \cup \mathsf{X} \cup \mathsf{T} \cup \mathsf{C} \cup \mathsf{P}$ be the compositional bijective representation of syntactic classes. For the sake of simplicity, ξ will be often omitted; therefore, with the same term we will denote a formula as well as its encoding in the LF signature; similarly we shall deal with sets of assumptions.

We represent the universal quantifier by the syntactic constructor $\forall : (\mathsf{X} \to \mathsf{P}) \to \mathsf{P}$ and hence we can take care of α-conversion of bound variables at the metalevel. Consequently, $\xi(\forall x p) = \forall(\lambda x.\xi(p))$, and, for instance, $\forall x\,[x := 0]\,(x = 0)$ is represented by $\forall(\lambda x : \mathsf{X}.\,[x := 0]\,(\mathsf{isId}(x) = 0))$.

Rules. Since $\mathcal{S}_{\mathrm{ND}}(\mathrm{DL})$ is in ND-style, most of the rules are encoded straightforwardly following the methodology of [9, 3], using as judgment $\mathsf{T} : \mathsf{P} \to \mathsf{Prop}$ (Fig.3). The intended meaning of $(\mathsf{T}\ p)$ is that the formula p holds.

In the following, we will briefly discuss some interesting points concerning the encoding of the most complex rules.

The infinitary rule *-I. Due the presence of *-I, the system $\mathcal{S}_{\mathrm{ND}}(\mathrm{DL})$ has to take into account infinite sets of premises. Hence we need to be able to refer to infinite sets of formulæ. We represent infinte sets of assumptions by a Coq term of type $\mathsf{nat} \to \mathsf{Prop}$. Thus, the version of the rule *-I we encode in Coq is the following:

$$^*\text{-I}\ \frac{\text{for all } n \in \mathbb{N} : I(c,p,n)}{[c^*]\,p} \quad \text{where} \quad \begin{array}{l} I : \mathbb{C} \to \mathbb{P} \to \mathbb{N} \to \mathbb{P} \\ I(c,p,0) = p, \;\; I(c,p,n+1) = [c]\,I(c,p,n) \end{array}$$

$$\wedge\text{-I} : \prod_{p,q:\mathsf{P}} (\mathsf{T}\ p) \to (\mathsf{T}\ q) \to (\mathsf{T}\ (p \wedge q)) \qquad ;\text{-I} : \prod_{p:\mathsf{P}} \prod_{c_1,c_2:\mathsf{C}} (\mathsf{T}\ [c_1][c_2]p) \to (\mathsf{T}\ [c_1;c_2]p)$$

$$\supset\text{-I} : \prod_{p,q:\mathsf{P}} ((\mathsf{T}\ p) \to (\mathsf{T}\ q)) \to (\mathsf{T}\ (p \supset q)) \qquad ;\text{-E} : \prod_{p:\mathsf{P}} \prod_{c_1,c_2:\mathsf{C}} (\mathsf{T}\ [c_1;c_2]p) \to (\mathsf{T}\ [c_1][c_2]p)$$

$$^*\text{-I} : \prod_{p:\mathsf{P}} \prod_{c:\mathsf{C}} \left(\prod_{n:\mathsf{nat}} (\mathsf{T}\ (\mathsf{I}\ c\ p\ n)) \right) \to (\mathsf{T}\ [c^*]p) \qquad \text{where } (\mathsf{I}\ c\ p\ 0) = p,$$

$$^*\text{-E} : \prod_{p:\mathsf{P}} \prod_{c:\mathsf{C}} (\mathsf{T}\ [c^*]p) \to \prod_{n:\mathsf{nat}} (\mathsf{T}\ (\mathsf{I}\ c\ p\ n)) \qquad (\mathsf{I}\ c\ p\ (S\ n)) = [c](\mathsf{I}\ c\ p\ n)$$

Fig. 3. Representation of some rules of $\mathcal{S}_{\mathrm{ND}}(\mathrm{DL})$ in the signature $\Sigma(\mathrm{DL})$.

$$:=\text{-I} : \prod_{A:\mathsf{X}\to\mathsf{P}} \prod_{x:\mathsf{X}} \prod_{t:\mathsf{Te}} \left(\prod_{y:\mathsf{X}} (\mathsf{isnotin}\ y\ \mathsf{P}\ \forall A) \to (\mathsf{isnotin}\ y\ \mathsf{Te}\ t) \to (\mathsf{T}\ (y = t)) \to (\mathsf{T}\ (A\ y)) \right)$$
$$\to (\mathsf{isnotin}\ x\ \mathsf{P}\ \forall A) \to (\mathsf{T}\ ([x := t](A\ x)))$$

$$:=\text{-E} : \prod_{A:\mathsf{X}\to\mathsf{P}} \prod_{q:\mathsf{P}} \prod_{x:\mathsf{X}} \prod_{t:\mathsf{Te}} \left(\prod_{y:\mathsf{X}} (\mathsf{isnotin}\ y\ \mathsf{P}\ \forall A) \to (\mathsf{isnotin}\ y\ \mathsf{Te}\ t) \to (\mathsf{isnotin}\ y\ \mathsf{P}\ q) \to \right.$$
$$\left. (\mathsf{T}\ (y = t)) \to (\mathsf{T}\ (Ay)) \to (\mathsf{T}\ q) \right) \to (\mathsf{isnotin}\ x\ \mathsf{P}\ \forall A) \to$$
$$(\mathsf{T}\ ([x := t]\ (A\ x))) \to (\mathsf{T}\ q)$$

Fig. 4. The LF encoding of the rules for assignment.

Therefore, using this encoding, we can refer only to premises which can be enumerated by a function provably total in PA^{ω}, pratically, this is more than enough.

The assignment rules. As remarked earlier, we cannot exploit higher-order syntax directly to encode $()^t_x$, the substitution operator, as was possible in [3, 9, 18]. The naïve encoding of the assignment constructor, $:=: \mathsf{Te} \to \mathsf{Te} \to \mathsf{C}$, could yield meaningless commands such as $0 := 1$. Substitution has to be dealt with differently from [9], rather in the style of [4]. The encodings of the rules :=-I and :=-E appear in Fig.4. We need to express the fact that an identifier is "fresh", i.e. that it is different from any other pre-existing identifier. To this end, we generalize Mason's idea [3] later expounded in [4, 19], and we introduce the two auxiliary judgments, isin, isnotin : $\mathsf{X} \to \prod_{A:\mathsf{Set}} A \to \mathsf{Prop}$. The intuitive meaning of (isin x A a) is "the identifier x appears in the phrase a whose type is A;" dually for isnotin. These two judgments are derivable by means of a simple set of rules which are polymorphic in the syntactic constructors (Fig.5). The inference of these judgments is completely syntax-driven: it is sufficient to look at the top-level constructor of the phrase for deciding which rule has to be applied. The premise (isnotin x P $\forall A$) of the :=-I rule enforces the fact that the context $A(\cdot)$ does not contain any occurrence of x. In both rules we have also to reify the "freshness condition" of variables locally quantified in premises. This is achieved by assuming suitable isnotin judgments. Such reified assumptions are needed to deal with "contexts" such as $A(\cdot)$ above, or the CongrId rule below.

$$\mathsf{isin\_x} : \prod_{x:\mathsf{X}} (\mathsf{isin}\ x\ \mathsf{X}\ x)$$

$$\mathsf{isin\_1} : \prod_{x:\mathsf{X}} \prod_{s_1,s_2:\mathsf{Set}} \prod_{op:s_1 \to s_2} \prod_{p:s_1} (\mathsf{isin}\ x\ s_1\ p) \to (\mathsf{isin}\ x\ s_2\ (op\ p))$$

$$\mathsf{isin\_2l} : \prod_{x:\mathsf{X}} \prod_{s_1,s_2,s_3:\mathsf{Set}} \prod_{op:s_1 \to s_2 \to s_3} \prod_{p_1:s_1} \prod_{p_2:s_2} (\mathsf{isin}\ x\ s_1\ p_1) \to (\mathsf{isin}\ x\ s_3\ (op\ p_1\ p_2))$$

$$\mathsf{isin\_2r} : \prod_{x:\mathsf{X}} \prod_{s_1,s_2,s_3:\mathsf{Set}} \prod_{op:s_1 \to s_2 \to s_3} \prod_{p_1:s_1} \prod_{p_2:s_2} (\mathsf{isin}\ x\ s_2\ p_2) \to (\mathsf{isin}\ x\ s_3\ (op\ p_1\ p_2))$$

$$\mathsf{isin\_n} : \prod_{s_1,s_2:\mathsf{Set}} \prod_{op:(\mathsf{X} \to s_1) \to s_2} \prod_{p:X \to s_1} \left(\prod_{y:\mathsf{X}} (\mathsf{isin}\ x\ s_1\ (p\ y)) \right) \to (\mathsf{isin}\ x\ s_2\ (op\ p))$$

$$\mathsf{isnotin\_symm} : \prod_{x,y:\mathsf{X}} (\mathsf{isnotin}\ y\ \mathsf{X}\ x) \to (\mathsf{isnotin}\ x\ \mathsf{X}\ y)$$

$$\mathsf{isnotin\_zero} : \prod_{x:\mathsf{X}} (\mathsf{isnotin}\ x\ \mathsf{Te}\ \mathsf{zero}) \qquad \mathsf{isnotin\_false} : \prod_{x:\mathsf{X}} (\mathsf{isnotin}\ x\ \mathsf{P}\ \mathsf{false})$$

$$\mathsf{isnotin\_1} : \prod_{x:\mathsf{X}} \prod_{s_1,s_2:\mathsf{Set}} \prod_{op:s_1 \to s_2} \prod_{p:s_1} (\mathsf{isnotin}\ x\ s_1\ p) \to (\mathsf{isnotin}\ x\ s_2\ (op\ p))$$

$$\mathsf{isnotin\_2} : \prod_{x:\mathsf{X}} \prod_{s_1,s_2,s_3:\mathsf{Set}} \prod_{op:s_1 \to s_2 \to s_3} \prod_{p:s_1} \prod_{p:s_2}$$
$$(\mathsf{isnotin}\ x\ s_1\ p_1) \to (\mathsf{isnotin}\ x\ s_2\ p_2) \to (\mathsf{isnotin}\ x\ s_3\ (op\ p_1\ p_2))$$

$$\mathsf{isnotin\_el} : \prod_{x,y:\mathsf{X}} \prod_{s:\mathsf{Set}} \prod_{p:s} (\mathsf{isnotin}\ x\ s\ p) \to (\mathsf{isin}\ y\ s\ p) \to (\mathsf{isnotin}\ y\ \mathsf{X}\ x)$$

$$\mathsf{isnotin\_n} : \prod_{s_1,s_2:\mathsf{Set}} \prod_{op:(\mathsf{X} \to s_1) \to s_2} \prod_{p:X \to s_1} \left(\prod_{y:\mathsf{X}} (\mathsf{isnotin}\ x\ \mathsf{X}\ y) \to (\mathsf{isnotin}\ x\ s_1\ (p\ y)) \right)$$
$$\to (\mathsf{isnotin}\ x\ s_2\ (op\ p))$$

Fig. 5. The rules for auxiliary judgments isin, isnotin of Σ(DL).

The congruence rules. The encodings of CONGR and CONGRID appear in Fig.6. In encoding CONGRID, we have to check that the context $A(\cdot)$ does not contain any occurrence of x, y. This is enforced as for :=-I, :=-E, via the premises (isnotin x P $\forall A$) and (isnotin y P $\forall A$) In encoding CONGR we have to check that the predicate A is command-free. This is easily achieved by introducing a new judgment BF : P $\to$ Prop, whose rules are the following:

$$\mathsf{BF\_false} : (\mathsf{BF}\ \mathsf{false}) \qquad \mathsf{BF\_forall} : \textstyle\prod_{p:\mathsf{X} \to \mathsf{P}} \left(\prod_{x:\mathsf{X}} (\mathsf{BF}\ (p\ x))\right) \to (\mathsf{BF}\ (\forall p)$$
$$\mathsf{BF\_eq} : \textstyle\prod_{t_1,t_2:\mathsf{Te}} (\mathsf{BF}\ (t_1 = t_2)) \qquad \mathsf{BF\_and} : \prod_{p,q:\mathsf{P}} (\mathsf{BF}\ p) \to (\mathsf{BF}\ q) \to (\mathsf{BF}\ (p \wedge q))$$
$$\mathsf{BF\_not} : \textstyle\prod_{p:\mathsf{P}} (\mathsf{BF}\ p) \to (\mathsf{BF}\ (\neg p)) \qquad \mathsf{BF\_imp} : \prod_{p,q:\mathsf{P}} (\mathsf{BF}\ p) \to (\mathsf{BF}\ q) \to (\mathsf{BF}\ (p \supset q))$$

Clearly, derivations of BF are syntax-driven and can be mostly automated in the Coq environment using the Auto tactic.

$$\text{CONGRID}: \prod_{x,y:\mathsf{X}} \prod_{A:\mathsf{X}\to\mathsf{P}} \prod_{w:U} (\mathsf{isnotin}\ x\ P\ \forall A) \to (\mathsf{isnotin}\ y\ P\ \forall A) \to$$
$$(\mathsf{T}\ (A\ x)) \to (\mathsf{T}\ ((\mathsf{isId}\ x) = (\mathsf{isId}\ y))) \to (\mathsf{T}\ (A\ y))$$

$$\text{CONGR}: \prod_{t_1,t_2:\mathsf{Te}} \prod_{A:\mathsf{Te}\to\mathsf{P}} (\mathsf{T}\ (A\ t_1)) \to (\mathsf{T}\ (t_1 = t_2)) \to (\mathsf{BF}\ (A\ t_2)) \to (\mathsf{T}\ (A\ t_2))$$

Fig. 6. The LF encoding of the congruence rules.

$$\forall\text{-I}: \prod_{A:\mathsf{X}\to\mathsf{P}} \left(\prod_{x:\mathsf{X}} (\mathsf{isnotin}\ x\ \mathsf{P}\ \forall A) \to (\mathsf{T}\ (A\ x)) \right) \to (\mathsf{T}\ (\forall A))$$

$$\forall\text{-E}: \prod_{A:\mathsf{X}\to\mathsf{P}} \prod_{q:\mathsf{P}} \prod_{t:\mathsf{Te}} \left(\prod_{x:\mathsf{X}} (\mathsf{isnotin}\ x\ \mathsf{Te}\ t) \to (\mathsf{isnotin}\ x\ \mathsf{P}\ q) \to (\mathsf{isnotin}\ x\ \mathsf{P}\ \forall A) \to \right.$$
$$\left. (\mathsf{T}\ (x = t)) \to (\mathsf{T}\ (A\ x)) \to (\mathsf{T}\ q) \right) \to (\mathsf{T}\ \forall A) \to (\mathsf{T}\ q)$$

Fig. 7. The LF encoding of the $\forall$-I, $\forall$-E rules.

The $\forall$-quantifier rules. The encoding of the rules for $\forall$ appearing in Fig.7, is not as straightforward as in the standard FOL case. We have to deal with side-conditions and reify "freshness" assumptions on the variables locally quantified in premises, as was the case for the :=-I and :=-E rules.

Adequacy of the encoding. The statement of the Adequacy Theorem for the encoding $\Sigma(\mathrm{DL})$ is more problematic than in the "paradigm case" of FOL [9], since we have to take into account infinite sets of formulæ. Clearly, this cannot be done in full generality and we will be able to state the Adequacy Theorem only with respect to *representable* sets of assumptions, i.e. sets of formulæ whose encodings can be enumerated in Coq. Formally, $\Gamma = \{p_n \mid n \in \mathrm{N}\}$ is *representable (in a context Δ)* if there exists a term G such that $\Delta \vdash_{\Sigma(\mathrm{DL})} G : \mathsf{nat} \to \mathsf{P}$ and for all $n \in \mathrm{N} : \Delta \vdash_{\Sigma(\mathrm{DL})} (G\ \bar{n}) = \xi(p_n)$

Given a representable set of assumptions Γ, in order to define $\gamma(\Gamma)$, the *Coq representation of Γ*, we proceed as follows. First of all, we assume, for each free identifier appearing in Γ, the identifier itself and the judgment asserting that it is different from any other identifier (notice that, for obvious reasons, we are interested in considering only a finite set of identifiers at any given time); we put

$$\iota(\Gamma) \stackrel{\text{def}}{=} \{x : \mathsf{X} \mid x \in \mathrm{FV}(\Gamma)\} \cup \{i_{xy} : (\mathsf{isnotin}\ x\ \mathsf{X}\ y) \mid x, y \in \mathrm{FV}(\Gamma), x \neq y\}$$

If $\Gamma = \{p_1, \ldots, p_n\}$ is finite then we put

$$\gamma(\{p_1, \ldots, p_n\}) = \iota(\Gamma) \cup \{u_1 : (\mathsf{T}\ \xi(p_1)), \ldots, u_n : (\mathsf{T}\ \xi(p_n))\}$$

Otherwise, if $\Gamma = \{p_n \mid n \in \mathrm{N}\}$ is infinite and representable by a term G in $\iota(\Gamma)$, we put $\gamma(\Gamma) = \iota(\Gamma) \cup \{U : \prod_{n:\mathsf{nat}} (\mathsf{T}\ (G\ n))\}$. Thus we have the following theorem, which is proved by induction.

Theorem 5 Adequacy of $\Sigma(\mathrm{DL})$. *Let Γ be a representable (in $\iota(\Gamma)$) set of assumptions. Then*

1. $\forall\Gamma$, *if* $\gamma(\Gamma) \vdash M : A$, *where* $A \in \{\mathsf{X}, \mathsf{Te}, \mathsf{B}, \mathsf{C}, \mathsf{P}\}$, *then*

$$(\exists u.\gamma(\Gamma) \vdash_{\mathcal{S}_{\mathrm{ND}}(\mathrm{DL})} u : (\mathsf{isin}\ x\ A\ M)) \iff x \in \mathrm{FV}(M)$$
$$(\exists u.\gamma(\Gamma) \vdash_{\mathcal{S}_{\mathrm{ND}}(\mathrm{DL})} u : (\mathsf{isnotin}\ x\ A\ M)) \iff x \notin \mathrm{FV}(M)$$

2. $\forall\Gamma, p: \quad \Gamma \vdash_{\mathcal{S}_{\mathrm{ND}}(\mathrm{DL})} p \iff \exists d.\ \gamma(\Gamma) \vdash_{\Sigma(\mathrm{DL})} d : (\mathsf{T}\ p)$.

2.2 The Encoding of $\mathcal{S}^a_{\mathrm{ND}}(\mathrm{DL})$: the Signature $\Sigma^a(\mathrm{DL})$

The new problematic issues is that of encoding proof rules. In fact, in the underlying theory there is no direct way of enforcing on a premise the condition that it is a theorem (i.e. that it depends on no assumptions) or, more generally, that a formula depends only on a given set of assumptions. The solution we give exploits again the possibility provided by the Logical Frameworks of considering locally quantified premises, i.e. general judgments in the terminology of Martin-Löf.

The basic judgment of $\Sigma^a(\mathrm{DL})$ is $\mathsf{U} : \mathsf{P} \to \mathsf{W} \to \mathsf{Prop}$ where W is a set with *no* constructors. Elements of W will be called *worlds* for suggestive reasons. We can now define a new signature for $\mathcal{S}_{\mathrm{ND}}(\mathrm{DL})$, namely $\Sigma_w(\mathrm{DL})$, whose rules are obtained from the corresponding rules of $\Sigma(\mathrm{DL})$ by just replacing T with U, and quantifying universally over the extra parameter; e.g.,

$$\supset\text{-I} : \prod_{p,q:\mathsf{P}} \prod_{w:\mathsf{W}} ((\mathsf{U}\ w\ p) \to (\mathsf{U}\ w\ q)) \to (\mathsf{U}\ w\ (p \supset q))$$

The CONVER rule can now be adequately encoded as follows:

$$\textsc{Conver} : \prod_{A:\mathsf{Te}\to\mathsf{P}} \prod_{c:\mathsf{C}} \prod_{t:\mathsf{Te}} \prod_{w:\mathsf{W}} \left(\prod_{w':\mathsf{W}} \prod_{x:\mathsf{X}} (\mathsf{U}\ w'\ (A\ t)) \to (\mathsf{isnotin}\ x\ \mathsf{P}\ \forall A) \to (\mathsf{isnotin}\ x\ \mathsf{C}\ c) \right.$$
$$\left. \to (\mathsf{U}\ w'\ (p\ (\mathsf{succ}\ (\mathsf{isld}\ x)))) \to (\mathsf{U}\ w'\ (\langle c\rangle\,(A\ (\mathsf{isld}\ x)))) \right) \to (\mathsf{U}\ w\ (\langle c^*\rangle\,(p\ 0)))$$

The idea behind the use of the extra parameter is that in making an assumption, we are forced to assume the existence of a world, say w, and to instantiate the judgment also on w. This judgment then appears as an hypothesis on w. Hence, deriving as premise a judgment, which is universally quantified with respect to W, amounts to estabilishing the judgment for a generic world on which no assumptions are made, i.e. on no assumptions. This simple encoding of the proof rule $[\cdot]$-I illustrates the point:

$$[\cdot]\text{-I} : \prod_{p:\mathsf{P}} \prod_{c:\mathsf{C}} \left(\prod_{w:\mathsf{W}} (\mathsf{U}\ w\ p) \right) \to \prod_{w:\mathsf{W}} (\mathsf{U}\ w\ [c]\,p)$$

$$\text{Ass}\ \frac{}{\Gamma \vdash \{p[t/x]\}x := t\{p\}} \qquad \text{Cons}\ \frac{\Gamma_1, p \vdash p_1 \quad \Gamma_2 \vdash \{p_1\}c\{q_1\} \quad q_1 \vdash q}{\Gamma_1, \Gamma_2 \vdash \{p\}c\{q\}}$$

$$\text{If}\ \frac{\Gamma_1 \vdash \{p \wedge b\}c_1\{q\} \quad \Gamma_2 \vdash \{p \wedge \neg b\}c_2\{q\}}{\Gamma_1, \Gamma_2 \vdash \{p\}\textbf{if } b \textbf{ then } c_1 \textbf{ else } c_2\{q\}} \qquad \text{While}\ \frac{\vdash \{p \wedge b\}c\{p\}}{\vdash \{p\}\textbf{while } b \textbf{ do } c\{p \wedge \neg b\}}$$

$$\text{Or}\ \frac{\Gamma \vdash \{p\}c_1\{q\} \quad \Gamma \vdash \{p\}c_2\{q\}}{\Gamma \vdash \{p\}c_1 + c_2\{q\}} \qquad \text{Comp}\ \frac{\Gamma_1 \vdash \{p\}c_1\{r\} \quad \vdash \{r\}c_2\{q\}}{\Gamma_1 \vdash \{p\}c_1; c_2\{q\}}$$

$$\text{While\_Termin}\ \frac{\vdash p(n+1) \supset b \quad \Gamma \vdash [p(n+1)]c[p(n)] \quad \vdash p(0) \supset \neg b}{\Gamma \vdash [p(n)]\textbf{while } b \textbf{ do } c[p(0)]}\ n \notin \mathrm{FV}(c)$$

Fig. 8. The rules of the system $\mathcal{S}_{\mathrm{ND}}(\mathrm{HL})$.

This idea, suitably generalized to take care of infinite sets of premises, can be used also to encode Scott's rule:

$$\mathsf{Sc}: \prod_{G:\mathsf{nat}\to\mathsf{P}} \prod_{p:\mathsf{P}} \prod_{c:\mathsf{C}} \left(\prod_{w:\mathsf{W}} \left(\prod_{n:\mathsf{nat}} (\mathsf{U}\ w\ (G\ n)) \right) \to (\mathsf{U}\ w\ p) \right) \to \prod_{w:\mathsf{W}} \left(\prod_{n:\mathsf{nat}} (\mathsf{U}\ w\ [c]\,(G\ n)) \right) \to (\mathsf{U}\ w\ [c]\,p)$$

This is a general methodology which allows to encode adequately arbitrary proper sequent-like rules. For lack of space we do not discuss adequacy formally; see [20, 12] for more details.

3 Derivation of Truth Hoare Logic

In this section we outline the derivation in Coq of the rules of a ND-style system for representing the truth CR for Hoare Logic $\Sigma(\mathrm{DL})$. The truth CR for Hoare Logic can be obtained from Definition 1 by istantiating the appropriate parameters, which appear in App.A.

For lack of space we cannot elaborate on the different CR's for Hoare Logic and on the formal systems for representing them. The area of truth CR's and ND-style systems for Hoare Logic is almost unexplored (see [11, 20]). Even the system in [3] is sound only wrt the validity CR. There are various possibilities of defining ND-style systems for Hoare Logic utilizing the *non-interference* judgements of [24]. Interesting systems, which successfully scale up to languages with procedures, arise also if we take seriously reasoning under assumptions. Such are conceptually appealing in that they connect naturally to the language of DL. We expect them to be practically significant. Here we consider the system $\mathcal{S}_{\mathrm{ND}}(\mathrm{HL})$, appearing in Fig.8, which is sound and complete for the truth CR.

Proposition 6. *The partial correctness rules of* $\mathcal{S}_{\mathrm{ND}}(\mathrm{HL})$ *are derivable in* $\mathcal{S}_{\mathrm{ND}}(\mathrm{DL}) \cup \{\mathrm{Sc}\}$; *the rule* While_Termin *is derivable in* $\mathcal{S}^{a}_{\mathrm{ND}}(\mathrm{DL}) \cup \{\mathrm{Sc}\}$.

Proof. (Sketch) We examine only the case of While (Fig.8). Recall that **while** b **do** $c \stackrel{\text{def}}{=} (b?; c)^*; \neg b?$, and suppose that $\pi_h : \vdash p \wedge b \supset [c]\,p$. Then, for all

$n \in \mathrm{N}, p \vdash [b?; c]^n\, p$, where $\pi_0 = p \vdash p$ and π_{n+1} is defined inductively:[3]

$$\dfrac{\dfrac{\dfrac{\begin{array}{c}(p)_2\\ \pi_n\\ {[b?;c]^n\, p}\end{array} \qquad \dfrac{\dfrac{p\;(b)_1}{p \wedge b} \quad \begin{array}{c}\emptyset\\ \pi_h\\ p \wedge b \supset [c]\,p\end{array}}{[c]\,p}}{[c]\,[b?;c]^n\, p}\,(2);\dagger}{[b?]\,[c]\,[b?;c]^n\, p}\,(1)}{[b?;c]\,[b?;c]^n\, p}$$

where † is an application of Sc for $\Gamma = \{p\}$. Then, the following derivation is a proof of WHILE in $\mathcal{S}_{\mathrm{ND}}(\mathrm{DL})$.

$$\dfrac{\dfrac{\dfrac{\dfrac{(p)_2\;(\neg b)_3}{p \wedge \neg b}}{[\neg b?]\,(p \wedge \neg b)}\,(3) \qquad \dfrac{\left\{\begin{array}{c|c}\begin{array}{c}(p)_1\\ \pi_n\\ {[b?;c]^n\, p}\end{array} & n \in \mathrm{N}\end{array}\right\}}{[(b?;c)^*]\,p}\,\dagger}{[(b?;c)^*]\,[\neg b?]\,(p \wedge \neg b)}\,(2);\ddagger}{\dfrac{[(b?;c)^*;\neg b?]\,(p \wedge \neg b)}{p \supset [(b?;c)^*;\neg b?]\,(p \wedge \neg b)}\,(1)}$$

where †, ‡ are sound applications of $*$-I and Sc respectively. □

The use of Sc is not essential, since this rule is admissible. However, the derivation of $\mathcal{S}_{\mathrm{ND}}(\mathrm{HL})$ is much easier if we assume Sc as an explicit rule of our system. In fact, due to the rules with discharged hypotheses, Coq does not allow for an inductive definition of the truth judgment U. Hence, we cannot reason inductively on proofs and derive in the system the admissibily of Sc.

The formal counterpart to Prop.6 has been carried out in Coq quite easily in the signature $\Sigma_w(\mathrm{DL}) \cup \{\mathrm{Sc}\}$.

4 Comparison with Related Work

To our knowledge, there is no published ND-style proof system for Dynamic Logic. Our approach was inspired by some unpublished notes by Colin Stirling [25], where a ND-style system for Deterministic Dynamic Logic is sketched. Stirling's fundamental idea is to "divorce the notion of free occurrence of a variable from that of substitution". The system deals with assertions of the form $p\theta$, where θ is called an *(explicit) substitution*: $\theta ::= \varepsilon \mid (^{t}_{x}\theta)$. A prefix of the form $^{t_1}_{x_1} \ldots ^{t_n}_{x_n}$ represents a sequence of "delayed" substitutions. Substitutions are not performed until the formula on which they are applied is command-free. This idea is inspiring but it is clearly impractical. $\mathcal{S}_{\mathrm{ND}}(\mathrm{DL})$ retains something of this idea, while it overcomes the "explicit substitution" problem in the assignment rules,

[3] The display of derivations is slightly non-standard but should be self explicatory.

by taking full advantage of assumptions, i.e. distributing the substitution in the proof context. Of course, this is sound only with respect to the truth consequence relation. The technique of treating substitutions by means of sets of assumptions has been introduced by Burstall and Honsell [4] and fully exploited in [19] in the context of encoding Natural Operational Semantics of programming languages in Type Theories.

A number of interesting issues arise if we compare the proof development environments generated by the signatures $\Sigma(\mathrm{DL})$ and $\Sigma_w(\mathrm{DL})$, to two remarkable examples of mechanized environments for program logics: the *Karlsruhe Interactive Verifier* (KIV) [10, 23] system and the implementation of Hoare Logic in the Cambridge HOL [6].

The KIV system is a tactical theorem prover based on (Deterministic) Dynamic Logic which realizes an environment for the development of verified software. In the tradition of the Edinburgh LCF, KIV provides a metalanguage which can be used for representing both the logic as well as the tactics and strategies for proof search and proof management. KIV is an Hilbert-style proof system: as in [7, 15], Dynamic Logic is axiomatised by means of several axioms and few rules. User-defined strategies and tactics make this unnatural calculus more user-friendly. The intended consequence relation of KIV is that of validity, not that of truth. As a consequence of this, KIV does not enjoy the Deduction Theorem ("$\Gamma, p_1 \vdash p_2 \iff \Gamma \vdash p_1 \supset p_2$" fails), which on the contrary is built in the system $\mathcal{S}_{\mathrm{ND}}(\mathrm{DL})$ which deals with "truth". Both KIV and the encodings of $\mathcal{S}_{\mathrm{ND}}(\mathrm{DL})$ represent the infinitary rule by means of a quantification over naturals, but while in the KIV system the quantification is at the level of the logic, in our approach it is at the meta-level (at the level of Coq). This makes our encoding closer in spirit to the original proof system. Furthermore, the higher order features of Coq provide "metavariables" for free: we can quantify over programs and carry out "schematic" proofs which can be reused.

The Hilbert-style proof system $\mathcal{S}_{\mathrm{H}}(\mathrm{HL})$ for Hoare Logic, implemented in the Cambridge HOL, among other aspects features a very interesting treatment of program variables: they are represented by objects of type *string*. This encoding provides naturally an infinite set of variables, different from one other, without the need of supplementary assumptions. This technique could be used to simplify our treatment of identifiers. However we still need the judgments isin, isnotin, to deal with, e.g., variables quantified locally to assumptions.

5 Final Remarks and Directions for Future Work

Pragmatics. Although the systems presented in this paper are quite powerful and rather natural, the proof development environments Coq-generated by their encodings are probably not yet effectively usable on large case studies. A serious pragmatic problem is that we have to duplicate at the level of the object logic (i.e. P), a lot of the machinery already present in Coq, and hence we cannot take full advantage of built-in tactics and strategies. However, it is still open whether it is possible to extend the formula-as-types paradigm to boxed formulæ of Dynamic Logic, or to explain them away using HOL constructs.

A possible pragmatic improvement of our approach would be that of automatizing derivations connected to side-condition judgments such as isin, isnotin, BF which are deterministically syntax-driven. This could be done using a logic programming language like Elf [21], or defining suitable tactics.

Systems of Dynamic Logic over other data types, beyond PA, should be investigated.

Finitary vs. Infinitary systems. Our systems are essentially infinitary, since we are interested in strongly complete representations of $\models$. It would be interesting to investigate the power of *finitary* proof systems. For instance, we could replace the *-I rule by the finitary *invariance rule*:

$$\overset{*}{f}\text{-I}\ \frac{\Gamma \vdash p \quad p \vdash [c]\,p}{\Gamma \vdash [c^*]\,p}$$

The system $\mathcal{S}_{\rm ND}{}^f(\text{DL}) \stackrel{\text{def}}{=} \mathcal{S}_{\rm ND}(\text{DL}) \setminus \{^*\text{-I}\} \cup \{\overset{*}{f}\text{-I}\}$ is incomplete, since it does not allow to derive the fundamental axiom of iteration ([15, Theor.3(7)]), i.e. $\not\vdash_{\mathcal{S}_{\rm ND}{}^f(\text{DL})} [c^*]\,p \supset [c]\,[c^*]\,p$. However, $\mathcal{S}_{\rm ND}{}^f(\text{DL}) \cup \{[c^*]\,p \supset [c]\,[c^*]\,p\}$ is strongly complete with respect to $\models \cap(\mathcal{P}_{<\omega}(\mathbb{P}) \times \mathbb{P})$.

Equivalences of Programs. An interesting application of the proof editor generated from the signature $\Sigma(\text{DL})$ using Coq is the possibility of proving formally the equivalences of programs. Following Meyer and Halpern [17], two programs $c, d \in \mathbb{C}$ are *equivalent* ($[\![c]\!] = [\![d]\!]$) if $\forall \mathcal{M} : [\![c]\!]_{\mathcal{M}} = [\![d]\!]_{\mathcal{M}}$. In other words, there is no model in which we can distinguish between the two programs. The encodings of $\mathcal{S}_{\rm ND}(\text{DL})$ could be particularly suited for *computer-assisted* proofs of equivalence of programs, since they naturally provide metalogical facilities such as quantifications on predicates (i.e. second-order quantifications) and proofs by induction on the structure of predicates.

Arithmetical Completeness. Completeness of Dynamic and Hoare Logics is usually discussed in terms of *arithmetical* (or *expressive*) models and *arithmetical* (*Cook's*) completeness [1, 8, 15]. A Hilbert-style system $\mathcal{S}_{\rm H}$ is Cook complete w.r.t. a class A of arithmetical models if $\forall \mathcal{M} \in A, \forall p : (\models_{\mathcal{M}} p \Rightarrow \text{Th}(\mathcal{M}) \vdash_{\mathcal{S}_{\rm H}} p)$, where $\text{Th}(\mathcal{M})$ denotes the collection of all command-free formulæ valid in the model $\mathcal{M}$. This means that completeness w.r.t. a particular model $\mathcal{M}$ is achieved by adding to the system *all* the first order properties of *that* model. This is different from our completeness results (Th.2, 3), where no extra axioms are needed. Indeed, the whole first order theory of N can be derived by $\mathcal{S}^a_{\rm ND}(\text{DL})$, due to the power of the infinitary rule *-I. On the other hand, Theorem 3 holds only for the special case of the standard model of arithmetic. If we want to give a natural deduction formulation of systems such as those of [1, 8, 15], we need to introduce an auxiliary unary predicate symbol, *isnat*, whose intended meaning is the set of standard integers (see [8, p.29]). In this case, the CONVER rule has to be modified as follows:

$$\text{CONVER}\ \frac{\emptyset \vdash (\mathit{isnat}(x) \wedge p_x^{x+1}) \supset \langle c\rangle\, p \quad \Gamma \vdash \mathit{isnat}(t) \supset p_x^t}{\Gamma \vdash \langle c^*\rangle\, p_x^0}\ x \notin \text{FV}(c)$$

A Syntax and Semantics of DL

Syntax and Semantics of PA. The language $\mathcal{L}(\text{PA})$ of Peano Arithmetic is defined as follows:

Identifiers	$\mathbb{X} : x ::= i_0 \mid i_1 \mid i_2 \mid i_3 \mid \ldots$
Terms	$\mathbb{T} : t ::= 0 \mid 1 \mid x \mid t + t \mid t * t$
Propositional Formulæ	$\mathbb{B} : b ::= t = t \mid t < t \mid b \supset b \mid b \wedge b \mid \neg b$
Formulæ	$\mathbb{P} : p ::= t = t \mid t < t \mid p \supset p \mid p \wedge p \mid \neg p \mid \forall x p$

The interpretation functions $\mathcal{T}[\![\cdot]\!]_{\mathcal{M}} : \mathbb{T} \to \mathbb{S}_{\mathcal{M}} \to \mathbb{D}_{\mathcal{M}}$, $\mathcal{F}[\![\cdot]\!]_{\mathcal{M}} : \mathbb{P} \to \mathcal{P}(\mathbb{S}_{\mathcal{M}})$ are defined in the style of Denotational Semantics over a model $\mathcal{M} = \langle D_{\mathcal{M}}, 0, 1, +, \cdot, \ldots \rangle$ for Peano Arithmetic. $\mathbb{S}_{\mathcal{M}} = \mathbb{X} \to D_{\mathcal{M}}$ is the domain of *environments* and it is ranged over by s, s_1, s_2. These two semantic functions are defined on the syntax of phrases in the obvious way. The semantics of formulæ is naturally extended to sets of formulæ: i.e. if $\Gamma \subseteq \mathbb{F}$ then $\mathcal{F}[\![\Gamma]\!]_{\mathcal{M}} \stackrel{\text{def}}{=} \bigcap_{p \in \Gamma} \mathcal{F}[\![p]\!]_{\mathcal{M}}$. Then, the usual Tarski's interpretation relation $\models_{\mathcal{M}} \subset \mathbb{S}_{\mathcal{M}} \times \mathbb{F}$ amounts to membership, i.e. $s \models_{\mathcal{M}} p \iff s \in \mathcal{F}[\![p]\!]_{\mathcal{M}}$.

Syntax and Semantics of Hoare Logic. Since in this paper we focus on PA, we give the definition of HL and DL only with respect to the first order theory of PA. The language $\mathcal{L}(\text{HL})$ is defined by restricting $\mathcal{L}(\text{PA})$ to quantifier-free formulæ and by introducing the new syntactic domains of *nondeterministic* **while** *programs*, *Hoare triples* and *assertions* as follows:

Non-deterministic While Programs	$\mathbb{W} : c ::= x := t \mid c; c \mid c + c$ $\mid$ **if** b **then** c **else** c $\mid$ **while** b **do** c	Hoare Triples Assertions	$\mathbb{H} : h ::= \{p\}C\{q\}$ $\mathbb{A} : a ::= p \mid h$

The semantics of Hoare Logic is given by naturally extending the interpretation to the new syntactic domains, i.e. $\mathcal{W}[\![\cdot]\!]_{\mathcal{M}} : \mathbb{W} \to \mathbb{S}_{\mathcal{M}} \to \mathcal{P}(\mathbb{S}_{\mathcal{M}})$, $\mathcal{H}[\![\cdot]\!]_{\mathcal{M}} : \mathbb{H} \to \mathcal{P}(\mathbb{S}_{\mathcal{M}})$, $\mathcal{A}[\![\cdot]\!]_{\mathcal{M}} : \mathbb{A} \to \mathcal{P}(\mathbb{S}_{\mathcal{M}})$. Hoare triples are interpreted as usual: $\mathcal{H}[\![\{p\}c\{q\}]\!]_{\mathcal{M}} \stackrel{\text{def}}{=} \{s \in \mathbb{S}_{\mathcal{M}} \mid s \in \mathcal{F}[\![p]\!]_{\mathcal{M}} \Rightarrow \mathcal{C}[\![c]\!]_{\mathcal{M}} s \subseteq \mathcal{F}[\![q]\!]_{\mathcal{M}}\}$.

Syntax and Semantics of DL. The language $\mathcal{L}(\text{DL})$ is defined by extending $\mathcal{L}(\text{PA})$ with a new formula constructor, $[\cdot]\cdot$, and by introducing the new syntactic domains, of *command-free formulæ* and of *regular programs*, as follows:

Command-free Formulæ	$\mathbb{F} : p ::= t = t \mid t < t \mid p \supset p \mid p \wedge p \mid \neg p \mid \forall x p$
Regular Programs	$\mathbb{C} : c ::= x := t \mid b? \mid c; c \mid c + c \mid c^*$
Formulæ	$\mathbb{P} : p ::= t = t \mid t < t \mid p \supset p \mid p \wedge p \mid \neg p \mid \forall x p \mid [c] p$

The semantics of DL is given by extending the interpretation to the domain $\mathbb{C}$. The function $\mathcal{C}[\![\cdot]\!]_{\mathcal{M}} : \mathbb{C} \to \mathbb{S}_{\mathcal{M}} \to \mathcal{P}(\mathbb{S}_{\mathcal{M}})$ is defined as follows (the composition operator is extended in the obvious way):

$$\mathcal{C}[\![x := t]\!]_{\mathcal{M}} \stackrel{\text{def}}{=} \lambda s.\{s[x \mapsto \mathcal{T}[\![t]\!]_{\mathcal{M}} s]\}$$

$$\mathcal{C}[\![c_1; c_2]\!] \stackrel{\text{def}}{=} \mathcal{C}[\![c_2]\!] \circ \mathcal{C}[\![c_1]\!] \qquad \mathcal{C}[\![c^*]\!] \stackrel{\text{def}}{=} \lambda s. \cup_{n \in \omega} \mathcal{C}[\![c]\!]^n s$$

$$\mathcal{C}[\![b?]\!] \stackrel{\text{def}}{=} \lambda s.\mathcal{F}[\![b]\!] \cap \{s\} \qquad \mathcal{C}[\![c_1 + c_2]\!] \stackrel{\text{def}}{=} \mathcal{C}[\![c_1]\!] \cup \mathcal{C}[\![c_2]\!]$$

Finally, the semantics of formulæ $\mathcal{F}[\![\cdot]\!]_{\mathcal{M}} : \mathbb{P} \to \mathcal{P}(\mathbb{S}_{\mathcal{M}})$ is extended in the extra case, by putting $\mathcal{F}[\![[c]\, p]\!]_{\mathcal{M}} \stackrel{\text{def}}{=} \{s \in \mathbb{S}_{\mathcal{M}} \mid \mathcal{C}[\![c]\!] s \subseteq \mathcal{F}[\![p]\!]\}$.

B Consequence Relations

Definition 7 CR. A *(single-conclusioned) Consequence Relation* on a set $\mathbb{F}$ of formulæ is a binary relation $\models \subseteq \mathcal{P}(\mathbb{F}) \times \mathbb{F}$ which satisfies the following properties:
Reflexivity: $p \models p$ for every formula $p \in \mathbb{F}$;
Transitivity, or "Cut": if $\Gamma_1 \models p$ and $\Gamma_2, p \models q$ then $\Gamma_1, \Gamma_2 \models p$.
Γ is called the *antecedent* or *set of assumptions*, and p is the *conclusion.* □

This definition differs from the one of [2] only in that we allow for possibly infinite sets of assumptions and exactly one conclusion.

CR's are usually defined in a completely abstract way, e.g. using semantics. Therefore, definitions of CR's are usually *ineffective*, and cannot be used in practice in order to establish consequences of formulæ from sets of assumptions. In order to use a CR one needs a *concrete* way of representing it. This is achieved by defining a *formal proof system* (called "calculus"). The objects of a formal proof systems usually are not simply formulæ of the logic, but can be formal representations of consequentiality (i.e. *sequents*, or even proofs of formulæ).

Definition 8 FPS. A *Formal Proof System* $\mathcal{S}$, or *Calculus*, for a CR $\models$ on a set $\mathbb{F}$ of formulæ is a method for defining a CR on $\mathbb{F}$, denoted by $\vdash_{\mathcal{S}}$.

1. $\vdash_{\mathcal{S}}$ is *sound (faithful)* if $\vdash_{\mathcal{S}} \subseteq \models$, that is, $\forall \Gamma, p : \Gamma \vdash_{\mathcal{S}} p \rightarrow \Gamma \models p$;
2. $\vdash_{\mathcal{S}}$ is *complete* if $\forall p : \emptyset \models p \rightarrow \emptyset \vdash_{\mathcal{S}} p$;
3. $\vdash_{\mathcal{S}}$ is *strongly complete* if $\models \subseteq \vdash_{\mathcal{S}}$, that is, $\forall \Gamma, p : \Gamma \models p \rightarrow \Gamma \vdash_{\mathcal{S}} p$. □

The assertion "$\Gamma \vdash_{\mathcal{S}} A$" is called *a (formal) sequent* and is read "A is derivable from Γ (in the system $\mathcal{S}$)."

Following [2], rules in ND-style calculi are general schemata of the form

$$\forall \Gamma_1, \ldots, \Gamma_n \frac{\Gamma_1, \Delta_1 \vdash p_1 \ldots \Gamma_n, \Delta_n \vdash p_n}{\Gamma_1, \ldots, \Gamma_n \vdash p} C$$

where C is a possible *side condition*, that is a restriction (max. level 2, in the terminology of [2]) on the applicability of the schemata.

References

1. K. R. Apt. Ten years of Hoare's logic: A survey — part I. *ACM Transactions on Programming Languages and Syms*, 3(4):431–483, Oct. 1981.
2. A. Avron. Simple consequence relations. *Inform. Comput.*, 92:105–139, Jan. 1991.
3. A. Avron, F. Honsell, I. A. Mason, and R. Pollack. Using Typed Lambda Calculus to implement formal systems on a machine. *Journal of Automated Reasoning*, 9:309–354, 1992.
4. R. Burstall and F. Honsell. Operational semantics in a natural deduction setting. In Huet and Plotkin [13], pages 185–214.
5. T. Coquand and G. Huet. The calculus of constructions. *Information and Control*, 76:95–120, 1988.
6. M. J. C. Gordon. Mechanizing program logics in higher order logic. In P. A. Subrahmanyam and G. Birtwistle, editors, *Current Trends in Hardware Verification and Automated Theorem Prover*, pages 387–439. Springer-Verlag, 1989.

7. D. Harel. *First-Order Dynamic Logic.* No.68 in LNCS. Springer-Verlag, 1979.
8. D. Harel. Dynamic logic. In D. Gabbay and F. Guenthner, editors, *Handbook of Philosophical Logic,* volume II, pages 497–604. Reidel, 1984.
9. R. Harper, F. Honsell, and G. Plotkin. A framework for defining logics. *J. ACM,* 40(1):143–184, Jan. 1993.
10. M. Heisel, W. Reif, and W. Stephan. A dynamic logic for program verification. In A. Meyer and M. Taitslin, editors, *Proc. of LFCS (Logic at Botik),* number 363 in Lecture Notes in Computer Science, pages 134–145. Springer-Verlag, 1989.
11. F. Honsell and M. Miculan. Encoding program logics in type theories. In J. Despeyroux, editor, *Deliverables of the TYPES Workshop* Proving Properties of Programming Languages, Sophia-Antipolis, Sept. 1993.
12. F. Honsell, M. Miculan, and C. Paravano. Encoding modal logics in Logical Frameworks. To appear, 1996.
13. G. Huet and G. Plotkin, editors. *Logical Frameworks.* CUP, June 1990.
14. INRIA, Rocquencourt. *The Coq Proof Assistant Reference Manual,* July 1995.
15. D. Kozen and J. Tiuryn. Logics of Programs. In J. van Leeuwen, editor, *Handbook of Theoretical Computer Science,* volume B, pages 789–840. North Holland, 1990.
16. Z. Luo, R. Pollack, and P. Taylor. *How to use LEGO (A Preliminary User's Manual).* Department of Computer Science, University of Edinburgh, Oct. 1989.
17. A. R. Meyer and J. Y. Halpern. Axiomatic definition of programming languages: A theoretical assessment. *J. ACM,* 29(2):555–576, Apr. 1982.
18. S. Michaylov and F. Pfenning. Natural Semantics and some of its Meta-Theory in Elf. In L.-H. Eriksson, L. Hallnäs, and P. Schroeder-Heister, editors, *Proceedings of the Second International Workshop on Extensions of Logic Programming,* number 596 in LNAI, pages 299–344, Stockolm, Sweden, Jan. 1991. Springer-Verlag.
19. M. Miculan. The expressive power of structural operational semantics with explicit assumptions. In H. Barendregt and T. Nipkow, editors, *Proceedings of TYPES'93,* number 806 in LNCS, pages 292–320. Springer-Verlag, 1994.
20. M. Miculan. *Encoding Logical Theories of Programs.* PhD thesis, Università di Pisa, 1997. To appear.
21. F. Pfenning. Elf: A language for logic definition and verified metaprogramming. In *Fourth Annual Symposium on Logic in Computer Science,* pages 313–322. IEEE, June 1989.
22. D. Prawitz. *Natural Deduction.* Almqvist & Wiksell, Stockholm, 1965.
23. W. Reif. The KIV system: Systematic construction of verified software. In D. Kapur, editor, *Proc. of CADE-11,* number 607 in Lecture Notes in Computer Science, pages 753–757. Springer-Verlag, 1992.
24. J. C. Reynolds. Syntactic control of interference. In *Conference Record of the Fifth Annual ACM Symposium on Principles of Programming Languages,* pages 39–46, Tucson, Oct. 1978. The Association for Computing Machinery.
25. C. Stirling. Logics for While Programs: Algorithmic/Dynamic Logics. Unpublished notes, 1985.
26. C. Stirling. Modal and Temporal Logics. In S. Abramsky, D. Gabbay, and T. Maibaum, editors, *Handbook of Logic in Computer Science,* volume 2, pages 477–563. Oxford University Press, 1992.
27. B. Werner. *Une théorie des constructions inductives.* PhD thesis, Université Paris 7, 1994.

An Algorithm for Checking Incomplete Proof Objects in Type Theory with Localization and Unification

Lena Magnusson

INRIA Sophia Antipolis

Lena.Magnusson@sophia.inria.fr

Abstract

A modular *type/proof checking algorithm* for incomplete proof objects is presented, where an incomplete proof object is represented as a term containing *placeholders* denoting the unfinished parts of the proof. The algorithm is designed for Martin-Löf's type theory with explicit substitutions, but the general ideas can be adapted to similar theories. It is the kernel of the proof editor ALF.

The algorithm handles incomplete terms in such a way that the type checking problem is reduced to a unification problem, i.e., the problem of finding instantiations to the placeholders in the term. Placeholders are represented together with their expected type and local context. We show that checking the correctness of instantiations can be optimized by *localization*, which means that it is enough to check an instantiation of a placeholder relative to its expected type and local context.

We present a unification algorithm which partially solves the unification problem, and we apply this unification algorithm to the type checking algorithm. We show that the type checking algorithm with unification and with localization is sound, and hence when all placeholders in a proof object are filled in and checked locally, we do not have to type check the global proof object again to ensure type correctness. Finally, we define two basic operations on a type checking problem, *insert* and *delete*, and we show that the basic tactics "intro" and "refine" can be defined in terms of *insert*. The *delete* operation provides a local undo mechanism which is unique for ALF. The operations are shown to preserve the validity of a partially solved type checking problem, and hence the proof editing facilities are proved to construct valid proofs.

1 Introduction

The basic idea behind type theory for developing proofs and programs is the Curry-Howard isomorphism between propositions and types [How80], as well as proofs and terms. If the typing relation is decidable, we can construct algorithms which check if a given proof object (term) is a proof of a given proposition (type). However, if our aim is to have systems in which we develop proofs and programs interactively, then we need a notion of *incomplete proof objects* to reflect the state of an unfinished proof/program. In this paper we will describe the basic ideas of an algorithm for type checking incomplete proof objects, which is a simplification of the algorithm used in the proof editor ALF ([MN94], [Mag95]). It is designed for Martin-Löf's type theory, but we believe the ideas can be carried over to other similar languages.

The algorithm has the following properties:

- The algorithm is a conservative extension of a type checking algorithm for complete terms, so the same algorithm can be used for both purposes.
- The algorithm is compositional, which means for instance that we can alter the unification strategy in the algorithm simply by replacing the unification function.
- The basic tactics "intro" and "refine" used in most proof assistants, can *both* be described in terms of replacing a placeholder (representing an unfinished part) by an incomplete term. The correctness of such a tactic is established by type checking.
- The type checking algorithm can be optimized by *localization*, which means that if we instantiate a placeholder in a term, it is enough to type check the instantiation relative to the placeholder's expected type in its local context. Hence, we need not type check the entire instantiated term again after each refinement.

The paper is organized in the following way; we start by outlining the type checking algorithm, and show the corresponding correctness result. Next, we describe localization and the correctness of this optimization. Then we will see how type checking can be improved by unification, and that localization can be applied here as well. Finally, we will see how the algorithm is applied in proof refinement.

2 Type checking

The basic idea of the type checking algorithm is that it transforms the type checking problem in three steps: from a type checking problem to a list of type equations which in turn is transformed into a list of term equations. The last transformation tries to solve or simplify the term equations. The point of these transformations is that when the term to be checked is complete (contains no placeholders), and if equality of terms in the underlying calculus is decidable, then we have a decision procedure for the type checking problem. If, on the other hand, the term is *incomplete* (contains placeholders), then the equations contain placeholders and we are faced with the problem of finding instantiations of these placeholders such that the equations are satisfied. Hence, in the latter case, we have a (generalized) unification problem. The type checking algorithm TC is thus a composition of the transformations GTE (Generate Type Equations), $TSimple$ (*Simplify Type equations*) and $Simple$ (*Simplify term equations*), that is

$$TC = Simple \circ TSimple \circ GTE.$$

The first two transformations are shown in the picture below:

Type checking: **Type equations:** **Term equations:**

$$e : \alpha \; \Gamma \quad \overset{GTE}{\Longrightarrow} \quad \begin{vmatrix} \alpha_1 = \alpha_1' \; \Gamma_1 \\ \vdots \\ ?_m : \alpha_m \; \Gamma_m \\ \vdots \\ \alpha_n = \alpha_n' \; \Gamma_n \end{vmatrix} \quad \begin{matrix} \overset{TConv}{\longrightarrow} \\ \\ \longrightarrow \\ \\ \overset{TConv}{\longrightarrow} \end{matrix} \quad \left. \begin{pmatrix} \begin{bmatrix} a_1^1 = b_1^1 : \alpha_1^1 \; \Gamma_1^1 \\ \vdots \\ a_1^k = b_1^k : \alpha_1^k \; \Gamma_1^k \end{bmatrix} \\ \vdots \\ ?_m : \alpha_m \; \Gamma_m \\ \vdots \\ \begin{bmatrix} a_n^1 = b_n^1 : \alpha_n^1 \; \Gamma_n^1 \\ \vdots \\ a_n^p = b_n^p : \alpha_n^p \; \Gamma_n^p \end{bmatrix} \end{pmatrix} \right\} \begin{matrix} \text{typed} \\ \text{unification} \\ \text{problem} \end{matrix}$$

$$\dashrightarrow \; T Simple$$
$$\dashrightarrow \; GE = TSimple \circ GTE$$

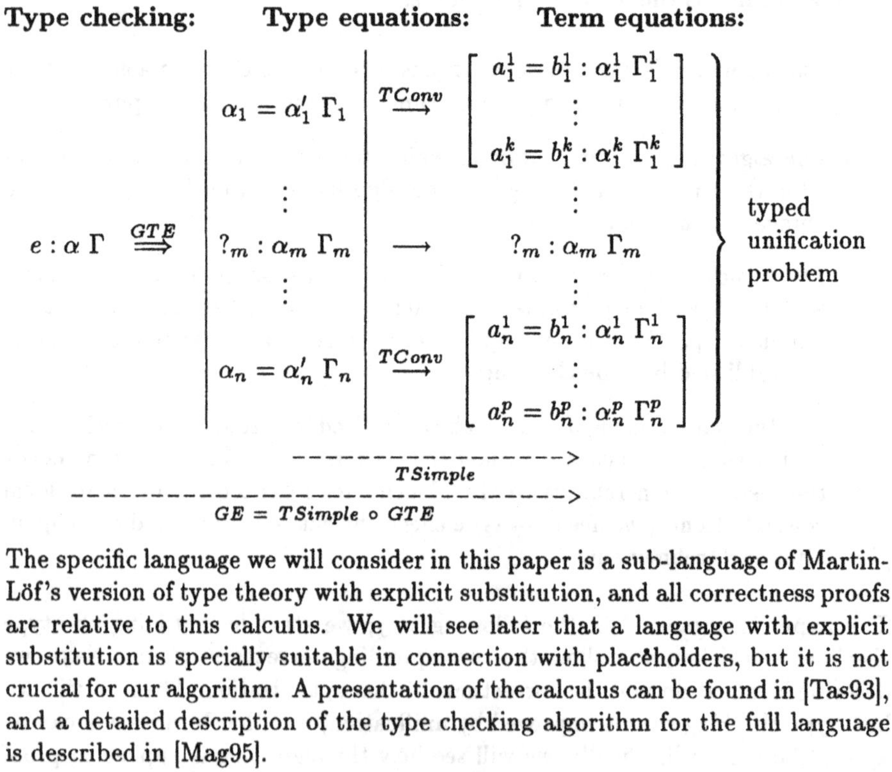

The specific language we will consider in this paper is a sub-language of Martin-Löf's version of type theory with explicit substitution, and all correctness proofs are relative to this calculus. We will see later that a language with explicit substitution is specially suitable in connection with placeholders, but it is not crucial for our algorithm. A presentation of the calculus can be found in [Tas93], and a detailed description of the type checking algorithm for the full language is described in [Mag95].

Martin-Löf's substitution calculus is a typed λ-calculus with dependent types and explicit substitution. We will *extend* the term language with a new syntactic category: the placeholders, which denotes "holes" intended to be filled in. We will call a term *complete* if it contains no placeholders. A (possibly incomplete) term e is defined by the following grammar

$$e ::= x \mid [x]e \mid (ee) \mid e\gamma \mid ?_n$$

where x is a variable, $[x]e$ denotes abstraction, (ee) application, $e\gamma$ the substitution γ applied to the term e and $?_n$ denotes a placeholder. Application is sometimes written $f(e)$, and $f(e_1, \ldots, e_n)$ is an abbreviation of $((\cdots(fe_1)\cdots)e_n)$. A type α is either *Set* or of the form *El*(A), where A is a term, or it is a function type $\alpha \to [x]\beta$ which denotes the function from α to the family $[x]\beta$ and where β may depend on x, or it is a family β applied to a term a (denoted βa). We will write $\alpha \to \beta$ as an abbreviation when β does not depend on x. Also, *El* is omitted when it is clear from the context that the type is meant rather than the term. Finally, a context is a list of variable bindings, where the type of a variable may depend on the previous variables.

2.1 Type checking incomplete terms

Since we have actually extended the language with placeholders, we must also give typing rules for placeholders to be able to type check terms in our extended language.

Placeholders and their declarations

A placeholder represents possibly an *open term*, and therefore a placeholder has a local context, where the variables it may depend on occur. The openness is important, since a placeholder may occur under a λ-binder, and we may use the bound variable in completing the placeholder. When viewed as an unfinished proof, the variables in the local context correspond to the assumptions we may use in completing the proof. Thus a placeholder declaration is the following:

Definition 2.1 A *placeholder declaration* is a placeholder $?_j$ together with an expected (incomplete) type α_j and an expected (incomplete) context Γ_j. We will write $?_j : \alpha_j \ \Gamma_j$ to denote a placeholder declaration.

The local context of a placeholder reflects its *scope*, and thus we can forget about the actual occurrence of the placeholder since the placeholder declaration contains all information about the placeholder we need. This fact is the basis of localization.

What does it mean for a placeholder to be type correct? Assume we have the following declaration

(1) $?_1 : \alpha_1 \ \Gamma_1$

and we want to type check

(2) $?_1 : \beta \ \Delta$.

A sufficient requirement is that the types α_1 and β are the same and that Γ_1 and Δ are the same, but we may weaken the requirement on the local contexts. It is enough that Γ_1 is a *sub-context* of Δ, since any term which is a solution in the smaller context is clearly a solution in the extended context, due to the thinning rule. Neither can the term contain any variables that are not in the smaller context, since then it would not be a solution. Therefore, we get the following two requirements:

(1) $\Gamma_1 \preceq \Delta$
(2) $\alpha_1 =_\beta \Delta$.

2.2 The algorithms

The standard typing rules of the calculus, are shown to the left in figure 1 below. In addition, there are rules for the sub-context relation, which are needed when placeholders are type checked. This kind of presentation of the typing relation is not directly suitable for a type checking algorithm, since it is not syntax-directed. The thinning rule and type-conversion rule are (almost) always applicable. Moreover, for the calculus considered here, the application rule is also problematic since, given an application, we can not always compute the type of the function (see [Sal88]).

On the right-hand side of the table we have defined another formulation of the typing relation, that we call *guarded typing*, denoted by

$$\Gamma \vdash_{tc} a : \alpha \ [\![\xi]\!]$$

where ξ is a guard. A guard consists of equations and declarations of the placeholders which occur in a. The idea is the following: If a is complete, then the typing relation $\Gamma \vdash a : \alpha$ holds iff the equations in the guard hold, and if a contains placeholders, then exactly the same instantiations validate the typing relation and the guard. The rules are purely structural on the term, and thus directly suitable for an algorithm. The type conversion rule is eliminated and distributed in the other rules where the type equality appears in the guards. Thinning can not always be avoided: to type check terms like $[x]([x]x)$ we need a thinning rule. Therefore our guarded typing rules will have a kind of thinning rule built in, but only where it is *necessary* and it chooses the *largest possible sub-context*. Hence, the unusual abstraction rule:

$$\frac{[\Delta, x : \alpha] \vdash_{tc} b : \beta x \ [\![\xi]\!]}{\Gamma \vdash_{tc} [x]b : \alpha \rightarrow \beta \ [\![\xi]\!]} \quad \begin{matrix} (\Delta = Sub(x, \Gamma)) \\ (\ FV(\alpha, \beta) \subseteq \Delta\ ) \end{matrix}$$

where $Sub(x, \Gamma)$ computes the largest sub-context of Γ *not containing* x. If $x \notin \Gamma$, we get the ordinary abstraction rule, since then $\Delta = \Gamma$ and the side conditions can be dropped.

The correctness of this rule relies on the following lemma where part (*iii*) is almost the inverse of the thinning rule:

Lemma 2.2 *Let x be a variable and Ψ be a valid context. Then*

(*i*)	*$Sub(x, \Psi)$ is a valid context*
(*ii*)	$Sub(x, \Psi) \preceq \Psi$
(*iii*)	*If $\Gamma \vdash a : \alpha$, $\Delta \preceq \Gamma$ and $FV(a, \alpha) \subseteq \Delta$ then $\Delta \vdash a : \alpha$.*

Typing rule	Guarded Typing rule
$\dfrac{}{\Gamma \vdash x : \alpha}\ (x : \alpha \in \Gamma)$	$\dfrac{}{\Gamma \vdash_{tc} x : \alpha\ [\![\alpha = \alpha'\ \Gamma]\!]}\ (x : \alpha' \in \Gamma)$
$\dfrac{[\Gamma, x : \alpha] \vdash b : \alpha'}{\Gamma \vdash [x]b : \alpha \to [x]\alpha'}$	$\dfrac{[\Delta, x : \alpha] \vdash_{tc} b : \beta x\ [\![\xi]\!]}{\Gamma \vdash_{tc} [x]b : \alpha \to \beta\ [\![\xi]\!]}\ \begin{matrix}(\Delta = Sub(x, \Gamma)) \\ (FV(\alpha, \beta) \subseteq \Delta)\end{matrix}$
$\dfrac{\Gamma \vdash f : \alpha \to \beta \quad \Gamma \vdash a : \alpha}{\Gamma \vdash (fa) : \beta a}$	$\dfrac{\Gamma \vdash_{tc} f : \alpha' \to \beta\ [\![\xi_1]\!] \quad \Gamma \vdash_{tc} a : \alpha'\ [\![\xi_2]\!]}{\Gamma \vdash_{tc} (fa) : \alpha\ [\![\xi_1, \xi_2, \beta a = \alpha\ \Gamma]\!]}$
$\dfrac{\Gamma \vdash a : \alpha \quad \Gamma \vdash \alpha = \alpha' : Type}{\Gamma \vdash a : \alpha'}$	–
$\dfrac{\Gamma \vdash a : \alpha \quad \Gamma \preceq \Delta}{\Delta \vdash a : \alpha}$	–
–	$\dfrac{}{\Gamma \vdash_{tc} ?_n : \alpha\ [\![?_n : \alpha_n\ \Gamma_n]\!]}\ (?_n \text{ new})$
–	$\dfrac{\Gamma_n \leq \Gamma\ [\![\xi']\!]}{\Gamma \vdash_{tc} ?_n : \alpha\ [\![\xi', \alpha = \alpha_n\ \Gamma]\!]}\ (?_n : \alpha_n\ \Gamma_n)$
$\dfrac{\Delta : Context}{[\,] \preceq \Delta}$	$\dfrac{}{[\,] \leq \Gamma\ [\![\,]\!]}$
$\dfrac{\Gamma \preceq \Delta \quad \Delta \vdash x : \alpha}{[\Gamma, x : \alpha] \preceq \Delta}$	$\dfrac{\Delta \leq \Gamma\ [\![\xi']\!]}{[\Delta, x : \alpha] \leq \Gamma\ [\![\xi', \alpha = \alpha'\ \Gamma]\!]}\ (x : \alpha' \in \Gamma)$

Figure 1: Typing rules

There is another solution to this problem in [Pol93], which is to distinguish between free and bound variables, and where the previously bound variable is renamed to a fresh parameter in the abstraction rule.

Finally, we do not solve the problem with the application rule, but instead we restrict the type checkable terms to the β-normal terms, and in this special case the type of the function-part in an application can always be computed. For reasons similar to the reasons why a β-redex can not be type checked, a term applied to a substitution can not either except in special cases, so for simplicity, we have left out the substitution rule completely.

The rest of the rules in figure 1 concern placeholders and the sub-context relation. The first placeholder rule states that if the placeholder is not previously declared, then it is simply declared to have the expected type and context. If it is known already, it is checked in the way explained in section 2.1. The guarded rules for sub-contexts are simply optimizations of the corresponding calculus rules.

Before we state the result of this section, relating the two systems of rules, we will have to make some definitions.

Definition 2.3 An *instantiation* σ is a set of assignments of terms to placeholders. We will call σ *complete* if all assigned terms in σ are complete.

Definition 2.4 We will say that a complete guard ξ *holds* if all equations in ξ are provable.

Proposition 2.5 *Let* Γ *be a valid context and* α *a valid type in* Γ. *Let* σ *be a complete instantiation assigning all placeholders in a term* e. *Then*
$\Gamma \vdash e\sigma : \alpha$ *if and only if* $\Gamma \vdash_{tc} e\sigma : \alpha \ [\![\xi]\!]$ *and* ξ *holds.*

Proof: By induction on the length of the respective derivations. □

2.2.1 The three transformations

The first transformation in the type checking algorithm, the generation of type equations, computes the guard in our guarded typing rules. The rules are designed to be syntax-directed and deterministic in the type checking direction, and the guard guarantees the type correctness. Thus, we have an algorithm
$GTE(a, \alpha, \Gamma) \Rightarrow \xi$
corresponding to the guarded typing rules. To be more exact, we have the following definitions:

Definition 2.6 A *typed unification problem* (TUP) is a list of incomplete equations together with a placeholder declaration for every placeholder occuring in the equations or in the expected types and contexts of the placeholder declarations. We will call a TUP with type (term) equations a type-TUP (term-TUP), respectively.

Definition 2.7 We will say that a TUP ξ *ensures* a statement if for instantiation σ such that $\xi\sigma$ holds, the corresponding statement the instantiation has been performed, is valid.

Hence, the *GTE* algorithm takes a type checking problem as input and produces a type-TUP as result.

The next transformation, the *TSimple* algorithm, takes as input a type-TUP and simplifies each equation with a type conversion algorithm. The result is a term-TUP since the type conversion produces term equations from one type equation. The type conversion proceeds by reducing both types to head-normal form, and then checks the reduced types structurally. The transformation relies on the following facts: (1) The reduction of a type to head-normal form terminates, and (2) if two types are provably equal then they have the same outermost head-normal form.

The final transformation, *Simple*, follows exactly the same structure as *TSimple*, but it simplifies term equations with the conversion algorithm instead. Thus it takes a term-TUP and produces a new term-TUP with simplified equations.

The conversion algorithm proceeds analogously to the type conversion, and is similar to the one described in [Coq91]. However, since the terms will be reduced, we need to know that the terms are well-typed to have termination. Since the terms may contain placeholders, we will have to relate the well-typedness to possible instantiations. Therefore we need a notion of well-formedness of the TUPs, relating the well-typedness of an equation to the previous equations and placeholder declarations. We will say that a TUP ξ extended by an equation is well-formed if any instantiation which satisfies ξ guarantees that the equation is well-typed.

Analogously as for type conversion we need the corresponding lemmas for terms to show correctness and termination of the conversion algorithm. We have not proved normalization for our reduction algorithm, so we will relate some of our results to these assumptions.

Reduction of incomplete terms will not change any termination conditions, since the reduction is simply suspended as soon as a placeholder appears as the head of the redex, that is if the head-redex is of the form $?_n$, $?_n\gamma$ or $?_n(a_1, \ldots, a_n)$. Once the placeholder is further instantiated, the reduction can continue until a new suspension or until the term is in head-normal form.

2.3 Correctness

When we talk about correctness of an incomplete proof term, we will always have to add the proviso that *there exists type correct instantiations of the remaining placeholders such that the equations hold.*

To show the correctness of the type checking algorithm, there are two properties we are interested in for the transformations:

(U) the set of unifiers (= valid instantiations) is preserved, and

(W) the well-formedness is preserved.

The (U) property is clear, since we want to solve the original problem, and the

(W) property is needed for conversion of terms as explained above.

We have the properties of the three transformations:

Proposition 2.8 (GTE-correct) *Let Γ be a valid context and α a valid type in Γ. If a is a β-normal term, then we have the following for any instantiation σ:*

(U) $\Gamma \vdash a\sigma : \alpha$ if and only if $GTE(a\sigma, \alpha, \Gamma) \Rightarrow \xi$ and ξ holds.
(W) ξ is well-formed.

Proof: (U) follows directly from proposition 2.5, and (W) is proved by induction on the derivation of $\Gamma \vdash_{tc} a\sigma : \alpha$ $[\![\xi]\!]$. □

Proposition 2.9 ($TSimple$-correct)
Let ξ be a well-formed type-TUP. If $TSimple\,\xi \Rightarrow C$ then
(U) $\xi\sigma$ holds iff $C\sigma$ holds, for any instantiation σ
(W) C is well-formed.

Proof: By induction on the length of C, using a lemma that type conversion preserves the set of unifiers and the well-formedness. □

Proposition 2.10 ($Simple$-correct)
Let C be a well-formed term-TUP. If $Simple\,C \Rightarrow C'$ then
(U) $C\sigma$ holds iff $C'\sigma$ holds, for any instantiation σ
(W) C' is well-formed.

Proof: By induction on the length of C, using a lemma that conversion preserves the set of unifiers and the well-formedness. □

Finally, we can state the main theorem, the correctness of type checking:

Theorem 1 (TC correct) *Let α be a type in context Γ, let a be a β-normal term, and σ an instantiation.*

If $TC(a\sigma, \alpha, \Gamma) \Rightarrow [\,]$, then $\Gamma \vdash a\sigma : \alpha$,

and assuming normalization of the head-normal reduction we also have

if $\Gamma \vdash a\sigma : \alpha$, then $TC(a\sigma, \alpha, \Gamma) \Rightarrow [\,]$

Proof: Follows directly from GTE-, $TSimple$- and $Simple$-correct. □

3 Localization

In this section we will describe an optimization of the previous type checking algorithm, which we call localization. The idea is that when we have an incomplete term which is type checked, and we want to instantiate a placeholder occurring in that term, it is enough to type check the instantiation relative to the placeholder's expected type and local context. This means that we can forget about the actual occurrence of the placeholder in the term, and we need no global type checking of the instantiated term, as illustrated on the left in the picture below:

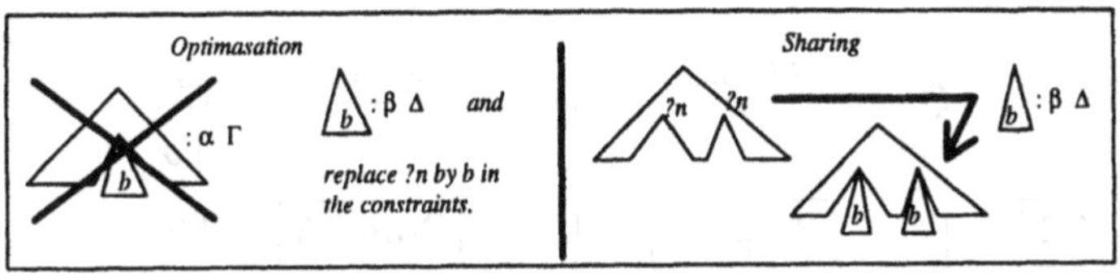

If the local type checking succeeds, we can safely replace the placeholder by the instantiation, and the local type checking guarantees the global correctness of the term. Clearly, the larger the term is, the greater the gain will be. Moreover, even if there are several occurrences of the placeholder in the term, they share the same placeholder declaration and are therefore checked only once.

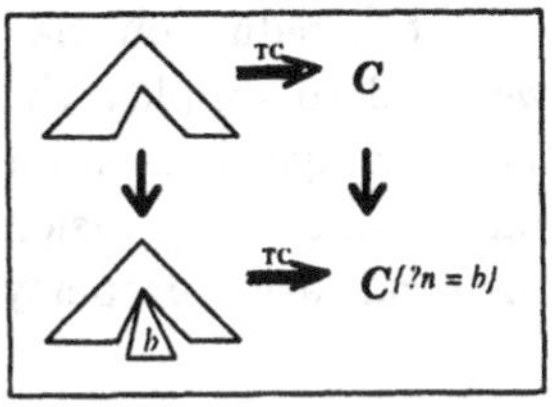

The reason we can localize the type checking, is that we get *exactly the same TUP* if we first instantiate a placeholder in the global term and then type check globally, as if we first type check the global term and then type check the instantiation locally relative to the placeholder declaration and replace the placeholder by its instantiation everywhere in the TUP. That is, type checking commutes with placeholder instantiations as is illustrated in the figure to the left.

The localization is feasible since we treat placeholders as "real open terms" and they carry their own local context which correspond to their respective scope in the global term. In the next section we will show the correctness of localization.

3.1 Correctness of localization

The main result of localization is the following:

If $TC(e,\alpha,\Gamma) \Rightarrow \mathcal{C}$, then $\Gamma \vdash e\sigma : \alpha$ iff $\mathcal{C}\sigma$ holds.

and it relies on the property that type checking commutes with instantiations, that is if $TC(e,\alpha,\Gamma) \Rightarrow \mathcal{C}$, then $TC(e\sigma,\alpha,\Gamma) \Rightarrow \mathcal{C}\sigma$, where $\mathcal{C}\{?_n{:=}b\}$ means the following: The placeholder declaration of $?_n$ in $\mathcal{C}$ is replaced by the result of type checking b with $?_n$'s expected type and local context, and in all equations and other placeholder declarations $?_n$ is replaced by b everywhere.

For technical reasons we must require the placeholders in the type checked term to be distinct, which is not a severe restriction at this point, to get the completeness result of localization. The soundness holds in either case. However, in the next section when we will define type checking with unification, we will only get soundness results since the unified terms do not satisfy this requirement.

What we need to show is that the third property, the localization property

(*L*) the transformation commutes with refinement instantiations,
is satisfied by the three transformations, that is we will show that the following diagram commutes:

$$\begin{array}{ccccccc}
e:\alpha\ \Gamma & \overset{GTE}{\Longrightarrow} & \xi & \overset{TSimple}{\longrightarrow} & C & \overset{Simple}{\longrightarrow} & C' \\
 & & & & & & \downarrow\sigma \\
\downarrow\sigma & \boxed{\text{Prop 3.1}} & \downarrow\sigma & \boxed{\text{Prop 3.2}} & \downarrow\sigma & \boxed{\text{Prop 3.3}} & C'\sigma \\
 & & & & & & \downarrow Simple_p \\
e\sigma:\alpha\ \Gamma & \overset{GTE}{\Longrightarrow} & \xi\sigma & \overset{TSimple}{\longrightarrow} & C\sigma & \overset{Simple}{\longrightarrow} & C''
\end{array}$$

Note that the last transformation, the simplification of term equations, does not commute directly with the application of instantiations, so we have to simplify again. The reason is that the equations in C' may not be possible to simplify further since a placeholder is blocking the reduction, but the reduction may proceed when the instantiation is performed. Thus we need to simplify the equations again after the instantiation. We get exactly the same equations either way, since the reduction of terms is completely deterministic, and a suspension simply postpones the reduction temporarily. We have the localization property for the three transformations:

Proposition 3.1 *Let Γ be a context and α a valid type in Γ. Let a be a β-normal term in which all placeholders are distinct. For any instantiation σ we have*

(*L*) *If* $GTE(a,\alpha,\Gamma) \Rightarrow \xi$ *then* (*L*) $GTE(e\sigma,\alpha,\Gamma) \Rightarrow \xi\sigma$

Proof: By induction on the length of derivation of $GTE(a,\alpha,\Gamma) \Rightarrow \xi$. □

Proposition 3.2 *For any instantiation σ:*

(*L*) *If* $TSimple(\xi) \Rightarrow C$, *then* $TSimple(\xi\sigma) \Rightarrow C\sigma$,

Proof: Induction on the length of $\xi\sigma$, using a lemma that type conversion respects localization. □

Proposition 3.3 *For any instantiation σ:*

(*L*) *If* $C \overset{S}{\longrightarrow} C'$ *and* $C\sigma \overset{S}{\longrightarrow} C''$, *then* $C'\sigma \overset{S}{\longrightarrow} C''$.

Proof: Induction on the length of C, using a lemma that conversion respects localization. □

Due to the compositional nature of the type checking algorithm, we get the main results simply by composing the corresponding result of the included algorithms:

Theorem 2 (*TC* with localization correct) *Let Γ be a context and α a valid type in Γ. Let a be a β-normal term. Assume $TC(a,\alpha,\Gamma) \Rightarrow C$. If all place-*

holders in a are distinct, we have

$\Gamma \vdash a\sigma : \alpha$ *if and only if* $C\sigma$ *holds*

In general, if the placeholders in a are not necessarily distinct, we get the soundness direction

if $C\sigma$ *holds, then* $\Gamma \vdash a\sigma : \alpha$

Proof: Follows directly by 3.1, 3.2, 3.3, 2.8, 2.9, and 2.10. □

4 Unification

Since the result of type checking is a unification problem, we can improve the algorithm by applying a unification algorithm to the result which will try to find instantiations to the placeholders. It is a higher order dependently-typed unification problem. There are complete unification algorithms for the $\lambda\Pi$-calculus, (see [Ell89], [Pym92], generalizations of [Hue75]). However, these algorithms do not apply here since they require the unknowns in the unification problem to be well-typed in a context. Thus, the equations depend on the types of the unknowns, but not the converse, which may be the case here. In [Dow93], a semi-decision unification algorithm for the type systems of Barendregt's cube ([Bar91]) is suggested. However, since the main application of our type checking algorithm is in an interactive proof editor, we prefer a simpler but safe algorithm that always terminates within a reasonable amount of time.

What we will present here is a first-order, open unification algorithm, that is solutions may contain placeholders. It is implemented in ALF. Simple equations are solved and the difficult ones are left as constraints, restricting future instantiations of the placeholders. There is no search involved so it will instantiate a placeholder automatically only when there is a unique solution.

4.1 Placeholders, explicit substitution and unification

The substitution calculus is not crucial for the work presented here, but the presence of explicit substitutions improves reduction of incomplete terms, that is "how far" the incomplete term could be reduced. For example, assume we want to reduce the term

$([x]f(x, ?_1))a$

where a is the argument to the function $[x]f(x, ?_1)$ which contains a placeholder $?_1$. Since $?_1$ is within the scope of the binder x, it may depend on x. Without explicit substitutions this term could not be reduced any further, but with explicit substitution we can safely reduce the term to

$f(a, ?_1\{x{:=}a\})$.

Since the unification algorithm finds instantiations by simplifying equations, and equations can only be simplified when they are reduced to the same form, further reduced terms may lead to more instantiations.

4.2 The unification algorithm

The goal of unification is to find instantiations of the placeholders such that the equations in the unification problem hold. Since our algorithm is first-order, it can only proceed when there is a solved equation in the list, that is an equation

$?_n = b : \beta \;\; \Delta.$

If the unification problem is well-formed, we know there is a declaration

$?_n : \alpha_n \;\; \Gamma_n$

defining the expected type and context of $?_n$. Clearly, to satisfy the equation $?_n$ must be b, but the question is whether b is type correct with respect to $?_n$'s declaration, that is if b is of type α_n in context Γ_n. We believe it is possible to prove that a well-formed unification problem ensures that

(1) α_n and β are equal types, and

(2) $\Gamma_n \preceq \Delta$,

but recalling lemma 2.2(*iii*), (1) and (2) are not sufficient to ensure type correctness since we do not know if $FV(b) \subseteq \Gamma_n$. Hence, we would still have to check the scope of a unification instantiation to guarantee soundness, as is shown in the following example:

Ex. Assume we have a relation $R : (A; A)Set$ over some set A, which is reflexive *refl* : $(x{:}A)R(x, x)$. We will try to show from these assumptions that $\exists x.\forall y.R(x, y)$. (This should not be possible since the statement is false for an arbitrary set only assuming reflexivity.) The statement can be represented by the unification problem with two placeholder declarations: $?x : A \;\; []$ and $?_1 : R(?x, y) \;\; [y : A]$. Now, if we try to solve the problem by using the reflexivity rule, we need to type check *refl*$(?_2) : R(?x, y) \;\; [y : A]$, which yields the new problem

$$\left[\begin{array}{c} ?x : A \;\; [] \\ ?_2 : A \;\; [y : A] \\ R(?x, y) = R(?_2, ?_2) \;\; [y : A] \end{array}\right] \xrightarrow{Unify} \left\{\begin{array}{c} ?x = y \\ ?_2 = y \end{array}\right\} \leftarrow \text{out of scope}$$

Here we can see that all equations are well-typed, but y is not in $?x$'s local context, so the solution is out of scope, and the type checking should fail.

Therefore, until we have proved (1) and (2), we must type check the unified term, which requires a notion of well-formedness on the unification problem in order to justify the precondition of the type checking algorithm. This is the reason why (so far) we will only have soundness and not completeness of the type checking algorithm with unification.

Since the detailed explanation of the unification algorithm is rather technical, we will only give an overview here (the details can be found in [Mag95]). The algorithm takes a unification problem and the result is a *partially solved unification problem* which is a pair of the remaining unification problem and an instantiation which contains the solved equations. The idea of the algorithm is simple: Find a solved equation in the unification problem and type check the instantiation. If this succeeds, move the instantiation to the solved part and apply it everywhere. Simplify the equations and call unification again. Thus, we have the following picture

$$\langle C,\{\}\rangle \overset{Unify}{\longrightarrow} \langle C_1,\theta_1\rangle \overset{Unify}{\longrightarrow} \cdots \overset{Unify}{\longrightarrow} \langle C_n,\theta_n\rangle$$

and the algorithm stops when there are no more solved equations in C_n.

We have the (U)-property of the unification algorithm, in the direction stating that the found solution is a correct solution, and that the algorithm preserves well-formedness (the (W)-property). These results are rather long and technical and therefore omitted.

Now we can define the type checking algorithm (with unification) for incomplete terms which is $TCU = \overset{Unify}{\longrightarrow_*} \circ TC$, and state the corresponding soundness property that the unification computes correct instantiations to the type checking problem: if $TCU(e,\alpha,\Gamma) \Rightarrow \langle C,\theta\rangle$ then C ensures $\Gamma \vdash e\theta : \alpha$.

4.3 Soundness of type checking with unification and localization

Just as for the type checking without unification, we want to apply our optimization of localizing the type checking. That is, we want to apply the instantiation directly to the unified problem, and not to the entire term, and then try to unify again. However, we do not have that an instantiation commutes with the unification. The reason is that after instantiation, we may have several solved equations concerning the same placeholder, and a different choice of equation gives a different new unification problem. However, we can still show soundness of the algorithm with unification and localization, by considering the sets of solutions rather than the actual problems. We need to define an order on unification problems:

Definition 4.1 We will say that $\langle C,\theta\rangle \geq_{\mathcal{U}} \langle C',\theta'\rangle$ if there is a θ'' such that

(i) $\theta' = \theta \circ \theta''$

(ii) $\mathcal{U}(C\theta'') \supseteq \mathcal{U}(C')$

where $\mathcal{U}(C)$ denotes the set of unifiers of C.

since ordinary set inclusion is not sufficient for our purposes. The intuition is that when $X \geq_{\mathcal{U}} Y$ then Y is essentially the same unification problem, but it may be more solved than X. What we are interested in finally, is that the unified problem gives correct solutions, so we have the following lemma:

Lemma 4.2 *If* $\langle C,\theta\rangle \geq_{\mathcal{U}} \langle C',\theta'\rangle$, *then* $\mathcal{U}\langle C,\theta\rangle \supseteq \mathcal{U}\langle C',\theta'\rangle$.

We also need to show that unification respects the order on unification problems, which is the following proposition:

Proposition 4.3 *Let $\langle C,\theta\rangle$ be a well-formed unification problem.*
If $\langle C,\theta\rangle \overset{Unify}{\longrightarrow}_* \langle C',\theta'\rangle$, then $\langle C,\theta\rangle \geq_{\mathcal{U}} \langle C',\theta'\rangle$.

Proof: By induction on the number of steps of $\overset{Unify}{\longrightarrow}$. □

The final proposition states that the order is preserved under application of an instantiation, that is it corresponds to the (L)-property of the earlier transformations:

Proposition 4.4 *Let $\langle C,\theta\rangle$ and $\langle C',\theta'\rangle$ be well-formed unification problems, and let σ be a instantiation such that $Dom(\sigma) \neq Dom(\theta)$.*
If $\langle C,\theta\rangle \geq_{\mathcal{U}} \langle C',\theta'\rangle$, then $\langle C\sigma,\theta\sigma\rangle \geq_{\mathcal{U}} \langle C'\sigma,\theta'\sigma\rangle$

Proof: Follows from the definition of $\geq_{\mathcal{U}}$, that well-formedness is preserved under instantiation, and theorem 2. □

The soundness result of localization is illustrated in the following picture, since with localization the algorithm takes the rightmost path and without the leftmost path, and the bottom line then states that the solutions found are correct ($=_{\mathcal{U}}$ denotes the same set of unifiers).

$$\begin{array}{ccccccc}
e:\alpha\ \Gamma & =_{\mathcal{U}} & \langle C,\{\}\rangle & \geq_{\mathcal{U}} & \langle C_0,\theta\rangle & & \\
\downarrow\sigma & \boxed{\text{Th. 2}} & \downarrow\sigma & \boxed{\text{Prop 4.4}} & \downarrow\sigma & & \\
e\sigma:\alpha\ \Gamma & =_{\mathcal{U}} & \langle C\sigma,\{\}\rangle & \geq_{\mathcal{U}} & \langle C_0\sigma,\theta\sigma\rangle & \geq_{\mathcal{U}} & \langle C_1,\theta_1\rangle \\
\downarrow\rho & \boxed{\text{Th. 2}} & \downarrow\rho & \boxed{\text{Prop 4.4}} & \downarrow\rho & \boxed{\text{Prop 4.4}} & \downarrow\rho \\
e\sigma\rho:\alpha\ \Gamma & =_{\mathcal{U}} & \langle C\sigma\rho,\{\}\rangle & \geq_{\mathcal{U}} & \langle C_0\sigma\rho,\theta\sigma\rho\rangle & \geq_{\mathcal{U}} & \langle C_1\rho,\theta_1\rho\rangle
\end{array}$$

The formal result that type checking with unification and localization is sound is the following:

Theorem 3 (*TCU* with localization sound) *Let α and Γ be a valid type and context, respectively, and let e be a term. Then we have the following soundness result:*

$$\text{If } TCU(e,\alpha,\Gamma) \Rightarrow \langle C,\theta\rangle \text{ then } C \text{ ensures } \Gamma \vdash e\theta : \alpha$$

Proof: Follows by propositions 4.3, 4.4 and theorem 2, since $TCU = \overset{Unify}{\longrightarrow}_* \circ TC$.
□

5 Application to proof refinement

In most interactive proof assistants, proof refinement is performed by successively refining a proof by applying tactics to the unfinished parts of the proof. That is with our terminology an incomplete term which is successively refined by giving instantiations to the placeholders in the term.

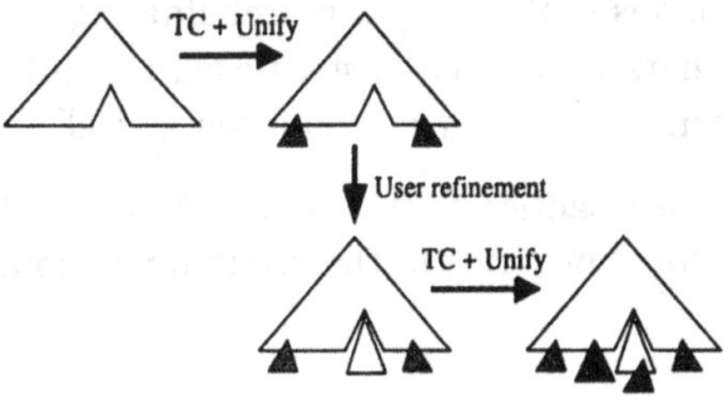

Hence proof refinement is a direct application of our type checking algorithm for incomplete terms, as is illustrated in the figure to the left. The correctness of the incomplete term is ensured by the unification problem we get by type checking the term. The correctness of the refinement is established by type checking the instantiation. Moreover, placeholders may be instantiated automatically by the unification, which is illustrated in the figure by the small grey triangles.

Hence we manipulate an incomplete term (with a type and context) together with a unification problem. We will call this a type checking problem. Naturally we want to benefit from the localization optimization of the type checking algorithm, so we will represent a partially solved type checking problem as a type checking problem together with a partially solved unification problem $\langle C, \theta\rangle$:

$$\langle e : \alpha \;\; \Gamma, \langle C, \theta\rangle\rangle.$$

We will say that the *partially solved type checking problem* $\langle e : \alpha \;\; \Gamma, \langle C, \theta\rangle\rangle$ *is valid* if $\langle C, \theta\rangle$ ensures $\Gamma \vdash e : \alpha$. The point of this representation is two-fold:

(1) We manipulate the unification problem, and *not* the incomplete proof term which tends to be rather large. If an instantiation is accepted, it is checked *locally* and simply updated in the proof term. The correctness is ensured by the new unification problem.

(2) User refinements are updated in the proof term, but unification instantiations are not, since they appear in the partially solved unification problem. This separation of instantiations is the reason we can provide a local undo mechanism which removes any subterm *as well as all its consequences*. The desire for such an operation has been expressed in [TBK92], and it can not be simulated by a state-undo.

5.1 Proof refinement operations

There are only two basic operations on a type checking problem, and from these other can be defined:

insert - replacing a placeholder by an incomplete term, and

delete - replacing a sub-term by a new placeholder.

The insert operation we have already defined, since it is exactly instantiating the placeholder with the term.

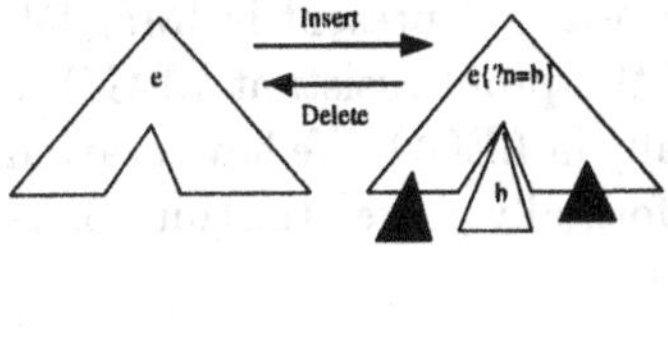

The idea is that the two operations insert and delete should be dual to each other as is illustrated in figure beside. For insert, the placeholder $?n$ in the incomplete term e is replaced by the term b, and for delete the sub-term b is replaced by a placeholder again. The filled triangles illustrate the placeholders which were instantiated by unification, that is the consequences of the term b, and they are removed as well.

We claimed in the introduction that the basic tactics "intro" and "refine" used in most proof assistants could both be defined in terms of the insert operation. This is the case, since we can define

$$intro = insert\ [x]?_1, \text{ and}$$
$$refine\ b = insert\ b(?_1, \ldots, ?_n)$$

where n is the difference in arity between the type of the goal and the type of b, which can always be computed.

The delete operation will "uninstantiate" a sub-term of the incomplete term. It removes the chosen sub-term in the global term and type checks the new global term, which means that all old unification instantiations are removed, and the result of the type checking is the new unification instantiations which exactly corresponds to the consequences of the new global term. It would be possible to localize the delete operation as well, but it would require much more overhead for the insert-operation. Hence, in favor of a faster insert-operation, we abandon localization of the delete-operation.

Finally, we can also show that the operations insert and delete perform valid transformations of a type checking problem:

Theorem 4 *The operations insert and delete preserves the validity of a partially solved type checking problem.*

Proof: Both operations respect the $\geq_{\mathcal{U}}$ relation by proposition 4.4 (for insert) and by proposition 4.3 and theorem 2 (for delete). Hence, we have that the unification problem ensures the type checking problem (by lemma 4.2), which means that the partially solved type checking problem is valid. □

6 Conclusion

We have presented a type checking algorithm for incomplete (and complete) terms, and shown how it can be optimized by localization. All algorithms are shown to be sound. We have seen that the operations used to edit proofs are defined in terms of the two basic operations (insert and delete) on incomplete terms. Hence, proof editing is reduced to type checking incomplete proof objects.

This paper is mainly a summary of the author's thesis work. However, the solution we suggested to handle the thinning rule, was not present in [Mag95]. In [MP93], the type/proof checking algorithm of the proof assistant LEGO is proved correct and the proofs are carried out formally in LEGO. We have started to formalize our proofs in ALF, and so far we have formally proved the soundness of the type checking algorithm for complete terms.

References

[Bar91] H. P. Barendregt. Introduction to Generalized Type Systems. *J. Functional Programming*, 1(2):125–154, April 1991.

[Coq91] Thierry Coquand. An algorithm for testing conversion in type theory. In *Logical Frameworks*. Cambridge University Press, 1991.

[Dow93] Gilles Dowek. A Complete Proof Synthesis Method for the Cube of Type Systems. *Journal of Logic and Computation*, 3(3):287–315, 1993.

[Ell89] Conal M. Elliot. Higher-order unification with dependent function types. In N. Dershowitz, editor, *Proceedings of the 3rd International Conference on Rewriting Techniques and Applications*, pages 121–136, April 1989.

[How80] W. A. Howard. The formulae-as-types notion of construction. In J. P. Seldin and J. R. Hindley, editors, *To H.B. Curry: Essays on Combinatory Logic, Lambda Calculus and Formalism*, pages 479–490. Academic Press, London, 1980.

[Hue75] Gérard Huet. A unification algorithm for typed λ-calculus. *Theoretical Computer Science*, 1(1):27–57, 1975.

[Mag95] Lena Magnusson. *The Implementation of ALF - a Proof Editor based on Martin-Löf's Monomorphic Type Theory with Explicit Substitution.* PhD thesis, Göteborg University and Chalmers University of Technology, January 1995.

[MN94] Lena Magnusson and Bengt Nordström. The ALF proof editor and its proof engine. In *Types for Proofs and Programs*, LNCS, pages 213–237, Nijmegen, 1994. Springer-Verlag.

[MP93] James McKinna and Randy Pollack. Pure type system formalized. In M. Bezem and J.F. Groote, editors, *Proceeding of the International Conference on Typed Lambda Calculi and Applications, TLCA'93*, pages 289–305. Springer-Verlag, LNCS 664, March 1993.

[Pol93] Randy Pollack. Closure under Alpha conversion. In *The Informal Proceeding of the 1993 Workshop on Types for Proofs and Programs*, May 1993.

[Pym92] David Pym. A unification algorithm for the logical framework. Technical Report ECS-LFCS-92-229, University of Edinburgh, August 1992.

[Sal88] Anne Salvesen. Polymorphism and Monomorphism in Martin-Löf's Type Theory. Technical report, Norwegian Computing Center, P.b. 114, Blindern, 0316 Oslo 3, Norway, December 1988.

[Tas93] Alvaro Tasistro. Formulation of Martin-Löf's Theory of Types with Explicit Substitution. Licentiate Thesis, Chalmers University of Technology and University of Göteborg, Sweden, May 1993.

[TBK92] L. Théry, Y. Bertot, and G. Kahn. Real Theorem Provers Deserve Real User-Interfaces. Technical Report 1684, INRIA Sophia-Antipolis, May 1992.

Decidability of All Minimal Models

Vincent Padovani

Université PARIS VII-C.N.R.S
U.R.A. 753
Equipe de Logique Mathématique
2 Place Jussieu - Case 7012
75251 PARIS CEDEX 05 - (FRANCE)
padovani@logique.jussieu.fr

Abstract. We consider a simply typed λ-calculus with constants of ground types, and assume that for one ground type o, there are finitely many constants of type o. We call *minimal model* the quotient by observational equivalence of the set of all closed terms whose type is of terminal subformula o. We show that this model is decidable: all classes of any given type are recursively representable, and observational equivalence on closed terms is a decidable relation. In particular, this result solves the question raised by R.Statman on the decidability of this model in the case of a unique ground type and two constants.

Observational equivalence on simply typed λ-terms is defined as the least binary relation $\|$ including β-equivalence and such that $t : A \to B \| t' : A \to B$ iff for all closed $u : A, u' : A$, if $u : A \| u' : A$ then $(t)u : B \| (t')u' : B$.

Suppose we are dealing with a simply typed λ-calculus with constants which are all of ground type, and assume for one ground type o there are finitely many constants of type o. Then, consider the set of all closed terms whose type is either o or of the form $A_1 \dots A_n \to o$. We call *minimal model* of simply typed λ-calculus the quotient of this set by observational equivalence.

We prove in this paper that this model is decidable *i.e* if we call *type* of a class the type of its elements then there are only finitely many classes of any given type, and there exists a computable function which, given an arbitrary type A, returns a set that contains a unique representative of each class of type A. We prove also that observational equivalence on closed terms is a decidable relation. In particular, this result solves the question raised by R.Statman on the decidability of this model in the case of a unique ground type and two constants. This question can be seen as a simplification of the *Lambda Definability* problem ([9], [10]) which is known to be undecidable ([5]).

The results presented here were found while studying the *Higher Order Matching* problem ([2], [6], [7], [8]) whose decidability is still open. As a corollary of the decidability of all minimal models, we prove also the decidability of a particular case of the higher order matching problem: the problem of solving finite sets of matching equations whose right-members are all constants of ground types.

1 Terms

We quote in this first part the definition of simply typed terms. The reader is assumed to be familiar with the notions of λ-term, α, β-conversions (see [4], [3] or [1]). We shall admit the well-known results of strong normalization and confluence of the β-reduction on simply typed terms.

1.1 Types

We let $\mathcal{F}$ be the set of all formulas of a language consisting of an arbitrary set of constants $\mathcal{O}$ and a binary connective $\rightarrow$:

$\mathcal{O} \subset \mathcal{F}$, and if $A, B \in \mathcal{F}$ then $(A \rightarrow B) \in \mathcal{F}$.

The formula $A = (A_1 \rightarrow (\ldots A_n \rightarrow \mathrm{o})\ldots)$ where $\mathrm{o} \in \mathcal{O}$ will be denoted as $A_1 \ldots A_n \rightarrow \mathrm{o}$. The constant o is called the *terminal subformula* (t.s.f.) of A. We call *order* of A the integer defined by:

if $n = 0$ then Ord $(A) = 1$, else $\mathrm{Ord}(A) = \sup_{i=1}^{n}(\mathrm{Ord}(A_i)) + 1$.

1.2 Simply Typed Terms

Assume that there is given:

- an infinite, countable set of variables, $x, y, z, \ldots$
- an infinite, countable set of constants, $a, b, c \ldots$
- an application from the set of all variables and constants to the set $\mathcal{F}$, mapping each symbol to a formula called its *type*, such that:
  - for each $A \in \mathcal{F}$, there exists an infinite number of variables of type A,
  - all constants are of ground type *i.e.* their types belong to $\mathcal{O}$.

We call *typed variables* all pairs of the form (x, A), written $x : A$, where A is the type of x, and *typed constants* all pairs of the form $a : \mathrm{o}$ where o is the ground type of a. The set of *simply typed terms* is defined as the least set $\mathcal{S}$ satisfying:

0. all typed variables and all typed constants belong to $\mathcal{S}$,
1. if $t : B \in \mathcal{S}$ and if $x : A$ is a typed variable, then $\lambda x\, t : A \rightarrow B \in \mathcal{S}$,
2. if $t : A \rightarrow B, u : A \in \mathcal{S}$ then $(t)u : B \in \mathcal{S}$.

The *context* of a typed term $t : A$ is defined as the set of all free variables and constants of t. We call *order* of $t : A$ the order of A. A *closed* term contains no free variable (*e.g.* a typed constant $a : \mathrm{o}$ is a closed term).

We denote as $\overline{\mathcal{S}}$ the quotient of $\mathcal{S}$ by α-equivalence *i.e.* renamings of bound variables by fresh variables of same type. By convention, elements of $\overline{\mathcal{S}}$ and $\mathcal{S}$ will be called *terms* and $\mathcal{S}$*-terms* respectively. Greek letters shall be used to denote arbitrary $\mathcal{S}$-terms. An $\mathcal{S}$-term τ of the α-class (the term) t will be called *a representative* of t.

2 Minimal Models

2.1 Observational Equivalence

Let t, t' be closed terms of type $A_1 \dots A_n \to o$. Let 0, 1 be distinct constants of type o. We say that t and t' are *observationally equivalent* if and only if for all closed $u_1 : A_1, \dots, u_n : A_n$ whose constants of type o belong to $\{1, 0\}$, $(t)u_1 \dots u_n \equiv_\beta (t')u_1 \dots u_n$[1]. We write $\|$ the relation thus defined.

Lemma 1. *Let t, t' be closed terms of type $A_1 \dots A_n \to o$. Then $t \| t'$ if and only if for all closed $u_1 : A_1, \dots, u_n : A_n$, $(t)u_1 \dots u_n \equiv_\beta (t')u_1 \dots u_n$.*

Proof. Suppose $u_1, \dots, u_n$ closed and such that $(t)u_1 \dots u_n \,\beta\, a$, $(t')u_1 \dots u_n \,\beta\, a'$ with $a \neq a'$. Let 0, 1 be distinct constants of type o. Call v_i the term obtained by the substitution in u_i of 1 for a, 0 for all other constants. Then $(t)v_1 \dots v_n$ is of normal form a or 1 while $(t')v_1 \dots v_n$ is of normal form a' or 0. □

Lemma 2. *$t \| t'$ if and only if for all u of ground type such that $u[t/x]$, $u[t'/x]$ are closed and well-typed, $u[t/x] \equiv_\beta u[t'/x]$.*

Proof. Suppose $t \| t'$ and $u[t/x]$ closed of ground type. We prove $u[t/x] \equiv_\beta u[t'/x]$ by induction on the length of the left-normalization of $u[t/x]$. The only case where we apply the hypothesis on t, t' is $u[t/x] = (t)u_1[t/x] \dots u_n[t/x]$. If $t \,\beta\, t'$ or if $t = \lambda y\, t_0$ then by induction hypothesis $u[t/x] \equiv_\beta (t)u_1[t'/x] \dots u_n[t'/x] = u_0[t'/x]$. By lemma 22 and by hypothesis on t and t', $u_0[t'/x] \equiv_\beta u[t/x]$. □

We denote as $[t : A]$ the class of observational equivalence of $t : A$, letting $App([u : A \to B], [v : A]) = [(u)v : B]$. It follows from lemma 2 that this notion of application of a class to another is well-defined.

2.2 Minimal Models

Let $\mathcal{C}$ be a finite, non-empty set of constants of same ground type o. For all types A of t.s.f. o, we write $\mathcal{T}(A, \mathcal{C})$ the set of all closed terms of type A whose constants of type o belong to $\mathcal{C}$. The quotient set $\mathcal{T}(A, \mathcal{C}) / \|$ is denoted as $\mathcal{M}(A, \mathcal{C})$.

The pair $\mathcal{M}_\mathcal{C} = (\{\mathcal{M}(A, \mathcal{C}) \mid \textit{t.s.f.}(A) = o\}, App)$ will be called a *minimal model* of simply typed λ-calculus. The present paper intends to show that *all minimal models are decidable* *i.e.* we shall prove that:

1. for all pairs $(A, \mathcal{C})$, $\mathcal{M}(A, \mathcal{C})$ is a finite set,
2. there exists a computable function which, given a pair $(A, \mathcal{C})$, returns a complete set of $\|$-representatives for $\mathcal{M}(A, \mathcal{C})$ *i.e.* returns a set that contains a unique representative of each element of $\mathcal{M}(A, \mathcal{C})$
3. $\|$ is a decidable relation.

[1] $\equiv_\beta$ denotes β-equivalence *i.e.* the reflexive and transitive closure of β-reduction.

3 Pure Types

Our first aim is to prove that if all minimal models are decidable in the particular case of $\mathcal{O} = \{o\}$, then all minimal models are decidable in the case where $\mathcal{O}$ is an arbitrary set.

3.1 Pure Forms

Definition 3. We call *pure form* of a type $B = B_1 \dots B_p \to o$ the type A satisfying:

1. if all ground types appearing in B are equal to o then $A = B$,
2. if *t.s.f.*$(B_j) \neq o$ then A is equal to the pure form of $B_1 ... B_{j-1} B_{j+1} ... B_p \to o$.
3. if *t.s.f.*$(B_1) = \dots =$ *t.s.f.*$(B_p) = o$ then $A = A_1 \dots A_p \to o$ where A_j is the pure form of B_j.

Remark. If $B_1 \dots B_p \to o$ is of pure form $A_1 \dots A_n \to o$, then there exists a unique sequence $I = (i_1, \dots, i_n)$ such that $1 \leq i_1 < \dots < i_n \leq n$, B_{i_k} is of pure form A_k and $\forall j \notin I$, *t.s.f.*$(B_j) \neq o$. Consequently, every type has a unique pure form.

Definition 4. We define *Nil* as a set that contains, for each $o \in \mathcal{O}$, a unique constant *nil* of type o. For any type A, we denote as $\lambda.nil : A$ the unique term of type A of the form $\lambda x_1 \dots x_n\ nil$ where $nil \in Nil$.

Definition 5. Let $A = A_1 \dots A_n \to o$. Let $B = B_1 \dots B_p \to o$ be a type of pure form A. Let $I = (i_1, \dots, i_n)$ such that $1 \leq i_1 < \dots < i_n \leq n$ with B_{i_k} of pure form A_k and $\forall j \notin I$, *t.s.f.*$(B_j) \neq o$.

1. (a) for any typed variable $Y : B$, let $Y_B^A = \lambda x_1 \dots \lambda x_n (Y) v_1 \dots v_p : A$ with
$$v_{i_k} = {x_k}_{A_k}^{B_{i_k}} \ (1 \leq k \leq n) \text{ and } v_j = \lambda.nil : B_j \ (j \notin I)$$
   (b) for any typed variable $X : A$, let $X_A^B = \lambda y_1 \dots \lambda y_p (X) w_1 \dots w_n : B$ with
$$w_k = {y_{i_k}}_{B_{i_k}}^{A_k} \ (1 \leq k \leq n).$$
2. (a) for any closed $t : B$, let $t_B^A : A = Y_B^A[t/Y]$,
   (b) for any closed $u : A$, let $u_A^B : B = X_A^B[u/X]$.

Lemma 6. Let B be a type of pure form A.

1. *For all closed $t : B$, $t \parallel (t_B^A)_A^B$.*
2. *For all closed $u : B$, $u \parallel (u_A^B)_B^A$.*

Proof. Suppose A, B and I are defined as they are in definition 5. We prove (1) and (2) by induction on B. If $p = 0$ *i.e.* if $B = \circ$ then $A = \circ$ and for all closed $t : \circ$, $u : \circ$, $t = t^{\circ}_{\circ}$, and $u = u^{\circ}_{\circ}$. Suppose $p > 0$.

1. Let $t : B$, $v_1 : B_1, \ldots, v_p : B_p$ be closed terms. Let $\overline{v}_{i_k} = (v_{i_k}{}^{A_k}_{B_{i_k}})^{B_{i_k}}_{A_k}$ $(1 \leq k \leq n)$. Let $\overline{v}_j = \lambda.nil : B_j$ $(j \notin I)$.
   - by definition, $(t)\overline{v}_1 \ldots \overline{v}_p \equiv_\beta ((t^A_B)^B_A)v_1 \ldots v_p$,
   - by induction hypothesis, for each $k \in [1 \ldots n]$, $\overline{v}_{i_k} \parallel v_{i_k}$ therefore, for all M such that $(\lambda z M)v_{i_k} : \circ$ be closed and well typed, $(\lambda z\, M)v_{i_k} \equiv_\beta (\lambda z\, M)\overline{v}_{i_k}$,
   - if $j \notin I$ then $t.s.f.(B_j) \neq \circ$ therefore, for all M such that $(\lambda z\, M)v_j : \circ$ be closed and well-typed, z cannot be free in the normal form of M and $(\lambda z\, M)v_j \equiv_\beta (\lambda z\, M)\overline{v}_j$.

   Thus $(t)v_1 \ldots v_p \equiv_\beta (t)\overline{v}_1 \ldots \overline{v}_p \equiv_\beta ((t^A_B)^B_A)v_1 \ldots v_p$. Since $v_1, \ldots, v_p$ are arbitrary, $t \parallel (t^A_B)^B_A$.

2. Let $u : A$, $w_1 : A_1, \ldots, w_n : A_n$ be closed terms. Let $\overline{w}_k = (w_k{}^{B_{i_k}}_{A_k})^{A_k}_{B_{i_k}}$ $(1 \leq k \leq n)$.
   - by definition, $(u)\overline{w}_1 \ldots \overline{w}_n \equiv_\beta ((u^B_A)^A_B)w_1 \ldots w_n$,
   - by induction hypothesis, for each $k \in [1 \ldots n]$, $\overline{w}_k \parallel w_k$ therefore, for all M such that $(\lambda z M)v_{i_k} : \circ$ be closed and well typed, $(\lambda z\, M)w_k \equiv_\beta (\lambda z\, M)\overline{w}_k$.

   Thus $(u)w_1 \ldots w_n \equiv_\beta (u)\overline{w}_1 \ldots \overline{w}_n \equiv_\beta ((u^B_A)^A_B)w_1 \ldots w_n$. Since $w_1, \ldots, w_p$ are arbitrary, $u \parallel (u^B_A)^A_B$.

□

Lemma 7. *Call* $\parallel$-compatible *every function F satisfying $F(t) \parallel F(t') \Leftrightarrow t \parallel t'$. Let B be an arbitrary type. Let A be the pure form of B. Then, for every finite, non-empty set of constants $\mathcal{C}$ of type t.s.f.(A):*

1. *$(u : A \mapsto u^B_A : B)$ is a $\parallel$-compatible function from $\mathcal{T}(A, \mathcal{C})$ to $\mathcal{T}(B, \mathcal{C})$.*
2. *$(t : B \mapsto t^A_B : A)$ is a $\parallel$-compatible function from $\mathcal{T}(B, \mathcal{C})$ to $\mathcal{T}(A, \mathcal{C})$.*

Proof. For all typed variables $X : A$, $Y : B$, the constants of Y^A_B, X^B_A belong to $Nil - \{nil : \circ\}$ hence, if $t \in \mathcal{T}(B, \mathcal{C})$ then $t^A_B \in \mathcal{T}(A, \mathcal{C})$ and if $u \in \mathcal{T}(A, \mathcal{C})$ then $u^B_A \in \mathcal{T}(B, \mathcal{C})$. It follows from definition 5 that if $u : A \parallel u' : A$ then $u^B_A \parallel u'^B_A$. By lemma 6(2), if $u^B_A \parallel u'^B_A$ then $u \parallel u'$. Similarly, if $t : B \parallel t' : B$ then $t^A_B \parallel t'^A_B$. By lemma 6(1), if $t^A_B \parallel t'^A_B$ then $t \parallel t'$. □

3.2 Reduction to the Case of a Unique Ground Type

Lemma 8. If all minimal models are decidable in the particular case of $\mathcal{O} = \{o\}$, then all minimal models are decidable in the case where $\mathcal{O}$ is an arbitrary set.

Proof. Let $\mathcal{R}$ be any function such that for all pairs $(A, \mathcal{C})$ where A contains a unique ground type, $\mathcal{R}(A, \mathcal{C})$ is a complete set of $\|$-representatives for $\mathcal{M}(A, \mathcal{C})$. Call $\mathcal{R}^*$ the function defined as follows:

> Let B be any type of t.s.f. o, let $\mathcal{C}$ be any non-empty, finite set of constants of type o, let A be the pure form of B. Let $\mathcal{R}^*(B, \mathcal{C}) = \{u_A^B : B \mid u \in \mathcal{R}(A, \mathcal{C})\}$.

Note that if $\mathcal{R}$ is computable the $\mathcal{R}^*$ is also computable. For all pairs $(B, \mathcal{C})$ with B of pure form A and for all $t \in \mathcal{T}(B, \mathcal{C})$, $(t_B^A)_A^B \| t$ and there exists $u \in \mathcal{R}(A, \mathcal{C})$ such that $(t_B^A)_A^B \| u_A^B$, hence, $\mathcal{R}^*(B, \mathcal{C})$ is a complete set of $\|$-representatives for $\mathcal{M}(B, \mathcal{C})$. Furthermore, for all t, $t' \in \mathcal{T}(B, \mathcal{C})$, $t \| t'$ if and only if $t_B^A \| t_B'^A$. Hence, if the relation $\|$ is decidable on the set $\mathcal{T}(A, \mathcal{C})$, then this relation is also decidable on the set $\mathcal{T}(B, \mathcal{C})$. □

4 Atomic Interpolation

Through sections 4, 5, 6 and 7, the set $\mathcal{O}$ is assumed to be equal to $\{o\}$. We shall give now the definition of an *(atomic) interpolation problem* and prove that for every closed term t, there exists an interpolation problem Φ of which t is a solution, and such that every solution of Φ is observationally equivalent to t.

Definition 9. An *interpolation equation* E is defined as an equation of the form $[(x)u_1 \dots u_n = a]$ where $u_1, \dots, u_n$ are closed terms and a is a constant. A *solution* of E is a closed term t such that $(t)u_1 \dots u_n \twoheadrightarrow_\beta a$. Two interpolation equations are *equivalent* if and only if they have the same set of solutions.

Remark. $[(x)u_1 \dots u_n = a]$ and $[(x)u_1' \dots u_n' = a]$ are equivalent $\Leftrightarrow$ for each i, $[(x_i)u_i = a]$ and $[(x_i)u_i'] = a$ are equivalent $\Leftrightarrow$ for each i, $u_i \| u_i'$.

Definition 10. An *interpolation problem* Φ is defined as a finite set of interpolation equations containing the same variable. A *solution* of Φ is a closed term which is a solution of each $E \in \Phi$.

Proposition 11. *Let $E = [(x)u_1 \dots u_n = a]$ be an interpolation equation. Let 0, 1 be two distinct constants. Let $E^* = [(x)u_1^* \dots u_n^* = a^*] = E[1/0, 0/1]$. Then, for all closed t:*

1. *If t is a solution of $\{E, E^*\}$ then for any constant b, $t[b/0, b/1]$ is a solution of $\{E, E^*\}$.*

2. If 0, 1 are not free in t then t is a solution of E ⇔ t is a solution of E^*.

Proof. 1. Suppose t is a solution of $\{E, E^*\}$. Let $t^* = t[2/0, 3/1]$ where $2, 3$ are two new constants. If, for instance, $(t^*)u_1 \ldots u_n \,\beta\, 2$ then $(t^*)u^* \ldots u^* \,\beta\, 2$ hence $(t)u_1 \ldots u_n \,\beta\, 0$, $a = 0$, $(t)u^* \ldots u^* \,\beta\, 0$ and $a^* = 0$, a contradiction. Similarly, the normal form of $(t^*)u_1 \ldots u_n$ cannot be 3, and the normal form of $(t^*)u_1^* \ldots u_n^*$ cannot be 2 nor 3. Consequently, for any constant b, $t[b/0, b/1] = t^*[b/2, b/3]$ is a solution of $\{E, E^*\}$.

2. Suppose 0, 1 are not free in t. Let $\sigma = [1/0, 0/1]$. Then $(t)u_1 \ldots u_n \,\beta\, a$ iff $\sigma((t)u_1 \ldots u_n) \,\beta\, \sigma(a)$ iff $(t)\sigma(u_1) \ldots \sigma(u_n) \,\beta\, \sigma(a)$ iff $(t)u_1^* \ldots u_n^* \,\beta\, a^*$. □

Lemma 12. *For any $(A, \mathcal{C})$, there exists a finite set P of interpolation problems satisfying:*

> *Let Φ be any element of P. If Φ is solvable, then there exists a solution of Φ that belongs to $\mathcal{T}(A, \mathcal{C})$.*
>
> *Let $\mathcal{R} \subset \mathcal{T}(A, \mathcal{C})$ be any set which contains a unique solution of each solvable problem in P. Then $\mathcal{R}$ is a complete set of $\|$-representatives for $\mathcal{M}(A, \mathcal{C})$.*

Proof. By induction of the order of A. If $A = \circ$ and $\mathcal{C} = \{a_1, \ldots, a_m\}$ then $P = \{\{[x = a_1]\}, \ldots, \{[x = a_m]\}\}$. Suppose $A = A_1 \ldots A_n \to \circ$. Let 0, 1 be two new constants. By induction hypothesis $\mathcal{M}_i(A_i, \{0, 1\})$ is finite. Let U_i be a complete set of $\|$-representatives for this latter set. Let F be the set of all functions from $U_1 \times \ldots \times U_n$ to $\mathcal{C} \cup \{0, 1\}$. Let P_0 be the set of all problems $\{[(x)u_1 \ldots u_n = f(u_1, \ldots, u_n)] \,|\, \forall i\, u_i \in U_i\}$ with $f \in F$. For all equations E, write E^* the equation $E[1/0, 0/1]$. We let P be the set of all problems $\Psi^* = \{E \,|\, E \in \Phi\} \cup \{E^* \,|\, E \in \Phi\}$ with $\Psi \in P_0$.

Let $\Psi^* \in P$. If Ψ^* is solved by a closed term t then: obviously, if $b \notin \mathcal{C} \cup \{0, 1\}$ then for any $a \in \mathcal{C}$, the term $t[a/b]$ is a solution of Ψ^* ; by proposition 11 (1) and by definition of Ψ^*, for any $a \in \mathcal{C}$, the term $t[a/1, a/0]$ is a solution of Ψ^*. Therefore, there exists a solution of Φ^* that belongs to $\mathcal{T}(A, \mathcal{C})$.

Furthermore, if $Q \in \mathcal{M}(A, \mathcal{C})$ then by definition of $\|$, there exists a unique problem $\Psi \in P_0$ of which all elements of Q are solutions; by proposition 11 (2), Ψ^* is also the unique element of P of which all elements of Q are solutions. □

Remark. The preceding lemma proves also that for each pair $(A, \mathcal{C})$, the quotient set $\mathcal{M}(A, \mathcal{C}) = \mathcal{T}(A, \mathcal{C}) / \|$ is a finite set.

5 Accessibility

The notion of *accessibility* of an address, in a simply typed term on η-long form, will be used extensively in section 6.

5.1 η-long Forms

Let $t = \lambda x_1 \dots x_m\,(u) v_1 \dots v_p : A_1 \dots A_n \to o$ where $m \leq n$ and u is either a variable, a constant or a term of the form $\lambda y\, w$. We call *η-long form* of t the unique term of same type of the form:

$\lambda x_1 \dots x_m x_{m+1} \dots x_n.(u^*) v_1^* \dots v_p^* x_{m+1}^* \dots x_n^*$, where:

- v_i^* is the η-long form of v_i,
- x_j^* is the η-long form of x_j,
- if u is a variable or a constant then $u^* = u$, else u^* is the η-long form of u.

In the remaining, all terms will be supposed to be on η-long form *i.e.* all terms will be assumed to belong to the least set $\overline{\mathcal{L}}$ satisfying:

0. all typed constants and all typed variables of ground type belong to $\overline{\mathcal{L}}$,
1. if $t : o \in \overline{\mathcal{L}}$ is of ground type and if $y_1 : A_1, \dots, y_n : A_n$ are typed variables then $\lambda y_1 \dots y_n.t : A_1 \dots A_n \to o \in \overline{\mathcal{L}}$,
2. if $t_1 : A_1, \dots, t_n : A_n \in \overline{\mathcal{L}}$ and if $x : A_1 \dots A_n \to o$ is a typed variable where o is a ground type, then $(x)\, t_1 \dots t_n : o \in \overline{\mathcal{L}}$,
3. if $t : A_1 \dots A_n \to o$, $u_1 : A_1, \dots, u_n : A_n \in \overline{\mathcal{L}}$ where o is a ground type then $(t)\, u_1 \dots u_n : o \in \overline{\mathcal{L}}$.

Remark. If $t : A \in \overline{\mathcal{S}}$ then $t\,\beta\, u$ if and only if $t^*\,\beta\, u^*$, where t^*, u^* are the η-long forms of t, u respectively. Furthermore, if $v : A \in \overline{\mathcal{L}}$ and if $v\,\beta\, w$ then $w : A \in \overline{\mathcal{L}}$. Therefore, we may assume whitout loss of generality that the set of simply typed terms is restricted to $\overline{\mathcal{L}}$.

5.2 Addresses

Definition 13. Let L be the set of all lists of integers. We let $(\tau, \Delta) \mapsto \tau/\Delta$ be the least application from $\mathcal{L} \times L$ to the set of all $\mathcal{L}$-terms of type o, which satisfies:

- $\lambda.\mathcal{Y}.\varepsilon/\langle\rangle = \varepsilon$,
- if $\tau = \lambda\mathcal{Y}.(\varepsilon_0)\varepsilon_1 \dots \varepsilon_n$ where $n > 0$ and ε_0 is a variable, a constant or an element of $\mathcal{L}$ then $\forall\, \Delta \in L$,

$$\tau/\langle i\rangle\Delta = \varepsilon_i/\Delta \quad \text{and} \quad \text{if } \varepsilon_0 \in \mathcal{L} \text{ then } \tau/\langle 0\rangle\Delta = \varepsilon_0/\Delta.$$

We call set of *addresses* in τ the set of all Δ such that τ/Δ is defined. We denote by $\mathit{Sub}(\tau, \Delta)$ the α-class of τ/Δ.

For any term t, we call set of *addresses* in t the set of addresses in any of its representatives and *depth* of t the maximal length of an address in t. We say that Δ is a *free occurrence* of the variable or constant z in t if and only if for every τ representative of t, τ/Δ is of the form $(z)\varepsilon_1 \ldots \varepsilon_n$. For any context Γ, we call *Γ-occurrences* in t all free occurrences of elements of Γ in t.

Definition 14. Let a be a constant. Let $\tau = \lambda\mathcal{Y}.(\varepsilon_0)\varepsilon_1 \ldots \varepsilon_n$. Let Δ be any address in τ. We call *pruning of τ by a at Δ* the $\mathcal{L}$-term $\tau(a/\Delta)$ defined by:

- $\tau(a/\langle\rangle) = \lambda\mathcal{Y}.a$,
- $\tau(a/\langle i\rangle\Delta)) = \lambda\mathcal{Y}.(\varepsilon'_0)\varepsilon'_1 \ldots \varepsilon'_n$ where
  $\varepsilon'_i = \varepsilon_i(a/\Delta)$ and $\varepsilon'_j = \varepsilon_j \quad (j \neq i)$.

Since $\tau \equiv_\alpha \tau'$ implies $\tau(a,\Delta) \equiv_\alpha \tau'(a,\Delta)$, we may define the *pruning of t by a at Δ* as $\tau(a/\Delta)$ where τ is an arbitrary representative of t.

For any set of constants $\mathcal{C}$, we call *$\mathcal{C}$-prunings* of t all terms obtained by successive prunings of t by elements of $\mathcal{C}$. A $\mathcal{C}$-pruning $\bar{t}$ is said to be *strict* if and only if at least one $\mathcal{C}$-occurrence in $\bar{t}$ is not a $\mathcal{C}$-occurrence in t.

5.3 Accessibility

Definition 15. An address Δ is said to be *β-accessible* in a term w iff:

> let $\overline{w}$ be the pruning of w at Δ by a constant a which does not appear in w. Then a appears in the normal form of $\overline{w}$.

Remark. If w is closed and if Δ is β-accessible in w, then for any a, the pruning of w by a at Δ is of normal form a.

6 Transferring Terms

We define now a class of closed terms of a simple structure, called *transferring terms*. The key-result presented in this section is the following: for every closed term t, there exists a transferring term observationally equivalent to t. As a corollary of this result, we will prove in section 7 the existence of an algorithm which takes as an input a pair $(A,\mathcal{C})$ and returns a set that contains a unique transferring representative of each element of $\mathcal{M}(A,\mathcal{C})$.

We give at first the definition of a transferring term. Next, we give the definition of an *approximation* of a solution of an interpolation problem. The links between these two definitions will be explained in section 6.2.

Definition 16. We say that a term $t : A$ is *transferring* if and only if t is closed, on normal form, and of the form:

1. $t = \lambda y_1 \ldots y_n.a$ where a is a constant, or,
2. $t = \lambda y_1 \ldots y_n.(y_i)v_1 \ldots v_p[w'/0, w''/1]$ where:
   (a) 0, 1 are constants,
   (b) $v_1 \ldots v_p$ are *closed* and their constants belong to $\{0, 1\}$
   (c) $\lambda y_1 \ldots y_n.w'$ et $\lambda y_1 \ldots y_n.w''$ are transferring.

Remark. If $t = \lambda\mathcal{Y}.w$ is transferring and if Δ is a $\mathcal{Y}$-occurrence in w then for every representative ε of w, all free variables of ε/Δ belong to $\mathcal{Y}$. Therefore, if t is a solution of $E = [(x)\, u_1 \ldots u_n = a]$ and if $\langle 0\rangle\Delta$ is β-accessible in $(t)u_1 \ldots u_n$ then $(\lambda\mathcal{Y}.\varepsilon/\Delta))u_1 \ldots u_n\, \beta\, a$.

6.1 Approximations

Definition 17. A *vector* is by definition a sequence $(t_1, \ldots, t_m)$ of closed terms of same type, denoted by $< t_1, \ldots, t_m >$. We call *type* of a vector the type of its elements. If $\overline{V} = (V_1, \ldots, V_n) = (< u_i^1, \ldots, u_i^m >)_{i=1}^n$, then:

- for $W =< a_1, \ldots, a_m >$, $[(x)\overline{V} = W]$ denotes the interpolation problem $\{[(x)u_1^j \ldots u_n^j = a_j] \mid j \in [1 \ldots m]\}$,
- for any closed $t : A_1 \ldots A_n \to o$ where A_i is the type of V_i, $[(x)\overline{V}][x \leftarrow t]$ denotes the normal form of $< (t)u_1^1 ... u_n^1, \ldots, (t)u_1^m ... u_n^m >$.

Definition 18. Let $W =< a_1, \ldots, a_m >$ be any vector of constants that contains at least two distincts elements. Let 0, 1 be two new constants. The set of *(0, 1)-approximations* of W is defined as the set of all elements of $\Pi_{j=1}^m\{a_j, 0, 1\}$ that contain at least two distinct constants.

We say that $< u_1, \ldots, u_m >$ of type $A_1 \ldots A_n \to o$ is *W-splitting* if and only if there exists in $\Pi_{j=1}^m \mathcal{T}(A_i, \{0, 1\})$ at least one $(v_1, \ldots v_n)$ such that the normal form of $< (u_1)v_1 ... v_p, \ldots, (u_m)v_1 ... v_p >$ is an approximation of W.

Definition 19. Let $\overline{V} = (< u_i^1, ..., u_i^m >)_{i=1}^n$. Let t be any closed term such that $[(x)\overline{V}][x \leftarrow t]$ is defined. Let $w_j = (t)u_1^j \ldots u_n^j$. An address Δ is said to be:

- *totally $\overline{V}$-accessible* in t iff for each j, $\langle 0\rangle\Delta$ is β-accessible in w_j,
- *partially $\overline{V}$-accessible* in t iff Δ is not totally $\overline{V}$-accessible in t and there exists j such that $\langle 0\rangle\Delta$ is β-accessible in w_j,
- *$\overline{V}$-inaccessible* otherwise.

Lemma 20. If $[(x)\overline{V}][x \leftarrow \lambda\mathcal{Y}.w]$ is a (0, 1)-approximation of W and if no strict $\{0, 1\}$-pruning of $\lambda\mathcal{Y}.w$ is a (0, 1)-approximation of W then: all partially $\overline{V}$-accessible addresses in $\lambda\mathcal{Y}.w$ are $\{0, 1\}$-occurrences; all constants of w belong to $\{0, 1\}$

Proof. Suppose $\overline{V} = (< u_i^1, ..., u_i^m >)_{i=1}^n$, $[(x)\overline{V}][x \leftarrow \lambda\mathcal{Y}.w] =< b_1, \ldots, b_m >$, $W =< a_1, \ldots, a_m >$. Let Δ be any partially $\overline{V}$-accessible address in $\lambda\mathcal{Y}.w$. Let j, k be such that $\langle 0\rangle\Delta$ be β-accessible in $(\lambda\mathcal{Y}.w)u_1^j \ldots u_n^j$ and be not β-accessible in $(\lambda\mathcal{Y}.w)u_1^k \ldots u_n^k$. Let $c = 1$ if $b_k \in \{0, a_k\}$, 0 otherwise. Let $\lambda\mathcal{Y}.\overline{w}$ be the c-pruning of $\lambda\mathcal{Y}.w$ at δ. Then $[(x)\overline{V}][x \leftarrow \lambda\mathcal{Y}.\overline{w}] =< c_1, \ldots c_m >$ where $\forall l\ c_l = \{b_l, 0, 1\}$, $c_k = b_k$ and $c_j = c$ with $c \neq c_k$. Hence, $< c_1, \ldots c_m >$ is still an approximation of W. By hypothesis. $\overline{w}$ is not a strict pruning of w, therefore Δ is a {0,1}-occurrence in w.

Since there exists at least one approximation of W, this vector contains at least two distinct constants. Therefore, all occurrences of a constant in $\lambda\mathcal{Y}.w$ are partially $\overline{V}$-accessible, and all constants of $\lambda\mathcal{Y}.w$ belong to $\{0, 1\}$. □

6.2 Existence of Transferring Representatives

We prove now that for every closed term t, there exists a transferring term observationally equivalent to t. If we assume that this property holds for all terms of depth at most $h - 1$, and consider a term t of depth h, then the next lemma proves that given an arbitrary interpolation problem Φ of which t is a solution, the problem Φ contains a splitting row; this latter property allows us to split Φ into two smaller interpolation problems Φ_0 and Φ_1, so that if we also assume the induction hypothesis that there exists transferring solutions of Φ_0 and Φ_1, then from these solutions and from this splitting row, one can build a transferring solution of Φ. The conclusion follows from the fact that for every t, there exists an interpolation problem such that every solution of this problem is observationally equivalent to t.

Lemma 21. *Let $t = \lambda y_1 \ldots y_n.(y_i)\lambda\mathcal{X}_1.v_1 \ldots \lambda\mathcal{X}_p.v_p = \lambda\mathcal{Y}.w$ where all $\lambda\mathcal{Y}\mathcal{X}_k.v_k$ are transferring. If t is a solution of $[(x)\overline{V} = W]$ where W contains at least two distinct constants, then at least one element of $\overline{V}$ is W-splitting.*

Proof. Let 0, 1 be two new constants. Let $\overline{t} = \lambda\mathcal{Y}.\overline{w}$ be the maximal $(0,1)$-pruning of t such that $[(x)\overline{V}][x \leftarrow \overline{t}]$ is an approximation of W. By lemma 20, all constants of $\overline{t}$ belong to $\{0, 1\}$, and every $\mathcal{Y}$-occurrence in $\overline{w}$ is totally $\overline{V}$-accessible.

We shall prove by induction on the number P of $\mathcal{Y}$-occurrences in $\overline{w}$ that at least one element of $(V_1, \ldots, V_n) = \overline{V}$ is W-splitting. If $P = 1$ then V_i is splitting. Suppose $P > 1$. Let $\Delta = \langle k\rangle\Delta'$ be any $\mathcal{Y}$-occurrence in w of non-null length. As $\lambda\mathcal{Y}\mathcal{X}_k.v_k$ is transferring, $Sub(\tau, \Delta)$ is of the form $(y_j)w_1 \ldots w_q[w'/0, w''/1]$ where $w_1, \ldots, w_m$ are closed and $\lambda\mathcal{Y}\mathcal{X}_k.w'$, $\lambda\mathcal{Y}\mathcal{X}_k.w''$ are transferring.

1. Since Δ is totally $\overline{V}$-accessible, if $w', w'' \in \{0, 1\}$ then $[(x)\overline{V}][x \leftarrow \lambda\mathcal{Y}.(y_j)w_1 ... w_q[w'/0, w''/1] = [(x)\overline{V}][x \leftarrow \overline{t}]$ and thereby V_j is W-splitting.

2. Otherwise, for instance, $w' \notin \{0,1\}$. By hypothesis on $\bar{t}$, there exists at least one 0-occurrence Δ_0 in $(y_j)w_1 \dots w_q$ such that $\Delta\Delta_0$ is totally $\overline{V}$-accessible in $\bar{t}$. Thereby $\forall\, u \in V_j$, $(u)w_1 \dots w_q\, \beta\, 0$ hence $(u)w_1 \dots w_q[w'/0, w''/1]\, \beta\, w'$.

   Let $\bar{t}' = \lambda\mathcal{Y}.\overline{w}'$ be the normal term obtained by the substitution at δ in $\overline{w}$ of any element of V_j for the free occurrence of y_j. Then $[(x)\overline{V}][x \leftarrow \bar{t}] = [(x)V][x \leftarrow \bar{t}']$, $\overline{w}'$ contains $(P-1)$ $\mathcal{Y}$-occurrences and by induction hypothesis at least one element of $\overline{V}$ is W-splitting. □

Theorem 22. *For any closed t, there exists a transferring term $t' \parallel t$.*

Proof. We assume that t is on normal form and of type $A = A_1 \dots A_n \to o$. Let $\mathcal{C}$ be the set of all constants of t if this set is not empty, $\{nil\}$ where nil is an arbitrary constant otherwise. Let P be a problem satisfying for the pair $(A, \mathcal{C})$ the conditions of lemma 12. Let $car(t)$ be the element of P of which t is a solution.

We shall prove by induction on (H, m) where H is the depth of t, that for every $\Phi \subset car(t)$ of cardinal at most m, there exists a transferring solution of Φ. This result is clear if all right-members of Φ are equal to a unique constant (in particular, if $|\Phi| \le 1$). Suppose $\Phi = [(x)V_1 \dots V_n = W] = \{E_1, \dots, E_m\}$ where W contains at least two distinct elements, with t of the form $\lambda\mathcal{Y}.(y_i)w_1 \dots w_p$.

By induction hypothesis on H, there exist transferring terms $\lambda\mathcal{Y}\, t_1, \dots, \lambda\mathcal{Y}\, t_p$ such that $\lambda\mathcal{Y}\, t_k \parallel \lambda\mathcal{Y}\, w_k$. By proposition 2, $\lambda\mathcal{Y}.(y_j)t_1 \dots t_p \parallel t$. By lemma 21, at least one element of $\overline{V} = \{V_1 \dots V_n\}$ is W-splitting.

Let $V_j =< u^1, \dots, u^m >$ be any W-splitting element of $\overline{V}$. Let 0, 1 be two new constants. Let $v_1 \dots v_p$ be closed terms whose constants belong to $\{0,1\}$ such that the normal form $< b_1, \dots, b_m >$ of $< (u^1)v_1 ... v_p, \dots, (u^m)v_1 ... v_p >$ is an approximation of W. Let Φ_0 be the problem which contains each E_j such that $\mathsf{D}_j = 0$, let Φ_1 be the problem which contains each E_j such that $\mathsf{D}_j = 1$. Since Φ_0 and Φ_1 contain at most $m-1$ equations, by induction hypothesis there exist $\lambda\mathcal{Y}.w'$ and $\lambda\mathcal{Y}.w''$ which are transferring solutions of Φ_0 and Φ_1 respectively. The term $\lambda\mathcal{Y}.(y_j)v_1 \dots v_p[w'/0, w''/1]$ is then a transferring solution of Φ. □

Remark. Theorem 22 is equivalent to the following property : every non-trivial, solvable interpolation problem contains at least one splitting row.

7 Computation of Transferring Representatives

It remains to prove, for every order N, the existence of a computable function which, given an arbitrary pair $(A, \mathcal{C})$ where A is of order at most N, returns a complete set of representatives for $\mathcal{M}(A, \mathcal{C})$. We prove the existence of such a function by giving constructive proofs of lemma 12 and theorem 22.

Lemma 23. *Let N be any integer. Let $\mathcal{C}$ be any finite, non-empty set of constants. Suppose that there exists a computable function $\mathcal{R}_{N-1}$ such that for all pairs $(B, \mathcal{C})$ where B is a type of order at most $N-1$, $\mathcal{R}_{N-1}(B, \mathcal{C})$ is a complete set of $\|$-representatives for $\mathcal{M}(B, \mathcal{C})$. Then,*

1. *There exists a computable function Car_N such that for all pairs $(A, \mathcal{C})$ where A is a type of order at most N, $Car_N(A, \mathcal{C})$ is a finite set of of interpolation problems satisfying:*

   each solvable problem in $Car_N(A, \mathcal{C})$ is solved by some element of $\mathcal{T}(A, \mathcal{C})$. Any set which contains, for each solvable problem $\Phi \in Car_N(A, \mathcal{C})$, a unique solution of Φ that belongs to $\mathcal{T}(A, \mathcal{C})$, is a complete set of $\|$-representatives for $\mathcal{M}(A, \mathcal{C})$.

2. *There exists a computable function which, given two terms t, $t' \in \mathcal{T}(A, \mathcal{C})$ where A is of order at most N, determines whether $t \| t'$ or not.*

Proof. For $A = A_1 \ldots A_n \to o$, the proof of (1) is similar to the proof of lemma 12 where $\mathcal{R}_{N-1}(B_i, \{0,1\})$ replaces U_i ($i \in [1 \ldots n]$). The set $Car_N(A, \mathcal{C})$ is then defined as the resulting set P. The second part of the lemma follows from the fact that for all t, $t' \in \mathcal{T}(A, \mathcal{C})$, then $t \| t'$ if and only if there exists $Car_N(A, \mathcal{C})$ such that t and t' are solutions of Φ. □

Lemma 24. *Let N be any integer. Let $\mathcal{C}$ be any finite, non-empty set of constants. If:*

> *there exists a computable function $\mathcal{R}_{N-1}$ such that for all pairs $(B, \mathcal{C})$ where B is a type of order at most $N-1$, $\mathcal{R}_{N-1}(B, \mathcal{C})$ is a complete set of $\|$-representatives for $\mathcal{M}(B, \mathcal{C})$,*

then

> *there exists a computable function $\mathcal{R}_N$ such that for all pairs $(A, \mathcal{C})$ where A is a type of order at most $N-1$, $\mathcal{R}_N(A, \mathcal{C})$ is a complete set of $\|$-representatives for $\mathcal{M}(A, \mathcal{C})$,*

Proof. For $A = A_1 \ldots A_n \to o$, let M be the maximal cardinal of all problems in $Car_N(A, \mathcal{C})$. For each $m \in [1 \ldots M]$, let $\mathcal{T}_m$ be the set defined as follows:

1. $\mathcal{T}_1$ is the set of all terms of the form $\lambda y_1 \ldots y_n.a : A$ where $a \in \mathcal{C}$.
2. for $m > 1$, $\mathcal{T}_m$ is equal to the union of $\mathcal{T}_{m-1}$ and the set of all terms of the form $\lambda y_1 \ldots y_n.(y_j)v_1 \ldots v_p[w'/0, w''/1]$ where:
   (a) 0, 1 are two new constants,
   (b) for $B_j = D_1 \ldots D_p \to o$, $\quad v_k \in \mathcal{R}_{N-2}(D_k, \{0,1\})$,
   (c) $\lambda y_1 \ldots y_n.w', \lambda y_1 \ldots y_n.w'' \in \mathcal{T}_{m-1}$

It follows from the proof of theorem 22 where we take $P = Car_N(A, \mathcal{C})$ and where for V_j of type $B_j = D_1 \dots D_p \to \mathrm{o}$, v_k is assumed to belong to $\mathcal{R}_{N-2}(D_k, \{0, 1\})$, that every solvable element of $Car_N(B, \Gamma)$ has a solution in $\mathcal{T}_M$. Therefore, $\mathcal{R}_N(B, \Gamma)$ can be defined as a set that contains, for each $\Phi \in Car_N(B, \Gamma)$ solved by some element of $\mathcal{T}_M$, a unique element of $\mathcal{T}_M$ which is a solution of Φ. □

8 Decidability of all Minimal Models

Theorem 25. *All minimal models are decidable.*

Proof. By lemma 8, it is sufficient to prove this result in the particular case of $\mathcal{O} = \{\mathrm{o}\}$. If we let $\mathcal{R}_1(\mathrm{o}, \mathcal{C}) = \mathcal{C}$ then from lemma 24 we infer the existence of a computable function which, given an arbitrary pair $(A, \mathcal{C})$ where A is a type and $\mathcal{C}$ is a finite, non-empty set of constants, returns a complete set of $\|$-representatives for $\mathcal{M}(A, \mathcal{C})$. By lemma 23 (2), there exists also a computable function which determines, given two closed terms, whether these terms are observationally equivalent or not. □

9 Decidability of Atomic Matching

Definition 26. An *atomic matching problem* Φ is defined as a finite set of equations of the form $[u = a]$ where a is a constant of ground type. Let $x_1 \dots x_n$ be the set of all free variables of Φ. We call *solution* of Φ every sequence of closed terms $(t_1 \dots t_n)$ such that t_i and x_i be of same type, and such that for every $[u = a] \in \Phi$, $u[t_1/x_1 \dots t_n/x_n]$ be of normal form a.

Remark. If a is of type o and x is of type A with *t.s.f.*$(A) = \diamond \neq \mathrm{o}$ then for any constant $b : \diamond$, $[u = a]$ and $[u[\lambda x_1 \dots x_n.b : A/x] = a]$ have same set of solutions. Thus, we may assume w.l.o.g that for every $[u = a] \in \Phi$, every free variable in u is of *t.s.f.* equal to the type of a. Consequently, we may also assume that all right-members of Φ are of same ground type, since Φ is solvable iff for each ground type o, $\Phi_{\mathrm{o}} = \{[u = a] \in \Phi \mid a \text{ is of type } \mathrm{o}\}$ is solvable.

Theorem 27. *Atomic Matching is decidable*

Proof. Let $\mathcal{C}$ be any finite, non-empty set of constants of type o. Let $x_1 : A_1, \dots, x_n : A_n$ be such that *t.s.f.*$(A_i) = \mathrm{o}$. By theorem 25, there exists a computable function that, given the pair $(A_i, \mathcal{C})$ returns a set $\mathcal{R}_i$ which is a complete set of $\|$-representatives for $\mathcal{M}(A_i, \mathcal{C})$ $(1 \leq n \leq n)$.

Let Φ be any atomic matching problem of free variables $x_1 \dots x_n$, such that all right-members of Φ belong to $\mathcal{C}$. Suppose $(w_1 \dots w_n)$ is a solution of Φ. We may assume that for each i, every constant of type o appearing in w_i belongs to

$\mathcal{C}$. Then for each i, there exists $t_i \in \mathcal{R}_i$ such that $w_i \parallel t_i$, and $(t_1 \ldots t_n)$ is still a solution of Φ. Thus, if Φ is solvable then $\mathcal{R}_1 \times \ldots \times \mathcal{R}_n$ contains at least one solution of Φ. □

References

1. Barendregt, H.: The Lambda Calculus, its Syntax and Semantics. North Holland (1981), (1984).
2. Dowek, G.: Third Order Matching is Decidable. Proceedings of Logic in Computer Science, Annals of Pure and Applied Logic (1993).
3. Hindley J.R., Seldin, J.P.: Introduction to Combinators and λ-Calculus. Cambridge University Press, Oxford (1986).
4. Krivine J.L.: Lambda Calculus, Types and Models. Ellis Horwood series in computer and their applications (1993) 1–66.
5. Loader, R.: The undecidability of λ-definability. Manuscript (1993).
6. Padovani, V.: On Equivalence Classes of Interpolation Equations. Proceedings of the second international conference on typed lambda-calculi and applications, Lecture Notes in Computer Science 902 (1995) 335–349.
7. Padovani, V.: Filtrage d'Ordre Supérieur. Thèse de doctorat, Université Paris VII (1996).
8. Padovani, V.: Decidability of Fourth Order Matching. Manuscript (1996).
9. Statman, R.: Completeness, invariance and λ-definability. Journal of Symbolic Logic, 47, 1 (1982).
10. Statman, R., Dowek, G.: On Statman's completeness theorem. Technical Report, CMU-CS-92-152, University of Carnegie Mellon (1992).

Circuits as Streams in Coq: Verification of a Sequential Multiplier

Christine Paulin-Mohring *

LIP, URA CNRS 1398
Ecole Normale Supérieure de Lyon
46 Allée d'Italie, 69364 Lyon cedex 07, France

Abstract. This paper presents the proof of correctness of a multiplier circuit formalized in the Calculus of Inductive Constructions. It uses a representation of the circuit as a function from the stream of inputs to the stream of outputs. We analyze the computational aspect of the impredicative encoding of coinductive types and show how it can be used to represent sequential circuits. We identify general proof principles that can be used to justify the correctness of such a circuit. The example and the principles have been formalized in the Coq proof assistant.

1 Introduction

1.1 Motivations

The formal proof of a circuits start with the choice of a model corresponding to an abstraction of the circuit. If the proof is intended to be checked on a computer, it is necessary to build a representation of this model inside the language of the theorem prover. Different programming languages ususally lead to different styles of encoding of data structures and algorithms. In the same way, each theorem prover is associated to a style for representing objects and proofs. For instance, in NQTHM [2, 3] circuits are represented as functions, and the inputs/outputs will be seen as finite lists while in HOL [10, 11] they are represented as relations. Coq contains both an impredicative logic and a functional programming language, it is consequentely natural to mix inside the specification both functional and relational notions. One can choose the most natural encoding or the most convenient associated proof methods. A feature of Coq with respect to the previously mentioned system is the interpretation of impredicative proofs as objects. We take advantadge of this for representing infinite structurs such as infinite lists (also called streams) and encode a circuit as a transformation on streams. These infinite lists are represented using a second-order existential quantification as was first proposed in [15] and also used in a proof of Eratosthenes's Sieve [14]. In this paper, we insist on the concrete interpretation of this encoding.

* This research was partly supported by ESPRIT Basic Research Action "Types" and by the GDR "Programmation" co-financed by MRE-PRC and CNRS.

1.2 Outline

The remaining part of this section is devoted to the introduction of Coq notations used in this paper. The section 2 gives a brief presentation of the impredicative representation of infinite objects in type theory. We emphasize the concrete aspect of this representation as a process. In section 3 we show how to represent a generic sequential circuit specified by the type of inputs, outputs and registers, and both the output and updating functions. We derive proof principles using invariants for this circuit. In section 4, a circuit is formalized, specified and finally proven using the methodology previously described. This circuit implements a multiplier and was taken as an example by M. Gordon [10] for the HOL theorem prover also studied in Coq [5] using a representation of the circuit by a primitive recursive function.

1.3 Notations

The developments presented in this paper have been completely formalised in the Coq proof assistant [4] and are available with the Coq distribution as a contribution.

To improve readibility, we shall not introduce and use the precise Coq notations but a more intuitive language.

The Calculus of Inductive Constructions which is the theoretical basis of the Coq system [4, 13] is an higher order typed lambda-calculus that is used both for the representation of functions in a ML-like language, of propositions and proofs.

The functional part The useful functional part of the Calculus corresponds to a second order lambda-calculus plus primitive inductive definitions.

Types The primitive types are "concrete" types representing algebraic structures specified by constructors. In this paper we shall use the types corresponding to the natural numbers, the booleans and a type *unit* with only one element *tt*.

Inductive *unit* : Set := *tt* : *unit*.
Inductive *bool* : Set := *true* : *bool* | *false* : *bool*.
Inductive *nat* : Set := O : nat | S : *nat*→*nat*.

Types can be composed to form new types :

$A \rightarrow B$ the type of functions from A to B
$A \otimes B$ the type of pairs (a, b) built from a of type A and b of type B
$A \oplus B$ the type of injections $(inl\ a)$ and $(inr\ b)$ with a of type A and b of type B

We shall also need type variables and universal quantification on such variables that will be written $(\forall X : \mathrm{Set})P$.

Terms Terms are built from variables and primitive constants using application and abstraction. The application of the term t to the term u is written $(t\ u)$ with $(t\ u_1 \ldots u_k)$ representing $(\ldots(t\ u_1)\ldots u_k)$. The abstraction of the term t with respect to the variable x of type A is written $[x : A]t$ with $[x_1, \ldots, x_k : A]t$ representing $[x_1 : A]\ldots[x_k : A]t$.

To the primitive types correspond methods of definition by pattern-matching and (restricted) recursion. We describe abstractly such functions by giving simple rewriting rules. The following functions will be used :

Predecessor	$O\dot{-}1 \rhd O$ $(S\,n)\dot{-}1 \rhd n$	Addition	$O+m \rhd m$ $(S\,n)+m \rhd (S\,(n+m))$
Projections	$(\mathit{fst}\,(x,y)) \rhd x$ $(\mathit{snd}\,(x,y)) \rhd y$	Conditional	$(\mathit{If\ true}\ x\ y) \rhd x$ $(\mathit{If\ false}\ x\ y) \rhd y$

The logical part As an atomic proposition we shall use equality between terms that will be written $t = u$. Proposition can be composed using usual quantifiers $A \Rightarrow B$, $A \wedge B$, $A \vee B$, $\neg A, (\forall x : T)A, (\exists x : T)A$.

Predicates Higher order quantification is also possible. A predicate is associated with an arity which is represented by a special type. If P is a predicate expecting n arguments of type $A_1, \ldots, A_n$ then one write $P : A_1 \rightarrow A_2 \rightarrow \cdots A_n \rightarrow \mathsf{Prop}$. The instance of the predicate P on objects $a_1, \ldots, a_n$ of the apropriate types is written $(P\ a_1 \ldots a_n)$. If P is a logical formula in which the variables $x_1, \ldots, x_n$ of type respectively $A_1, \ldots, A_n$ occurs free $[x_1 : A_1] \ldots [x_n : A_n]P$ is a predicate with arity $A_1 \rightarrow \cdots A_n \rightarrow \mathsf{Prop}$ such that $([x_1 : A_1] \ldots [x_n : A_n]P\ a_1 \ldots a_n)$ is equivalent to P in which x_i was substituted by a_i. Quantification over a predicate variable with arity α is written $(\forall P : \alpha)Q$.

Accessibility We shall use the a notion of accessibility for a relation. Let R be a relation on a type A (ie $R : A \rightarrow A \rightarrow \mathsf{Prop}$) then an object x of type A is accessible for the relation R (we shall write $(Acc\ R\ x)$ if any object y such that $(R\ y\ x)$ is itself accessible. This is a possible way to represent the fact that there is no infinite decreasing sequence starting from x. A relation is well-founded if ans only if any element is accessible.

Definitions We introduce formal notations the following way:

$$\textbf{Def}\ f[x_1 : A_1; \ldots; x_n : A_n]\ :\ B\ :=\ t$$

$$\begin{aligned} \textbf{Def}\ f\ :\ B\ :=\ & (f\ p_1^1 \ldots p_k^1) \rhd t^1 \\ & \ldots \\ & (f\ p_1^n \ldots p_k^n) \rhd t^n \end{aligned}$$

In the first case f is an abreviation for the term $[x_1 : A_1] \ldots [x_n : A_n]t$ of type $A_1 \rightarrow \cdots A_n \rightarrow B$, in the second case, f represents a function definable using pattern-matching and possibly recursion which is completely specified by the given equations.

2 Representation of infinite objects

2.1 Encoding of infinite objects

In [12], T. Hagino introduced a simply typed lambda-calculus extended with primitive types corresponding to categorical structures like natural numbers or infinite lists. In [15], G. Wraith showed that these types could be encoded in the second order polymorphic lambda-calculus.

Greatest fixed points in Coq In the following, F stands for any type transformer (ie. an object, possibly a variable, such that for any type X, $(F\ X)$ is a type). We assume F is a monotonic operator (ie a covariant functor), it means that for each term f of type $A \to B$ one can build a term $(Fmon\ f)$ of type $(F\ A) \to (F\ B)$. This construction can be automatically computed if X occurs only positively in $(F\ X)$.

Building the greatest fixed point of F corresponds to finding a type nu for which we have an object Out of type $nu \to (F\ nu)$ and an object $Intro$ of type $(F\ nu) \to nu$. These two operators witnesses the fact that nu is a fixed point. We require also the existence of an object $CoIter$ of type $(X \to (F\ X)) \to X \to nu$ representing the fact that nu is a greatest fixed point (actually post-fixed point of F). A possible representation of nu in Coq is given as the following concrete definition:
Inductive $nu : \mathsf{Set} := CoIter : (\forall X : \mathsf{Set})(X \to (F\ X)) \to X \to nu.$
This type generalizes the algebraic structures like natural numbers. It is a type with only one constructor which is indexed by any type X. This type can be seen as an encoding of the second-order existential quantifier $(\exists X : \mathsf{Set})(X \to (F\ X)) \otimes X$. We shall give a more precise computational interpretation of this type in the section 2.3. A closed normal object of this type can always be written $(CoIter\ A\ f\ x)$ with $A : \mathsf{Set}$, $f : A \to (F\ A)$, and $x : A$.

From this definition, we get directly the operator $CoIter$ with the expected type. We get also elimination principles. These are used both at the logical level to prove properties of objects in nu, and at the computational level to build functions depending on objects in nu.

At the logical level, assume we have an object $m : nu$ and a predicate P with arity $nu \to \mathsf{Prop}$. In order to prove $(P\ m)$ it is enough to prove $(P\ (CoIter\ X\ f\ x)$ with X, f, x fresh variables $(X : \mathsf{Set}, f : X \to (F\ X), x : X)$.

At the computational level , assume P is a type and H is a term of type $(\forall X : \mathsf{Set})(X \to (F\ X)) \to X \to P$ then it is possible to define a function H_{nu} of type $nu \to P$ such that the following equivallence holds : $(H_{nu}\ (CoIter\ X\ f\ x)) \equiv (H\ X\ f\ x)$

The operators $Intro$ and Out can be deduced using the following terms :
Def $Out\ :\ nu \to (F\ nu)\ :=\ (Out\ (CoIter\ X\ f\ x)) \rhd (Fmon\ (CoIter\ X\ f)\ (f\ x))$
Def $Intro\ [p : (F\ nu)]\ :\ nu\ :=\ (CoIter\ (F\ nu)\ (Fmon\ Out)\ p).$
This general pattern can be instantiated with different covariant functors in order to represent possibly infinite natural numbers or binary trees. These examples are briefly presented in section 2.3. One important application is the type of infinite lists also called streams that is presented now.

2.2 Streams

A typical example of a type built this way is the type Str_A of streams (infinite lists of objects in a given type A). It is obtained with the operator $F \equiv [X : \mathsf{Set}](A \otimes X)$.

In that case, the function $Fmon$ can be defined as :
Def $Fmon\ :\ (X \to Y) \to A \otimes X \to A \otimes Y\ :=\ (Fmon\ f\ (a, x)) \rhd (a, (f\ x))$.
From the function Out of type $Str_A \to A \otimes Str_A$ and the projections, we get easily the two functions $Hd : Str_A \to A$ and $Tl : Str_A \to Str_A$ giving respectively the head and tail of a stream. The following computational rules hold :

$$(Hd\ (CoIter\ X\ f\ x)) \equiv (fst(f\ x))$$
$$(Tl\ (CoIter\ X\ f\ x)) \equiv (CoIter\ X\ f\ (snd\ (f\ x)))$$

2.3 Concrete representation of coinductive constructions

We explain now the computational aspect of this representation of infinite objects.

As we said before, a closed normal term of type *nu* is equal to $(\mathit{CoIter}\ X\ f\ x)$. It means that it is a structure with three elements: a type X, an object x of type X and a function f of type $X \rightarrow (F\ X)$.

We can represent this object with a picture :

$x : X$
$f : X \rightarrow (F\ X)$

We call this object a process, X is the type of the state variable whose value is x and f is the transformation function that can give rise to new processes built on the same type and to various "observational" values. This type behaves like an abstract data type, which means that if we have an object s of type Str_A we know it has the form $(\mathit{CoIter}\ X\ f\ x)$ for some arbitrary type X but we cannot access this type. In particular, when building from s an object in a type T, T cannot mention X.

Pictorial specification of streams In case of the type of streams, the *Hd* and *Tl* functions can be represented the following way :

$x : X$	$\xrightarrow{Tl}$	$(\mathit{snd}\ (f\ x)) : X$
$f : X \rightarrow A \otimes X$		$f : X \rightarrow A \otimes X$
$Hd \downarrow$		
$(\mathit{fst}\ (f\ x)) : A$		

Other coinductive types

Infinite integers Assume F is $[X : \mathsf{Set}](\mathit{unit} \oplus X)$ then $Nw = (nu\ F)$ represents the type of possibly infinite integers.

Given a finite integer n of type *nat* one can represent the corresponding infinite integer by the process :

$n : \mathit{nat}$
$f : \mathit{nat} \rightarrow \mathit{unit} \oplus \mathit{nat} := (f\ O) \triangleright (\mathit{inl}\ tt)$ $(f\ (S\ p)) \triangleright (\mathit{inr}\ p)$

The infinite integer can be represented by the simple process :

$tt : \mathit{unit}$
$\mathit{inl} : \mathit{unit} \rightarrow \mathit{unit} \oplus \mathit{unit}$

The *Out* function gives from an object in *Nw* an object in $\mathit{unit} \oplus Nw$ representing the predecessor.

When this object is a left injection, it means that the process represents 0 and taking the predecessor has the effect to end the process, when it is a right injection we obtain the process representing the predecessor.

Pictorially we have one of the two situations :

$$\boxed{\begin{array}{c} x : X \\ \hline p : X \to unit \oplus X \end{array}} \longrightarrow \; () \qquad\qquad \text{when } (p\,x) = (inl\ tt)$$

$$\boxed{\begin{array}{c} x : X \\ \hline p : X \to unit \oplus X \end{array}} \longrightarrow \boxed{\begin{array}{c} y : X \\ \hline p : X \to unit \oplus X \end{array}} \text{when } (p\,x) = (inr\ y)$$

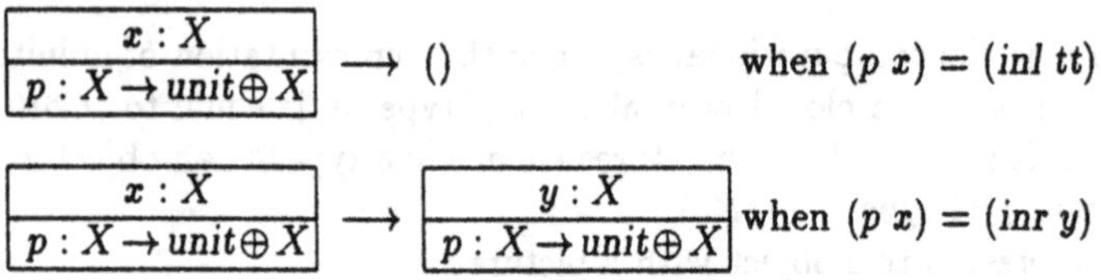

Infinite binary trees Assume F is $[X : Set](A \otimes (X \otimes X))$ the type $Trw = (nu\ F)$ represents the type of infinite binary trees. The *Out* function gives from an object in Trw an object in $A \otimes Trw \otimes Trw$ built from the label in the node and the left and right sons of the tree.

More computationally, applying an *Out* step to an object in Trw raises the label of type A plus two new processes of the same sort.

$$\boxed{\begin{array}{c} x : X \\ \hline p : X \to A \otimes (X \otimes X) \end{array}} \longrightarrow \boxed{a : A}$$
$$\downarrow \qquad \downarrow \qquad\qquad \text{when } (p\,x) = (a, (l, r))$$
$$\boxed{\begin{array}{c} l : X \\ \hline p : X \to A \otimes X \otimes X \end{array}} \boxed{\begin{array}{c} r : X \\ \hline p : X \to A \otimes (X \otimes X) \end{array}}$$

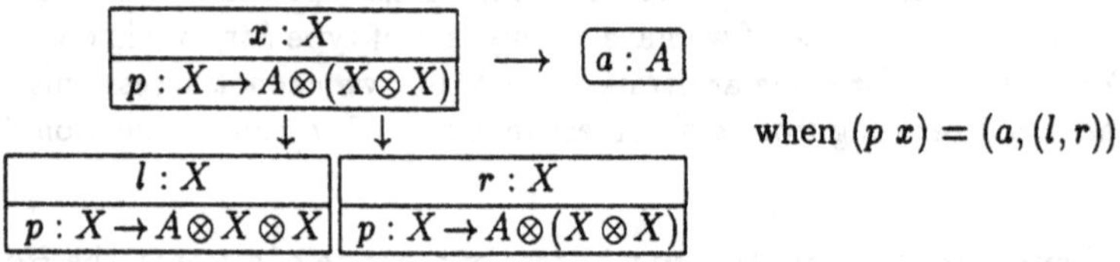

2.4 Co-iteration vs Co-recursion

We can remark that the *Out* step applied to an object of type $M \equiv (nu\ F)$ seen as a process produces a composite object in which may appear one or several objects of type M which are processes sharing the original implementation. It means that the type X of the implementation and the transformation function are the same. Only the state, that is the particular value of type X changes.

If we see a stream as a process then any tail of the stream will represent the same process but at various stages of its life.

Sometimes this way of building streams is too limited. For instance, how can we build the concatenation of an element a of type A in front of a stream s ? We want the first *Out* step should give the pair (a, s) and the next *Out* steps should behave like the *Out* steps of s.

Using the *CoIter* operator, one can implement the concatenation function by adding a boolean information for the identification of the first step. The following stream implements the concatenation of a to s:

$$\boxed{\begin{array}{l} \qquad\qquad (true, s) : bool \otimes Str_A \\ \hline f \;:\; bool \otimes Str_A \;\to\; A \otimes (bool \otimes Str_A) \;:=\; (f\,(true, s)) \rhd (a, (false, s)) \\ \qquad\qquad\qquad\qquad\qquad\qquad\qquad\qquad\quad (f\,(false, s)) \rhd (Hd\ s, (false, Tl\ s)) \end{array}}$$

but it is not a very efficient implementation because each step tests whether it is the first one...

One may prefer to use a more powerful scheme *CoRec* known as co-recursion which has type $(X : Set)(X \to A \otimes (Str_A \oplus X)) \to X \to Str_A$.

If a stream s is built from $(CoRec\ X\ f\ x)$ then $(f\ x)$ has type $A \otimes (Str_A \oplus X)$ If $(f\ x)$ is $(a, inl\ s')$ with $s' : Str_A$, we expect $(Tl\ s)$ to be s'. If $(f\ x)$ is $(a, inr\ y)$ with $y : X$, we expect $(Tl\ s)$ to be $(CoRec\ X\ f\ y)$.

Computationally, it means that the transformation step may not only modify the current value of the state like in the iterative case, but instead it may provide a new process built on a new implementation.

Pictorially, if a stream defined as $(CoRec\ X\ f\ x)$ is represented by

$$\begin{array}{|c|}\hline x : X \\ \hline f : X \rightarrow A \otimes (Str_A \oplus X) \\ \hline \end{array}$$

we have one of the two following situations :

$$\begin{array}{|c|}\hline x : X \\ \hline f : X \rightarrow A \otimes (Str_A \oplus X) \\ \hline \end{array} \xrightarrow{Tl} \begin{array}{|c|}\hline s : Str_A \\ \hline \end{array} \qquad \text{when } (snd\ (f\ x)) = (inl\ s)$$

$$\begin{array}{|c|}\hline x : X \\ \hline f : X \rightarrow A \otimes (Str_A \oplus X) \\ \hline \end{array} \xrightarrow{Tl} \begin{array}{|c|}\hline y : X \\ \hline f : X \rightarrow A \otimes (Str_A \oplus X) \\ \hline \end{array} \text{when } (snd\ (f\ x)) = (inr\ y)$$

The *cons* operation becomes trivial when using the co-recursion scheme. Given $a : A$ and $s : Str_A$ it can be implemented efficiently as:

$$\begin{array}{|c|}\hline tt : unit \\ \hline [x : unit](a, inl\ s) : unit \rightarrow A \otimes (Str_A \oplus unit) \\ \hline \end{array}$$

General co-recursion More generally, for an arbitrary functor F the type of the recursion scheme $CoRecis\ (X : \mathrm{Set})(X \rightarrow (F\ (nu \oplus X))) \rightarrow X \rightarrow nu$
As was noticed by H. Geuvers [7], one can easily build a coinductive type enjoying a co-recursion scheme instead of a co-iteration scheme :

Inductive $nur : \mathrm{Set} := CoRec : (X : \mathrm{Set})(X \rightarrow (F\ (nur \oplus X))) \rightarrow X \rightarrow nur.$

This approach has the drawback that our inductive definition mechanism should accept the occurrence of nur to be positive in $(F\ (nur \oplus X))$.

With this definition we can easily build the *Outr* function of type $nur \rightarrow (F\ nur)$ and a function *Intror* of type $(F\ nur) \rightarrow nur$ assuming $(Fmon\ (f \circ g)) \equiv (Fmon\ f) \circ (Fmon\ g)$ and $(Fmon\ [x : X]x\ m) \equiv m$ it is possible to check that $(Outr\ (Intror\ m))$ is convertible with m.

We shall not use this type in our encoding of circuits for which the iterative representation is computationally more relevant.

Anyway it is well-known that a kind of co-recursion operator can be mimicked with the iterative version of coinductive types. Given $X : \mathrm{Set}$, $f : X \rightarrow (F\ (nu \oplus X))$ and $x : X$, an object of type nu representing an object defined by co-recursion $(CoRec\ X\ f\ x)$ can be implemented as :

$$\begin{array}{|lcl|}\hline \multicolumn{3}{|c|}{(inr\ x) : nu \oplus X} \\ \hline f\ :\ (nu \oplus X) \rightarrow (F\ (nu \oplus X)) & := & (f\ (inl\ m)) \triangleright (Fmon\ inl\ (Out\ m)) \\ & & (f\ (inr\ x)) \triangleright (f\ x) \\ \hline \end{array}$$

However, this operator does not enjoy exactly the expected reduction rules. The corresponding equalities are only provable in an extensional way (we can only prove that the two streams generates equal values).

Streams versus functions There is a correspondence between streams of elements of a type A and functions from *nat* to A. It is easy to build a function *nth* which takes an integer n and associates to an arbitrary stream the $n+1$-th element of this stream. We first define iteratively the function which takes the n-th tail of a stream.

$$\textbf{Def}\ nthtl : Str_A \to \mathbf{nat} \to Str_A := \begin{array}{ll} (nthtl\ s\ O) & \rhd s \\ (nthtl\ s\ (S\ n)) & \rhd (Tl\ (nthtl\ s\ n)) \end{array}$$

$$\textbf{Def}\ nth\ [s : Str; n : \mathbf{nat}] : A := (Hd\ (nthtl\ s\ n))$$

Reciprocally, given a function f there is a uniform way to build a stream s such that $(nth\ s\ n)$ reduces to $(f\ n)$ for instance : $(CoIter\ \mathbf{nat}\ [n : \mathbf{nat}]((f\ n), (S\ n)))$.

The two representations do not have the same computational behavior. The computation of the n-th value of s using an eager evaluation always computes the sequence $(f\ 0) \ldots (f\ (n-1))$ which may not be very efficient. On the other side, assume f is defined in a primitive recursive way, $((f\ 0) = x_0\ \ (f\ (n{+}1)) = (g\ n\ (f\ n)))$ such that the computation of $(f\ n)$ takes n steps. In order to compute the sequence $(f\ 0) \ldots (f\ (n-1))$ with a functional representation it will take n^2 steps. But if we choose a clever stream representation as

$$(CoIter\ A \otimes \mathbf{nat}\ [x : A \otimes \mathbf{nat}]((fst\ x), (g\ (snd\ x)\ (fst\ x)), (S\ (snd\ x)))\ (x_0, O))$$

then the cost of the computation of the sequence will be linear.

The co-iterative representation of streams seems perfectly adequate for the encoding of circuits and we shall experiment it in Coq.

3 Circuits

We shall now describe the representation of a circuit as a stream transformer. In that case, streams defined using the co-iteration principle suits perfectly.

3.1 Specification of a sequential circuit

A circuit realizes a function from the set of inputs to the set of outputs. When we have a combinational circuit, the function which is realized depends only on the structure of the circuit.

When the circuit contains registers (sequential circuit), the output is computed from the inputs and the current value of registers, the new value of registers is also obtained from the old values of registers and the current value of inputs. So the function which is realized depends in general on the value of the registers. The value of the registers is itself a function which depends on the structure of the circuit, the initial value of the register and the finite list of previous values of inputs. One way to represent the function realized by a sequential circuit is to add as an extra parameter an integer n representing the current stage of the circuit.

From the structure of the circuit we can deduce two functions one (called *outp*) computing the output from the input and registers, the other one (called *upd*) updating the registers from the inputs and current values of registers. Let us call *TI* the type of inputs, *TO* the type of outputs and *TR* the type of registers, we have $outp : TI \to TR \to TO$ and $upd : TI \to TR \to TR$.

Circuits as functions It is possible to represent the inputs as a function *input* : $nat \rightarrow TI$. Assume the initial value of registers is r_0. We can define a function *register* : $nat \rightarrow TR$ representing the value of registers at each time and finally the function *circuit* : $nat \rightarrow TO$ representing the value of outputs. These functions can be defined in a primitive recursive way by :

Def *register* : $nat \rightarrow TR$:= $(register\ O) \quad \triangleright r_0$
$\qquad (register\ (S\ n)) \triangleright (upd\ (input\ n)\ (register\ n))$

Def *circ* $[n : nat]$: TO := $(outp\ (input\ n)\ (register\ n))$

This approach is taken in [5] for the verification of the multiplier circuit in Coq.

3.2 Representing a circuit as a stream transformer

In this paper we represent the circuit as a function from the stream of inputs to the stream of outputs whose implementation makes reference to the type of registers.

More precisely the previous circuit will be represented as a process built on the type $Str_{TI} \otimes TR$. Assume the current state is a pair (s, r), the process will first consume the stream of inputs s to produce the current input i and the stream of remaining inputs t, the output will be $(outp\ i\ r)$ and the next value of the state will be $(t, (upd\ i\ r))$. We introduce the function corresponding to the transition step :

Def *trans* : $(Str_{TI} \otimes TR) \rightarrow (TO \otimes (Str_{TI} \otimes TR))$:=
$(trans\ (s, r)) \triangleright (outp\ (Hd\ s)\ r, (Tl\ s, upd\ (Hd\ s)\ r))$

Definition 1. The Coq code for a circuit of entry type *TI*, output type *TO*, updating function *upd* and output function *outp* is the following :

Def *circ* $[ri : TR; siStr_{TI}]$: Str_{TO} := $(CoIter\ Str_{TI} \otimes TR\ trans\ (si, ri))$

It corresponds to $\dfrac{(si, ri) : Str_{TI} \otimes TR}{trans : (Str_{TI} \otimes TR) \rightarrow (TO \otimes (Str_{TI} \otimes TR))}$

3.3 Reasoning on circuits

This representation suggests particular proof methods.

One property to be checked for circuits is "given two circuits, prove that they realize the same relation between inputs and outputs". Usually one circuit represents the implementation to be checked and the other one the specification which is another implementation using a less efficient but more comprehensible circuit. Another verification can be to check that a circuit satisfies a certain logical property.

Usually, assume we have a circuit specified by the functions *outp* and *upd* as before. Let us call *circ* the same function of type $TR \rightarrow Str_{TI} \rightarrow Str_{TO}$ as defined above in definition 1. Given an input stream I and an initial value for register R, we denote by *CIRC* the object of type Str_{TO} built as $(circ\ R\ I)$. We want to prove that a certain relation holds on outputs that will depend on the stream input I and also on a time parameter. From now on we write $s[n]$ instead of $(nth\ s\ n)$. We assume given a property $Q : nat \rightarrow TO \rightarrow \mathsf{Prop}$. And we expect to prove:

$$(\forall n : nat)(Q\ n\ CIRC[n])$$

This property can be proven, as an instance of a more general scheme applicable to any iteratively defined function.

3.4 Properties of iteratively defined functions

Assume we have a type X, a function f of type $X \rightarrow X$, and x of type X, one can define a function *iter* of type $nat \rightarrow X$ such that $(iter\ n)$ iterates n times f from x.

Let Q be a property of type $nat \rightarrow X \rightarrow \text{Prop}$. We are interested in proving two kinds of properties of Q with respect to *iter*. The first one is $(\forall n : nat)(Q\ n\ (iter\ n))$ and the second one is $(\exists n : nat)(Q\ n\ (iter\ n))$. Both can be proven using the existence of an invariant *Inv* with type $nat \rightarrow X \rightarrow \text{Prop}$.

Lemma 2. Let $\text{Inv} : \text{nat} \rightarrow X \rightarrow Prop$, *such that:*

1. $(\forall n : \text{nat})(\forall y : X)(\text{Inv}\ n\ y) \Rightarrow (Q\ n\ y) \wedge (\text{Inv}\ (S\ n)\ (f\ y))$
2. $(\text{Inv}\ O\ x)$

then there is a proof of $(\forall n : \text{nat})(Q\ n\ (iter\ n))$.

PROOF: It follows from $(\forall n : nat)(Inv\ n\ (iter\ n))$ proved by induction on n. □

Lemma 3. Let $\text{Inv} : \text{nat} \rightarrow X \rightarrow Prop$, $Rel : \text{nat} \otimes X \rightarrow nat \otimes X \rightarrow Prop$ *such that:*

1. $(Acc\ Rel\ (O, x))$ *(cf 1.3)*
2. $(\forall n : \text{nat})(\forall y : X)(\text{Inv}\ n\ y) \Rightarrow (Q\ n\ y) \vee ((\text{Inv}\ (S\ n)\ (f\ y)) \wedge (Rel\ (S\ n, f\ y)\ (n, y)))$
3. $(\text{Inv}\ O\ x)$

then there is a proof of $(\exists n : \text{nat})(Q\ n\ (iter\ n))$.

One first proves $(\forall p : \text{nat})(Acc\ Rel\ (p, x)) \Rightarrow (\text{Inv}\ p\ x) \Rightarrow (\exists n : \text{nat})(Q\ (p{+}n)\ (iter\ n)))$ by well-founded induction on (p, x) from which the result follows. □

Remark The fact that *nat* is involved in the well-founded relation may seem unnecessarily complicated. It is actually very useful, for instance in order to express that the object of type X will decrease only after a finite number of steps.

3.5 Application to streams and circuits

Universal properties

Lemma 4. Let $Q : \text{nat} \rightarrow A \rightarrow Prop$ *and* $s : Str_A$. *If there exists* $\text{Inv} : \text{nat} \rightarrow Str_A \rightarrow Prop$ *such that:*

1. $(\forall n : \text{nat})(\forall s : Str_A)(\text{Inv}\ n\ s) \Rightarrow (Q\ n\ (Hd\ s)) \wedge (\text{Inv}\ (S\ n)\ (Tl\ s))$
2. $(\text{Inv}\ O\ s)$

then we have : $(\forall n : \text{nat})(Q\ n\ s[n])$.

PROOF: Lemma 2 with $f := Tl$ and the predicate $[n : \text{nat}][s : Str_A](Q\ n\ (Hd\ s))$. □

Invariant on implementation If we know the implementation of the stream, then we can derive a more precise principle using an invariant on the implementation itself.

Lemma 5. *Let* $Q : \mathrm{nat} \to A \to Prop$, *X be a type,* $f : X \to A \otimes X$ *and* $x_0 : X$. *If there exists* $\mathrm{Inv} : \mathrm{nat} \to X \to Prop$ *such that:*

1. $(\forall n : \mathrm{nat})(\forall x : X)(\mathrm{Inv}\ n\ x) \Rightarrow (Q\ n\ (fst\ (f\ x))) \wedge (\mathrm{Inv}\ (S\ n)\ (snd\ (f\ x)))$
2. $(\mathrm{Inv}\ O\ x_0)$

then we have : $(\forall n : \mathrm{nat})(Q\ n\ (CoIter\ X\ f\ x_0)[n])$

Proof: Lemma 2 with the function $[x : X](snd\ (f\ x))$ and the predicate $[n : \mathrm{nat}][x : A](Q\ n\ (fst\ (f\ x)))$. □

Invariant on a circuit In the case of a circuit we furthermore can use the properties :

$$(Hd\ (circ\ s\ r)) \equiv (outp\ (Hd\ s)\ r)$$
$$(Tl\ (circ\ s\ r)) \equiv (circ\ (Tl\ s)\ (upd\ (Hd\ s)\ r))$$

Corollary 6. *Let* $\mathrm{inv} : \mathrm{nat} \to Str_{TI} \to TR \to Prop$ *such that:*

1. $(\forall n : \mathrm{nat})(\forall s : Str_{TI})(\forall r : TR)$
   $(inv\ n\ r) \Rightarrow (Q\ n\ (outp\ (Hd\ s)\ r)) \wedge (inv\ (S\ n)\ (Tl\ s)\ (upd\ (Hd\ s)\ r))$
2. $(inv\ O\ I\ R)$

then we have: $(\forall n : \mathrm{nat})(Q\ n\ CIRC[n])$

Proof: We apply lemma 5 with $X = Str_{TI} \otimes TR$, $x_0 = (I, R)$ and the invariant $[n : \mathrm{nat}][x : Str_{TI} \otimes TR](inv\ n\ (fst\ x)\ (snd\ x))$. □
We can use the fact that the stream of inputs is the input stream I at time n.

Corollary 7. *If there exists an invariant* $inv : \mathrm{nat} \to TR \to Prop$ *such that:*

1. $(\forall n : \mathrm{nat})(\forall r : TR)(inv\ n\ r) \Rightarrow (Q\ n\ (outp\ I[n]\ r)) \wedge (inv\ (S\ n)\ (upd\ I[n]\ r))$
2. $(inv\ O\ R)$

then we can prove: $(\forall n : \mathrm{nat})(Q\ n\ CIRC[n])$

Proof: We apply the previous corollary with the invariant: $[n : nat][s : Str_{TI}][r : TR](s{=}(nthtl\ I\ n)) \wedge (inv\ n\ r)$ □

Existential properties We can apply the lemma 3 to various instances in order to get proofs that the property Q will be reached. We only give here the counterpart of the lemma 7.

Lemma 8. *If there exists an invariant* $inv : \mathrm{nat} \to TR \to Prop$ *and a relation Rel :* $\mathrm{nat} \otimes TR \to \mathrm{nat} \otimes TR \to Prop$ *such that:*

1. $(\forall n : nat)(\forall r : TR)(inv\ n\ r)$
$\Rightarrow (Q\ n\ (outp\ I[n]\ r)) \vee ((inv\ (S\ n)\ (upd\ I[n]\ r)) \wedge (Rel\ (S\ n, upd\ I[n]\ r)\ (n, r)))$
2. $(inv\ O\ R)$
3. $(Acc\ Rel\ (O, R))$

then $(\exists n : nat)(Q\ n\ CIRC[n])$ *is provable.*

PROOF: We apply the lemma 3 to:
- the function implementing the circuit,
- the invariant : $[n : nat][p : Str_{TI} \otimes TR]((fst\ p)=(nthtl\ I\ n)) \wedge (inv\ n\ (snd\ p))$,
- the property $[n : nat][p : Str_{TI} \otimes TR](Q\ n\ (outp\ (Hd\ (fst\ p))\ (snd\ p)))$,
- the relation $[p, q : nat \otimes (Str_{TI} \otimes TR)](Rel\ ((fst\ p), (snd\ (snd\ p)))\ ((fst\ q), (snd\ (snd\ q))))$

4 The multiplier circuit

We study a very simple example introduced in [10] which implements a multiplier.

4.1 Graphical description of the multiplier

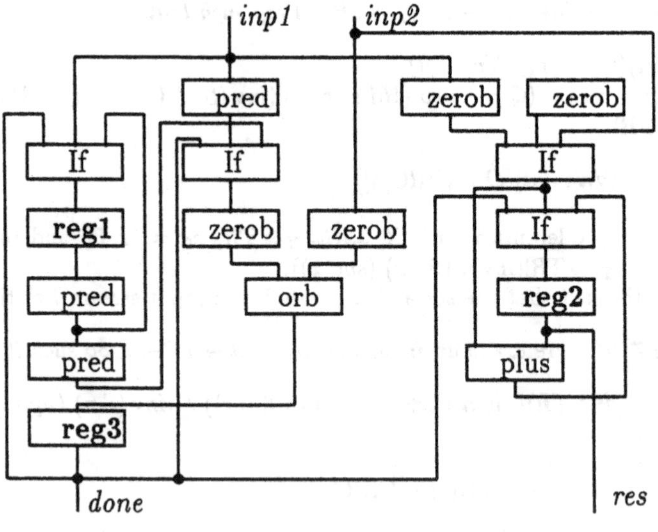

4.2 Representation

Each combinational part of the circuit can be interpreted as a COQ function working on natural numbers and booleans. For the definition and the specification of the circuit, we use the basic operations (*orb*, *zerob*) on booleans with their properties. Now we can introduce the functions for computing the outputs and updating the registers.

Each function depends a priori on the values of the inputs *inp*1 and *inp*2 of type *nat* and of the values of the registers *reg*1, *reg*2 of type *nat* and *reg*3 of type *bool*.

Def *upd1* $[i1, r1 : \mathrm{nat}; r3 : \mathit{bool}]$: *nat* := $(\mathit{If}\ r3\ i1\ (r1{-}1))$.
Def *upd2* $[i1, i2, r2 : \mathrm{nat}; r3 : \mathit{bool}]$: *nat* :=
$(\mathit{If}\ r3\ (\mathit{If}\ (\mathit{zerob}\ i1)\ O\ i2)\ ((\mathit{If}\ (\mathit{zerob}\ i1)\ O\ i2) + r2))$.
Def *upd3* $[i1, i2, r1 : \mathrm{nat}; r3 : \mathit{bool}]$: *bool* :=
$(\mathit{orb}\ (\mathit{zerob}\ (\mathit{If}\ r3\ (i1 \dot{-} 1)\ ((r1 \dot{-} 1) \dot{-} 1)))\ (\mathit{zerob}\ i2))$.
The types for registers, entries and outputs are defined using the macro command Record which is equivalent to the definition of a n-ary product but with explicit given names for the n-uple constructor and the projections.
Record *TR* : Set := *reg* {*reg*1 : nat; *reg*2 : nat; *reg*3 : nat}.
Record *TI* : Set := *inp* {*inp*1 : nat; *inp*2 : nat}.
Record *TO* : Set := *out* {*res* : nat; *done* : *bool*}.
The initial values for *reg*1 and *reg*2 can be arbitrary, we call them *ri1*,*ri2*. The initial value of *reg*3 needs to be *true*. The *upd* and *outp* function can easily be defined, as well as the initial value.
Def *update* $[i : \mathit{TI}; r : \mathit{TR}]$: *TR* :=
(*reg* (*upd*1 (*inp*1 *i*) (*reg*1 *r*) (*reg*3 *r*))
(*upd*2 (*inp*1 *i*) (*inp*2 *i*) (*reg*2 *r*) (*reg*3 *r*))
(*upd*3 (*inp*1 *i*) (*inp*2*i*) (*reg*1 *r*) (*reg*3 *r*))).
Def *output* $[i : \mathit{TI}; r : \mathit{TR}]$: *TO* := (*out* (*reg*2 *r*) (*reg*3 *r*)).
Def *init* [*TR*] : (*reg ri1 ri2 true*) := .
Def *circ_mult* $[si : \mathit{Str}_{TI}]$: Str_{TO} := (*circ outp upd init si*).

4.3 Specification

The informal specification of the circuit is the following: assume the values of *inp*1 and *inp*2 are constants equal to X and Y then the next time *done* will be *true*, the value of *out* will be equal to $X \times Y$.

In order to express the specification, we introduce the property *stable* with type $\mathit{nat} \to \mathsf{Prop}$ which means that for all $k < n$, $I[k] = (\mathit{inp}\ X\ Y)$. We shall use the following properties of this predicate.

$(\mathit{stable}\ O)$
$(n : \mathrm{nat})(\mathit{stable}\ (S\ n)) \Rightarrow (\mathit{stable}\ n)$
$(n : \mathrm{nat})(\mathit{stable}\ (S\ n)) \Rightarrow I[n]{=}(\mathit{inp}\ X\ Y)$.

The property to be proved for this circuit is :
Def *Q* $[n : \mathrm{nat}; o : \mathit{TO}]$: Prop :=
$(\mathit{stable}\ n) \Rightarrow n{\neq}O \Rightarrow (\mathit{done}\ o){=}\mathit{true} \Rightarrow (\mathit{res}\ o){=}(X \times Y)$.
For the invariant, we use the construction *IfProp* with type $\mathsf{Prop} \to \mathsf{Prop} \to \mathit{bool} \to \mathsf{Prop}$ such that $(\mathit{IfProp}\ A\ B\ b)$ is equivalent to $(b{=}\mathit{true} \to A) \wedge (b{=}\mathit{false} \to B)$. The invariant is defined as:
Def *InvM* $[n : \mathrm{nat}; r : \mathit{TR}]$: Prop :=
$(\mathit{stable}\ n) \Rightarrow$
$(\mathit{IfProp}\ (n{\neq}O) \Rightarrow (\mathit{reg2}\ r){=}(X \times Y)$
$((\mathit{reg1}\ r) \dot{-} 1){\neq}O \wedge X{\neq}O \wedge ((((\mathit{reg1}\ r) \dot{-} 1) \times Y) + (\mathit{reg2}\ r)){=}(X \times Y)$
$(\mathit{reg3}\ r))$.
Formally we have to check the two properties stated in proposition 7. The second condition which checks that the invariant is satisfied by the initial state of the circuit is trivially true by absurdity because at the initial stage *r3* is equal to *true* and $n{=}O$.

4.4 Proof of termination

It is not enough to prove that we get the expected result when *done* is equal to *true*, one need also to show that at some point *done* will be equal to *true*.

For this, it is enough to apply the lemma 8 with the property $[n : nat][o : TO]n \neq O \wedge (done\ o){=}true$. We have to find both a decreasing relation and an invariant. It is easy to remark that for the register r if $(reg3\ r){=}false$ then $(reg1\ r) \neq O$ and consequently $(reg1\ r)$ decreases strictly. This is true except for the first step, consequently we can take the order:

Def *Rel* $[p : \mathbf{nat} \otimes TR; q : \mathbf{nat} \otimes TR]$: Prop :=
$(lt\ (fst\ q)\ (fst\ p)) \wedge ((lt\ O\ (fst\ q)) \Rightarrow (lt\ (reg3\ (snd\ p))\ (reg3\ (snd\ q))))$

This order can be proven to be well-founded. The invariant will be $[n : nat][r : TR](reg3\ r){=}false \Rightarrow (reg1\ r) \neq O$ which satisfies the expected properties.

5 Related work and Conclusion

Many experiments in hardware verification have been done with the NQTHM or HOL theorem provers. In NQTHM, circuits are represented as functions and proofs are done using induction and computation over functions, while in HOL they are represented as relations and proofs are done at the logical level. In Coq, we can freely choose one or the other representations as well as mixing them together or use other representation like the streams suggested in this paper. Few experiments have been performed on this topic, and further investigations remains to be done in order to see the advantages of Coq in this area.

S. Coupet and L. Jakubiec [6] have first investigated proving simple circuits in Coq (factorial, and the multiplier studied here). Further experiments prooving microprocessors using Coq have been done by L. Arditi [1].

The system Coq now provides primitive co-inductive definitions [8, 9] but when we started this study, it was only possible to encode these infinite structures using an impredicative encoding. However this encoding appears to be well-suited for the representation of processes.

In this paper, we first showed the concrete representation of coinductive definitions (encoded impredicatively) as a simple process and we applied this representation to the type of streams. We showed principles using invariants for proving that a property holds for any element of the stream or for one of them. Finally we showed how to represent a sequential circuit as a function from a stream of inputs to a stream of outputs starting from functions describing how to update the registers and produce the outputs. Using this representation and the proof principles over streams, we completely derived the proof of a simple multiplier circuit.

The type of streams of objects of type A is isomorphic to the type of functions from *nat* to A. Consequently the development we made and principles we proved could equivalently have been done with functions like in [5]. The difference between the two types is intentional, a stream is a process which iteratively produces values while a function is an arbitrary method to produce outputs from inputs. The streams are an interesting model for circuits that could suggest alternative proof methods : proving the equivalence of two circuits using a bisimulation or developing a circuit starting from its specification using parameterized streams as in [14].

Acknowledgments We thank the team on hardware verification at Université de Provence in Marseille, especially S. Coupet and L. Pierre for fruitful discussions on the way circuits were represented for formal verification. These discussions suggested the study of this example.

References

1. L. Arditi. Formal verification of microprocessors : a first experiment with the Coq proof assistant. Research report, I3S, Université de Nice - Sophia Antipolis, 1996. To appear.
2. R. S. Boyer and J. S. Moore. *A computational logic*. ACM Monograph. Academic Press, 1979.
3. R. S. Boyer and J. S. Moore. *A computational logic handbook*. Academic Press, 1988.
4. C. Cornes, J. Courant, J.-C. Filliâtre, G. Huet, P. Manoury, C. Muñoz, C. Murthy, C. Parent, C. Paulin-Mohring, A. Saïbi, and B. Werner. The Coq Proof Assistant Reference Manual version 5.10. Rapport Technique 0177, INRIA-Rocquencourt-CNRS-ENS Lyon, July 1995. Available by anonymous ftp on ftp.inria.fr.
5. S. Coupet-Grimal and L. Jakubiec. Verification formelle de circuits avec Coq. In *Journée du GDR-Programmation*, Lille, September 1994. Also available as a Coq contribution.
6. S. Coupet-Grimal and L. Jakubiec. Coq and hardware verification : a case study. In *International Conference on Theorem Proving in Higher Order Logics (TPHOL'96)*, Turku, Finland, August 1996. To appear.
7. H. Geuvers. Inductive and coinductive types with iteration and recursion. Faculty of Mathematics and Informatics, Catholic University Nijmegen, 1991.
8. E. Giménez. Co-inductive types in Coq. Technical report, Projet Coq, INRIA Rocquencourt, CNRS ENs Lyon, July 1995. To appear.
9. E. Giménez. Implementation of co-inductive types in Coq: an experiment with the alternating bit protocol. Rapport de recherche, LIP-ENS Lyon, 1995. In preparation.
10. M. Gordon. Why higher-order logic is a good formalism for specifying and verifying hardware. In G. Milne and P. A. Subrahmanyam, editors, *Formal Aspects of VLSI Design*, 1986. also issued as University of Cambridge Computer Laboratory Technical Report No. 77, 1985.
11. M.J.C. Gordon and T. F. Melham. *Introduction to HOL. A theorem proving environment for higher order logic*. University of Cambridge, 1993.
12. T. Hagino. A typed lambda-calculus with categorical type constructors. In D.H. Pitt, A. Poigné, and D.E. Rydeheard, editors, *Category in Computer Science*, volume 283 of *Lecture Notes in Computer Science*. Springer-Verlag, September 1987.
13. G. Huet, G. Kahn, and C. Paulin-Mohring. The Coq proof assistant - a tutorial. Rapport Technique 0178, Projet Coq-INRIA Rocquencourt-ENS Lyon, July 1995. Available by anonymous ftp on ftp.inria.fr.
14. F. Leclerc and C. Paulin-Mohring. Programming with streams in Coq. a case study : The sieve of eratosthenes. In H. Barendregt and T. Nipkow, editors, *Types for Proofs and Programs, Types' 93*, volume 806 of *LNCS*. Springer-Verlag, 1994.
15. G. C. Wraith. A note on categorical data types. In D.H. Pitt, D.E. Rydeheard, P. Dybjer, A.M. Pitts, and A. Poigné, editors, *Category Theory and Computer Science*, volume 389 of *Lecture Notes in Computer Science*, pages 118–126. Springer-Verlag, September 1989.

Context-Relative Syntactic Categories and the Formalization of Mathematical Text

Aarne Ranta

Department of Philosophy, P.O.Box 24
00014 University of Helsinki, Finland.

The format of grammar presented by Montague (1974) is widely applied in the study of the logical structure of informal language. Thus it is natural to try how it works in the analysis of language in which logical content is uncontroversially a prominent part of meaning, the language of mathematics. In Ranta 1995, we presented a system of syntactic categories obtained from categories of Montague style by adding domain parameters; semantically, this corresponds to the transition from simple type theory to a type theory with multiple domains of individuals and dependent function types. In this paper, we shall generalize the system of categories further, by adding context parameters. In this way, it becomes possible to express arbitrarily complex quantificational structures in English. We go on by defining a category of proof texts, which are interpreted as type-theoretical proof objects. A system of introduction and elimination rules will be presented for the logical constants, as well as some mathematical proof rules.

The rules presented in this paper are a fragment of a grammar implemented in the proof editor ALF. A similar grammar has been implemented for French, too. The implementation can be used as an interactive proof text editor, so that the user chooses proof steps, wordings, and grammatical structures, and the system checks that the text is both mathematically and grammatically correct.

1 Introduction

A mathematical text can be considered from two points of view, linguistic and logical. From the linguistic point of view, a mathematical text is made up from sentences, which, in turn, are made up from nouns and verbs and adjectives, according to the same rules of grammar as any other text. From the logical point of view, a mathematical text is an expression of a theorem or of a proof, made up by applications of logical constants and proof constructors, and by bindings of variables.

Let us consider an example:

> *If f is a differentiable function, then if f is increasing, $f'(x) > 0$ for every x.*

Linguistically, this is an English sentence with some symbols used as constituents, in a way that is normal in mathematical writing. It is a conditional whose antecedent is formed from a noun phrase and a verb phrase; the noun phrase is a single symbol f and the verb phrase is the copula *is* attached to an indefinite noun phrase. In this way, we can enter deeper and deeper in the grammatical structure of the sentence, eventually to find the way in which it is made up from words and suffixes and symbols, and conclude that it is a well-formed English sentence.

Logically, the sentence expresses the proposition

$$(\forall f : R \to R)(\Pi z : (\forall x : R)\mathrm{Diff}(f, x))$$
$$(\mathrm{Incr}(f) \supset (\forall x : R)(D(f, x, \mathrm{ap}(z, x)) > 0)).$$

This formalization is in constructive type theory, where the propositions-as-types principle is applied to express the dependence of the term $f'(x)$ on the proof that f is differentiable at x. Thus it is somewhat more accurate than a formalization in predicate calculus. What it is intended to show is the mathematical content of the sentence—the logical role it plays in a theory in which it occurs.

These two analyses of the sentence are very different and, in a sense, complementary: they are both essential for a full understanding of the sentence as a piece of mathematical text. A mathematical text is not correct if it does not conform to both grammatical and logical rules. A complete system of rules for building mathematical texts should thus incorporate both kinds of information. Both linguistic and logical analysis of language ignore some relevant distinctions.

That logical analysis ignores linguistic distinctions is shown clearly by the possibility of expressing a given proposition by hundreds or thousands of different sentences: that the proposition is the same for all of them means that the linguistic differences are suppressed in the proposition. (That there can be so many linguistic expressions is easy to apprehend: if a formula is made up from ten operators and each operator is expressible in two ways, there are 1024 expressions for the proposition.)

That linguistic analysis, on the other hand, usually ignores logical distinctions is perhaps still better known to mathematicians. Two aspects can be pointed out in the example above. First, the formation of sentences from nouns and verbs and adjectives is often presented as much more liberal than what is mathematically meaningful. Both of the sentences

the function f is increasing,
the number x is increasing,

are grammatically well-formed, but only the former one makes mathematical sense. This is because the predicate Incr is only defined for functions, not for numbers. Second, different statuses of symbols are ignored. In our example, the first occurrence of the symbol f is in a *declaration*, corresponding to its use in the quantifier prefix $(\forall f : R \to R)$: this declaration creates a context in which the symbol can be used as a referring expression. The other two occurrences of f are normal uses of the symbol in the context in which it has been declared.

These logical phenomena, although sometimes ignored, are certainly often discussed in modern linguistic theory, under the titles of *selectional restrictions* and *discourse representation*, respectively. In Ranta 1995, we presented a way of making selectional restrictions—logically, domain distinctions—explicit in grammar, by relativizing grammatical categories to domains. For instance, the category PN of proper names was replaced by the family of categories PN(A), where A : dom. The expressions of each category are *syntax trees*, type-theoretical objects that can be effectively both *interpreted* as ordinary mathematical objects and *sugared* into ordinary English expressions—that is, into strings of characters.

In this paper, we shall present a further relativization of grammatical categories to contexts, to be able to give a full analysis of mathematical texts.

2 Context-Relative Categories

The general form of a grammatical rule is

$$\frac{a_1 : \alpha_1 \quad \cdots \quad a_n : \alpha_n}{\begin{array}{l} C(a_1,\ldots,a_n) : \alpha \\ C(a_1,\ldots,a_n)^\star \;=\; F(a_1^\star,\ldots,a_n^\star) \\ C(a_1,\ldots,a_n)^\circ \;=\; G(a_1^\circ,\ldots,a_n^\circ) \end{array}}$$

Some of the types $\alpha_1,\ldots,\alpha_n$ are grammatical categories, some of them ordinary type-theoretical categories. The corresponding arguments $a_1,\ldots,a_n$ of C are called syntactic and semantic arguments, respectively. In sugaring, the semantic arguments are erased, but they are indispensable for interpretation, and, indeed, for the very formation of the syntax tree. If the grammatical categories are $\alpha_{i_1},\ldots,\alpha_{i_k}$, the rule above corresponds to the phrase structure rule

$$\alpha \to \alpha_{i_1} \ \ldots \ \alpha_{i_k}.$$

The semantic arguments of a grammatical construction include domain and context information. For domains, we shall use the ordinary notation for sets of lower-level type theory, as presented in Martin-Löf 1984. For contexts, we shall use a notation stemming from Per Martin-Löf's lectures on substitution calculus in 1992. (Tasistro 1993 uses a slightly different notation, but gives a presentation of the same structure.) In the ALF implementation, the types cont and dom are encoded as inductively defined universes. (So is, consequently, prop, which is the same as dom.)

By writing

$$\Gamma : \text{cont},$$

we mean that Γ is a sequence of hypotheses, of the form

$$x_1 : A_1, \ \ldots, \ x_n : A_n,$$

where $n = 0,1,2,\ldots$ and each A_k is a set depending on the hypotheses up to $n = k-1$. We write

$$J/\Gamma$$

for a judgement J, of any of the four forms of Martin-Löf (1984), when made in the context Γ. We think of contexts as being defined inductively by the rules

$$() : \text{cont}, \qquad \frac{\Gamma : \text{cont} \quad A : \text{dom}/\Gamma}{(\Gamma, x : A) : \text{cont}},$$

where x is a fresh variable.

We can now generalize the category S of sentences to the family of categories

$$\mathrm{S}(\Gamma),$$

where Γ : cont, of sentences in the context Γ. Expressions of $\mathrm{S}(\Gamma)$ are interpreted as propositional functions

$$A : \mathrm{prop}/\Gamma.$$

The variables of Γ may thus occur free in A. (The old category S is now obtained as the special case $\mathrm{S}(())$, the category of sentences in the empty context.)

A typical example of a sentence in a non-empty context is the succedent of a conditional. The ordinary phrase structure rule,

$$\mathrm{S} \rightarrow \textit{if}\ \mathrm{S}\ \textit{then}\ \mathrm{S},$$

presents the conditional as a mere concatenation of two sentences. But the sentence

if a number is even then it is divisible by 2

cannot be understood as the mere concatenation of the sentences *a number is even* and *it is divisible by* 2, because the second sentence depends on the first sentence: the pronoun *it* is interpreted as the number given in the context of the first sentence. The precise grammatical rule for the conditional, which makes this dependence explicit, is

$$\frac{\Gamma : \mathrm{cont} \quad A : \mathrm{S}(\Gamma) \quad B : \mathrm{S}((\Gamma,\ x : A^{\star}))}{\begin{array}{l} \mathrm{if}(\Gamma, A, B) : \mathrm{S}(\Gamma) \\ \mathrm{if}(\Gamma, A, B)^{\star} = (\Pi x : A^{\star})B^{\star} \\ \mathrm{if}(\Gamma, A, B)^{\circ} = \textit{if}\ A^{\circ}\ \textit{then}\ B^{\circ} \end{array}}$$

The category PN of proper names, which was first generalized to the family $\mathrm{PN}(A)$ of proper names of type A, is now generalized to the family

$$\mathrm{PN}(\Gamma, A),$$

where Γ : cont and $A : \mathrm{dom}/\Gamma$, of proper names of type A in the context Γ. Expressions of $\mathrm{PN}(\Gamma, A)$ are interpreted as elements of A depending on Γ, that is, as objects

$$a : A/\Gamma.$$

A typical example is the anaphoric pronoun *it*,

$$\frac{\Gamma : \mathrm{cont} \quad A : \mathrm{dom}/\Gamma \quad a : A/\Gamma}{\begin{array}{l} \mathrm{Pron}(\Gamma, A, a) : \mathrm{PN}(\Gamma, A) \\ \mathrm{Pron}(\Gamma, A, a)^{\star} = a \\ \mathrm{Pron}(\Gamma, A, a)^{\circ} = \textit{it} \end{array}}$$

The corresponding phrase structure rule

$$\mathrm{PN} \rightarrow \textit{it}$$

is particularly unrevealing as for the conditions of use of the pronoun:

> The anaphoric pronoun *it* may be used as a name referring to any individual of any type given in the context.

(Cf. Ranta 1994, chapter 4, for more discussion about the use of anaphoric pronouns. Their use in mathematical text is often avoided if the uniqueness of interpretation is in danger.)

More complicated examples of a proper names in a context are

the inverse of the function f,
the derivative of f *at* x,
the intersection point of l *and* m.

They are, superficially, similar to the proper names

the square of the number x,
the value of the polynomial P *at* x,
the greatest common divisor of 51 *and* 85.

But logically, the examples are different. Each of the former ones hides a *presupposition*, a condition whose proof must be given in the context. In the first example, f must be bijective; in the second one, f must be differentiable at x; and in the third one, the lines l and m must intersect. The proofs are provided by semantical arguments of the grammatical constructions. For instance, the third example is produced by the rule

$$\frac{\Gamma : \text{cont} \quad A, B : \text{dom}/\Gamma \quad C : (A)(B)\text{prop}/\Gamma \quad D : \text{dom}/\Gamma \qquad f : \text{F4}(\Gamma, A, B, C, D) \quad a : \text{PN}(\Gamma, A) \quad b : \text{PN}(\Gamma, B) \quad c : C(a^\star, b^\star)/\Gamma}{\begin{array}{l}\text{DRAW}(\Gamma, A, B, C, D, f, a, b, c) : \text{PN}(\Gamma, D) \\ \text{DRAW}(\Gamma, A, B, C, D, f, a, b, c)^\star = f^\star(a^\star, b^\star, c) \\ \text{DRAW}(\Gamma, A, B, C, D, f, a, b, c)^\circ = \textit{the } f^\circ \textit{ of } a^\circ \textit{ and } b^\circ.\end{array}}$$

(Cf. Ranta 1995, section 8, where the same rule is given without dependence on a context, thus requiring a constant proof of the presupposition.)

The generalization of most of the categories and rules of Ranta 1995 is straightforwardly done pointwise. The following table shows the context-relative versions of some of the main categories.

category	of	where	is interpreted
$\text{S}(\Gamma)$	sentences	Γ : cont	prop/Γ
$\text{CN}(\Gamma)$	common nouns	Γ : cont	dom/Γ
$\text{PN}(\Gamma, A)$	proper names	Γ : cont, A : dom/Γ	A/Γ
$\text{NP}(\Gamma, A)$	noun phrases	Γ : cont, A : dom/Γ	$((A)\text{prop})\text{prop}/\Gamma$
$\text{V1}(\Gamma, A)$	intransitive verbs	Γ : cont, A : dom/Γ	$(A)\text{prop}/\Gamma$
$\text{V2}(\Gamma, A, B)$	transitive verbs	Γ : cont, A, B : dom/Γ	$(A)(B)\text{prop}/\Gamma$

The first rule of predication,

$$\text{S} \rightarrow \text{NP V1}$$

becomes

$$\frac{\Gamma : \text{cont} \quad A : \text{dom}/\Gamma \quad Q : \text{NP}(\Gamma, A) \quad F : \text{V1}(\Gamma, A)}{\begin{array}{l}\text{SUBJ}(\Gamma, A, Q, F) : \text{S}(\Gamma) \\ \text{SUBJ}(\Gamma, A, Q, F)^\star = Q^\star(F^\star) \\ \text{SUBJ}(\Gamma, A, Q, F)^\circ = Q^\circ\, F^\circ.\end{array}}$$

Basic expressions, that is, lexical items, are generalized, accordingly, to expressions usable in any context. Their interpretations do not effectively depend on the context. For instance,

$$\frac{\Gamma : \text{cont}}{\begin{array}{l}\text{zero}(\Gamma) : \text{PN}(\Gamma, N) \\ \text{zero}(\Gamma)^\star = 0 \\ \text{zero}(\Gamma)^\circ = 0\end{array}}$$

(One might first think of basic expressions as expressions in the empty context, but this would not accord with the pointwise relativization of other forms of expression. Moreover, basic expressions would then not be readily usable in nonempty contexts.)

The really significant use of context-relative categories is made in the description of progressive structures, in rules that extend the context. We have already mentioned the progressive implication; the conjunction is analogous, interpreted in terms of Σ rather than just &. Yet another device of extending a context is an assumption made in the course of a proof text. As we shall see in Section 6, an assumption extends the context until it is discharged.

3 Explicit Variables

What we have considered so far might be called the implicit context of an expression: the variables appear in the syntax tree and in the logical interpretation, but they are not visible in the English string itself, after sugaring. In the language of mathematics, explicit variables are used as well. In the statement

if n is a number, then $n + 1$ is divisible by itself,

the antecedent introduces the explicit variable n, of type N, which is then used in the succedent. In the statement

if l and m are intersecting lines, then l contains the intersection point of l and m,

there are two explicit variables, l and m of type Ln, and one implicit variable, a proof that l intersects m. All these variables are used in the succedent.

In the grammatical analysis of a mathematical text, one must keep track not only of the context, but of what part of the context is explicit. It is clear that explicit context can also be used in the same way as implicit context: in the statement *if n is a number, then the successor of it is divisible by itself,*

the reference to the number n is made by using the pronoun *it*. But implicit variables can only be used as hidden, semantical arguments.

To formalize the distinction between explicit and implicit variables, we extend the inductive definition of contexts, which was given in the previous section, by the clause

$$\frac{\Gamma : \mathrm{cont} \quad A : \mathrm{dom}/\Gamma \quad t : \mathrm{Str}}{(\Gamma,\ x_t : A) : \mathrm{cont}},$$

where x is a fresh variable. The string t is the variable name to be used in the text; the difference to the implicit variable declaration is that such a text name is provided, not only a theory-internal name. (To guarantee the freshness of t with respect to the text names introduced earlier, we may either demand t to be fresh, or add a sufficient number of primes to it in sugaring.)

There is no semantic difference between $(\Gamma,\ x_t : A)$ and $(\Gamma,\ x : A)$. That is, they are satisfied by exactly the same substitutions, namely

$$(\gamma, x = a),$$

where γ satisfies Γ and $a : A\gamma$. The distinction is used in the definition of the syntactic category

$$\mathrm{VAR}(\Gamma, A)$$

of explicit variables of type A in the context Γ. The interpretation of such an explicit variable is an element of A in Γ,

$$a : A/\Gamma.$$

(In fact, it will always be one of the variables declared in Γ.)

The first rule of formation of explicit variables says that whenever a context Γ is extended to $(\Gamma,\ x_t : A)$, we may form an expression of the category $\mathrm{VAR}((\Gamma,\ x_t : A), A)$, a *new variable*, interpreted as x and sugared to t,

$$\frac{\Gamma : \mathrm{cont} \quad A : \mathrm{dom}/\Gamma \quad t : \mathrm{Str}}{\begin{array}{l} \mathrm{NVAR}(\Gamma, A, t) : \mathrm{VAR}((\Gamma,\ x_t : A), A) \\ \mathrm{NVAR}(\Gamma, A, t)^{*} = x \\ \mathrm{NVAR}(\Gamma, A, t)^{\circ} = t. \end{array}}$$

The explicit variables of a context are inherited by all extensions of the context. This is expressed by the grammatical rule for *ancient variables*,

$$\frac{\Gamma : \mathrm{cont} \quad A, B : \mathrm{dom}/\Gamma \quad v : \mathrm{VAR}(\Gamma, A)}{\begin{array}{l} \mathrm{AVAR}(\Gamma, A, B, v) : \mathrm{VAR}((\Gamma,\ x : B), A) \\ \mathrm{AVAR}(\Gamma, A, B, v)^{*} = v^{*} \\ \mathrm{AVAR}(\Gamma, A, B, v)^{\circ} = v^{\circ} \end{array}}$$

This rule is also valid for the extension of Γ by an explicit variable. (In the notation that we are using, there is a slight difficulty in the interpretation of

NVAR(Γ, A, t): it is defined to be x, which is not shown in the syntax tree itself, but only in the type of the tree. In the metamathematical definition of contexts used in the ALF implementation, an extended context is a code of a set ot the form $(\Sigma x : G)A(x)$, and the interpretation of the last variable of the context is the function $(z)q(z)$ defined on this set. The interpretation of an ancient variable AVAR(Γ, A, B, v) is $(z)v^\star(p(z))$.)

The grammatical representation of an English explicit variable, a syntax tree of type VAR(Γ, A), changes as the context grows, although the sugaring does not change. The syntax trees of explicit variables are, in fact, a version of the *indices* of de Bruijn (1972), indicating the *reference depth* of variables: the last, the one before the last, etc.

In de Bruijn's original work, the indices are bare numerals. Their formal definition in type theory forces them to have context and domain arguments, and the string argument permits their sugaring to the symbols actually used in the text. But we can introduce a system of abbreviations reminiscent of de Bruijn's notation, in which AVAR operators are conceived as successors, and the context and domain arguments are hidden:

$$
\begin{aligned}
0(t) &= \mathrm{NVAR}(t),\\
1(t) &= \mathrm{AVAR}(\mathrm{NVAR}(t)),\\
2(t) &= \mathrm{AVAR}(\mathrm{AVAR}(\mathrm{NVAR}(t))),\\
&\text{etc.}
\end{aligned}
$$

4 Mathematical Symbolism in English Text

The variant of English that we are describing could be called, following de Bruijn, the Mathematical Vernacular, "the very precise mixture of words and formulas used by mathematicians in their better moments" (de Bruijn 1994, p. 865). It is possible to use formulae as sentences and terms as proper names, as in many of the examples already given. But it is against the rules of mathematical writing to use English proper names as parts of terms, or sentences as parts of formulae. The mathematical symbolism has its own internal grammar and an interface into the English grammar.

The small fragment of symbolism that we need in arithmetic and geometry comprises formulae (FML) built from terms (TRM) by infix predicates (PRD) such as $=, <, >$,

$$\mathrm{FML} \rightarrow \mathrm{TRM}\ \mathrm{PRD}\ \mathrm{TRM}$$

$$\frac{\Gamma : \mathrm{cont} \quad A, B : \mathrm{dom} \quad a : \mathrm{TRM}(\Gamma, A) \quad F : \mathrm{PRD}(A, B) \quad b : \mathrm{TRM}(\Gamma, B)}{\mathrm{PRED}(\Gamma, A, B, a, F, b) : \mathrm{FML}(\Gamma)}$$

$$
\begin{aligned}
\mathrm{PRED}(\Gamma, A, B, a, F, b)^\star &= F^\star(a^\star, b^\star)\\
\mathrm{PRED}(\Gamma, A, B, a, F, b)^\circ &= a^\circ\ F^\circ\ b^\circ
\end{aligned}
$$

Terms are either variables or constants, or built from given terms by various well-known operators, such as prefixes, postfixes, and infixes, or by more specific ones such as the derivative:

TRM $\to$ TRM INF TRM

$$\frac{\Gamma : \mathrm{cont} \quad f : \mathrm{TRM}(\Gamma, R \to R) \quad x : \mathrm{TRM}(\Gamma, R) \quad c : \mathrm{Diff}(f^\star, x^\star)/\Gamma}{\begin{array}{l} \mathrm{DER}(\Gamma, f, x, c) : \mathrm{TRM}(\Gamma, R) \\ \mathrm{DER}(\Gamma, f, x, c)^\star = D(f^\star, x^\star, c) \\ \mathrm{DER}(\Gamma, f, x, c)^\circ = f^{\circ\prime}(x^\circ) \end{array}}$$

The interface of the symbolism to English is defined by two rules:

S $\to$ FML.

$$\frac{\Gamma : \mathrm{cont} \quad A : \mathrm{FML}(\Gamma)}{\begin{array}{l} \mathrm{FORMULA}(\Gamma, A) : \mathrm{S}(\Gamma) \\ \mathrm{FORMULA}(\Gamma, A)^\star = A^\star \\ \mathrm{FORMULA}(\Gamma, A)^\circ = \$A^\circ\$ \end{array}}$$

PN $\to$ TRM.

$$\frac{\Gamma : \mathrm{cont} \quad A : \mathrm{dom}/\Gamma \quad a : \mathrm{TRM}(\Gamma, A)}{\begin{array}{l} \mathrm{TERM}(\Gamma, A, a) : \mathrm{PN}(\Gamma, A) \\ \mathrm{TERM}(\Gamma, A, a)^\star = a^\star \\ \mathrm{TERM}(\Gamma, A, a)^\circ = \$a^\circ\$ \end{array}}$$

Sugaring in these rules produces LaTeX code, in which dollar signs are used for delimiting passages typeset in a special "math font".

Some authors prefer to embed symbolic expressions in English text by means of some extra words, writing A *holds* instead of bare A and *the* A a instead of bare a, but we shall here stay content with plain symbolic sentences and proper names. Notice that, in order for the sugaring *the* A° a° of the term proper name to make sense, the premise $A : \mathrm{dom}/\Gamma$ would have to be strengthened to $A : \mathrm{CN}(\Gamma)$.

5 Explicit quantifiers

A common structure in which the context is extended in a mathematical text is an explicit quantifier, either universal or existential:

S $\to$ *for all* CN VAR, S

$$\frac{\Gamma : \mathrm{cont} \quad A : \mathrm{CN}(\Gamma) \quad t : \mathrm{Str} \quad B : \mathrm{S}((\Gamma,\ x_t : A^\star))}{\begin{array}{l} \mathrm{forall}(\Gamma, A, t, B) : \mathrm{S}(\Gamma) \\ \mathrm{forall}(\Gamma, A, t, B)^\star = (\forall x : A^\star)B^\star \\ \mathrm{forall}(\Gamma, A, t, B)^\circ = \textit{for all } A^\circ(\mathrm{pl})\ t, B^\circ \end{array}}$$

S $\to$ *there exists a* CN VAR *such that* S

$$\frac{\Gamma : \mathrm{cont} \quad A : \mathrm{CN}(\Gamma) \quad t : \mathrm{Str} \quad B : \mathrm{S}((\Gamma,\ x_t : A^\star))}{\begin{array}{l} \mathrm{exists}(\Gamma, A, t, B) : \mathrm{S}(\Gamma) \\ \mathrm{exists}(\Gamma, A, t, B)^\star = (\exists x : A^\star)B^\star \\ \mathrm{exists}(\Gamma, A, t, B)^\circ = \textit{there exists } \mathrm{INDEF}(A^\circ)\ t \textit{ such that } B^\circ \end{array}}$$

(In the former rule, the parameter pl of the sugaring of A produces the plural. In the latter rule, the operation INDEF produces the article *a* or *an*, depending on A°.)

Equipped with the two rules of explicit quantification, as well as the rules of progressive implication and conjunction (see Section 2), our fragment of mathematical English can now express any proposition of the form

$$(Q_1 x_1 : A_1)(Q_2 x_2 : A_2) \cdots (Q_n x_n : A_n)A,$$

where each Q_i is either universal or existential, each A_i is expressible by a sentence or by a common noun, and A is expressible by a sentence.

Of course, there are other forms of explicit quantification in natural language, for instance, ones by which whole lists of variables can be declared at the same time. But we can already find an expression for the proposition stated in Section 1,

> *for all functions f, if f is differentiable, then if f is increasing, then for all points x, $f'(x) > 0$.*

Assuming it unproblematic how to define an operator VARPREDA1 with the effect

$$\text{S} \rightarrow \text{VAR } \textit{is} \text{ AI}$$

(cf. Ranta 1995, sections 7 and 11, for predication rules), we build the syntax tree

$$\text{forall(function}, f, \text{if(VARPREDA1(0}(f)\text{), differentiable)},$$
$$\text{if(VARPREDA1(1}(f)\text{), increasing), forall(point}, x, \text{FORMULA(PRED}(\Gamma,$$
$$\text{DER(VARIABLE(3}(f))\text{), VARIABLE(0}(x)\text{), ap}(z, v)), >, \text{zero}_R))))))$$

with the desired interpretation and sugaring. We have hidden the semantic arguments of the tree, except the context of the last sentence, which is decisive for the well-formation of the term $f'(x)$, the four-hypothesis context

$$\Gamma = (y_f : R \rightarrow R,\ z : (\forall x : R)\text{Diff}(y, x),\ u : \text{Incr}(y),\ v_x : R).$$

(Observe, furthermore, the operator VARIABLE, which takes a variable into a term, the commoun noun *point* interpreted as R, the 0 of the reals zero_R, and the interpretation of the adjective differentiable as the property of being everywhere differentiable.)

6 Proof Texts

The proof editor Coq has an interface facility of rewriting formal proofs as English texts (see Coscoy *et al.* 1995). The rewriting procedure is a direct translation of a λ term. As such, it resembles the sugaring procedure presented in Ranta 1994, which takes type-theoretical formulae directly into strings of words. As we now prefer an indirect approach based on syntax trees, we introduce the new syntactic category

$$\mathrm{PROOF}(\Gamma, A),$$

where Γ : cont and A : prop/Γ, of proofs of the proposition A in the context Γ. A syntax tree of type PROOF(Γ, A) is interpreted as a proof object

$$a : A/\Gamma.$$

The category PROOF(Γ, A) is thus semantically equal to the category PN(Γ, A) of proper names, even though the superficial difference is big: proper names are typically the smallest units of language, whereas proof texts are very large units.

There are lots of rules for building proof texts. What we shall show here are rules corresponding to Gentzen's natural deduction rules for predicate calculus. (Mathematicians, of course, usually prefer much more compressed rules.) We shall mainly follow the wordings of Coscoy *et al.* 1995. Sometimes we shall have to change them because we also sugar the expressions of propositions: Coscoy *et al.* only sugar the proof steps, leaving the propositions formal. The interpretations of the logical constants, as well as the set-theoretical notation, are from Martin-Löf 1984.

All punctuation is defined by the sugaring rules, and so is the use of capitals: passages starting with capital letters are underlined. The font used for English expressions is changed from italic to roman, to conform with the usual practice of mathematical writing.

Conjunction introduction. $\dfrac{A \quad B}{A \& B}$

$$\frac{\Gamma : \mathrm{cont} \quad A, B : \mathrm{S}(\Gamma) \quad a : \mathrm{PROOF}(\Gamma, A^\star) \quad b : \mathrm{PROOF}(\Gamma, B^\star)}{\begin{array}{l}\mathrm{ConjI}(\Gamma, A, B, a, b) : \mathrm{PROOF}(\Gamma, A^\star \& B^\star) \\ \mathrm{ConjI}(\Gamma, A, B, a, b)^\star = (a^\star, b^\star) \\ \mathrm{ConjI}(\Gamma, A, B, a, b)^\circ = a^\circ.\ \underline{b^\circ}.\ \text{Altogether, } A^\circ \text{ and } B^\circ\end{array}}$$

Conjunction elimination. $\dfrac{A \& B}{A} \quad \dfrac{A \& B}{B}$

$$\frac{\Gamma : \mathrm{cont} \quad A : \mathrm{S}(\Gamma) \quad B : \mathrm{prop}/\Gamma \quad c : \mathrm{PROOF}(\Gamma, A^\star \& B)}{\begin{array}{l}\mathrm{ConjEl}(\Gamma, A, B, c) : \mathrm{PROOF}(\Gamma, A^\star) \\ \mathrm{ConjEl}(\Gamma, A, B, c)^\star = p(c^\star) \\ \mathrm{ConjEl}(\Gamma, A, B, c)^\circ = c^\circ.\ \text{A fortiori, } A^\circ\end{array}}$$

$$\frac{\Gamma : \mathrm{cont} \quad A : \mathrm{prop}/\Gamma \quad B : \mathrm{S}(\Gamma) \quad c : \mathrm{PROOF}(\Gamma, A \& B^\star)}{\begin{array}{l}\mathrm{ConjEr}(\Gamma, A, B, c) : \mathrm{PROOF}(\Gamma, B^\star) \\ \mathrm{ConjEr}(\Gamma, A, B, c)^\star = q(c^\star) \\ \mathrm{ConjEr}(\Gamma, A, B, c)^\circ = c^\circ.\ \text{A fortiori, } B^\circ\end{array}}$$

The grammatical rules for conjunction elimination are perhaps stronger than expected: in the left rule, the second premise is $B : \mathrm{prop}/\Gamma$ instead of $B : \mathrm{S}(\Gamma)$, and in the right rule, the first premise is weakened correspondigly. Thus the conjunct that is not the conclusion of the rule can be any proposition in Γ, not necessarily one expressible by a sentence. The reason is that only the conclusion is used in the sugaring rule. Following the principle that syntactic arguments are not deleted in sugaring (Ranta 1995, section 6), we treat the other conjunct as a semantic argument of the rule.

Implication introduction. $$\frac{\begin{array}{c}(A)\\ B\end{array}}{A \supset B}$$

$$\frac{\Gamma : \mathrm{cont} \quad A, B : \mathrm{S}(\Gamma) \quad t : \mathrm{Str} \quad b : \mathrm{PROOF}((\Gamma,\ x_t : A^\star), B^\star)}{\begin{array}{l}\mathrm{ImplI}(\Gamma, A, B, t, b) : \mathrm{PROOF}(\Gamma, A^\star \supset B^\star)\\ \mathrm{ImplI}(\Gamma, A, B, t, b)^\star = (\lambda x) b^\star\\ \mathrm{ImplI}(\Gamma, A, B, t, b)^\circ = \text{assume}\end{array}}$$

A°. (t)

$\underline{b^\circ}$. Hence, if A°, then B°

Several things are to be observed about implication introduction. First, the hypothesis is marked by an explicit variable, which makes it possible to refer to the assumption later in the course of the proof. Second, the rule is easy to strengthen to having the progressive implication

$$(\Pi x : A^\star) B^\star$$

in its conclusion; the third premise is then

$$B : \mathrm{S}((\Gamma,\ x : A^\star)).$$

(An analogous generalization is possible for the conjunction rules.) Third, Coscoy *et al.* 1995 suggest, for stylistic reasons, the omission of the conclusion from the sugaring. The argument B is then not used in sugaring, and it can be weakened to a semantic argument.

Implication elimination. $$\frac{A \supset B \quad A}{B}$$

$$\frac{\begin{array}{l}\Gamma : \mathrm{cont} \quad A : \mathrm{prop}/\Gamma \quad B : \mathrm{S}(\Gamma)\\ c : \mathrm{PROOF}(\Gamma, A \supset B^\star) \quad a : \mathrm{PROOF}(\Gamma, A)\end{array}}{\begin{array}{l}\mathrm{ImplE}(\Gamma, A, B, c, a) : \mathrm{PROOF}(\Gamma, B^\star)\\ \mathrm{ImplE}(\Gamma, A, B, c, a)^\star = \mathrm{ap}(c^\star, a^\star)\\ \mathrm{ImplE}(\Gamma, A, B, c, a)^\circ = c^\circ.\ \underline{a^\circ}.\ \text{We deduce that } B^\circ\end{array}}$$

Observe, again, that A is a semantic argument not used in sugaring.

Disjunction introduction. $\dfrac{A}{A \vee B} \qquad \dfrac{B}{A \vee B}$

$$\frac{\Gamma : \text{cont} \quad A, B : \mathrm{S}(\Gamma) \quad a : \mathrm{PROOF}(\Gamma, A^\star)}{\begin{array}{l}\mathrm{DisjIl}(\Gamma, A, B, a) : \mathrm{PROOF}(\Gamma, A^\star \vee B^\star) \\ \mathrm{DisjIl}(\Gamma, A, B, a)^\star = i(a^\star) \\ \mathrm{DisjIl}(\Gamma, A, B, a)^\circ = a^\circ.\ \text{A fortiori, } A^\circ \text{ or } B^\circ\end{array}}$$

$$\frac{\Gamma : \text{cont} \quad A, B : \mathrm{S}(\Gamma) \quad b : \mathrm{PROOF}(\Gamma, B^\star)}{\begin{array}{l}\mathrm{DisjIr}(\Gamma, A, B, b) : \mathrm{PROOF}(\Gamma, A^\star \vee B^\star) \\ \mathrm{DisjIr}(\Gamma, A, B, b)^\star = j(b^\star) \\ \mathrm{DisjIr}(\Gamma, A, B, b)^\circ = b^\circ.\ \text{A fortiori, } A^\circ \text{ or } B^\circ\end{array}}$$

Disjunction elimination. $\dfrac{A \vee B \quad \begin{array}{c}(A)\\ C\end{array} \quad \begin{array}{c}(B)\\ C\end{array}}{C}$

$$\frac{\begin{array}{l}\Gamma : \text{cont} \quad A, B : \mathrm{S}(\Gamma) \quad C : \mathrm{S}(\Gamma) \\ c : \mathrm{PROOF}(\Gamma, A^\star \vee B^\star) \\ t : \mathrm{Str} \quad d : \mathrm{PROOF}((\Gamma,\ x_t : A^\star), C^\star) \\ u : \mathrm{Str} \quad e : \mathrm{PROOF}((\Gamma,\ y_u : B^\star), C^\star)\end{array}}{\begin{array}{l}\mathrm{DisjE}(\Gamma, A, B, C, c, t, d, u, e) : \mathrm{PROOF}(\Gamma, C^\star) \\ \mathrm{DisjE}(\Gamma, A, B, C, c, t, d, u, e)^\star = D(c^\star, (x)d^\star, (y)e^\star) \\ \mathrm{DisjE}(\Gamma, A, B, C, c, t, d, u, e)^\circ = c^\circ.\ \text{Hence we have two cases. First, assume}\end{array}}$$

A°. (t)

$\underline{d^\circ}$. Second, assume

B°. (u)

$\underline{e^\circ}$. Thus C°, in both cases

Absurdity elimination. $\dfrac{\bot}{C}$

$$\frac{\Gamma : \text{cont} \quad C : \mathrm{S}(\Gamma) \quad c : \mathrm{PROOF}(\Gamma, \bot)}{\begin{array}{l}\mathrm{AbsE}(\Gamma, C, c) : \mathrm{PROOF}(\Gamma, C^\star) \\ \mathrm{AbsE}(\Gamma, C, c)^\star = R_0(c^\star) \\ \mathrm{AbsE}(\Gamma, C, c)^\circ = c^\circ.\ \text{Hence } C^\circ\end{array}}$$

Universal introduction. $\dfrac{\begin{array}{c}(x : A)\\ B(x)\end{array}}{(\forall x : A)B(x)}$

$$\frac{\Gamma : \text{cont} \quad A : \text{CN}(\Gamma) \quad t : \text{Str} \quad B : \text{S}((\Gamma,\ x_t : A^\star)) \quad b : \text{PROOF}((\Gamma,\ x_t : A^\star), B^\star)}{\begin{array}{l}\text{UnivI}(\Gamma, A, t, B, b) : \text{PROOF}(\Gamma, (\forall x : A^\star)B^\star) \\ \text{UnivI}(\Gamma, A, t, B, b)^\star = (\lambda x)b^\star \\ \text{UnivI}(\Gamma, A, t, B, b)^\circ = \text{consider an arbitrary } A^\circ\ t.\ \underline{b^\circ}.\ \text{We have proved that, for all } t,\ B^\circ, \text{ since } t \text{ is arbitrary}\end{array}}$$

Just as in the case of implication introduction, Coscoy *et al.* 1995 suggest the omission of the statement of the conclusion. This means the weakening of B to a semantic argument.

Universal elimination. $$\frac{(\forall x : A)B(x) \quad a : A}{B(a)}$$

$$\frac{\Gamma : \text{cont} \quad A : \text{dom}/\Gamma \quad t : \text{Str} \quad B : \text{S}((\Gamma,\ x_t : A)) \quad c : \text{PROOF}(\Gamma, (\forall x : A)B^\star) \quad a : \text{PN}(\Gamma, A)}{\begin{array}{l}\text{UnivE}(\Gamma, A, t, B, c, a) : \text{PROOF}(\Gamma, B^\star(x = a^\star)) \\ \text{UnivE}(\Gamma, A, t, B, c, a)^\star = \text{ap}(c^\star, a^\star) \\ \text{UnivE}(\Gamma, A, t, B, c, a)^\circ = c^\circ.\ \text{In particular, } B^\circ \text{ holds for } t \text{ set to } a^\circ\end{array}}$$

Here there is an alternative sugaring, which is even more natural:

c°. In particular, $B^\circ[a^\circ/t]$

That is, t is replaced by a° in B°. But a can then not be just any proper name: it must be a symbolic term, since the variable symbol t may have occurrences inside formulae. The explicit substitution style is thus more general.

Existential introduction. $$\frac{a : A \quad B(a)}{(\exists x : A)B(x)}$$

$$\frac{\Gamma : \text{cont} \quad A : \text{CN}(\Gamma) \quad t : \text{Str} \quad B : \text{S}((\Gamma,\ x_t : A^\star)) \quad a : A^\star/\Gamma \quad b : \text{PROOF}(\Gamma, B^\star(x = a))}{\begin{array}{l}\text{ExistI}(\Gamma, A, t, B, a, b) : \text{PROOF}(\Gamma, (\exists x : A^\star)B^\star) \\ \text{ExistI}(\Gamma, A, t, B, a, b)^\star = (a, b^\star) \\ \text{ExistI}(\Gamma, A, t, B, a, b)^\circ = b^\circ.\ \text{Thus there exists INDEF}(A^\circ)\ t \text{ such that } b^\circ\end{array}}$$

Observe that a is a semantic argument not used in sugaring.

Existential elimination. $$\frac{(\exists x : A)B(x) \quad \begin{array}{c}(x : A, B(x)) \\ C\end{array}}{C}$$

$$\frac{\begin{array}{l}\Gamma : \text{cont} \quad A : \text{CN}(\Gamma) \quad t : \text{Str} \quad B : \text{S}((\Gamma,\ x_t : A^\star)) \\ C : \text{S}(\Gamma) \quad c : \text{PROOF}(\Gamma, (\exists x : A)B^\star) \\ u : \text{Str} \quad d : \text{PROOF}(((\Gamma,\ x_t : A^\star),\ y_u : B^\star), C^\star)\end{array}}{\begin{array}{l}\text{ExistE}(\Gamma, A, t, B, C, c, u, d) : \text{PROOF}(\Gamma, C^\star) \\ \text{ExistE}(\Gamma, A, t, B, C, c, u, d)^\star = E(c^\star, (x, y)d^\star) \\ \text{ExistE}(\Gamma, A, t, B, C, c, u, d)^\circ = c^\circ.\ \text{Consider an arbitrary } A^\circ\ t \text{ such that} \\ \qquad\qquad\qquad\qquad\qquad\qquad B^\circ.\ (u) \\ \qquad\qquad\qquad\qquad\qquad \underline{d^\circ}.\ \text{Thus } C^\circ,\ \text{independently of } t\end{array}}$$

We have now shown how proof texts are built from smaller proof texts by rules that correspond to the natural deduction rules of predicate calculus. Sometimes a proof required as a constituent is just a proof by assumption, which is provided by the following rule.

Assumption.

$$\frac{\Gamma : \text{cont} \quad A : \text{S}(\Gamma) \quad v : \text{VAR}(\Gamma, A^\star)}{\begin{array}{l}\text{Ass}(\Gamma, A, v) : \text{PROOF}(\Gamma, A^\star) \\ \text{Ass}(\Gamma, A, v)^\star = v^\star \\ \text{Ass}(\Gamma, A, v)^\circ = \text{by the assumption } v^\circ,\ A^\circ\end{array}}$$

It is certainly not common to build proofs with so small steps as the rules of natural deduction. To generate more advanced proofs, we need lots of compressed rules, beginning from double and triple universal introduction, Modus Tollens, de Morgan laws, etc. We also need other rules than those concerning logical constants. As an example, consider the proof rules corresponding to the inductive definition of Even and Odd,

$$\text{Even}(0) \qquad \frac{\text{Even}(a)}{\text{Odd}(s(a))} \qquad \frac{\text{Odd}(a)}{\text{Even}(s(a))}$$

$$\frac{\Gamma : \text{cont}}{\begin{array}{l}\text{evax1}(\Gamma) : \text{PROOF}(\Gamma, \text{Even}(0)) \\ \text{evax1}(\Gamma)^\star = \text{evz} \\ \text{evax1}(\Gamma)^\circ = \text{by the first axiom of evenness, 0 is even}\end{array}}$$

$$\frac{\Gamma : \text{cont} \quad a : \text{PN}(\Gamma, N) \quad b : \mathit{PROOF}(\Gamma, \text{Even}(a^\star))}{\begin{array}{l}\text{evax2}(\Gamma, a, b) : \text{PROOF}(\Gamma, \text{Odd}(0)) \\ \text{evax2}(\Gamma, a, b)^\star = \text{ods}(a^\star, b^\star) \\ \text{evax2}(\Gamma, a, b)^\circ = b^\circ.\ \text{By the second axiom of evenness, the} \\ \qquad\qquad\qquad\qquad \text{successor of } a^\circ \text{ is odd}\end{array}}$$

$$\frac{\Gamma : \text{cont} \quad a : \text{PN}(\Gamma, N) \quad b : PROOF(\Gamma, \text{Odd}(a^\star))}{\begin{array}{ll} \text{evax3}(\Gamma, a, b) : \text{PROOF}(\Gamma, \text{Even}(0)) & \\ \text{evax3}(\Gamma, a, b)^\star = \text{evs}(a^\star, b^\star) & \\ \text{evax3}(\Gamma, a, b)^\circ = b^\circ. \text{ By the third axiom of evenness, the successor of } a^\circ \text{ is even} & \end{array}}$$

(The three natural deduction rules are formalized by the three constants evz, ods, and evs.)

As the last example, consider the principle of mathematical induction, in the usual form, which compresses together type-theoretical N elimination and universal introduction:

Mathematical induction.
$$\frac{C(0) \qquad \begin{array}{c}(x : N, C(x)) \\ C(s(x))\end{array}}{(\forall x : N)C(x)}$$

$$\frac{\begin{array}{l}\Gamma : \text{cont} \quad t : \text{Str} \quad C : \text{S}((\Gamma,\ x_t : N)) \\ d : \text{PROOF}(\Gamma, C^\star(x = 0)) \\ u : \text{Str} \quad e : \text{PROOF}(((\Gamma,\ x_t : N),\ y_u : C^\star), C^\star(x = s(x)))\end{array}}{\begin{array}{l}\text{Ind}(\Gamma, t, C, d, u, e) : \text{PROOF}(\Gamma, (\forall x : N)C^\star) \\ \text{Ind}(\Gamma, t, C, d, u, e)^\star = (\lambda x)R(x, d^\star, (x, y)e^\star) \\ \text{Ind}(\Gamma, t, C, d, u, e)^\circ = \text{we proceed by induction. First, } d^\circ. \text{ Second, consider an arbitrary } t \text{ such that} \\ \qquad C^\circ.\ (u) \\ \underline{e^\circ}. \text{ So we have proved that, for all } t,\ C^\circ\end{array}}$$

7 Proof Text Editor

We have defined a system of syntax trees together with sugarings into English and interpretations as mathematical objects. But we have not shown how to perform *parsing*—to take English strings into syntax trees—and *phrasing*—to take mathematical objects into syntax trees. We have already noticed that sugaring and interpretation destroy information, so that parsing and phrasing are, essentially, search procedures. They can have multiple outcomes or none at all. (Phrasing, typically, has multiple outcomes: a given mathematical object can be expressed in several ways. For parsing, the opposite is typical, since there are so many meaningless strings.) But it should be possible to define search algorithms for limited fragments as solutions to the parsing and phrasing problems, which can be stated in type theory as follows:

$$\text{list}((\exists y : \text{S}(()))I(\text{Str}, y^\circ, x)) \ \ (x : \text{Str}),$$
$$\text{list}((\exists y : \text{S}(()))I(\text{prop}, y^\star, x)) \ \ (x : \text{prop}).$$

A translation of a proof term into a text could then be defined as phrasing followed by sugaring.

But there is another way of seeing the task of generating proof text, namely as an interactive process. Users of Coq and ALF are used to building proof terms interactively, rather than striving after automatic theorem provers. Now, if someone wants to get not only a formal proof but a corresponding text, he can try to build a syntax tree of type PROOF interactively. From this, he will obtain both a text and a formal proof. He can make decisions concerning the text, so that he can, for example, choose different expressions for one and the same proposition in different places, to avoid monotony. The proof text editor checks both mathematical and grammatical correctness all the time.

The top level of the proof text editor can be defined as the function

$$\begin{array}{rcl} \multicolumn{3}{l}{\mathrm{ThmWithProof} : (A : \mathrm{S}(()))(a : \mathrm{PROOF}((), A^{*}))\mathrm{Str}} \\ \mathrm{ThmWithProof}(A, a) & = & \text{Theorem. } \underline{A^{\circ}}. \\ & & \text{Proof. } \underline{a^{\circ}}. \end{array}$$

The user can start editing a proof text by refining an unspecified string with ThmWithProof. He then gets the subgoals

$$A = ? : \mathrm{S}(()),\ a = ? : \mathrm{PROOF}((), A^{*}).$$

The example shown below has been created by using ALF in this way. The corresponding proof tree is

$$\dfrac{\dfrac{E(0)}{E(0) \vee O(0)}\,\vee Il \qquad \dfrac{\begin{matrix}3.\\ E(x) \vee O(x)\end{matrix} \quad \dfrac{\dfrac{\begin{matrix}1.\\ E(x)\end{matrix}}{O(s(x))}\,\text{ods}}{E(s(x)) \vee O(s(x))}\,\vee Ir \quad \dfrac{\dfrac{\begin{matrix}2.\\ O(x)\end{matrix}}{E(s(x))}\,\text{evs}}{E(s(x)) \vee O(s(x))}\,\vee Il}{E(s(x)) \vee O(s(x))}\,\vee E, 1., 2.}{(\forall x : N)(E(x) \vee O(x))}\,\text{Ind}, 3.$$

Acknowledgements

I am grateful to Yann Coscoy and to Gilles Kahn for the stimulating exchange of ideas.

Example Proof Text Produced by Machine

Theorem. Every number is even or odd.

Proof. We proceed by induction. First, by the first axiom of evenness, 0 is even. A fortiori, 0 is even or 0 is odd. Second, consider an arbitrary number n such that

$$n \text{ is even or odd. } (a)$$

By the assumption a, n is even or odd. So we have two cases. First, assume

$$n \text{ is even. } (b)$$

By the assumption b, n is even. By the second axiom of evenness, the successor of n is odd. A fortiori, the successor of n is even or the successor of n is odd. Second, assume

$$n \text{ is odd. } (c)$$

By the assumption c, n is odd. By the third axiom of evenness, the successor of n is even. A fortiori, the successor of n is even or the successor of n is odd. Hence, the successor of n is even or odd in both cases. So we have proved that, for all n, n is even or odd.

References

N.G. de Bruijn. Lambda calculus notation with nameless dummies, a tool for automatic formula manipulation, with application to the Church-Rosser theorem. *Indagationes Mathematicae* 34, pages 381–392, 1972. Reprinted in R. Nederpelt, editor, *Selected Papers on Automath*, pages 375–388. North-Holland, Amsterdam, 1994.

N.G. de Bruijn. The mathematical vernacular, a language for mathematics with typed sets. R. Nederpelt, editor, *Selected Papers on Automath*, pages 865–935. North-Holland, Amsterdam, 1994.

Yann Coscoy, Gilles Kahn and Laurent Théry. Extracting text from proofs. Rapport de recherche n.2459, INRIA, Sophia-Antipolis, 1995.

Lena Magnusson and Bengt Nordström. The ALF Proof Editor and Its Proof Engine. In H. Barendregt and T. Nipkow, editors, *Types for Proofs and Programs*, pages 213–237. *Lecture Notes in Computer Science* 806, Springer-Verlag, Heidelberg, 1994.

Per Martin-Löf. *Intuitionistic Type Theory*. Bibliopolis, Naples, 1984.

Richard Montague. *Formal Philosophy*. Yale University Press, New Haven, 1974. Collected papers edited by Richmond Thomason.

Aarne Ranta. *Type Theoretical Grammar*. Oxford University Press, Oxford, 1994.

Aarne Ranta. Syntactic categories in the language of mathematics. In P. Dybjer, B. Nordström, and J. Smith, editors, *Types for Proofs and Programs*, pages 162-182, *Lecture Notes in Computer Science* 996, Springer-Verlag, Heidelberg, 1995.

A Simple Model Construction for the Calculus of Constructions

M. Stefanova[1] and H. Geuvers[2*]

[1] Faculty of Mathematics and Informatics
University of Nijmegen, The Netherlands
e-mail: milena@cs.kun.nl
[2] Faculty of Mathematics and Informatics
University of Eindhoven, The Netherlands
e-mail: herman@win.tue.nl

Abstract. *We present a model construction for the Calculus of Constructions (CC) where all dependencies are carried out in a set-theoretical setting. The Soundness Theorem is proved and as a consequence of it Strong Normalization for CC is obtained. Some other applications of our model constructions are: showing that CC + Classical logic is consistent (by constructing a model for it) and showing that the Axiom of Choice is not derivable in CC (by constructing a model in which the type that represents the Axiom of Choice is empty).*

1 Introduction

In the literature there are many investigations on the semantics of polymorphic λ-calculus with dependent types (see for example [12, 11, 10, 1, 5, 13]). Most of the existing models present a semantics for systems in which the inhabitants of the impredicative universe (*types*) are "lifted" to inhabitants of the predicative universe (*kinds*) (see [16]). Such systems are convenient to be modeled by locally Cartesian-closed categories having small Cartesian-closed subcategories. A well-known instance of these categorical models is the category of ω-sets (or D-sets) and its subcategory of modest sets, which is isomorphic to the category of partial equivalence relations (PER). Then the types are interpreted as PERs and then "lifted" through an isomorphism to modest sets and hence to ω-sets.

In practical applications, however, one prefers to use a different simple syntactical presentation of type systems - the so-called *Pure Type Systems* (PTSs). A semantics of such a system is usually obtained by implicitly or explicitly encoding the system into the system with "lifted" types, so the types are interpreted in the same way. The resulting semantics, even the one presented by concrete models (see [12, 13]) is still complicated as it gives an indirect meaning of PTSs. Moreover, most concrete models of such type systems are extensional in the sense that the interpretation of a type is a set with an equivalence relation on it with the equivalence relation on the function space defined as the extensional equality

* Part of this research was performed while the author was working at the University of Nijmegen, on the ESPRIT BRA project 'Types for Proofs and Programs'

of functions. As the syntax is not extensional, these models are less suitable for showing non-provability of various statements in PTSs.

This paper presents a new class of concrete models for the *Calculus of Constructions* (CC) presented as a PTS. The models are intensional - semantical objects are equal iff they are equal in the underlying weakly-extensional combinatory algebra. (So, two functions of the same type that have the same graph are not necessarily equal).

Furthermore, a new direct meaning is assigned to the typable expressions of CC, without "lifting" the interpretations of types to interpretations in the predicative universe. There are three disjoint collections of semantical objects in each model: *elements* (of the underlying combinatory algebra) to interpret *objects* (inhabitants of types), *poly-functionals* to interpret *constructors* (inhabitants of kinds) and *predicative sets* to interpret kinds. A special case of poly-functionals are specific sets, called *polysets*. Types are interpreted as polysets. This corresponds to the fact that types form a subclass of the collection of constructors. The poly-functionals are restricted set-theoretical functionals or sets, and the predicative sets are sets having poly-functionals as their elements. The restrictions on poly-functionals are a consequence from the fact that polymorphism is not set-theoretical in the classical sense (see [14]). However, two poly-functionals or two predicative sets are equal if they are set-theoretically equal. Two elements are equal if they are equal via the equality of the underlying weakly-extensional combinatory algebra.

The three collections of semantical objects are built simultaneously, by induction on the structure of typable terms. This is in line with the fact that objects and types cannot be defined separately for systems with dependent types. In such a way a proper direct meaning is obtained for dependent types without disregarding any dependencies.

Impredicativity is modeled in a proper way as well, by using the notion of polystructure over the underlying combinatory algebra. Polystructures poses similar closure properties as PERs, namely closed under products defined on them and intersections, but are simpler - they are just collections of subsets of the combinatory algebra.

An interesting aspect of the models that we obtain is that it is now relatively easy to find counter-models (for proving properties about the syntax). In a separate section we give some applications of this. For example we show that the Axiom of Choice (AC) is not derivable in CC by constructing a model where the type representing AC is interpreted as the empty set. Furthermore, we show how the property of *strong normalization* can be derived directly from a particular model of CC.

2 Some Basic Definitions

2.1 Calculus of Constructions

In this section a precise definition of the Calculus of Constructions (CC) is presented. We adopt the same syntax for CC as in [8, 3]. To present the derivation rules for CC we first fix the set of *pseudoterms* from which the derivation rules select the (typable) terms.

Definition 2.1 The set of pseudoterms, $\mathcal{T}$, is defined by

$$\mathcal{T} ::= \star \mid \Box \mid \mathbf{Var}^{*} \mid \mathbf{Var}^{\Box} \mid \Pi\mathbf{Var} : \mathcal{T}.\mathcal{T} \mid \lambda\mathbf{Var} : \mathcal{T}.\mathcal{T} \mid \mathcal{T}\mathcal{T},$$

where $\mathbf{Var}^{*}$ and $\mathbf{Var}^{\Box}$ are countable disjoint sets of variables and $\mathbf{Var} = \mathbf{Var}^{*} \bigcup \mathbf{Var}^{\Box}$.

Definition 2.2 The Calculus of Constructions is a typed λ-calculus with the following derivation rules:

(axiom)	$\vdash * : \Box$	
(Var)	$\dfrac{\Gamma \vdash T : s}{\Gamma, v{:}T \vdash v : T}$	$s \in \{*, \Box\}$, $v \in \mathbf{Var}^{s} \setminus FV(\Gamma)$
(weak)	$\dfrac{\Gamma \vdash T : s \quad \Gamma \vdash M : U}{\Gamma, v{:}T \vdash M : U}$	$s \in \{*, \Box\}$, $v \in \mathbf{Var}^{s} \setminus FV(\Gamma)$
$(\prod)$	$\dfrac{\Gamma \vdash T : s_1 \quad \Gamma, v{:}T \vdash U : s_2}{\Gamma \vdash \Pi v : T.U : s_2}$	$s_1, s_2 \in \{*, \Box\}$
(λ)	$\dfrac{\Gamma, v{:}T \vdash M : U \quad \Gamma \vdash \Pi v : T.U : s}{\Gamma \vdash \lambda v : T.M : \Pi v : T.U}$	$s \in \{*, \Box\}$
(app)	$\dfrac{\Gamma \vdash M : \Pi v : T.U \quad \Gamma \vdash N : T}{\Gamma \vdash MN : U[N/v]}$	
(conv)	$\dfrac{\Gamma \vdash M : T \quad \Gamma \vdash U : s}{\Gamma \vdash M : U}\ T =_{\beta} U$	$s \in \{*, \Box\}$

For the informal explanation of these rules see, for example, [8, 3]. The set of terms of CC is defined by

$$\mathbf{Term} = \{A \mid \exists \Gamma, B[\Gamma \vdash A : B \vee \Gamma \vdash B : A]\}.$$

It is convenient to divide the typable terms into subsets ([3, 8]) in the following way:

$$\begin{aligned} \mathbf{Kind} &:= \{A \in \mathcal{T} \mid \exists \Gamma\ (\Gamma \vdash A : \Box)\ \} \\ \mathbf{Constr} &:= \{C \in \mathcal{T} \mid \exists \Gamma, A\ (\Gamma \vdash C : A : \Box)\ \} \\ \mathbf{Type} &:= \{\sigma \in \mathcal{T} \mid \exists \Gamma\ (\Gamma \vdash \sigma : *)\ \} \\ \mathbf{Obj} &:= \{t \in \mathcal{T} \mid \exists \Gamma, \sigma\ (\Gamma \vdash t : \sigma : *)\ \} \end{aligned}$$

Here, $\Gamma \vdash t : \sigma : *$ abbreviates $\Gamma \vdash t : \sigma \wedge \Gamma \vdash \sigma : *$ and $\Gamma \vdash C : A : \Box$ abbreviates $\Gamma \vdash C : A \wedge \Gamma \vdash A : \Box$.

We use x, y and z to denote variables of $\mathbf{Var}^{*}$, also called *object variables*, and we use α, β, and γ to denote variables of $\mathbf{Var}^{\Box}$, also called *constructor variables*. The small Greek letters will denote types, the letters A, B, C, P, Q - kinds or constructors and the letters t, m, n - objects.

2.2 Combinatory Algebras

Combinatory algebras are used to model the set of pseudoterms of CC. Below we list the definitions of some notions used in the present paper. Most of the definitions in this section are taken from [2] and [6].

Definition 2.3 A *combinatory algebra* (ca) is an applicative structure $\mathcal{A} = \langle \mathbf{A} , . , \mathbf{k} , \mathbf{s} , =_A \rangle$ with distinguished elements $\mathbf{k}$ and $\mathbf{s}$ satisfying

$$(\mathbf{k}.x).y =_A x , \qquad ((\mathbf{s}.x).y).z =_A (x.z).(y.z)$$

The application (.) is usually not written.

Definition 2.4 The set of *terms over* $\mathcal{A}$ (notation $\mathcal{T}(\mathcal{A})$) is defined as follows.

$$\mathcal{T} ::= \mathbf{Var} \mid \mathbf{A} \mid \mathcal{T}\mathcal{T}$$

Every ca is *combinatory complete*, i.e., for every $T \in \mathcal{T}(\mathcal{A})$ with $\mathrm{FV}(T) \subset \{x\}$, there exists an $f \in \mathbf{A}$ such that

$$f.a =_A T[a/x] \qquad \forall a \in \mathbf{A}.$$

Such an element f will be denoted by $\Delta x.T$ in the sequel. For example, as explained in [2], one can define Δ as the standard abstraction λ^* with the help of the combinators $\mathbf{k}$ and $\mathbf{s}$. In the sequel we refer to Δ as an arbitrary abstraction operation on $\mathbf{A}$, which exists due to combinatory completeness.

The set Λ of pure lambda terms is a combinatory algebra, viz.,

$$\Lambda = \langle \Lambda , . , \lambda xy.x , \lambda xyz.xz(yz) , =_\beta \rangle.$$

One can choose in this case Δ to be just the abstraction operation λ on pure terms.

There is a natural mapping from Λ to any other combinatory algebra $\mathcal{A}$. Let $\rho : \mathbf{Var} \to \mathbf{A}$. The interpretation $[\ ]_\rho$ of the lambda-terms into $\mathbf{A}$ is defined as follows.

$$\begin{aligned} [v]_\rho &= \rho(v) \\ [T_1T_2]_\rho &= [T_1]_\rho[T_2]_\rho \\ [\lambda v.T]_\rho &= \Delta v.[T]_{\rho[v:=v]}. \end{aligned}$$

As was pointed out to us by Th. Altenkirch, it is not true in general that, if $T_1 =_\beta T_2$, then $[T_1]_\rho =_A [T_2]_\rho$. In [2] it is shown that this holds for a special case of combinatory algebras - the so called λ-models where Δ is chosen to be λ^* and in which additional axioms hold (see [2], page 94-95). If one considers an arbitrary abstraction Δ (as we do), then it is convenient to take weakly-extensional combinatory algebras to model Λ.

Let $\sim$ be a binary relation on $\mathbf{A}$. For $T_1, T_2 \in \Lambda$ we say that $T_1 = T_2$ is true in the ca $\mathcal{A}$ w.r.t. $\sim$ (notation $\mathcal{A}, \sim \models T_1 = T_2$), if for every valuation ρ, $[T_1]_\rho \sim [T_2]_\rho$. The above notion of satisfaction is easily extended to arbitrary first-order equational formulas over Λ.

Definition 2.5 The equivalence realtion $\sim$ is *weakly-extensional* over $=_A$ if,

- $=_A \subseteq \sim$;
- if $a_1 \sim a_2$ and $b_1 \sim b_2$, then $a_1a_2 \sim b_1b_2$;
- $\mathcal{A}, \sim \models \forall x(T_1 = T_2) \to \lambda x.T_1 = \lambda x.T_2$.

Now we can prove the following lemma.

Lemma 2.6 Let $\mathcal{A}$ be a ca and $\sim$ a weakly-extensional relation over $=_{\mathcal{A}}$. Then, for all ρ,

$$\text{if } T_1, T_2 \in \Lambda \text{ and } T_1 =_\beta T_2, \text{ then } [T_1]_\rho \sim [T_2]_\rho.$$

Examples 2.7 – The relation $\sim = \mathbf{A} \times \mathbf{A}$ is weakly-extensional over $=_{\mathcal{A}}$, because it relates all elements of $\mathbf{A}$;

- Let Δ be the abstraction λ^* defined with the help of **k** and s (see [2], page 90). Any congruence relation which contains $=_{\mathcal{A}}$ and satisfies the equations $\mathbf{A}_\beta$ and Meyer-Scott axiom (see [2], page 94-95) is weakly-extensional over $=_{\mathcal{A}}$;
- In the combinatory algebra $\Lambda = \langle \Lambda , \cdot , \lambda xy.x , \lambda xyz.xz(yz) , =_\beta \rangle$, the β-equality is weakly-extensional over itself (if Δ is taken to be λ).

3 The Model Construction

The notion of *CC-structure* and the interpretations of the typable terms of CC are explained informally in the next paragraphs. For more details about the intuition see [15].

The typable terms of CC are mapped into a (set-theoretical) hierarchical structure (called CC-structure) according to their classification as objects, constructors or kinds. The predicative universe of CC is interpreted as a collection $\mathcal{U}^\square$ of sets (*predicative structure*) and every kind is mapped to a predicative set. Predicative structures are closed under set-theoretical dependent products. The impredicative universe $*$ is interpreted as a collection $\mathcal{U}^*$ of subsets of the underlying ca. We call this collection *polystructure* and its elements *polysets*. $\mathcal{U}^*$ itself is an element of $\mathcal{U}^\square$ and is closed under non-empty intersections and dependent products (to be defined). Constructors are interpreted as elements of $\bigcup_{X \in \mathcal{U}^\square} X$ ($\bigcup \mathcal{U}^\square$ in short). Their interpretations are called *poly-functionals*. In particular, types are mapped to polysets.

Due to the various dependencies in CC, kinds have two other interpretations, as polysets and as elements of the underlying ca, and constructors have a second interpretation as elements of the ca. Three interpretation functions are defined by simultaneous induction on the structure of typable terms: $[\![\ ]\!]^\square$ to map kinds to predicative sets, $[\![\ ]\!]^*$ to map constructors and kinds to polyfunctionals, and $(\!|\ |\!)$ to map kinds, constructors and objects to elements of the ca. For these interpretations the following Soundness result is proved:

$$\begin{array}{lll}
\Gamma \vdash A : \square & \Rightarrow [\![A]\!]^\square_{\xi,\rho} \in \mathcal{U}^\square & [\![A]\!]^*_{\xi,\rho} \in \mathcal{U}^* \\
\Gamma \vdash P : A : \square & \Rightarrow [\![P]\!]^*_{\xi,\rho} \in [\![A]\!]^\square_{\xi,\rho} & (\!|P|\!)_\rho \in [\![A]\!]^*_{\xi,\rho} \\
\Gamma \vdash \sigma : * & \Rightarrow [\![\sigma]\!]^*_{\xi,\rho} \in \mathcal{U}^* & \\
\Gamma \vdash t : \sigma : * & \Rightarrow (\!|t|\!)_\rho \in [\![\sigma]\!]^*_{\xi,\rho} &
\end{array}$$

Here, ξ and ρ are valuations: ξ assigns a *poly-functional* to every constructor variable and ρ assigns an element of $\mathbf{A}$ to every constructor variable and object variable.

Now we are ready to give a formal definition of a class of mathematical structures which constitute models of CC. Let $\mathcal{A}$ be a ca in the sequel.

Definition 3.1 The operation of *dependent product* $\Pi_{\mathcal{A}}$ on $\mathcal{A}$ takes as arguments a subset X of $\mathbf{A}$ and a function $F : X \to \wp(\mathbf{A})$ and is defined as:

$$\prod_{\mathcal{A}}(X, F) := \{f \in \mathbf{A} \mid \forall n \in X(f.n \in F(n))\}$$

Note that $X = \emptyset$ implies $\prod_{\mathcal{A}}(X, F) = A$, and if $X \neq \emptyset$ and $F(x) = \emptyset$ for some $x \in X$ then $\prod_{\mathcal{A}}(X, F) = \emptyset$. For convenience $\prod_{\mathcal{A}}(X, F)$ will be denoted by $\prod_{\mathcal{A}} x \in X.F(x)$. Like in CC, if F is a constant function on X, say $F(x) = Y$, then we denote $\prod_{\mathcal{A}}(X, F)$ as a function space $X—Y$, which is defined as $\{f \in \mathbf{A} \mid \forall n \in X(f.n \in Y)\}$.

The impredicative universe of CC is interpreted as a *polystructure*. The impredicativity (or polymorphism) is modeled by requiring polystructures to be closed under arbitrary intersections.

Definition 3.2 Let $\mathcal{A}$ be a ca and $\star \in \mathbf{A}$. A *sufficient* subset of $\mathbf{A}$ w.r.t. $\star$ is a set $\overline{\mathbf{A}}$, such that

1. $\emptyset \subsetneq \overline{\mathbf{A}} \subseteq \mathbf{A}$;
2. If $t[a] \in \overline{\mathbf{A}}$ for some $a \in \mathbf{A}$, then $\Delta x.t[x] \in \overline{\mathbf{A}}$;
3. If $\overrightarrow{a} \in \overline{\mathbf{A}}$, then $\star\overrightarrow{a} \in \overline{\mathbf{A}}$;
4. If $t[a] \in \overline{\mathbf{A}}$, $a \in \overline{\mathbf{A}}$, then $(\Delta x.t[x])a \in \overline{\mathbf{A}}$.

Examples 3.3 The set $\mathbf{A}$ is a sufficient subset of itself (taking for $\star$ an arbitrary element of $\mathbf{A}$). Furthermore, $\mathbf{SN}$, the set of β-strongly-normalizing pure λ-terms, is a sufficient subset of Λ w.r.t. x, for any variable x. To show this, take the ca $\langle \Lambda, \cdot, \lambda xy.x, \lambda xyz.xz(yz), =_\beta \rangle$ and Δ to be λ.

Definition 3.4 Let $\mathcal{A}$ be a ca, $\star \in \mathbf{A}$ and $\overline{\mathbf{A}}$ a sufficient subset of $\mathbf{A}$ w.r.t. $\star$. A *polystructure* over $\mathcal{A}$, $\overline{\mathbf{A}}$ and $\star$ is a collection $\mathcal{P} \subseteq \wp(\overline{\mathbf{A}})$, such that the following conditions hold.

(i) $\overline{\mathbf{A}} \in \mathcal{P}$;
(ii) $\mathcal{P}$ is closed under dependent products, i.e. for every $X \in \mathcal{P}$ and every function $F : X \to \mathcal{P}$, $\prod_{\mathcal{A}} x \in X.F(x) \in \mathcal{P}$.
(iii) $\mathcal{P}$ is closed under non-empty intersections, i.e., if I is a nonempty set and $X_i \in \mathcal{P}$ for every $i \in I$ then $\bigcap_{i \in I} X_i \in \mathcal{P}$;
(iv) for all $X \in \mathcal{P}$, if $t[a] \in X$ for some $a \in \overline{\mathbf{A}}$, then $(\Delta x.t[x])a \in X$;
(v) for all $X \in \mathcal{P}$, if $a \in X$ and $b \in \overline{\mathbf{A}}$, then $\mathbf{k}ab \in X$.

The elements of a polystructure are called *polysets*.

Remark 3.5 If $\emptyset \in \mathcal{P}$, then $\overline{\mathbf{A}} = \mathbf{A}$ due to the requirements that $\mathcal{P} \subseteq \wp(\overline{\mathbf{A}})$ and that polystructures should be closed under dependent products, since $\emptyset — \overline{A} = \mathbf{A}$.

Examples 3.6 Let $\mathcal{A}$ be a ca.

1. A *saturated set* is a set X of strongly normalizing λ-terms such that $y\overrightarrow{P} \in X$ for every variable y and $\overrightarrow{P} \in \mathbf{SN}$ and, if $M[Q/y]\overrightarrow{P} \in X$ and $Q \in \mathbf{SN}$.

then $(\lambda y.M)Q\vec{P} \in X$. The set of saturated sets is denoted by **SAT** . **SAT** is a polystructure over the ca $\langle \Lambda, \cdot, \lambda xy.x, \lambda xyz.xz(yz), =_\beta \rangle$, **SN** and x (for any variable x).

2. The set $\{\emptyset, \mathbf{A}\}$ is a polystructure over $\mathcal{A}$, $\mathbf{A}$ and $\star$, for any element $\star \in \mathbf{A}$.
3. The set $\mathcal{P} := \{X \subseteq \mathbf{A} \mid X \text{ is closed under } =_A\}$ is a polystructure over $\mathcal{A}$, $\mathbf{A}$ and $\star$, for any element $\star \in \mathbf{A}$.

We shall often be concerned with 'simple' kinds of polystructures, like the ones in the last two examples, where all the polysets are closed under $=_A$ and the sufficient subset is just $\mathbf{A}$ itself. We therefore give the following definition.

Definition 3.7 Let $\mathcal{A}$ be a ca. A *simple polystructure* over $\mathcal{A}$ is a collection $\mathcal{P} \subseteq \wp(A)$, such that the following conditions hold.
(i) $\mathbf{A} \in \mathcal{P}$;
(ii) $\mathcal{P}$ is closed under arbitrary nonempty intersections;
(iii) $\mathcal{P}$ is closed under dependent products;
(iv) Every element of $\mathcal{P}$ is closed under the equivalence relation $=_A$.

If one just works with simple polystructures, the relation $=_A$ is not really necessary; instead one could just look at the quotient algebra $\mathbf{A}/=_A$. (We are also interested in the polystructure of saturated sets, which is not simple.) Note that simple polystructures are still intensional: if X and Y are polysets and $f, g \in X \to Y$, then $\forall x \in X[fx =_A gx]$ does not necessarily imply $f =_A g$.

The predicative universe $\square$ is interpreted as a *predicative structure*. The necessary properties of predicative structures are derived from the rules of CC. A predicative structure contains a polystructure as an element and is closed under a restricted set-theoretical product.

Definition 3.8 Let $\mathcal{A}$ be a ca and $\sim$ a binary relation on $\mathcal{A}$. The operation $\tilde{\Pi}$ takes as arguments a subset X of $\mathbf{A}$ and a function $F : X \to SET$, and is defined by:

$$\tilde{\Pi}(X, F) := \{f \in \Pi x \in X.F(x) \mid \forall x_1, x_2 \in X(x_1 \sim x_2 \Longrightarrow f(x_1) = f(x_2))\}$$

Here, $\Pi x \in X.F(x)$ denotes the set of functions f such that for all $x \in X$, $f(x) \in F(x)$ (the set-theoretical dependent product).

Note that, if $X = \emptyset$ then $\tilde{\Pi}(X, F) = \{\emptyset\}$, where $\emptyset$ ambiguously denotes the empty function. Furthermore, if $X \neq \emptyset$ and $F(x) = \emptyset$ for some $x \in X$, then $\tilde{\Pi}(X, F) = \emptyset$. (The same holds if $F(x_1) \bigcap F(x_2) = \emptyset$ for some $\sim$-related elements x_1 and x_2.) For convenience, $\tilde{\Pi}(X, F)$ will be denoted by $\tilde{\Pi} x \in X.F(x)$.

Definition 3.9 A *predicative structure over a polystructure* $\mathcal{P}$ *and a relation* $\sim$ (on $\mathcal{A}$) is a collection of sets $\mathcal{N}$ such that
(i) $\mathcal{P} \in \mathcal{N}$;
(ii) $\mathcal{N}$ is closed under set-theoretical dependent product, Π, i.e. if $B \in \mathcal{N}$ and $F : B \to \mathcal{N}$, then $\Pi b \in B.F(b) \in \mathcal{N}$
(iii) $\mathcal{N}$ is closed under $\tilde{\Pi}$ for *$\sim$-preserving functions*, i.e. if $X \subseteq \mathbf{A}$ and $F : X \to \mathcal{N}$ such that $\forall x_1, x_2 \in X.x_1 \sim x_2 \Longrightarrow F(x_1) = F(x_2)$, then

$$\tilde{\Pi} x \in X.F(x) \in \mathcal{N}.$$

An example of a predicative structure is the collection SET of all sets.

For convenience we introduce some notations. If $f(b) \in F(b)$ for all $b \in B$, then $\lambda\, b \in B.\ f(b)$ denotes the function $b \longmapsto f(b)$. If $g(b) \in F(b)$ and $g(b_1) = g(b_2)$ whenever $b_1 \sim b_2$, then $\tilde{\lambda}\, x \in B.\ g(x)$ denotes the function $b \longmapsto g(b)$.

Now we are ready to give the definition of CC-structures and to define the interpretations of typable terms into such CC-structures.

Definition 3.10 A *CC-structure* is a tuple $\mathcal{M} = \langle \mathcal{A}, \overline{\mathbf{A}}, \star, \sim, \mathcal{U}^{*}, \mathcal{U}^{\Box} \rangle$, where

1. $\mathcal{A}$ is a ca;
2. $\overline{\mathbf{A}}$ is a sufficient subset of $\mathbf{A}$ w.r.t. $\star$;
3. $\star$ is a fixed element of $\mathbf{A}$;
4. $\sim$ is a weakly-extensional equivalence relation over $=_{\mathcal{A}}$ (see def.2.5); [3].
5. $\mathcal{U}^{*}$ is a polystructure over $\mathcal{A}$, $\overline{\mathbf{A}}$ and $\star$;
6. $\mathcal{U}^{\Box}$ is a predicative structure over $\mathcal{U}^{*}$ and $\sim$;

Definition 3.11 An *atom-valuation* of constructor and object variables is any map $\rho\ :\ \mathbf{Var}^{*} \bigcup \mathbf{Var}^{\Box} \ \rightarrow\ \mathbf{A}$. A *constructor-valuation* of constructor variables is a map $\xi : \mathbf{Var}^{\Box} \rightarrow \bigcup_{X \in \mathcal{N}} X$.

Definition 3.12 The *atom-interpretations* of the typable terms under an atom-valuation ρ are defined as follows

$$\boxed{\begin{aligned} (\!| * |\!)_\rho &:= \star \\ (\!| v |\!)_\rho &:= \rho(v) \quad \text{if } v \text{ is a variable} \\ (\!| T_1 T_2 |\!)_\rho &:= (\!| T_1 |\!)_\rho . (\!| T_2 |\!)_\rho \\ (\!| \lambda v : T_1.T_2 |\!)_\rho &:= \mathbf{k}.(\Delta v.(\!| T_2 |\!)_{\rho[v:=v]}).(\!| T_1 |\!)_\rho \\ (\!| \prod v : T_1.T_2 |\!)_\rho &:= \star.(\!| T_1 |\!)_\rho .(\Delta v.(\!| T_2 |\!)_{\rho[v:=v]}) \end{aligned}}$$

Remark 3.13 As usual (see [2]), $(\!| T |\!)_{\rho[v:=v]}$ denotes the term over $\mathcal{A}$ obtained from T by applying the map $(\!|\ |\!)_{\rho'}$ to it, where $\rho' : \mathbf{Var} - \mathcal{T}\ (\mathbf{A})$ is defined as

$$\rho'(u) = \begin{cases} \rho(u) & \text{if } u \neq v, \\ v & \text{if } u = v \end{cases}$$

Fact 3.14 Due to the fact that $\sim$ simulates the equality on a weakly extensional combinatory algebra, the following holds:

1. If $m_1, m_2 \in \mathbf{A}$ and $m_1 \sim m_2$, then $(\!| T |\!)_{\rho[v:=m_1]} \sim (\!| T |\!)_{\rho[v:=m_2]}$.
2. If $T_1 =_\beta T_2$, then $(\!| T_1 |\!)_\rho \sim (\!| T_2 |\!)_\rho$.
3. $(\!| T_1[T_2/v] |\!)_\rho = (\!| T_1 |\!)_{\rho[v:=(\!| T_2 |\!)_\rho]}$.

Definition 3.15 Let ρ be an atom-valuation and ξ a constructor-valuation. The $\mathcal{U}^{*}$*-interpretation* of kinds and constructors

$$[\![\ ]\!]^{*}_{\xi,\rho}\ :\ \{\Box\} \cup \mathbf{Kind}\ \cup \mathbf{Constr}\ \longrightarrow \bigcup \mathcal{U}^{\Box}$$

and the $\mathcal{U}^{\Box}$*-interpretation* of kinds

$$[\![\ ]\!]^{\Box}_{\xi,\rho}\ :\ \{\Box\} \cup \mathbf{Kind}\ \longrightarrow \mathcal{U}^{\Box}$$

[3] Note that we do not require $s \not\sim k$, i.e. $A/_\sim$ is not necessarily a (weakly-extensional) ca.

are defined simultaneously by induction on the structure of terms as follows.

$$\llbracket * \rrbracket^{\square}_{\xi,\rho} := \llbracket \square \rrbracket^{\square}_{\xi,\rho} := \mathcal{U}^{*}$$
$$\llbracket \Pi\alpha : A.B \rrbracket^{\square}_{\xi,\rho} := \Pi\, a \in \llbracket A \rrbracket^{\square}_{\xi,\rho}.\ \tilde{\Pi}\, m \in \llbracket A \rrbracket^{*}_{\xi,\rho}.\llbracket B \rrbracket^{\square}_{\xi[\alpha:=a],\rho[\alpha:=m]} \quad \text{if } A, B \in \mathbf{Kind}$$
$$\llbracket \Pi x : \sigma.B \rrbracket^{\square}_{\xi,\rho} := \tilde{\Pi}\, m \in \llbracket \sigma \rrbracket^{*}_{\xi,\rho}.\llbracket B \rrbracket^{\square}_{\xi,\rho[x:=m]} \quad \text{if } \sigma \in \mathbf{Type}\ ,\ B \in \mathbf{Kind}$$

$$\llbracket * \rrbracket^{*}_{\xi,\rho} := \llbracket \square \rrbracket^{*}_{\xi,\rho} := \overline{\mathbf{A}}$$
$$\llbracket \alpha \rrbracket^{*}_{\xi,\rho} := \xi(\alpha) \quad \text{if } \alpha \in \mathbf{Var}^{\square}$$
$$\llbracket \Pi\alpha : A.B \rrbracket^{*}_{\xi,\rho} := \bigcap_{a \in \llbracket A \rrbracket^{\square}_{\xi,\rho}} \prod\nolimits_{A} m \in \llbracket A \rrbracket^{*}_{\xi,\rho}.\llbracket B \rrbracket^{*}_{\xi[\alpha:=a],\rho[\alpha:=m]} \quad \text{if } A \in \mathbf{Kind}$$
$$\llbracket \Pi x : \sigma.B \rrbracket^{*}_{\xi,\rho} := \prod\nolimits_{A} m \in \llbracket \sigma \rrbracket^{*}_{\xi,\rho}.\llbracket B \rrbracket^{*}_{\xi,\rho[x:=m]} \quad \text{if } \sigma \in \mathbf{Type}$$
$$\llbracket PQ \rrbracket^{*}_{\xi,\rho} := \llbracket P \rrbracket^{*}_{\xi,\rho}(\llbracket Q \rrbracket^{*}_{\xi,\rho})((\!| Q |\!)_{\rho}) \quad \text{if } P, Q \in \mathbf{Constr}$$
$$\llbracket Pt \rrbracket^{*}_{\xi,\rho} := \llbracket P \rrbracket^{*}_{\xi,\rho}((\!| t |\!)_{\rho}) \quad \text{if } P \in \mathbf{Constr}\ ,\ t \in \mathbf{Obj}$$
$$\llbracket \lambda\alpha : A.P \rrbracket^{*}_{\xi,\rho} := \lambda\, a \in \llbracket A \rrbracket^{\square}_{\xi,\rho}\,.\ \tilde{\lambda}\, m \in \llbracket A \rrbracket^{*}_{\xi,\rho}.\ \llbracket P \rrbracket^{*}_{\xi[\alpha:=a],\rho[\alpha:=m]}$$
$$\text{if } A \in \mathbf{Kind}\ ,\ P \in \mathbf{Constr}$$
$$\llbracket \lambda x : \sigma.P \rrbracket^{*}_{\xi,\rho} := \tilde{\lambda}\, m \in \llbracket \sigma \rrbracket^{*}_{\xi,\rho}.\ \llbracket P \rrbracket^{*}_{\xi,\rho[x:=m]} \quad \text{if } \sigma \in \mathbf{Type}\ ,\ P \in \mathbf{Constr}$$

Remark 3.16 The interpretations $\llbracket\ \rrbracket^{\square}_{\xi,\rho}$ and $\llbracket\ \rrbracket^{*}_{\xi,\rho}$ may be undefined. For example, if the first argument of the operation $\tilde{\Pi}$ is not a subset of $\mathbf{A}$ or the abstraction $\tilde{\lambda}$ has the wrong arguments. We will show that, for well-typed terms, the interpretations are well-defined indeed.

For these interpretations the substitution property, which is stated in the next lemma, holds. The relation $\cong$ is 'Kleene-equality'.

Lemma 3.17 Let $t \in \mathbf{Obj}$, $Q \in \mathbf{Constr}$, $T \in \mathbf{Kind} \bigcup \mathbf{Constr}$ and $s \in \{*, \square\}$. Then:

$$\llbracket T[Q/\alpha] \rrbracket^{s}_{\xi,\rho} \cong \llbracket T \rrbracket^{s}_{\xi[\alpha:=\llbracket Q \rrbracket^{*}_{\xi,\rho}],\rho[\alpha:=(\!| Q |\!)_{\rho}]} \text{ and } \llbracket T[t/x] \rrbracket^{s}_{\xi,\rho} \cong \llbracket T \rrbracket^{s}_{\xi[x:=(\!| t |\!)_{\rho}],\rho[x:=.]}$$

Definition 3.18 The constructor valuations ξ and the atom valuation ρ *satisfy the context* Γ (notation $\xi, \rho \vDash \Gamma$) if

(i) for every constructor variable α and kind A such that $(\alpha : A) \in \Gamma$,
$$\xi(\alpha) \in \llbracket A \rrbracket^{\square}_{\xi,\rho} \text{ and } \rho(\alpha) \in \llbracket A \rrbracket^{*}_{\xi,\rho}.$$
(ii) for every object variable x and type σ , such that $(x : \sigma) \in \Gamma$,
$$\rho(x) \in \llbracket \sigma \rrbracket^{*}_{\xi,\rho}.$$

Definition 3.19 We say that the CC-structure $\mathcal{M}$ *models* $\Gamma \vdash M : T$ (notation $\Gamma \vDash_{\mathcal{M}} M : T$) iff for every $\xi, \rho \vDash \Gamma$,

(i) If $M \in \mathbf{Kind}$, then $\llbracket M \rrbracket^{\square}_{\xi,\rho} \in \mathcal{U}^{\square}$, $\llbracket M \rrbracket^{*}_{\xi,\rho} \in \mathcal{U}^{*}$, $(\!| M |\!)_{\rho} \in \overline{\mathbf{A}}$;
(ii) If $M \in \mathbf{Constr}$ then $\llbracket M \rrbracket^{*}_{\xi,\rho} \in \llbracket T \rrbracket^{\square}_{\xi,\rho}$ and $(\!| M |\!)_{\rho} \in \llbracket T \rrbracket^{*}_{\xi,\rho}$;
(iii) If $M \in \mathbf{Obj}$ then $(\!| M |\!)_{\rho} \in \llbracket T \rrbracket^{*}_{\xi,\rho}$.

Definition 3.20 If $\Gamma \vdash M_i : T, i = 1,2$ and $M_1 =_\beta M_2$,we say that the CC-structure $\mathcal{M}$ *models* $M_1 =_\beta M_2$ (notation $\Gamma \models_{\mathcal{M}} M_1 =_\beta M_2$) if for all ξ, ρ such that $\xi, \rho \models \Gamma$,

$$(\!|M_1|\!)_\rho \sim (\!|M_2|\!)_\rho,$$
$$[\![M_1]\!]^s_{\xi,\rho} \cong [\![M_2]\!]^s_{\xi,\rho},$$

for applicable $s \in \{*, \Box\}$.

Definition 3.21 Let $m_1, m_2 \in \mathbf{A}$, $v \in \mathbf{Var}$. We say that m_1 and m_2 are v-*compatible* in the CC-structure $\mathcal{M}$ with respect to $\Gamma \vdash M : T$ (notation $\Gamma, v := m_1, m_2 \models_{\mathcal{M}} M : T$) if for all valuations ξ and ρ, such that $\xi, \rho[v := m_i] \models \Gamma$ $(i = 1,2)$,

$$(\!|M|\!)_{\rho[v:=m_1]} \sim (\!|M|\!)_{\rho[v:=m_2]},$$
$$[\![M]\!]^s_{\xi,\rho[v:=m_1]} \cong [\![M]\!]^s_{\xi,\rho[v:=m_2]},$$

for applicable $s \in \{*, \Box\}$.

The next theorem says that every CC-structure is a *model* of CC, namely it models every legal judgment of CC.

Theorem 3.22 (Soundness) Let $\mathcal{M}$ be a CC-structure and let Γ be a context and M and T terms such that $\Gamma \vdash M : T$. Then the following holds.

(i) $\Gamma \models_{\mathcal{M}} M : T$;
(ii) for every $m_1, m_2 \in \mathbf{A}$, such that $m_1 \sim m_2$, $\Gamma, v := m_1, m_2 \models_{\mathcal{M}} M : T$;
(iii) if $M \to_\beta N$, then $\Gamma \models_{\mathcal{M}} M =_\beta N$.

Proof. The proof of (i)-(ii) is by simultaneous induction on derivations. The non-trivial cases are: the (λ)-rule, where property (iii) of polystructures is applied (see def.3.4); the ($\prod$)-rules, where the closure of $\mathcal{U}^*$ under non-empty intersections and dependent products and the closure of $\mathcal{U}^\Box$ under set-theoretical products and under $\tilde{\Pi}$ are used. Furthermore, in the conversion rule the following property is essential. Two typable terms are β-equal (as pseudoterms) iff they are equal via a reduction-expansion path through the set of well-typed terms. (This property follows from Church-Rosser for β and Subject Reduction for β.) In the end, note that to prove the condition (iii) of the Soundness Theorem, Subject Reduction for β is necessary. □

4 Applications

In this section we treat some examples of models of CC that fit in the framework described above. Our main goal hereby is to prove properties about the syntax by employing the models. Typical statements that we can prove in this way are e.g. that the Axiom of Choice is not derivable in CC and that Classical Logic is a consistent extension of CC. The first is proved by constructing a model in which the type that represents the Axiom of Choice is empty and the second is proved by constructing a model in which the type representing the double negation law is inhabited and the interpretation of $\perp$ is empty. The examples that we show are in the same realm (and sometimes the same) as the ones in [17]. We think (and hope) however that in many cases counterexamples can be constructed more easily using our model construction.

Before going into details, we first compute the interpretations of some logical formulas to observe that their interpretation in the model expresses - roughly - what the formula states. For example, it is easy to check that the interpretation of $\exists x{:}\sigma.\tau$ is not empty iff there exists an element t in $[\![\sigma]\!]^*_{\xi,\rho}$ such that $[\![\tau]\!]^*_{\xi,\rho[x:=t]} \neq \emptyset$.

In this section we restrict ourselves to simple polystructures. (So, $\overline{\mathbf{A}} = \mathbf{A}$, $\emptyset \in \mathcal{P}$ and all polyset are closed under $=_A$.)

Lemma 4.1 In CC-structures with simple polystructures the following holds.

1. $[\![\exists x{:}\sigma.\tau]\!]^*_{\xi,\rho} \neq \emptyset$ iff there exists $t \in [\![\sigma]\!]^*_{\xi,\rho}$ such that $[\![\tau]\!]^*_{\xi,\rho[x:=t]} \neq \emptyset$.
2. If CL is the statement $\Pi\alpha{:}*.\neg\neg\alpha\to\alpha$ of Classical Logic, then $[\![\mathrm{CL}]\!]^*_{\xi,\rho} \neq \emptyset$ iff $\bigcap_{X\in\mathcal{U}^*}((X\to\emptyset)\to\emptyset)\to X \neq \emptyset$.
3. $[\![t =_\sigma q]\!]^*_{\xi,\rho} \neq \emptyset$ iff $(\!|t|\!)_\rho \sim (\!|q|\!)_\rho$, where $=_\sigma$ represents Leibniz equality on σ.
4. The statement PI of Proof-Irrelevance is defined as $\Pi\alpha{:}*.\Pi x,y{:}\alpha.x =_\alpha y$. Then $[\![\mathrm{PI}]\!]^*_{\xi,\rho} \neq \emptyset$ iff for all $t,q \in \mathbf{A}$, $t \sim q$.

It is not true that every formula of higher order predicate logic has such a direct interpretation in the models. As an example we look at the statement of extensionality for propositions, EXT. It is defined as

$$\mathrm{EXT} := \Pi\alpha,\beta{:}*.(\alpha\leftrightarrow\beta)\to\alpha =_* \beta.$$

Here, $=_*$ denotes Leibniz equality on the kind $*$. The interpretation of EXT is

$$\bigcap_{X,Y\in\mathcal{U}^*}\prod\nolimits_A m,n\in\mathbf{A}.(X\leftrightarrow Y)\to\bigcap_{Q\in\mathcal{U}^*\to\mathbf{A}\to\mathcal{U}^*}(\mathbf{A}\to\mathbf{A})\to QXm\to QYn\,.$$

$$[\![\mathrm{EXT}]\!]^*_{\xi,\rho} \neq \emptyset \text{ iff } \bigcap_{X,Y\in\mathcal{U}^*}(X\leftrightarrow Y)\to\prod\nolimits_A m,n\in\mathbf{A}.\bigcap_{Q\in\mathcal{U}^*\to\mathbf{A}\to\mathcal{U}^*} QXm\to QYn \neq \emptyset$$
$$\text{iff } \sim = \mathbf{A}\times\mathbf{A} \text{ and } \mathcal{U}^* = \{\emptyset,\mathbf{A}\}.$$

The fact that $\mathcal{U}^* = \{\emptyset,\mathbf{A}\}$ indeed somehow expresses extensionality of propositions in the model, but $\sim = \mathbf{A}\times\mathbf{A}$ does not in any way.

4.1 Classical Logic and Proof-irrelevance

Adding Classical Logic to CC is done by putting $x : \Pi\alpha{:}*.\neg\neg\alpha\to\alpha$ as a declaration in the context. It is not difficult to find a polystructure in which $[\![\mathrm{CL}]\!]^*_{\xi,\rho}$ is nonempty, while $[\![\bot]\!]^*_{\xi,\rho}$ is empty ($\bot = \Pi\alpha{:}*.\alpha$). Consider the polystructure $\mathcal{U}^* := \{\emptyset,\mathbf{A}\}$. In this model, $[\![\mathrm{CL}]\!]^*_{\xi,\rho} = \mathbf{A}$, because $((\mathbf{A}\to\emptyset)\to\emptyset)\to\mathbf{A} = \mathbf{A}$ and $((\emptyset\to\emptyset)\to\emptyset)\to\emptyset = \mathbf{A}$.

Lemma 4.2 x : CL is a consistent context of CC.

The statement of Proof-Irrelevance, PI, says that every two elements of a type are equal. Above we have seen that $[\![\mathrm{PI}]\!]^*_{\xi,\rho} \neq \emptyset$ iff $\forall t,q \in \mathbf{A}[t \sim q]$ Now consider the polystructure $\mathcal{U}^* := \{\emptyset,\mathbf{A}\}$ where $\mathbf{A}$ is a weakly-extensional ca and $\sim$ is simply the equality $=_A$ on $\mathbf{A}$, so it does not identify all elements. We find that $[\![\mathrm{PI}]\!]^*_{\xi,\rho} = \emptyset$. Hence we can conclude the following.

Lemma 4.3 In CC there is no term M such that $\vdash M$: PI. Moreover, there is no term M such that $\vdash M$: CL→PI.

The second part of this Lemma can also be reversed. Consider therefore the polystructure $\mathcal{U}^* := \{X \subset \mathbf{A} \mid X \text{ closed under } =_A\}$ and let the equivalence relation $\sim$ be the relation that identifies all elements ($\sim = \mathbf{A} \times \mathbf{A}$). (This makes that $\mathbf{A}/\sim$ is a degenerate λ-algebra, but that is no problem for our construction.) Now, $[\![\mathrm{PI}]\!]^*_{\xi,\rho} \neq \emptyset$, because $\sim$ relates all elements. On the other hand, $[\![\mathrm{CL}]\!]^*_{\xi,\rho} = \emptyset$: take X and Y such that $\emptyset \subsetneq X, Y \subsetneq \mathbf{A}$ and $X \cap Y \neq \emptyset$; then $((X \to \emptyset) \to \emptyset) \to X = \mathbf{A} \to X$ and $((Y \to \emptyset) \to \emptyset) \to Y = \mathbf{A} \to Y$, so $[\![\mathrm{CL}]\!]^*_{\xi,\rho} \subset (\mathbf{A} \to X) \cap (\mathbf{A} \to Y) = \emptyset$. We have obtained the following result.

Lemma 4.4 In CC there is no term M such that $\vdash M$: CL. Moreover, there is no term M such that $\vdash M$: PI→CL.

In [4], it is shown that there is a term M such that

$$x{:}\mathrm{EXT}, \alpha{:}*, c, c'{:}\alpha, h{:}c \neq_\alpha c' \vdash M{:}\text{'every } f{:}\alpha \to \alpha \text{ has a fixed point'}.$$

The statement that 'every $f{:}\alpha \to \alpha$ has a fixed point' is written formally as $\Pi f{:}\sigma \to \sigma. \exists x{:}\sigma. fx =_\sigma x$. In the models we are looking at here, this is even stronger: we can show that $[\![\mathrm{EXT} \to \mathrm{PI}]\!]^*_{\xi,\rho}$ is not empty (and from $[\![\mathrm{PI}]\!]^*_{\xi,\rho} \neq \emptyset$ it easily follows that 'every function has a fixed point' is true in the model). We have seen that $[\![\mathrm{EXT}]\!]^*_{\xi,\rho} \neq \emptyset$ iff $\sim = \mathbf{A} \times \mathbf{A}$ and $\mathcal{U}^* = \{\emptyset, \mathbf{A}\}$. Furthermore, we have seen in Lemma 4.1 that $[\![\mathrm{PI}]\!]^*_{\xi,\rho} \neq \emptyset$ iff for all $t, q \in \mathbf{A}$, $t \sim q$. So, we can conclude that, if $[\![\mathrm{EXT}]\!]^*_{\xi,\rho} \neq \emptyset$, then $[\![\mathrm{PI}]\!]^*_{\xi,\rho} \neq \emptyset$. Hence $[\![\mathrm{EXT} \to \mathrm{PI}]\!]^*_{\xi,\rho} \neq \emptyset$.

The interpretation of 'every $f{:}\sigma \to \sigma$ has a fixed point' is (writing Y for $[\![\sigma]\!]^*_{\xi,\rho}$) $\prod_A g \in Y \to Y. [\![\exists x{:}\sigma. fx =_\sigma x]\!]^*_{\xi,\rho[f:=g]}$.

If $[\![\mathrm{PI}]\!]^*_{\xi,\rho} \neq \emptyset$ in the model, then for all $t \in Y$ and $g \in Y \to Y$ we have $[\![fx =_\sigma x]\!]^*_{\xi,\rho[x,f:=t,g]}$, simply because $[\![y =_\sigma x]\!]^*_{\xi,\rho[x,y:=t,q]} \neq \emptyset$ for all $t, q \in \mathbf{A}$.

So, from $[\![\mathrm{PI}]\!]^*_{\xi,\rho} \neq \emptyset$ we conclude that every $f{:}\sigma \to \sigma$ (for any σ) has a fixed point.

Lemma 4.5 The sets $[\![\mathrm{PI} \to \text{'for every type } \sigma \text{ every } f{:}\sigma \to \sigma \text{ has a fixed point'}]\!]^*_{\xi,\rho}$ and $[\![\mathrm{EXT} \to \mathrm{PI}]\!]^*_{\xi,\rho}$ are not empty in our models.

4.2 Axiom of Choice

We now show that the Axiom of Choice is not inhabited in CC by giving a model in which the type AC (representing the Axiom of Choice) is empty. Define

$$\mathrm{AC} := (\Pi x{:}\sigma. \exists y{:}\tau. Rxy) \to (\exists f{:}\sigma \to \tau. \Pi x{:}\sigma. Rx(fx)).$$

Here, σ and τ are two inhabited types and R is a variable of type $\sigma \to \tau \to *$. (We could have formalized AC in a more general way, by abstracting over σ, τ and R, but if AC above is not inhabited, then a more abstract version of the Axiom of Choice is also not inhabited.) To simplify notation we write AC_1 for $\Pi x{:}\sigma. \exists y{:}\tau. Rxy$ and AC_2 for $\exists f{:}\sigma \to \tau. \Pi x{:}\sigma. Rx(fx)$.

We consider the combinatory algebra $\mathbf{A} := \Lambda/\beta\eta$, consisting of $\beta\eta$-equivalence classes of λ-terms. Take as polystructure $\mathcal{U}^* := \{\emptyset, \mathbf{A}\}$ and let $\sim \subset \mathbf{A} \times \mathbf{A}$ be equality (of $\beta\eta$-equivalence classes). Now,

$$\begin{aligned}[\![\mathrm{AC}_1]\!]^*_{\xi,\rho} = \mathbf{A} \ &\text{iff } \textstyle\prod_A m \in [\![\sigma]\!]^*_{\xi,\rho}.[\![\exists y{:}\tau.Rxy]\!]^*_{\xi,\rho[x:=m]} = \mathbf{A} \\ &\text{iff for all } m \in \mathbf{A},\ [\![\exists y{:}\tau.Rxy]\!]^*_{\xi,\rho[x:=m]} = \mathbf{A} \\ &\text{iff for all } m \in \mathbf{A} \text{ there is a } t \in \mathbf{A} \text{ with } \xi(R)(m,t) = \mathbf{A}\end{aligned}$$

(Note that $[\![\sigma]\!]^*_{\xi,\rho} = \mathbf{A}$, because σ is inhabited and furthermore note that, if for all $m \in \mathbf{A}$, $P(m) = \mathbf{A}$, then $\prod_A m \in \mathbf{A}.P(m) = \mathbf{A}$.) We also find that

$$[\![\mathrm{AC}_2]\!]^*_{\xi,\rho} = \mathbf{A} \text{ iff for some } f \in \mathbf{A}\rightarrow\mathbf{A},\ \xi(R)(m, fm) = \mathbf{A} \text{ for all } m \in \mathbf{A}.$$

If we define $\xi(R)(m,t) := \mathbf{A}$ iff $m \neq t$, then $\forall m \in \mathbf{A}\exists t \in \mathbf{A}[m \neq t]$, so $[\![\mathrm{AC}_1]\!]^*_{\xi,\rho} = \mathbf{A}$, but not $\exists f \in \mathbf{A}\rightarrow\mathbf{A}\forall m \in \mathbf{A}[fm \neq m]$ (because of the fixed point theorem for the lambda calculus), so $[\![\mathrm{AC}_2]\!]^*_{\xi,\rho} = \emptyset$. We conclude that $[\![\mathrm{AC}]\!]^*_{\xi,\rho} = \emptyset$ in this model.

Lemma 4.6 There is no closed term of type AC in CC.

One may wonder what happens if one makes the type AC more concrete, e.g. is AC inhabited for all *closed* types σ and τ and all *closed* predicates R? By adapting the construction above a little bit it can be shown that this question has to be answered in the negative.

Consider the model described above (with $\mathbf{A} = \Lambda/\beta\eta$, $\mathcal{U}^* = \{\emptyset, \mathbf{A}\}$ and $\sim$ the equality between $\beta\eta$-equivalence classes). Take for both σ and τ the type of Church numerals, N, and take for R the predicate $\lambda x, y{:}N.x \neq_N y$. The interpretation of N is $\mathbf{A}$ and, using Lemma 4.1 we see that for $m, t \in \mathbf{A}$, $[\![Rxy]\!]^*_{\xi,\rho[x,y:=m,t]} = \mathbf{A}$ iff $m \neq t$. Similarly as above, we find that $[\![AC_1]\!]^*_{\xi,\rho} \neq \emptyset$ and $[\![AC_2]\!]^*_{\xi,\rho} = \emptyset$.

Lemma 4.7 There are closed types σ and τ and a closed predicate R such that there is no closed term of type AC.

Of course, this still leaves the question open whether the Axiom of Choice holds as a rule, that is, whether the following holds. If $\vdash M : \Pi x{:}\sigma.\exists y{:}\tau.Rxy$, is there a closed term N of type $\exists f{:}\sigma\rightarrow\tau.\Pi x{:}\sigma.Rx(fx))$? This question is not addressed here.

5 Strong Normalization

In this subsection we explain how strong normalization can be proved by using a specific model of CC. The approach used here differs from the ones in [10] and [1], where strong normalization is also derived from particular models. Hyland and Ong (see [10]) point out that there are some complications resulting from the fact that $\langle \mathbf{SN}, =_\beta\rangle$ is not a conditional partial combinatory algebra (c-pca). Hence, instead of considering β-equality they work with so-called 'conditionally-weak equality', which is the equality relation generated from the reduction relation $\rightarrow_{cw}$, defined by (β) and the rule 'if $M \rightarrow_{cw} N$ and $C[-]$ is a term-with-hole such that no free variable of M becomes bound in $C[M]$, then $C[M] \rightarrow_{cw} C[N]$'. So, $\rightarrow_{cw}$ is not compatible with abstraction; in fact $\rightarrow_{cw}$ is a way of restricting the reduction 'under a λ'. This leads to much additional work for studying properties of cw-equality and the c-pca $\langle \mathbf{SN}, =_{cw} \rangle$, while the only equality we are really interested in is the β-equality. Moreover,in [10] models which contain the empty set as a possible interpretation of a type are excluded.

Altenkirch [1] presents a simpler solution, by taking the intersection of the collection of partial equivalence relations over the pure λ-terms and the collection of saturated sets (with a modified definition of the notion of 'saturated set', slightly different from 3.6) as interpretation of $*$.

Our approach is based on the fact that the full collection of saturated sets (see 3.6, or [3]) is a polystructure over the set of pure λ-terms Λ. $v\overrightarrow{P} \in X$: The following CC-structure is used to prove strong normalization.

$$\mathcal{M} = \langle \Lambda \bigcup \{\star\}, \ \mathbf{SN}, \ \star, \ =_\beta, \ \mathbf{SAT}, \ SET \rangle,$$

where Λ is the set of untyped λ-terms and **SN** is the set of β-strongly-normalizing λ-terms. In 3.3 it is shown how **SN** can be seen as a sufficient subset of Λ. This CC-structure models CC according to the Soundness Theorem 3.22.

Theorem 5.1 (Strong Normalization for CC). If $\Gamma \vdash M : T$, then $M \in SN$.

Proof. We define a maximum element of $[\![A]\!]^{\square}_{\xi,\rho}$ for every kind A in the following way.

$$\begin{aligned} max(\mathbf{SAT}) &= \mathbf{SN} \\ max([\![\textstyle\prod \alpha : A.B]\!]^{\square}_{\xi,\rho}) &= \lambda\, a \in [\![A]\!]^{\square}_{\xi,\rho}\,.\,\tilde{\lambda}\, m \in [\![A]\!]^{*}_{\xi,\rho}.\ max([\![B]\!]^{\square}_{\xi[\alpha:=a].\rho[\alpha:=m]}) \\ max([\![\textstyle\prod x : \sigma.B]\!]^{\square}_{\xi,\rho}) &= \tilde{\lambda}\, m \in [\![\sigma]\!]^{*}_{\xi,\rho}.\ max([\![B]\!]^{\square}_{\xi,\rho[x:=m]}) \end{aligned}$$

Let $\rho(v) = v$ for every variable v, and $\xi(\alpha) = max([\![A]\!]^{\square}_{\xi,\rho})$ for every $(\alpha : A) \in \Gamma$. (This is possible due to the linearity of the legal contexts). It is immediately verified that, for all terms N, $N \in \mathbf{SN}$ iff $(\!|N|\!)_\rho \in \mathbf{SN}$. Furthermore, the so-chosen valuation ρ and ξ obviously satisfy Γ. From the Soundness Theorem it follows that $(\!|M|\!)_\rho \in [\![T]\!]^{*}_{\xi,\rho} \subseteq \mathbf{SN}$. Hence $(\!|M|\!)_\rho \in \mathbf{SN}$, and so $M \in \mathbf{SN}$. □

For a more detailed presentation of the proof of strong normalization see [15].

6 Related Research

The present paper combines and develops further the ideas in [7] and [15]. This results in constructing a relatively simple set-theoretical notion of model of CC being a PTS. It has been shown how syntactical properties of the system can be studied in a semantical way. Furthermore, such an essential property as SN has been shown to be in a close relation with the semantics of CC. The resulting proof of SN is very flexible in a sense that it can be adapted in a modular way to various extensions of CC, such as inductive types and kinds (see [15]). An interesting question is whether the whole model construction can be extended in a modular way to give semantics of richer systems than CC.

We compare our notion of model with the following.

- **Categorical Models**(see for example [11]). We do not use the abstract machinery of category theory and instead present a simple, intuitively grounded notion of model for CC being a PTS.

- **Standard Realizability Models** (see [12, 13]). The differences here are conceptual. As has been mentioned before, realizability models are a convenient tool for describing semantics for impredicative systems in which the type-dependency rule $(*, \Box)$ of PTSs is "encoded" by explicit "lifting" of every type to a special small kind (see [16, 1]. Such models are usually extensional. A semantics of the PTS CC can be obtained from these models via a syntactic mapping from CC-PTS-style to CC-with-lifting. The model described here is intensional and presents a direct meaning of the Calculus of Construction *as a PTS*.

- **Abstract non-categorical model-constructions.** The only such model-construction we know is the one described in [1]. It is a non-trivial presentation of categorical models without using categorical tools. A non-trivial instance of it is the class of standard realizability models. Note, that this abstract notion of model is also for a system with "lifted" types.

In fact the principle difference between our notion of model and the above three classes of models is that we give a direct interpretation of the rules of Pure Type Systems. We present a new class of concrete models, which are intensional. This makes us believe that these models cannot be viewed as a particular instance of the abstract scheme, as for example presented in [1]. In fact we have tried to organize these concrete models in a more general scheme to cover the PERs as well, but we have so far not succeeded. However one can use PERs instead of polystructures as interpretations of $*$ and 'redo' the rest of the construction.

- **Other (partial) models of the PTS CC** (see [8, 4]). In the literature there are models of CC employed for proving strong normalization, in which CC is interpreted via an explicit or implicit syntactical mapping into Girard's system $F\omega$ (see [9, 8]) . Furthermore, there are models in which type-dependencies are not fully disregarded as in [4] where dependencies are eliminated only in the interpretation of kinds. The interpretations in such models are not straightforwardly extendible to richer systems, for example with inductive types, and our notion of models is more flexible in this sense.

Acknowledgments

We would like to thank Thorsten Altenkirch for some illuminating discussions on the subject of (weakly extensional) combinatory algebras. We are also very grateful to Henk Barendregt, Erik Barendsen and Stefano Berardi for helpful discussions on topics related to the subject of this paper. Further, the comments of the two anonymous referees have been very helpful for us to improve the contents of this paper. Finally, we want to thank Erik Barendsen for his help with LaTeX.

References

1. T. Altenkirch. *Constructions, Inductive Types and Strong Normalization.* PhD thesis, Laboratory for the Foundations of Computer Science, University of Edinburgh, 1993.

2. H. P. Barendregt. *The Lambda Calculus: Its Syntax and Semantics.* North-Holland, Amsterdam, second, revised edition, 1984.
3. H. P. Barendregt. Typed lambda calculi. In Abramski, editor, *Handbook of Logic in Computer Science.* Oxford University Press, 1992.
4. S. Berardi. Encoding of data types in pure construction calculus: a semantic justification. In G. Plotkin and G. Huet, editors, *Logical Enviroments*, pages 30–60, Edinburgh, 1992.
5. S. Berardi. An application of per models to program extraction. *Mathematical Structures in Computer Science*, 3:309–331, 1993.
6. I. Bethke and J. W Klop. Collapsing partial combinatory algebras. Technical report, CWI, The Netherlands, 1995.
7. J. H. Geuvers. Semantics for dependent types (the calculus of constructions) by a 'double' model construction. Technical report, Department of Computer Science, University of Eindhoven, 1995.
8. J. H. Geuvers. A short and flexible proof of strong normalization for the calculus of constructions. In P. Dybjer, B. Nordström, and J. Smith, editors, *Types for Proofs and Programs, Int. Workshop TYPES '94, Båstad, Sweden, LNCS 996*, pages 14–38, Edinburgh, 1995.
9. J.H. Geuvers and M.J. Nederhof. A modular proof of strong normalization for the calculus of constructions. *Journal of Functional Programming*, 1(2):155–189, 1991.
10. J .M. E. Hyland and C.-H. L. Ong. Modified realizability and strong normalization proofs. In M. Bezem and J. F. Groote, editors, *Typed Lambda Calculi and Applications*, 1993.
11. J. M. E. Hyland and M. Pitts. The theory of constructions: Categorical semantics and topos-theoretic models. In Boulder, editor, *AMS notes*, 1987.
12. G. Longo and E. Moggi. Constructive natural deduction and its 'ω-set' interpretation. *Mathematical Structures in Computer Science*, 1:215–254, 1991.
13. Z. Luo. A higher-order calculus and theory abstraction. *IC*, 90:107–137, 1991.
14. J. C. Reynolds. Polymorphism is not set-theoretic. In G. Kahn, D. B. McQueen, and G. Plotkin, editors, *Lecture Notes in Computer Science 173*, 1984.
15. M.T. Stefanova. Schematic proof of strong normalization for barendregt's-cube, 1995. Submitted, also available at http://www.cs.kun.nl/~milena.
16. T. Streicher. *Semantics of Type Theory. Correctness, Completeness and Independence Results.* Progress in Theoretical Computer Science. Birkhäuser, Boston, 1991.
17. T. Streicher. Independence of the induction principle and the axiom of choice in the pure calculus of constructions. *TCS*, 103(2):395–409, 1992.

Optimized Encodings of Fragments of Type Theory in First Order Logic

Tanel Tammet and Jan M. Smith

Department of Computing Science,
Chalmers University of Technology and Univ. of Göteborg,
S-41296 Göteborg, Sweden.
e-mail: {tammet, smith}@cs.chalmers.se

Abstract. The paper presents sound and complete translations of several fragments of Martin-Löf's monomorphic type theory to first order predicate calculus. The translations are optimised for the purpose of automated theorem proving in the mentioned fragments. The implementation of the theorem prover Gandalf and several experimental results are described.

1 Introduction

The subject of this paper is the problem of automated theorem proving in Martin-Löf's monomorphic type theory [16, 8], which is the underlying logic of the interactive proof development system ALF [2, 11].

In the scope of our paper the task of automated theorem proving in type theory is understood as demonstrating that a certain type is inhabited by constructing a term of that type. The problem of inhabitedness of a type A is understood in the following way: given a list of judgements Γ (these may be constant declarations, explicit definitions and defining equalities), find a term a such that $a \in A$ is derivable from Γ. The term a is explicitly constructed and, hence, the judgement $a \in A$ can be checked by ALF.

Direct usage of type theory for automated reasoning poses serious problems due to the higher-order nature of the theory, requiring the use of higher-order unification. Since the latter is undecidable, theorem provers for higher-order logics use either an incomplete unification procedure or special incremental techniques. However, it is often the case that large parts of the theories represented in the type framework are essentially first-order. We argue that in such cases it is advantageous to use first-order techniques, due to the higher efficiency of specialised first order proof search methods as compared to methods usable in the general higher-order case.

We consider the question of axiomatizing the problem of inhabitedness of a type as a formula both in the Horn fragment of the standard first-order logic (where classical and intuitionistic logic coincide) and in full first-order intuitionistic logic, denoted later by F_1 and F_2. The presented translations are shown to be sound and complete.

Translations of Martin-Löf's type theory to theories based on predicate logic have been considered earlier by Aczel [1] and Smith [17], but with purposes different from automated theorem proving. Our translation is also similar to the translation given by Felty and Miller [9] of the logical framework LF to the logic hh^{ω} of hereditary Harrop formulas with quantification at all non-predicate types. However, our work differs from theirs in that we consider translations of fragments of type theory into first order logic and that our main interest is in optimizing the translation for enhancing the efficiency of automated proof search for the problem of inhabitedness.

While it is not realistic to expect that fully automated methods will manage most of the hard tasks in theorem-proving, we believe that the automated methods can be used as a powerful tool when developing proofs interactively in a proof sytem like ALF. T. Tammet has implemented a resolution-based theorem prover for the fragments F_1 and F_2 described in the paper. The prover takes advantage of the optimised translations we introduce and is designed for use together with the system ALF, which incorporates the pattern-matching extension of the underlying monomorphic type theory [8, 11]. Pattern-matching is implemented in the special part of the prover devoted to searching for structural induction proofs.

The paper is structured as follows: the sections 2 and 3 give a brief overview of Martin-Löf's type theory and the resolution method. Section 4 is the central part of the paper, starting with the basic translation to the Horn fragment of first order predicate calculus and finally introducing our optimisations to the translation. Section 5 describes the implementation of the equality predicate and section 6 extends the translation from Horn clauses to the full intuitionistic logic. Finally, section 7 presents experiments with the implementation.

2 Martin-Löf's Type Theory

In type theory we can form judgements of the forms

- A *type*, A is a type,
- $A = B$, A and B are equal types,
- $a \in A$, a is an object in the type A,
- $a = b \in A$, a and b are equal objects in the type A.

In general, a judgement is made in a context, i.e., a list of assumptions $x_1 \in A_1, \ldots, x_n \in A_n$ where for $j \leq n$, A_j may depend on $x_1, \ldots, x_{j-1}$.

There are basically two ways of introducing types in Martin-Löf's type theory: function types and inductively defined sets. Because of the possibility of introducing sets by induction, type theory is an open theory; it is in this sense that the theory may serve as a logical framework.

We denote the type of sets by Set. Given a set A we may form the type $El(A)$ of its elements; hence we have the rule $\dfrac{A \in \mathsf{Set}}{El(A)\ type}$ We will write A instead of

El(A), since it will always be clear from the context whether we mean A as a set (i.e., as an object in Set) or as a type.

If A is a type and B is a family of types for $x \in A$, then we can form the type of functions $(x \in A)B$ from A to B.

$$\frac{A \textit{ type} \qquad B \textit{ type } [x \in A]}{(x \in A)B \textit{ type}}$$

All free occurrences of x in B become bound in $(x \in A)B$. Given a function in $(x \in A)B$ we may apply it on an object in A:

$$\frac{c \in (x \in A)B \qquad a \in A}{c(a) \in B\{a/x\}}$$

where $B\{a/x\}$ denotes the result of substituting a for all free occurances of x in B. A basic way of forming functions is by abstraction:

$$\frac{b \in B \;\; [x \in A]}{[x]b \in (x \in A)B}$$

A function applied on an object is defined by the ordinary β-rule.

$$\frac{a \in A \qquad b \in B \;\; [x \in A]}{([x]b)(a) = b\{a/x\} \in B\{a/x\}}$$

We also have the usual η-, α- and ξ-rules as well as substituition rules. We will often use the notation $(A)B$ when B does not contain any free occurrences of x. In order to increase the readability, we will write $(x_1 \in A_1; \ldots; x_n \in A_n)B$ instead of $(x_1 \in A_1) \ldots (x_n \in A_n)B$ and $b(a_1, \ldots, a_n)$ instead of $b(a_1) \ldots (a_n)$. Similarly, we will write $[x_1] \ldots [x_n]e$ as $[x_1, \ldots, x_n]e$.

The generality of type theory as a logical framework comes from the possibilities of introducing new constants. It is in this way that we can introduce the usual mathematical objects like natural numbers, functions, tuples etc. as well as sets expressing propositions. There are two kinds of constants: *primitive* and *defined*.

A set is defined by its introduction rules, i.e., by giving a collection of primitive constants with appropriate types. For example, the set of natural numbers is defined by declaring the constants $\mathsf{N} \in \mathsf{Set}$, $0 \in \mathsf{N}$, $\mathsf{succ} \in (\mathsf{N})\mathsf{N}$.

A defined constant can either be *explicitly* or *implicitly* defined. We declare an explicitly defined constant c by giving a definition of it: $c = a \in A$ For instance, we can make the following explicit definitions: $1 = \mathsf{succ}(0) \in \mathsf{N}$, $I_{\mathsf{N}} = [x]x \in (\mathsf{N})\mathsf{N}$ and define $I = [A, x]x \in (\mathsf{A} \in \mathsf{Set}; \mathsf{A})\mathsf{A}$ as the monomorphic identity function which when applied to an arbitrary set A yields the identity function on A.

We declare an implicitly defined constant by showing what definiens it has when we apply it to its arguments. An implicit definition may be recursive. The implicit constant $+$, expressing addition of natural numbers, is introduced by $+ \in (\mathsf{N}; \mathsf{N})\mathsf{N}$, $+(0, \mathsf{y}) = \mathsf{y}$, $+(\mathsf{succ}(\mathsf{x}), \mathsf{y}) = \mathsf{succ}(+(\mathsf{x}, \mathsf{y}))$.

The definition of + is an example of an implicit constant defined by pattern-matching on the possible constructors of the set N. In Martin-Löf's original formulation, implicitely defined constants were only possible to introduce by primitive recursion schemes. We will, however, use the more general formulation with pattern-matching, proposed by Coquand [7]. For our approach to automated theorem proving in type theory, pattern-matching is important since it often makes it possible to avoid higher order functions.

A basic idea of type theory is the so called Curry-Howard correspondence between propositions and sets: a proposition is represented as the set of its proofs. Hence, the type of propositions is identified with the type Set. Variables are used as names of assumptions and constants are used as rules. To apply a rule to a number of subproofs is done by applying a constant to the corresponding subproof objects.

A theory is presented by a list of typings and definitions of constants. When we read the constant as a name of a rule, then a primitive constant is usually a formation or introduction rule, an implicitly defined constant is an elimination rule (with the contraction rule expressed as the step from the definiendum to the definiens) and finally, an explicitly defined constant is a lemma or derived rule.

3 The Resolution Calculus

We will define some standard notions of the resolution method, restricting us to the Horn fragment where classical and intuitionistic provability coincide. For further details see, for example, [6] or [4].

An *atom* is a predicate symbol applied to zero or more terms. A *positive literal* is an atom. A *negative literal* is an atom preceded by the negation sign. A *clause* is a finite set of literals. All variables in a clause are interpreted as being universally quantified. In classical logic a clause $\{L_1, L_2, \ldots, L_n\}$ is interpreted as the disjunction $L_1 \vee L_2 \vee \ldots \vee L_n$. A clause, literal, atom or a term is said to be *ground* if it contains no variables. A clause is said to be a *singleton clause* if it only contains a single literal. A *Horn clause* is a clause which contains at most one positive literal. We will often write Horn clauses as *sequents*, since this interpretation suits intuitionistic logic; a sequent $L_1, \ldots, L_n \Rightarrow L$ is considered to be the same as a clause $\{\neg L_1, \ldots, \neg L_n, L\}$.

New clauses are derived by the rule of hyperresolution

$$\frac{L_1, \ldots, L_n \Rightarrow L \qquad \Rightarrow L'_1 \qquad \ldots \qquad \Rightarrow L'_n}{\Rightarrow L\sigma} \quad \sigma = mgu(L_1, L'_1) \ldots mgu(L_n, L'_n)$$

where $mgu(L, L')$ denote the most general unifier of the terms or literals L and L'.

4 Translating Non-Nested Function Types

In this section we will consider the fragment F_1 of type theory which corresponds to Horn clauses. Our goals are:

1. give a sound and complete translation of the fragment F_1 to Horn clauses,
2. optimise the translation for the purposes of automated theorem proving, keeping soundness and completeness,
3. extend the translation to a wider fragment than F_1, taking full first order intuitionistic logic as target logic.

A *function type* is a type of the form $(x_1 \in A_1; \ldots; x_n \in A_n)B$, where $n > 0$.

Definition *A type C belongs to the type fragment F_1 if either C does not contain function types or C has the form $(x_1 \in A_1; \ldots; x_n \in A_n)B$ where none of A_i and B is or contains a function type.*

We say that a judgement belongs to the judgement fragment F_1 if the type of the judgement belongs to F_1. When we speak about the fragment F_1 in the following, it will always be clear from the context whether we mean the type fragment or the judgement fragment.

Example 1. The type $(\mathsf{X} \in \mathsf{Set}; \mathsf{x} \in \mathsf{X}; \mathsf{y} \in \mathsf{X})\mathsf{X}$, corresponding to the implication $\mathsf{X} \to (\mathsf{X} \to \mathsf{X})$, is in F_1. The type $(\mathsf{X} \in \mathsf{Set}; \mathsf{x} \in \mathsf{X}; \mathsf{y} \in (\mathsf{z} \in \mathsf{X})\mathsf{X})\mathsf{X}$, corresponding to $\mathsf{X} \to ((\mathsf{X} \to \mathsf{X}) \to \mathsf{X})$ contains a function type $(\mathsf{z} \in \mathsf{X})\mathsf{X}$ in its third argument, thus it is not in the fragment F_1.

4.1 Translating Judgements and the Goal

We use a two-place first-order predicate In and a first-order equality predicate $=$ to translate judgements.

The intended meaning of $In(a, A)$ is that the term a is an element of the set denoted by the term A, i.e., $a \in A$. Each judgement in F_1 is encoded as a clause in the Horn fragment of first-order logic without quantifiers. All the (first-order) variables in a clause are understood as being universally quantified.

- **Application terms.** An application term $a \equiv f(g_1, \ldots, g_n)$ is translated by full uncurrying. So, in case f is a composite term $h(l_1, \ldots, l_k)$, then one step of uncurrying gives a term $h(l_1, \ldots, l_k, g_1, \ldots, g_n)$ for a. For instance, the term $\mathsf{f}(\mathsf{x}, \mathsf{y})(\mathsf{g}(\mathsf{x}))$ is translated as $f(x, y, g(x))$.
  Notice that in the fragment F_1, all the occurrences of a function symbol in the translated terms will have the same number of arguments. The last fact justifies the syntactic correctness of the translation into first-order language without an extra layer of encoding for application terms.
- **Expressions declaring primitive constants.** A primitive constant $f \in (x_1 \in A_1; \ldots; x_n \in A_n)B$ such as $\mathbf{suc} \in (N)N$ is translated as the clause $In(x_1, A'_1), \ldots, In(x_n, A'_n) \Rightarrow In(f(x_1, \ldots, x_n), B')$, where each x_i is a variable, f is a constant symbol, A'_i and B' are translations of A_i and B, respectively.
  The only variables in the resulting clause are x_i $(1 \leq i \leq n)$. Notice that in the translation of an expression in the fragment F_1, the leftmost symbol of each subterm is a function symbol. This justifies the syntactic correctness of the translation into first-order language.

- **Expressions defining implicit constants.** The definition $f(t_1, \ldots, t_n) = g(h_1, \ldots, h_k)$, of an implicit constant f, is translated as the clause $\Rightarrow F' = G'$, where F' and G' are translations of $f(t_1, \ldots, t_n)$ and $g(h_1, \ldots, h_k)$, respectively.
- **Explicit definitions and equality of types.** Explicit definitions $c = a \in A$ and judgements of the form $A = B$ where A and B are types are not translated at all. Instead, all the type theory expressions containing occurrences of the left side c of some explicit definition or the left side A of an asserted equality of types are normalized by expanding the definition and reducing the resulting redexes before doing the translation.
- **The inhabitedness problem:** Given a list of judgements Γ, show the inhabitedness of a type $G \equiv (x_1 \in A_1; \ldots; x_n \in A_n)B$. We are moreover only interested in the case when B is not the constant Set.

  In order to avoid n explicit abstraction steps in the final part of the derivation, we use the pattern-matching formulation of the abstraction term inhabiting G. Thus we assume that G is a type of a (new) implicitly defined constant g. The constant g is essentially the name of the function term we use instead of the explicit lambda-term $\lambda x_1, \ldots, x_n.t$. Our goal is to construct a term t (corresponding to the body of the abstraction term) for the right hand side of the equation $g(x_1, \ldots, x_n) = t$ which defines a function inhabiting G.

  Let $\sigma \equiv \{c_1/x_n, \ldots, c_n/x_n\}$ be a substitution replacing the variables in G by new constant symbols (Skolem constants) $c_1, \ldots, c_n$ not occurring anywhere in G or in any of the judgements in Γ. The goal will be encoded as the problem of deriving a substitution instance of the clause $\Rightarrow In(x, B'\sigma)$ from the set of clauses $\Gamma' \cup E \cup A'$, where B' is the translation of B, Γ' is the set of translations of all the elements of Γ, E is the standard axiomatization of equivalence and substitutivity of equality for $\Gamma' \cup A' \cup B'$, and A' is the set of clauses

$$\Rightarrow In(c_1, A'_1\sigma), \ldots, \Rightarrow In(c_n, A'_n\sigma),$$

  where each A'_i is a translation of A_i. The variable x in $\Rightarrow In(x, B'\sigma)$ is the variable to be unified, i.e., at the place of x we will obtain the inhabiting term. The operation of replacing the variables in G by the new constants is a specific instance of the Skolemization procedure and, unlike full Skolemization, is correct for intuitionistic logic, see [12] and [13].

  A substitution instance of $\Rightarrow In(x, B'\sigma)$ is derivable from the set $\Gamma' \cup E \cup A'$ if and only if the clause set $\Gamma' \cup E \cup A' \cup \{In(x, B'\sigma) \Rightarrow\}$ is refutable. We will say that the translation of the goal type G is the clause set $A' \cup \{In(x, B'\sigma) \Rightarrow\} \cup E'$, where E' is the set of equality substitution axioms for the function symbols in $A \cup B$.

  There are well-known techniques enabling us to always construct the required substitution instance of $\Rightarrow In(x, B'\sigma)$ from the resolution refutation of Horn clause sets like $\Gamma' \cup E \cup A' \cup \{In(x, B'\sigma) \Rightarrow\}$; see [6] and [5]. It is easy to see that any refutation from a Horn clause set Γ where $In(x, B'\sigma) \Rightarrow$ is a single clause containing no positive literals will end with the hyperresolution

step with premisses being the input clause $In(x, B'\sigma) \Rightarrow$ and some derived clause $\Rightarrow In(t, r)$. Due to the specific form of the clause sets obtained by the translations of type theory judgements, the terms t and r will moreover always be ground.
After finding the refutation we thus have an instance of the clause $\Rightarrow In(x, B'\sigma)$ with a ground term t replacing the variable x. The function body g is built of t by replacing the Skolem constant symbols $c_1, \ldots, c_n$ in t by the variables $x_1, \ldots, x_n$, respectively.

Example 2. In this example, we introduce an inductively defined predicate Leq, expressing the less than or equal relation on the natural numbers (we will add numbers for easier reference).

$$\mathsf{N} \in \mathsf{Set} \tag{1}$$
$$\mathsf{0} \in \mathsf{N} \tag{2}$$
$$\mathsf{s} \in (\mathsf{x} \in \mathsf{N})\mathsf{N} \tag{3}$$
$$\mathsf{Leq} \in (\mathsf{x}, \mathsf{y} \in \mathsf{N})\mathsf{Set} \tag{4}$$
$$\mathsf{leq_0} \in (\mathsf{x} \in \mathsf{N})\mathsf{Leq}(\mathsf{0}, \mathsf{x}) \tag{5}$$
$$\mathsf{leq_s} \in (\mathsf{x}, \mathsf{y} \in \mathsf{N}; \mathsf{z} \in \mathsf{Leq}(\mathsf{x}, \mathsf{y}))\mathsf{Leq}(\mathsf{s}(\mathsf{x}), \mathsf{s}(\mathsf{y})) \tag{6}$$

We denote these declarations by Γ. Consider the task of finding a term inhabiting the following type C:

$$(\mathsf{x} \in \mathsf{N})\mathsf{Leq}(\mathsf{s}(\mathsf{0}), \mathsf{s}(\mathsf{s}(\mathsf{s}(\mathsf{x}))))$$

The translation $Tr(\Gamma)$ of Γ is the following clause set:

1: $\Rightarrow In(N, Set)$
2: $\Rightarrow In(0, N)$
3: $In(x, N) \Rightarrow In(s(x), N)$
4: $In(x, N), In(y, N) \Rightarrow In(Leq(x, y), Set)$
5: $In(x, N) \Rightarrow In(leq_0(x), Leq(0, x))$
6: $In(x, N), In(y, N), In(z, Leq(x, y)) \Rightarrow In(leq_s(x, y, z), Leq(s(x), s(y)))$

where x, y and z are the only variables. The translation of the goal is the following clause set C':

7: $\Rightarrow In(c, N)$
8: $In(u, Leq(s(0), s(s(s(c))))) \Rightarrow$

where u is a variable and c is a new constant symbol. We want to show that the clause set $Tr(\Gamma) \cup C'$ is refutable and find a term t such that the set $Tr(\Gamma) \cup C'\{t/u\}$ would also be refutable. Indeed, there exists the following resolution refutation:

9 (from 3,7): $\Rightarrow In(s(c), N)$
10 (from 3,9): $\Rightarrow In(s(s(c)), N)$

11 (from 5,10): $\Rightarrow In(leq_0(s(s(c))), Leq(0, s(s(c))))$
12 (from 6,2,10,11): $\Rightarrow In(leq_s(0, s(s(c)), leq_0(s(s(c)))), Leq(s(0), s(s(s(c)))))$
13 (from 8,12): $\Rightarrow$

giving us the term $leq_s(0, s(s(c)), leq_0(s(s(c))))$ as the required substitution instance for u in $In(u, Leq(s(0), s(s(s(c)))))$. By replacing the new constant c with a variable x we get the term $leq_s(0, s(s(x)), leq_0(s(s(x))))$ as the body of a function inhabiting the type $(\mathsf{x}\in\mathsf{N})\mathsf{Leq}(\mathsf{s}(0), \mathsf{s}(\mathsf{s}(\mathsf{s}(\mathsf{x}))))$.

We will below present an optimization leading to a smaller input clause set which will avoid the explicit derivation of 9, 10 and 11 in the present example.

4.2 Translating Derivation Rules

Type Formation Rules For our purposes, the set of assumptions and the goal can be assumed to be already correctly formed types. Because the derivation rules of type theory preserve type correctness, we can ignore type formation rules without losing soundness.

Notice that our translation preserves the subformula structure. Concerning completeness, we see that we may ignore type construction rules as long as we only need types that are syntactically subtypes of the assumptions and the goal. Since F_1 corresponds to a fragment of first-order logic and since the normal form of any derivation in first-order logic has the subformula property, we may, hence, ignore type construction rules.

The Application rule and the Substitution Rules These are the main rules for our purposes. It is easy to see that for the fragment F_1 the application rule

$$\frac{c\in(x\in A)B \quad a\in A}{c(a)\in B\{a/x\}}$$

can be assumed to have a "multiple form" instantiating all the arguments of a function at once:

$$\frac{c\in(x_1\in A_1;\ldots;x_n\in A_n)B \quad a_1\in A_1 \ \ldots\ a_n\in A_n}{c(a_1,\ldots,a_n)\in B\{a_1/x_1,\ldots,a_n/x_n\}}$$

Indeed, since in F_1 function types do not occur as argument types of functions, if the result of a single-step application rule is a function, then this function can only be used as a left premiss of an application rule.

The translated form of the multiple application rule is:

$$\frac{\begin{array}{c} In(x_1, A_1),\ldots,In(x_n, A_n) \Rightarrow In(c(x_1,\ldots,x_n), B) \\ \Rightarrow In(a_1, A_1) \\ \ldots \\ \Rightarrow In(a_n, A_n) \end{array}}{\Rightarrow In(c(a_1,\ldots,a_n), B\{a_1/x_1,\ldots,a_n/x_n\})}$$

The last rule is an instance of the hyperresolution rule combining multiple modus ponens with limited substitution – only most general unifiers can be substituted:

$$\frac{F_1,\ldots,F_n \Rightarrow F \qquad \Rightarrow F_1' \qquad \ldots \qquad \Rightarrow F_n'}{\Rightarrow F\sigma} \sigma = mgu(F_1,F_1')\ldots mgu(F_n,F_n')$$

4.3 Soundness and Completeness of the Translation

We will denote the result of translating a judgement or a list of judgements A as $Tr(A)$. We will denote the set of clauses obtained by translating a goal type A as $Trg(A)$.

We will show soundness and completeness of the translation and the hyperresolution calculus with respect to the fragment F_1 of type theory. By soundness we mean that if there is a hyperresolution refutation of $Trg(G) \cup Tr(\Gamma)$ for a goal type G and a list of judgements Γ, then there is a term t and type theory proof of $t \in G$ from Γ. By completeness we mean that if there is a type theory proof from Γ showing that some term inhabits a certain type G, then there is a hyperresolution refutation of $Trg(G) \cup Tr(\Gamma)$.

Lemma 1. *Removing all the equality rules of type theory except β-conversion (see section 2) preserves completeness for the fragment* F_1.

Proof. All the equality rules except β-conversion are covered by the standard first-order axiomatization of equivalence and substitutivity properties of the first-order equality predicate.

Lemma 2. *The type theory calculus obtained by removing the abstraction rule and the β-conversion rule preserves completeness for the fragment* F_1.

Proof. It is easy to see that for the fragment F_1 the abstraction rule is unnecessary. The reason is that F_1 corresponds to a fragment of first-order logic, and since the latter is cut-free, we have the subformula property, guaranteeing completeness without introducing any assumptions which are not subformulas of the conclusion.

Since we do not have assumptions, that is, formulas of the form $b \in B[x \in A]$ in the fragment F_1, and the abstraction rule is unnecessary, then the β-conversion rule (corresponding to the cut rule in first-order logic)

$$\frac{a \in A \quad b \in B[x \in A]}{((x)b)(a) = b\{a/x\} \in B\{a/x\}}$$

is also unnecessary.

The following is the standard *lifting lemma* of the theory of resolution calculus. (see e.g. [6]):

Lemma 3. *Let A and B be two clauses $A \equiv \{A_1, \ldots, A_n\}$ and $B \equiv \{B_1, \ldots, B_n\}$. Let A' and B' be two clauses with the following properties: $A' = A\sigma \cup A''$, $B' = B\rho \cup B''$ where σ and ρ are substitutions, A'' and B'' are arbitrary clauses. Whenever a new clause C' can be derived from A' and B' by resolution, there exists a clause C derivable from A and B such that $C' = C\mu \cup C''$, where μ is a subsitution and C'' is a clause.*

Lemma 4. *The hyperresolution rule applied to the translation of type theory judgements is sound and complete for type theory with only application and substitution as derivation rules.*

Proof. The proof of soundness is by induction on the size of derivation. The base case is immediate. The induction step is also obvious, since every hyperresolution application corresponds to a derivation in type theory containing only substitutions and applications.

The proof of completeness is also by induction on the size of derivation. Again, the base case is obvious. For the induction step, assume that we have a substitution or application in type theory from premisses Γ with conclusion F. We have to show that there is a corresponding hyperresolution derivation from the clause set $Tr(\Gamma')$ giving a clause $Tr(F')$ such that Γ is a set of substitution instances of Γ' and F is a substitution instance of F'. The substitution step is obvious: take the translation of the unchanged premiss of the substitution derivation. The application step follows from the lifting lemma.

Theorem 5. *The translation and hyperresolution are sound and complete with respect to the fragment F_1 of type theory.*

Proof. Follows from the previous lemmas in this section.

4.4 Optimizing the Translation

We introduce two optimizations of our translation of the fragment F_1. The optimized translations do not allow to get a proof term directly. However, from the proof of the optimized translation it is possible to efficiently construct the proof of the unoptimized translation, which gives the required proof term. Such an algorithm is implemented in our prover Gandalf.

The First Optimization: O_1 Let Γ be a list of type theory judgements in the fragment F_1 and let G be a goal type in the fragment F_1. Observe that all the positive singleton clauses in $Tr(\Gamma) \cup Trg(G)$ are ground and all the variables in a positive literal of any non-singleton clause C in $Tr(\Gamma) \cup Trg(G)$ occur as first arguments in the negative literals of C. Therefore any nonemtpy clause derived from $Tr(\Gamma) \cup Trg(G)$ by hyperresolution is a singleton ground clause.

We present an optimization O_1 for translations of type theory judgements, which is crucial for improving the efficiency of automated proof search. The point of O_1 is allowing the derivation of non-ground singleton clauses, each covering a possibly infinite set of ground singleton clauses derivable from the non-optimized clause set.

The optimization O_1 is obtained by replacing all atoms with the binary predicate In by an atom with a unary predicate Inh, always discarding the first argument of In.

The encoded goal clause $G \equiv \ \Rightarrow In(x, B\sigma)$ turns into a ground clause $O_1(G) \equiv \ \Rightarrow Inh(B\sigma)$. After we have found a first-order derivation of the clause $O_1(G)$ from the set of optimized assumption clauses $O_1(\Gamma)$, we construct the corresponding derivation of a substitution instance of the non-optimized G from the set of non-optimized assumptions Γ.

Example 3. Consider the set of judgements A obtained by translating the type theory judgements in example 2. The optimization O_1 applied to the clauses in example 2 will give the following clause set $O_1(A)$.

1': $\Rightarrow Inh(Set)$
2': $\Rightarrow Inh(N)$
3': $Inh(N) \Rightarrow Inh(N)$
4': $Inh(N), Inh(N) \Rightarrow Inh(Set)$
5': $Inh(N) \Rightarrow Inh(Leq(0, x))$
6': $Inh(N), Inh(N), Inh(Leq(x, y)) \Rightarrow Inh(Leq(s(x), s(y)))$
7': $\Rightarrow Inh(N)$
8': $Inh(Leq(s(0), s(s(s(c))))) \Rightarrow$

There exists the following resolution refutation from $O_1(A)$:

11' (from 2',5'): $\Rightarrow Inh(Leq(0, x)$
12' (from 2',2',11',6'): $\Rightarrow Inh(Leq(s(0), s(x)))$
13' (from 8',12'): $\Rightarrow$

The crucial importance of the optimization O_1 stands in that whereas hyperresolution derives only ground clauses from the the unoptimised translation, then from the optimised translation it is possible to derive new clauses containing variables. Such clauses stand for generally infinite sets of ground clauses derivable from the unoptimised translation.

In the example above, we can derive a non-ground clause $\Rightarrow Inh(leq(s(0), s(x)))$ from the clauses 2', 5' and 6', covering the infinite set of clauses $\Rightarrow In(p_1, leq(s(0), s(0))), \Rightarrow In(p_2, leq(s(0), s(s(0)))), \Rightarrow In(p_3, leq(s(0), s(s(s(0))))), \ldots\}$ derivable from A.

We now build a new clause set A^i from the unoptimized clause set A in the example above by replacing the clause $8: \ In(u, leq(s(0), s(s(s(c))))) \Rightarrow$ with the clause $8^i: \ In(u, leq(s(0), s^i(c))) \Rightarrow$ where $s^i(c)$ stands for the term where s is applied i times. The shortest hyperresolution refutation of A^i consists of $i+3$ hyperresolution steps. The shortest hyperresolution refutation of $O_1(A^i)$ consists always of 3 steps, regardless of i. Due to the optimization we avoid deriving the previously necessary sequent $\Rightarrow In(s^i(c), N)$.

Let Γ be a clause set in the fragment F_1, let G be a goal type in F_1. $Tr(\Gamma)$ is a translated form of Γ and $Trg(G)$ is the translated form of G. $O_1(Tr(\Gamma))$ is the optimized form of $Tr(\Gamma)$.

For the simplicity of presentation we will assume that equality is not present in Γ or G and that $Trg(G)$ consists of a sole negative singleton clause. The case with the equality will be treated later in Section 5. It is always possible to reformulate G and Γ as G' and Γ' by assuming that all the positive singleton clauses in the original $Trg(G)$ are members of $Tr(\Gamma')$. The reformulated $Trg(G')$ then consists of a sole negative singleton clause, which can be used in the hyperresolution refutation of $Tr(\Gamma') \cup Trg(G')$ only for the last inference, the derivation of the empty clause.

Soundness and completeness of the optimization O_1 The first order language of $Tr(\Gamma)$ is not typed. However, due to the construction of $Tr(\Gamma)$, all the terms occurring in the clauses of $Tr(\Gamma)$ can be seen as being typed by Γ. Every variable x occuring in a clause C in $Tr(\Gamma)$ occurs in a literal $In(x, t_x)$ in C, corresponding to a judgement $x \in t_x$ in Γ.

In the following we consider all the variables, constants, function symbols and terms (briefly: *objects*) in $Tr(\Gamma)$ to be typed. The type of an object in $Tr(\Gamma)$ is determined by Γ. The type of an object in $O_1(Tr(\Gamma))$ is the same as the type of a corresponding object in $Tr(\Gamma)$. A term t constructed from objects in $Tr(\Gamma)$ is *type-correct* iff the term t' corresponding to t in type theory is type-correct in the context of Γ.

By $\Delta \vdash_{h*} C$ we denote that a clause C is derivable from the clause set Δ by hyperresolution. Since any clause C such that $Tr(\Gamma) \vdash_{h*} C$ is ground, it is easy to see that C is type-correct.

Differently from $Tr(\Gamma)$, it is possible to derive non-ground clauses from $O_1(Tr(\Gamma))$. We extend the notion of type-correctness to clauses C such that $O_1(Tr(\Gamma)) \vdash_{h*} C$. Each variable x occurring in C can be traced (renaming taken into account) through the derivation tree of C to the occurrence of some variable y in $O_1(Tr(\Gamma))$. Thus we can say that it has a type of the variable y and we will extend the notion of type-correctness to the clauses derived from $O_1(Tr(\Gamma))$.

Lemma 6. *Consider a variable x occurring inside $O_1(Tr(\Gamma))$. Either x occurs as an argument of the predicate Inh, in which case it has a universal type* Set *or x is an argument a_i of some term $f(a_1, \ldots, a_n)$ occurring inside $O_1(Tr(\Gamma))$. In the last case the type of x is determined by the function symbol f, the position i of a_i in the term and and a subset of arguments $\Delta \subset \{a_1, \ldots, a_n\}$ such that $a_i \notin \Delta$. There exists a reflexive ordering $\succeq_d$ of the elements of $\{a_1, \ldots, a_n\}$, such that whenever $a_k \succeq_d a_l$ $(1 \leq k, l \leq n)$, the type of a_l cannot depend on the type of a_k.*

Proof. Follows from the rules of monomorphic type theory as a syntactic property.

Theorem 7. *The optimization O_1 preserves soundness and completeness.*

Proof. Let Γ be a clause set in the fragment F_1, let $Tr(\Gamma)$ be a translated form of Γ and let $O_1(Tr(\Gamma))$ be the optimized form of $Tr(\Gamma)$.

Completeness: if $Tr(\Gamma) \vdash_{h*} C$ holds, then there is such a clause C' and such a substitution σ that $C = C'\sigma$ and $O_1(Tr(\Gamma)) \vdash_{h*} O_1(C')$ holds. Consequently, if $Tr(\Gamma) \cup Trg(G)$ is refutable, then $O_1(Tr(\Gamma)) \cup O_1(Trg(G))$ is refutable.

The proof is easy, since O_1 does nothing but removes the first argument of each predicate symbol. Let D be a hyperresolution derivation of C from $Tr(\Gamma)$. Construct a new derivation D' by removing the first arguments from each occurrence of the predicate Inh in D and replacing Inh with In. Then D' is a substitution instance of a derivation giving $O_1(C')$ from $O_1(Tr(\Gamma))$. Therefore, due to the completeness of hyperresolution, $O_1(Tr(\Gamma)) \vdash_{h*} O_1(C')$ holds.

Soundness: If $O_1(Tr(\Gamma)) \vdash_{h*} C$ holds, then C is type-correct.

Hence (due to the completeness of $Tr(\Gamma)$ for type theory), if $O_1(Tr(\Gamma)) \cup O_1(Trg(G))$ is refutable, then $Tr(\Gamma) \cup Trg(G)$ is refutable.

Proof. We use induction over the hyperresolution derivation for the optimized case. The proof relies on that we are using monomorphic type theory where the previous lemma holds and that any applied substitution is a most general unifier of two existing terms.

Base case: obvious.

Induction step. Consider the hyperresolution rule:

$$\frac{L_1, \ldots, L_n \Rightarrow L \quad \Rightarrow L_1' \quad \ldots \quad \Rightarrow L_n'}{\Rightarrow L\sigma} \sigma = mgu(L_1, L_1') \ldots mgu(L_n, L_n')$$

The literal L has a form $Inh(r)$. The induction step is proved by showing that $r\sigma$, hence also $L\sigma$, is type-correct.

The proof is by induction over the substitution σ which is ordered by the dependency ordering $\succeq_d$. Base case is obvious, we proceed to proving the induction step.

As an induction hypothesis we assume that there is a subset ρ of σ such that $r\rho$ is type-correct and for each $\{s/v\}$ in ρ and $\{p/u\}$ in $\sigma - \rho$ holds $v \succeq_d u$. Essentially, we construct the substitution by starting from the $\succeq_d$-smallest variables and proceeding according to the ordering $\succeq_d$.

An element t/x of $\sigma - \rho$ is obtained by unifying a variable x in a literal $L_i\rho$ with the term t in $L_i'\rho$, where $\rho \subset \sigma$. We have:

$$\forall u, p, v, s.(\{p/u\} \subset (\sigma - \rho) \ \& \ \{s/v\} \subset \rho) \Rightarrow u \succeq_d v$$

The variable x either occurs as a sole argument in the literal $Inh(x)$, in which case x has a universal type Set or as an argument a_i of some surrounding term $f(a_1, \ldots, a_n)$.

In the first case also t occurs as a sole argument of $Inh(t)$, the type of t is Set and thus $r\rho\{t/x\}$ is type-correct.

Consider the second case. Here also the term t occurs as an i-th argument of a surrounding term $f(a_1', \ldots, a_n')$. Both the leading function symbol f and the position index i in the surrounding term are the same for x and t. Thus either both the types of x and t do no depend on other terms or they both depend on a subset of arguments in the surrounding term. Consider the case where the types of x and t do not depend on other terms. In that case the type of t is the same as the type of x and thus $r\rho\{t/x\}$ is type-correct.

Consider the case where the types of x and t depend on other terms. Due to the previous lemma all these depended-upon terms form a subset of pairwise corresponding arguments D of $f(a_1, \ldots, a_n)$ and D' of $f(a'_1, \ldots, a'_n)$. The previous lemma shows that there exists a dependency ordering $\succeq_d$ so that the types of the elements of D and D' do not depend on the types of x and t. Thus we can assume that $D = D' = D\sigma = D'\sigma$, i.e, the terms corresponding to D and D' in L_i and L'_i are already unified by ρ. Hence the type of t in $L'_i\rho$ is the same as the type of x in $L_i\rho$, thus $r\rho\{t/x\}$ is type-correct.

Observe that in some sense the unrestricted substitution rule (i.e. a substitution rule which uses arbitrary substitutions, not only these obtained by unification) would make the optimized calculus unsound in respect to the type theory, although the refutability of a set $O_1(Tr(\Gamma))$ with unrestricted substitution added as a derivation rule would still be equivalent to the refutability of $Tr(\Gamma)$.

The Second Optimization: O_2 The second optimization O_2 is applicable only to such clause sets which have been already optimized by O_1. O_2 is obtained by removing certain clauses and some atoms on the left sides of other clauses. It is essentially a preprocessing phase pre-applying obvious hyperresolution steps and removing redundant clauses and literals.

Definition *We say that a type* $f \in (x_1 \in A_1; \ldots; x_n \in A_n)\mathsf{Set}$ *is* essentially independent *in a given list of judgements iff it can be shown that* $f(x_1, \ldots, x_n)\rho$ *is inhabited for any substitution* ρ *such that* $f(x_1, \ldots, x_n)\rho$ *is correctly formed regarding types. We will call such* f *an* essentially independent constructor

For example, the special type Set, the type of natural numbers $\mathsf{N} \in \mathsf{Set}$, $0 \in \mathsf{N}$, $\mathsf{s} \in (\mathsf{x} \in \mathsf{N})\mathsf{N}$ and the parameterized list type $\mathsf{List} \in (\mathsf{x} \in \mathsf{Set})\mathsf{Set}$, $\mathsf{nil} \in (\mathsf{x} \in \mathsf{Set})\mathsf{List}(\mathsf{x})$, $\mathsf{cons} \in (\mathsf{x} \in \mathsf{Set}; \mathsf{y} \in \mathsf{x}; \mathsf{z} \in \mathsf{List}(\mathsf{x}))\mathsf{List}(\mathsf{x})$ are easily shown to be *essentially independent.* As a negative example, the type Leq used in the previous examples is not essentially independent.

The optimization O_2 takes a set of assumptions of the form given by the optimization O_1. It returns a modified set of assumptions and the goal where for any input judgement clause $s \equiv Inh(A_1), \ldots, Inh(A_m) \Rightarrow Inh(B)$ the following is done:

- if B is a composite term with an essentially independent constructor as a leading function symbol, remove the clause s.
- remove any premiss $Inh(A_i)$ such that A_i has an essentially independent constructor as a leading function symbol.

Example 4. Take the O_1-optimized clause set S from the example 3. You may also want to look at the original untranslated list of type theory judgements and the goal in the example 2. The result of the optimization S_2 applied to S is the following set of three clauses:

5": $\Rightarrow Inh(Leq(0, x))$
6": $Inh(Leq(x, y)) \Rightarrow Inh(Leq(s(x), s(y)))$
8": $Inh(Leq(s(0), s(s(s(c))))) \Rightarrow$

The last clause set has a short refutation:

1 (from 6", 5") $\Rightarrow Inh(Leq(s(0), s(x))$
2 (from 8", 1) $\Rightarrow$

In case the type term A in the goal clause $G \equiv \Rightarrow Inh(A)$ has an essentially independent leading function symbol, then the problem of constructing an element of A reduces to the simple problem of using the procedure of checking essential independency for constructing an element of A.

Soundness and completeness of the optimization O_2 follow from the definition of essentially independent types.

5 Building In Equality

For the Horn fragment where the translation of the F_1 class belongs, the explicit axiomatization of the equality predicate (except the reflexivity axiom $x = x$ which must be preserved) can be replaced by the following restricted form of paramodulation without losing completeness (see eg. [10]).

$$\frac{\Rightarrow L[t] \quad \Rightarrow t' = g}{\Rightarrow L[g]\sigma} \sigma = mgu(t, t')$$

where $L[g]$ is obtained by replacing one occurrence of the term t in $L[t]$ by the term g. The term t (the term *paramodulated into*) in the paramodulation rule is prohibited to be a variable. The equality predicate in the rule is assumed to be commutative, i.e., $t' = g$ is the same as $g = t'$.

The *definitional* equality predicate $=$ in type theory extended with pattern-matching (as in Alf) is always assumed to define a terminating and confluent rewrite relation E. Thus we do not lose completeness in case we treat such equality axioms as rewrite rules, ie. if we rewrite any term in any derived first-order clause modulo the rewriting relation E. See [10]). However, we will still need to keep the paramodulation rule to guarantee completeness.

The soundness and completeness of using the paramodulation (or rewrite rules) for the O_1-optimized translations of type theory judgements is proved analogously to the earlier proof of soundness and completeness of the O_1-optimized translation.

Note that the other type of equality often used in the applications of type theory, the *propositional* equality Id, is not definable in F_1. However, we can build the propositional equality directly into the first order calculus.

We will use the following special form of the paramodulation rule along with the reflexivity axiom $\Rightarrow Id(A,x,x)$ instead of the standard equivalence and substitution rule schemes for Id:

$$\frac{\Rightarrow L[t] \quad \Rightarrow Id(A,t',g)}{\Rightarrow L[g]\sigma} \sigma = mgu(t,t')$$

where $L[g]$ is obtained by replacing one occurrence of the term t in $L[t]$ by the term g. The terms t and t' in the paramodulation rule are prohibited to be variables. Id is assumed to be commutative, i.e., $Id(A,t',g)$ is the same as $Id(A,g,t')$.

6 Translating Nested Function Types

6.1 The General Case

Consider full type theory. We obtain the translation Tri by modifying and extending the translation Tr given for the fragment F_1 to the implicational fragment of first-order intuitionistic logic as a target logic.

- **Application terms.** $f(g_1, g_2, \ldots, g_n)$ is translated as $ap(\ldots ap(ap(Tri(f), Tri(g_1)), Tri(g_2)), \ldots), Tri(g_n))$, where $Tri(t)$ denotes the result of the translation of t.
- **Abstraction terms.** An abstraction term $[x]t$ is translated by Schönfinkel's abstraction algorithm:
  $[x]x \rightarrow I$
  $[x]M \rightarrow ap(K, Tri(M))$ if M is a variable or constant, $M \neq x$.
  $[x](MN) \rightarrow ap(ap(S, [x]Tri(M)), [x]Tri(N))$.
  where I, S, K are special constants.
- **Type judgements.** A judgement $t \in (x \in A)B$ is translated as $\forall x.Tri(x \in A) \Rightarrow Tri(ap(t,x) \in B)$. A judgement $t \in C$ where C is not a function type is translated as $Inh(Tri(t), Tri(C))$. Constants and variables remain unchanged by the translation.
- **Goal.** The goal $G_1, \ldots, G_n \vdash_{tt} ? \in B$ of finding a term inhabiting B in the context of judgements $G_1, \ldots, G_n$ is translated as a formula $Tri(G_1) \Rightarrow (\ldots(Tri(G_n) \Rightarrow \exists x.Tri(x \in B))\ldots)$.
- **Target logic.** An implicational fragment of first-order intuitionistic logic with the equality predicate plus the standard equalities $S_=, K_=, I_=$ for combinators S, K, I: $ap(I,x) = x$, $ap(ap(K,x),y) = x$, $ap(ap(ap(S,x),y),z) = ap(ap(x,z), ap(y,z))$.

It is known (see [3]) that the Schönfinkel's abstraction algorithm combined with the beforementioned equality rules for S, K, I simulates weak β-reduction of lambda calculus $([x]MN) = M\{N/x\}$ but not the ξ rule: $M = M' \Rightarrow [x]M = [x]M'$.

From the view of automated theorem proving the main problem with using the equalities $S_=, K_=, I_=$ stands in that these equalities significantly expand the search space of proving a type theory goal. In the following we will consider a fragment where $S_=, K_=, I_=$ can be avoided without resorting to higher order unification.

6.2 Translating Types with Independent Nested Function Types

The following fragment F_2 is a superset of the previously considered fragment F_1. The motivation for considering F_2 stems from the fact that the problems arising in the general case disappear, but since F_2 corresponds to the implicational fragment of full first-order intuitionistic logic, it is strong enough to allow synthesis of conditional programs.

Definition *An* independent function type *is a type with the form* $(x \in A)B$ *such that* x *does not occur in* B.

A type C *in type theory belongs to the type fragment* F_2 *iff* C *is either not a function type or it has a form* $(x \in A)B$ *such that the following two cases hold:*

1. B *belongs to the type fragment* F_2
2. A *is not a function type or* A *is an independent function type and* x *does not occur in* B.

A type theory judgement C *belongs to the judgement fragment* F_2 *if* C *does not contain a type outside the type fragment* F_2.

The translation Tr' for F_2 is obtained from the previously considered translation Tri by applying an optimization O_1 (literals of the form $In(t, g)$ are converted to the form $Inh(g)$). Soundness and completeness proofs of the translation are obtained from the analogous proofs for the fragment F_1. The most convenient way to extend these proofs is to use the resolution method for intuitionistic logic proposed by G.Mints, see [14] and [15].

In addition to the optimization O_1, we will apply the analogue of the optimization O_2 to the formula given by the translation Tri.

We note that the introduction and elimination rules for disjunction and conjunction can be defined in F_2. These connectives will be on the different level than implication, but we can enhance the efficiency of the prover by building these connectives into the target logic, much like we can build propositional equality into target logic.

Since quantifiers cannot be defined in F_2, we can handle those only by building them into the target logic, ie. considering full intuitionistic logic instead of the implicational fragment.

7 Experiments with the Implementation

T.Tammet has implemented an automated theorem prover Gandalf, which looks for type theory proofs in the fragments F_1 and F_2. It uses all the optimizations presented in the paper and (for the fragment F_1) builds the proof term which can be later checked by the ALF proofchecker. In order to be able to build the proof term, Gandalf keeps track of all the necessary information while looking for the first order proofs. In essence, the proof of the optimized version of the problem is used for constructing the proof of the unoptimized version, and the proof term is obtained from the latter.

Gandalf is written in Scheme and compiled to C. The timings presented in the following are obtained by running Gandalf on a SUN SS-10.

Gandalf takes a file containing type theory judgements and possibly several goal types, written in ALF syntax. It converts the judgements and goals to first order language using the translation and optimizations described in the previous sections. After that it starts looking for proofs. Gandalf organizes proof search by iterative deepening on runtime. Suppose the input file contains a list of judgements Γ and a list of goal types $G_1, \ldots, G_n$. Gandalf will take the first time limit t_1 and allocate t_1/n seconds for the attempt to prove G_1. In case it fails, Gandalf will proceed to G_2, etc. In case it succeeds, all the following proof search subtasks will treat G_1 as a judgement, the remaining time from t_1 will be divided between goals $G_2, \ldots, G_n$ and Gandalf will proceed to the next goal G_2. In case a proof search attempt has been conducted for each goal $G_1, \ldots, G_n$ and for some of these no proof is found, Gandalf will take a new time limit $t_2 = f * t_1$ for some factor f and will perform a new interation for yet unproved goals with the new time limit t_2.

Consider the task of proving a separate subgoal G: $(x_1 \in A_1; \ldots; x_n \in A_n)B$. Gandalf will attempt to use structural induction, i.e., pattern-matching, for proving G. It will consider each argument type A_i in G, finding all these judgements in Γ which are introduction rules for A_i, that is, which are of the form $(y_1 \in B_1; \ldots; y_n \in B_m)C$ with C and A_i being unifiable. It will then generate a set T of different proof search tasks for G, each element of T corresponding to a subset of variables $x_1, \ldots, x_n$ being inducted upon. To every element (induction case) of the task in T it adds the induction assumptions. Induction assumptions are generated from the subterms of the pattern of the inductive case at hand. Only these assumptions are considered which are structurally smaller than the pattern of the particular induction case.

A certain amount of time will be allocated for proof search for each element of T. In case Gandalf manages to prove some element E of T, it has found the proof for G and it will continue with the next open goal from the set $G_1, \ldots, G_n$.

Consider the task of proving an element E in the set of proof search tasks for G. Each such element generally consists of a number of pure first order proof tasks $R_1, \ldots, R_k$, each R_i corresponding to one case of structual induction. E is proved only if each of $R_1, \ldots, R_k$ has been proved.

In case Gandalf finds a proof for some goal G_i, it will construct a sound type theory proof of G_i, using the ALF syntax. Each inductive case will have its own separate proof. Each such separate proof is constructed from the proof found for the corresponding first order clause set. In order to make this possible, Gandalf keeps track of all the necessary information while looking for the first order proofs.

The current implementation of Gandalf is only able to to construct type theory proofs for the fragment F_1. The part constructing type theory proofs from the resolution proofs for the intuitionistic fragment F_2 is being worked upon.

Gandalf does not attempt to construct lemmas. Thus it is completely up to the user to include all the necessary lemmas in the input file. Selecting lemmas to be proved (and later used for the main proof) is one of the main mechanisms available to the user in order to guide the blind search of Gandalf.

In addition to the selection of lemmas, there are a number of flags and parameters the user can give to Gandalf in order to guide the proof search. For example, it is possible to indicate that no induction should be used for a certain goal or that a certain subset of variables has to be inducted upon, etc.

7.1 Example. Correctness of Toy Compiler

The following example encodes the problem of proving correctness of a simple compiler. The example is presented in [8] with a proof created by a human user (C.Coquand) in interaction with the ALF system. We present a proof found by the Gandalf system using a number of crucial *hints* given to Gandalf by the human user.

We want to compute a polynomial expression build of multiplication, addition, basic integers and one variable on a simple stack machine. The instructions for this machine are:

- Duplication of the top of the stack.
- Reversal of the top items on the stack.
- Replacement of the top items on the stack by an item that is their sum (resp. product).
- Replacement of the top item n on the stack by a given item n_0.

The problem is to compile a given polynomial expression $e(x)$ to a list l of intructions such that if we execute l on the stack, then the result of this computation is the stack with the value of the expression $e(x)$ pushed to the top.

The evaluation function is represented as a type theoretic function $\mathsf{Eval} \in (\mathsf{Expr}; \mathsf{N})\mathsf{N}$ such that $\mathsf{Eval}(\mathsf{e}, \mathsf{n})$ gives the value of the expression e when its unique variable is set equal to value n. The execution function which computes a final stack from the input stack and a list of instructions is represented as an inductively defined relation EXEC between a list of instructions and two stacks, reflecting operational semantics. This definition uses an auxiliary relation Exec between a single instruction and two stacks.

The proof of the main theorem thm requires a lemma showing that EXEC is a transitive relation. Gandalf does not attempt to create lemmas automatically, thus lemma is present in the input file along with the assumption that it is already proved.

```
N : Set,  0 : N,  s : (N)N
plus : (N;N)N,   mult : (N;N)N

List : (Set)Set
  nil : (t:Set)List(t)
  cons : (t:Set; x:t; y:List(t))List(t)

Stack : Set,   null: Stack,   push:(N;r)Stack

Instr : Set

Dup : Instr, Rev : Instr, Add : Instr, Mul : Instr, Lit : (N)Instr

Expr : Set,
  Sum : (Expr;Expr)Expr,
  Pro : (Expr;Expr)Expr
  Num : (N)Expr
  Arg : Expr

Eval : (Expr;N)N
  Eval(Sum(e1,e2),n)=plus(Eval(e1,n),Eval(e2,n))
  Eval(Pro(f1,f2),n)=mult(Eval(f1,n),Eval(f2,n))
  Eval(Num(n1),n)=n1
  Eval(Arg,n)=n

append : (List(Instr);List(Instr))List(Instr)
  append(nil(Instr),x)=x
  append(cons(Instr,x,y),z)=cons(Instr,x,append(y,z))
  append(x,nil(Instr))=x

Exec : (Instr;Stack;Stack)Set
 Exec_Dup : (n:N;r:Stack)
            Exec(Dup,push(n,r),push(n,push(n,r)))
 Exec_Rev : (n1,n2:N;r:Stack)
            Exec(Rev,push(n1,push(n2,r)),push(n2,push(n1,r)))
 Exec_Add : (n1,n2:N;r:Stack)
            Exec(Add,push(n1,push(n2,r)),push(plus(n1,n2),r))
 Exec_Mul : (n1,n2:N;r:Stack)
            Exec(Mul,push(n1,push(n2,r)),push(mult(n1,n2),r))
 Exec_Lit : (n,m:N;r:Stack)
            Exec(Lit(n),push(m,r),push(n,r))

Program = List(Instr)  : Set

EXEC : (Program; Stack; Stack)Set
```

```
exec_nil : (r:Stack)EXEC(nil(Instr),r,r)
exec_seq : ( i:Instr; p:Program; r1,r2,r3:Stack;
             Exec(i,r1,r2); EXEC(p,r2,r3) )
           EXEC(cons(Instr,i,p),r1,r3)

Comp : (e:Expr)Program
 Comp(Sum(e1,e2)) =
   cons(Instr,
        Dup,
        append(Comp(e2),
               append(cons(Instr,Rev,nil(Instr)),
                  append(Comp(e1),cons(Instr,Add,nil(Instr))) )))
 Comp(Pro(f1,f2)) =
   cons(Instr,
        Dup,
        append(Comp(f2),
               append(cons(Instr,Rev,nil(Instr)),
                  append(Comp(f1),cons(Instr,Mul,nil(Instr))) )))
 Comp(Num(n)) =
   cons(Instr,Lit(n),nil(Instr))
 Comp(Arg) = nil(Instr)


lemma : ( p1,p2:Program; s1,s2,s3:Stack;
          EXEC(p1,s1,s2); EXEC(p2,s2,s3) )
        EXEC(append(p1,p2),s1,s3)

thm : (e:Expr; r:Stack; n:N)
      EXEC(Comp(e),push(n,r),push(Eval(e,n),r))

  thm(e,r,n) = ?(forceind(e),noind(r,n),method(both-ends))
```

The expression thm(e, r, n) =?(forceind(e), noind(r, n), method(both-ends)) gives hints for the search of the proof of thm. The expressions forceind(e) and noind(r, n) tell Gandalf that it is necessary to use induction on the variable e, while it is prohibited to use induction on the variables r and n. In case we do not provide Gandalf with these two hints, it will spend a lot of time attempting to use induction schemas which are of no use when proving thm, and the proof is found only after a one-hour search.

The expression method(both-ends) tells Gandalf that it should look for proof by reasoning from both ends, i.e. doing both forward reasoning and backward reasoning simultaneously (implemented as binary unit resolution).

Consider the definition of append used in the formulation of the problem. The current version of the proof checker ALF does not allow overlapping patterns, thus it fails to type-check the third case append(x, nil(Instr)) = x. However, this case preserves confluency of the definition of append. We have preferred to add it to the definition of append, since the extended rewriting relation clears up a noticeable amount of search space and enables the prover to find the proof faster. Alternatively, we could consider proving the equality $Id(List(Instr), append(x, nil(Instr)), x)$ as a separate lemma, which will have the same efficiency-boosting effect in case the prover is able to orient this equality to a rewriting rule.

The following is a proof found by Gandalf. We have deleted five arguments of essentially independent type from each application of the functions lemma and exec_seq in order to shorten the proof.

The proof is found in ca two and a half minutes. The first two induction cases thm(Sum(x4, x5), r, n) and thm(Pro(x2, x3), r, n) are both proved in one minute (five thousand clauses derived, four thousand of these kept), the last two cases thm(Num(x1), r, n) and thm(Arg, r, n) are proved in a fraction of a second (resp. 21 and 14 clauses derived), half a minute is wasted on an initial attempt to prove thm(Sum(x4, x5), r, n) with a half-minute time limit.

```
thm(Sum(x4,x5),r,n) =
  lemma(exec_seq(ExecDup(n,r),
                 thm(x5,push(n,r),n)),
       lemma(exec_seq(Exec_Rev(Eval(x5,n),n,r),
                      thm(x4,push(Eval(x5,n),r),n)),
            exec_seq(Exec_Add(Eval(x4,c),Eval(x5,n),r),
                exec_nil(push(plus(Eval(x4,n),Eval(x5,n)),r)))))

thm(Pro(x2,x3),r,n) =
  lemma(exec_seq(Exec_Dup(n,r),
                 thm(x3,push(n,r),n)),
        lemma(exec_seq(Exec_Rev(Eval(x3,n),n,r),
                       thm(x2,push(Eval(x3,n),r),n)),
            exec_seq(Exec_Mul(Eval(x2,n),Eval(x3,n),r),
                exec_nil(push(mult(Eval(x2,n),Eval(x3,n)),r)))))

thm(Num(x1),r,n) =
  exec_seq(Exec_Lit(x1,n,r),
           exec_nil(push(x1,r)))

thm(Arg,r,n) = exec_nil(push(n,r))
```

In the example above we instructed Gandalf to use forward reasoning and backward reasoning simultaneously (implemented as unit resolution). However, the default strategy of Gandalf is using pure forward reasoning (implemented as hyperresolution). The latter, while being a good choice for a large class of problems, is ill suited for the current problem. It takes Gandalf almost two hours (deriving 337008 clauses) to prove even a single induction case thm(Sum(x4, x5), r, n) of the general theorem thm(e, r, n) when using pure forward reasoning.

We are planning to implement a heuristic module of Gandalf which would automatically make choices between reasoning methods.

References

1. Peter Aczel. The strength of Martin-Löf's type theory with one universe. In *Proceedings of the Symposium on Mathematical Logic, Oulu, 1974*, pages 1–32. Report No 2, Department of Philosophy, University of Helsinki, 1977.
2. L. Augustsson, T. Coquand, and B. Nordström. A short description of Another Logical Framework. In *Proceedings of the First Workshop on Logical Frameworks, Antibes*, pages 39–42, 1990.
3. H. Barendregt. *The Lambda Calculus*. North Holland, 1981.
4. T.Tammet C.Fermüller, A.Leitsch and N.Zamov. *Resolution Methods for the Decision Problem*, volume 679 of *Lecture Notes in Artificial Intelligence*. Springer-Verlag, Berlin Heidelberg, 1993.
5. C.Green. Application of theorem-proving to problem solving. In *Proc. 1st Internat. Joint. Conf. Artificial Intelligence*, pages 219–239, 1969.
6. C.L.Chang and R.C.T Lee. *Symbolic Logic and Mechanical Theorem Proving*. Academic Press, 1973.
7. Thierry Coquand. Pattern matching with dependent types. In *Proceeding from the logical framework workshop at Båstad*, June 1992.
8. Thierry Coquand, Bengt Nordström, Jan M. Smith, and Björn von Sydow. Type theory and programming. *EATCS*, 52, February 1994.
9. A. Felty and D. Miller. Encoding a Dependent-type λ-Calculus in a Logic Programming Language. In *Proceedings of CADE-10*. Lecture Notes in Artificial Intelligence 449, Springer Verlag, 1990.
10. G.Peterson. A technique for establishing completeness results in theorem proving with equality. *SIAM J. of Comput*, 12:82–100, 1983.
11. Lena Magnusson. The new Implementation of ALF. In *The informal proceeding from the logical framework workshop at Båstad, June 1992*, 1992.
12. D. Miller. *Proofs in Higher Order Logics*. Ph.D. thesis, Carnegie Mellon University, 1983.
13. D. Miller. A compact representation of proofs. *Studia Logica*, 46(4), 1987.
14. G. Mints. Gentzen-type systems and resolution rules. part i. propositional logic. In *COLOG-88*, volume 417 of *Lecture Notes in Computer Science*, pages 198–231. Springer Verlag, 1990.
15. G. Mints. Resolution strategies for the intuitionistic logic. In *Constraint Programming*, volume 131 of *NATO ASI Series F*, pages 289–311. Springer Verlag, 1994.
16. Bengt Nordström, Kent Petersson, and Jan M. Smith. *Programming in Martin-Löf's Type Theory. An Introduction*. Oxford University Press, 1990.
17. Jan Smith. An interpretation of Martin-Löf's type theory in a type-free theory of propositions. *Journal of Symbolic Logic*, 49(3):730–753, 1984.

Organization and Development of a Constructive Axiomatization

Jan von Plato
vonplato@cc.helsinki.fi
University of Helsinki

1 Introduction

The following is a record of experiences in the constructive axiomatization of parts of basic mathematics. In the foundational debates of this century, constructive mathematics has been closely tied to the number systems. One starts from the natural numbers, then introduces the basic mathematical structures, the rationals, reals, real functions, and so on. Constructivity is driven back, in the end, to calculation with natural numbers. The peculiar character of a piece of constructive mathematics is brought out nicely in constructive analysis (as in Bishop and Bridges 1985). But the basic properties, say, the undecidability of equality of reals, are consequences of the quantificational structures in the definitions. Thus, it is not always so clear which among the various properties of objects in a constructive theory should come first in order if axiomatized directly.

Such a direct approach is taken in our (1995) work on constructive elementary geometry. It has few precedents in the literature on constructive mathematics. Heyting in 1925 was able to lay down some fundamental principles, but even he was largely motivated by the aim of leading the properties of the constructive geometrical plane back to the constructive real number arithmetic. This, then, is the present question: If we grant a purely abstract approach to constructive mathematics, freed of natural numbers as the ultimate ground, how should the constructive axiomatization be organized? Second, what are the ways of developing a constructive axiomatization? Initial experience with constructive geometry has led to a recipe that has been successfully used in such fields as the theory of order and combinatorial topology. We shall show this basic structure in Section 2, and then try to illustrate by various examples the generality of the formula.

Apart from the methodological discussion, new results in this paper are: Derivation of the general uniqueness axiom III of our (1995) from a formulation in terms of a constructor; Exact location of the place where constructive geometry calls for an extra basic concept in comparison to the classical one; Axioms for the oriented affine plane and an elementary derivation of the Jordan property for half-planes from these.

2 Basic Structure of a Constructive Axiomatization

The basic structure of a constructive axiomatization, as espoused here, contains: a proper choice of constructive basic concepts, the general properties that these basic concepts enjoy, the realization of the classical ideal situation through construction postulates, the properties and uniqueness of constructed objects, and compatibility among the various concepts and constructions.

1. Choice of basic concepts: A set is discrete if it has a decidable equality relation, otherwise it is continuous. In the discrete case, we can infer constructively equality from the impossibility of its negation. With a continuous set, the double negation cannot be eliminated; The realization that with constructive real numbers one has to start with an *apartness* relation and define equality as its negation, was Brouwer's. Heyting in 1925 generalized this to points and lines in his work on intuitionistic projective geometry.

The more general idea is to choose 'finitely precise' basic concepts when dealing with continuous sets. For example, instead of incidence of a point with a line, we choose the apartness of a point from a line and define the former 'ideal' situation as its negation.

2. General axioms for basic concepts: The above will be the semantical basis for the justification of general properties of the basic concepts. Example: Let Pt be the set of points, let $a,\ b\ :\ Pt$, and let $DiPt$ be a two place relation on points, with the sugaring

$$DiPt(a,b) \rhd a \text{ and } b \text{ are distinct points }.$$

Let $DiPt(a,b)$ and let $c\ :\ Pt$. If we fail to decide whether $DiPt(b,c)$ (resp. $DiPt(a,c)$), then, since $DiPt(a,b)$ is a 'finitely precise' proposition, we may infer $DiPt(a,c)$ (resp. $DiPt(b,c)$). Therefore we have the principle

$$\text{I} \quad DiPt(a,b) \rightarrow DiPt(a,c) \vee DiPt(b,c),$$

the apartness axiom for distinct points. Equality of points, in the sense of coincidence, is defined by $EqPt(a,b) \equiv \sim DiPt(a,b)$. Once we have named a point a, we refer by a to precisely that point, which is expressed by the axiom

$$\text{II} \quad \sim DiPt(a,a).$$

With I and II, we say $DiPt$ is an apartness relation. Substituting a for c in I, we get $DiPt(a,b) \rightarrow DiPt(a,a) \vee DiPt(b,a)$. We have by II $EqPt(a,a)$, therefore $DiPt(a,b) \rightarrow DiPt(b,a)$. Taking contrapositions, we obtain $EqPt(a,b) \rightarrow EqPt(b,a)$ and $EqPt(a,b)\ \&\ EqPt(a,c) \rightarrow EqPt(b,c)$. An apartness relation is one whose negation is an equivalence relation.

Other relations analogous to apartness relations, but enjoying somewhat different properties, can be found in our (1995).

3. Construction postulates for ideal concepts: The ideally precise is effected by construction postulates. It is laid down axiomatically what the properties of such constructed objects are. An obvious but instructive example is the construction of a connecting line in constructive geometry. We can write it as a rule of inference, where Ln is the set of lines.

$$\frac{a\ :\ Pt \quad b\ :\ Pt \quad \vdash DiPt(a,b)}{ln(a,b)\ :\ Ln}$$

The construction depends on the truth of the condition that a and b are distinct points.

4. Properties of constructed objects: We want to express that $ln(a,b)$ goes precisely through the points a and b. Classically one says a and b are incident with line $ln(a,b)$. To express this constructively, we introduce the basic concept Apt, with

$$Apt(a,l) \rhd \text{ point } a \text{ is apart from line } l,$$

and define the old concept of incidence as $Inc(a,l) \equiv \sim Apt(a,l)$. Obviously, Apt is again a 'positive' concept. To prove $Inc(a,l)$, we must show that any proof of $Apt(a,l)$ can be converted into an impossibility. The ideal properties of the connecting line construction are that

$$DiPt(a,b) \rightarrow Inc(a, ln(a,b)),$$

$$DiPt(a,b) \rightarrow Inc(b, ln(a,b)).$$

5. Uniqueness of the constructions: Classically, we require that an object sharing the properties of a constructed object, is equal to it. With $EqLn$ expressing equality of two lines, we would put

$$5.1. \quad DiPt(a,b) \;\&\; Inc(a,l) \& Inc(b,l) \rightarrow EqLn(l, ln(a,b)).$$

The constructive version is, with $DiLn$ an apartness relation sugared as

$$DiLn(l,m) \rhd l \text{ and } m \text{ are distinct lines},$$

$$5.2. \quad DiPt(a,b) \;\&\; DiLn(l, ln(a,b)) \rightarrow Apt(a,l) \vee Apt(b,l).$$

(Naturally we put $EqLn \equiv \sim DiLn$.) Semantical considerations justify this principle. But it turns out that such constructive uniqueness axioms for constructions can be expressed in a more general form. Principle 5.2 is actually equivalent to an apparently more general one that doesn't mention the connecting line construction:

$$5.3. \quad DiPt(a,b) \;\&\; DiLn(l,m) \rightarrow Apt(a,l) \vee Apt(a,m) \vee Apt(b,l) \vee Apt(b,m).$$

It is clear that 5.3 implies 5.2. To see the converse, assume $DiPt(a,b)$ and $DiLn(l,m)$, then construct $ln(a,b)$. By the apartness axiom for distinct lines, $DiLn(l, ln(a,b)) \vee DiLn(m, ln(a,b))$. It is now immediate to apply 5.2 to both cases separately. From $DiLn(l, ln(a,b))$, we conclude $Apt(a,l) \vee Apt(b,l)$, from $DiLn(m, ln(a,b))$ in turn $Apt(a,m) \vee Apt(b,m)$, so that the consequent of 5.3 follows. Principle 5.3 also gives the uniqueness of the intersection point construction.

6. Compatibility axioms: We need constructive forms of the substitution principles for equals. Typical such an axiom is

$$6.1. \quad Apt(a,l) \rightarrow DiPt(a,b) \vee Apt(b,l).$$

Note the constructive motivation: If $Apt(a,l)$, if you are unable to decide whether $DiPt(a,b)$, you can 'safely' infer $Apt(b,l)$. The classical principle

$$6.2. \quad Inc(a,l) \;\&\; EqPt(a,b) \rightarrow Inc(b,l)$$

is weaker, it follows by contraposition from 6.1 but not the other way around. Substitution principles for the constructed objects should come out as theorems.

We have now illustrated the structure of a constructive axiomatization: There are sets of objects, 'finitely precise' basic relations on these, constructions of ideal objects, ideal properties of these latter objects, general principles that entail the uniqueness of the constructions, and constructive principles permitting the substitution of equals in the basic relations.

3 Development of a Constructive Axiomatization

We can develop a constructive axiomatization in at least two ways: By *extension* and *refinement*. The latter is the more challenging one, but let us look at the former first.

7. Extension: We want to add the concept of parallel lines to the constructive incidence geometry sketched in Section 2. The property is ideal, therefore we introduce a concept *Con* that has to satisfy the condition

$$7.1. \quad Par(l,m) = \sim Con(l,m).$$

It is routine to see that the axioms for *convergent* lines are

$$7.2. \quad \sim Con(l,l),$$

$$Con(l,m) \rightarrow Con(l,n) \vee Con(m,n).$$

The second principle is particularly intuitive. The concept of convergent lines has been lurking behind much of the writing on geometry, say as in Hilbert's "intersecting lines", but was never spelled out before.

The corresponding construction postulate for the ideal situation is

$$\frac{a : Pt \quad l : Ln}{par(l,a) : Ln}$$

The ideal properties are

$$7.3. \quad Inc(a, par(l,a)),$$

$$Par(l, par(l,a)).$$

The uniqueness of the constructed parallel is expressed constructively by

$$7.4. \quad DiLn(par(l,a),m) \rightarrow Apt(a,m) \vee Con(l,m).$$

Again, as in paragraph 5, this result follows from a more general uniqueness principle that does not mention the parallel line construction:

$$7.5. \quad DiLn(l,m) \rightarrow Apt(a,l) \vee Apt(a,m) \vee Con(l,m).$$

Taking contrapositions in 7.4, we get the classical uniqueness of the parallel line construction.

Convergence of two lines will also appear in the condition for the intersection point construction:

$$\frac{l : Ln \quad m : Ln \quad \vdash Con(l,m)}{pt(l,m) : Pt}$$

For details, see our (1995).

Next we must check through the previous concepts for compatibility. This will lead to adding the principle

$$7.6. \quad Con(l,m) \rightarrow DiLn(l,n) \vee Con(m,n).$$

Substituting m for n, we get

$$7.7. \quad Con(l,m) \rightarrow DiLn(l,m).$$

Contraposition is

$$7.8. \quad EqLn(l,m) \rightarrow Par(l,m).$$

It seems like an innocent convention to say that equal lines are parallel. But the constructive version shows that the implication is substantial. With $Con(l,m)$, we can construct $pt(l,m) : Pt$ in affine geometry, with $DiLn(l,m)$ not. The usual classical definition of parallelism is

$$7.9. \quad Par(l,m) = EqLn(l,m) \vee (\forall x)(\sim Inc(x,l) \vee \sim Inc(x,m)).$$

And then it is trivial that $EqLn(l,m) \rightarrow Par(l,m)$. Not so constructively: The implication $Con(l,m) \rightarrow DiLn(l,m)$ comes from compatibility axiom 7.6.

Heyting in 1959 continues doing geometry with three basic concepts, defining parallelism of distinct lines l and m through $(\forall x)(\sim Inc(x,l) \vee \sim Inc(x,m))$. The constructive principle is given by formula 7.5 (also axiom A2 in our 1995)

$$DiLn(l,m) \rightarrow Apt(a,l) \vee Apt(a,m) \vee Con(l,m).$$

But here the universal quantifier cannot be driven inside the disjunction constructively, so the consequent does not state that any two distinct lines are parallel or convergent: We do have, assuming $DiLn(l,m)$,

$$7.10. \quad (\forall x : Pt)(Apt(x,l) \vee Apt(x,m) \vee Con(l,m)),$$

whereas

$$7.11. \quad (\forall x : Pt)(Apt(x,l) \vee Apt(x,m)) \vee Con(l,m)$$

fails. That is why constructive geometry needs one more basic concept in comparison to the classical one.

Further illustrations of extension of an axiomatization can be found in our (1995). We shall now turn to refinement.

8. Refinement: Let us think of the concept of linear order from a constructive point of view. We have a set L, pictured as a directed line, and points $a, b, c, \dots$ in

L. An infix notation is adequate at this stage as there is no dependency structure at the level of informal axiomatization. Classically, one begins with a weak order relation $\leq$, then defines strict order by

$$8.1. \quad a < b \equiv a \leq b \;\&\; \sim a = b$$

But constructively we would have an apartness relation instead; so assume this to be the case. Then, if $a \# b$, it is decidable whether $a < b$ or $b < a$. We have the constructive refinement

$$8.2. \quad a \# b = a < b \vee b < a.$$

of the apartness relation. The task is to axiomatize strict order constructively so that 8.2 appears as a definition of apartness, with its properties provable. Moreover, the concept in refinement is so chosen that the disjuncts appear incompatible:

$$8.3. \quad \sim(a < b \;\&\; b < a).$$

It follows, in particular, that

$$8.4. \quad a < b \rightarrow \sim b < a,$$

$$\sim a < a.$$

By the propositional equivalence of $(A \vee B) \rightarrow C$ and $(A \rightarrow C)\&(B \rightarrow C)$, we can split axioms in which the apartness relation appears in the assumptions. We get

$$8.5. \quad a < b \rightarrow a < c \vee c < a \vee b < c \vee c < b,$$

$$b < a \rightarrow a < c \vee c < a \vee b < c \vee c < b.$$

By commutativity of disjunction, we can bring these to exactly the same form with a and b just interchanged. Next, since the assumption was strengthened, we check if the conclusion could permit some asymmetry, too. So, if we can't decide whether $a < c$, $c < a$ cannot be inferred, but $c < b$ instead can. By incompatibility, $b < c$ is impossible. This leaves us

$$8.6. \quad a < b \rightarrow a < c \vee c < b,$$

an ordered version of the apartness axiom. The constructive theory of linear order is axiomatized by 8.3 and 8.6. It is interesting to note that transitivity is a theorem. Weak order is defined by

$$8.7. \quad a \geq b \equiv \sim a < b.$$

It has the usual properties.

The classical law

$$8.8. \quad \sim\sim a < b \rightarrow a < b$$

is an abstract version of Markov's principle (cf. Bridges 1989).

The above was fairly straightforward, for there were no constructions nor dependency structures. We shall look at a refinement of constructive geometry that displays these, namely, one where the lines of the constructive geometrical plane are *directed*. The basic relation *Apt* is at once refined into

$$8.9. \quad Apt(a,l) = L(a,l) \vee R(a,l)$$

(for Left, Right). Once we have $Apt(a,l)$ established, the disjunction 8.9 is 'observable'. We get as our first axiom of the ordered geometrical plane the exclusion principle

$$8.10. \quad \sim(L(a,l) \ \& \ R(a,l)).$$

Going through the axioms of constructive incidence geometry in 2, we notice that compatibility of distinct points with *Apt* gives us the axioms

$$8.11. \quad L(a,l) \rightarrow DiPt(a,b) \vee L(b,l),$$
$$R(a,l) \rightarrow DiPt(a,b) \vee R(b,l).$$

Assume now $L(a,l)$, $R(b,l)$. By 8.10, $\sim L(b,l)$ so we get at once from 8.11 the conclusion $DiPt(a,b)$: Points on different sides of a line are distinct. Statements of this principle in the literature invariably miss to indicate how it should be proved. At most there is an axiom stating that if three distinct points are not incident with a line, at least two of them are on the same side of it. Note that this follows immediately from our definition 8.9 and axiom 8.10, but is obviously inadequate for its intended purpose, the derivation of the Jordan property for a line. Let us show how one arrives at that property in a construcive and elementary manner:

With $L(a,l)$, $R(b,l)$, we conclude that $DiPt(a,b)$ so we can now construct the line $ln(a,b)$. It is easy to prove, from $Apt(a,l)$, that $DiLn(l, ln(a,b))$. Uniqueness axiom 7.5 gives

$$8.12. \quad DiLn(l, ln(a,b)) \rightarrow Apt(b,l) \vee Apt(b, ln(a,b)) \vee Con(l, ln(a,b)).$$

Collecting the assumptions and noting that $Inc(b, ln(a,b))$, this simplifies into

$$8.13. \quad DiPt(a,b) \ \& \ Apt(a,l) \rightarrow Apt(b,l) \vee Con(l, ln(a,b)).$$

The refinement 8.9 gives

$$8.14. \quad DiPt(a,b) \ \& \ L(a,l) \rightarrow (L(b,l) \vee R(b,l)) \vee Con(l, ln(a,b)),$$
$$DiPt(a,b) \ \& \ R(a,l) \rightarrow (L(b,l) \vee R(b,l)) \vee Con(l, ln(a,b)),$$

and it is routine to arrive at the strengthened forms

$$8.15. \quad DiPt(a,b) \ \& \ L(a,l) \rightarrow L(b,l) \vee Con(l, ln(a,b)),$$
$$DiPt(a,b) \ \& \ R(a,l) \rightarrow R(b,l) \vee Con(l, ln(a,b)).$$

This is the constructive formulation of the uniqueness of the parallel line construction in ordered plane affine geometry. We get at once the result that

$$8.16. \quad L(a,l) \ \& \ R(b,l) \rightarrow DiPt(a,b) \ \& \ Con(l, ln(a,b)),$$

that is, the connecting line of a and b intersects the dividing line l. Now the intersection point condition has been proved, and we can construct $pt(l, ln(a,b)) : Pt$. Further basic topological properties of the geometrical plane follow with equal naturalness.

4 Formalization

Our way of approaching constructive axiomatization is one where constructions are brought back to constructive mathematics. This fact is somewhat hidden in the notation; For example, we used just the turnstile in the condition for the connecting line construction rule. The properties of constructed objects are expressed with a condition, as in $DiPt(a,b) \rightarrow Inc(a, ln(a,b))$. Here the consequent is a proposition only if the antecedent is true, so the writing actually hides a structure with dependent types. There is no uniform way of writing such axioms in first-order form. Constructions with conditions invite one to use type theory in formalization. Further, as type theory is constructive, it is directly suitable for formalizing constructive mathematics. Once we have written out an axiomatization in the notation of type theory, the computer implementations of type theory, such as Alf or Coq, are available for proof editing purposes, . All the theorems and geometric constructions of our (1995) have been proof edited in Coq in Kahn (1995). We give here only a sample session of type-theoretical formalization:

9. Formalization in type theory: The first interesting thing in type theoretical formalization happens with constructions that have conditions. We have

$$Pt : Set, Ln : Set,$$

$$DiPt : (Pt)(Pt)Set,$$

$$Apt : (Pt)(Ln)Set,$$

$$ln : (a : Pt)(b : Pt)(w : DiPt(a,b))Ln.$$

The connecting line construction for two points a, b has as third argument a proof w that a and b are distinct. To implement the axiom

$$DiPt(a,b) \rightarrow Inc(a, ln(a,b))$$

we put

$$inc\_ln : (a : Pt)(b : Pt)(w : DiPt(a,b))Not(Apt(a, ln(a,b,w))).$$

Compare this to a two-sorted first order axiomatization (with upper case letters for points, lower case for lines)

$$\forall X \forall Y (X \# Y \rightarrow \exists z Inc(X,z)).$$

There is no way of coding the computational information for $X\#Y$ in the incidence proposition if the existential quantifier is used. Further, with the use of constructions, all axioms are expressed in a quantifier-free form.

Let us look at the axioms of linear order. The principle

$$\sim (a < b \;\&\; b < a)$$

can be formalized as follows:

$$L : Set,$$

$$<: (L)(L)Set,$$

$$incom : (a : L)(b : L)(<(a,b))(<(b,a))(A : Set)A.$$

Explicit logic seems to be as absent as it is in informal mathematics. We just declare a function *incom* that converts proofs $v :< (a,b)$ and $w :< (b,a)$ into a proof of any proposition, $incom(a,b,v,w,A) : A$. The rule of *ex falso quodlibet* can be given directly, no separate logical negation or absurdity proposition is needed. Other logical operations can be treated similarly (cf. our 1995, sec. 10).

Finally, we note that in the present scheme of constructive axiomatization, the addiction of the law of double negation will make the axiomatizations fall back into classical ones.

References:

Bishop, E. and D. Bridges (1985) *Constructive Analysis*, Springer.

Bridges, D. (1989) The constructive theory of preference relations on a locally compact space, *Proceedings of the Koninklijke Nederlandse Akademie van Wetenschappen*, Ser. A92, pp. 141–165.

Heyting, A. (1925) *Intuitionistische Axiomatik der Projektieve Meetkunde*, P. Nordhoff, Groningen.

Heyting, A. (1959) Axioms for intuitionistic plane affine geometry, in L. Henkin et al. (eds.) *The Axiomatic Method*, pp. 160–173, North-Holland, Amsterdam.

Kahn, G. (1995) Constructive geometry according to Jan von Plato, report, INRIA, Sophia-Antipolis.

von Plato, J. (1995) The axioms of constructive geometry, *Annals of Pure and Applied Logic*, vol. 76, pp. 169-200.

Lecture Notes in Computer Science

For information about Vols. 1–1083

please contact your bookseller or Springer-Verlag

Vol. 1084: W.H. Cunningham, S.T. McCormick, M. Queyranne (Eds.), Integer Programming and Combinatorial Optimization. Proceedings, 1996. X, 505 pages. 1996.

Vol. 1085: D.M. Gabbay, H.J. Ohlbach (Eds.), Practical Reasoning. Proceedings, 1996. XV, 721 pages. 1996. (Subseries LNAI).

Vol. 1086: C. Frasson, G. Gauthier, A. Lesgold (Eds.), Intelligent Tutoring Systems. Proceedings, 1996. XVII, 688 pages. 1996.

Vol. 1087: C. Zhang, D. Lukose (Eds.), Distributed Artificial Intelliegence. Proceedings, 1995. VIII, 232 pages. 1996. (Subseries LNAI).

Vol. 1088: A. Strohmeier (Ed.), Reliable Software Technologies – Ada-Europe '96. Proceedings, 1996. XI, 513 pages. 1996.

Vol. 1089: G. Ramalingam, Bounded Incremental Computation. XI, 190 pages. 1996.

Vol. 1090: J.-Y. Cai, C.K. Wong (Eds.), Computing and Combinatorics. Proceedings, 1996. X, 421 pages. 1996.

Vol. 1091: J. Billington, W. Reisig (Eds.), Application and Theory of Petri Nets 1996. Proceedings, 1996. VIII, 549 pages. 1996.

Vol. 1092: H. Kleine Büning (Ed.), Computer Science Logic. Proceedings, 1995. VIII, 487 pages. 1996.

Vol. 1093: L. Dorst, M. van Lambalgen, F. Voorbraak (Eds.), Reasoning with Uncertainty in Robotics. Proceedings, 1995. VIII, 387 pages. 1996. (Subseries LNAI).

Vol. 1094: R. Morrison, J. Kennedy (Eds.), Advances in Databases. Proceedings, 1996. XI, 234 pages. 1996.

Vol. 1095: W. McCune, R. Padmanabhan, Automated Deduction in Equational Logic and Cubic Curves. X, 231 pages. 1996. (Subseries LNAI).

Vol. 1096: T. Schäl, Workflow Management Systems for Process Organisations. XII, 200 pages. 1996.

Vol. 1097: R. Karlsson, A. Lingas (Eds.), Algorithm Theory – SWAT '96. Proceedings, 1996. IX, 453 pages. 1996.

Vol. 1098: P. Cointe (Ed.), ECOOP '96 – Object-Oriented Programming. Proceedings, 1996. XI, 502 pages. 1996.

Vol. 1099: F. Meyer auf der Heide, B. Monien (Eds.), Automata, Languages and Programming. Proceedings, 1996. XII, 681 pages. 1996.

Vol. 1100: B. Pfitzmann, Digital Signature Schemes. XVI, 396 pages. 1996.

Vol. 1101: M. Wirsing, M. Nivat (Eds.), Algebraic Methodology and Software Technology. Proceedings, 1996. XII, 641 pages. 1996.

Vol. 1102: R. Alur, T.A. Henzinger (Eds.), Computer Aided Verification. Proceedings, 1996. XII, 472 pages. 1996.

Vol. 1103: H. Ganzinger (Ed.), Rewriting Techniques and Applications. Proceedings, 1996. XI, 437 pages. 1996.

Vol. 1104: M.A. McRobbie, J.K. Slaney (Eds.), Automated Deduction – CADE-13. Proceedings, 1996. XV, 764 pages. 1996. (Subseries LNAI).

Vol. 1105: T.I. Ören, G.J. Klir (Eds.), Computer Aided Systems Theory – CAST '94. Proceedings, 1994. IX, 439 pages. 1996.

Vol. 1106: M. Jampel, E. Freuder, M. Maher (Eds.), Over-Constrained Systems. X, 309 pages. 1996.

Vol. 1107: J.-P. Briot, J.-M. Geib, A. Yonezawa (Eds.), Object-Based Parallel and Distributed Computation. Proceedings, 1995. X, 349 pages. 1996.

Vol. 1108: A. Díaz de Ilarraza Sánchez, I. Fernández de Castro (Eds.), Computer Aided Learning and Instruction in Science and Engineering. Proceedings, 1996. XIV, 480 pages. 1996.

Vol. 1109: N. Koblitz (Ed.), Advances in Cryptology – Crypto '96. Proceedings, 1996. XII, 417 pages. 1996.

Vol. 1110: O. Danvy, R. Glück, P. Thiemann (Eds.), Partial Evaluation. Proceedings, 1996. XII, 514 pages. 1996.

Vol. 1111: J.J. Alferes, L. Moniz Pereira, Reasoning with Logic Programming. XXI, 326 pages. 1996. (Subseries LNAI).

Vol. 1112: C. von der Malsburg, W. von Seelen, J.C. Vorbrüggen, B. Sendhoff (Eds.), Artificial Neural Networks – ICANN 96. Proceedings, 1996. XXV, 922 pages. 1996.

Vol. 1113: W. Penczek, A. Szałas (Eds.), Mathematical Foundations of Computer Science 1996. Proceedings, 1996. X, 592 pages. 1996.

Vol. 1114: N. Foo, R. Goebel (Eds.), PRICAI'96: Topics in Artificial Intelligence. Proceedings, 1996. XXI, 658 pages. 1996. (Subseries LNAI).

Vol. 1115: P.W. Eklund, G. Ellis, G. Mann (Eds.), Conceptual Structures: Knowledge Representation as Interlingua. Proceedings, 1996. XIII, 321 pages. 1996. (Subseries LNAI).

Vol. 1116: J. Hall (Ed.), Management of Telecommunication Systems and Services. XXI, 229 pages. 1996.

Vol. 1117: A. Ferreira, J. Rolim, Y. Saad, T. Yang (Eds.), Parallel Algorithms for Irregularly Structured Problems. Proceedings, 1996. IX, 358 pages. 1996.

Vol. 1118: E.C. Freuder (Ed.), Principles and Practice of Constraint Programming — CP 96. Proceedings, 1996. XIX, 574 pages. 1996.

Vol. 1119: U. Montanari, V. Sassone (Eds.), CONCUR '96: Concurrency Theory. Proceedings, 1996. XII, 751 pages. 1996.

Vol. 1120: M. Deza. R. Euler, I. Manoussakis (Eds.), Combinatorics and Computer Science. Proceedings, 1995. IX, 415 pages. 1996.

Vol. 1121: P. Perner, P. Wang, A. Rosenfeld (Eds.), Advances in Structural and Syntactical Pattern Recognition. Proceedings, 1996. X, 393 pages. 1996.

Vol. 1122: H. Cohen (Ed.), Algorithmic Number Theory. Proceedings, 1996. IX, 405 pages. 1996.

Vol. 1123: L. Bougé, P. Fraigniaud, A. Mignotte, Y. Robert (Eds.), Euro-Par'96. Parallel Processing. Proceedings, 1996, Vol. I. XXXIII, 842 pages. 1996.

Vol. 1124: L. Bougé, P. Fraigniaud, A. Mignotte, Y. Robert (Eds.), Euro-Par'96. Parallel Processing. Proceedings, 1996, Vol. II. XXXIII, 926 pages. 1996.

Vol. 1125: J. von Wright, J. Grundy, J. Harrison (Eds.), Theorem Proving in Higher Order Logics. Proceedings, 1996. VIII, 447 pages. 1996.

Vol. 1126: J.J. Alferes, L. Moniz Pereira, E. Orlowska (Eds.), Logics in Artificial Intelligence. Proceedings, 1996. IX, 417 pages. 1996. (Subseries LNAI).

Vol. 1127: L. Böszörményi (Ed.), Parallel Computation. Proceedings, 1996. XI, 235 pages. 1996.

Vol. 1128: J. Calmet, C. Limongelli (Eds.), Design and Implementation of Symbolic Computation Systems. Proceedings, 1996. IX, 356 pages. 1996.

Vol. 1129: J. Launchbury, E. Meijer, T. Sheard (Eds.), Advanced Functional Programming. Proceedings, 1996. VII, 238 pages. 1996.

Vol. 1130: M. Haveraaen, O. Owe, O.-J. Dahl (Eds.), Recent Trends in Data Type Specification. Proceedings, 1995. VIII, 551 pages. 1996.

Vol. 1131: K.H. Höhne, R. Kikinis (Eds.), Visualization in Biomedical Computing. Proceedings, 1996. XII, 610 pages. 1996.

Vol. 1132: G.-R. Perrin, A. Darte (Eds.), The Data Parallel Programming Model. XV, 284 pages. 1996.

Vol. 1133: J.-Y. Chouinard, P. Fortier, T.A. Gulliver (Eds.), Information Theory and Applications II. Proceedings, 1995. XII, 309 pages. 1996.

Vol. 1134: R. Wagner, H. Thoma (Eds.), Database and Expert Systems Applications. Proceedings, 1996. XV, 921 pages. 1996.

Vol. 1135: B. Jonsson, J. Parrow (Eds.), Formal Techniques in Real-Time and Fault-Tolerant Systems. Proceedings, 1996. X, 479 pages. 1996.

Vol. 1136: J. Diaz, M. Serna (Eds.), Algorithms – ESA '96. Proceedings, 1996. XII, 566 pages. 1996.

Vol. 1137: G. Görz, S. Hölldobler (Eds.), KI-96: Advances in Artificial Intelligence. Proceedings, 1996. XI, 387 pages. 1996. (Subseries LNAI).

Vol. 1138: J. Calmet, J.A. Campbell, J. Pfalzgraf (Eds.), Artificial Intelligence and Symbolic Mathematical Computation. Proceedings, 1996. VIII, 381 pages. 1996.

Vol. 1139: M. Hanus, M. Rogriguez-Artalejo (Eds.), Algebraic and Logic Programming. Proceedings, 1996. VIII, 345 pages. 1996.

Vol. 1140: H. Kuchen, S. Doaitse Swierstra (Eds.), Programming Languages: Implementations, Logics, and Programs. Proceedings, 1996. XI, 479 pages. 1996.

Vol. 1141: H.-M. Voigt, W. Ebeling, I. Rechenberg, H.-P. Schwefel (Eds.), Parallel Problem Solving from Nature – PPSN IV. Proceedings, 1996. XVII, 1.050 pages. 1996.

Vol. 1142: R.W. Hartenstein, M. Glesner (Eds.), Field-Programmable Logic. Proceedings, 1996. X, 432 pages. 1996.

Vol. 1143: T.C. Fogarty (Ed.), Evolutionary Computing. Proceedings, 1996. VIII, 305 pages. 1996.

Vol. 1144: J. Ponce, A. Zisserman, M. Hebert (Eds.), Object Representation in Computer Vision. Proceedings, 1996. VIII, 403 pages. 1996.

Vol. 1145: R. Cousot, D.A. Schmidt (Eds.), Static Analysis. Proceedings, 1996. IX, 389 pages. 1996.

Vol. 1146: E. Bertino, H. Kurth, G. Martella, E. Montolivo (Eds.), Computer Security – ESORICS 96. Proceedings, 1996. X, 365 pages. 1996.

Vol. 1147: L. Miclet, C. de la Higuera (Eds.), Grammatical Inference: Learning Syntax from Sentences. Proceedings, 1996. VIII, 327 pages. 1996. (Subseries LNAI).

Vol. 1148: M.C. Lin, D. Manocha (Eds.), Applied Computational Geometry. Proceedings, 1996. VIII, 223 pages. 1996.

Vol. 1149: C. Montangero (Ed.), Software Process Technology. Proceedings, 1996. IX, 291 pages. 1996.

Vol. 1150: A. Hlawiczka, J.G. Silva, L. Simoncini (Eds.), Dependable Computing – EDCC-2. Proceedings, 1996. XVI, 440 pages. 1996.

Vol. 1151: Ö. Babaoğlu, K. Marzullo (Eds.), Distributed Algorithms. Proceedings, 1996. VIII, 381 pages. 1996.

Vol. 1153: E. Burke, P. Ross (Eds.), Practice and Theory of Automated Timetabling. Proceedings, 1995. XIII, 381 pages. 1996.

Vol. 1154: D. Pedreschi, C. Zaniolo (Eds.), Logic in Databases. Proceedings, 1996. X, 497 pages. 1996.

Vol. 1155: J. Roberts, U. Mocci, J. Virtamo (Eds.), Broadbank Network Teletraffic. XXII, 584 pages. 1996.

Vol. 1156: A. Bode, J. Dongarra, T. Ludwig, V. Sunderam (Eds.), Parallel Virtual Machine – EuroPVM '96. Proceedings, 1996. XIV, 362 pages. 1996.

Vol. 1157: B. Thalheim (Ed.), Conceptual Modeling – ER '96. Proceedings, 1996. XII, 489 pages. 1996.

Vol. 1158: S. Berardi, M. Coppo (Eds.), Types for Proofs and Programs. Proceedings, 1995. X, 296 pages. 1996.

Vol. 1159: D.L. Borges, C.A.A. Kaestner (Eds.), Advances in Artificial Intelligence. Proceedings, 1996. XI, 243 pages. (Subseries LNAI).

Vol. 1160: S. Arikawa, A.K. Sharma (Eds.), Algorithmic Learning Theory. Proceedings, 1996. XVII, 337 pages. 1996. (Subseries LNAI).

Vol. 1161: O. Spaniol, C. Linnhoff-Popien, B. Meyer (Eds.), Trends in Distributed Systems. Proceedings, 1996. VIII, 289 pages. 1996.

Vol. 1162: D.G. Feitelson, L. Rudolph (Eds.), Job Scheduling Strategies for Parallel Processing. Proceedings, 1996. VIII, 291 pages. 1996.